A GUIDE TO
Microsoft® Windows® 98

Michael Jang

ONE MAIN STREET, CAMBRIDGE, MA 02142

an International Thomson Publishing company I(T)P®

Cambridge • Albany • Bonn • Boston • Cincinnati • London • Madrid • Melbourne • Mexico City
New York • Paris • San Francisco • Singapore • Tokyo • Toronto • Washington

A Guide to Microsoft Windows 98 is published by Course Technology.

Associate Publisher:	Kristen Duerr
Senior Acquisitions Editor:	Stephen Solomon
Senior Product Manager:	Jennifer Normandin
Product Manager:	David George
Production Editor:	Catherine G. DiMassa
Development Editor:	Ann Shaffer
Technical Editor:	Steve Thomas
Composition House:	GEX, Inc.
Text Designer:	GEX, Inc.
Cover Designer:	Wendy J. Reifeiss
Marketing Manager:	Susan Ogar

© 1999 by Course Technology—I(T)P®

For more information contact:

Course Technology
One Main Street
Cambridge, MA 02142

ITP Europe
Berkshire House 168-173
High Holborn
London WCIV 7AA
England

Nelson ITP Australia
102 Dodds Street
South Melbourne, 3205
Victoria, Australia

ITP Nelson Canada
1120 Birchmount Road
Scarborough, Ontario
Canada M1K 5G4

International Thomson Editores
Seneca, 53
Colonia Polanco
11560 Mexico D.F. Mexico

ITP GmbH
Königswinterer Strasse 418
53227 Bonn
Germany

ITP Asia
60 Albert Street, #15-01
Albert Complex
Singapore 189969

ITP Japan
Hirakawacho Kyowa Building, 3F
2-2-1 Hirakawacho
Chiyoda-ku, Tokyo 102
Japan

All rights reserved. This publication is protected by federal copyright law. No part of this publication may be reproduced, stored in a retrieval system, or transmitted in any form or by any means, electronic, mechanical, photocopying, recording, or otherwise, or be used to make a derivative work (such as translation or adaptation) without prior permission in writing from Course Technology.

Trademarks

Course Technology and the Open Book logo are registered trademarks and CourseKits is a trademark of Course Technology. Custom Edition is a registered trademark of International Thomson Publishing.

I(T)P®   The ITP logo is a registered trademark of International Thomson Publishing.

Some of the product names and company names used in this book have been used for identification purposes only and may be trademarks or registered trademarks of their respective manufacturers and sellers.

Disclaimer

Course Technology reserves the right to revise this publication and make changes from time to time in its content without notice.

ISBN 0-7600-1075-7

Printed in Canada

2 3 4 5 6 7 8 9 WC 02 01 00 99

Brief Table of Contents

PREFACE	xiii
CHAPTER 1 Introduction to Windows 98	1
CHAPTER 2 Planning and Installing Windows 98	31
CHAPTER 3 The Windows 98 Registry	65
CHAPTER 4 Managing Windows 98 Users, Profiles, and Policies	101
CHAPTER 5 Networking and the Internet	143
CHAPTER 6 Windows 98 Communications and Mobile Computing	183
CHAPTER 7 Windows 98 Server Services	217
CHAPTER 8 Managing Windows 98 System Resources	253
CHAPTER 9 Managing Windows 98 Applications	295
CHAPTER 10 Monitoring, Tuning, and Optimizing Windows 98	331
CHAPTER 11 Security, Access Controls, and Fault Tolerance	379
CHAPTER 12 Advanced Windows 98 Installation Options	407
CHAPTER 13 Advanced Windows 98 Networking Topics	461
CHAPTER 14 Troubleshooting	505
APPENDIX A Online Resources and Bibliography	563
APPENDIX B The Windows 98 Command-Line Environment	569
GLOSSARY	579
INDEX	600

TABLE OF CONTENTS

PREFACE	xiii

CHAPTER 1
Introduction to Windows 98 — 1
Microsoft Operating Systems	2
A Brief History of Windows on the Desktop	2
Meet Windows 98	4
Windows 98 Architecture	6
Key Features of Windows 98	8
Windows 98 Hardware and Architectural Features	8
Power and Usability	11
Robustness and Reliability	12
Increased Internet Integration	15
Chapter Summary	16
Key Terms	17
Review Questions	23
Hands-on Projects	26
Case Projects	29

CHAPTER 2
Planning and Installing Windows 98 — 31
Windows 98 System Requirements	32
Planning Your Windows 98 Configuration	32
File Systems	32
Networking Model	36
Security Strategies	40
Installation Approaches	42
Installation Types	42
Installation Options	43
Chapter Summary	55
Key Terms	56
Review Questions	59
Hands-on Projects	62
Case Projects	63

CHAPTER 3
The Windows 98 Registry — 65
An Overview of the Windows 98 Registry	66
Benefits of the Windows 98 Registry	66
Windows 98 Registry Files	67

Windows 98 Registry Access and Usage	68
Hardware Profiles	70
User Profiles	70
System Policies	72
Using Registry Checker and Registry Editor	72
Registry Safety	72
Registry Editor	74
The Structure of the Windows 98 Registry	74
Plug and Play and the Windows 98 Registry	79
Additional Registry Tools and Utilities	81
Simple, Safe Registry Tools	82
Advanced Registry Tools	82
System Policy Editor	82
Chapter Summary	83
Key Terms	84
Review Questions	88
Hands-on Projects	91
Case Projects	99

CHAPTER 4
Managing Windows 98 Users, Profiles, and Policies — 101

The Role of the User in Windows 98	102
Usernames and Passwords	102
Passwords and Networks	103
Password Lists	103
Password List Editor	106
User Environments in Windows 98	107
User Profiles	107
Hardware Profiles	116
System Policies	118
Chapter Summary	131
Key Terms	133
Review Questions	135
Hands-on Projects	138

CHAPTER 5
Networking and the Internet — 143

The Language of Networking	144
Basic Networking	145
Installing Multiple Protocols	146
TCP/IP	147
Modems and Network Cards	148
Configuring TCP/IP	149

Connecting to the Internet	151
Internet Connection Options	153
Internet Connection Wizard	154
Other ISPs	160
The Internet	160
Chapter Summary	167
Key Terms	167
Review Questions	172
Hands-on Projects	174
Case Projects	182

CHAPTER 6
Windows 98 Communications and Mobile Computing — 183

The Windows Telephony API	184
Modems and Related Devices	184
Installation Wizards	185
Configuring Global Modem Properties	185
Configuring Dialing Properties	188
Remote Access with Dial-Up Networking	190
Installing and Configuring ISDN Devices	193
Multilink Connections	195
Compression	195
Internet Access via a LAN Gateway	196
Overcoming Phone Line Transmission Problems	197
Faster Connections	197
Troubleshooting Connection Problems	198
HyperTerminal	199
Phone Dialer	200
Mobile Computing and Windows 98	200
PC Card Support	201
Power Management	201
Hot Docking and Port Replication Support	202
Managing Files with the Briefcase	203
Direct Cable Connection	204
Chapter Summary	205
Key Terms	206
Review Questions	208
Hands-on Projects	211
Case Projects	215

CHAPTER 7
Windows 98 Server Services — 217

Personal Web Server	218
Comparative Features	218
Installing Personal Web Server	219

Personal Web Manager	223
Web Sharing	230
Connecting Your Web Site	231
Remote Access Server	232
Comparisons	233
Installing RAS for Windows 98	233
Configuring Remote Access Server for Windows 98	234
Sharing Resources Through Windows 98 RAS	236
RAS Authentication and Access Controls	239
Chapter Summary	240
Key Terms	240
Review Questions	242
Hands-on Projects	246
Case Projects	251

CHAPTER 8
Managing Windows 98 System Resources — 253

Shared resources in the Windows 98 environment	254
Assigning Access Permissions to Shared Folders	255
User-level Versus Share-level Permissions	255
Setting Up User-level Security	255
Sharing Resources with User-level Security	256
Create, Share, and Monitor Network Resources	257
Shared Fax Modems	258
Integrating Telephones into a Network	259
Printing in the Windows 98 Environment	260
Managing Windows 98 Hard Disks	265
Disk Partitioning	266
Enabling Large Disk Support	268
FAT32 Drive Converter	269
Disk Compression	270
Disk Defragmenter	272
Purge the Recycle Bin	273
Multimedia and Windows 98	274
Ring Architecture	274
Multimedia Architecture	275
DirectX Media Components	279
DirectX Multimedia Applications	280
Media Player	280
Chapter Summary	281
Key Terms	282
Review Questions	284
Hands-on Projects	289
Case Projects	292

CHAPTER 9
Managing Windows 98 Applications — 295

- 32-Bit System and Memory Architecture — 296
  - Definitions — 296
  - Virtual Machines — 298
  - Virtual Memory — 299
  - Memory Management — 301
  - CPU Access — 302
- Inside the System Virtual Machine — 304
  - Windows 98 and Win16 Applications — 304
  - Running Win32 Applications in Windows 98 — 306
  - 32-Bit Components vs. 16-Bit Components — 306
  - Thunking — 307
  - Separate Message Queues — 307
  - Long Filename Support — 307
- Support for MS-DOS Applications in Windows 98 — 308
  - Benefits of Windows 98 for MS-DOS Applications — 308
  - MS-DOS Mode — 309
  - Memory Protection — 309
  - Operational Defaults — 310
  - Running MS-DOS Applications in Windows 98 — 315
- File Systems and the Win32 Driver Model — 315
  - Virtual Device Drivers — 315
  - The Windows 32-bit Driver Model — 316
  - The Installable File System Manager — 317
- Chapter Summary — 319
- Key Terms — 320
- Review Questions — 322
- Hands-on Projects — 326
- Case Projects — 330

CHAPTER 10
Monitoring, Tuning, and Optimizing Windows 98 — 331

- Taking Stock: System Inventory and Overview — 332
  - Microsoft System Information — 332
  - Device Manager — 337
  - Third-Party Alternatives — 337
- Understanding Windows 98 Performance — 338
  - Establishing a Baseline — 338
  - Baselines and Bottlenecks — 338
  - Cache Management — 340
  - Measuring Performance — 341
  - Diagnosing Problems — 341

Performance Monitoring in Windows 98	342
System Monitor Features	342
Using System Monitor	349
Using Trial and Error	351
Microsoft System Information Tools	351
Optimizing Windows 98	356
Optimizing the CPU	356
Memory Management	357
Hard Disk Management	358
Optimizing CD-ROM and Digital Video Disc Drives	364
Removable Media	365
Graphics	365
Printing	366
Network Optimization	367
System Configuration Utility	368
Optimization Utilities	369
Chapter Summary	369
Key Terms	370
Review Questions	372
Hands-on Projects	375
Case Projects	378

CHAPTER 11
Security, Access Controls, and Fault Tolerance   **379**

An Overview of Windows 98 Security	380
Pass-through Security and Windows 98	381
Creating and Documenting Your Security Plan	381
Administering User-level Security from a Windows 98 Computer	381
Third-party Authentication and Security Tools	384
Fault Tolerance in Windows 98	384
FAT32 Boot Sector Backups	385
Preventative Maintenance Utilities	385
Backup	387
System Recovery Strategies and Techniques	390
Fault Tolerance in Earlier Versions of Windows	392
Fault Tolerance in Windows NT	392
Intellimirror	393
Chapter Summary	393
Key Terms	394
Review Questions	396
Hands-on Projects	400
Case Projects	405

CHAPTER 12
Advanced Windows 98 Installation Options — 407
Windows 98 Setup in Detail — 408
    Preparing the Setup Wizard — 408
    User Input and Copying Files — 408
    Detecting Hardware — 409
    Smart Recovery — 409
    Setup Options — 409
    Boot Disks — 409
    CD-ROM Drivers — 411
    Using the Boot Disk — 412
    Uninstalling Windows 98 — 413
Batch Mode Installation — 414
    Installing Microsoft Batch 98 — 414
    Collecting Registry Settings — 415
    General Setup Options — 416
    Network Options — 423
    Optional Components — 431
    Internet Explorer Options — 431
    Advanced Options — 435
    Multiple Machine-Name Files — 437
    Saving Your Batch Settings — 438
    The Batch File — 439
Installing Windows 98 Across a Network — 439
    Basic Network Installation — 440
    Windows NT Push Installation — 440
    Novell NetWare Push Installation — 443
    Pull Installations — 444
Managing Dual or Multiboot Machines — 444
    Setting up Partitions — 444
    Third-party Boot Managers — 445
Chapter Summary — 446
Key Terms — 447
Review Questions — 448
Hands-on Projects — 453
Case Projects — 459

CHAPTER 13
Advanced Windows 98 Networking Topics — 461
The Installable File System Manager and File Requests — 462
Binding — 463
Network Clients as Redirectors — 463
    Preparing the Message — 464
    Client for Microsoft Networks — 464
    Client for NetWare Networks — 466

Dual-Protocol Clients	468
Working with Novell Client Software and Windows 98	468
Configuring a Windows 98 NetWare Client	469
Configuring and Managing Windows 98 Protocols	470
TCP/IP	471
The IPX/SPX-compatible Protocol	479
DLC	482
NetBEUI	482
Fast Infrared	483
Network Driver Interface Specification (NDIS)	483
Open Datalink Interface (ODI)	484
A Focus on Hardware	484
Network Cards	484
Hardware on the Network	485
Types of Networks	485
Configuring Windows 98 as a Server—Using File and Printer Sharing	489
Configuring a Windows 98 Computer as a Browser	489
File and Printer Sharing for NetWare	490
Net Watcher	490
Workgroups and Domains	492
Chapter Summary	492
Key Terms	493
Review Questions	495
Hands-on Projects	499
Case Projects	504

CHAPTER 14
Troubleshooting   **505**

Troubleshooting 101: Basic Skills and Approaches	506
Identifying the Problem	506
Forming a Theory	507
Testing Your Solution	508
Regular Maintenance	508
Troubleshooting the Windows 98 Installation	509
Automated Setup Documentation	509
Incompatible Compression Regimes	512
Conventional Memory Requirements	513
Troubleshooting the Startup and Shutdown Processes	513
Startup and Shutdown Troubleshooter	514
Startup Menu and Safe Mode	516
Emergency Startup Disk	517
Conflicts	519
System Configuration Utility	520
System File Checker	526

Cables and Connections	528
Printer Troubleshooting	529
MSInfo and Print Problems	529
Printer Spool	530
Printer Memory	531
Printer Properties	532
Troubleshooting Disk and File System Problems	536
Hard Disks	536
File Systems	537
Microsoft System Information (MSInfo)	538
Automatic Skip Driver Agent	539
Windows Report Tool	539
Troubleshooting the Network Configuration	540
Troubleshooting NetBEUI	540
Troubleshooting the IPX/SPX-compatible Protocol	541
Troubleshooting Other Devices	544
Other Sources for Troubleshooting Information	548
Chapter Summary	550
Key Terms	551
Review Questions	552
Hands-on Projects	556
Case Projects	561

APPENDIX A
Online Resources and Bibliography   563

Web Sites	563
Media-based Windows 98 Web Sites	564
General Windows 98 Web Sites	565
MCSE Web Sites	566
Books	566
Microsoft Books	568

APPENDIX B
The Windows 98 Command-Line Environment   569

Command-line Entries for Windows 98 Utilities	570
MS-DOS Commands	571
Networking Commands	574
System Commands	575
Setup Switches	576

GLOSSARY   579

INDEX   600

PREFACE

Windows 98 is a feature-rich operating system designed to work well alone or on a network. In this book, you learn about a broad variety of tools to install, configure, manage, monitor, and troubleshoot this operating system. You also gain the knowledge you need to prepare for the Microsoft Windows 98 certification exam, #70-098, Implementing and Supporting Microsoft Windows 98. When you pass this exam, you become certified as a Microsoft Certified Professional. It is also one of the exams that you need on the road towards becoming a Microsoft Certified Systems Engineer (MCSE).

One bonus you receive when you learn Windows 98 is that it is effectively an introduction to the Windows NT 5.0 Server and Workstation operating systems. Microsoft has designed the structure and format of Windows 98 to be as compatible as possible with NT 5.0. When you learn Windows 98, you learn the structure of the operating system that could very well be at the center of computing for the foreseeable future.

As you go through this book, you will learn concepts and practice them on your computer in a broad variety of hands-on projects.

In **Chapter 1**, "Introduction to Windows 98," you learn the basics of what Microsoft Windows 98 can do, as a system and as a client on a network. In **Chapter 2**, "Planning and Installing Windows 98," you get a chance plan and install Windows 98 as a new system or as an upgrade.

In **Chapter 3**, "The Windows 98 Registry," you learn about the Registry and its role as the central configuration database for Windows 98. In **Chapter 4**, "Managing Windows 98 Users, Profiles, and Policies," you learn to control what different users can do with their Windows 98 computers, whether they be stand-alone, or part of a Windows NT or Novell NetWare network.

To simplify your introduction to Windows 98 networking, you learn about TCP/IP in the context of connecting to an Internet Service Provider in **Chapter 5**, "Networking and the Internet." While **Chapter 6**, "Windows 98 Communications and Mobile Computing," is focused on the Windows 98 tools to help you manage a laptop computer, it is written to allow anyone with a modem to learn the techniques. In **Chapter 7**, "Windows 98 Server Services," you learn how to create a Web site with Personal Web Server, as well as how to set up your Windows 98 computer as a Remote Access Server.

Now that you have set up Windows 98 and made it useful with network connections, you are ready for **Chapter 8**, "Managing Windows 98 System Resources." In this chapter, you learn to manage a variety of resources: Windows NT or Novell NetWare networks, hard disks, and multimedia applications.

In **Chapter 9**, "Managing Windows 98 Applications," you learn about how Windows 98 actually works, and how it manages different programs. In **Chapter 10**, "Monitoring, Tuning, and Optimizing Windows 98," you use the System Monitor to measure the behavior of your computer. In **Chapter 11**, "Security, Access Controls, and Fault Tolerance," you begin to manage your computer with tools such as ScanDisk and Disk Defragmenter.

Now that you have learned how to install Windows 98 and what it can do, you learn how to automate and customize the process for different configurations in **Chapter 12**, "Advanced Windows 98 Installation Options." With what you know by the time you reach **Chapter 13**, "Advanced Windows 98 Networking Topics," you learn how Windows 98 can be integrated on a network. Although you learn about troubleshooting various components throughout the book, you can learn to solve many common problems in **Chapter 14**, "Troubleshooting."

This book is intended to be just the beginning of your study. **Appendix A**, "Online Resources and Bibliography," includes a number of books and Web sites where you can learn more about Windows 98. **Appendix B**, "The Windows 98 Command Line Environment," provides a list of the more common commands that you can use to call up Windows 98 utilities, as well as some of the more common MS-DOS commands. It also lists some of the options that you can use to set up Windows 98.

FEATURES

To aid you in fully understanding Windows 98 concepts, there are many features in this book designed to improve its pedagogical value.

- **Chapter Objectives.** Each chapter in this book begins with a detailed list of the concepts to be mastered within that chapter. This list provides you with a quick reference to the contents of that chapter, as well as a useful study aid.

- **Illustrations and Tables.** Numerous illustrations of Windows 98 screens and components aid you in the visualization of common steps, theories, and concepts. In addition, many tables provide details and comparisons of both practical and theoretical information.

- **Hands-on Projects.** Although it is important to understand the theory behind operating system and networking technology, nothing can improve upon real-world experience. To this end, along with theoretical explanations, each chapter provides numerous hands-on projects aimed at providing you with real-world implementation experience.

- **Chapter Summaries.** Each chapter's text is followed by a summary of the concepts it has introduced. These summaries provide a helpful way to recap and revisit the ideas covered in each chapter.

- **Review Questions.** End-of-chapter assessment begins with a set of review questions that reinforce the ideas introduced in each chapter. These questions not only ensure that you have mastered the concepts, but are written to help prepare you for the Microsoft certification examination.

- **Case Projects.** At the end of each chapter, you are given opportunities to put yourself in a real-world situation. Instead of reciting the book, this is your chance to implement the skills and knowledge gained in the chapter through real-world setup and administration scenarios.

Preface   xv

TEXT AND GRAPHIC CONVENTIONS

Wherever appropriate, additional information and exercises have been added to this book to help you better understand what is being discussed in the chapter. Icons throughout the text alert you to additional materials. The icons used in this textbook are described below.

The **Note** icon is used to present additional helpful material related to the subject being described.

Each hands-on activity in this book is preceded by the **Hands-On** icon and a description of the exercise that follows.

Tips are included from the author's experience and provide extra information about how to attack a problem, or what to do to in certain real-world situations.

The **Cautions** are included to help you anticipate potential mistakes or problems so you can prevent them from happening.

Case Project icons mark the running case project. These are more involved, scenario-based assignments. In this extensive case example, you are asked to implement independently what you have learned.

INSTRUCTOR'S MATERIALS

The following supplemental materials are available when this book is used in a classroom setting. All of the supplements available with this book are provided to the instructor on a single CD-ROM.

Electronic Instructor's Manual. The Instructor's Manual that accompanies this textbook includes:

- Additional instructional material to assist in class preparation, including suggestions for lecture topics, suggested lab activities, tips on setting up a lab for the hands-on assignments, and alternative lab setup ideas in situations where lab resources are limited.

- Solutions to all end-of-chapter materials, including the Project and Case assignments.

Course Test Manager 1.2. Accompanying this book is a powerful assessment tool known as the Course Test Manager. Designed by Course Technology, this cutting-edge Windows-based testing software helps instructors design and administer tests and pre-tests. In addition to being able to generate tests that can be printed and administered, this full-featured program also has an online testing component that allows students to take tests at the computer and have their exams automatically graded.

PowerPoint presentations. This book comes with Microsoft PowerPoint slides for each chapter. These are included as a teaching aid for classroom presentation, to make available to students on the network for chapter review, or to be printed for classroom distribution. Instructors, please feel at liberty to add your own slides for additional topics you introduce to the class.

TRANSCENDER CERTIFICATION TEST PREP SOFTWARE

Bound into the back of this book is a CD-ROM containing Transcender Corporation's Implementing and Supporting Microsoft Windows 98 certification exam preparation software with one full exam that simulates the Microsoft exam (Exam 70-098).

ACKNOWLEDGEMENTS

The craft of making a book today is much more than just sitting alone typing into a computer. As trite as it sounds, it is a team effort. Many thanks go to Ann Shaffer, our Developmental Editor, for helping me make my writing better in a timely fashion. Thanks to the team at Course Technology: Kristen Duerr, Jennifer Normandin, Dave George, Stephen Solomon, Cathie DiMassa, and John Bosco for just about everything else. Thank you, Steve Thomas, for your careful readings. Thank you, Dave Johnson, for backing me up when I needed it. If I missed anyone, thank you too. Thanks to my colleagues at Boeing who taught me to write clearly and rigorously. And thank you, Ed Tittel. You brought me into this business, you sang my praises to others. Thank you, Ed, for getting CT to ask me to finish this book.

Finally, thank you, Nancy, my love and partner, for giving me the emotional support that I needed to become an author and to get through this venture.

PREPARING FOR MICROSOFT CERTIFICATION

Microsoft offers a program called the Microsoft Certified Professional (MCP) program. Becoming a Microsoft Certified Professional can open many doors for you. Whether you want to be a network engineer, product specialist, or software developer, obtaining the appropriate Microsoft Certified Professional credentials can provide a formal record of your skills to potential employers. Certification can be equally effective in helping you secure a raise or promotion.

The Microsoft Certified Professional program is made up of many courses in several different tracks. Combinations of individual courses can lead to certification in a specific track. Most tracks require a combination of required and elective courses. One of the most common tracks for beginners is the Microsoft Certified Product Specialist (MCPS). By obtaining this status, your credentials tell a potential employer that you are an expert in a specialized computing area such as Personal Computer Operating Systems on a specific product, like Microsoft Windows 98.

HOW CAN TRANSCENDER'S TEST PREP SOFTWARE HELP?

To become a Microsoft Certified Professional, you must pass rigorous certification exams that provide a valid and reliable measure of technical proficiency and expertise. The CD-ROM contained in this book, Transcender Corporation's Limited Version certification exam preparation software, can be used in conjunction with the book to help you assess your progress in the event you choose to pursue Microsoft Professional Certification. The Transcender CD-ROM presents a series of questions that were expertly prepared to test your readiness for the official Microsoft Certification examination on Implementing and Supporting Windows 98 (Exam 70-098). These questions were taken from a larger series of practice tests produced by the Transcender Corporation—practice tests that simulate the interface and format of the actual certification exams. Transcender's complete product also offers explanations for all questions. The rationale for each correct answer is carefully explained, and specific page references are given for Microsoft Product Documentation and Microsoft Press reference books. These page references enable you to study from additional sources.

Practice test questions from Transcender Corporation are acknowledged as the best available. In fact, with their full product, Transcender offers a money-back guarantee if you do not pass the exam. If you have trouble passing the practice examination included on the enclosed CD-ROM, you should consider purchasing the full product with additional practice tests and personalized feedback. Details and pricing information are available at the back of this book. A sample of the full Transcender product is on the enclosed CD-ROM, including remedial explanations.

The Transcender product is a great tool to help you prepare to become certified. If you experience technical problems with this product, please e-mail Transcender at *course@transcender.com* or call (615) 726-8779.

WANT TO KNOW MORE ABOUT MICROSOFT CERTIFICATION?

There are many additional benefits to achieving Microsoft Certified status. These benefits apply to you as well as to your potential employer. As a Microsoft Certified Professional (MCP), you will be recognized as an expert on Microsoft products, have access to ongoing technical information from Microsoft, and receive special invitations to Microsoft conferences and events. You can obtain a comprehensive, interactive tool that provides full details about the Microsoft Certified Professional program online at *www.microsoft.com/train_cert/cert/certif.htm*. For more information on texts at Course Technology that will help prepare you for certification exams, visit our Web site at *www.course.com*.

When you become a Certified Product Specialist, Microsoft sends you a Welcome Kit that contains:

- An 8-1/2 x 11" Microsoft Certified Product Specialist wall certificate. Also, within a few weeks after you have passed any exam, Microsoft sends you a Microsoft Certified Professional Transcript that shows which exams you have passed.
- A Microsoft Certified Professional Program membership card.
- A Microsoft Certified Professional lapel pin.
- A license to use the Microsoft Certified Professional logo. You are licensed to use the logo in your advertisements, promotions, proposals, and other materials, including business cards, letterheads, advertising circulars, brochures, yellow page advertisements, mailings, banners, resumes, and invitations.
- A Microsoft Certified Professional logo sheet. Before using the camera-ready logo, you must agree to the terms of the licensing agreement.
- A Microsoft TechNet CD-ROM.
- A 50% discount toward a one-year membership in the Microsoft TechNet Technical Information Network, which provides valuable information via monthly CD-ROMs.
- Dedicated forums on CompuServe (GO MECFORUM) and The Microsoft Network, which enable Microsoft Certified Professionals to communicate directly with Microsoft and one another.
- A one-year subscription to Microsoft Certified Professional Magazine, a career and professional development magazine created especially for Microsoft Certified Professionals.
- A Certification Update subscription. Certification Update is a bimonthly newsletter from the Microsoft Certified Professional program that keeps you informed of changes and advances in the program and exams.
- Invitations to Microsoft conferences, technical training sessions, and special events.
- Eligibility to join the Network Professional Association, a worldwide association of computer professionals. Microsoft Certified Product Specialists are invited to join as associate members.

A Certified Systems Engineer receives all the benefits mentioned above as well as the following additional benefits:

- Microsoft Certified Systems Engineer logos and other materials to help you identify yourself as a Microsoft Certified Systems Engineer to colleagues or clients.
- Ten free incidents with the Microsoft Support Network and a 25% discount on purchases of additional 10-packs of Priority Development and Desktop Support incidents.
- A one-year subscription to the Microsoft TechNet Technical Information Network.
- A one-year subscription to the Microsoft Beta Evaluation program. This benefit provides you with up to 12 free monthly beta software CDs for many of Microsoft's newest software products. This enables you to become familiar with new versions of Microsoft products before they are generally available. This benefit also includes access to a private CompuServe forum where you can exchange information with other program members and find information from Microsoft on current beta issues and product information.

CERTIFY ME!

So you are ready to become a Microsoft Certified Professional. The examinations are administered through Sylvan Prometric (formerly Drake Prometric) and are offered at more than 700 authorized testing centers around the world. Microsoft evaluates certification status based on current exam records. Your current exam record is the set of exams you have passed. To maintain Microsoft Certified Professional status, you must remain current on all the requirements for your certification.

Registering for an exam is easy. To register, contact Sylvan Prometric, 2601 West 88th Street, Bloomington, MN, 55431, at (800) 755-EXAM (3926). Dial (612) 896-7000 or (612) 820-5707 if you cannot place a call to an 800 number from your location. You must call to schedule the exam at least one day before the day you want to take the exam. Taking the exam automatically enrolls you in the Microsoft Certified Professional program; you do not need to submit an application to Microsoft Corporation.

When you call Sylvan Prometric, have the following information ready:

- Your name, organization (if any), mailing address, and phone number.
- A unique ID number (e.g., your Social Security number).
- The number of the exam you wish to take (#70-098 for the Implementing and Supporting Microsoft Windows 98 exam).
- A payment method (e.g., credit card number). If you pay by check, payment is due before the examination can be scheduled. The fee to take each exam is currently $100.

Upgrade to the full version of Win98Cert 5.0

What you get with the full version:

- Three full-length exams, including simulation questions
- Detailed Score History
- Expanded Printing Options
- Detailed answer explanations and citations for every question
- Money Back if You Don't Pass Guarantee★

  ★ *See our Web site for guarantee details*

To upgrade to the full version:

1. Install Win98Cert 5.0 Limited Version on the computer system on which you intend to use the full version.

2. When the program starts, choose "Order Full Version."

3. To upgrade immediately, enable your Internet connection, and go to
   http://www.transcender.com/upgrade/limited/win98cert5.

4. Follow the instructions posted at the above listed URL.

5. If you do not wish to purchase your upgrade online, mail us the completed coupon below (no reproductions or photocopies please). Enclose a check or money order, payable to Transcender Corporation, for $129, plus $6 shipping ($25 outside U.S.).

Terms and Conditions:

Maximum one upgrade per person. Pre-payment by check, money order, or credit card is required. For your own protection, do not send currency through the mail.

Send to: Upgrade Program
Transcender Corporation
242 Louise Avenue
Nashville, TN 37203

Please send me the Win98Cert 5.0 Upgrade. Enclosed is my check or credit card number, payable to Transcender Corporation for $129 plus $6 ($25 outside U.S.). TN residents add $10.64 for sales tax.

Name _____ School _____

Address _____ Credit Card: VISA MC AMEX DISC

City _____ State _____ CC# _____

Zip _____ Country _____ Expiration _____

Phone _____ Name on Card _____

E-Mail _____ Signature _____

CRS1198

Transcender Corporation

SINGLE-USER LICENSE AGREEMENT

IMPORTANT. READ THIS LICENSE AGREEMENT (THE "AGREEMENT") CAREFULLY BEFORE OPENING THE SOFTWARE PACK. YOU AGREE TO BE LEGALLY BOUND BY THE TERMS OF THIS LICENSE AGREEMENT IF YOU EITHER (1) OPEN THE SOFTWARE PACK, OR (2) IF YOU INSTALL, COPY, OR OTHERWISE USE THE ENCLOSED SOFTWARE. IF YOU DO NOT AGREE WITH THESE TERMS, DO NOT OPEN THE SOFTWARE PACK AND DO NOT INSTALL, COPY, OR USE THE SOFTWARE. YOU MAY RETURN THE *UNOPENED SOFTWARE* TO THE PLACE OF PURCHASE WITHIN FIFTEEN (15) DAYS OF PURCHASE AND RECEIVE A FULL REFUND. NO REFUNDS WILL BE GIVEN FOR SOFTWARE THAT HAS AN OPENED SOFTWARE PACK OR THAT HAS BEEN INSTALLED, USED, ALTERED, OR DAMAGED.

Grant of Single-User License. **YOU ARE THE ONLY PERSON ENTITLED TO USE THIS SOFTWARE.** This is a license agreement between you (an individual) and Transcender Corporation whereby Transcender grants you the non-exclusive and non-transferable license and right to use this software product, updates (if any), and accompanying documentation (collectively the "Software"). ONLY YOU (AND NO ONE ELSE) ARE ENTITLED TO INSTALL, USE, OR COPY THE SOFTWARE. Transcender continues to own the Software, and the Software is protected by copyright and other state and federal intellectual property laws. All rights, title, interest, and all copyrights in and to the Software and any copy made by you remain with Transcender. Unauthorized copying of the Software, or failure to comply with this Agreement will result in automatic termination of this license, and will entitle Transcender to pursue other legal remedies. IMPORTANT, under the terms of this Agreement:

> YOU MAY: (a) install and use the Software on only one computer or workstation, and (b) make one (1) copy of the Software for backup purposes only.
>
> YOU MAY NOT: (a) use the Software on more than one computer or workstation; (b) modify, translate, reverse engineer, decompile, decode, decrypt, disassemble, adapt, create a derivative work of, or in any way copy the Software (except one backup); (c) sell, rent, lease, sublicense, or otherwise transfer or distribute the Software to any other person or entity without the prior written consent of Transcender (and any attempt to do so shall be void); (d) allow any other person or entity to use the Software or install the Software on a network of any sort (these require a separate license from Transcender); or (e) remove or cover any proprietary notices, labels, or marks on the Software.

Term. The term of the license granted above shall commence upon the earlier of your opening of the Software, your acceptance of this Agreement or your downloading, installation, copying, or use of the Software; and such license will expire three (3) years thereafter or whenever you discontinue use of the Software, whichever occurs first.

Warranty, Limitation of Remedies and Liability. If applicable, Transcender warrants the media on which the Software is recorded to be free from defects in materials and free from faulty workmanship for a period of thirty (30) days after the date you receive the Software. If, during this 30-day period, the Software media is found to be defective or faulty in workmanship, the media may be returned to Transcender for replacement without charge. YOUR SOLE REMEDY UNDER THIS AGREEMENT SHALL BE THE REPLACEMENT OF DEFECTIVE MEDIA AS SET FORTH ABOVE. EXCEPT AS EXPRESSLY PROVIDED FOR MEDIA ABOVE, TRANSCENDER MAKES NO OTHER OR FURTHER WARRANTIES REGARDING THE SOFTWARE, EITHER EXPRESS OR IMPLIED, INCLUDING THE QUALITY OF THE SOFTWARE, ITS PERFORMANCE, MERCHANTABILITY, OR FITNESS FOR A PARTICULAR PURPOSE. THE SOFTWARE IS LICENSED TO YOU ON AN "AS-IS" BASIS. THE ENTIRE RISK AS TO THE SOFTWARE'S QUALITY AND PERFORMANCE REMAINS SOLELY WITH YOU. TRANSCENDER'S EXCLUSIVE AND MAXIMUM LIABILITY FOR ANY CLAIM BY YOU OR ANYONE CLAIMING THROUGH OR ON BEHALF OF YOU ARISING OUT OF YOUR ORDER, USE, OR INSTALLATION OF THE SOFTWARE SHALL NOT UNDER ANY CIRCUMSTANCE EXCEED THE ACTUAL AMOUNT PAID BY YOU TO TRANSCENDER FOR THE SOFTWARE, AND IN NO EVENT SHALL TRANSCENDER BE LIABLE TO YOU OR ANY PERSON OR ENTITY CLAIMING THROUGH YOU FOR ANY INDIRECT, INCIDENTAL, COLLATERAL, EXEMPLARY, CONSEQUENTIAL, OR SPECIAL DAMAGES OR LOSSES ARISING OUT OF YOUR ORDER, USE, OR INSTALLATION OF THE SOFTWARE OR MEDIA DELIVERED TO YOU OR OUT OF THE WARRANTY, INCLUDING WITHOUT LIMITATION, LOSS OF USE, PROFITS, GOODWILL, OR SAVINGS, OR LOSS OF DATA, FILES, OR PROGRAMS STORED BY THE USER. SOME STATES DO NOT ALLOW THE EXCLUSION OR LIMITATION OF INCIDENTAL OR CONSEQUENTIAL DAMAGES, SO THE ABOVE LIMITATIONS MAY NOT APPLY TO YOU.

Restricted Rights. If the Software is acquired by or for the U.S. Government, then it is provided with Restricted Rights. Use, duplication, or disclosure by the U.S. Government is subject to restrictions as set forth in subparagraph (c)(1)(ii) of The Rights in Technical Data and Computer Software clause at DFARS 252.227-7013, or subparagraphs (c)(1) and (2) of the Commercial Computer Software Act—Restricted Rights at 48 CFR 52.227-19, or clause 18-52.227-86(d) of the NASA Supplement to the FAR, as applicable. The contractor/manufacturer is Transcender Corporation, 242 Louise Avenue, Nashville, Tennessee 37203-1812.

General. This Agreement shall be interpreted and governed by the laws of the State of Tennessee without regard to the conflict of laws provisions of such state, and any legal action relating to this Agreement shall be brought in the appropriate state or federal court located in Davidson County, Tennessee, which venue and jurisdiction you agree to submit to, and the prevailing party in any such action shall be entitled to recover reasonable attorneys' fees and expenses as part of any judgment or award. This Agreement is the entire Agreement between us and supersedes any other communication, advertisement, or understanding with respect to the Software. If any provision of this Agreement is held invalid or unenforceable, the remainder shall continue in full force and effect. All provisions of this Agreement relating to disclaimers of warranties, limitation of liability, remedies, or damages, and Transcender's ownership of the Software and other proprietary rights shall survive any termination of this Agreement.

CHAPTER ONE

INTRODUCTION TO WINDOWS 98

This chapter provides a whirlwind tour of Windows 98, and prepares you for the more detailed chapters that follow. Here you will learn about the development of Windows 98 and the basic features of the Windows 98 environment. You will become familiar with the elements that make up its basic structure, or architecture. You will also learn how Windows 98 compares to other Microsoft operating systems, such as Windows 95 and Windows NT. This chapter also covers the integration of Windows 98 with the Internet Explorer Web browser (which Microsoft presently includes as part of Windows 98).

AFTER READING THIS CHAPTER AND COMPLETING THE EXERCISES YOU WILL BE ABLE TO:

- Describe the various Microsoft operating systems
- Explain the history of the Microsoft Windows operating systems
- Describe the differences between Windows 98 and other Microsoft operating systems
- Describe the Windows 98 architecture
- Describe the key features of Windows 98

Microsoft Operating Systems

An **operating system** (OS) is the software that allows a computer to run applications (such as word-processing and spreadsheet programs), store data, and communicate with other computers via a network. Over the years, Microsoft has developed numerous operating systems to accommodate systems ranging from standalone desktop computers to huge networks spanning multiple locations.

Today, Microsoft offers three major types of operating systems: servers, workstations, and clients. A **server** operating system, such as **Windows NT Server**, includes a broad range of features that allow a networked computer to provide services (such as applications and access to files and printers) to other computers on the network. This type of operating system takes its name from the kind of computer on which it runs—a server, which is a powerful, multi-user personal computer (PC) that is attached to a network and that provides services for other users elsewhere on the network.

A **workstation** operating system, such as **Windows NT Workstation**, has many of the same powerful features as a server operating system, but lacks the collection of network services and applications that would allow it to provide a wide variety of services to other computers on a network. This kind of operating system generally appeals to power users, network administrators, and other heavy-duty network users for whom purchasing a high-end, heavily loaded PC (known as a workstation) makes good economic sense.

Finally, a **client** operating system (such as Windows 98, Windows 95, or even earlier versions of Windows) is aimed at everyday computer users, who only need access to modest applications such as an e-mail program, a word processor, a spreadsheet, and a Web browser. On a network, such machines are known as clients, because they get the files, applications, and other services they need from servers. Such computers are sometimes also referred to as **desktops**, because they fit on top of a desk.

A Brief History of Windows on the Desktop

Like the early mainframes and minicomputers, the first personal computers (or PCs) of the 1980s commonly relied on a text-based operating system called **DOS** (disk operating system). The appearance (or interface) of the DOS screen, with its complex and sometimes arcane text commands, was difficult to master. The Microsoft implementation of DOS was known as **MS-DOS**.

To make computers more approachable, and easier to use, researchers began to develop **graphical user interfaces** (GUIs), which used a pictorial format, rather than text commands. These efforts began to show real promise in the 1970s, well before PCs were first introduced. At that time a group of researchers at the Xerox Palo Alto Research Center (PARC) developed the Alto, the first GUI-based computer. The Alto provided a "What You See Is What You Get" (WYSIWYG) display on the computer's monitor that used graphics rather than text commands. On a visit to PARC in 1979, Steven Jobs (CEO and founder of Apple Computer) recognized the possibilities of a picture-based interface that would be easy for the average consumer to master. Much of the interface of Apple's early computers consists of a GUI interface similar to the one developed at PARC.

Introduction to Windows 98 3

Apple developed the mouse as a point-and-click device that could be used to navigate a GUI interface. The fact that this GUI was so easy to use made Apple computers popular among schools, artists, and designers. Realizing the potential for this type of operating system, Microsoft produced Windows, one of the first DOS-based GUIs for the PC. With Windows, users no longer had to remember cryptic DOS commands such as "dir" and "cd." However, Windows did not make DOS programs obsolete. On the contrary, DOS programs generally ran well in early Windows environments, because DOS still functioned as the primary "behind the scenes" operating system. The Windows interface was designed to look like the top of a desk, with applications and files represented by graphics (or icons) on the desktop. Figure 1-1 illustrates a typical MS-DOS screen, with its black and white text. Figure 1-2 illustrates a typical Windows 98 desktop.

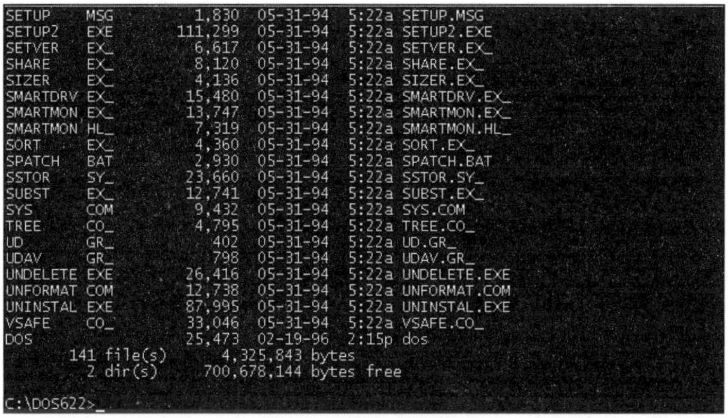

Figure 1-1 MS-DOS screen

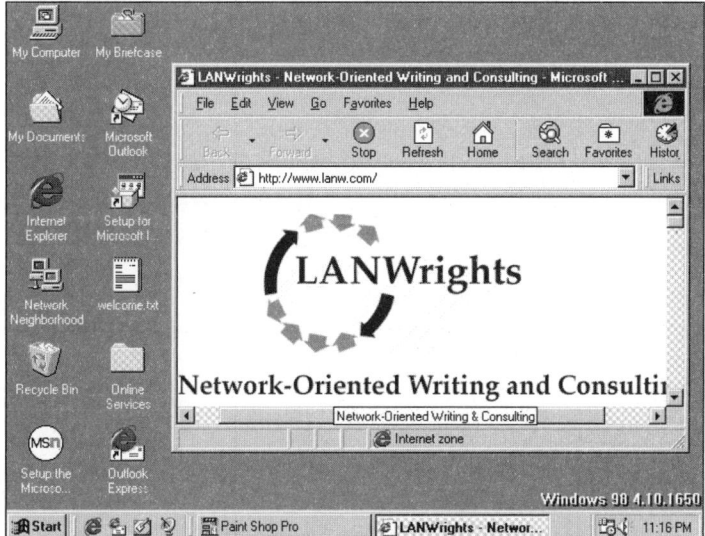

Figure 1-2 Windows desktop

Windows went through three major versions between 1985 and 1990, but it wasn't until the release of Windows 3.0 in 1990 that Windows finally became the default desktop environment for PCs in homes, offices, and corporations. **Windows 3.x**, as its multiple versions are sometimes called, was a 16-bit operating system, which means that it processed elements of computer information (known as bits) in groups of 16.

Windows 95 was released in July 1995 as a major step forward in Windows desktop technology. Many components of Windows 95 were 32-bit, which meant that it processed information in groups of 32. This allowed Windows 95 to perform some tasks, such as printing, faster than Windows 3.x. Even better, the 32-bit components allowed Windows 95 to run multiple applications (a process known as multitasking) more efficiently.

It is important to note, however, that Windows 95 was not entirely a 32-bit operating system. Behind the scenes, Windows 95 continued to incorporate key components of an updated version of DOS, which remained true to its 16-bit heritage. (Although this updated version of MS-DOS is sometimes referred to as "MS-DOS 7.0," it was not a separate operating system like earlier versions of MS-DOS.)

Windows 95 supported a variety of **network protocols** (that is, the formal rules that computers use to communicate with one another). Thus, it could easily be integrated into a variety of networks. In addition, the Windows 95 desktop was easier to use than earlier versions of Windows, in part because of the **Start menu**, which simplified the process of starting applications and opening files, and the **taskbar**, which made it easy to switch among active applications. Better still, Windows 95 took advantage of a new technology called **Plug and Play**, which allows the operating system to automatically "sense" the hardware (such as a printer or modem) installed on a PC.

While Windows 3.1 was designed for entry-level users, Windows NT 3.1 was created for power users. But the lack of commonality between these systems made upgrading from Windows to Windows NT difficult. When developing Windows 95 and Windows NT 4.0, Microsoft focused on giving the two operating systems the same "look and feel." As a result, some programs do work on both systems. But the operating systems still do not share many drivers. In addition, they have different file systems (NTFS and FAT32). Thus, upgrading is still difficult. One of Microsoft's goals for Windows 98 and Windows NT 5.0 is to make sure that they share file systems and as many drivers as possible. More shared elements will make upgrading easier.

Meet Windows 98

Windows 98 is more than merely a new and improved rendition of Windows 95. For one thing, while Windows 95 still uses MS-DOS along with 16-bit elements for certain operations, Windows 98 was designed from top to bottom as a 32-bit operating system. It is no longer necessary to rely on a separate copy of MS-DOS once a computer starts up and begins normal operations.

Because Windows 98 is a 32-bit operating system, it can support more powerful applications and larger numbers of applications simultaneously. Another advantage of Windows 98 has to do with how it interacts with a computer's memory, or random access memory (**RAM**), which is the physical component in which a computer stores data and applications. When a computer does not have enough physical RAM for certain operations, Windows 98 can make use of virtual memory. **Virtual memory** is a software component that acts like an extension to physical RAM and resides in a reserved space on the hard disk.

In addition, Windows 98 makes multitasking (running more than one program simultaneously) easier. It also provides more support for programs that can run multiple activities, or execution threads, simultaneously (a process called **multithreading**).

The multitasking and multithreading capabilities of Windows 98 represent a profound break from Windows 95, which blended older 16-bit technologies with newer 32-bit technologies, thus limiting both memory management and multitasking capabilities. Because Windows 98 does a better job of reclaiming used memory and other system resources when an application or a driver fails, it is more stable and reliable than Windows 95.

Another advantage of Windows 98 is the way it interacts with drivers. A **driver** (or **device driver**) is hardware or software that permits the operating system to communicate with hardware devices such as disk drives, the keyboard, and so forth. Under Windows 3.x and Windows 95, each new version of the operating system required new drivers. Finding exactly the right drivers for a new version of Windows could be difficult and time-consuming. Once Windows NT 5.0 is released, finding the right driver will no longer be an issue, because Microsoft is developing Windows NT 5.0 around nearly the same architecture as the one developed for Windows 98. As a result, hardware and software vendors can create a single driver for their products that will work with both Windows 98 and Windows NT. This, in turn, makes it easier for users to locate and install the drivers they need, because they have fewer options to choose from.

The new 32-bit drivers follow the specifications of the Windows Driver Model (WDM). WDM drivers support the Plug and Play capabilities of Windows 98 by helping the operating system recognize new devices and configuration settings without requiring users to restart (or reboot) their machines (as is currently necessary with Windows 95 and Windows NT 4.0).

The final advantage of Windows 98 relates to the type of file systems it supports. A **file system** is the overall structure or organization an operating system uses to name, store, and organize files. A **file system driver** permits an operating system like Windows 98 to use a file system in order to store and retrieve data and applications. Windows 98 supports the same kind of installable 32-bit file system drivers used by Windows NT, including support for a variety of hard disk and CD-ROM file formats. As in Windows NT, Windows 98 file system drivers also support access to shared file systems and resources on the network, so that a single file system interface can handle local hard disks and CD devices, plus access to shared file systems elsewhere on the network.

In many ways, Windows 98 has more in common with Windows NT than it does with Windows 95 and earlier Windows desktop operating systems. This is by design; some industry sources believe that the code (the vast collection of software components that make up any operating system or large application) for these two versions of Windows will probably converge some time in the next two to four years.

WINDOWS 98 ARCHITECTURE

The general structure of an operating system is known as its architecture. The major building blocks of the Windows 98 architecture are shown in Figure 1-3.

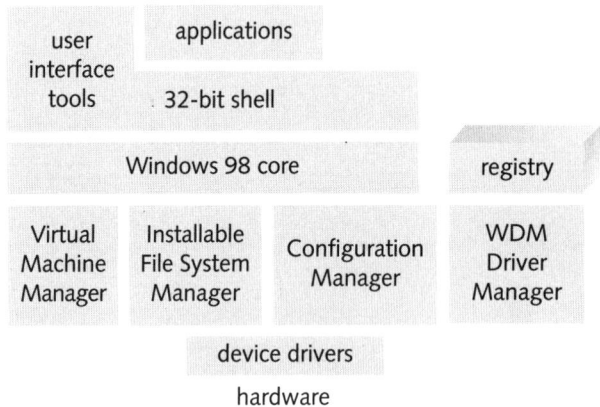

Figure 1-3 Windows 98 architecture

The following list briefly describes each of the elements of the Windows 98 architecture from bottom to top, as they appear in Figure 1-3. You will learn more about these elements in subsequent chapters.

- **Hardware**: At the bottom of the Windows 98 architecture is the hardware, with which the operating system must communicate. The term hardware refers to physical devices, such as a disk drive, tape drive, mouse, keyboard, graphics card, or monitor.

- **Device drivers**: This is software that communicates directly with hardware devices. The device drivers then interact with Windows 98 to provide the operating system with the information it needs about the physical computer. In essence, device drivers function as translators between the hardware and the Windows 98 operating system. Windows 98 can interact with both older 16-bit device drivers and with newer 32-bit drivers that conform to the 32-bit Windows Driver Model (WDM).

- **Virtual Machine Manager**: This component sets up private workspaces, called virtual machines, for all applications that run on a Windows 98 computer. Each virtual machine is assigned its own special names and memory addresses.

- **Installable File System (IFS) Manager**: This component interacts with all the various file system drivers and creates a single file system interface for applications and the operating system to use. The IFS Manager allows Windows 98 to support multiple file systems and network access through a single consistent interface.

- **Configuration Manager:** This component manages all aspects of the computer's general setup, or configuration, including its hardware and software components. It accepts and responds to all messages that originate from both the PC's hardware and from the **BIOS** (the program that actually gets a computer up and running). The Configuration Manager provides the operating system with a single point of access for hardware configuration data and for information from all the device drivers.

- **WDM Driver Manager:** This component allows 32-bit Windows drivers that adhere to the Windows Driver Model (and therefore work with both Windows 98 and Windows NT 5.0) to communicate with the computer's hardware.

- **Windows 98 core:** The heart of the operating system. Controls and coordinates all system activity. The core consists of three layers: user, GDI (graphical device interface), and kernel. Windows 98 incorporates both 16-bit and 32-bit components for each layer. The Windows 98 core routes information from lower-level system components to upper-level ones. Ultimately, it also oversees the storage of data, and manages the applications that access hardware and the network.

- **32-bit shell:** In Figure 1-3, this element is enclosed in an L-shaped box along with the user interface tools, to indicate that they are really two facets of the same component. Together, they constitute the part of the operating system that the user interacts with on a daily basis. (The user interface tools are discussed as a separate item in this list.) The 32-bit shell, in the bottom part of the L, is available only to applications and system services. It provides the necessary underpinnings for key system utilities that users interact with directly—such as **Windows Explorer** (the utility used for file management) and **My Computer** (the utility used for accessing files and applications). Thanks to the 32-bit shell, you can maneuver among files and applications by double-clicking the appropriate icon. The icons are, in turn, part of the user interface tools, which are explained next.

- **User interface tools:** The user interface tools provide a standard set of graphical items, such as browsers, toolbars, taskbars, icons, and so forth, that the user can manipulate in order to interact with utilities, applications, and the operating system. These items are used consistently by all utilities and applications, and give all software running under Windows 98 a common look and feel.

- **Applications:** Applications are the programs that allow the user to create documents, view Web pages, edit graphics, and so on. They can include built-in Windows 98 tools and utilities (such as System Monitor and WordPad), Microsoft programs (such as Word and Excel), and third-party programs (such as WinZip and Corel WordPerfect Suite).

- **Registry:** The Windows 98 Registry is a comprehensive database of information about a Windows 98 system that includes all the application, operating system, and hardware configuration data necessary for the system to function. The Registry also includes system security data, and user-related preferences and settings, and it keeps track of all configuration data while the system is running.

Because of its built-in networking capabilities and support for limited network services (including a so-called Personal Web Server, or PWS), Windows 98 can be used as a stand-alone computer, as a peer in a **peer-to-peer network** (a type of network in which each computer can be a client or a server), and as a client machine on a network.

You will learn more about the Windows 98 architecture throughout the rest of this book.

KEY FEATURES OF WINDOWS 98

The key features of Windows 98 fall into four broad categories:

- Hardware and architectural features
- Power and usability features
- Robustness and manageability features
- Internet integration features

Windows 98 Hardware and Architectural Features

You have already learned about two important hardware and architectural features: Plug and Play and the related Configuration Manager. These features enable Windows 98 to recognize a broad range of hardware interfaces and devices. Several other important hardware and architectural features are described in the following sections.

Win32 Driver Model (WDM)

As you learned earlier in this chapter, the **Win32 Driver Model (WDM)** supports both Windows 98 and Windows NT. (This includes the forthcoming Windows NT 5.0, which is expected to ship some time in mid-1999.) WDM drivers work equally well for Windows 98 and Windows NT 5.0, which greatly simplifies driver development for device vendors. To make this possible, Microsoft has embedded Windows NT code into a special Windows 98 WDM device driver named NTKERN.VXD. This permits new generation drivers to run alongside existing VXDs (virtual device drivers) developed for Windows 95, and allows Windows 98 to maintain support for older 16- and 32-bit device drivers. In other words, Windows 98 provides support for newer technologies, while maintaining backward compatibility with older technologies (and the older drivers that come with them).

FAT32 File System and Conversion Utility

FAT32 is a 32-bit file system. (The term "**FAT**" is an acronym of "file allocation table," which refers to the database that tracks the location of specific files within the file system. You'll learn more about the file allocation table in Chapter 2.) Much like the 32-bit NT File System (NTFS) native to Windows NT, FAT32 supports more advanced features (such as larger drives and improved reliability) than earlier versions of FAT.

To facilitate upgrades from earlier versions of FAT, Windows 98 also includes a graphical FAT32 conversion utility, called Drive Converter. To use Drive Converter, click the Start button, point to Accessories, point to System Tools, and then click Drive Converter (FAT32).

 Note that converting from an earlier version of FAT to FAT32 is a one-way process. You cannot reverse a conversion. In order to return a drive to an earlier FAT format, you would have to back up the files on another drive, reformat the original drive to an earlier FAT format, and then restore those files to the reformatted drive.

Enhanced Power Management

Following the latest industry standard proposed by Microsoft, Intel, and Toshiba, Windows 98 offers built-in support for the Advanced Configuration and Power Interface, known by its acronym as **ACPI**. ACPI defines a standard set of hardware interfaces for managing power on hardware devices, including monitors and other energy-intensive devices on ordinary desktop machines.

Likewise, Windows 98 supports the Advanced Power Management (**APM**) 1.2 extensions to ACPI, which define a thorough set of controls for battery-powered devices such as laptop and notebook computers, including suspend and sleep modes (which permit laptops to suspend operations temporarily or to deactivate themselves more completely), disk spindown (which turns off power to a laptop's hard disk), PC card power management, modem power down, and resume on ring or keyboard/mouse events. All these Windows 98 features help laptops make the most of limited battery resources when operating in undocked modes.

Multiple Displays

Windows 98 can recognize multiple graphics cards in a single PC, and it provides controls to "distribute" the desktop across a variety of multiple display devices. This provides a dramatic increase in workspace for those who can afford to install multiple displays on a single PC, including desktop publishers, Web developers, video and multimedia producers, and others. With multiple displays, the Windows 98 desktop icons, an e-mail package, a Web browser, and other support tools can reside on one display, while the user's primary applications occupy the other.

Next-Generation Hardware

The three years that have passed between the introduction of Windows 95 and that of Windows 98 have witnessed a proliferation of high-speed interfaces and special-purpose PC hardware. Windows 98 incorporates support for this next generation of hardware standards and devices, including the following:

- **Universal serial bus (USB)**: A medium-speed serial bus designed to handle up to 127 peripheral devices through a single port, including mice, keyboards, modems, telephones, scanners, and joysticks.

- **IEEE 1394**: Similar to USB, but designed for higher-bandwidth applications such as multimedia and video. Also known as **firewire**.

- **Accelerated graphics port (AGP)**: A special-purpose graphics interface that speeds up information transfer from Pentium-class processors to graphics adapters.
- **Digital Video Disc (DVD) standard**: A new standard that promises to revolutionize CD-based information delivery with up to 18 GB of data on a single disc and extremely fast access and transfer rates.

Support for PC Card and PCMCIA

A **PC card** is a small adapter interface used for laptop and other portable PC computers. The PC Card standard defines a standard slide-in card interface for laptop interface cards of all kinds. The PC Card standard replaces the Personal Computer Memory Card International Association's (**PCMCIA**'s) earlier definition. In addition to recognizing and handling on-the-fly extraction and insertion of such cards, Windows 98 supports other PC Card handling features, including:

- **PCCard32**: Also known as Cardbus, this feature delivers a 32-bit wide interface for PC Cards and enables such cards to support high-speed video and 100 Mbps network interfaces.
- **3.3 volt operation**: In keeping with manufacturers' desires to lower voltage consumption, this feature supports PC Cards that operate at the same voltage level as modern high-speed CPUs, and lowers power requirements and extends battery life for laptop and other portable computers.
- **Multifunction card support**: Earlier versions of Windows were not completely compatible with multifunction PC Cards, such as combination modem/network interface cards. Windows 98 includes broad support for multifunction cards.

Taken in combination, these capabilities make Windows 98 laptop-friendly and well suited for mobile computing.

Point-to-Point Tunneling Protocol Support

Point-to-Point Tunneling Protocol (PPTP) permits users to make secure connections to private networks through public networks such as the Internet. Windows 98 includes built-in support for PPTP and allows users to employ dial-up networking (explained in Chapter 4) and remote access services (explained in Chapter 7) to connect to private networks using any **Internet Service Provider (ISP)**. (An ISP is an organization that maintains a constant presence on the Internet, and divides up and resells available Internet connections at different speeds to customers who seek to connect to the Internet at large.) Via such connections, users can access e-mail, printers, and other resources, just as if they were attached locally to the network.

ActiveMovie

Media-streaming is a technology for delivering data across a network. **ActiveMovie** is the media-streaming component of Windows 98. It permits a computer to play back the front end of an incoming file even while the remainder of the file may be en route from a server elsewhere on the network. ActiveMovie promises to deliver high-quality multimedia video to the desktop, and should allow users to access video conferencing, training materials, and entertainment materials across the network. ActiveMovie supports the majority of available multimedia data formats as well.

POWER AND USABILITY

In addition to its hardware and architecture features, Windows 98 sports a user interface that is designed to be easier to use than the Windows 95 interface. It puts more power at the user's fingertips, providing instant access to resources, visual controls, and system capabilities. Some of the most useful elements in this category are covered in the following sections.

Integrated Internet Shell

The Integrated Internet Shell may be among the most useful capabilities included with Windows 98. However, this capability relies on Microsoft's bundling of Internet Explorer 4.0 with Windows 98, which has occasioned a great deal of legal maneuvering of late. Such considerations aside, the Internet shell makes access to Internet resources part and parcel of the standard Windows 98 shell. It allows you to use either the My Computer interface or the Explorer utilities to access local, networked, and Internet resources. In other words, you can use a single interface to view information on the local network, on an intranet, or on the Internet.

Taskbars and Toolbars

The Windows 98 taskbar shows icons for all currently active applications. Windows 98 also provides a collection of predefined toolbars that include network addresses, Internet links, desktop elements, and so-called "Quick Launch" selections as default elements on the desktop. Windows 98 also makes it possible to create and use customized toolbars for all kinds of specialized activities and to aggregate taskbars and toolbars more or less at will. This translates into a desktop that's easy to configure and lay out so that it meets your needs precisely, while keeping important resources no more than a single mouse click away.

The Windows Scripting Host

Windows 98 includes built-in support for scripts, which allow you to automate routine or repetitive tasks consisting of a mixture of keyboard input, desktop navigation, and mouse clicks. Among other things, you can create scripts for creating shortcuts, connecting to network servers or mapping shared drives, and accessing printers. The **Windows Scripting Host (WSH)** handles Visual Basic and Java scripts. WSH also allows third parties to build ActiveX scripting engines that should ultimately support other scripting languages as well.

Display Settings and Controls

In Windows 98, screen resolution and color depth changes can be configured to take immediate effect. Windows 98 also allows for a greater variety of graphics adapter settings than does Windows 95. Thanks to Plug and Play, monitors (and other display devices) can configure themselves automatically.

Supercharged Setup Program

Windows 98 recognizes and preserves settings (such as desktop layout settings) from previous Windows 95 installations. Because Windows 98 can "read" existing values during the setup process, it can skip steps in which user input might otherwise be necessary. Windows 98 also easily incorporates older hardware that fails to conform to Plug and Play standards. In addition, Windows 98 setup permits you to back up system files on your hard disk so that Windows 98 can be uninstalled and Windows 95 reinstated. Finally, Windows 98 includes an option to generate an **Emergency Startup Disk** (**ESD**) as part of the setup process. You can use the ESD to recover from many, if not all, hard disk boot failures in which the floppy drive remains bootable.

Start Menu Enhancements

The Start Menu Organizer Wizard helps you organize and control the contents of the Start Menu. For example, you can create menu options simply by dragging an **.exe** file (an executable file that launches a program) or desktop icon onto any level of the Start Menu.

Dial-Up Networking (DUN)

The **Dial-Up Networking (DUN)** feature permits you to combine two or more modems, ISDN (Integrated Services Digital Network) devices, or other dial-up devices of the same type, and aggregate their bandwidth to achieve faster communications. (An **ISDN** connection provides a digital alternative to standard voice telephone connections. ISDN is widely available in North America and Europe, and supports one or two 64-kbps channels for data or voice connections.)

In addition, Windows 98 DUN also supports **Dial-Up Scripting**, which helps automate connecting to bulletin boards or other online services. The DUN Wizard also offers a smart interface that can handle most of the details involved when setting up and using dial-up connections for the first time. DUN is explained in detail in Chapter 6.

Online Services Folder

The default Windows 98 desktop includes a desktop folder that contains links to the most popular online service providers, ready to be configured and used immediately. At the time of this writing, the providers represented include the Microsoft Network (MSN), America Online (AOL), AT&T WorldNet, CompuServe, and Prodigy. This makes it easy to establish Internet access, and provides a broad range of options to the average user.

ROBUSTNESS AND RELIABILITY

In the section on the Windows 98 architecture, you learned about some features that contribute to the reliability of Windows 98—specifically, the absence of a DOS kernel running in the background, improved virtual memory and resource management, and the virtual machine architecture. The following sections describe some other Windows 98 features that add to the system's robustness and reliability.

Internet System Update

The **Windows Update** option, at the top of the Start menu, launches Internet Explorer under a set of controls that perform an inventory of your system, compare what they find to the latest set of official updates on the Microsoft Web site, and present you with a menu of possible choices to bring your system as up to date as possible. Individual users can thereby update their systems on a daily basis. Perhaps more importantly, system administrators can monitor available updates and schedule regular deployments to workstations across the network as needed.

System File Checker

System File Checker is a utility that checks the integrity and consistency of Windows 98 system files, including files that end with extensions such as:

- **.dll**: Used for Microsoft Windows executable code modules
- **.com**: Used for executable command files
- **.vxd**: Used for special virtual device drivers
- **.drv**: Used for 32-bit device drivers
- **.ocx**: Used for ActiveX controls
- **.inf**: Used for files that contain hardware or device driver configuration or installation information
- **.hlp**: Used for help system files

System File Checker can restore original versions of system files that have changed, either by using the original Windows 98 installation CD or by downloading versions of newer files from the Microsoft Web site. System File Checker appears to be a valuable system integrity tool and should make it easy to roll back from unwanted updates or other system changes. To start System File Checker, click the Start menu, point to Programs, point to Accessories, point to System Tools, and then click System File Checker.

Microsoft System Information

The **Microsoft System Information** (**MSI**) utility presents information gleaned from the Configuration Manager and the Windows 98 Registry, thus providing a comprehensive overview of hardware and software installed on a particular Windows 98 PC. MSI not only documents hardware configuration information, but also reports on applications that are loaded and on tasks that are running at any given moment. This appears to be an extremely useful system configuration and operations monitoring tool. To start MSI, click the Start menu, point to Programs, point to Accessories, point to System Tools, and then click Microsoft System Information.

System Monitor

System Monitor can track and display usage information about dial-up adapters, disk caches, the file system, the operating system kernel, the memory manager, and the Microsoft Network client. While it's by no means as comprehensive as the Windows NT Performance Monitor, System Monitor promises to be a useful monitoring and troubleshooting tool for desktop machines.

Dr. Watson

Dr. Watson is a utility that captures information about application faults and errors. For developers, Dr. Watson is an essential debugging tool; for ordinary administrators or users it comes in most handy when gathering data during the troubleshooting process. While its output in Windows 98 requires detailed programming knowledge to decipher, Dr. Watson provides some useful analysis and interpretation of application faults.

Windows 98 Backup

Unlike Windows 95 and earlier versions of Windows, Windows 98 includes a simple but effective Backup utility. The Windows 98 implementation supports a number of backup formats, and is covered thoroughly in Chapter 11. If you use Windows 98 on a standalone PC, the built-in Backup utility should suffice for most needs, but for those on a network or with larger disk drives, commercial backup software is probably worth further investigation.

Disk Optimization Tools

The disk optimization tools included with Windows 98 simplify the process of disk maintenance. **ScanDisk** examines directory and file structures for errors and is capable of repairing any minor errors it finds. Scandisk can repair both FAT and FAT32 partitions. You can use the Disk Defragmentation tool to address the problem of large files that, over time, have been divided into small pieces, scattered in various places on a disk. The Disk Defragmentation tool takes files scattered across multiple locations on a hard disk and reassembles them in a single location. These disk optimization tools can be accessed via the Tools tab of the Properties dialog box, as explained in Chapter 8. The Backup program (discussed in the previous section) is also accessed via the Tools tab.

This combination of disk checking, backup, and defragmentation tools is well organized on the Tools tab, and should be adequate for most users' needs. You can use the Windows Tune-Up Wizard (explained in the next section), to automate the process of disk optimization. You will learn more about the disk optimization tools in Chapter 8.

Windows Tune-Up Wizard

The Windows Tune-Up Wizard guides you through a series of questions that determine the optimization your system requires. It also permits you to schedule weekly automated tune-ups. In addition, you can use the Tune-Up Wizard to schedule ScanDisk and Disk Defragmenter sessions. Finally, the Tune-Up Wizard can clean up unwanted or unnecessary files on its own.

INCREASED INTERNET INTEGRATION

In the sections that follow, you will learn about the advanced browsing and information gathering capabilities of Windows 98, its Internet communication tools, and its ability to customize and schedule regular information deliveries from selected Internet or intranet sites.

Advanced Internet Browsing

Microsoft's inclusion of Internet Explorer (IE) 4.0 with Windows 98 makes it easy to browse the Web for all kinds of resources. Advanced features found in IE 4.0 include the following:

- Product Update, which delivers automatic updates for Internet Explorer and helps keep this important application current and up to date

- Advanced browser controls such as AutoComplete (which can automatically complete **URLs**, or web page addresses, for you), Web searching tools, multilevel folder organization and categorization for Favorites (URLs saved as bookmarks), navigation histories on Forward and Back buttons, and page-printing facilities

- Support for all major Internet and Web standards, including HTML, Java, ActiveX, JavaScript, and Visual Basic, plus major security standards such as the Secure Sockets Layer (SSL) and SOCKS (for use of Windows Sockets applications through a firewall or proxy server, as explained in Chapter 4)

- Advanced Web technologies that include Dynamic HTML, XML, and other code speedups

Taken together, these capabilities make IE 4.0 one of the most powerful and user-friendly browsers around. IE 4.0 is covered in greater detail in Chapter 13.

Internet Communication Tools

In addition to IE 4.0, Windows 98 includes other tools designed to improve communications online:

- Microsoft Outlook Express, which supports both e-mail and newsgroup access through a single, simple user interface

- Microsoft NetMeeting, which provides an Internet conferencing tool that can handle audio, data, or video conferences

- Microsoft NetShow, which delivers live or recorded broadcasts across the Internet or an intranet; its streaming data capabilities permit users to view information even while downloads are still underway, without slowing overall network behavior

- Microsoft FrontPage Express, which provides a visual HTML editor based on the full-blown standalone FrontPage 98 HTML editor and publication tool

- Personal Web Server and an accompanying Web Publishing Wizard, which permit any Windows 98 user to publish limited-access Web pages for intranet or Internet access

In short, there's a great deal more to the Internet communications capabilities of Windows 98 than just Web browsing, including content creation and delivery and client software for most of the popular Internet-based services and information resources. The services side of this capability is covered in Chapter 7, while other Internet connectivity options are covered in Chapters 1 and 2.

Personalized Information Delivery

To help with the problem of information overload, Window 98 also provides a tool to help you select and schedule downloads of the information you wish to track regularly. This includes a built-in "channel selector" that appears on the Windows 98 desktop to help you select, position, and manage those data channels that you wish to make active on your desktop. It also includes a series of notification settings on IE 4.0 Favorites that will notify you whenever a site changes, and that can automatically download new versions of designated pages.

CHAPTER SUMMARY

- An operating system (OS) is the software that allows a computer to run applications, store data, and communicate with other computers via a network. Microsoft offers three major types of operating systems: those for servers (such as Windows NT Server), workstations (such as Windows NT Workstation), and clients (such as Windows 98). A client operating system is aimed at everyday computer users. Client computers get the files, applications, and other services they need from servers. Windows 98 has its roots in the first personal computers (or PCs) of the 1980s, which relied on the text-based operating system called MS-DOS (Microsoft Disk Operating System). To make computers more approachable, and easier to use, researchers developed graphical user interfaces (GUIs), which use a pictorial format, rather than text commands. Microsoft eventually introduced the Windows operating system as one of the first DOS-based GUIs for the PC. It soon became the standard desktop operating system for PCs. Then, in July 1995, a much-improved version, called Windows 95, was released.

- Many components of Windows 95 were 32-bit, which meant that it processed information in groups of 32. This allowed Windows 95 to perform some tasks, such as printing, faster than earlier 16-bit versions of Windows. Also, Windows 95 could be easily integrated into a variety of networks. In addition, Windows 95 took advantage of a new technology called Plug and Play, which allows the operating system to automatically "sense" the hardware (such as a printer or modem) installed on a PC. Windows 98 is more than merely a new and improved rendition of Windows 95. For one thing, Windows 98 was designed from top to bottom as a 32-bit operating system, which means it can support more powerful applications, and larger numbers of applications simultaneously. In addition, Windows 98 makes multitasking and multithreading easier. Windows 98 also makes it easy for users to find the right driver for their hardware, because all new 32-bit drivers follow the specifications of the Windows Driver Model (WDM). WDM drivers support the Plug and Play capabilities of Windows 98 by helping the operating system recognize new devices and configuration settings without requiring users to restart their machines. The final advantage of Windows 98 is that it supports the same kind of installable 32-bit file system drivers used by Windows NT, which includes support for a variety of hard disk and CD-ROM file formats.

- The general structure of an operating system is known as its architecture. At the bottom of the Windows 98 architecture is the computer's hardware, with which the operating system must communicate. The device drivers are the software that conveys information between the hardware and the operating system. The Virtual Machine Manager sets up private workspaces, called virtual machines, for all applications that run on a Windows 98 computer. The Installable File System (IFS) Manager interacts with all the various file system drivers and creates a single file system interface for applications and the operating system to use. The Configuration Manager manages all aspects of the computer's general setup, or configuration, including its hardware and software components. The WDM Driver Manager allows 32-bit Windows drivers that adhere to the Windows Driver Model to communicate with the computer's hardware. The Windows 98 core controls and coordinates all system activity.

- Higher up in the architecture, the 32-bit shell and the user interface tools make up the part of operating system that the user interacts with on a daily basis. The applications are the programs that allow the user to create documents, view Web pages, edit graphics, and so on. Finally, the Windows 98 Registry is a comprehensive database of information about a Windows 98 system that includes all the application, operating system, and hardware configuration data necessary for the system to function.

- The key features of Windows 98 fall into four broad categories: hardware and architectural features, power and usability features, reliability and manageability features, and Internet integration features. The hardware and architectural features include a FAT32 file system conversion utility and enhanced power management. The power and usability features include the Windows Scripting Host and the Setup program. The reliability and manageability features include the Internet System Update and the System File Checker. Finally, the Internet integration features include advanced Internet browsing and personalized information delivery.

KEY TERMS

- **32-bit shell** — The underpinnings for the user interface in the Windows 98 environment, this software provides a default user interface that appears on the desktop after system bootup.

- **ACPI (Advanced Configuration and Power Interface)** — An extended and enhanced version of the APM originally defined by Intel and Microsoft to improve battery life and power management for laptops and other portable computing devices.

- **Active Desktop** — A special view of the Windows 98 desktop that integrates Internet and network resources with purely local resources, and provides single-click access to all resources within its purview.

- **ActiveMovie** — The media-streaming component of Windows 98. It permits a computer to play back the front end of an incoming file even while the remainder of the file may be en route from a server elsewhere on the network.
- **ActiveX** — Microsoft standards that support interactive content on the Internet. With the Windows Scripting Host, ActiveX can support interactive Web content.
- **AGP (accelerated graphics port)** — An Intel-defined specification designed to speed up communications between Pentium processors and the graphics processors usually found on graphics adapter cards, or other specialized image-processing devices.
- **APM (Advanced Power Management)** — A predecessor to the ACPI, the APM represented an initial effort from Microsoft and computer manufacturers to define power-conserving and management interfaces for desktop and portable computers.
- **applications** — The programs that allow the user to create documents, view Web pages, edit graphics, and so on.
- **BIOS (basic input/output system)** — The software that defines the most basic set of PC system capabilities that are used during system startup to access a hard drive or floppy disk to load a master boot record, and then to load the operating system that actually makes the computer work. Even after bootup, BIOS routines play a key role in handling basic system input and display behavior.
- **client** — A desktop or portable computer used to access network resources.
- **.com** — A common Windows or DOS file extension that indicates an executable command file.
- **Configuration Manager** — The Windows 98 architectural component that manages all aspects of the computer's general setup, or configuration, including its hardware and software components.
- **desktop** — A computer that fits on top of a desk and is used to conduct everyday work. Also used to refer to the main Windows interface, which looks like the top of a desk.
- **device driver** — A special operating system software component that mediates information exchange between a computer and some attached device, be it a graphics or network adapter; a keyboard, mouse, or other input device; or a CRT, LCD, or some other display device.
- **Dial-Up Scripting** — The scripting language supported by Microsoft Dial-Up Networking (DUN), which is used to automate the process of establishing a connection when dialing into a bulletin board, e-mail system, or some other communication provider's online services.
- **Digital Video Disc (DVD) standard** — A new standard that promises to revolutionize CD-based information delivery with up to 18 GB of data on a single disc and extremely fast access and transfer rates.

- **.dll (dynamic link library)** — A Microsoft Windows executable code module that is loaded on demand and is often used to define common or shared system functionality in Windows runtime environments.
- **DOS (disk operating system)** — A generic name for a class of 16-bit PC operating systems made popular by IBM's adoption of Microsoft DOS (*see also* MS-DOS) in the early 1980s.
- **driver** — *See* device driver.
- **.drv** — A common Windows NT or Windows 98 file extension that indicates a 32-bit device driver.
- **Dr. Watson** — A Windows 98 utility that captures information about application faults and errors.
- **Dial-Up Networking (DUN)** — Microsoft's collection of telephony, modem-handling, and remote communications services, designed to make it easy for users to access and interact with online information providers in the Windows 95, Windows 98, and Windows NT operating systems.
- **Emergency Startup Disk (ESD)** — A Windows 98 installation feature that permits users to create a special-purpose boot floppy disk that can be used to start up the computer should the boot information on the hard disk become damaged or otherwise corrupted.
- **.exe** — A common Windows or DOS file extension for a binary executable file, most often a program of some kind.
- **FAT (file allocation table)** — A table of file names, directory entries, and disk location information known as a file allocation table gives the FAT file system its name, as well as describing its organization. This file system has been part of Microsoft operating systems since the first implementation of DOS in the 1980s.
- **FAT32 (32-bit FAT)** — A 32-bit version of the FAT file system.
- **file system** — The overall structure or organization an operating system uses to name, store, and organize files. A file system is a physical disk structure that permits a computer operating system to allocate hard disk storage, to associate storage regions with named entities called files and folders or directories, and to read and write such entities upon user or application demand.
- **file system driver** — The software component that permits an operating system like Windows 98 to use a file system in order to store and retrieve data and applications.
- **FireWire** — *See* IEEE 1394.
- **graphical user interface (GUI)** — Any of a number of windows-oriented user interfaces, commonly associated with modern operating systems such as the Macintosh Operating System (MacOS) and Microsoft Windows. GUI may also be used more generically to describe any program that uses a graphical user interface, irrespective of the operating system involved.

- **hardware** — The physical devices, such as a disk drive, tape drive, mouse, keyboard, graphics card, or monitor, with which the operating system must communicate. The hardware is at the bottom of the Windows 98 architecture.

- **.hlp** — A common Windows file extension for a help system file.

- **IEEE 1394** — Also known as firewire. An official standard for a 100 Mbps serial interface specified by the Institute of Electrical and Electronics Engineers (IEEE). Supports 100 Mbps data rates, and can handle cables up to 4.5 meters (approximately 15 feet). This serial interface was designed with high-end consumer electronics, video, and networking requirements in mind.

- **.inf** — A common Windows file extension for a file that contains hardware or device driver configuration or installation information.

- **.ini** — A common Windows 3.x or Windows 95 file extension that indicates a file that contains startup or initialization settings for hardware or software components on a PC.

- **Installable File System (IFS) Manager** — The Windows 98 architectural component that interacts with the various file system drivers and creates a single file system interface for applications and the operating system to use. The IFS Manager allows Windows 98 to support multiple file systems and network access through a single consistent interface.

- **Internet service provider (ISP)** — An organization that maintains a constant presence on the Internet, and divides up and resells available Internet connections at different speeds to customers who seek to connect through their point of Internet presence to the Internet at large.

- **ISDN (Integrated Services Digital Network)** — A digital alternative to standard voice telephone connections, ISDN is widely available in North America and Europe, and supports one or two or 64-kbps channels for data or voice connections.

- **kernel** — *See* Windows 98 core.

- **Microsoft System Information (MSI)** — A utility that presents information gleaned from the Configuration Manager and the Windows 98 Registry, thus providing a comprehensive overview of hardware and software installed on a particular Windows 98 PC.

- **MS-DOS** — The Microsoft version of the DOS operating system (*see* DOS).

- **multitasking** — The ability to run more than one program at the same time.

- **multithreading** — The ability of a computer's operating system and hardware to execute multiple pieces of code (or threads) from a single application simultaneously; this is what permits applications like MS Word to manage text input on the display while performing spelling or grammar checks in the background.

- **My Computer** — One of two primary resource navigation tools that are included in the default shell for Windows 95, Windows 98, and Windows NT.

- **network protocols** — The rules that govern message formats and sequences that computers use to communicate with one another over a network. Examples of network protocols include NetBEUI and TCP/IP, which will be discussed in later chapters.

- **.ocx** — A common Windows 95, Windows 98, and Windows NT file extension that designates a file that contains one or more ActiveX controls.
- **operating system (OS)** — Software that makes it possible for a computer to run applications, store data, and communicate across a network.
- **PC card** — A common, small adapter interface used for laptop and other portable PCs.
- **PCMCIA (Personal Computer Memory Card International Association)** — The original name of the industry consortium that developed the small adapter interface for laptop and other portable PCs known as the PC Card.
- **peer-to-peer network** — A type of networking in which each computer can be a client to other computers, and act as a server as well.
- **Plug and Play** — A set of specifications that permits hardware and system components to identify themselves during installation and configuration, and that allows software to sense addition and removal of system components on the fly.
- **Point-to-Point Tunneling Protocol (PPTP)** — PPTP provides a secure, encrypted communications technique that permits the Internet and other public communications carriers to transport information between remote clients and private networks without fear of interception and decoding of traffic across insecure links.
- **RAM (random access memory)** — RAM provides the working storage that computers use to manipulate programs and data while they're executing; in many ways, the amount of RAM on a PC, also known as physical memory, helps to determine its overall performance and multitasking capabilities.
- **Registry** — The core Windows 98 repository for all system, software, and hardware configuration information, and more. The Windows 98 Registry is covered in detail in Chapter 3.
- **ScanDisk** — A management utility that scans hard disks to check FAT integrity, verify folder/directory structures, and check files to ensure their proper sequence and construction.
- **server** — A networked computer that responds to client requests for network resources.
- **Start menu** — The main menu, which appears when you click the Start button in the lower-left corner of the Windows 95, Windows 98, or Windows NT display. Applications, documents, services, and other system management activities may be launched at will from this menu.
- **System File Checker** — A utility that checks the integrity and consistency of the Windows 98 system files, including files that end with extensions such as .dll, .com, .vxd, .drv, .ocx, .inf, and .hlp.
- **System Monitor** — A Windows 98 utility that can track and display usage information about dial-up adapters, disk caches, the file system, the operating system kernel, the memory manager, and the Microsoft Network client.

- **taskbar** — A special desktop construct within Windows 98 that appears within the Start menu frame at the bottom of the display, and provides an immediate method to toggle among active applications (the Alt-Tab key combination represents an equivalent keyboard shortcut).

- **User interface tools** — The part of the 32-bit shell with which the user interacts. Provides a standard set of graphical items, such as browsers, toolbars, taskbars, icons, and so forth, that the user can manipulate in order to interact with utilities, applications, and the operating system. These items are used consistently by all utilities and applications, and give all software running under Windows 98 a common look and feel.

- **universal serial bus (USB)** — A medium-speed serial bus designed to handle up to 127 peripheral devices through a single port, including mice, keyboards, modems, telephones, scanners, and joysticks.

- **URL (Uniform Resource Locator)** — A special naming convention used to identify transport protocols and information resources available through a Web browser. Sometimes referred to as a Web page address.

- **USB** — *See* Universal serial bus.

- **Virtual Machine Manager** — The Windows 98 architectural component that sets up private workspaces, called virtual machines, for all applications that run on a Windows 98 computer.

- **virtual memory** — A software component that acts like an extension to physical RAM and resides in a reserved space on the hard disk. Virtual memory is a hallmark of most modern operating systems, including Windows 95, Windows 98, and Windows NT.

- **.vxd** — A common Windows 95, Windows 98, and Windows NT file extension that indicates a special virtual device driver.

- **Windows Driver Model (WDM)** — A common 32-bit device driver architecture that permits vendors to write a single device driver that will work both for Windows 98 and Windows NT 5.0 without alteration. Also referred to as Win32 Driver Model.

- **WDM Driver Manager** — The Windows 98 architectural component that allows 32-bit Windows drivers that adhere to the Windows Driver Model (and therefore work with both Windows 98 and Windows NT) to communicate with the computer's hardware.

- **Windows 3.x** — A generic way to refer to various implementations of Windows version 3, including Windows 3.0, Windows 3.1, Windows 3.11, and Windows for Workgroups.

- **Windows 98** — The latest iteration of Microsoft's most popular desktop operating system, and the primary focus of this book.

- **Windows 98 core** — The heart of the operating system; controls and coordinates all system activity. Consists of user, GDI, and kernel layers.

- **Windows Explorer** — One of two primary desktop and resource navigation tools supplied as part and parcel of the 32-bit shell in Windows 95, Windows 98, and Windows NT.

- **Windows NT Server** — The highest-powered version of Windows NT currently available from Microsoft. Includes a broad range of network services and applications that make it uniquely well-suited to deliver file, print, and application services to network clients of many kinds.

- **Windows NT Workstation** — The most powerful desktop operating system currently available from Microsoft. Windows NT Workstation shares a common fundamental architecture with Windows NT Server, but lacks the collection of network services and applications that would make it able to function as a general-purpose network server on its own (Windows NT Workstation is also subject to a maximum of 10 simultaneous logged-in users, while Windows NT Server is subject to no such limitation, except for user licensing considerations).

- **Windows Scripting Host (WSH)** — A scripting facility included with Windows 98. WSH makes it possible to automate and schedule routine tasks of all kinds, including command lines sequences, keystrokes, and mouse events.

- **Windows Update** — The automatic, Internet-based software update utility included as a part of the Windows 98 operating system. Windows Update makes it possible to keep Windows 98 current at all times with only minimal effort.

- **workstation** — A synonym for user computer. The term "workstation" also carries more of a connotation of power and capability than does the term "client." Historically, hardware vendors differentiated between workstation computers and personal computers, to emphasize a difference in speed, power, and cost. Today, this distinction is almost meaningless.

REVIEW QUESTIONS

1. Windows 98 supports backward compatibility with DOS and older Windows applications. True or False?

2. Windows 98 uses a combination of physical RAM and disk space for its memory. What is this kind of memory system called?
   a. flat memory model
   b. virtual memory
   c. private memory
   d. computer memory

3. Which of the following characteristics best describes the Windows 98 core components?
   a. remain resident in memory at all times, and control and coordinate system activity
   b. run only at startup, to load the entire operating system
   c. run only when needed, when an active process blocks for I/O, or an interrupt occurs
   d. none of the above

4. Windows 98 supports only cooperative multitasking. True or False?
5. Windows 98 supports only the FAT32 file system. True or False?
6. Windows 98 works well in heterogeneous networking environments. True or False?
7. Which of the following reliability features appear in Windows 98? (Choose all correct answers.)
    a. robust multitasking
    b. ScanDisk checks the hard disk for problems each time the system boots.
    c. better ability to reuse system resources freed by failed applications
    d. A built-in backup utility makes it easier to capture and restore a system's contents.
8. Of the following, which describes Plug and Play? (Choose all correct answers.)
    a. a technique for adding and removing system hardware
    b. a standard that permits system components to be self-describing for easy installation and configuration
    c. a technology to accommodate any kind of system hardware components without human intervention
    d. a standard device registration technology that automatically senses when components are added to or removed from a system
9. Which of the following best describes the characteristics of the Windows Driver Model?
    a. a standard driver architecture for all versions of Windows
    b. a 32-bit driver specification that's equally compatible with Windows NT 5.0 and Windows 98
    c. a set of hardware interface specifications that support automatic registration of hardware with Windows 98
    d. a revised set of driver software that makes older devices compatible with Plug and Play
10. Of the following capabilities, which are provided when using an installable file system on Windows 98? (Choose all correct answers.)
    a. support for hard disk file systems
    b. network redirectors for access to shared resources
    c. CD-ROM access
    d. transparent access to modems and other communications devices
11. Of the following file extensions, which is the most likely to identify a Windows 98 virtual device driver?
    a. .drv
    b. .inf
    c. .ocx
    d. .vxd

12. The two file systems supported in Windows 98 are FAT and _____.
13. Windows 98 runs on top of DOS. True or False?
14. If a file system is converted from FAT to FAT32, how can you restore that file system to its original format?
    a. use the Drive Converter utility to switch from FAT32 back to FAT
    b. reformat the partition in FAT format; the files will automatically be converted
    c. back up the FAT32 partition to another drive, reformat to FAT, then recopy the files to the reformatted partition
    d. none of the above
15. Windows 98 can handle multiple graphics displays, provided the right hardware is available and properly configured. True or False?
16. Windows 98 includes support for which of the following next-generation device standards or formats? (Choose all correct answers.)
    a. USB
    b. firewire
    c. AGP
    d. SMDS
17. Which of the following PC Card capabilities appear in Windows 98?
    a. PCCard32
    b. 2.2 volt operation
    c. improved multifunction card support
    d. PC Card IV support
18. Of the following capabilities, which does the Point-to-Point Tunneling Protocol enable? (Choose all correct answers.)
    a. remote access to corporate networks
    b. access to any TCP/IP-based network resource
    c. secure, encrypted communications across a public communications carrier for private client/server communications
    d. none of the above
19. Of the following scripting languages, which does the Windows Scripting Host currently support? (Choose all correct answers.)
    a. TCL
    b. Perl
    c. Java
    d. Visual Basic
20. Windows 98 includes a built-in system update facility that downloads operating system updates directly from the Internet. True or False?

HANDS-ON PROJECTS

The system requirements for the hands-on projects in the chapter are all the same. You must have access to a PC that is either attached to a network, or that has a modem attached, with Windows 98 already installed. For Project 1-1, a working link to the Internet must be available to permit use of the Windows Update utility.

PROJECT 1-1

In this project you will examine the Internet system update feature. This project provides steps for using a Microsoft Web page. Keep in mind that Web pages change frequently, and as a result the steps described in this project may not work exactly as described. In any case, you should be able to follow the instructions on the Web page to update your system.

1. Click the **Start** button on the taskbar, and then click **Windows Update**. The Welcome to Windows Update Web page opens.
2. If you are on a computer with a modem not currently connected to the Internet, a Dial-up connection dialog box appears. Click **Connect** to connect your computer to the Internet. You will learn how to set up Internet connections in Chapter 6.
3. Click **Product Update**.
4. In the left-hand pane, click **Critical Updates**, then, if necessary, click **Yes** in the Security Warning dialog box to accept content from Microsoft.
5. In the Windows Update dialog box, click **Yes**.
6. In the left-hand pane, click **Picks of the Month**. Review the listing in the right-hand pane. Repeat with Recommended Updates and Additional Features.
7. In the left-hand pane, click **Device Drivers**. This opens up the Windows Update dialog box.
8. Click **OK** to have the Windows update Web site look through your computer for current Windows 98 drivers. The results appear in a new Internet Explorer window.
9. Press **Alt+Tab** to return to the first Internet Explorer window.
10. In the left-hand pane, click **Member Services**.
11. Click **Technical Support** to review lists of frequently asked questions (FAQs) or information about common problems and solutions related to Windows 98.
12. Click **Site Feedback** to send e-mail to Microsoft about the update pages and their contents.

Introduction to Windows 98   27

PROJECT 1-2

In this project you will examine the Windows 98 disk optimization tools.

1. Click the **Start** button on the taskbar, click **Programs**, and then click **Windows Explorer**. The Windows Explorer window opens. As you will learn in Chapter 8, you can use Windows Explorer to gain access to the Windows 98 disk optimization tools. The left-hand pane displays all the system resources visible through Windows Explorer, with hard drives, folders, and other items represented by icons. The right-hand pane displays the contents of whatever item is selected in the left-hand pane.

2. In the left-hand pane, click on a hard drive icon to select it, as shown in Figure 1-4.

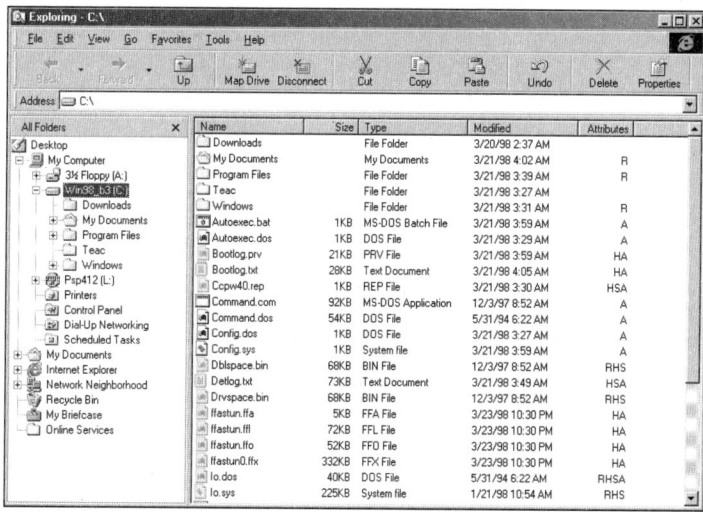

Figure 1-4   Selecting a hard drive in Windows Explorer

3. Click **File** on the menu bar, and then click **Properties**. The Properties dialog box opens.
4. If necessary, click the General tab. The General tab shows the proportions of used and unused space on the drive, as in Figure 1-5.

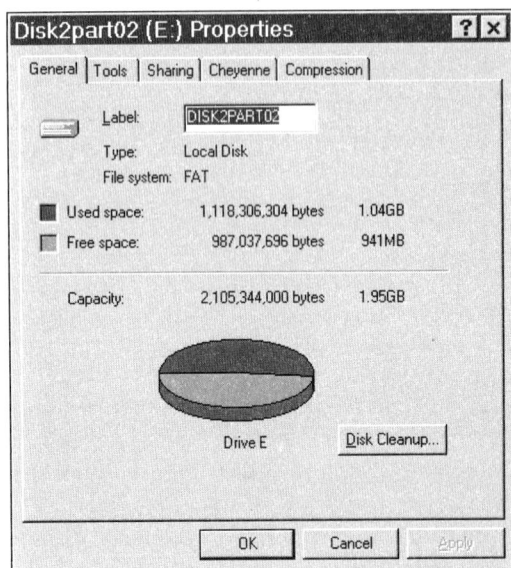

Figure 1-5 General tab of the Properties dialog box

5. Click the **Tools** tab. Your dialog box should now look similar to Figure 1-6. This tab allows you to check a hard drive for errors (using the Check Now button), make backup copies of files (using the Backup Now button), and take files scattered across multiple locations on a hard disk and reassemble them in a single location (using the Defragment Now button).

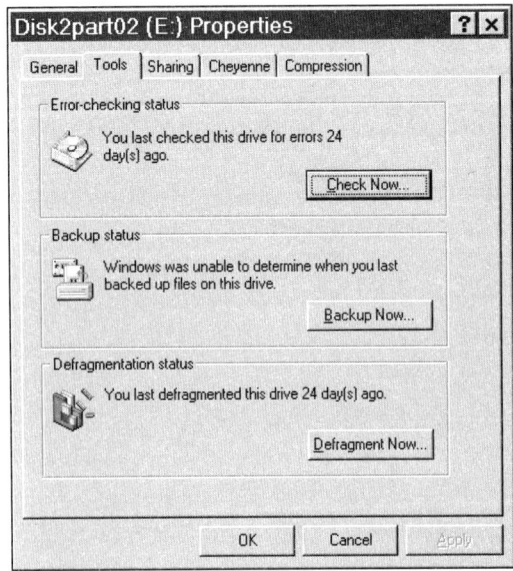

Figure 1-6 Tools tab of the Properties dialog box

6. Explore each of these options in turn. (If no backup device is attached to your computer, you will not be able to experiment with the Backup utility. But you can try the other two without damaging your computer.)

7. When you've finished, close any open windows, including Windows Explorer.

CASE PROJECTS

1. You have chosen Windows 98 as the new standard desktop operating system for your employer, the New Dawn Corporation. You've been asked to justify this selection in terms of the operating system's capabilities, especially those that relate to robustness and reliability. In two or three paragraphs describe the features of Windows 98 that relate to robustness and reliability, and explain the advantages they offer your company.

2. You work for a pharmacy chain that uses networked kiosks located in stores across the nation. Management is seeking a new operating system for these remote locations that can easily be kept up to date. Why is Windows 98 a good choice for such a situation? Which two features of this operating system can work together to make it easy to schedule automatic operating system updates on a weekly basis? What kinds of connections would the kiosks need for such a strategy to work?

CHAPTER TWO

PLANNING AND INSTALLING WINDOWS 98

Deploying Windows 98 is a multifaceted process, whether one intends to install it on a single workstation, within a workgroup, or across an entire enterprise-wide network spanning multiple locations.

In this chapter you will learn the system requirements for Windows 98, including the type of processor and the amount of memory required to allow Windows 98 to work most efficiently. Then you will take some time to plan your Windows 98 system. Finally, you will learn how to install and configure Windows 98.

AFTER READING THIS CHAPTER AND COMPLETING THE EXERCISES YOU WILL BE ABLE TO:

- Describe the Windows 98 system requirements
- Choose an appropriate file system, networking model, and security strategies
- Install Windows 98 as a new installation, as an upgrade, or as part of a dual-boot configuration

Windows 98 System Requirements

When you install any kind of software, including an operating system, you need to determine whether the software will run properly on your computer. Most software manufacturers provide a list of minimum requirements (for example, that you need at least 8 megabytes of RAM) for their products. For Windows 98, Microsoft says you need a minimum of a 66 megahertz (MHz) 80486DX processor, 16 megabytes (MB) of RAM, and 200 MB of free space on your hard drive. For Windows 98 to perform at its best, however, you should use at least a Pentium processor, and at least 24 MB of RAM. Also, if you choose to install many optional components, you may need between 250 MB and 300 MB of free space on your hard drive.

If you are upgrading from Windows 95 and choose to back up your Windows 95 system files during setup, reserve another 50 MB on your hard drive. And finally, make sure there will be enough hard disk space left over for a swap file. The **swap file** is a reserved area on a hard disk that Windows 98 uses to store elements of virtual memory that are not currently in active use. (Data constantly moves back and forth from this file, into and out of RAM. The continual swapping of information gives the swap file its name.) The size of the swap file fluctuates and is dependent on the amount of real memory on your PC and on the memory demands of the applications you run. In Windows 98, the operating system itself manages the swap file and makes use of as much free disk space for virtual memory as it thinks it needs. The Windows 98 swap file is named Win386.swp and resides in the C:\Windows directory. For more information about the swap file and how to configure it manually, see Chapter 10.

Planning Your Windows 98 Configuration

When planning your Windows 98 system, you must weigh your own needs and work environment against the features and configurations that Microsoft describes as ideal. Among the features you must consider are the file system, the networking model, and security strategies. These items are explained in the following sections. You will actually learn how to implement these features later in this book, after you have installed Windows 98.

File Systems

A **file system** defines the general organization of files and folders on a hard disk, and also provides the structure within which files may be named, stored, deleted, copied, moved, and so forth. The amount of space that you have on your hard disk after installation depends on the file system that you choose. As you will learn in this chapter, Windows 98 gives you a choice between two different file systems, each with its own advantages and disadvantages.

All Microsoft operating systems can use some version of the File Allocation Table (**FAT) file system**. This system takes its name from the special list, called the file allocation table (or FAT), in which the operating system stores information about the location of files. Your disk is divided into a fixed number of storage cells. FAT contains pointers to every one of these cells. Some files are large enough to take up multiple cells. Under the FAT system, when you load a particular file, the operating system first looks in the file directory to identify the cell where the beginning of the file is stored. Then it checks the file allocation table to find out if the file is stored in more than one location, and then retrieves the file. In the file allocation table, each file is represented by a sequence of numbers that identifies where each part of the file is located. The file allocation table is similar to a card catalog at the library. You need the card catalog to find out where a specific book (or file) is located. The twist is that parts of the book may be located in different parts of the library.

FAT is sometimes also referred to as FAT16, because it uses 16-bit locator IDs in its file allocation table to identify files. FAT16 is a **real-mode** file system, which means that it cannot use extended memory. Under FAT16, file names can be no longer than eight characters.

A new 16-bit FAT file system called VFAT, which was introduced with Windows 95, allows for **long filenames** of up to 255 characters (with a total of 260 characters for the complete path name). Today, Windows NT and Windows 95 both support VFAT, as does Windows 98. But Windows 98 also supports a 32-bit implementation of the FAT file system called FAT32.

As its name implies, FAT32 uses 32-bit entries in its file allocation tables, and can therefore identify many more files and disk locations than FAT16. (You'll learn why in the next section.)

FAT32 is a **protected-mode** file system. A protected-mode system can use extended memory, which means that it can access large amounts of storage more efficiently than is possible in 16-bit environments. A protected mode file system maximizes the performance of hard drives, CD-ROMs, and network resources and supports multitasking. FAT32 also allows for long filenames.

The next section discusses each file system's characteristics and merits.

Understanding the FAT and FAT32 File Systems

FAT32 was designed to overcome a number of limitations of FAT16. First of all, as mentioned earlier, FAT16 uses 16-bit entries in its file allocation tables, and therefore cannot identify as many files and disk locations as FAT32.

To fully understand this limitation of FAT16, you need to understand some terminology pertaining to storage devices such as hard disk drives. Each hard disk is divided into areas of constant size called **sectors**. A group of sectors makes up a **cluster**. Each cluster has a unique locator ID, called an address, which is listed in the file allocation table. These addresses are 16 bits long for FAT16 and 32 bits long for FAT32. In other words, while a FAT16 drive can theoretically be divided into $2^{16} = 65,536$ clusters, a FAT32 drive can be divided into approximately $2^{32} = 4,294,967,926$ clusters.

Physical hard drives may be divided into separate sections, called **partitions**. Each partition has its own FAT. The size of each partition is the number of clusters multiplied by the size of each cluster. The largest possible FAT16 or FAT32 cluster is 32 KB. Since there are 65,536 FAT16 clusters, the biggest FAT16 partition is 2 GB. If you are using FAT16 with a hard drive larger than 2 GB, you need more than one partition. Since there are 4.3 billion FAT32 clusters, the biggest FAT32 partition is theoretically 140 TB. Windows 98 actually limits FAT32 partitions to 2 TB, a limit the largest hard drives probably won't reach for years.

Although there is only one FAT per partition, each partition can include one or more separate **logical drives**, each with their own drive letter (such as C:, D:, or E:).

FAT32 can also create much smaller clusters on large drives than FAT16. This is important because each file stored on the hard disk consumes at least one cluster, no matter how small a file may be. Thus, if a hard drive contains many small files, it's especially wise to use correspondingly small clusters. (It might be helpful to think of clusters as containers in a refrigerator and files as different flavors of fruit juice. If you use only 2-gallon containers, you won't be able to fit many flavors inside the refrigerator. By using many 8-ounce containers instead, you can store a great many more flavors within the same refrigerator.)

Suppose you have a FAT16 drive on which clusters take up 32 KB each. If you saved a 10-KB file to that drive, it would take up a full 32-KB cluster, even though it only really required 10 KB. Thus, 22 KB of that cluster would be unavailable to other files, and would therefore be wasted space. FAT32, on the other hand, could use clusters as small as 4 KB. This means the same 10 KB file would consume two entire clusters (8 KB) and half of a third cluster (2 KB), with only 2 KB of wasted space. Compare this to the 22 KB wasted under FAT16.

The size of clusters varies, depending on the size of the physical hard drive or partition. Table 2–1 compares the cluster sizes associated with different partitions for FAT16 and FAT32 volumes.

Table 2-1 Cluster Sizes of FAT16 and FAT32

Drive or Partition Size	FAT16 Cluster Size	FAT32 Cluster Size
260 MB–511 MB	8 KB	not supported
512 MB–1023 MB	16 KB	4 KB
1024 MB–2 GB	32 KB	4 KB
2 GB–8 GB	not supported	4 KB
8 GB–16 GB	not supported	8 KB
16 GB–32 GB	not supported	16 KB
32 GB–127 GB	not supported	32 KB
more than 127 GB	not supported	64 KB

Because of its ability to use smaller clusters, the FAT32 file system can be as much as 20–30% more efficient than a FAT16 file system of similar size. On average, the typical gain in efficiency is more like 10–15%.

In addition to allowing for a more efficient use of space, smaller-sized clusters increase the speed of the operating system. When searching for a file, the operating system has to skip over less wasted space, and so can read more information from the same amount of disk surface faster. When coupled with the Windows 98 Disk Defragmenter utility, small clusters can result in applications that load up to 50% faster than in a FAT16 system. (As you'll learn in Chapter 8, the Disk Defragmenter consolidates information stored on a hard drive to eliminate spaces between units of data.)

FAT32 is also better at responding to hardware failure (such as a malfunctioning hard drive, or a power surge) without loss of data. This ability to overcome failure is known as a system's **fault tolerance**. One important measure of any system's fault tolerance is its ability to keep copies, or backups, of important files. FAT32 maintains backups of a hard drive's **boot sector** (the part of the hard drive where the special programs that start up a computer are stored); FAT16 does not. In addition, FAT32 expands the information in the **boot record** (which is the first entry in the boot sector, and tells the computer where to look for key boot information and related programs) to include a backup of crucial data structures.

Both FAT16 and FAT32 make backups of the file allocation table, but only FAT32 can switch to the backup copy on the fly if the original becomes damaged or is otherwise unreadable. And finally, FAT32 can also relocate the root directory (which contains the basic structures for all files and directories on a disk partition) elsewhere on the hard disk to avoid bad sectors; FAT16 cannot. These features of FAT32 reduce the chance that a failure could cause a hard drive to become unusable.

Another advantage of the Windows 98 file system is that it makes it easy to use **utility software** (software that, among other things, is used to rearrange and streamline the contents of a hard disk, or perhaps to delete unwanted or unneeded files). When one of these disk utilities is accessing the disk, no other application is allowed to save files. This prevents data from becoming corrupted. At the same time, it allows you to run disk cleanup or optimization utilities in the background, without stopping work in other running applications. However, keep in mind that many 16-bit utilities will not work in a FAT32 file system.

Choosing an Appropriate File System

If you simply want to pick the most advanced technology, FAT32 is the clear winner. However, here are some other variables you must consider:

- **Disk size**: FAT32 only supports drives from 512 MB up to 2 TB in size. If your drive is smaller than 512 MB, you must use FAT16. On logical drives of 256 MB or less, FAT16 is actually quite efficient, both in speed and storage.

- **Operating system compatibility**: Windows 98, Windows 95 OSR2, and Windows NT 5.0 (projected to be released in 1999) can use FAT16 or FAT32. However, MS-DOS, Windows 3.1, Windows NT 4.0, and most other operating systems use FAT16 instead, and cannot read from a FAT32 drive. This is important to keep in mind if you have a dual- or multiboot computer—that is, a computer that runs two or more operating systems. On such a computer, the multiple operating systems may share the same partition. If they share partitions, you need a FAT that works with both operating systems. (Dual- and multiboot configurations are explained in more detail later in this chapter.) You can only share files between FAT32 computers and FAT16 computers over a network.

- **Reversibility**: Microsoft provides a converter wizard that can convert your system from FAT16 to FAT32 without erasing the contents of your hard disk. Note, however, that it is *not* possible to revert back to FAT16 without backing up files, reformatting the drive, and restoring the files. To open the converter wizard, click Start, point to Programs, point to Accessories, point to System Tools, and then click Drive Converter (FAT32).

- **Software already installed on your computer**: While Microsoft makes efforts to maintain backward compatibility in FAT32 for most applications, you may need to upgrade older disk utility software. Check with the software's vendor. Also, when converting to FAT32, you should turn off virus protection software that is installed in the BIOS, or that uses older, 16-bit real-mode drivers. This is because the conversion process modifies the boot sector. In addition, on a hard drive that has been compressed using the Microsoft DriveSpace 3 disk compression utility, which squeezes files and directories into smaller versions of themselves, you must decompress that drive before converting to FAT32, because DriveSpace 3 does not work with FAT32.

If the preceding considerations do not prevent you from using FAT32, you will benefit from its reliability, resource conservation, improved speed, and increased capacity.

Networking Model

When planning a Windows 98 installation, you also need to consider whether you will be integrating the computer into a network, and, if so, the particular type of network involved. You can integrate Windows 98 into most popular networks right out of the box. In some cases, third parties supply add-ons to permit Windows 98 to participate in other, less common types of networks. The built-in components of Windows 98 include a broad range of protocols (languages computers use to communicate with one another). You will learn more about protocols in Chapter 5. For now, just keep in mind that these protocols include:

- **Network transport protocols**: Used to move data across particular types of networks. Examples include TCP/IP and IPX/SPX.
- **Communications protocols**: Used to request specific services from a network, such as browsing for computer names or resources (such as shared directories or printers). Examples include NetBIOS.

Windows 98 is also designed to suit two widely used standards for network interfaces:

- **Network Device Interface Specification (NDIS)**: (Microsoft's standard driver architecture used in Windows operating systems of many kinds
- **Open Datalink Interface (ODI)**: Novell's equivalent of NDIS, used for NetWare clients

The particular **networking model** you follow can be anything from a simple standalone workstation with a modem used for remote networking and Internet access, to a small group of desktop workstations on a peer-to-peer network, to a large group of workstations that share one or more dedicated servers or domain controllers. The following sections explore each of these alternatives and the impact they have on the installation process.

Standalone vs. Networked

A **standalone** workstation is one that operates without any kind of connection to a network. If you are installing Windows 98 on standalone workstations, you will probably use the installation CD (or if Microsoft provides a 3½-inch disk-based version, the disks) included in the Windows 98 box. On a networked workstation you can also connect to a shared directory where the installation files are stored.

Installation from a network directory has several advantages. Because the Windows Registry remembers the location of the network directory where the installation files reside, those files remain available should you later need to add a device or change your Windows configuration. On standalone workstations, whenever Windows 98 requests additional support files, the user must insert the installation CD. (As an alternative, you could keep a copy of the installation files on the local hard disk for direct access when necessary.) Thus, modifying a PC in a networked environment is faster and easier and uses fewer resources (no wasted hard disk space, no need for multiple 3½-inch disks or CDs) than for standalone workstations.

Workgroups and Domains

If you are installing Windows 98 in a network environment, you must understand how modern Microsoft operating systems, such as Windows 98, interact with a network. Microsoft offers two primary models for networking: the workgroup model and the domain model. These models, which define how resources are shared and accessed on a network, are briefly explained in the following sections. For more information on networking options, see *A Guide to Networking Essentials*, published by Course Technology.

The Workgroup Model.
The first of Microsoft's networking models is the **workgroup model**. Any machine in a workgroup can act as a client to other machines in the same workgroup, but the same machine may act as a server to other machines in the workgroup as well. To be specific, machines in a workgroup can share directories and printers with one another, and all machines can act as both clients and servers. Because all machines in a workgroup are more or less equal in their capabilities, this kind of network model is sometimes called peer-to-peer networking.

Workgroups are designed to accommodate small numbers of users who work together on a regular basis, and who therefore often need to share data and resources. Access to shared resources (such as files or printers) is controlled on a per resource basis. (The shared resources are often simply referred to as "shares.") Microsoft calls this approach **share-level security**. Under share-level security, you generally need to provide a password for each resource you want to access. Each member of the workgroup is responsible for managing the resources on his or her machine. This means that to access a directory share on Bob's machine, you might need to know one password, and to access a printer on Bob's machine, you might need to know yet another password.

If you use share-level security with a group of five or more machines, each with multiple resources to share, the number of passwords users have to remember can get out of hand quickly. In general, the more users who participate in a workgroup, the greater the potential for chaos. For this reason, Microsoft recommends that workgroups should seldom exceed five participant machines. For groups of ten or more users, the workgroup model is inappropriate. When the number of users to manage gets large, or when more centralized control over resources and security is desirable, the domain model fits that bill much better than the workgroup model.

The Domain Model. A **domain** is a group of networked workstations and servers. It is managed as a group of user accounts. This is different from the Internet definition of domain, which (in the United States) is the three-letter designator at the end of an Internet address, such as "com". The **domain model** for networking relies on the presence of one or more specialized Windows NT servers, called **domain controllers**. These machines provide centralized network logon services and control access to resources. In the domain model, each user has a user account, which is assigned rights to particular resources on the network. The user only has to provide one password (and a username) in order to log on to the entire network. After the user has logged on, all the user's requests for resources are channeled through the domain controller, which then determines whether or not the user has the right to access that particular resource.

The type of security that the domain model provides is called **user-level security**, because it depends on a user entering a valid password and username in order to gain access to the domain in the first place.

Because at least one server is required to support a domain, the domain model is more expensive to install and more complex to use than the workgroup model. But it is also much more secure and more convenient for network administrators to manage. Most Microsoft networks larger than 10 machines include a Windows NT server acting as a domain controller.

Domains can be as small as a single office or department, or as large as an entire organization. The maximum number of users that a domain can handle is a subject of some controversy, but most experts agree that several thousand users in a single domain do not overtax the ability of Windows NT to function as a domain controller.

However, larger networks are usually divided into multiple domains as a matter of convenience and to increase security. (For example, the sales department computers might be in one domain, while the personnel computers are in another.) When a user in one domain requests access to a resource (such as a printer) in another domain, that request is passed through a security provider, such as Windows NT. (NetWare can also provide domain services, although they differ somewhat from those of Windows NT.) For more information on domains, see *A Guide to Windows NT Server 4.0 in the Enterprise*, published by Course Technology.

Choosing an Appropriate Network Model

If you choose to install Windows 98 on a standalone computer, you do not have to concern yourself with selecting a network model, because there's no network involved. But if the machine on which you're installing Windows 98 is attached to a network, you must decide whether to configure the machine as a workgroup member or a domain member during the installation process. Fortunately, it's reasonably easy to switch from one model to another after installation, but chances are that you won't be making such a switch very often.

There are advantages and disadvantages to both the workgroup model's share-level security and the domain model's user-level security. The advantage of share-level security is that it permits you to grant access to a broad range of users simply by giving them the password to the shared resource. But this convenience results in decreased security—a password may be widely distributed and used indiscriminately.

Whereas user-level security grants precise control over resources, and even permits personal accountability, the resources and maintenance required are greater. You must include a security provider to act as a domain controller—such as a Windows NT or NetWare server—and that server must accommodate a separate, uniquely named account for each user who requires access to domain resources. Even then, you must also grant such users (or the group they belong to) explicit access to the resources they need; sometimes, you must also deny them access to those resources you don't want them to be able to use.

When choosing a network model, remember that share-level access is appropriate for relatively small peer-to-peer networks, in which individual workstations share directories, printers, and other resources with the rest of their peers. By itself, Windows 98 cannot support user-level security. If all computers on a network use Windows 98, a workgroup model with peer-to-peer networking and share-level security is the only possible networking option.

User-level access is best suited for larger networks with one or more domain controllers, and for environments where security is important. Also, if you use only a NetWare server to administer a domain, you can only offer user-level access, because NetWare does not support share-level access. In environments where a Windows NT domain controller is present, it is also possible for workgroup-based computers and domain-based computers to interact and exchange data. However, crossing this boundary requires extra effort on the part of the network administrator. For example, domain users need access to a valid share-level password, while workgroup users need valid user accounts in the domain.

Understanding Naming Issues

Windows 98 requires each computer on a network to be assigned a workgroup name and a unique computer name, regardless of what type of networking software is in use. If you install networking software during the Windows 98 Setup, you will be asked to supply these names. You may, however, alter either the computer or workgroup name, or both, after Setup is complete.

To change the computer and workgroup name after Windows 98 has been installed, right-click the Network Neighborhood icon on the desktop, and then click Properties on the shortcut menu. When the Network dialog box opens, click the Identification tab. There you will see three text boxes for the computer's name, the name of the workgroup, and the computer description. When entering this information, follow the rules explained in Table 2-2.

Table 2-2 Computer Identification Settings

Setting	Description
Computer name	A unique alphanumeric string of text up to 15 characters long. May not include spaces but can include any of the following special characters: ! @ # $ % ^ & ( ) - _ ' { } . ~
Workgroup	Follows the same conventions as those for computer names, except that workgroup names needn't be unique
Computer Description	Displayed as a comment next to a computer name when a user browses the network. May be up to 48 characters long.

SECURITY STRATEGIES

When planning your installation of Windows 98, you also need to consider how you want to ensure the security of your computer, whether it's operating as a standalone or as part of a network. The goal of computer security is to ensure that the hardware, software, and data are protected from damage, theft, and unauthorized usage. At the same time, the security system should interfere as little as possible with authorized use of the computer.

In the previous section you learned about Windows 98 security as it pertains to the workgroup and domain models. Both of these models use a **logon method** to establish security controls and access rights, which means that a user must enter a name and a password every time she or he logs on. In addition, the name and password combination must be recognized as valid, either by the Windows 98 machine with a resource to share (for the workgroup model) or by a domain controller (for the domain model). With the right settings, the act of logging onto a system unlocks a password cache that automatically accesses other shared resources with previously entered passwords. The password cache is explained in detail in Chapter 4.

But username and password validation is just one security tool provided by Windows 98. In this section you will learn about the security benefits of modifying system policies and creating user profiles. You will also learn about the security aspects of the password cache.

System Policies

System policies are predefined rules that control what users can and cannot do on their desktop computers and on the network. You manage system policies via a program called the System Policy Editor (SPE). Chapter 5 discusses system policies and the SPE in detail. The remainder of this section explains what you need to know in order to plan your Windows 98 system.

When you change settings in the SPE, you are actually changing settings in the Registry. You can use the SPE to restrict what Control Panel settings users can configure. It also allows you to customize what users can view in their Network Neighborhood windows, Start menus, or other parts of the desktop, and to configure network settings from a central location.

The System Policy Editor provides a simplified and comprehensive interface for changing many common Registry settings for an individual computer. You can then save these changes in a system policy file that can be loaded on other computers in order to impose the same changes upon them. Windows 98 provides a standard set of policies that you can use to specify settings for others, but you can also create custom policies for any Windows application that uses the Registry. If you use a program company-wide that must be configured a certain way for everyone, a custom policy can be a real time-saver.

In a networked environment with a domain controller, the system policy file is stored on the server and is loaded whenever a user logs on to the network. System policies can be applied on a user-by-user basis, or you can take advantage of groups already defined on your NetWare or NT network by applying group policies to named groups of users.

Several of the Windows 98 policies are specifically designed to enforce **password security,** which means that you can define additional requirements on passwords to help improve their security. For example, you can require a minimum password length, or require that passwords be composed of a combination of letters and numbers. You can also deny users access to the Windows 98 user interface if they do not provide a valid name and password. This last option has two benefits: it prevents unauthorized access to the PC as well as to the network, and it teaches novice users that they must log on properly instead of merely clicking "cancel" at the logon screen. If the user is not logged on properly, he or she may not be able to perform some important tasks, such as printing.

User Profiles

A **user profile** is a collection of files containing preferences and configuration settings specific to a single user. For example, a user profile can define a user's customized desktop. Chapter 5 discusses user profiles in detail. The remainder of this section explains what you need to know in order to plan your Windows 98 system.

Each user profile is stored in its own folder, under the user's username. User profile folders are stored in the Profiles directory, which in turn can be found in the Windows directory. (For example, the profile information for a user with an account named "BobS" would reside in C:\Windows\Profiles\BobS.)

When user profiles are enabled, multiple users on a single computer can maintain their own personal desktop settings independently. User profiles can be made mandatory, and used to enforce specific user settings on particular machines.

Although mandatory user profiles and system policies accomplish some of the same goals, they are not identical, nor should they be used for the same reasons. Microsoft recommends that you choose one method or the other. Table 2-3 describes the differences between user profiles and system policies:

Table 2-3 Differences Between User Profiles and System Policies

User Profiles	System Policies
Affects user-specific settings only	Controls both user- and computer-specific settings
Controls every user-specific setting	May selectively control certain user settings, yet leave others under a user's control

Password Cache

As discussed earlier, Windows 98 security for file and printer sharing can be based on user-level access or share-level access. In both methods, the user must enter a password and username before accessing the desktop. However, the password and username are processed in different ways for each type of security. In user-level security, the usernames and passwords are passed to a domain controller, which compares them to a list of users, and then either accepts or rejects the logon attempt.

But in a workgroup with share-level access, the user ID and password serve to unlock a password cache file associated with each user in a Windows directory. The **password cache** stores all passwords that have been entered onto the machine in one place, as a convenience for the user. Chapter 4 discusses the password cache in detail. The remainder of this section explains what you need to know in order to plan your Windows 98 system.

The first time a user accesses a share-level resource, the password to that resource is saved in the password cache, so the user only needs to enter that password once. From then on, unless the password is changed or the password list is edited, the user will always obtain immediate access to that shared resource as long as he or she logged on correctly at startup. Note that if the user has never logged on to a workstation before, a new password cache is created.

The password cache is not accessible until the user logs on. Once the cache is unlocked, the user may delete individual passwords via a utility called the Password List Editor. Note that the user can never view the passwords in the cache, because they remain encrypted at all times.

Resource sharing with user-level access is easier to administer than with share-level access. Despite the convenience of password-caching, share-level access invariably spawns a confusing number of passwords on a network, with a different password required for each shared resource. Should an employee ever leave your company, you'd be forced to change passwords for all resources that the departed employee used. In addition, you would have to communicate the new passwords to other employees, so they could update their password caches. In a user-level security environment, you could simply delete the employee's account from the domain controller. No further action would be necessary.

INSTALLATION APPROACHES

In the previous sections you've learned about the issues you will have to consider when installing Windows 98. Now you can learn exactly how to install the operating system.

By now, you should have verified that the systems on which you intend to install Windows 98 meet or exceed Microsoft's minimum hardware requirements. You should also know which file system or file systems and which network and security models you wish to use, or which ones are already deployed. If you've chosen names for your computers and workgroups, you should also verify that those computer names are unique, and that workgroup names meet organizational standards and structures.

Next, you have to decide which Windows 98 components you want to install. The type of installation you choose determines which components are installed, as explained in the following section.

INSTALLATION TYPES

Windows 98 offers four types of installation, and each type represents a collection of components that differs slightly from the other types. These types are as follows:

- **Typical**: Includes the most commonly required components of Windows 98, and should suffice for most desktop installations.

- **Portable**: Includes a subset of components aimed at laptop users. Works well for most laptop installations.

- **Compact**: Includes the minimum number of components that will result in a working Windows 98 installation. Use this only when disk space and memory are at an absolute premium. Normally, this applies only to older laptops and desktops that just barely meet the minimum hardware requirements for Windows 98. This type is not recommended.

- **Custom**: Aimed at expert users. Allows an expert to examine all of the component categories for Windows 98 (and their constituent files), and then manually select any and all elements that should be included in a particular installation. This option is most often selected for automated installations, or for bulk installations, where testing has permitted an information systems (IS) professional to select exactly which components to include. This kind of installation is explained in more detail in Chapter 12.

For most installations, the Typical installation is probably the safest option.

After deciding which type of installation you want (and, therefore, which components you want to install), you must decide whether you wish to perform a new installation, an upgrade from Windows 3.x to Windows 98, or an upgrade from Windows 95 to Windows 98. These options are explained in the next section.

INSTALLATION OPTIONS

The Windows 98 installation program is known as Windows 98 Setup, or sometimes just **Setup.** There are two environments from which to run Setup: from MS-DOS, or from within Windows 95. The method you choose depends on your current configuration. If you have Windows 95 and want to keep the settings when you upgrade to Windows 98, run Setup from within Windows 95. If you have Windows 3.1 or Windows for Workgroups on your machine, run Setup from MS-DOS. If you are planning a new installation (that is, an installation on a computer not already running some version of Windows), you also have to run Setup from MS-DOS.

Here are some other reasons why you might run Setup from MS-DOS:

- You don't want your Windows 95 settings to carry over into Windows 98.
- Setup failed when you ran it from Windows 95.
- You want to install Windows 98 to a new directory.

For all configurations, make sure that antivirus software and other **terminate-and-stay-resident** (**TSR**) programs are not running when you launch Setup. TSR programs include any kind of software that's instantly available with a hot-key sequence (such as Starfish Software's SideKick) as well as some device drivers in the DOS and Windows 3.x environments. These programs are called TSRs because they remain locked into your PC's memory, ready to be activated at any time, even when they're not actually running. That is, the program terminates, or ends, but stays in memory. TSR programs can interfere with installations of any kind, but they are particularly likely to interfere when you are installing a new operating system. For example, some anti-virus programs ask you to approve all file changes made by executable programs such as Setup, one by one, a process that can involve thousands of files. Therefore, Microsoft recommends that you disable them before attempting to install Windows 98.

The easiest way to make sure that a system is booting up without TSRs (or other software that you might normally load at startup) is to boot from a bootable MS-DOS 3½-inch disk that includes only the barest minimum of drivers and software necessary to boot the machine and access the CD-ROM drive. This is called a "clean boot" because it bypasses all the add-ons and other features that can sometimes interfere when you install or upgrade an operating system.

New Installation

A new installation of Windows 98 begins at the MS-DOS prompt. Before you begin, you need the following information or equipment:

- The name of the directory where you plan to install Windows 98.
- The computer name, workgroup name, and computer description (such as "Sales department workstation"). Computer names and workgroup names are each limited to 15 alphanumeric characters; the computer description is limited to 48 alphanumeric characters.
- The MS-DOS driver for either your network drive or your CD-ROM drive. Which driver you need depends on where the Windows 98 installation files are located. Note that you do not need these drivers if you are installing from 3½-inch disks.
- A blank, formatted 3½-inch disk that you will use to create an emergency recovery disk, called the Emergency Startup Disk.

After you have compiled this information and equipment, you are ready to begin installing Windows 98.

The following steps walk you through a new installation of Windows 98. Read the steps to familiarize yourself with the process. Then, in the following sections, you will learn about installing Windows 98 as an upgrade. The discussion in those sections assumes that you are already familiar with the steps involved in a new installation. In the hands-on projects at the end of this book, you will have a chance to perform the type of installation that is appropriate for your system, using the files from the installation CD. (Network installation is covered in Chapter 12.)

The following steps assume that you already have a bootable 3½-inch disk for your operating system that contains your real-mode CD driver or that gives you access to your real-mode CD driver on your hard disk. You will learn how to create a bootable floppy in Chapter 12.

If you are working from Windows 95, you may not have any real-mode CD-ROM drivers installed. Consult the documentation for your CD-ROM drive. If you do not have 3½-inch disks from your manufacturer associated with the installation of your CD-ROM drive, you may be able to get the appropriate drivers from their Web site.

Planning and Installing Windows 98   45

 For most users, a new installation is probably not necessary, and introduces needless complexity. If you already have Windows 95 installed on your computer, installing Windows 98 as an upgrade should work fine. However, if you want to avoid any possibility of errors resulting from TSRs, or legacy drivers, consider performing a new installation.

 The installation process may be slightly different for you depending on the configuration of your computer.

To perform a new installation of Windows 98:

1. Boot the machine from a bootable DOS 3½-inch disk. Once the bootup process is complete, the A:\ DOS prompt appears on the screen.

2. Switch to the drive that contains the Windows 98 Setup program, whether it is on a 3½-inch disk or CD. If you are using a disk, type A: and then press Enter. If you are using a CD, type the CD-ROM drive letter, and press Enter.

3. Type Setup and press Enter. You see a warning indicating that Setup is going to perform a routine check on your system. Press Enter to continue. A diagnostic utility called ScanDisk performs a routine check on your file system. ScanDisk won't allow the installation to proceed if it finds any problems, but this should not be an issue for a new installation.

4. After ScanDisk completes its check of the system, highlight Exit, then press Enter to leave ScanDisk. Setup Wizard, the program that will walk you through the installation process, begins loading. You see a welcome screen, as shown in Figure 2-1.

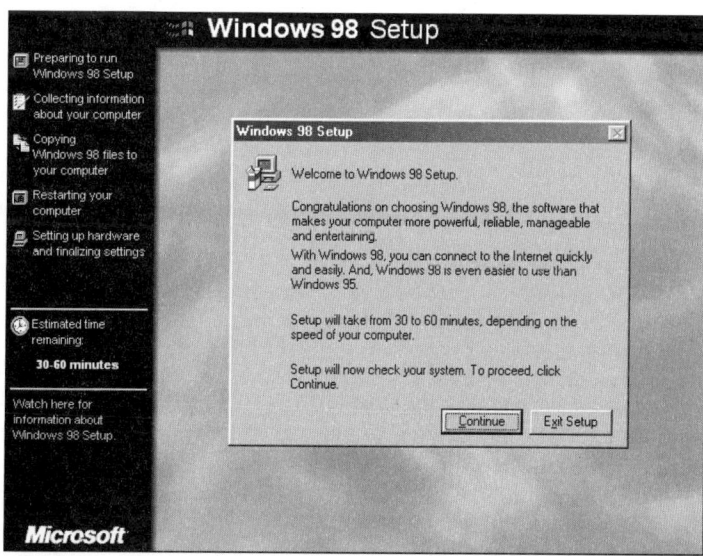

Figure 2-1   Windows 98 Setup welcome screen

5. Click Continue. A license agreement appears, as shown in Figure 2-2.

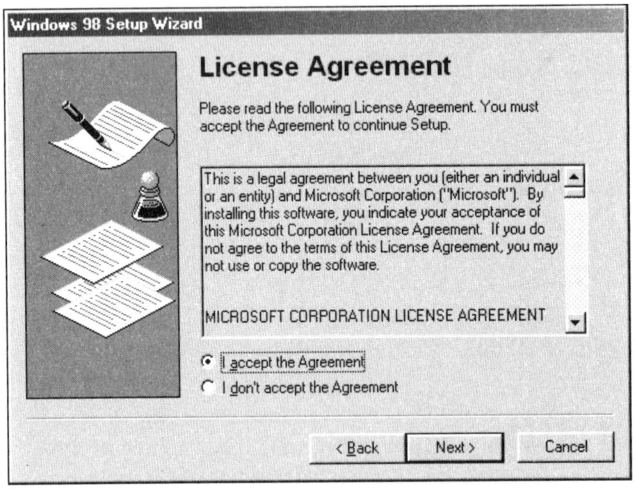

Figure 2-2 Windows 98 License Agreement

6. Click the I accept the Agreement option button, and then click Next. Unless your organization operates under a Microsoft site license, the Product Identification dialog box opens. If your network is set up under a Microsoft site license, Setup automatically skips to Step 8.

7. In the Product Key dialog box, enter the product ID number from your Windows 98 disks or your Certificate of Authenticity. The product ID will contain a set of 5 groups of letters and numbers that look something like this: ABCD1-EFGHI-JKL23-45MNO-PQ678. (If you are not using an English language keyboard, click Help. Then use the Keyboard Helper option to enter characters using the mouse.) Click Next.

8. The Select Directory dialog box appears. Here you can specify the directory in which you want to install Windows 98. By default, Setup selects the C:\Windows directory. For most normal installations, this works fine. However, you may select another directory if you wish, by clicking the Other directory option button, as explained in the next step.

9. Click Next to accept the C:\WINDOWS directory. Or click the Other directory option button, enter an alternate directory name, and then click Next.

10. The Preparing Directory dialog box appears, as shown in Figure 2-3, while Setup prepares the Windows 98 directory structures, along with all necessary sub-folders. At the same time, Setup also checks for already-installed Windows 98 components, and checks for adequate free disk space. This step may take several minutes. As long as Setup finds sufficient disk space, this step completes automatically.

Planning and Installing Windows 98   47

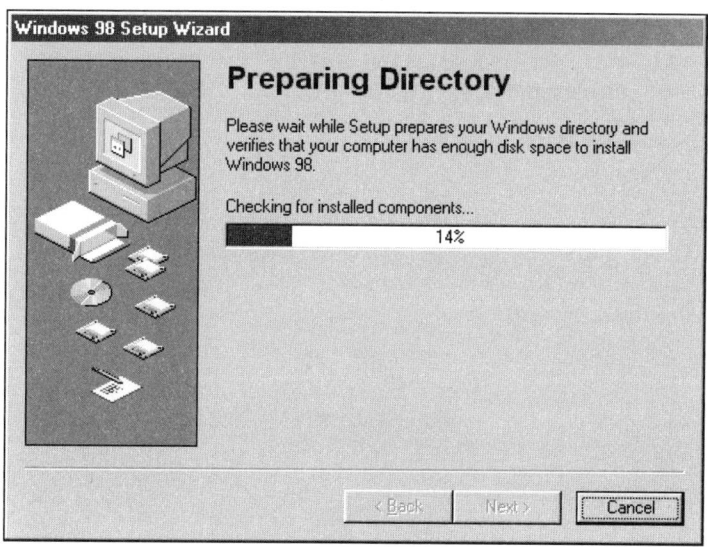

Figure 2-3 Preparing Directory dialog box

11. Once the directory structures are ready, the Setup Options dialog box opens, as shown in Figure 2-4. Here you must select which predefined set of Windows 98 components to install. The choices are: Typical, Portable, Compact, and Custom. As explained earlier, in most cases you will use the Typical option, which is selected by default.

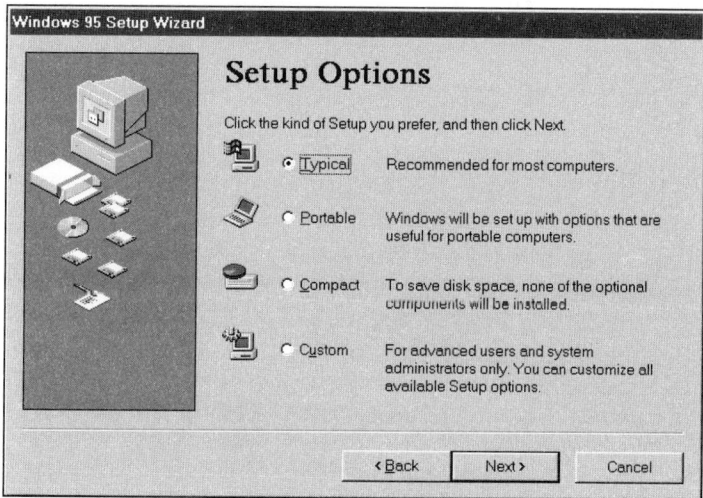

Figure 2-4 Setup Options dialog box

12. Unless you have particular needs that require another choice, click Next to accept the default option, Typical. The User Information dialog box opens next.

13. Enter your name and your company's name in the appropriate text boxes.

14. Click Next to continue the installation.

15. The Windows Components dialog box appears next. Here you can choose to install the most common components or customize what you install. Select the "Show me the list of components so I can choose" option and click Next.

16. The Select Components dialog box opens, as shown in Figure 2-5. Here you can select the Windows 98 components you want to install.

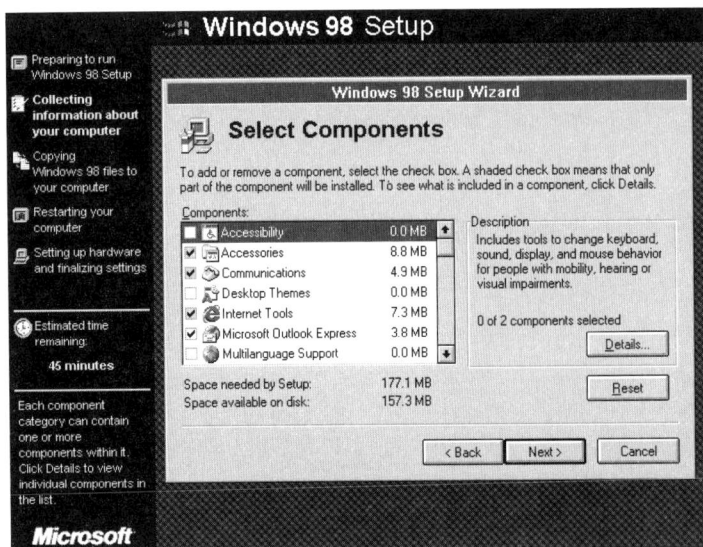

Figure 2-5 Select Components dialog box

17. To view a description of any Windows 98 component, select the component in the Components list box, and then view its description in the Description box. To learn even more about the selected component, click Details.

18. After you have read the descriptions of some or all of the components, you need to select which components you want to install. Components with checked boxes (such as the Microsoft Outlook Express box, in Figure 2-5) will be installed in their entirety. Components with empty check boxes (such as the Desktop Themes box, in Figure 2-5) will not be installed. Components with greyed, but checked boxes (such as the Internet Tools box, in Figure 2-5), will install only a subset of the available components for that category. For ordinary purposes the defaults work fine, but for the purposes of this book, you will probably want to select everything. A box is considered selected if it contains a simple check mark, with no grey background. (Thus, to select greyed, but checked boxes, you need to click once to uncheck the box, and then click again to select the entire category's contents.)

19. Select the components you want and click Next. The Identification dialog box opens. The information you enter here will identify your computer to the network. (If you are already connected to a network, skip to Step 21. You will enter identification data during hardware detection in Step 28.)

20. Type the appropriate information in the three text boxes, keeping in mind the naming rules described in Table 2-2 earlier in this chapter. Remember, all user and computer names in a domain must be unique. Figure 2-6 shows the Identification dialog box with sample entries.

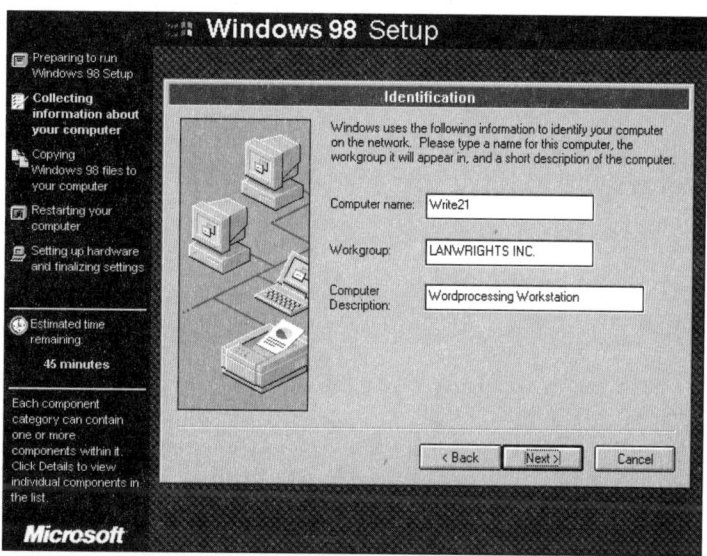

Figure 2-6 Identification dialog box

21. The Establishing Your Location dialog box appears next. Here you can select the country from which you would like to see channels listed on your computer. After you select a country, Windows 98 automatically picks a group of related channels that will appear on your desktop. A channel is a Web page that is updated continuously on the desktop.

22. Select a country, and then click Next. The Insert Disk dialog box opens, on top of the Emergency Startup Disk dialog box, as shown in Figure 2-7.

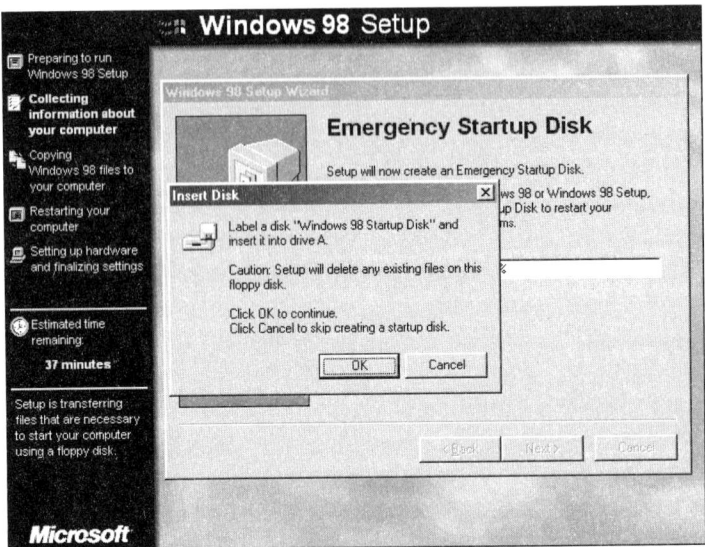

Figure 2-7 Insert Disk dialog box on top of the Emergency Startup Disk dialog box

23. At this point in the installation process, Setup allows you to create an Emergency Startup Disk (ESD). The ESD incorporates a collection of troubleshooting commands and utilities. You can use the ESD to boot your system if its hard disk ever becomes unbootable. It is especially important to create an ESD if you convert your boot drive to FAT32, because pre-Windows 98 boot disks cannot read FAT32 drives. To begin creating an ESD, follow the directions in the Insert Disk dialog box for labeling a blank floppy disk, insert the floppy disk into the disk drive, and then click OK. The installation process pauses for 30 to 60 seconds while Setup creates the ESD. The ESD contains a real-mode CD-ROM driver that works with many, but not all, CD drives.

24. Click Next. The Start Copying Files dialog box, shown in Figure 2-8, opens, indicating that Setup has collected all the information it needs to begin the actual installation.

Planning and Installing Windows 98   51

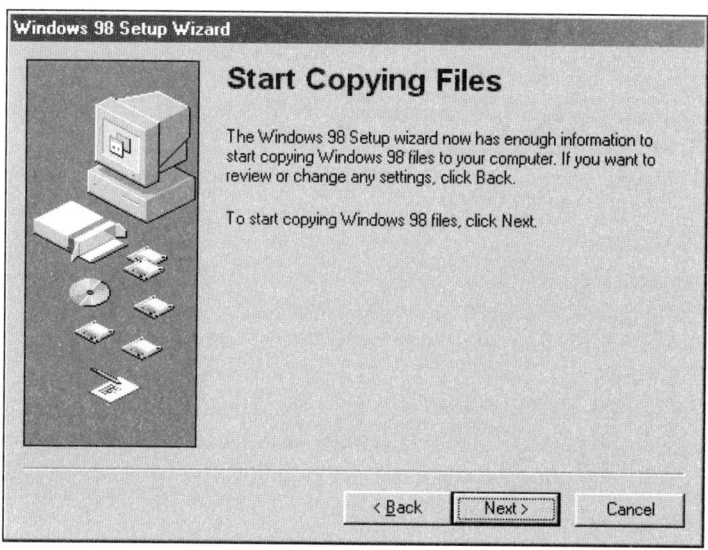

Figure 2-8   Start Copying Files dialog box

25. Click Next. Setup begins copying Windows 98 files to your computer's hard drive. Setup requires no input during this phase, and should not be disturbed.

If you interrupt Setup during this process, you will need to start the entire process again. Otherwise you may not have the proper files to start your computer.

26. Once all the necessary files are copied, Setup begins a 15-second countdown prior to restarting the computer. You may skip the delay by clicking Restart.
27. After a moment, you see a message that reads "Getting ready to run Windows 98 for the first time."
28. After Windows 98 finishes restarting, Setup begins its final installation phase, in which it detects hardware and finalizes settings. You may need to select a time zone for your computer. Windows 98 may restart during hardware detection.

If you are familiar with Windows 95, you might be interested to learn that, in Windows 95 Setup, the hardware detection process occurred before files were copied to the hard drive. Microsoft has since learned that the hardware detection process runs more smoothly if it occurs after files have been copied to the hard drive.

29. After the hardware detection phase is complete, Setup restarts your computer again. The first thing you see is the Enter Windows Password dialog box. Enter a user name and password in the appropriate text boxes. If you do not want to be prompted for logon each time you start Windows 98, do not enter a password. If your computer is connected to a network, you may be asked for a domain name and a password. (You will start learning about domains in Chapter 5.) Windows 98 setup is then complete. At this point, you should be ready to run Windows 98.

Windows 3.x Upgrade

The process of installing Windows 98 as an upgrade to Windows 3.1 is virtually identical to the new installation process, which is explained in the previous section. Keep in mind that you must boot directly to MS-DOS; do not launch Windows 3.1. (If your startup sequence automatically launches Windows, use the CTRL+C keyboard combination to stop Windows from loading.) Any MS-DOS drivers for your CD-ROM must already be installed if you intend to install Windows 98 from a CD; likewise, MS-DOS network drivers must also be installed if you intend to install Windows 98 from a network drive.

Once you've launched the Windows 98 Setup program, you will encounter a few minor differences from the steps described in the previous section. You will see the Save System Files dialog box, shown in Figure 2-9. Here you can choose to save a backup copy of the old system files, should you ever need to uninstall Windows 98.

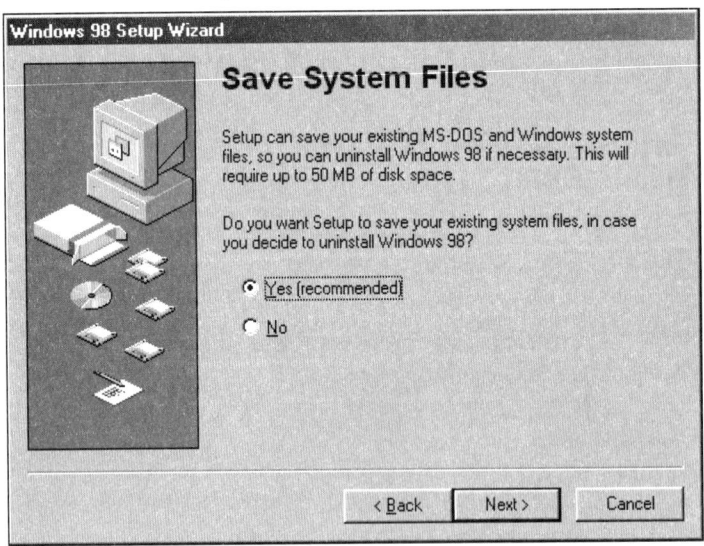

Figure 2-9   Save System Files dialog box

Click the "Yes (recommended)" option button, unless you're sure there isn't enough disk space to back up files. These backup files consume as much as 75 MB of disk space when the operating system replaced is Windows 95. However, Windows 3.1 seldom requires more than 10 MB of disk space.

Windows 95 Upgrade

Before upgrading from Windows 95, it is important to have a working Emergency Startup Disk and a backup of your Registry. If the upgrade stops in the middle for any reason, your Windows 95 Registry could easily be unusable. One approach is to use the Regedit command. In Windows 95, click Start, point to Programs, then click MS-DOS prompt. At the C:\ prompt, type "Regedit /e regback.txt". If you then run into a problem and have to restart with the Windows 95 Emergency Startup Disk, all you need to do to restore your Windows 95 Registry from your A:\ prompt is to type "Regedit /c c:\regback.txt". Be extremely cautious when using the Regedit command. Type the command exactly as you see it here, and do not attempt to experiment or you could render your Windows 95 Registry unusable.

To upgrade from Windows 95, click the Start button, click Run, and then type "*x:*\setup", where *x* represents the letter for the drive where Setup resides. Press Enter to begin the installation process.

You will be greeted with the Welcome to Windows 98 Setup dialog box (shown previously, in Figure 2-1). When you click Continue, Setup prepares its wizard to guide you through the rest of the process. After a few moments, you see the License Agreement dialog box (shown previously in Figure 2-2).

When you get to Step 8, however, you will *not* be allowed to choose an alternate target directory for Windows 98. Instead, Setup defaults to the current Windows 95 directory. Next, you will see the Checking Your System dialog box, shown in Figure 2-10. While this dialog box is visible, Setup runs ScanDisk in the background, but omits performing a surface scan. You won't notice ScanDisk unless it finds some error.

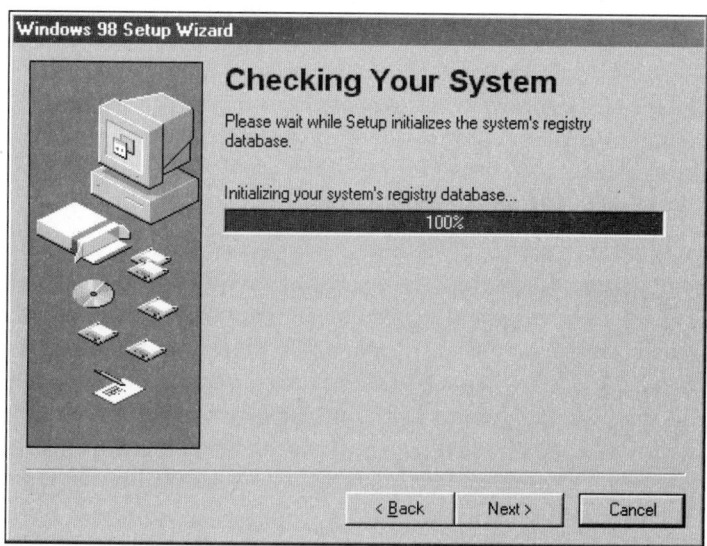

Figure 2-10 Checking Your System dialog box

Next, Setup checks the Windows Registry by running the Windows 98 Registry Scanner. (The Windows 98 Registry and related tools are discussed in Chapter 3.)

Next, Setup prepares the Windows 98 directory structure with all its required subfolders. Then, Setup gives you the option of saving system files, just as in the Windows 3.1 installation process. Once again, this permits you to store the complete set of Windows 95 files for subsequent restoration, should you decide to uninstall Windows 98 at some later date.

The steps for selecting components are unnecessary when upgrading from Windows 95 because Setup can glean the required installation information from the current Windows 95 Registry. The steps for setting up hardware and finalizing settings remain identical, subject only to one exception: Windows 98 does not attempt to identify any device that is not Plug and Play compatible. Rather, it assumes that the settings in the Windows 95 Registry for non-Plug-and-Play components are already correct. If that is not true, you must rectify any problems once Setup completes the upgrade.

Uninstalling Windows 98

You can restore a previous Windows configuration by uninstalling Windows 98, provided that these qualifications are met:

- You have answered "Yes" during the Windows 98 installation when prompted to Save System Files.
- You have not converted your boot drive to FAT32 nor compressed it with DriveSpace. Either action will cause uninstall to fail, even if previous system files are available.

Windows 98 uses two backup files to save previous systems. The first is named **WINUNDO.DAT**, and can consume as much as 75 MB of disk space. The second file is named **WINUNDO.INI**, and contains a map to the original locations for the files stored in WINUNDO.DAT. Delete these only when you are certain you will no longer need them. Better yet, copy them to a Zip disk, or a network server, if you can.

Dual-boot Configurations

When a computer can boot to two operating systems—usually by presenting a menu of options available early in the boot process—it is said to be a **dual-boot machine**. If a computer can boot more than two operating systems, it is usually said to be a **multiboot machine**. Windows 95, Windows 98, and Windows NT all include a boot loader (a piece of software that controls the process when a computer starts up and loads an operating system) that permits users to pick which operating system they want to boot, when more than one operating system is available. OS/2 provides similar capabilities, and third-party companies such as V Communications offer special-purpose software that can boot a large number of operating systems on a single machine.

Windows 98 can be installed on any boot drive that has a FAT16 partition with sufficient free space available. Simply install Windows 98 to its own directory, rather than copying it into an existing Windows directory. (For instance you could instruct Setup to place the

Windows 98 files in a directory named C:\Win98.) Windows 98 needs around 130 MB for a typical installation. You can configure your computer to dual boot with Windows NT, Windows 3.1, or MS-DOS 5.0 or later versions. You cannot dual boot Windows 98 and Windows 95, because Windows 98 is intended as an upgrade to Windows 95, and both operating systems would try to use the same boot file.

For dual-boot configurations with either Windows 3.1 or Windows NT and Windows 98, applications must be installed twice—once for each operating system. They may be installed into the same application directories to conserve disk space, but each version of Windows must be allowed to put its configuration files, DLLs, and Registry entries where it expects to find them. For more information on dual- or multiboot configurations, see Chapter 12 of this book. You can also go to *http://www.microsoft.com/kb/*, and search for "Dual boot configurations." Unfortunately, the Microsoft Web servers are often quite busy. If you do not find this page the first time you look, try again in a few hours. Alternate sources are noted in the Appendix for "Online Resources and Bibliography."

CHAPTER SUMMARY

- For Windows 98, Microsoft says you need a minimum of a 66 MHz 80486DX processor, 16 MB of RAM, and 200 MB of free space on your hard drive. For Windows 98 to perform at its best, however, you should use at least a Pentium processor, 24 MB of RAM, and (depending on the configuration you choose) 350 MB of free space or more on your hard drive.

- When planning your installation of Windows 98, you must consider which file system you want to use, the best networking model for your situation, and the available security strategies. A file system defines the general organization of files and folders on a hard disk, and also provides the structure within which files may be named, stored, deleted, copied, moved, and so forth. Windows 98 allows you to choose between the older FAT16 file system and a new file system, called FAT32. For modern, large hard drives, FAT32 is faster and more efficient than FAT16, primarily because FAT32 can use smaller clusters than FAT16. However, you need to consider numerous variables before selecting a file system.

- In addition to the file system, you need to consider whether you will be integrating the computer into a network, and, if so, the particular type of network involved. The workgroup model provides share-level security, which generally requires users to provide a password for each resource they want to access. The domain model for networking provides centralized network logon services and controls access to resources via user-level security. On small networks, share-level security requires less administration, but can be less secure, than user-level security. User-level security provides more control, but is more expensive to implement and maintain than share-level security. By itself, Windows 98 cannot support user-level security. Windows 98 requires each computer on a network to be assigned a workgroup name and a unique computer name, regardless of what type of networking software is in use.

- When planning your installation of Windows 98, you also need to consider how you want to ensure the security of your computer. In addition to the logon requirements of share-level and user-level security, you can take advantage of other security features, including system policies, user profiles, and the password cache.

- Before actually installing Windows 98, you need to decide which Windows 98 components you want to install. Windows 98 offers four types of installation; each type represents a collection of components. For most installations, the Typical installation is probably the safest option.

- After deciding which components you want to install, you must decide what kind of Windows 98 installation you wish to perform. You have a choice of performing a new installation, an upgrade from Windows 3.x to Windows 98, or an upgrade from Windows 95 to Windows 98. Note that it is possible to uninstall Windows 98, and that you can configure your system to boot multiple operating systems, only one of which is Windows 98.

KEY TERMS

- **boot record** — The first entry in the boot sector. Tells the computer where to look for key boot information and related programs.

- **boot sector** — A special area on a bootable hard disk containing a series of instructions and code that tells a computer where one or more operating systems are located on the disk, and how to start up (boot) each one.

- **cluster** — A storage area on a hard disk consisting of a group of sectors.

- **compact installation** — One of the options presented by the Windows 98 Setup program. Copies only the minimum files and components necessary to create a working version of Windows 98. Designed to consume as little disk space as possible. Unless disk space is at a premium, this option is not recommended.

- **custom installation** — One of the options presented by the Windows 98 Setup program. Allows an expert to examine all of the component categories for Windows 98 (and their constituent files) and then manually select any and all elements that should be included in a particular installation. This option is most often selected for automated installations, or for bulk installations, where testing has permitted an IS professional to select exactly which components to include.

- **domain** — A group of users and computers. Many organizations divide their users and computers according to the internal structure of the company. For example, the Marketing employees might all be assigned to the Marketing domain. Domains are often used to assign different levels of access to confidential data. This definition of a domain is different from the Internet definition of domain, which (in the United States) is the three-letter designator at the end of an Internet address, such as "com".

- **domain controllers** — Specialized Windows NT Servers that provide centralized network logon services and control access to resources. *See also* Domain model.

- **domain model** — One of two Microsoft models for networking access and security. Depends on the presence of a server called a domain controller that stores a database of user accounts, group information, and access rights to network and server resources, thereby providing a single logon to the domain, and centralized security and access control mechanisms. *Compare to* Workgroup model.

- **dual-boot machine** — A computer that can boot to two operating systems.

- **FAT file system** — Any of a number of file systems that use a file allocation table as the primary means of organizing data on a hard disk. MS-DOS and Windows 3.11 through Windows for Workgroups use a simple 16-bit FAT file system (FAT16) that supports only eight-character filenames. A new 16-bit FAT file system called VFAT was introduced with Windows 95 that could also handle long filenames. Today, Windows NT and Windows 95 both support VFAT, as does Windows 98. But Windows 98 also supports a 32-bit implementation of the FAT file system called FAT32.

- **fault tolerance** — The ability of a computer system to withstand element or component failures. Also refers to a design and deployment strategy for computer systems that systematically seeks to eliminate any single factors that could cause system failures or data loss.

- **file system** — The part of the operating system that defines the general organization of files and folders on a hard disk, and also provides the structure within which files may be named, stored, deleted, copied, moved, and so forth. *See also* FAT file system.

- **logical drive** — The software counterpart of a physical disk drive. Each logical drive is assigned a letter (such as C, D, or E). Physical disk drives can be split into partitions, each with their own File Allocation Table (FAT). Partitions can be split into multiple logical drives.

- **logon method** — The process of supplying a user account name and a password when prompted for such information, when a user tries to gain access to a Windows computer; the addition of third-party software may impose additional checks or input requirements (such as thumbprint or retinal scans, multiple password checks, and so forth).

- **long filenames** — Filenames of up to 255 characters (with a total of 260 characters for the complete path name).

- **multiboot machine** — A computer that can boot to three or more operating systems.

- **networking model** — The kind of network access and security controls that apply to specific Microsoft network implementations; the models supported include the workgroup model and the domain model.

- **partition** — A section of a hard drive. Each partition has its own File Allocation Table (FAT). Partitions can be further divided into logical drives.

- **password cache** — A list of passwords for individual users who use share-level security to access resources on a specific Windows workstation, maintained locally in a .pwl file on that machine.

- **password security** — The use of a password to grant access to some specific resources; in the domain model for security, the domain controller requires a valid account name and password before a user is permitted to log on to a machine or access any domain resources, and handles all authentication requests thereafter; in the workgroup model for security, individual resources carry password checks, and users must remember and use individual passwords on a per resource basis.

- **portable installation** — One of the options presented by the Windows 98 Setup program. Tailored for use on a portable or laptop computer, and therefore omits certain items that may not be of interest to portable computer users, while including a complete collection of communications and remote access tools.

- **protected mode** — A mode of DOS operation in which memory addresses beyond the 1 MB "high-water" mark required for real-mode operation may be accessed; protected-mode operation is the norm for newer versions of Windows NT and Windows 95.

- **real mode** — A mode of DOS operation in which the original constraints of the 80286 processor architecture are rigidly enforced, and in which only the lower 1 MB of RAM may be directly addressed. This distinction is important because it relates to the method in which certain device drivers operate, and because switching between real and protected mode, or vice versa, is a time-consuming and therefore "expensive" operation in terms of system overhead and performance.

- **sector** — A portion of a hard drive.

- **Setup** — The Windows 98 installation program. Officially known as "Windows 98 Setup."

- **share-level security** — A security strategy for Windows 98 in which individual network-accessible resources, called shares, are managed independently, and each requires its own password for access.

- **standalone** — A computer that operates without a direct network attachment of any kind.

- **standalone workstation** — A workstation that operates without any kind of connection to a network.

- **swap file** — A reserved area on a hard disk that Windows 98 uses to store elements of virtual memory that are not currently in active use. Data constantly moves back and forth from this file, into and out of RAM. The continual swapping of information gives the swap file its name.

- **system policy** — A set of restrictions on user access, resources, desktop attributes, and application access that may be applied on a per user, per computer, or per group basis. Windows 98 includes a tool called the System Policy Editor, which must be used to create or modify such policies.

- **terminate-and-stay-resident program (TSR)** — A special type of DOS program, such as a driver, that loads into memory and remains present even when not in use, so as to be available whenever it's needed. (For example, to handle incoming data from a network interface, or to send outgoing data through such an interface.) One of the greatest advantages of Windows 98 is that it can load and unload drivers as they're needed, rather than consuming precious system resources with TSRs.

- **Typical installation** — The default installation option presented by the Windows 98 Setup program. Should suffice for most ordinary users, for either desktop or laptop computers.

- **user-level security** — A form of network security that establishes system and resource access on the basis of a password and username provided by the user. The domain controller checks this information against a list of usernames and passwords, and then either accepts or rejects the logon attempt. This is the highest level of security currently available to Windows 98 users, and is only possible on networks including a domain controller.

- **user profile** — A collection of files containing preferences and configuration settings specific to a single user.

- **utility software** — Software used to rearrange and streamline the contents of a hard disk, or perhaps to delete unwanted or unneeded files.

- **WINUNDO.DAT** — A kind of "suitcase file" (that is, a file that contains multiple original files in a restorable format) that is created when the Uninstall option is selected when installing Windows 98 as an upgrade. Contains the complete set of files that constituted the previous version of Windows.

- **WINUNDO.INI** — A map file that records the contents of WINUNDO.DAT and the original locations of the files it contains. Should you ever choose to uninstall Windows 98, this file unpacks the contents of WINUNDO.DAT and indicates where its component files should reside.

- **workgroup model** — One of two security models supported for Windows 98, the workgroup model depends on share-level security and peer-to-peer interaction to make network resources available to users. This model works best for small groups of users who normally work together. *Compare to* domain model.

Review Questions

1. Which of the following does not meet the minimum requirements for Windows 98?
    a. 66 MHz 80486DX CPU
    b. 12 MB of RAM
    c. 200 MB available disk space

2. Which of the following file formats does Windows 98 support? (Choose all correct answers.)

   a. NTFS
   b. FAT
   c. HPFS
   d. FAT32

3. On a multiboot machine, you must use FAT16 on partitions that Windows NT 4.0 needs to access. True or False?

4. Which of the following items is not an advantage of FAT32 over FAT16?

   a. long filename support
   b. support for smaller disk clusters
   c. ability to access backup FAT and boot records
   d. support for larger disk drives

5. For drives smaller than 512 MB, FAT32 is not a viable disk format. True or False?

6. Which networking protocol is the best choice for a standalone Windows 98 machine?

   a. TCP/IP
   b. NetBEUI
   c. NWLink
   d. none of the above

7. Which of the following apply to the Workgroup model? (Choose all correct answers.)

   a. works best for large numbers of users
   b. allows for user-level security
   c. Workgroup names limit the number of PCs immediately visible in Network Neighborhood.
   d. sometimes called peer-to-peer networking

8. Which of the following apply to the Domain model? (Choose all correct answers.)

   a. works best for larger numbers of users
   b. requires a domain controller
   c. allows for user-level security
   d. good for small networks where administrative costs have to be kept as low as possible

9. A domain model is best when security is relatively important. True or False?

10. A workgroup model is best when security is relatively unimportant. True or False?

11. Of the following characters, which may appear in Windows 98 computer names? (Choose all correct answers.)
    a. letters (a-z, A-Z)
    b. numbers (0-9)
    c. colon (:)
    d. forward slash (/)
12. Windows 98 and Windows NT can both read FAT32 files. True or False?
13. A disk partition is the same as a logical drive. True or False?
14. You can use a protected-mode driver when installing Windows 98 from the DOS command prompt. True or False?
15. How do you back up a Windows 95 Registry when preparing to upgrade to Windows 98?
    a. click Start, click Run, type regback
    b. click Start, point to Programs, point to Accessories, point to System Tools, click on Regback
    c. copy the default Registry from the Windows 95 installation CD
    d. click Start, point to Programs, point to MS-DOS Prompt, type Regedit /e regback.txt
16. Which of the following operating systems use a Registry? (Choose all correct answers.)
    a. Windows 3.x
    b. Windows 95
    c. Windows 98
    d. MS-DOS
17. A password cache represents a potential security threat. True or False?
18. If you want to retain current desktop settings and preferences from Windows 95, which Windows 98 installation option should you use?
    a. new installation
    b. upgrade installation
    c. network installation
    d. CD-ROM installation
19. If you want to eliminate current desktop settings and preferences from Windows 95, which Windows 98 installation option should you use?
    a. new installation
    b. upgrade installation
    c. network installation
    d. CD-ROM installation

20. Which of the following explain why you cannot dual boot Windows 95 and Windows 98? (Choose all correct answers.)
    a. Windows 98 is intended as an upgrade to Windows 95.
    b. Windows 95 and Windows 98 both use the same boot file.
    c. Windows 95 and Windows 98 are not compatible.
    d. none of the above

Hands-on Projects

Project 2-1

In this project, you will install Windows 98 as a new installation from the installation CD. To complete this project you need a computer that meets the minimum hardware requirements for Windows 98, plus a CD-ROM drive, and a hard drive with at least 150 MB of free space available. Windows 95 should not be installed on this system. You should already have installed MS-DOS 6.22 and the drivers for your CD-ROM and 3½-inch disk drives. You will also need a 3½-inch disk to create the Emergency Startup Disk.

1. Review the steps for a new installation provided in the chapter.
2. Compile the information you need to install Windows 98 (such as the computer name), as explained in the chapter.
3. Install Windows 98 as a new installation, as described in the chapter, using the files provided on the installation CD.

Project 2-2

In this project, you will install Windows 98 as an upgrade from Windows 95, using the files provided on the installation CD. To complete this project you need a computer that meets the minimum hardware requirements for Windows 98, plus a CD-ROM drive, and a hard drive with at least 150 MB of free space available. You should already have installed Windows 95. You will also need a 3½-inch disk to create the Emergency Startup Disk.

1. Review the discussion of installing Windows 98 as an upgrade, provided in the chapter.
2. Compile the information you need to install Windows 98 (such as the computer name), as explained in the chapter.
3. Install Windows 98 as an upgrade to Windows 95, as described in the chapter, using the files provided on the installation CD.

CASE PROJECTS

1. As the administrator at Helpful Design, a small industrial design company with 10 employees, you've been asked to upgrade all three of the company's computers to Windows 98. Each computer has different operating systems installed: MS-DOS 6.2, Windows 3.1, and Windows 95. You have two weeks to complete this project. Each of the target machines meets the basic Windows 98 hardware, memory, and disk space requirements. All machines include a CD-ROM drive. Discuss the differences in installation requirements. What should you back up on each system before installing Windows 98? Should you transfer the settings from your old operating system?

2. Your boss has heard that FAT32 is the best file system to use with Windows 98. He thinks that all 20 computers in your office should be upgraded to Windows 98 because of what FAT32 can do. Write a short report to your boss discussing the advantages and disadvantages of FAT32. Why will FAT32 save you disk space over FAT16? What happens if you have to uninstall Windows 98 back to Windows 95 OSR2? What if you're uninstalling to Windows 3.1?

3. As a network administrator, you're required to be familiar with all operating systems in use at your company, and to troubleshoot operating system problems. You can't afford a new machine for exclusive use of Windows 98. How might you add Windows 98 to an existing PC running Windows 95? What issues do you need to consider? If you were adding Windows 98 to an existing PC running Windows NT Workstation, what file system would you use and why?

CHAPTER THREE

THE WINDOWS 98 REGISTRY

The **Registry** is the central configuration database for Windows 98. It acts as an interface between the user and just about every setting related to the operating system. The Registry encompasses information about all users who log on to a specific Windows 98 computer, and stores configuration and settings information for external devices, plus information about all the internal hardware and system components in any modern PC. During the Windows 98 boot process, the Registry provides essential data that permits a PC to start up and commence operations, and stores information about new devices or components that may be added to a system once Windows 98 is running.

Because the Registry is so vital to the workings of Windows 98, editing it can be dangerous. One wrong move and you may need to reload the entire operating system. To minimize the danger, Windows 98 is designed so that the vast majority of users will never have to edit the Registry directly. For example, when installing programs, or hardware, the user is provided with special safe tools that prevent direct interaction with the Registry. The disadvantage of these tools is that they make assumptions about preferred settings that may not be appropriate for every user. As a Windows 98 expert, you may be asked to edit some of these settings by editing the Registry directly.

> **AFTER READING THIS CHAPTER AND COMPLETING THE EXERCISES YOU WILL BE ABLE TO:**
>
> - Understand the structure and functions of the Windows 98 Registry
> - Identify major keys and subkeys in the Registry
> - Back up and restore the Registry
> - Use direct and indirect Registry maintenance tools, including Control Panel utilities, Registry checkers, and the Windows 98 Registry Editor
> - Locate and identify significant user, hardware, and policy or profile data files

In this chapter, you will become familiar with the structure of the Registry, learn how to modify specific values in the Registry, and learn how to back up and restore the Registry. You will learn about the role of the Registry in the Windows 98 architecture in Chapter 9.

An Overview of the Windows 98 Registry

The Windows 98 Registry contains thousands of variables regarding the computer system, and individual users. Each variable is called a **key**. Windows 98 organizes these keys into a hierarchical database of information. (A **hierarchical database** is a database in which information is organized in an upside-down tree-like structure, where the lower levels contain successively greater detail.) One key may specify which programs appear in your Start menu, while another specifies the resolution of your monitor, and yet another specifies the fonts used for your printer. Because the size of the Registry can easily exceed 1 MB, Windows 98 loads into RAM only the portions of the Registry related to dynamic data (that is, data that is regularly updated). As you will learn later in this chapter, dynamic data helps Windows 98 manage time-sensitive information such as network and performance settings. The Registry incorporates many of the functions of Windows 3.x configuration files, such as Autoexec.bat, Config.sys, and Win.ini. These files exist in Windows 98 solely to support those legacy programs that cannot communicate through the Registry.

The Registry plays two primary roles in the Windows 98 operating system:

1. The Registry maintains a database of installed hardware and uses **Plug and Play (PnP)** to update this database whenever you add or remove hardware. This updating process is known as **enumeration**. You will learn more about PnP later in this chapter.

2. The Registry maintains a snapshot (called a **User Profile**) for each user who logs on to a specific Windows 98 machine. Every user can add different programs and icons to his or her User Profile. As you will learn in Chapter 4, a systems administrator can use User Profile management tools to limit how much users can customize their profiles.

Although the Windows 98 Registry is structurally similar to the Windows 95 Registry, Microsoft has added several new features. First, the Windows 98 Registry includes some self-correcting mechanisms. During the startup sequence, Windows 98 checks the contents and integrity of the Registry. Some errors are fixed automatically, while others may require you to restore the Registry from a backup.

Benefits of the Windows 98 Registry

The Registry offers fast access to standard Windows 32-bit programs and drivers via built-in application programming interfaces (APIs). The 32-bit **Registry APIs** allow a variety of applications to interact consistently with the operating system. Thanks to the APIs built into the Registry, the Windows 98 Registry is more reliable than the Windows 95 Registry. Unfortunately, the benefits do not extend to legacy 16-bit programs. Other benefits of the

Windows 98 Registry are described in the following list. Note that many of these benefits are made possible by the Registry Checker utility, which is explained later in this chapter.

- **Improved system performance**: Through increased use of the Registry, Windows 98 takes better advantage of 32-bit memory than Windows 95.

- **Improved caching**: Caching, a process by which the Registry stores part of its information in RAM, allows the operating system to access this information faster. Windows 98 caches time-sensitive information such as Plug and Play and performance data in RAM.

- **More reliable code sharing**: Because Windows 98 Registry keys no longer have a size limit, more applications can use the same Dynamic Link Libraries (DLLs). A DLL is a group of programming functions that are used by multiple programs simultaneously. Fewer DLLs mean that Windows 98 spends less time searching for other programs.

- **Efficient size**: On startup, the Registry Checker minimizes the size of the Registry files. A smaller Registry means that applications can load more efficiently.

- **Better protection against corruption**: The Windows 98 start sequence checks the Registry for potential corruption. For example, if you accidentally pull the plug on your computer, Windows 98 will use the Registry Checker to check for problems when you restart.

- **Automated backup and restore**: Daily backups are automated. Windows 98 can address more problems by restoring the last known working backup. Windows 98 usually keeps five working backups. If no backups are available, the Registry Checker attempts to repair the damage.

- **Remote management**: Network administrators can manage the Registry settings of remote computers over a network. You will learn more about remote Registry management in Chapter 11.

- **Customizable by user**: Roaming profiles can be set up on a network server. A user with a roaming profile can have the same Windows 98 "look and feel" on any computer on that network. You will learn more about roaming profiles in Chapter 4.

- **Customizable by hardware setup**: Multiple hardware profiles can be set up in the Registry. This means that a user with a laptop and docking station does not have to change hardware settings every time he or she removes the laptop from the docking station. You will learn more about hardware profiles in Chapter 4.

- **Customizable by user group**: Network administrators can create consistent settings for a group through system policies. You will learn more about system policies in Chapter 4.

WINDOWS 98 REGISTRY FILES

The Windows 98 Registry is a single **logical database**, which means that it functions as if it were a single contiguous source of information. However, it is actually stored in two separate files: System.dat and User.dat. The **System.dat** file specifies a computer's hardware and software configuration. It is customized and stored on the computer with that particular configuration. The **User.dat** file specifies settings related to particular users. Because users can log on to different computers, Windows 98 allows you to store the User.dat file on a central server, where it is available to all users. The following sections describe these Registry files in more detail.

User-related Registry Data

The User.dat file contains user-specific information. If you have set up your Windows 98 computer for multiple logons, different User.dat files are created for each user. This file can be stored in one of three places. If logons are not set up, the User.dat file can be found in the \Windows directory. If you have set up a Windows 98 machine for multiple users, their User.dat files are stored in different \Windows\Profiles subdirectories. If your Windows 98 machine allows for roaming profiles on a network (as explained in Chapter 4), the User.dat file is stored on a network server. Wherever it is stored, the User.dat file is combined with the System.dat file to create the Registry for that session.

Hardware-related Registry Data

Because the System.dat file includes the hardware data of the Registry, it is sometimes known as the hardware profile. It also includes Plug and Play and configuration data. System.dat can be found in the \Windows directory of the local machine. Do not copy this file to another machine unless you know that the configurations are identical; if something goes wrong, you may need to reload Windows 98 from scratch.

Registry Policies

As a network administrator, you can use the Policy.pol file to override settings from the User.dat or System.dat files. It is common to apply one policy to a group of users or computers. Although policy files can be stored in a local \Windows directory, the more secure location is in a limited-access network server.

As a network administrator, you can use registry policies to control how users interact with their computers. Policies can be set for individuals or for user groups known as domains. (Strictly speaking, a **domain** consists of a group of computers. However, because a domain is managed by groups of users, the term "domain" is often defined as a group of computers and users.) Common domains in a business include Sales, Engineering, Marketing, and Manufacturing. Different policies can be specified for different domains. For more details on domain management, please consult *A Guide to Windows NT Server 4.0 in the Enterprise,* published by Course Technology.

WINDOWS 98 REGISTRY ACCESS AND USAGE

In this section, you will learn when and how Windows 98 interacts with the Registry. Most often, Windows 98 interacts with the Registry via special utilities or applets. (An **applet** is a program embedded in another program, such as the utilities in the Control Panel.)

For example, you can safely modify Registry settings relating to the "look and feel" of your desktop by using the Control Panel Display applet. To open the Display applet, click Start, point to Settings, click Control Panel, and then double-click the Display applet. The Appearance tab of the Display applet is shown in Figure 3-1. The "Scheme" that appears in the middle of this window controls several Registry keys. If you change the display scheme, Windows will change the related Registry keys for you. If you want a display scheme that is not included in one of the Display applet options, you may need to edit the Registry directly, using the Registry Editor. You will learn about the Registry Editor later in this chapter.

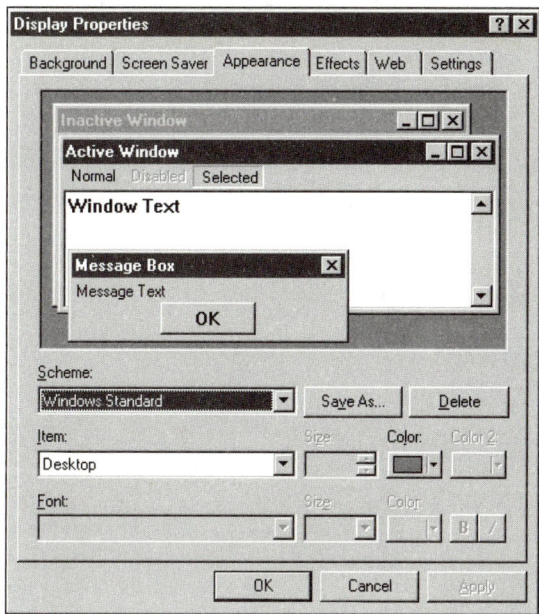

Figure 3-1 Appearance tab of the Display dialog box

Windows 98 starts interacting with the Registry as soon as you start your computer. As Windows 98 loads, it compares the hardware listed in the Registry keys with the hardware actually installed on your computer. If they don't match, Windows 98 calls on Plug and Play to install the new hardware. Plug and Play revises the Registry as it installs the components that are new to your system.

To the Registry, loading a program is similar to loading Windows 98. Programs use the Registry to set up everything from printers to the default file folders. When you install a new program on your system, a setup or installation wizard revises the Registry to match your preferences.

The Windows 98 Registry includes special keys, called dynamic keys, used to manage real-time information. **Dynamic keys** are commonly used to measure network and system performance. Through dedicated storage locations in RAM, they provide quick access to real-time programs such as performance monitors. These dynamic keys are not stored in the permanent Registry files.

Although the standard methods for installing programs and hardware modify the Registry automatically, you usually need to restart Windows 98 before these Registry changes can take effect.

In the sections that follow, you will learn about some of the primary methods for organizing or controlling major parts of the Registry, including hardware profiles, user profiles, and system policies.

HARDWARE PROFILES

A **hardware profile** is the set of keys, drivers, and settings associated with each installed component. You can define a hardware profile through the Hardware Profiles tab of the System applet, shown in Figure 3-2. Laptop users with docking stations need two hardware profiles—one for the undocked computer, and one for the docked computer. With the proper hardware configurations, you can start your laptop, and Windows 98 will pick the profile that matches your current configuration. If there is a problem, Windows 98 will prompt you to choose the closest match. Hardware profiles are explained in more detail in Chapter 4.

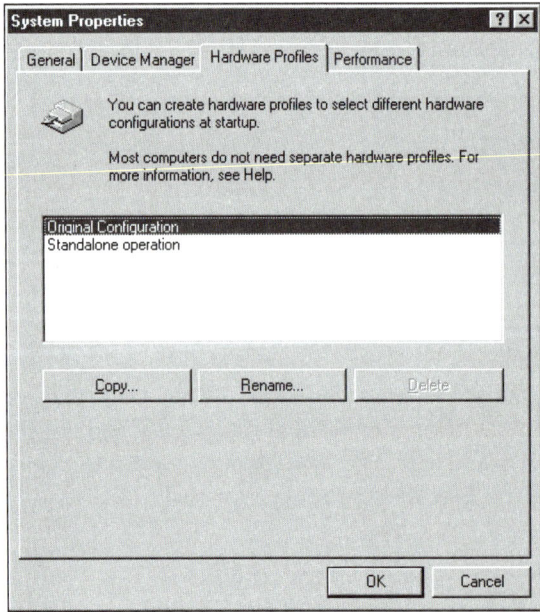

Figure 3-2 The Hardware Profiles tab of the System Properties dialog box

USER PROFILES

A user profile takes the settings you have customized in Windows 98 (such as the desktop colors or the programs on the Start menu) and stores them in the User.dat file. As explained earlier, if you are the only user on your system, the User.dat file is stored on the local C:\Windows directory. When you create a second user account on a Windows 98 machine, User.dat files are stored in individual subdirectories in the local \Windows\Profiles directory.

Two Control Panel applets are used to customize a user profile. As shown in Figure 3-3, you can choose what you customize on the desktop through the Personalized Items Settings dialog box. As shown in Figure 3-4, you can force all local users to share the same desktop settings through the User Profiles tab in the Passwords applet. You will learn more about user profiles in Chapter 4; for this chapter, all you need to know is that a Windows 98 user profile creates a special collection of Registry keys for each user.

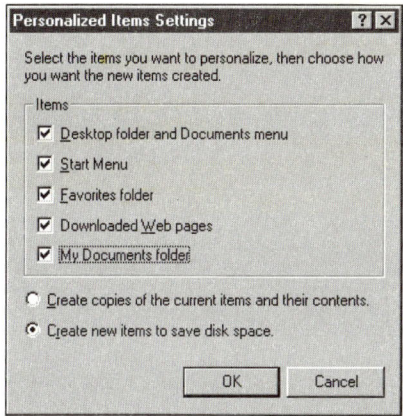

Figure 3-3 Personalized Items Settings dialog box

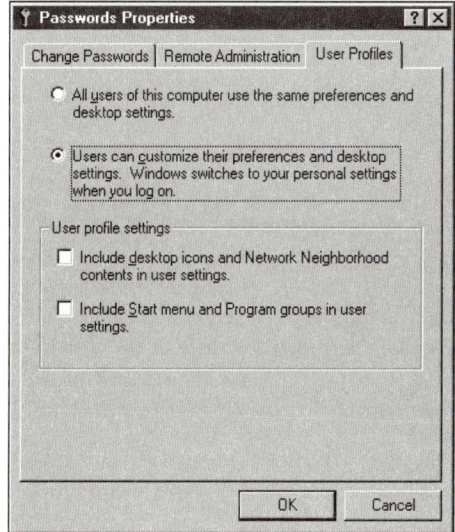

Figure 3-4 User Profiles tab of the Passwords Properties dialog box

System Policies

Windows 98 supports a rich array of settings, all created through a **system policy**, which allow you to control what users or computers can do on a network. Policies are collected in a Policy.pol file. After you create a system policy (and associated Policy.pol file), Windows 98 changes your Registry files accordingly, the next time you log on. You will learn more about policies in Chapter 4. For now, all you need to know is that system policies impose restrictions on a range of Registry values. Restrictions can limit the ability of users to interact with their desktops and applications and to access network resources. You can use the System Policy Editor to define the following kinds of policies:

- **User policy**: Apply to individual user accounts.
- **Group policy**: Apply to all users in a network-based domain.
- **Computer policy**: Similar to user policies, but while user policies apply to user accounts, computer policies apply to a specific computer name on the network.
- **Global policy**: Apply to all Windows 98 computers in a domain. This is the most powerful way to establish a policy for an entire network.

Using Registry Checker and Registry Editor

In this section you will learn about the basic tools used to manage the Registry directly: the **Registry Checker** and the **Registry Editor**. These tools are designed to help you back up, restore, and even repair the Registry as safely as possible. You will use the Registry Editor to examine the contents of the Registry later in this chapter.

Registry Safety

Any time you attempt to interact with the Registry, you take on the risk of making your system inoperable. Thus, before you attempt to use the Registry Checker and the Registry Editor, you should take the following precautions:

- First, make sure that the Emergency Startup Disk (ESD) that you created in Chapter 2 actually works. When used in conjunction with the Registry Checker and the Registry Editor, the ESD ensures that you can recover from almost any failure.
- Next, you should complete the first three Hands-on Projects at the end of this chapter, in which you back up the Registry, restore the Registry from a backup copy, and then scan the Registry for errors. Once you are comfortable with these exercises, you will be able to recover from almost any Registry problem.

It is critical to learn to back up and restore the Registry. If you have a catastrophic failure, reloading Windows 98 will be the least of your problems. To return your system to its pre-catastrophic state, you will also need to reload all your applications.

Once you are certain that you can recover from any Registry problems, you are ready to examine the two main Registry tools, as explained in the following sections.

Registry Checker

Upon startup, Windows 98 uses Registry Checker to check for problems in the Registry. In the event of a Registry error, the Registry Checker can restore a previous working backup. If there is no backup, it can repair some Registry problems. If there is no problem, Registry Checker simply performs regular backups. Windows 98 provides two versions of this utility:

- **Scanreg.exe**: You can only operate this powerful, 16-bit version of Registry Checker after booting into MS-DOS mode. Windows 98 uses Scanreg to check and scan the Registry upon each startup. When appropriate, Scanreg automatically backs up and restores the Registry. Figure 3-5 shows the Scanreg /FIX command at the DOS command line, which can sometimes repair the Registry. This command could be crucial if you have to reboot with the ESD and do not have a working backup Registry.

```
C:\windows>scanreg /?

Windows Registry Checker

Usage: SCANREG [/<option>]

<option>
    ?              : Displays usage.
    BACKUP         : Backup the registry and related system configuration files.
    RESTORE        : Choose a backup to restore.
    FIX            : Repair the registry.
    COMMENT="<comment>"
                   : Adds the specified comment to the CAB file while backing up.

C:\windows>_
```

Figure 3-5 DOS Registry Checker

- **Scanregw.exe**: The regular 32-bit version of the Registry Checker is less powerful than Scanreg. Its job is to scan the Registry. When complete, it allows you to create a Registry backup. This version of the Registry Checker cannot restore to a backup or fix errors. If Scanregw shows a problem, you should reboot into MS-DOS mode and then use Scanreg.

Over time, the Registry tends to increase in size. Bigger Registries take more time to scan. Because almost everything in Windows 98 depends on the Registry, this affects performance. To help prevent problems due to an overly large Registry, each time Windows 98 boots, Scanreg compacts the Registry whenever free space in the Registry files exceeds a certain level.

REGISTRY EDITOR

Once you have completely backed up the Registry, and have practiced restoring it, you are ready to open the Registry Editor, as explained in the next section.

Before you continue, complete the first three Hands-on Projects at the end of this chapter. Even though you will not change any Registry values when examining them, you should still know how to recover from a Registry error before even attempting to open the Registry Editor.

Once the Registry Editor is open, you must proceed with caution. Do not make changes just to see what happens. Be sure you know what you're doing at all times, and don't succumb to the temptation to experiment unless you're ready to deal with the consequences.

The Registry Editor includes no built-in integrity checks, nor will it warn you that certain changes can have serious repercussions. Worse yet, the Registry Editor includes no "Undo" key—once you make a change, the only way to restore the Registry to its prior state is to do so by configuring individual settings by hand. Any change or addition made using the Registry Editor takes effect immediately, and this information is written to User.dat or System.dat the very next time the Registry cache is **flushed**, or written to disk.

The Registry Editor is compatible with Remote Procedure Call (RPC), a Windows 98 feature that allows a program on one computer to use a different program on another computer connected through a network. Thus, you can use the Registry Editor to edit the Registry on local or remote machines. You will learn about remote administration of the Registry in Chapter 11.

In the remainder of this chapter, you will open up the Registry Editor in order to examine the major Registry keys. You will have the opportunity to change a Registry value in the Hands-on Projects at the end of this chapter.

THE STRUCTURE OF THE WINDOWS 98 REGISTRY

The Registry is a hierarchically organized group of settings for your computer. You can view this structure in the Registry Editor. There are six major Registry keys, known as root keys. A number of **subkeys** are grouped below each root. The left pane of the Registry Editor shows key names, while the right pane lists the actual settings. Figure 3-6 shows the branching, tree-like structure of the Registry subkeys.

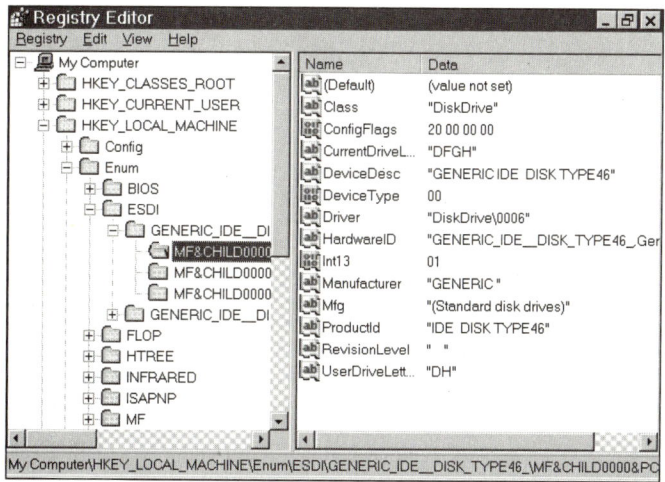

Figure 3-6 Subkeys of the root key HKEY_LOCAL_MACHINE

There are six root keys in the Registry. Together, these keys specify everything about the current hardware and software setup and configuration of your computer. Data from the three hardware configuration root keys (HKEY_LOCAL_MACHINE, HKEY_CURRENT_CONFIG, and HKEY_CLASSES_ROOT) is stored in the System.dat file. Data from the two user profiles root keys (HKEY_USERS and HKEY_CURRENT_USER) is stored in the User.dat file. The sixth root key (HKEY_DYN_DATA) maintains and monitors the performance of your computer while it is in operation; the data from this key is not stored when you shut down your computer. Two root keys, HKEY_LOCAL_MACHINE and HKEY_USERS, are considered master root keys because the information in the other root keys is derived from them.

The following list provides brief descriptions of each root key.

- **HKEY_LOCAL_MACHINE**: Contains local hardware and software configuration data. Applies to all users. Stored in the System.dat file.

- **HKEY_CURRENT_CONFIG**: Defines the current hardware configuration. Stored in System.dat.

- **HKEY_CLASSES_ROOT**: Supports the Windows 98 graphical user interface and backward compatibility with OLE (object linking and embedding) of data between programs and 16-bit applications. Stored in System.dat.

- **HKEY_DYN_DATA**: RAM-based Registry data to support real-time data collection such as performance and network monitoring. Not stored.

- **HKEY_USERS**: Global and user-specific settings for all users. Stored in the User.dat file.

- **HKEY_CURRENT_USER**: Configuration data for the current user. Stored in the User.dat file.

Note that, for the sake of brevity, root keys are usually referred to without the "HKEY" prefix. So for example, HKEY_LOCAL_MACHINE is often referred to simply as LOCAL_MACHINE.

In the following sections, you will learn more about the root keys. You may want to open up your Registry Editor in order to view the contents of these keys. Since you have your ESD, and Registry backups, and know how to restore the Registry, you can start learning to become a Registry expert with a minimum of fear.

To open the Registry Editor, click Start, click Run, type regedit in the Run text box, and then press Enter. You will see a two-pane window that appears similar to Windows Explorer. To view a subkey, click the plus (+) sign to the left of a root key in the left-hand pane. As you progress in this chapter, follow along on your Windows 98 Registry Editor. Keep Figure 3-7 handy to help you understand the relationships between Registry keys. As you can see in this figure, the two master root keys are USERS and LOCAL_MACHINE. The other keys draw their information from the master root keys.

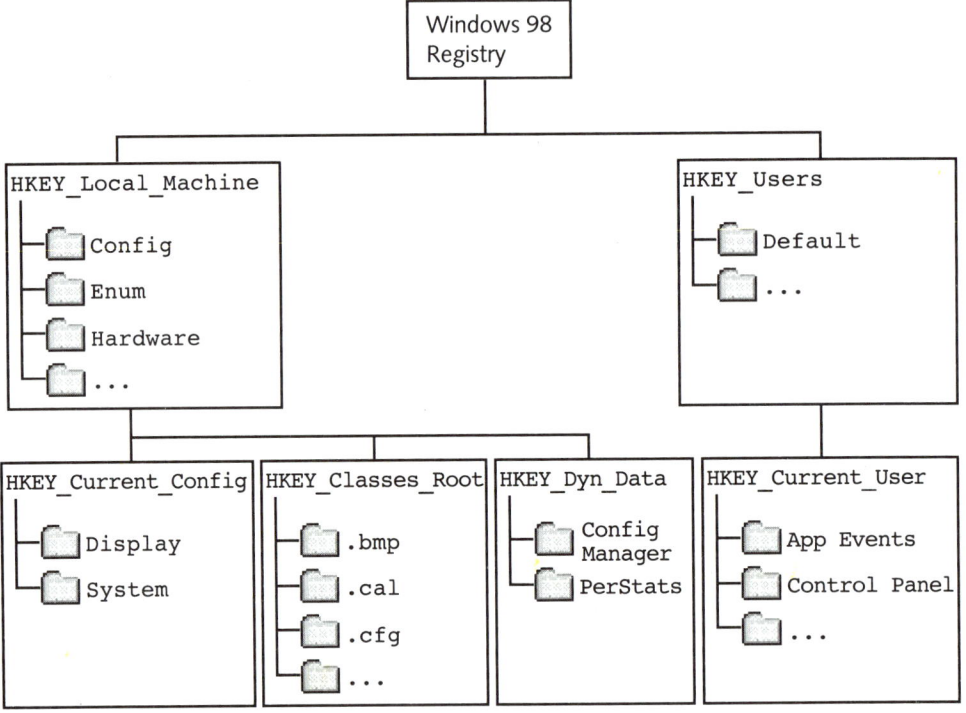

Figure 3-7 Relationships among Registry root keys

HKEY_LOCAL_MACHINE

One of two master root keys in the Registry, HKEY_LOCAL_MACHINE includes configuration data for the local computer, device drivers, and applications. Data for the

HKEY_CURRENT_CONFIG root key is drawn from this master root key to establish a current working configuration for the machine.

Windows 98 interacts with LOCAL_MACHINE whenever the hardware on your system interacts with Plug and Play (PnP). PnP checks for hardware when Windows 98 starts up and when you use the Add New Hardware Control Panel applet. On startup, Windows 98 verifies the current configuration in LOCAL_MACHINE. If there is no match, it starts PnP to find and configure the changes in your system. The most important subkeys in HKEY_LOCAL_MACHINE are described in Table 3-1.

Table 3-1 HKEY_LOCAL_MACHINE Subkeys

Subkey	Description
Config	If you have one hardware configuration, the Config key has only one subkey. On startup, the subkey that matches your configuration is turned into the HKEY_CURRENT_CONFIG root key.
Enum	Hardware is attached to your system via connections known as **buses**. Windows 98 includes a set of bus enumerators that checks for active hardware attached to each bus. When enumeration finds hardware (such as a printer), it lists the device type, hardware ID, manufacturer, and drivers for that device.
Hardware	Contains data for processor and COM ports
Network	Contains information about user network logons, including username, primary network provider, server validation status, and active system policies
Security	Contains network security and provider information, and available remote administration facilities
Software	Contains configuration data for all software as installed
System	By default, this key has one subkey, CurrentControlSet. This subkey manages Windows 98 startup, device drivers, and interfaces, such as language support.

HKEY_CURRENT_CONFIG

Although the CURRENT_CONFIG root key is taken from LOCAL_MACHINE, the Registry uses it to govern all Windows 98 interactions with your hardware. If you have created multiple hardware configurations, the default is in the HKEY_LOCAL_MACHINE\Config\0001 subkey. The second configuration is located in HKEY_LOCAL_MACHINE\Config\0002. On startup, Windows 98 analyzes the hardware on your system. It then chooses the subkey that most closely resembles the current configuration. You will learn how to create and manage multiple hardware configurations in Chapter 6.

HKEY_CLASSES_ROOT

The CLASSES_ROOT key supports three functions: program links to registered file types, backward compatibility with 16-bit programs, and the requirements of OLE (object linking and embedding) and DDE (dynamic data exchange). An example of a program link is the association between .doc files and Microsoft Word. When you double-click on a .doc file, CLASSES_ROOT directs your system to open up that file with a certain word processor. The backward compatibility of CLASSES_ROOT generally makes the 16-bit support of traditional Windows 3.x files, such as Win.ini, obsolete. **OLE** allows the contents of one program file, such as an Excel spreadsheet, to be linked to another file, such as a Microsoft Word document. When the data in your spreadsheet changes, DDE reflects this change in your Word document. **DDE** is the legacy version of OLE.

HKEY_DYN_DATA

For best performance, some Registry data is assembled and stored in RAM. Functions such as network communications, performance monitoring, and video access can't wait for hard disk access. This time-sensitive data is organized in the DYN_DATA root key. DYN_DATA includes two subkeys, related to hardware settings and active network components.

The **Config Manager** subkey is a snapshot of the current system configuration. It includes currently active drivers (installed and loaded), as well as devices or drivers that failed to load at startup or during installation. This subkey is rebuilt every time a Windows 98 system starts up, and is updated each time a device is added to or removed from the system. The **PerfStats** subkey includes data that describes active network components and services.

HKEY_USERS

The USERS root key includes all user preferences in Windows 98. It contains current user information, as well as subkeys for individual users that have been set up on the system. If only one user has been created, the user subkey is .Default. Otherwise, the subkey will reflect the username. When a user logs on to a computer, Windows 98 creates the CURRENT_USER root from the appropriate subkey.

HKEY_CURRENT_USER

This root contains profile data for the current user. The settings describe a complete Windows 98 user environment. These settings include application preferences, screen colors, and security information. Settings in CURRENT_USER supersede any conflicting settings in LOCAL_MACHINE. You will learn to create and manage users in Chapter 4. The most important subkeys are described in Table 3-2.

Registry Data Types

You've just examined all of the major types of keys in the Registry. Each of these keys is associated with a number or setting, which is actually a variable. There are three different kinds of Registry data types: text, binary, and DWORD, as described in Table 3-3.

Table 3-2 HKEY_CURRENT_USER Subkeys

Subkey	Description
AppEvents	Specifies the path and filename for sound files associated with certain system events such as shutdown. Sound labels are located in the EventLabels subkey; the associated .wav files are located in the Schemes subkey. For example, the default Registry tells Windows 98 to play "recycle.wav" when you empty your recycle bin.
Control Panel	Specifies Control Panel settings, including Display, Accessibility, Keyboard, and Power Management
InstallLocationsMRU	Specifies locations from which software was most recently installed. (**MRU** is short for "most recently used.") If you rerun a setup utility for a new program, this key determines where Windows 98 looks for updated files.
Keyboard layout	Contains settings corresponding to the keyboard that is currently active. You can choose from a number of different keyboards for different languages and alphabets. For example, for a U.S. keyboard, the HKEY_CURRENT_USER/keyboard layout/preload/1 key has a value of 00000409.
Network	Contains subkeys describing recent and persistent network connections
RemoteAccess	Contains address and profile subkeys used for remote network access or dial-up networking
Software	Contains software settings for the current user. Includes .ini access data for programs that need 16-bit Windows code.

Table 3-3 Registry Data Types

Data Type	Explanation
Text	Variable-length string of characters always ending with the ASCII null character
Binary	Variable-length string of hexadecimal digits. Hexadecimal is base 16. In our world of base 10 numbers, the sixteen digits are: 0, 1, 2, 3, 4, 5, 6, 7, 8, 9, A, B, C, D, E, and F.
DWORD	A single 32-bit value expressed as an 8-digit hexadecimal number. In computer jargon, 4 bits are known as a "nibble," 8 bits are known as a "byte," 16 bits are known as a "word," and 32 bits are known as a "DWORD" (or double word).

PLUG AND PLAY AND THE WINDOWS 98 REGISTRY

As you learned in Chapter 2, PnP is a feature that simplifies the process of installing and removing devices from a computer, sometimes even while the computer is running. The Registry contains the hardware-specific information necessary to make PnP work. In fact, the Registry is the primary source of device configuration information for PnP.

Three elements are required for PnP to work most efficiently. First, you need an operating system that is compatible with PnP, such as Windows 98. Next, you need a motherboard with a PnP **basic input/output system (BIOS)** to start the PnP process before your system loads Windows 98. Finally, you need PnP-compatible hardware to connect to your system. If your computer is new enough to include only PnP components, installing new hardware in Windows 98 is usually hassle free.

On systems where the operating system, BIOS, and hardware devices are all incompatible with PnP, installation works just as on older PCs—which means you may have to spend a lot of time making adjustments until you have properly configured the device. However, most systems lie somewhere between these two extremes, requiring you to understand the configuration settings and parameters of so-called "legacy devices" (those too old to adhere to PnP), to make sure they can coexist peacefully with newer PnP-compatible devices. If what you add is PnP-compatible, Windows 98 configures the device automatically. If it is not PnP-compatible, Windows 98 provides a Setup Wizard to assist with manual installation and configuration.

Within the HKEY_LOCAL_MACHINE root key, the Enum subkeys are most involved in the process of detecting and establishing hardware configurations for a Windows 98 machine. The Enum subkeys specify a variety of system and device characteristics, as described in Table 3-4.

Windows 98 actually uses two separate processes to find hardware on a computer: detection and enumeration. During the **detection** process, which is part of the initial Windows 98 setup process, the operating system searches for and attempts to recognize non-PnP devices. After you install Windows 98, detection can be activated through the Add New Hardware applet in the Control Panel. Windows 98 does not attempt to detect non-PnP hardware every time it starts.

During **enumeration**, Windows 98 scans each bus and driver class to find existing or new PnP devices. Windows 98 goes through the enumeration process during Windows 98 setup, each time Windows 98 starts up, and whenever Windows 98 is notified that a device has been added to or removed from the system. Once Windows 98 collects PnP data through enumeration, it is organized as a part of the Registry in the HKEY_DYN_DATA root key.

Table 3-4 Relationship Between Enum Subkeys and Plug and Play

Subkey	Description
ACPI	Short for "Advanced Configuration and Power Interface." Required only for battery-powered systems (e.g., laptop computers). This key describes the power interface of your laptop. You will learn more about ACPI in Chapter 6.
BIOS	On computers with a PnP BIOS, this key lists the interface between your BIOS and a variety of devices including your CPU, your COM port, and your printer port. Each subkey begins with the string *PnP and is followed by a four-digit number that groups components by classes. Numbered subkeys contain configuration information for each device.
ESDI	Configuration data for **IDE** (Integrated Device Electronics) controllers, a common, inexpensive hard drive interface technology. **ESDI** (Enhanced Small Device Interface) controllers are obsolete if you have Windows 98.
FLOP	Configuration data for the floppy disk controller
ISAPNP	Configuration data for PnP-compatible ISA cards. The ISA (Industry Standard Architecture) expansion slot was updated in 1993 to accommodate PnP.
Infrared	Configuration data for infrared devices, including designated LPT and COM ports
Monitor	Information for the monitors installed on your system
Network	Configuration data on the network setup in your computer, including protocols, redirectors, and services such as Client for Microsoft Networks.
PCI	Includes PnP data for all PCI devices on your system. A PCI device is usually a 32-bit local PC adapter bus designed by Intel.
PCMCIA	PnP data for any PC Cards attached to your (typically) laptop computer. You will learn more about PC Cards in Chapter 6.
Root	PnP data that describes communication between the core components of your system BIOS, motherboard, and COM and LPT ports, as well as core legacy devices.
SCSI	Configuration data for installed SCSI (Small Computer Systems Interface) devices. Like IDE and PCI, SCSI is used to connect to computer peripherals.

ADDITIONAL REGISTRY TOOLS AND UTILITIES

Several Windows 98 programs allow you to interact with the Registry, either directly or indirectly. You have already learned about the Registry Checker and the Registry Editor. In this section, you'll learn about some indirect Registry tools. In the Hands-on Projects, you'll have a chance to put this knowledge to work, as you experiment with several of these utilities. Likewise, in other chapters in this book—for instance, in the section on the Network applet in Chapter 4—you will examine or manipulate the Registry as you check and set a variety of system and software configuration parameters for Windows 98.

Simple, Safe Registry Tools

Not surprisingly, Microsoft recommends that you do not use the Registry Editor unless it is absolutely necessary. The following tools are safer and easier to use than the Registry Editor.

- **Control Panel applets**: There are a number of programs in Control Panel that provide access to a broad range of system, hardware, and software settings. When you modify these settings, you are modifying the Registry. For example, if you use the Display applet to change the number of pixels shown on your display from 640 x 480 to 800 x 600, the values in the HKEY_CURRENT_CONFIG\Display\Settings key will change accordingly.

- **System Policy Editor**: The System Policy Editor provides controls for system settings (computer policies), user settings (user and group policies), or both (global policies). As you will learn in Chapter 4, user profiles permit different users to customize their desktops and work environments, even when multiple users share a single Windows 98 machine. The System Policy Editor is explained in more detail later in this chapter.

- **Setup programs or Installation Wizards**: When you install a new program, you are actually making a number of changes and additions to the Registry. One example is the association of a file extension such as .abc with a specific program.

Advanced Registry Tools

Despite the large number of indirect Registry tools, there are limits to what these tools can do. Sometimes the only way to make the change you need is through the Registry Editor.

For example, it would make sense to use the Registry Editor on a laptop with a built-in infrared adapter. If you use the Control Panel applet to enable infrared communication, it will check for infrared connections every few seconds. When you restart Windows 98, infrared detection becomes an implied startup program, documented only in the Registry. Whether or not the infrared monitor actually detects a device, it will write the result to the Registry. By default, the Registry flushes to the System.dat file every 10 seconds. This is frequent enough to prevent an essential tool such as ScanDisk from ever completing its job. In this case, the only way to allow ScanDisk to finish is to deactivate the infrared monitor in the Registry startup settings for your system.

In general, the Registry defines a comprehensive database of configuration information about a machine and its operating system, hardware and software components, and desktop layout. But some Registry settings are not shown; a number of working keys do not explicitly appear in the Registry. In other words, before you can change the value of certain keys, you need to add them to the Registry.

System Policy Editor

The System Policy Editor generates and manages policy files. It is not installed by default. You will learn how to use and install the System Policy Editor in Chapter 4.

System policies can have a profound impact on the Windows 98 Registry, and act primarily to restrict access to certain applications, desktop settings, or other system features, by changing related Registry settings. Because system policies are sensitive files, they usually are stored on network servers in secure directories. Editing a system policy file usually requires administrative access to the applicable Policy.pol file for the user, computer, or group of your choice.

Once you create a policy file, you may install it on a local computer or on a network server. When a subject user logs on, the policy file is downloaded from the local or network server computer. After the file is downloaded, the policy modifies the Registry of that user. However, any changes related to the System.dat file will not take effect until that user logs on the next time, using the revised Registry.

Chapter Summary

- The Registry is the ultimate source of all operating system, hardware, software, and desktop-related information for all users who share a Windows 98 computer. As the main repository for this critical information, the Registry plays a key role whenever hardware, software, or users are added to—or removed from—a Windows 98 computer. Because Registry errors can have profound consequences, even rendering a machine unusable, you need to approach changing the Registry with caution, and only after learning to back up and restore the contents.

- Most of the Registry is stored in two files: User.dat, which contains user-specific information, and System.dat, which contains system and software configuration data. As a network administrator, you can change the settings in these files by creating a Policy.pol file through the System Policy Editor. Policies can be set up to affect individual users, computers, or groups as designated through a network domain.

- The benefits of the Windows 98 Registry include direct access to Registry data during **system bootup**, which accommodates the automatic configuration of Plug and Play hardware. As hardware or software is added to or removed from a Windows 98 machine, the Registry monitors and maintains relevant configuration data. The Windows 98 Registry is better than the Windows 95 Registry for several reasons: regular compacting of Registry files improves access time and performance, flexible key size helps more applications share DLLs, and the Registry Checker can scan and repair errors or corrupt data. Windows 98 even supports remote procedure call APIs to allow network administrators to manage a Registry remotely over a network.

- In Windows 98, Registry information can be collected in ways that accommodate flexible configuration. These include hardware profiles, which permit a computer to identify and select among multiple possible hardware configurations. User profiles allow individual users on the same Windows 98 computer to establish their own unique, customized desktop settings. Network administrators can use these options to simplify system and user management.

- There are a number of indirect tools that allow you to manage the Registry safely. Setup programs add their settings to the Registry without direct user editing. Control Panel applets can manage a broad range of registry settings and values. When required,

- the Registry Checker is available to back up, restore, and repair its contents. Through system policy files, the System Policy Editor can impose restrictions on what users and groups can do, how computers behave, and even network access to applications and resources.
- As with any critical resource, it is wise to approach the Registry with caution and respect. But it is impossible to ignore how vital the Registry really is to Windows 98.

KEY TERMS

- **applet** — Literally, this means "a small application." It refers to programs that are run from inside other programs. For example, the Control Panel contains numerous applets.
- **application programming interface (API)** — A set of common tools, protocols, and program routines that provide a common interface to a major component such as the Registry.
- **basic input/output system (BIOS)** — The software that actually gets a computer up and running. A Plug and Play BIOS matches installed hardware with available system resources, such as COM and LPT ports. A Plug and Play BIOS is usually stored in a flash memory chip that can be updated as required.
- **binary** — The number system with two unique digits, 1 and 0. Some Registry keys are described as binary data.
- **bus** — A set of connections between your CPU or RAM and other hardware components. On startup, the Registry commands the BIOS to check all buses to identify configured and unconfigured Plug and Play hardware.
- **caching** — The process of storing data that provides quick future access to that data. Windows 98 stores part of the Registry in what is known as a RAM cache. Caching speeds up access to Registry key data.
- **Config Manager** — A subkey of the HKEY_DYN_DATA Registry tree, which stores configuration data on all active devices in RAM, thereby speeding up access for PnP and other Windows 98 subsystems.
- **detection** — The process of searching for legacy hardware. Windows 98 performs detection when you first set up Windows 98 and run the Add New Hardware applet in Control Panel.
- **domain** — A group of users and computers, as defined in a network that uses a server such as Windows NT server or Novell Netware to verify user logons.
- **DWORD** — A type of Registry data. A DWORD is a group of bits. There are 4 bits in a nibble, 8 bits in a byte, 16 bits in a word, and 32 bits in a DWORD. In the Registry, a DWORD is represented as eight hexadecimal (base 16) digits.
- **Dynamic Data Exchange (DDE)** — A process by which two applications can share the same data. See OLE for the current standard for data sharing.

- **dynamic key** — A type of Windows 98 Registry value that is stored in RAM, and is not explicitly written to any of the Registry files. Dynamic Registry keys map the current settings for plug and play hardware, the network and system performance.
- **enumeration** — The process of searching all connections (buses and devices) on a PC during startup for Plug and Play (PnP) devices. When a PnP-compatible device or driver is added to or removed from a Windows 98 PC, the Registry uses enumeration to update the system.
- **ESDI (Enhanced Small Device Interface)** — A hard disk interface used on small computers. ESDI standard drives have generally been replaced by IDE and SCSI systems. The ESDI Registry subkey contains IDE drive configuration data.
- **flush** — The process by which Registry data is written to the hard disk.
- **hardware profile** — The set of keys, drivers, and settings associated with each installed component. Windows 98 supports multiple hardware profiles on a single computer. This can accommodate setups such as a laptop that runs in "docked" mode in a docking station or "undocked" mode when you use the laptop out of the office. Different hardware profiles are stored in the HKEY_LOCAL_CONFIG\Config\000n key. The first configuration has a subkey of 0001, the second configuration has a subkey of 0002, and so on.
- **hierarchical database** — A database in which information is organized in a tree-like structure, where the lower levels contain successively greater detail. Used to describe the structure of the Registry, because it consists of a set of nested keys, beginning with the root keys.
- **HKEY_CLASSES_ROOT** — A Registry root key that provides backward compatibility information for OLE and 16-bit applications, but also includes Registry values used to control drag-and-drop operations, shortcuts, and various aspects of the Windows 98 GUI. This root key is associated with the HKEY_LOCAL_MACHINE\Software\Classes subkey.
- **HKEY_CURRENT_CONFIG** — A Registry root key that contains information about the current hardware and software configuration for a Windows 98 machine. This root key is associated with the HKEY_LOCAL_MACHINE\Config subkey to provide quick, easy access to configuration data for PnP and other hardware management services in Windows 98.
- **HKEY_CURRENT_USER** — A Registry root key that defines the desktop settings, menus, shortcuts, and resource mappings in effect for the user currently logged on to the system. This key is associated with the HKEY_USERS subkey for that user's account name. If there is only one user on the local system, this root key maps to the .Default subkey.
- **HKEY_DYN_DATA** — A Registry root key that stores all its values in RAM to support faster access. It also contains a copy of the current hardware configuration (in the Config Manager subkey) and active performance counters (in the PerfStats) subkey.

- **HKEY_LOCAL_MACHINE** — A Registry master root key that is associated with the System.dat Registry file, and stores all hardware- and software-related configuration data.
- **HKEY_USERS** — A Registry master root key that is associated with the User.dat Registry file. This key contains elements such as user preferences, desktop settings, shortcuts, menus, and taskbars. Individual user profiles set up as roaming profiles will usually reside on a network server, rather than on an individual machine (although a local copy will be cached to enable access when the network server is down).
- **IDE (Integrated Device Electronics)** — A common, inexpensive hard drive interface technology widely used on many PCs to this day; an enhanced version known as EIDE (Enhanced IDE) is far more common today, because it supports larger, faster drives. One commonly advertised technology is Ultra ATA, which is a version of EIDE.
- **ISA (Industry Standard Architecture)** — The adapter card bus introduced with the IBM PC/AT. The 16-bit ISA bus is still a widely used standard PC bus architecture.
- **key** — A named value within the Registry database; in the Windows 98 Registry Editor, keys appear in the left-hand pane of the Registry Editor display.
- **logical database** — A single contiguous source of information. The Windows 98 Registry is a logical database. Although it resides in multiple physical files, it behaves like a single, coherent collection of information.
- **MRU** — Short for "most recently used." The InstallLocationsMRU Registry key stores the drive or network address where the Windows 98 Setup program last found installation files.
- **object linking and embedding (OLE)** — A means by which two programs can share the same data. For example, when you import a picture into a Microsoft Word document, OLE links the picture to the designated picture-editing program. If you make a change to the picture, OLE allows Microsoft Word to reflect the change.
- **PCI (Peripheral Component Interconnect)** — A 32-bit local PC adapter bus designed by Intel; since PCI is much faster and more capable than ISA, it is the more common bus for video and network adapter cards.
- **PerfStats** — A dynamic Registry key used to store real-time counters and performance data about the current state of a Windows 98 system.
- **Plug and Play (PnP)** — A design specification created to permit a properly equipped PC BIOS and operating system to automatically detect and configure PnP-compatible devices. PnP works during system installation and startup, or as devices are added to or removed from an active system.
- **Regedit** — Another name for the Registry Editor.
- **Registry** — The hierarchical database that stores all user, hardware, software, and operating system configuration information about a Windows 98 system.

- **Registry API (or 32-bit Registry API)** — The standard programming interface that allows for consistency among system tools, install wizards, setup programs, and other software that interacts with the Registry.

- **Registry Checker** — The application that checks the integrity of the Registry. Each time Windows 98 starts up, Registry Checker can back up, restore, or repair the Registry as directed, or if damage or corruption is detected during startup. There are two versions of Registry Checker: the Windows 98 DOS version, Scanreg.exe, is more powerful than the GUI version, Scanregw.exe.

- **Registry Editor** — The high-risk tool used to directly inspect and edit the Registry. Regedit.exe can be found in the Windows 98 root directory, usually C:\Windows.

- **remote procedure call (RPC)** — A Windows 98 feature that allows a program on one computer to use a different program on another computer connected through a network. Microsoft RPCs allow a network administrator to remotely manage a remote Registry through a local Registry Editor.

- **Scanreg.exe** — The 16-bit DOS-based implementation of Registry Checker that runs each time Windows 98 starts up. If you are in the Windows 98 GUI, you need to restart your computer in MS-DOS mode to execute this program. You can use it to back up, restore, or repair a Registry.

- **Scanregw.exe** — The 32-bit Windows implementation of Registry Checker that may be run from the standard Windows 98 desktop. It is not as powerful as Scanreg.exe.

- **subkey** — A Registry key one or more levels down from another Registry key.

- **system bootup** — The process that occurs when a computer is first powered on, such as when Windows 98 starts. A PnP BIOS will check the system for existing and new PnP devices. This information is reflected in the hardware configuration in the Registry.

- **system policy** — A collection of Registry controls that may be used to control system access and appearance for individual users, groups, computers, or entire networks.

- **System.dat** — One of two primary Windows 98 Registry files. The System.dat file includes data on operating system configuration, hardware components, and installed software. This file is always stored on the local computer.

- **user profile** — A collection of user preference data that includes details such as desktop settings, shortcuts, menus, and toolbars. Individual user profiles are located in a subkey of the HKEY_USERS root key. User profile data is stored in the User.dat file.

- **User.dat** — One of two primary Windows 98 Registry files, User.dat contains user profile information for all users known to a system. It also includes default settings and related information for new users.

REVIEW QUESTIONS

1. Which of the following phrases describes the Windows 98 Registry? (Choose all correct answers.)
   a. the central configuration database for configuration data for Windows 98
   b. a hierarchical database of operating system, hardware, software, and user data
   c. a replacement for multiple configuration files used in DOS and earlier versions of Windows
   d. a database containing only binary variables

2. Of the following statements, which two describe the primary roles of the Registry?
   a. acts as a single, consistent database of hardware configuration information
   b. contains only data related to software configuration
   c. contains a snapshot of user data, called a user profile, for each named user with rights to log on to a specific Windows 98 system
   d. is modified by user profiles but not system policies

3. There are no tools available to help you manage the Registry safely. True or False?

4. Which of the following Windows 98 system components benefit from the Registry APIs? (Choose all correct answers.)
   a. Autoexec.bat
   b. 32-bit Windows programs
   c. Config.sys
   d. all 16-bit applications

5. By default, how many backup copies of the Registry does Windows 98 maintain?
   a. 2
   b. 5
   c. 7
   d. 10

6. What happens when you restart Windows 98 after an improper shutdown?
   a. The Registry Checker will always restore a previously backed up Registry.
   b. Scanreg checks the Registry for corruption.
   c. Scanregw checks the Registry for corruption.
   d. You need to rebuild the Registry from scratch.

7. Which of the following do not contain a significant amount of Registry data? (Choose all correct answers.)
   a. user profiles
   b. workgroup profiles
   c. hardware profiles
   d. system policies

8. Although the Windows 98 Registry acts like a single logical database, it is stored in multiple files. True or False?
9. Windows 98 uses which two of the following files to store Registry data?
   a. Policy.pol
   b. Common.adm
   c. User.dat
   d. System.dat
10. Which of the following Registry files must be stored locally on a Windows 98 machine?
    a. Policy.pol
    b. Common.adm
    c. User.dat
    d. System.dat
11. Which of the following Registry-related files contains information about system policies?
    a. Policy.pol
    b. Common.adm
    c. User.dat
    d. System.dat
12. The User.dat file for a roaming user profile is most likely to be stored on:
    a. a local machine
    b. a remote server
    c. a floppy disk
    d. the Registry
13. On a Windows 98 machine with multiple user profiles, where are individual user profiles stored?
    a. \Windows
    b. \Windows\System
    c. \Windows\Profiles
    d. \Windows\System32
14. Which of the following methods are safe ways to manipulate the Registry? (Choose all correct answers.)
    a. Control Panel applets
    b. setup programs or install wizards
    c. Registry Checker
    d. Registry Editor

15. Which of the following choices accurately describe dynamic Registry keys? (Choose all correct answers.)
    a. stored only in memory, not written to disk
    b. help to support rapid access to configuration data for the PnP subsystem
    c. provide temporary storage for transient data
    d. provide storage for performance-related counters and data
16. Which of the following elements can be part of a user profile? (Choose all correct answers.)
    a. desktop settings
    b. preferences
    c. application drivers
    d. application access
17. To manage the type of access allowed to a particular user on a certain Windows 98 machine, what kind of system policy would you use?
    a. user policy
    b. group policy
    c. computer policy
    d. global policy
18. Master root keys derive their settings from subkeys. True or False?
19. Which of the following Windows 98 root keys are master keys?
    a. HKEY_LOCAL_MACHINE
    b. HKEY_DYN_DATA
    c. HKEY_CURRENT_CONFIG
    d. HKEY_USERS
20. Which of the following is not a type of Registry data?
    a. floating point
    b. text
    c. binary
    d. DWORD
21. Which of the following is the name of the process by which Windows 98 finds legacy devices installed on the system?
    a. inspection
    b. enumeration
    c. detection
    d. selection

22. Which of the following tools can you use to repair a damaged Registry or restore a Registry backup?
    a. Regrest
    b. ScanDisk
    c. Scanreg
    d. Scanregw
23. Before working with the Registry Editor, it is unnecessary to back up the Registry, because you can always use the "Undo" function to reverse unwanted changes. True or False?

HANDS-ON PROJECTS

For all of these Hands-on Projects, you will need access to a computer with Windows 98 installed, preferably one not connected to a network. If you have a User.dat file on the local machine, then it is possible to do these projects with a Windows 98 computer on the network.

PROJECT 3-1

In this project, you will learn how to perform the single most important activity related to the Windows 98 Registry—backing it up. Check with your instructor to see if you will back up to a directory on the hard drive, or to a floppy disk, and adjust the following instructions accordingly.

1. Click **Start**, point to **Programs**, and then click **Windows Explorer**.
2. Click **Start**, point to **Find**, and then click **Files or Folders**. The Find Files dialog box opens.
3. Make sure the C: drive is selected in the Look in box. Then type **rb*.cab** in the Named text box, and click **Find Now**. Figure 3-8 shows these current Registry files and backups in the Find Files dialog box.

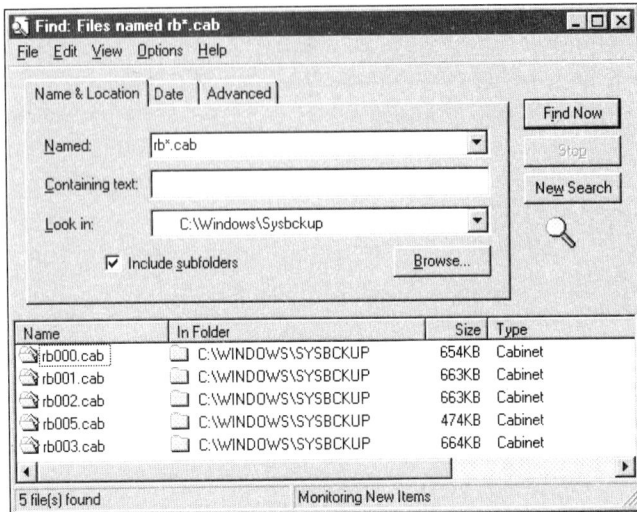

Figure 3-8 Backup Registry files

4. In the Find Files dialog box, click **File** on the menu bar, and then click **Save Search**. An icon entitled "Files named rb@.cab.fnd" appears on your desktop.

5. Click **Start**, and then click **Shut Down**. The Shut Down Windows dialog box opens, as shown in Figure 3-9.

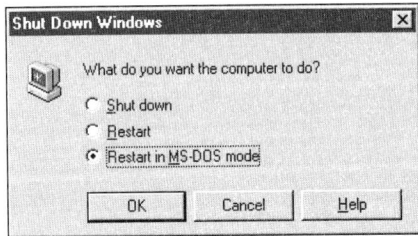

Figure 3-9 Shut Down Windows dialog box

6. Click the **Restart in MS-DOS mode** option button, and then click **OK**. Your computer shuts down and then restarts in MS-DOS mode, as indicated by the MS-DOS prompt.

7. Type **scanreg /?** then press **Enter** to display Help information about the DOS version of the Registry Checker.

8. Review the Help information.

9. Type **scanreg /backup /comment="Lab Test"** at the MS-DOS prompt, then press **Enter**. This completes the process of backing up the Registry.

10. Restart your computer.

11. Double-click the "**Files named...**" icon that you created on your desktop in Step 4, then click **Find Now** in the Find Files dialog box.
12. Compare the results with your previous search. As shown in Figure 3-10, the list has changed slightly: the oldest file has disappeared, and a new rb00n.cab file has been created.

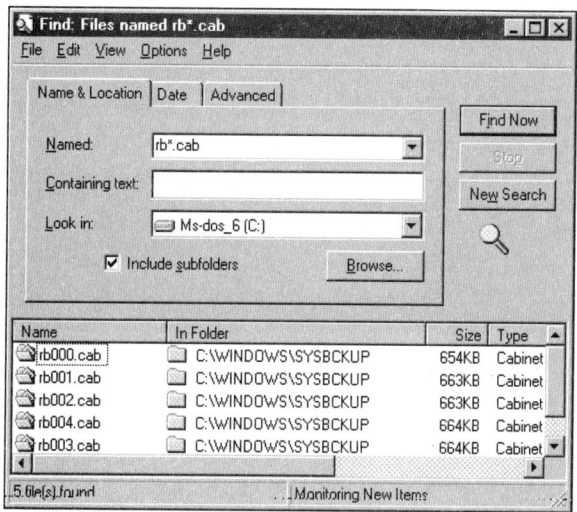

Figure 3-10 Change in Backup Registry files

13. Close the Find Files dialog box.
14. Delete the desktop icon that you created in Step 4.

PROJECT 3-2

In this project, you will restore the Registry that you backed up in Project 3-1. To use the Scanreg tool to restore a Windows 98 Registry, you must reboot your machine into DOS, and run the Scanreg.exe command. To better simulate an emergency situation, have the Emergency Startup Disk (ESD) ready that you created in Chapter 2. An Emergency Startup Disk is highly recommended. If you do not have an ESD, click Start, point to Settings, click Control Panel, double-click the Add/Remove Programs icon, click the Startup Disk tab, then click Create Disk. Insert a 3½-inch disk as prompted (as well as your Windows 98 installation CD, if necessary). Follow any remaining prompts to finish creating the ESD. Then click OK to close the Add/Remove Programs Properties.

1. Put your ESD into the 3½-inch disk drive.
2. Restart your computer.
3. You can find the scanreg file in your C:\Windows\System directory. Type **C:**, press **Enter**, type **CD\Windows\System**, and press **Enter** again. At the MS-DOS prompt, type **scanreg /restore**. A screen similar to the one shown in Figure 3-11 appears.

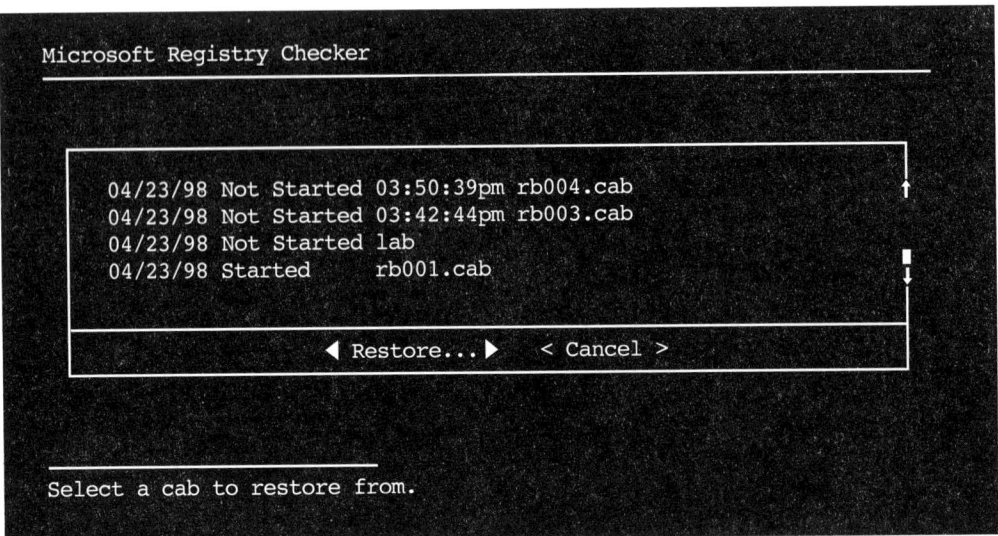

Figure 3-11 Registry Checker Restore options

4. Use the up and down arrow keys to select the Restore option with the most current time stamp.
5. Press the **R** key to initiate the Registry Restore operation. Once the Restore operation is finished, you will see a screen indicating that the Registry Restore command was executed successfully.
6. Press the **R** key to restart the computer. The computer restarts in normal Windows 98 mode.

PROJECT 3-3

In this project, you will apply the /Fix parameter to Scanreg, to practice repairing a damaged or corrupted Registry. Of course, your Registry isn't damaged, so what you see in this project won't exactly match the process of repairing a damaged Registry—but at least you will become familiar with the general process. Because Scanreg runs automatically each time a Windows 98 system boots up, you probably will never have to do this yourself. However, it is nice to know, "just in case." As with Projects 3-1 and 3-2, you will reboot your machine into the DOS mode of Windows 98.

1. Click **Start**, and then click **Shut Down**. The Shut Down Windows dialog box opens.
2. Click the **Restart in MS-DOS mode** option button.
3. Click **OK**. Your computer shuts down and then restarts in MS-DOS mode, as indicated by the MS-DOS prompt.

4. At the MS-DOS prompt, type **scanreg /fix**. A screen like the one shown in Figure 3-12 appears. The Scanreg function requires no user interaction, but it does update the display to show you which step is active, beginning with the bottom step, "Rebuilding system registry," as indicated by the » symbol to the left of that text.

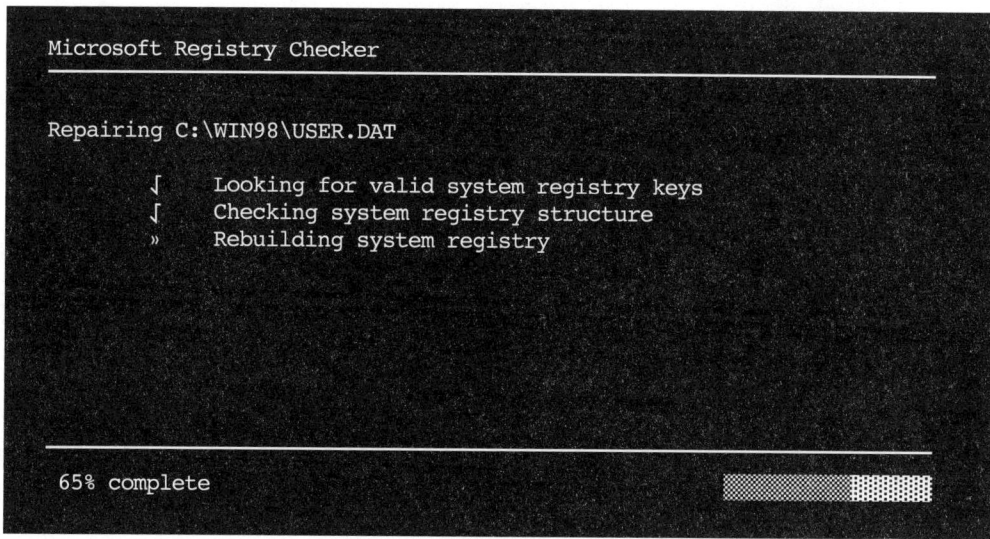

Figure 3-12   Scanreg fixing the Registry

5. Once the first phase is complete, the program begins to check the system Registry structure (that is, the contents of the System.dat file). During this phase of the process, a screen like the one shown in Figure 3-13 appears.

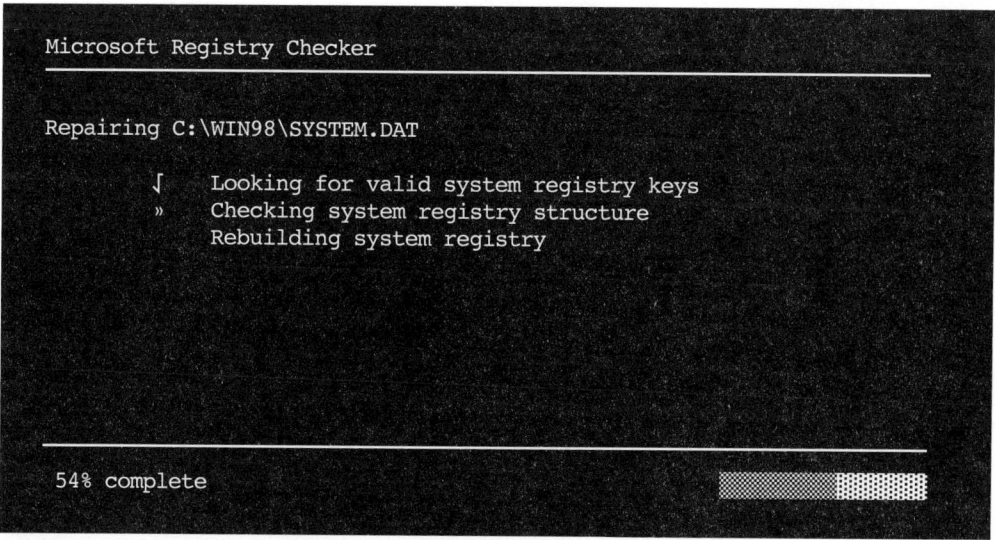

Figure 3-13   Scanreg checking the Registry structure

6. During the final phase, Scanreg checks the validity of all the Registry keys. Because your Registry is not damaged, Scanreg reports success, as shown in Figure 3-14.

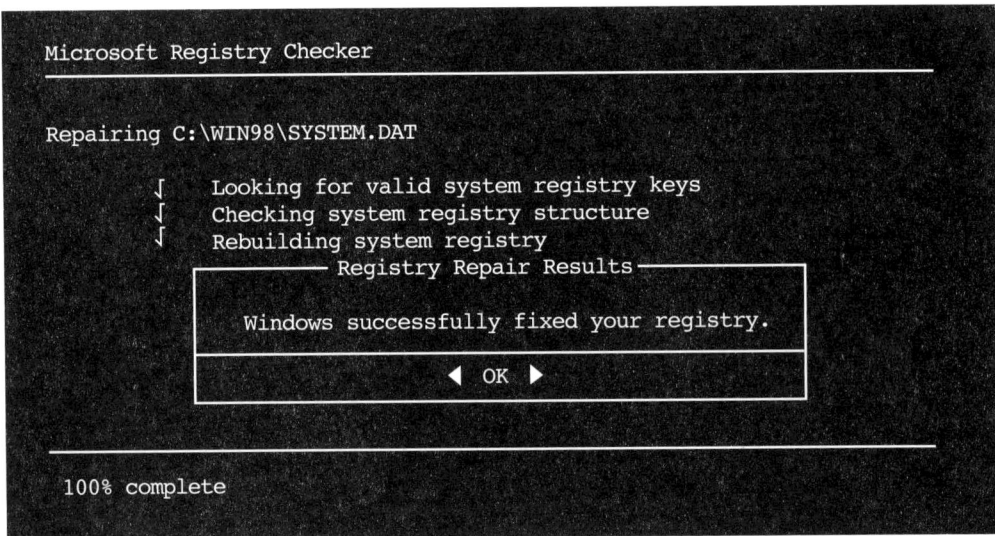

Figure 3-14 Successful completion of a Registry check

7. To return to the regular Windows 98 GUI mode, press **Ctrl + Alt + Del** simultaneously. The machine reboots.

PROJECT 3-4

In this project, you will use the Registry Editor to export a subkey to a hard disk file. You can use this technique to back up parts of the Registry. Although Scanreg/ backup (which you performed in Project 3-1) is the preferred method, as a network administrator, you may need to back up part of a computer Registry on a network using the Registry Editor.

Do not attempt to complete this project until you have completed Projects 3-1 through 3-3.

1. Click **Start**, click **Run**, type **Regedit** in the Open text box, and then click **OK**. The Registry Editor opens.
2. In the left-hand pane, click the **plus sign (+)** to the left of the HKEY_CURRENT_USER key, to expand its subkeys. Use the same technique to expand the Control Panel subkey, and then open the Appearance subkey beneath Control Panel, as shown in Figure 3-15. The details in the Registry Editor on your computer may differ from Figure 3-15.

The Windows 98 Registry   97

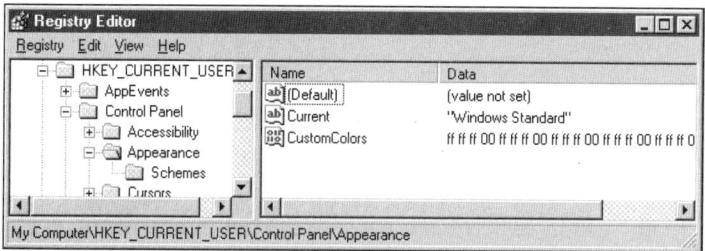

Figure 3-15   The HKEY_CURRENT_USER/Control Panel/Appearance subkey

3. To save the contents of the Appearance subkey, click **Registry** on the menu bar, and then click **Export Registry file**. This opens the Export Registry File dialog box.
4. Type **appearance.reg** in the File name text box, as shown in Figure 3-16.

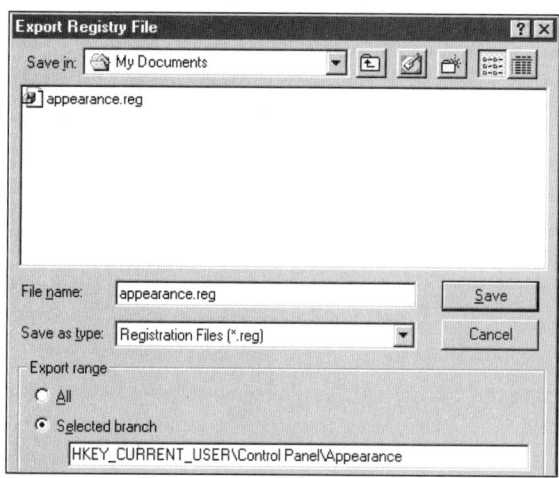

Figure 3-16   Exporting one Registry subkey

5. Click **Save** to save the file to the default directory, My Documents.
6. If you don't plan to complete Hands-on Project 3-5, exit the Registry Editor by clicking the Close button in the upper-right corner of the Registry Editor window. Do not exit the application if you plan to complete Project 3-5 next.

PROJECT 3-5

In this project, you will learn how to import a saved Registry, or a saved portion of the Registry, using the Windows 98 Registry Editor. This project assumes you have completed Project 3-4. If you just completed Project 3-4, start with Step 3; otherwise, begin with Step 1.

1. Click **Start**, click **Run**, type **Regedit** in the Open text box, and then click **OK**. The Registry Editor window opens.

2. In the left-hand pane, click the **plus sign (+)** to the left of the HKEY_CURRENT_USER key, to expand its subkeys. Use the same technique to expand the Control Panel subkey, and then select the Appearance subkey beneath Control Panel. Your screen should look similar to Figure 3-16.

3. To import the saved version of this Registry subkey, click **Registry** on the menu bar, and then click **Import Registry File**. The Import Registry File dialog box opens.

4. Type **appearance.reg** in the File name text box, click **OK**, and then click **OK** again. The current contents of the Appearance subkey are replaced by values from the file you previously exported in Project 3-4. In this case the values are identical to the values in the Registry, but if you are performing this task in a real-life situation, they probably won't be.

5. Exit the Registry Editor by clicking the **Close** button in the upper-right corner of the Registry Editor window.

PROJECT 3-6

In this project, you will add a new key to the Registry that will speed up how quickly submenus display when you work with any application that uses cascading menus (such as the Start menu and its many submenus). This change provides a quick and easy "performance boost" to Windows 98, because it lets you navigate around your desktop a bit more quickly than the default menu speed setting.

Do not attempt to complete this project until you have completed Projects 3-1 through 3-4. Do not make any changes to the Registry other than the one described in the following steps.

1. Click **Start**, click **Run**, type **Regedit** in the Open text box, and then click **OK**. The Registry Editor window opens.

2. In the left-hand pane, click the **plus sign (+)** to the left of the HKEY_CURRENT_USER key, to expand its subkeys. Use the same technique to expand the Control Panel and Desktop subkeys. Then click the desktop subkey to open it. Next, you will add a new value to the Desktop subkey named MenuShowDelay.

3. Click **Edit** on the menu bar, click **New**, and then click **String Value**. A new value named "NewValue#1" appears in the right-hand pane, as shown in Figure 3-17. (If the commands on the Edit menu are greyed out, you did not open the desktop subkey in Step 2.)

The Windows 98 Registry   99

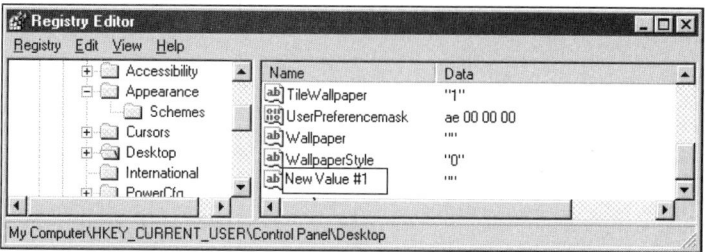

Figure 3-17 Activating a Registry key with a new value

4. Type **MenuShowDelay** to replace the string "NewValue#1", then press **Enter**.
5. Click **Edit** on the menu bar, and then click **Modify**. The Edit String dialog box opens, as shown in Figure 3-18. Here you can assign a value for the data associated with this named Value. The acceptable range of values for this setting is from 0 (fastest) to 10 (slowest). Most users find that 0 is too fast, so you will try the "1" setting.

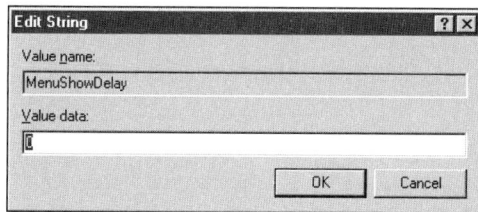

Figure 3-18 Entering a new value in a Registry key

6. Type **1**, and then click the **OK** button.
7. Close the Registry Editor by clicking the **Close** button in the upper-right corner of the Registry Editor Window. Next, you will examine the results of this change to your Registry.
8. Click **Start**; then navigate through some submenus. You should notice an increase in the speed at which these menus pop up when you drag to the right of a menu with a cascading submenu.

CASE PROJECTS

1. Because you need to add some special desktop controls to several Windows 98 desktops, you have no choice but to use the Registry Editor to add these values. Explain what your first step in adding these keys should be, and why this step is absolutely essential to the ongoing health and well-being of the systems you must manage.

2. At Telepad Inc., two Windows 98 machines in the corporate library contain a top-secret database, which should only be accessed at those machines. Explain how you might restrict users from accessing this data across the network, and what kind of tool you might employ to prevent users who are permitted to access the network from copying files from this machine across the network. Why might this not be the best approach for someone's everyday desktop machine?

3. Your boss has experimented with the Registry in Windows 95 with disastrous results. He has heard that Windows 98 is even more dependent on the Registry and fears the worst. Explain to your boss what you can do to protect and back up the Registries. Tell him what additional backup programs are available. Explain what you can and cannot safely do to the Registry. Explain how to prevent unauthorized users from attempting to edit the Registry. Because Windows 98 is more dependent on the Registry then Windows 95, explain how the performance of the Registry has been optimized in Windows 98.

CHAPTER FOUR

Managing Windows 98 Users, Profiles, and Policies

Windows 98 gives users a great deal of control over their operating system. These controls range from the ability to customize the desktop to the ability to restrict the functions of a particular computer. The look, feel, and functionality of Windows 98 as customized by a user is also known as the user environment. In this chapter, you will learn about most of the Windows 98 features that allow you to control the user environment.

AFTER READING THIS CHAPTER AND COMPLETING THE EXERCISES YOU WILL BE ABLE TO:

- Describe the multiuser environment of Windows 98
- Enable multiple user profiles with Windows 98
- Create and manage both user preferences and mandatory profiles
- Deploy roaming profiles over a Windows NT or NetWare network
- Create and use hardware profiles
- Create and deploy system policies

On a standalone Windows 98 computer, you can create a separate user environment for each user by employing user profiles. On a networked Windows 98 computer, you can create a separate user environment for each user by employing user profiles and policies. In order to implement user profiles and policies, the network must contain a server running Windows NT Server or Novell NetWare.

Understanding the various options offered by profiles and policies can be difficult. At the end of this chapter, you will find a list summarizing these options. As you learn each kind of profile and policy, you may want to refer to this list to help you keep the differences straight.

THE ROLE OF THE USER IN WINDOWS 98

Windows 98 is a **multiuser operating system,** which means that it performs two major roles. As an operating system, Windows 98 integrates the functions of and interactions among your hardware components. As a multiuser system, it also stores and manages separate environments for multiple users.

There are actually two types of multiuser operating systems. Operating systems such as Windows 98 load one of several customized user environments for each user as he or she logs on, but only allows one logged-on user per computer. The other type of system—UNIX, for example—allows different users to log on simultaneously in different environments. Through time-sharing, UNIX can distribute its resources on demand. Multiple users can log on to different UNIX terminals, each with his or her own environment.

Multiuser operating systems maintain separate accounts for each user. A **user account** is a logical identifier that the operating system employs to identify individuals, to associate a specific user with his or her preferred environment, and to manage the access of each user to system resources. In the following section, you will learn to manage multiple user accounts on a standalone system. You will also learn what it takes to manage multiple accounts on a server-based network.

By default, Windows 98 is configured as a one-user system. In this chapter, you will learn to implement a multiuser environment in Windows 98. In the Hands-on Projects at the end of this chapter, you will actually configure multiple users.

USERNAMES AND PASSWORDS

In this chapter, you will learn to configure Windows 98 to require passwords. When password use is required, a user who boots into a Windows 98 computer will see the "Welcome to Windows" dialog box requesting a valid username and password. Unless a user enters this logon information, the default user environment will appear. In a multiuser system, the default user environment typically provides limited or no access to computer and network resources. You will need a computer with Windows 98 installed, connected to a Windows NT network. You will learn to set up user-level security on your computer in Chapter 8.

A username can be up to 128 alphanumeric characters (letters or digits) long. A password is a security device used to allow only the authorized user into each account. By default,

Windows 98 places no restrictions on what can be used as a password. You could, for instance, choose to use no characters as your password, but such a password would not make your system very secure.

 If you do not see a Change Password tab, you have not logged on to your Windows 98 computer. Restart Windows 98 and log on. If you are not given a chance to log on, click Start, point to Settings, click Control Panel, and then double-click the Network applet. In the Primary Network Logon box, choose Client for Microsoft Networks or Client for NetWare Networks and click OK. If neither of these options is available, you will learn to enable them later in this chapter.

By employing a system policy, you can create minimum requirements for passwords. You can specify a minimum length or require that each password have a combination of letters, numbers, and punctuation. (You will learn more about system policies later in this chapter). A secure password is not based on slang or dictionary words. It is at least six characters long and consists of some combination of upper- and lowercase letters, numerals, and punctuation.

PASSWORDS AND NETWORKS

Passwords are central to permissions for Windows 98, both when it is installed on a standalone computer and on a network. On a network, there are two standard types of permissions, known as share-level and user-level security. Each type of permission entails its own password, as you will see in Chapter 7. This chapter assumes you are using share-level security.

Share-level security means that you have a password for each resource (or share), such as file folders and printers. You can specify different passwords for each resource. You do not need to create or administer users on a network. However, the number of different passwords can become unwieldy in a large network. All an outsider needs to access your network is the right password.

Under **user-level security,** you need a username and a password on a Windows NT or Novell NetWare server to log on to the network. A network administrator can give permissions to resources such as files and printers to specific users or groups of users. The user name and password associated with user-level security should not be confused with the user name and password that can be required in order to log on to a local Windows 98 computer. Network administrators cannot assign permissions to files and printers for users on a standalone Windows 98 computer. However, to simplify the logon process, it is common to use the same username and password for logging onto the local Windows 98 computer, and onto the network under user-level security.

PASSWORD LISTS

At a Windows 98 client machine on a network, users may have to log on twice or more: once onto the local Windows 98 computer, then onto one or more networks. Then, once users are logged on to the network, they may have to provide a password for each resource (such as printers or files) they want to access.

You can reduce the number of required logons in two ways. First, you can employ the same password for both local and network access, in which case Windows 98 will only require you to log on once in order to access both the local Windows 98 computer and the network. Second, you can use the Windows 98 password cache to prevent users from having to enter passwords every time they want to access a resource. The **password cache** is a list of resources and encrypted versions of their associated passwords. The password cache can allow you to log on to specified network resources automatically when you log on to Windows 98.

Note that using the same password to log on to Windows 98 and the network decreases the security of your network. Using the password cache also decreases security. But there is a practical limit to the number of passwords that most users can remember. If these measures keep users from posting their passwords next to their computer, they may be worth the risk.

The password cache is stored in a **password list file (PWL)** located in the main Windows directory (e.g., C:\Windows*username*.pwl). Your Windows 98 system keeps a separate password cache for each user. This file is encrypted to prevent unauthorized users from deciphering your other passwords. You can even use a system policy to prevent users from seeing this encrypted file.

To change a password stored in the Windows 98 password cache, you can use the Password Properties applet, which is accessed via the Passwords icon in the Control Panel. The Passwords Properties applet has three tabs—Change Passwords, Remote Administration, and User Profiles. The Remote Administration tab is discussed in Chapter 11. The User Profiles tab is discussed later in this chapter. The Change Passwords tab, shown in Figure 4-1, offers you the option of changing either your Windows logon password or other passwords, such as your network access or resource passwords.

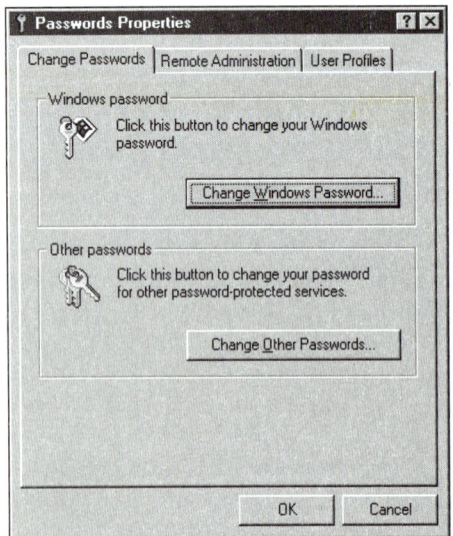

Figure 4-1 The Change Passwords tab of the Passwords applet

The following steps show you how to change your Windows 98 password, and at the same time change your network access password to match your new Windows 98 logon password. The subsequent instructions show you how to simply change your network access or resource passwords.

To change a network or resource password to match your new Windows logon password:

1. Click Start, point to Settings, click Control Panel, double-click the Passwords icon, and then click the Change Passwords tab.

2. Click Change Windows Password. The Change Windows Password dialog box appears, giving you the option of changing other known passwords to match your Windows 98 logon password.

 If you see Old Password, New Password, and Confirm New Password text boxes, your computer has not been set up to log on to a Microsoft Windows NT network. You will learn how to set up your computer to log on to a Windows NT network in Chapter 13.

3. Select the check boxes beside each network or resource whose password you wish to change, and then click OK. Another Change Windows Password dialog box opens.

4. In the Old password text box, type your old password.

5. In the New password text box, type your new password.

6. In the Confirm new password text box, type your new password again.

7. Click OK. The Windows 98 logon password and the passwords for other selected systems are changed to match the password you entered in Step 5.

The Change Other Passwords button on the Change Passwords tab allows you to assign different passwords to different resources. If your computer is not set up to connect to a Windows NT or Novell NetWare network, you will not be able to perform these steps. You will learn to set up your computer to log on to a Windows NT and a Novell NetWare network later in this chapter. To change passwords for other resources:

1. Click Start, point to Settings, click Control Panel, double-click the Passwords icon, and then click the Change Passwords tab.

2. Click Change Other Passwords. The Select Password dialog box opens.

3. In the Select Password dialog box, select the passwords you want to change, and then click Change. The Change Password dialog box opens.

4. You'll be prompted to type in your old password once, then the new password twice.

5. Click OK. The password for the selected system is changed.

Windows NT provides a much broader range of password restrictions than those offered by Windows 98. The **Password Policy** of Windows NT allows limits on minimum and maximum length and age. In addition, you can prevent a user from switching between the same two or three passwords. By applying Service Pack 3 to Windows NT, a network administrator can require passwords to contain at least three of the following types of characters: uppercase letters, lowercase letters, numerals, and punctuation.

When Windows 98 computers are clients of Windows NT servers, you can use Windows NT password rules for network access. You can also use system policies to regulate local logons to Windows 98 machines.

PASSWORD LIST EDITOR

Sometimes the owners of network resources change their passwords. In that case, the password in your password cache will no longer work. Then it makes sense to delete the password from your cache, using a utility known as the Password List Editor. After you delete the password from the password cache, you can access the resource again, using the new password, at which point Windows 98 will give you the option of saving the new password. The process of saving the password sends your new password to the cache.

The **Password List Editor** is shown in Figure 4-2. You can install this utility only after you install Windows 98, using the Windows Setup tab of the Control Panel Add/Remove Programs applet and the files on the Windows 98 installation CD in the \Tools\Reskit\Netadmin\Pwledit directory. You'll have a chance to practice installing the Password List Editor in the Hands-on Projects at the end of this chapter.

You cannot display or edit passwords in the Password List Editor. The Password List Editor simply allows you to display the networks and resources in your cache. If you need to delete a password, you simply select the resource or network whose password you want to delete, and click Remove.

Keep in mind that every resource on the password cache list is at risk if an unauthorized user discovers the associated password. If you want to minimize your risk, you can disable password caching through a system policy. If you do choose to disable password caching, you will have to enter a password every time you need to access a resource.

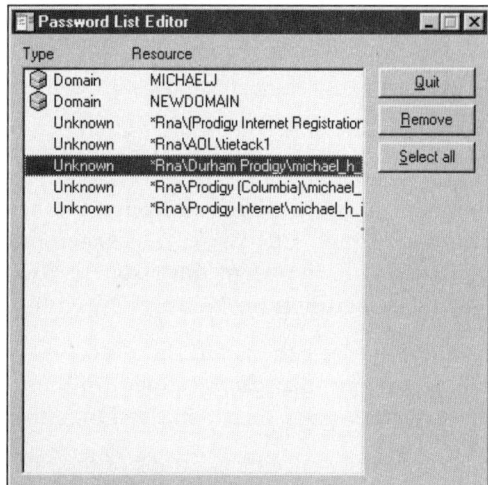

Figure 4-2   The Password List Editor

USER ENVIRONMENTS IN WINDOWS 98

The Windows 98 **user environment** is more than just the visible desktop and available network resources. The user environment also encompasses a broad collection of permissions, preferences, configurations, restrictions, and security limitations. Each of these components of the user environment is discussed in the following sections.

USER PROFILES

A **user profile** is a collection of preferences and configuration settings specific to a single user. A user profile stores desktop settings, Start menu layout, color and sound schemes, screen saver settings, and network drive mappings. In addition to these appearance-related settings, a user profile also includes settings for the following items, which are described in more detail in other chapters:

- **User.dat**: This file contains the parts of the Registry that are user-specific.
- **Application Data**: This folder includes the Address Book used by the Internet Explorer Mail program, the Quick Launch toolbar adjacent to the Start button, and the Windows 98 Welcome screen that you see at least the first time you install Windows 98.
- **Cookies**: This folder holds cookies, which include details pertinent to visiting a particular Web site.
- **Desktop**: This folder holds the contents and settings for the Active Desktop.
- **Favorites**: This folder contains information regarding the user's preferred Web sites. To access the contents of this folder, click Start, and then point to Favorites.

- **History**: This folder contains information regarding the Web sites most recently accessed via Internet Explorer. The contents of this folder are only available through Internet Explorer.
- **My Documents**: This folder opens by default when a user attempts to save a document from within an application.
- **NetHood**: This folder maintains a list of network drive mappings. Whenever you link to a drive on another computer through a network, your system maps (or associates) an unused drive letter, such as E, F, or G to this resource. You will learn more about this in Chapter 13, in the discussion on Network Neighborhood.
- **Recent**: This folder holds shortcuts to at least the last 12 files accessed by the user. Shortcuts are links to a file or program that can be stored on the desktop. To get to these shortcuts, click the Start menu, and then point to Documents.
- **Start Menu**: This folder maintains the user-specific portions of the Start menu.
- **Temporary Internet Files**: This folder stores cache files for Internet Explorer. The most recent data accessed from the Internet is stored in these files. You can specify the amount of disk space used by this folder via the Internet Options command on the View menu in Internet Explorer.

Multiple User Profiles

By default, Windows 98 is configured to store only one user profile. If there are multiple users on the same Windows 98 client, any change made by one user will affect all other users. To allow different users to manage their own configurations, you need to enable multiple user profiles.

Keep in mind that Windows 98 stores multiple user profiles differently from the default user profile. The default profile, including User.dat and associated folders, is stored in the main Windows 98 directory (C:\Windows). When multiple user profiles exist, Windows stores each profile in a directory named C:\Windows\Profiles\<*username*>, where <*username*> represents a specific account name. This scheme prevents the settings of one user profile from affecting the settings of another. Windows NT 4.0 uses the same scheme to store user profiles.

Because of the difference between these two storage methods, it is important to decide early on whether or not to enable multiple user profiles on a newly installed Windows 98 client. Otherwise, multiple users will start either with the full history and preferences of the original user, or with a "bare bones" group of settings.

Multiple user profiles are enabled through the Password applet of the Control Panel. The User Profiles tab of this applet contains two option buttons, as shown in Figure 4-3. To specify a single, universal profile, click the "All users of this computer use the same preferences and desktop settings" option button. To allow for multiple, individual profiles, click the "Users can customize their preferences and desktop settings. Windows switches to your personal settings whenever you log on" option button.

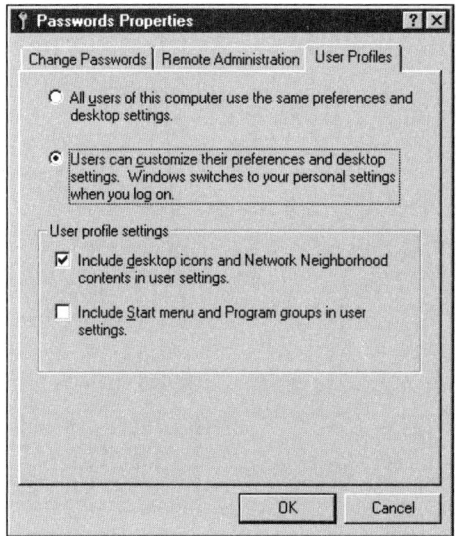

Figure 4-3 User Profiles tab of the Passwords Properties dialog box

When you choose the second option (i.e., multiple profiles), two check boxes are available:

- Include desktop icons and Network Neighborhood contents in user settings.
- Include Start menu and Program groups in user settings.

By default, multiple profiles allow users to control desktop icons, the Network Neighborhood contents, the Start menu, and Program groups. If you do not want different users to control which icons are on their desktops or what they see on the network through Network Neighborhood, deselect the first check box. If you do not wish individual users to manage their own Start menus, deselect the second check box. You will have the chance to enable multiple user profiles in the Hands-on Projects at the end of this chapter.

If you are working in a multiple user profile environment, any changes you make to the user environment are written to your user profile. The next time you log on, you see the same Windows 98 desktop and environment that you had when you logged off.

It is possible to switch from a multiple-user system back to a single-user system. Simply disable multiple user profiles through the User Profiles tab of the Passwords applet by selecting the "All users of this computer use the same preferences and desktop settings." option button. Although none of the stored profiles will be deleted, all users will start again with the same Windows 98 desktop and environment.

In the remainder of this chapter, you will work with local and network variations of profiles and policies. Before any of these profiles or policies can take effect, you need to enable multiple user profiles.

Network and Local Users

All users are first local users, which is to say that all users must first log on to a local computer. In addition, some local users have network privileges, and can log on to the network from the local computer. Users with network privileges are known as **network users**. You create network user accounts through a network domain controller such as a Windows NT server. (A domain, as introduced in Chapter 3, is a special group of users and computers.) You create local user accounts on the local Windows 98 computer. Users who only have access to the local computer, and no access to the network, are sometimes referred to as **local-only users**.

Network users can log on to a network via a Windows 98 machine by providing correct authentication information (username, password, and domain name). These users also have local privileges on that Windows 98 machine.

To enable local users to log on to a Windows 98 machine, open the Network applet from the Control Panel, click the Configuration tab, and examine the Primary Network Logon list box. This box provides options: Client for Microsoft Networks, Client for NetWare Networks, and Windows Logon. If the first two options are not already there, you will learn to activate them later in this chapter. You can activate Microsoft Family Logon using the same technique. If you want the local user to be able to log on to the Windows 98 machine, select the Windows Logon option. If you do not select this option, user logon requests will be routed (or passed) over the network to the Windows NT or NetWare domain controller, to check your username and password. Because the domain controller knows nothing about local Windows 98 user accounts, any local logon attempts will be refused. As a result, only users with valid network user accounts will be able to access that Windows 98 computer.

Network user accounts can only be created through the domain controller. Once the accounts are created, the users of those accounts can log on to a Windows 98 machine connected to that network. If multiple user profiles are enabled, a new Windows 98 user profile is created for each network user new to that computer. If that user enters the same password for Windows 98 and the network, he or she will not have to log on to that Windows 98 computer again. As discussed earlier in this chapter, this convenience poses a possible security risk.

You can create local Windows 98 user accounts, and manage existing user accounts through the User Settings applet accessible from the Control Panel, shown in Figure 4-4. If you have not set up users before, you are sent directly to the Add New User wizard. To create new accounts, click New User. The Add User Wizard opens, requesting a new username and password. Next, the Add User Wizard displays the Personalized Items Settings dialog box, as shown in Figure 4-5. Here you can select the items you want to include in the new user account profile (such as a specific Start menu or Favorites folder). You can also specify whether to copy or create new versions of these items.

Managing Windows 98 Users, Profiles, and Policies   111

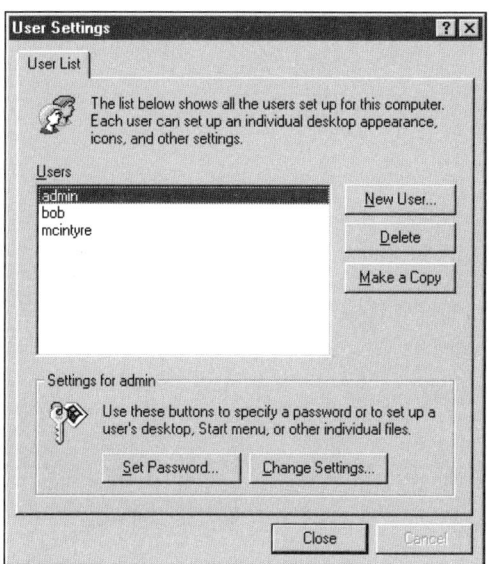

Figure 4-4   User Settings dialog box

Figure 4-5   Add User Wizard, Personalized Items Settings dialog box

The decision regarding how the new items are created (whether by copying or by creating) is important. If you choose to use the copy method, the contents of the selected items from the currently logged-on user will be duplicated in the profile for the new user. If you choose to create new items from scratch, the result will be a series of empty folders for each selected item. Among other things, this means that the resulting Start menu will be nearly empty; even Windows Explorer will not be included. Additional features must be added either via a system policy or by a user.

By default, anyone logged on to a Windows 98 computer can open the Users applet. Unless restricted by a system policy, any user can create new accounts, and make other changes such as altering and deleting local profiles. Later in this chapter, you will learn how to create a system policy to disable access to different features, including the Users applet.

Roaming and Local Profiles

By default, all user profiles are local. This is true for profiles associated with both local-only Windows 98 users and users who access a network through a Windows 98 client. User profiles created on one Windows 98 computer are not available on any other computer.

If you want a user profile to be available on more than one computer, you can transform a local profile into a **roaming profile**. A roaming profile is simply a local profile that is stored on a shared network drive. Roaming profiles are available on any computer connected to the network on which the profile is stored. Thus, no matter which workstation a user logs on to, his or her personal profile will be available from the network. Each time a user logs off, any changes made to his or her profile will be stored on the network share. Naturally, roaming profiles are available only to network users.

 In Microsoft terminology, a roaming profile is also called a **roving profile**.

Windows 98 user profiles are not compatible with Windows NT Workstation user profiles. If your roaming profile does not work on your local computer, you get the default environment for that system. Because of the differences between Windows 98 and Windows 95, Microsoft does not recommend using a Windows 95 profile on a Windows 98 client, or vice versa.

Roaming profiles are enabled through the domain controller of the attached network. However, there are several issues that you should consider before enabling roaming profiles for Windows 98 users:

- **The networking client**: A 32-bit protected-mode client software program such as Client for Microsoft Networks or Client for NetWare Networks is required to connect to the network.
- **Long file name (LFN) support**: The network server that stores roaming user profiles must support long file names (LFN). A LFN can have up to 255 characters. If LFNs are not supported, only the User.dat file will be downloaded to the clients. Because the other parts of the profile (e.g., Temporary Internet Files) do not correspond to the standard 8.3 filename format (e.g., abcdefgh.doc), they are not loaded on a non-LFN-compatible server.
- **Network home directory on a Microsoft network**: On Microsoft networks, a home directory is required for each user in the \Users folder of the networked NT server. The roaming profile will be stored in that directory.
- **Network home directory on a NetWare network**: On a Novell NetWare network, roaming profiles are stored in the \Sys\Mail\User_id directory. The NetWare User_id is a unique 8-digit number that is not otherwise related to a username.

- **Consistent client-server interface**: Each of the Windows 98 clients must be installed so that the main Windows directory name is the same for all clients and uses the same drive letter. For example, if the main Windows directory is defined as C:\Windows on one client and D:\Win98 on another, then portions of the profile will either not read correctly or will not be copied to the network server.

- **User profile support**: As explained earlier in this chapter, user profiles must be enabled on each Windows 98 client, using the User Profiles tab of the Control Panel Passwords applet.

Once these requirements are met, you may enable roaming profiles on your Windows NT, NetWare, or other type of network, as explained in the following sections.

Enabling Roaming Profiles in Windows NT.
If Windows 98 uses Client for Microsoft Networks to access a Windows NT network, you can enable roaming profiles. This section describes the configuration steps that you must complete on a Windows 98 computer, and gives general instructions for the steps you must complete on the Windows NT server. Access to a Windows NT server is not required to understand this process. You should have a Windows 98 computer connected and logged on to a Windows NT network that has not already been configured for mandatory profiles. (A mandatory profile is a user profile that does not store any changes made by a user. You will learn more about mandatory profiles later in this chapter.) If possible, the Windows NT server should also be configured to share the C:\Users directory. Because this could put user information at risk, you should not access user profile information on a Windows NT server without the permission (and ideally, supervision) of your instructor or network administrator.

1. On the Windows 98 computer, click Start, point to Settings, click Control Panel, and double-click the Network icon. The Network dialog box opens.

2. If necessary, click the Configuration tab. In the "The following network components are installed" box, you should see "Client for Microsoft Networks". If not, refer to the following Note for instructions on installing this client.

 Client for Microsoft Networks can be installed from the Configuration tab of the Network applet in the Control Panel. In this tab, click Add. In the Select Network Component Type dialog box, double-click Client. In the Select Network Clients dialog box, select Microsoft as a manufacturer, and double-click Client for Microsoft Networks. Click OK as required to exit the Network applet. You will probably be prompted to restart your computer to complete the installation.

3. In the Primary Network Logon list box, select Client for Microsoft Networks, and then click Properties. If it is not already selected, select the "Log on to Windows NT domain" option, then enter the name of your domain in the Windows NT Domain text box. If you do not know the domain name of your network, consult your instructor or Network Administrator. Click OK to return to the Network dialog box, then click OK in the Network dialog box.

4. If necessary, restart your computer as prompted to complete this installation.

5. Next, you need to connect to the main directory of the Windows NT server through your networked Windows 98 computer. Click Start, Programs, and then click Windows Explorer.

6. In the left-hand pane, click the plus sign (+) to the left of Network Neighborhood, and then click the plus sign to the left of Entire Network.

7. Click the computer name of your Windows NT server.

8. Create a home directory on the Windows NT server that matches your username (e.g., C:\Users\BobT for Bob Tynan, C:\Users\Admin for the Admin account, and so forth).

The next time a roaming user logs off the Network, a Windows 98 profile will be copied to the home directory share. Specifically, the User.dat file from the local Windows 98 computer will be copied to the Windows NT directory that you just created. Each time the user logs off thereafter, any profile changes are written to the user's roaming profile.

Enabling Windows 98 Roaming Profiles in NetWare. Before configuring a roaming profile on a NetWare network, you need to install and configure Client for NetWare Networks. To perform the steps in this section, you need a Windows 98 machine connected to a NetWare network, version 3.1 or higher. The NetWare server must be set up to share its Mail subdirectory. With appropriate client software, roaming profiles can also be enabled on other networks. For NetWare, the steps are as follows:

1. On the Windows 98 computer, click Start, point to Settings, click Control Panel, and double-click the Network icon.

2. If necessary, click the Configuration tab. In the "The following network components are installed" box, you should see "Client for NetWare Networks". If not, see the paragraph introducing these steps.

3. In the Primary Network Logon list box, select Client for NetWare Networks, and then click Properties. In the Client for NetWare Networks Properties dialog box, click the General Tab, then enter the name of the main NetWare server on your network. If you do not know the name of the appropriate NetWare server, consult your instructor or network administrator. Click OK to return to the Network dialog box, then click OK in the Network dialog box.

4. If necessary, restart your computer as prompted, to complete this installation.

5. Next, you need to connect to the main directory of the NetWare server through your networked Windows 98 computer. Click Start, Programs, and then click Windows Explorer.

6. In the left-hand pane, click the plus sign (+) to the left of Network Neighborhood, and then click the plus sign to the left of Entire Network.

7. Click the name of your NetWare server.

8. Instead of the Users subdirectory, you are looking for the \sys\mail\user_id subdirectory. Unlike Windows NT, in NetWare the subdirectory is created for you. For our purposes, the user_id is a random 8-digit number.

The next time that user logs off, a Windows 98 profile will be copied to the Mail directory share. In other words, the User.dat file will be copied from the local Windows 98 computer to the NetWare directory associated with your username. Any changes made to that profile during subsequent sessions will be written to that share when the user logs off.

Mandatory Profiles

The profiles discussed so far are user-configurable. This means that users can modify such profiles simply by changing their user environments. The changes made by the user are automatically stored in his or her user profile.

You can restrict this freedom through the use of mandatory profiles. A **mandatory profile** is a user profile that does not store any changes made by a user. Mandatory profiles do not prevent users from changing their environments; however, any changes made by a user are not saved to the mandatory profile at logoff. In other words, a user subject to a mandatory profile gets the same user environment every time he or she logs on.

To create a mandatory profile, first create a user profile with all desired settings and preferences. For example, if you are creating a mandatory profile for support staff, you might want to remove database applications from the Start menu, and add a Microsoft Word shortcut to the desktop. When you are satisfied with the configuration, log off, and then log on the new user. Rename the new User.dat file to User.man. The specific steps are as follows:

1. Enable roaming profiles as described earlier in this chapter.

2. Create a new user account in the domain that you want to be subject to the mandatory profile. (For example, create a user account named SalesTemp to represent the Sales domain.)

3. Log on to Windows 98 with this new user account.

4. Modify the user environment as desired. For example, you may want to change the Start menu, desktop settings, colors, sounds, application installation, or drive mappings.

5. Log off, and then log on using the new account. This action writes your profile changes to the User.dat file for your temporary user.

6. Find the User.dat file for the new user (SalesTemp) in your Windows NT or NetWare server. In a NetWare environment, this file is stored in the Home\Mail\User_id directory; in a Windows NT environment, it is stored in the \Users*username* (in this example, \Users\SalesTemp) directory.

7. Change this filename to User.man.

For either a NetWare or a Windows NT network, you can copy the contents of the mandatory profile into the profile directory for each desired user. However, this would be time-consuming with a large number of users. Another option in a Windows NT network is to change the home directory for each user to the mandatory profile directory. Although this is easier, when there is a large number of users, any personal data on this server directory would no longer be available to each user.

If you want to make subsequent changes to a mandatory profile, you need to follow this sequence:

1. Rename User.man back to User.dat.
2. Log on as that user.
3. Make all necessary changes.
4. Log off.
5. Rename User.dat to User.man.

Unless every user has been configured to log on over a network through one mandatory profile directory, these steps require that you copy the new mandatory profile into each of the affected user profile directories.

Troubleshooting Profiles

In the Windows 98 environment, user profiles are fairly simple and straightforward. But this does not imply that user profiles are foolproof and free of technical difficulties. If you discover that user profiles are not functioning correctly, consult the following checklist:

- Verify that multiple user profiles are enabled on each Windows 98 client.
- Verify that the correct network client is defined as the Primary Network Logon.
- Verify that roaming profiles are stored in the correct network share.
- Synchronize the time, date, and time zone for clients and servers.
- Re-create briefcases that existed before user profiles were set up. Briefcase does not automatically update locations for files when the location of a profile changes. You will learn more about briefcases in Chapter 6.

If, after working through this checklist, you still cannot resolve the problem, reconfigure and reenable profiles. You may have skipped a step or mistyped a name or a parameter.

HARDWARE PROFILES

Hardware profiles tell Windows 98 which set of drivers to load for a particular hardware configuration. Specifically, a **hardware profile** is a collection of device settings and drivers that correspond to a known computer or device configuration. In most cases, the hardware attached to a Windows 98 computer does not change frequently. However, where hardware configurations do change, hardware profiles eliminate any need to remove and install drivers each time a device is added or removed from the computer.

Hardware profiles are used most often with notebook computers or other computers with hot-swappable components such as PC Cards (previously called PCMCIA Cards), or docking stations. Hardware profiles are not strictly required on systems that are fully Plug-and-Play-compatible, but they do provide tremendous convenience.

Managing Windows 98 Users, Profiles, and Policies

Hardware profiles function as follows:

- During bootup, Windows 98 polls all attached devices for their identifier (ID number, serial number, make, model, type, and so on). This information is used to match all detected or enumerated hardware to any defined hardware profiles.
- If a match is found, Windows 98 automatically selects that profile and uses its configuration to boot.
- If no match is found, Windows 98 prompts the user to select a profile from its collection of all known hardware profiles.

You create and manage hardware profiles through the Hardware Profiles tab in the Control Panel System applet, shown in Figure 4-6. By default, a single hardware profile named "Original Configuration" always appears. This profile contains the current hardware configuration.

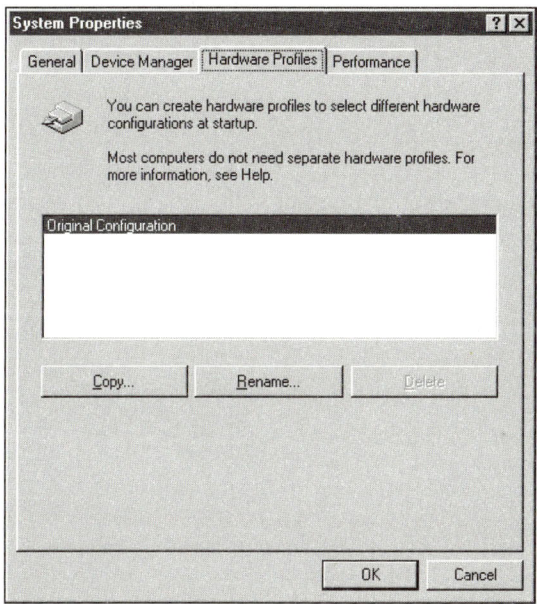

Figure 4-6 Hardware Profiles tab of the System applet

To create a new hardware profile, follow these general steps:

1. Click Start, point to Settings, click Control Panel, double-click the System icon, and then click the Hardware Profiles tab.

2. Select an existing profile and then click Copy. The Copy Profile dialog box opens.

3. Enter a new name for your profile. It is a good idea to use descriptive names that refer to some significant feature of a hardware profile (for example, modem, network, or docking station).

4. Click OK. The new profile appears in the list of profiles in the Hardware Profiles tab.

5. Reboot your computer. In the initial bootup of Windows 98, you will be prompted to select which profile you want to use.

6. Type the number for your new profile and then press Enter to continue restarting Windows 98. Now that your new profile is in effect, you can change this new profile to reflect your desired hardware configuration, as explained in the remaining steps.

7. Power down your computer.

8. Change the hardware devices to meet your requirements for the new hardware profile.

9. Reboot your computer. During the boot process, you will be prompted to select your new profile.

10. Once Windows 98 boots, make any changes to device drivers and configurations. The new profile is stored automatically when the machine is restarted or shut down.

The next time Windows 98 boots, it will attempt to match the connected hardware with some hardware profile. If a match is found, that profile is loaded. Once Windows 98 is running, check the active profile in the Hardware Profiles tab of the Control Panel System applet. If your changes were successful, your new profile will be highlighted.

You can disable device drivers that you may not be using in a specific hardware configuration as follows: Click Start, point to Settings, click Control Panel, double-click System, click the Hardware Profiles tab, then highlight the configuration that you want to change. Click the Device Manager tab, then click "View devices by type" if required. Click the plus sign adjacent to the hardware that you are disabling, highlight the driver, then click Properties. In the device usage area of the General tab, click Disable in this hardware profile.

You can use the Hardware Profiles tab of the Control Panel System applet to rename or delete existing hardware profiles. However, once you delete a hardware profile, it is completely removed from the system. It is not possible to undelete a hardware profile. The only way to back up a hardware profile is by backing up the Registry. Thus, before deleting a hardware profile, you should back up the Registry, just in case you change your mind. You learned about backing up the Registry in Chapter 3.

SYSTEM POLICIES

In addition to user profiles and hardware profiles, you can also use system policies to control the Windows 98 user environment. A **system policy** is a tool that places limits on the user environment. It can be set up for individual users or computers, or for groups of users known as domains. As discussed in Chapter 3, most of the user environment is controlled and maintained by the HKEY_CURRENT_USER key in the Registry. System policies enforce their restrictions by overwriting specific portions of the Registry each time a subject user logs on.

System policies and user profiles can both be used to modify the user environment. It's important to understand the distinction between the two. As you learned earlier in this chapter, user profiles include elements such as icons and recently used files. In contrast, the effect of a system policy is limited to the settings in the Registry. For example, system policies may be used to:

- Reduce access to Control Panel applets
- Remove functionality from the desktop and basic Windows 98 utilities, such as the Registry Editor
- Enforce specific desktop features, such as standards for wallpaper or icons
- Preconfigure network settings

System policies can be applied in three ways: to individual users, to groups such as domains, or to a specific computer. These applications are known as **user policies**, **group policies**, and **computer policies**, respectively. Once created, these policies are saved in a single file, **Config.pol**, in your network logon directory. There are several limitations on system policies:

- If a user policy exists, then no group policies may be applied to that user.
- Multiple group policies may be defined, but they should be given a priority order.
- Groups may only be defined on a network domain controller.
- Computer policies apply to all users of the computers to which they apply.
- Windows 98 policies are not compatible with Windows NT policies.

In the following sections, you will learn to use the System Policy Editor. This utility provides a series of policy templates that can be customized for different computers, users, or groups. You will then learn how single and multiple system policies can be implemented in a network.

The System Policy Editor

You create and edit system policies with the **System Policy Editor**. This utility is not installed by default, but must be manually installed using the files on the Windows 98 installation CD. You will have a chance to install the System Policy Editor in the Hands-on Projects at the end of this chapter.

Once installed, the System Policy Editor appears as an option on the Start menu. To open it, click Start, point to Programs, point to Accessories, point to System Tools, and then click System Policy Editor.

The System Policy Editor can be used to modify the Registry directly. Note that the File menu of the System Policy Editor includes an Open Registry command. Use this command at your peril. However, despite the danger associated with this command, it is safer than the Registry Editor discussed in Chapter 3. Unlike the Registry Editor, the System Policy Editor does not make any changes until you save and exit. On the other hand, the System Policy Editor does not allow you to customize a user environment in as much detail as does the Registry Editor.

The relatively safe way to use the System Policy Editor is through policy files. Because a policy file can be made specific to a user, group, or computer, you can test a policy on a sample user before implementing it for groups on a network.

There are two file types associated with the System Policy Editor: administrative (.adm) and policy (.pol) files. These files are explained in further detail in the sections that follow.

- **.adm files**: These are the administrative template files that may be modified and transformed into actual policy files. You can use more than one administrative file at a time in System Policy Editor. Different .adm files are available to create different policies.

- **.pol files**: These are actual policy files. Microsoft refers to two basic policy files: Config.pol and Policy.pol. They are often used interchangeably. Config.pol is the file you actually save on a server. This file then modifies the Registry whenever a user to whom the policy applies logs on.

System Policy .adm files. .adm files are templates used to create .pol policy files. The policy that you create can only be as detailed as the administrative files that you load into System Policy Editor. The .adm files essentially provide programming code to define parameters used to modify the Registry. The System Policy Editor loads .adm files, then saves .pol files. The .adm file that you choose determines the settings that you can change. You can load more than one .adm file; the number of settings that you can change is based on the combined .adm files. You can create custom .adm files using a text editor. However, the syntax is complex and specific.

Several .adm files are included with the System Policy Editor. They are not copied by default and can be found on the Windows installation CD in the \Tools\Reskit\Netadmin\Poledit directory. These administrative files determine what you can change in the System Policy Editor. As you look over the following list, think in terms of the policies that can be created with each administrative file.

- **Appsini.adm**: Settings to allow installation of programs over a network
- **Chat.adm**: Relates to Microsoft Chat
- **Common.adm**: Blank by default. Used to store custom items.
- **Conf.adm**: Relates to NetMeeting
- **Inetresm.adm**: Relates to Internet Explorer information services access
- **Inetsetm.adm**: Relates to general Internet Explorer configuration
- **Oem.adm**: Relates to Outlook Express
- **Shellm.adm**: Relates to Windows Explorer and other Desktop items
- **Subsm.adm**: Relates to Internet Explorer Channels and subscriptions
- **Windows.adm**: Contains the default items used in a system policy

To understand the details of what a policy file can do, it is instructive to look through the programming code for the Oem.adm administrative file. This file relates to Outlook Express, which is the mail manager for Internet Explorer. The basic purpose of Oem.adm is to provide policies designed to reduce mail and newsgroup support costs. Explanations are included in italics after each group of programming commands. Do not be concerned if the following information seems overwhelming. Once you gain some experience in network administration, you will be able to use this kind of code to create special administrative policies. For now, simply review the code in order to become familiar with its general format. After each section of code, you'll find an explanation of the code you've just read.

```
; oem.adm
"
;
"
;;;;;;;;;;;;;;;;;;;;;;;;;
CLASS USER ;;;;;;;;;;;;;;
;;;;;;;;;;;;;;;;;;;;;;;;;

CATEGORY !!OutlookExpress
    KEYNAME "Software\Microsoft\Outlook Express"
    POLICY !!Zones
        PART !!RestSite CHECKBOX
        VALUENAME "Security Zone"
        VALUEON NUMERIC 4
        VALUEOFF NUMERIC 3
        END PART
    END POLICY
```

The previous settings relate to Outlook Express which uses the Security Zones associated with Internet Explorer. When the VALUEON NUMERIC equals 4, all mail is placed in the Restricted Sites zone, which filters mail from all but explicitly trusted Web sites.

```
    POLICY !!HTMLMail
        PART !!DisableHTMLinMail CHECKBOX
        KEYNAME "Software\Microsoft\Outlook Express\Mail"
        VALUENAME "Message Send HTML"
        VALUEON NUMERIC 0
        VALUEOFF NUMERIC 1
        END PART
```

```
            PART !!DisablePlaininNews CHECKBOX
            KEYNAME "Software\Microsoft\Outlook Express\News"
            VALUENAME "Message Send HTML"
            VALUEON NUMERIC 1
            VALUEOFF NUMERIC 0
            END PART
        END POLICY
    END CATEGORY
```

The previous settings specify whether HTML (Hypertext Markup Language) is to be used with mail and news messages. You are strongly encouraged to retain these default settings whereby mail can be written in HTML and news is always in plaintext.

```
    CATEGORY !!OENav
        KEYNAME "Software\Microsoft\Outlook Express\"
        POLICY !!Navigation
            PART !!OutlookBar CHECKBOX
            VALUENAME "OutBar"
            VALUEON NUMERIC 1
            VALUEOFF NUMERIC 0
            END PART
```

The previous settings relate to customization features within Outlook Express.

```
            PART !!FolderView CHECKBOX
            VALUENAME "Tree"
            VALUEON NUMERIC 0
            VALUEOFF NUMERIC 1
            END PART
```

The previous setting turns off the Explorer style tree view of folders.

```
            PART !!FolderBar CHECKBOX
            VALUENAME "FolderBar"
            VALUEON NUMERIC 1
            VALUEOFF NUMERIC 0
            END PART
```

The previous setting turns off the folder bar, the horizontal line associated with each Outlook Express folder.

```
                PART !!TipofDay CHECKBOX
                    VALUENAME "Tip of the Day"
                    VALUEON NUMERIC 0
                    VALUEOFF NUMERIC 1
                END PART
            END POLICY
    END CATEGORY
    [strings]
    OutlookExpress="General Settings"
    OENav="View Customization"
    ServerSettings="Mail, news, and directory server settings"
    Zones="Mail and news security zones"
    RestSite="Put mail and news in the Restricted Sites zone
    (instead of the Internet zone)"
    HTMLMail="HTML mail and news composition settings"
    DisableHTMLinMail="Mail: Make plain text message composition
    the default for mail messages (instead of HTML mail)"
    DisablePlaininNews="News: Make HTML message composition the
    default for news posts (instead of plain text)"
    Navigation="Folder and Message Navigational Elements"
    OutlookBar="Turn on Outlook Bar"
    FolderView="Turn off Folder List (tree view of folders)"
    FolderBar="Turn on Folder Bar (horizontal line that displays
    the selected folder's name)"
    TipofDay="Turn off the Tip of the Day"
```

Remember, the settings that you can control in the System Policy Editor are only as complete as the .adm files that you load. Before you can add or remove .adm files, you need to close all open policies in the System Policy Editor. The specific steps for adding or removing current .adm files are as follows:

These steps assume you have already installed the System Policy Editor, following the steps provided in the Hands-on Projects at the end of this chapter.

1. Click Start, point to Programs, point to Accessories, point to System Tools, and then click System Policy Editor.

2. Click File on the menu bar, and then click Close to ensure that no .adm files are active.

3. Click Options on the menu bar, and then click Policy Template. The Policy Template Options dialog box opens, as shown in Figure 4-7. If this is the first time that you have opened the System Policy Editor after installation, this dialog box displays the two default .adm files: Common.adm and Windows.adm. If other .adm files are included, you may need your Windows 98 Installation CD.

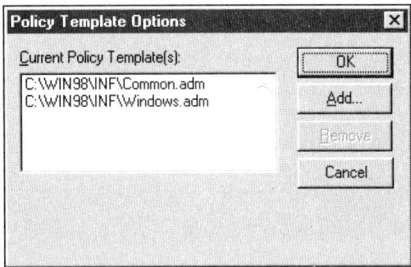

Figure 4-7   Policy Template Options dialog box

4. To add a new policy template, click Add. The Open Template File dialog box appears, where you can locate and load new .adm files. These .adm files can be found on your Windows 98 installation CD, in the \Tools\Reskit\Netadmin\Poledit folder.

5. To remove a system policy, select the policy in the Current Policy Template(s) list, and then click Remove.

6. Click OK to close the Policy Template Options dialog box and return to the System Policy Editor.

System Policy .pol files.   The System Policy Editor can use one or more .adm files to create a single Config.pol file. Config.pol is the one policy file for Windows 98. This file contains each of the user, group, and computer policies defined through the System Policy Editor. The Config.pol file greatly simplifies the administrative duties associated with system policies. Config.pol is created when you select File, Save from the System Policy Editor menu bar.

There are two sample policy files available on your Windows 98 installation CD, Standard.pol and Maximum.pol. These files are also located in the \Tools\Reskit\Netadmin\Poledit folder on the Windows 98 installation CD. The two sample policies depict different levels of control over users.

Default System Policies

Generally, when you save a policy file, you want it to include settings for only specific users, computers, and groups. You will learn to add specific users, computers, and groups to a policy in the next section. It is dangerous to include the Default User and Default Computer icons with the policy that you save, as these settings apply to all users, even to the Registries of network administrators.

Managing Windows 98 Users, Profiles, and Policies 125

The general process for creating a policy is as follows. As described in this section, first you load the .adm files that you need. Then, click File on the System Policy menu bar, and then click New. This creates icons for the Default User and Default Computer policies. The settings in these policies are based on your choice of .adm files, and will apply to every user on the system unless you specify otherwise by creating additional polices. To help prevent unauthorized users from altering the default policies, you can delete these default icons. They are just icons; the settings that you created via the .adm files will still exist even if you delete the icons. In the next section, you will learn to add specific users, computers, and groups to the template that you created. Then you can modify the policies of your choice. In the following section, you then learn to save your new policy to the config.pol file in the appropriate location. When this process is complete, the policy of your choice will apply to the users, computers, and groups of your choice, not to everyone.

1. Click Start, point to Programs, point to Accessories, point to System Tools, and then click System Policy Editor.

2. Select and load the desired .adm template files, as discussed in the previous section.

3. Click File on the menu bar, and then click New. Two default policy icons appear in the System Policy Editor display area—Default Computer and Default User, as shown in Figure 4-8.

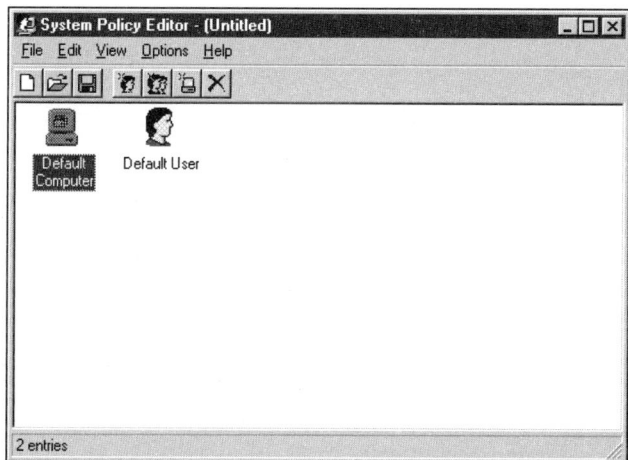

Figure 4-8 Default policy icons in the System Policy Editor

If you change the wrong setting in one of these default policies and then save the default policies in the appropriate locations, Windows 98 could become inoperable. Every time you load the System Policy Editor, you load the new versions of default policies that caused you trouble before. If this happens, the only way to restore the system is to reinstall Windows 98. If you create such a "DOA" policy and place it on your network, each and every Windows 98 client will be affected by your negligence and require reinstallation.

It is useful to study the structure of a default policy before creating one of your own. The following discussion will help you gain a full understanding of what controls are available, and how altering these controls can affect user environments.

A computer policy is a system policy that applies to only one computer. To begin examining the Default Computer policy, double-click the Default Computer icon in the System Policy Editor. This opens a Default Computer Properties dialog box similar to Figure 4-9.

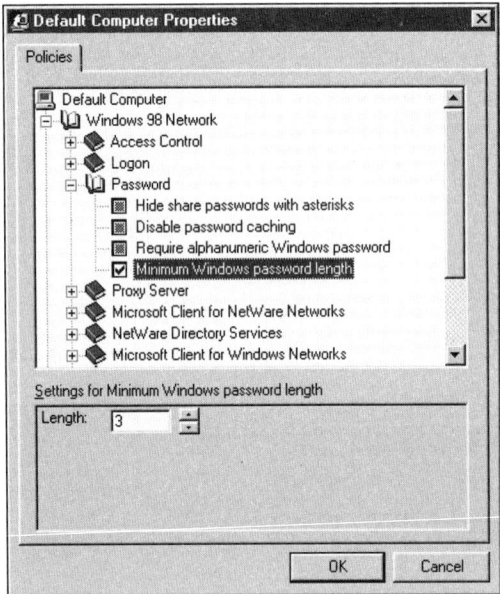

Figure 4-9 Default Computer Properties dialog box

The Default Computer Properties dialog box organizes policy settings in a tree-like, outline structure. This dialog box works similarly to Windows Explorer, in that clicking a plus sign (+) next to a heading displays subordinate headings. The individual settings appear next to check boxes.

A Windows 98 check box allows for three settings:

- **Gray:** A gray check box means that nothing has been added to this setting.
- **Empty:** An empty check box means that a setting is disabled or cleared. In the System Policy Editor, this can change an associated setting in the Registry.
- **Checked:** A selected check box means that a setting is enabled. Within a policy, an enabled setting will overwrite any conflicting setting in the Registry.

The **Default Computer policy** is a system policy that applies to a computer if a specific computer policy is not defined. It includes settings for everything from network security to allowable programs. Once the default profile is installed, the settings change your Registry. As shown in Figure 4-9, these settings are divided into two main headings—Windows 98 Network and Windows 98 System. The line between these two categories is not clear; for some administrative files, both categories contain network-related parameters. The best way to learn about the possibilities is to open the Default Computer and Default User dialog boxes for each .adm file, one at a time. Figure 4-9 shows a policy in which the minimum password length is 3 characters.

The **Default User policy** is a system policy that applies to a user if a specific user policy is not defined. If you display the Default User policy in the Properties dialog box, you will see the same two major categories as in the Default Computer policy. However, the specific settings are different. The original version of the Default User policy allows you to limit the use of file and print sharing. The original version of the Default User policy allows you to customize the following desktop settings:

- **Shell, Custom Folders:** Customizes the contents of the Programs menu, Start menu, Startup folder, and Network Neighborhood. Customizes the icons on your desktop.

- **Shell, Restrictions:** Deactivates Windows 98 functions such as the Start menu Run and Find commands. Prevents access to major utilities such as My Computer and Network Neighborhood.

- **Control Panel:** Prevents access to Display, Network, Passwords, Printers, and System applets

- **Desktop Display:** Specifies wallpaper; limit changes in color schemes

- **Restrictions:** Disables MS-DOS mode, disables Registry editing, and limits applications to Windows

As strange as it sounds, the settings of the Default User and Default Computer policies are not specified by default. In this case, "Default" means that the policy is applicable to all users by default; there are many possible customizable "Default," or global, policies. (You learned about these global policies in Chapter 3.)

In the following section, you will learn how to take these policies and customize them for specific users, computers, or groups.

Creating, Editing, and Deleting System Policies

You have learned about the different .adm files on which you can base a policy. You have also created Default User and Default Computer policy icons in the System Policy Editor. Unless you want a policy that applies to all users, you should delete these icons. You will have the chance to delete these icons in the following steps, in which you create specific policies for the Users, Computers, and Groups of your choice. To create a new system policy:

1. Click Start, point to Programs, point to Accessories, point to System Tools, and then click System Policy Editor.

2. Click Options on the menu bar, click Policy Templates, and then verify that the desired .adm template files are loaded. If necessary, repeat steps 3–6 from the section entitled "System Policy .adm files." These steps are located after the programming code for the Oe.adm file.

3. Click File on the menu bar, and then click New. This automatically creates Default User and Default Computer policy icons. As discussed in the previous section, these default policies are not defaults in the usual sense, in that they contain prespecified settings. Instead, they are policies that would be enforced by default throughout the network. To prevent unnecessary risk to your system, you should delete these icons, as explained in the next step.

4. Highlight one default policy icon, click Edit on the menu bar, then click Remove, then click Yes to confirm the deletion. Repeat for the remaining default policy icon.

5. Click Edit on the menu bar, and then click Add User, Add Group, or Add Computer. Whichever you choose, a dialog box opens prompting you for the name of the specific user, Computer, or group.

6. Type the name of the User, Computer, or Group. The User name that you enter should match the name used to log on to the computer or the network. The Computer name can be found in the Identification tab of the Network dialog box. The Group name corresponds to a local or a global group on a Windows NT or Novell NetWare network. For more information on local and global groups, consult *A Guide to Microsoft Windows NT Server 4.0 in the Enterprise*, published by Course Technology.

7. Click OK.

Before you can make Group policies work, you need to install them on each affected Windows 98 computer. To do so, click Start, point to Control Panel, double-click Add/Remove Programs, and then click the Windows Setup tab. In this tab, highlight System Tools, click Details, check the box next to Grouppol, click OK to return to the Add/Remove Programs Properties dialog box, click OK in the Properties dialog box, then insert your Windows 98 Installation CD when prompted.

8. A new icon with the name of the User, Computer or Group appears in the System Policy Editor.

At this point, you have created a policy template for a specific user, computer, or group. To begin changing its settings, double-click the policy's icon to open a Properties dialog box similar to the one you saw in Figure 4-9. The exact settings you see in the Properties dialog box will depend on the .adm file you loaded before creating the policy. The following steps guide you through the process of examining your new system policy to see which settings you can change. After completing your changes, you can save it as a .pol file.

1. In the System Policy Editor, double-click the icon for the policy you want to edit. This opens a Properties dialog box, similar to the one shown previously in Figure 4-9.

2. Click the plus sign next to the first major item you want to change. Continue expanding the subordinate items, until you display the check boxes you need to edit.

3. Check or uncheck individual settings as desired.

4. Click OK to close the Properties dialog box. Now that your policy template meets your specifications, you can save it as a .pol file, as described in the next step.

5. Click File on the menu bar, and then click Save As. The Save As dialog box opens. To apply this policy on your local computer, save it as C:\Windows\Config.pol. In the next section, you will learn where to store this policy on a Windows NT or Novell NetWare network.

That completes the process of creating a new system policy. Keep in mind that you will need to create individual policies for each computer, group, and user that you want to restrict.

Remember that changes to a policy are not saved until you use the Save As command on the System Policy Editor File menu.

Sometimes, it will make sense to delete a policy. Deleting policies is fairly simple:

1. Click Start, point to Programs, Accessories, System Tools, then click System Policy Editor.

2. To open the policy that you just created, click File on the menu bar, then click Open Policy. The Open Policy dialog box appears.

3. Open the config.pol file you just created, which should be located in the C:\Windows directory.

4. In the System Policy Editor, select the icon for the policy you want to delete.

5. Click Edit on the menu bar, click Remove, then click OK in the warning dialog box to confirm the deletion.

Storing Policies

As mentioned earlier, a system policy is a single Config.pol file that contains multiple user, group, and computer policies. A Windows 98 machine on a network automatically looks for this Config.pol file each time a user logs on. Windows 98 searches for this file in three places, in the following order:

- Locally, in the main Windows subdirectory (C:\Windows).
- On an NT Server, in the Netlogon directory share and the home directory of the user. The Netlogon directory share is the \Netlogon folder of the NT Server that verifies your username and password for network access. The home directory of the user is the \Users*user_name* directory on that same NT Server, where *user_name* stands for your logon username.
- On a Novell NetWare server, in the Mail\user_id directory and the Sys\Public directories. As you learned earlier, the NetWare user_id is a seemingly random 8-digit number.

Only the first copy of Config.pol found by Windows 98 will be used. Therefore you should maintain firm control over where this file is stored and how it is updated.

Multiple Group Policies

Multiple group policies can be defined and applied to a single user. If no user-specific profile is defined, then group policies apply. On a Windows NT network, users can belong to multiple groups (or domains). Any and all group policies will be applied to all members of each group. This can result in two or more group policies that apply to a single user. Because group policies may conflict, Windows 98 uses a priority system. As the system administrator, you can specify which policies have priority. To do so, open the System Policy Editor, click Group Priority on the menu bar, and then click Options. This opens the Group Priority dialog box, shown in Figure 4-10.

The policies in the Group Order list box are applied in reverse order, from the bottom up. In Figure 4-10, the lowest priority policy (Temp) would be applied first, then the Admin policy, and then the Sales policy. Each time a policy is applied, it overwrites the previously read lower priority policy. Ultimately, the highest priority policy (in Figure 4-10, the Sales policy) takes precedence by overwriting all other group policies.

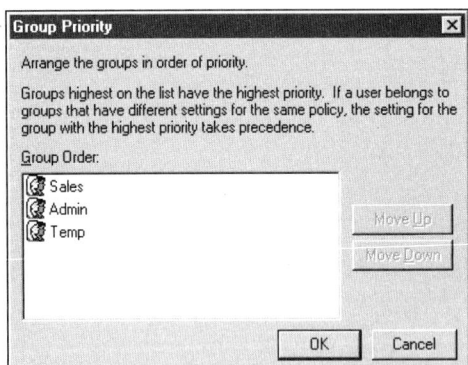

Figure 4-10   Group Priority dialog box

Applying Multiple Policies

Once you begin creating system policies, each and every user is subject to at least the Default User and Default Computer policies. As you create specific policies for users, groups, and computers, you may have difficulty remembering which policies apply in each situation. If you do become confused, consult the following list, which explains the order in which system policies are applied.

1. A user-specific policy is applied, if one exists.
2. The Default User policy is applied if a user-specific profile does not exist.
3. No group policies are applied if a user-specific profile exists.
4. All relevant group policies (for groups the user belongs to) are applied from lowest priority to highest priority.
5. A computer-specific policy is applied if one exists.

6. The Default Computer policy is applied if a computer-specific profile does not exist.

If the Config.pol file cannot be located, or the server where the file resides is not available, Windows 98 uses the current Registry settings.

System Policy Deployment

Deploying system policies on your network is not difficult. However, you must pay attention to detail. Always test your policies thoroughly before deploying them across your entire network. The safest way to test a policy is by setting up an individual user or computer profile for a sample user or computer. For the test, store your Config.pol file locally. The general steps required to deploy system policies for Windows 98 clients are as follows:

1. Enable user profiles, as described earlier in this chapter.
2. Decide which policy issues or restrictions should be controlled for each client computer.
3. Decide which policy issues or restrictions should be controlled for each group.
4. Decide which policy issues or restrictions should be controlled for each user.
5. Install the System Policy Editor, following the steps provided in the Hands-on Projects at the end of this chapter.
6. Create any additional .adm template files that may be necessary.
7. After examining existing templates, load all appropriate .adm template files into the System Policy Editor.
8. Create all required group policies.
9. Create all required computer policies.
10. Create all required user policies.
11. Edit the Default User and Default Computer policies as necessary.
12. Save the system policy as Config.pol.
13. Test this system policy on several computers.
14. Once test results are satisfactory, place this file in a network location accessible to Windows 98 machines.

CHAPTER SUMMARY

- Windows 98 is a multiuser operating system. As a multiuser system, Windows 98 supports multiple local users and can be a client computer for multiple network users. However, Windows 98 is only able to support a single user logon at a time. Unlike systems such as UNIX, Windows 98 does not support multiple simultaneous local logons.

- Windows 98 identifies users by a username and password. To obtain access to Windows 98 locally or to use Windows 98 as a network client, you must respond to the logon prompt with a valid username and password. Windows 98 can use the same password for local logons and network logons. All passwords used on a Windows 98 system are stored by default in the password cache. The password cache is an encrypted .pwl file. Changing passwords is performed through the Password applet, but passwords may be deleted from the cache using the Password List Editor tool.

- The user environment of Windows 98 includes the visible desktop and utilities and the networking infrastructure and the underlying system configuration. Thus, the user environment represents a broad collection of permissions, preferences, configurations, restrictions, and security limitations.

- User profiles provide a powerful way to control the user environment within Windows 98. A user profile represents the stored collection of preferences and configuration settings specific to a single user. A profile includes the Start menu, desktop icons, drive mappings, color schemes, and more. By default, Windows 98 maintains only a single user profile for all users who log on to a machine. But through the User Profiles tab of the Passwords applet, a profile for each individual user can be created and maintained.

- Users with access to only the local Windows 98 machine are managed through the Users applet. Windows 98 users with access to a Windows NT or NetWare network are managed through the network's domain controller or directory server.

- Windows 98 profiles may be stored on a network share to create roaming profiles. A roaming profile is a profile that "follows" a user from one client machine to another. Roaming profiles are enabled on the network domain controller by defining a user account's home directory. Windows 98 profiles are not compatible with Windows NT profiles.

- Mandatory profiles can be used to enforce a specific profile or to prevent changes to an existing profile. Any profile can be transformed into a mandatory profile by renaming the User.dat file in the main level of the profile to User.man. Once this is complete, changes made by a user are not added to the profile.

- Hardware profiles provide another way to control the Windows 98 environment. Hardware profiles simplify management of computer systems with dynamic device configurations. Typically, hardware profiles define multiple configurations for notebook computers with PC Card slots or docking bays. Hardware profiles are managed through the Hardware Profiles tab in the System applet. Once a new hardware profile is created, you can boot into that profile and make any modifications to match a specific hardware/device configuration. During each subsequent reboot, Windows 98 will detect the hardware present and attempt to choose a matching hardware profile. If this cannot be resolved automatically, you will be prompted to select a profile.

- Another key component for managing both user and computer environments is system policies. A system policy restricts the Windows 98 environment, unlike user profiles, which define the environment preferences for a single user. A system policy controls a user environment at the Registry level by overwriting parts of the Registry.

- The System Policy Editor (SPE) is used to create and manage system policies. Template files (.adm) are used to provide the basic structure for any system policy. The SPE is used to create user-, group-, and computer-specific policies based on such templates. A system policy is stored as a Config.pol file. Windows 98 loads this file during each bootup and logon, and all applicable policy items are applied.

- The following list should help you understand the basic concepts associated with profiles and policies:

    - **Logon Requirements**: Separate usernames and passwords can be stored on Windows 98 computers and the network. They can be synchronized for convenience.

    - **Share-level security**: A type of security in which passwords are assigned to resources such as file folders and printers. Can lead to a large number of passwords. Logins are not required.

    - **User-level security**: A type of security in which permission to use resources are assigned by domains, at the Windows NT or Novell NetWare Server level. Logins and passwords are required.

    - **User profiles**: When user profiles are implemented, a User.dat file exists for every user who can log on.

    - **.Adm files**: Templates with a list of settings that can be imported into the System Policy Editor.

    - **Default policy**: Created when you load one or more .adm files. If saved as part of a Config.pol file, it affects all users. There are many possible default policies.

    - **User policy**: Applies to users, as identified by logon username.

    - **Computer policy**: Applies to users, as identified by the Computer name in the Identification tab in the Network dialog box.

    - **Group policy**: Applies to groups, as identified in a NT Server or Novell NetWare domain.

KEY TERMS

- **.adm files** — Text-based system policy template files.
- **computer policy** — A system policy that applies to a single computer.
- **Config.pol** — The standard default name for the system policy file.
- **default computer policy** — A system policy that applies to a computer if a Computer policy is not defined.
- **default user policy** — A system policy that applies to a user if a User policy is not defined.

- **group policy** — A system policy that applies to each member of a group.
- **hardware profile** — Represents the collection of connected hardware, drivers, and settings specific to a particular hardware configuration.
- **local-only users** — Users who only have access to the local computer, with no access to a network.
- **local profile** — A user profile that exists only on a local client. By default, all profiles are initially local profiles.
- **mandatory profiles** — A user profile that does not record user environment changes. To create a mandatory profile, rename User.dat to User.man.
- **multiuser operating system** — A software product that integrates the functions and interactions between hardware components in separate environments for multiple users.
- **network users** — User accounts defined by a domain controller that can log on to any workstation within the network, including Windows 98.
- **password cache** — *See* password list file (.pwl).
- **Password List Editor** — A simple tool used to remove passwords from the Windows 98 password list file.
- **password list file (.pwl)** — The files stored in the main Windows 98 subdirectory where all passwords are stored. This file is encrypted.
- **password policy** — Refers to Windows NT rules on passwords for age, content, and repetition. Applies to Windows 98 systems that verify logons through a Windows NT-based network.
- **.pol files** — System policy files created by the System Policy Editor.
- **roaming profile** — A user profile that is stored on a network share so that it can be used on any network client.
- **roving profile** — Another term for a roaming profile.
- **system policies** — A control tool that restricts or limits the operational environment for users, groups, or computers. System policies work by overwriting the local Registry each time a user logs on.
- **System Policy Editor** — The administrative tool used to create and modify system policies.
- **user accounts** — Logical identifiers used by the operating system to identify specific individuals, associate their user environments with them, and track and control their resource access.
- **User.dat** — The portion of a user profile that contains the Registry portions specific to all users on a particular Windows 98 machine.
- **user environment** — The collection of user preferences and administrative limitations that determine how the user interface looks and operates.

- **user.man** — The filename that applies to a mandatory user profile (instead of User.dat).
- **user policy** — A system policy that applies to a single user.
- **user profile** — A stored collection of preferences and configuration settings specific to a single user.

REVIEW QUESTIONS

1. Which of the following types of users are supported in Windows 98? (Choose all correct answers.)
   a. local users
   b. universal users
   c. network users
   d. nonauthenticated users

2. How many simultaneous users is Windows 98 designed to support?
   a. one
   b. two
   c. four
   d. sixteen

3. Windows 98 is configured to support multiple user profiles by default. True or False?

4. By what mechanism does Windows 98 associate a user with a specific profile?
   a. retinal scan
   b. NetBIOS computer name
   c. user account
   d. Windows 98 does not associate a human being with a profile.

5. The Users applet in the Control Panel is used to create and manage network user accounts, just like Windows NT User Manager for Domains. True or False?

6. By what mechanism is a password policy enforced on Windows 98?
   a. through the Password applet
   b. using Novell NetWare
   c. via user settings in Windows NT Server
   d. with a system policy

7. Where are passwords stored in Windows 98?
   a. in the Registry
   b. in Username.pwl files
   c. in plaintext files in the user policy directory
   d. Passwords are not stored by default in Windows 98.

8. By what means can a password be changed in Windows 98? (Choose all correct answers.)
   a. the System Policy Editor
   b. the Passwords applet
   c. the password command line utility
   d. the Password List Editor
9. Your local Windows 98 password and your networking logon password can be set to the same string of characters. True or False?
10. Which tools are not installed by default into Windows 98? (Choose all correct answers.)
    a. System Policy Editor
    b. Users applet
    c. Password List Editor
    d. Passwords applet
11. Which of the following items are stored in a user profile? (Choose all correct answers.)
    a. Desktop icons
    b. Start menu layout
    c. network drive mappings
    d. color and sound scheme
12. Which of the following items are stored in the profiles directory for each user? (Choose all correct answers.)
    a. Application Data folder
    b. Favorites folder
    c. History folder
    d. NetHood folder
13. The configuration, settings, and contents of the Active Desktop are not stored within a user profile. True or False?
14. In which directory are multiple local profiles stored by Windows 98?
    a. C:\Windows\Users
    b. C:\Users
    c. C:\Windows\Profiles
    d. C:\Windows\Inf
15. Which of the following are configuration settings for user profiles on the User Profiles tab of the Password applet? (Choose all correct answers.)
    a. Include desktop icons and Network Neighborhood contents in user settings.
    b. Include Internet Explorer configuration settings and files in user settings.

c. Include drive mappings and printer shares in user settings.

d. Include Start menu and Program groups in user settings.

16. When a multiprofile Windows 98 system is configured back to supporting only a single profile for all users, the profiles stored for the multiple users are automatically deleted. True or False?

17. Windows 98 can alter the settings, group memberships, and home directory locations of network users via the Users applet. True or False?

18. What type of profile can "follow" a user from one Windows 98 client to another? (Choose all correct answers.)

   a. local mandatory

   b. local user preferences

   c. roaming mandatory

   d. roaming user preferences

19. The server hosting roaming profiles does not need to support long filenames. The LFN to 8.3 conversion algorithm is used by profiles to maintain compatibility. True or False?

20. All of the Windows 98 clients must have a similar installation configuration (i.e., main Windows directory name and drive letter) for network-based profiles to function properly. True or False?

21. How do you identify a mandatory profile?

   a. its storage on a network share

   b. It contains the Common Files folder.

   c. the User.man file

   d. the presence of a System.dat file

22. Windows 98 is able to automatically select and boot with a hardware profile if the devices present during bootup are previously known in their current configuration. True or False?

23. A specific user policy, all group policies (of which the user is a member), and the computer policy for the client in use are applied to each user when he or she logs on to Windows 98. True or False?

24. Which of the following types of system policies does Windows 98 support? (Choose all correct answers.)

   a. user

   b. group

   c. domain

   d. computer

25. Both .adm files and .pol files are created using the System Policy Editor. True or False?

Hands-on Projects

Project 4-1

In this project, you will configure your Windows 98 computer to support multiple local users. To minimize data requirements, it would be better (but not absolutely necessary) to complete this project with a standalone computer just after installing Windows 98. In the following steps, you will use the Enable Multi-user Settings Wizard, which is made up of several successive dialog boxes, or pages.

1. Click **Start**, point to **Settings**, click **Control Panel**, and then double-click the **Users** icon. If users have been set up before, the User Settings page of the Enable Multi-user Settings wizard opens. Otherwise, the Enable Multi-user Settings dialog box opens; in this case, skip to Step 3.
2. Click **New User**. The Add User page of the Enable Multi-user Settings Wizard opens. Click **Next**.
3. In the New User text box, type the username of the currently logged on user. In other words, type your username.
4. Click **Next**. The Enter New Password page opens.
5. In the Password text box, type the password of your choice. You will use this password in the future in order to access Windows 98.
6. Click **Next**. The Personalized Items Settings page opens.
7. Select all five check boxes in the Items list (Desktop folder and Documents menu, Start Menu, Favorites folder, Downloaded Web pages, and My Documents folder).
8. Select the **Create copies of the current items and their content** option button, and then click **Next**. The Ready to Finish page opens.
9. Click **Finish**. If you see a message indicating that Password caching has been disabled, it was disabled in a policy file, possibly on a network server beyond your control. You can do this on other Windows 98 computers through your System Policy Editor file, in the Computer Policy for the Windows 98 Network.
10. When prompted, click **Yes** to reboot your Windows 98 computer.

Project 4-2

In this project, you will install and use the Password List Editor. To complete this project, you need to have a computer with Windows 98 installed. You will also need the Windows 98 installation CD.

1. Insert the Windows 98 Installation CD into the CD-ROM drive.

2. Click **Start**, point to **Settings**, click **Control Panel**, and then double-click the **Add/Remove Programs** icon.
3. Click the **Windows Setup** tab.
4. Click **Have Disk**. The Install From Disk dialog box opens.
5. Click **Browse**. The Open dialog box appears.
6. Use the Drives drop-down list to switch to your CD-ROM drive.
7. In the Folders display area, scroll down, open the **Tools** folder, open the **Reskit** folder, open the **Netadmin** folder, and then open the **Pwledit** folder.
8. Click **OK**. The Install From Disk dialog box now displays the path *<CD-ROM drive letter>*:\Tools\Reskit\Netadmin\Pwledit, where "*<CD-ROM drive letter>*" stands for the letter associated with your CD-ROM drive.
9. Click **OK**. The Have Disk dialog box displays the available components from the defined path.
10. Select the **Password List Editor** check box.
11. Click **Install**. Windows 98 loads the necessary files and installs the Password List Editor. You return to the Add/Remove Programs Properties dialog box.
12. Click **OK**.
13. Close the Control Panel. Now you can open the Password List Editor.
14. Click **Start**, point to **Programs**, point to **Accessories**, point to **System Tools**, and then click **Password List Editor**. The type and related resource for each password currently stored in the cache (other than the Windows 98 local logon password) is displayed in the PLE. You could delete any of these passwords by selecting them and then clicking Remove. If you do not see anything in this list, you may not have stored any passwords, or another user may have disabled caching through a policy file.
15. Click **Quit** to exit the Password List Editor.

PROJECT 4-3

In this project, you will enable multiple user profiles. To complete this project, you need a computer with Windows 98 installed.

1. Click **Start**, point to **Settings**, click **Control Panel**, and then double-click the **Passwords** icon.
2. Click the **User Profiles** tab.
3. Click the **Users can customize their preferences and desktop settings. Windows switches to your personal settings whenever you log on** option button.
4. Select both of the check boxes that appear when you select the option button in the previous step.

5. Click **OK**, and then reboot the computer. Now you can log on to Windows 98 using the username and password that you just created in Project 4-1.

Project 4-4

In this project, you will install the System Policy Editor. To complete this project, you need a computer with Windows 98 installed. You will also need the Windows 98 Installation CD.

1. Insert the Windows 98 Installation CD into the CD-ROM drive.
2. Click **Start**, point to **Settings**, click **Control Panel**, and then double-click the **Add/Remove Programs** icon.
3. Click the **Windows Setup** tab.
4. Click **Have Disk**. The Install From Disk dialog box opens.
5. Click **Browse**. The Open dialog box appears.
6. Use the Drives drop-down list to switch to your CD-ROM drive.
7. In the list of folders, double-click the **Tools folder**, double-click the **Reskit** folder, double-click the **Netadmin** folder, and then double-click the **Poledit** folder.
8. In the list of filenames, click **Poledit.inf**.
9. Click **OK**. The Install From Disk dialog box now displays the path *<CD-ROM drive letter>*:\Tools\Reskit\Netadmin\Poledit, where "*<CD-ROM drive letter>*" stands for the letter associated with your CD-ROM drive.
10. Click **OK**. The Have Disk dialog box displays the available components from the defined path.
11. Select the **System Policy Editor** check box.
12. Click **Install**. Windows 98 loads the necessary files and installs the System Policy Editor. Eventually, you return to the Add/Remove Programs Properties dialog box.
13. Click **OK**.
14. Close the Control Panel.

Project 4-5

In this project, you will use the System Policy Editor to create a user policy. To complete this project, you need to have a computer with Windows 98 and the System Policy Editor installed.

1. Click **Start**, point to **Programs**, point to **Accessories**, point to **System Tools**, and then click **System Policy Editor**. The System Policy Editor window opens.
2. Click **File** on the menu bar, and then click **New Policy**. The Default Computer and Default User profile icons are displayed, as shown earlier in the chapter, in Figure 4-8.

Highlight each icon and press the **Delete** key on your keyboard. Click **Yes** to confirm each deletion.

3. Click **Edit** on the menu bar, and then click **Add User**. The Add User dialog box opens.
4. Type **Bob**, and then click **OK**. The Bob user policy icon is displayed in the System Policy Editor.
5. Double-click the **Bob user policy** icon. The Bob Properties dialog box opens.
6. Click the **plus sign** beside "Windows 98 Network" to expand its contents.
7. Click the **plus sign** to the left of "Sharing" to expand its contents.
8. Click the **"Disable file sharing controls"** check box and the **"Disable print sharing controls"** check box, so that a check mark appears in both check boxes.
9. Click the **plus sign** beside "Windows 98 System" to expand its contents.
10. Click the **plus sign** beside "Shell" to expand its contents.
11. Click the **plus sign** beside "Restrictions" (below "Shell") to expand its contents.
12. Click the **"Disable Shut Down command"** check box so that a check mark appears in the check box.
13. Click the **plus sign** beside "Restrictions" (below Windows 98 System) to expand its contents.
14. Click the **"Disable Registry editing tools"** check box so that a check mark appears in the check box.
15. Click **OK** at the bottom of the Properties dialog box. You return to the SPE.
16. Click **File** on the menu bar, and then click **Save As**. The Save As dialog box opens.
17. In the File Name text box, type **Test.pol**.
18. Click **Save**. You return to the SPE. If you get a message stating that an error occurred writing the Registry, you may need to save the file in another folder or disk.
19. Click **File** on the menu bar, and then click **Exit**.

PROJECT 4-6

In this project, you will use the System Policy Editor to create three dummy group policies. Then you will specify their relative priority. To complete this project, you need to have a computer with Windows 98 and the System Policy Editor installed.

1. Click **Start**, point to **Programs**, point to **Accessories**, point to **System Tools**, and then click **System Policy Editor**. The System Policy Editor window opens.
2. Click **File** on the menu bar, and then click **New Policy**. The Default Computer and Default User policy icons are displayed.
3. Click **Edit** on the menu bar, and then click **Add Group**. The Add Group dialog box opens.

4. Type **Sales**, and then click **OK**. The Sales group policy icon is displayed in the System Policy Editor.
5. Repeat Steps 3 and 4 to create two other groups named Admin and Marketing.
6. Click **Options** on the menu bar, and then click **Group Priority**. The Group Priority dialog box opens.
7. Select the Admin group by clicking **Admin** in the Group Order list.
8. Click the **Move Up** button once. The Admin group now appears above the Sales group. The Admin group now has top priority.
9. Select the Sales group by clicking **Sales** in the Group Order list.
10. Click the **Move Down** button once. The Sales group now appears below the Marketing group. The Sales group now has lowest priority.
11. Click **OK**. You return to the System Policy Editor.
12. Click **File** on the menu bar, and then click **Exit**.
13. Click **No** when asked if you want to save your changes.

CASE PROJECTS

1. You need to explain the user environment of Windows 98 to your manager. Write a three- to four-paragraph report explaining the various aspects of the user environment and how these aspects can be controlled.

2. You have a desktop computer with several hot-swappable devices, three PC Card slots, a USB port, and multiple interchangeable SCSI devices. Write a one- to two-paragraph report explaining how Windows 98 supports hardware configurations that vary between bootups.

3. There are 25 Windows 98 computers in your office network. Three groups of 25 users work on the network in 8-hour work shifts. Thus, these computers are used 24 hours a day. Users rarely work on the same Windows 98 client two shifts in a row. You want to grant users the ability to customize their user environments and retain that environment throughout their employment. Write a three- to four-paragraph report explaining how this is possible in Windows 98.

4. Several computers are located in public areas of a large office building. These computers provide temporary places for visitors to access public data and to create brief reports. You do not wish changes to the user environment to be recorded between logons. Write a one- to two-paragraph report explaining how Windows 98 makes this possible.

5. Because of recent system crashes, management at your company has demanded that users be restricted from editing the Registry, from sharing local resources, and from launching MS-DOS applications on Windows 98 computers. Write a three- to four-paragraph report explaining whether or not Windows 98 can perform these tasks and, if so, by what mechanisms this may be accomplished.

CHAPTER FIVE

NETWORKING AND THE INTERNET

This book covers Windows 98 networking in four chapters. This chapter introduces basic networking concepts in the context of connecting to the Internet. In Chapter 6, you will learn about the world of mobile computing, from modem installation to dial-up networking. In Chapter 7, you will learn about the other Internet-related features of Windows 98, namely Front Page Express, Personal Web Server, and Remote Access Server. After several chapters related to architecture and security, you will be ready for Chapter 13, where you will learn to configure and use Windows 98 primarily on a local area network.

AFTER READING THIS CHAPTER AND COMPLETING THE EXERCISES, YOU WILL BE ABLE TO

- Discuss basic features of Windows 98 networking
- Understand the role of protocols, especially TCP/IP
- Configure and use a new Internet connection
- Understand the features available in Internet Explorer 4.0
- Connect to an FTP server

This chapter starts with a basic introduction to networking. It continues with a discussion of TCP/IP, the language of the Internet, and then focuses on the way Windows 98 works with TCP/IP. Because the language of networking often seems quite different from standard English, you will then review some networking key terms. You will then learn to set up connections through the Internet Connection Wizard, and use the basic Microsoft Internet tools included in Windows 98: Internet Explorer, Outlook Express, and NetMeeting.

Because of the way Windows 98 is organized, connecting to the Internet is similar to connecting to a local area network (LAN). Details of connecting a Windows 98 computer to a LAN are more complex and will be covered in the discussion of advanced networking in Chapter 13.

THE LANGUAGE OF NETWORKING

Networks are managed through a series of protocols. A **protocol** is a standard, or set of rules, for data communication; among other things, protocols govern how data travels over modems and network adapters. For two computers to communicate, they need to share a set of protocols. There are three basic protocol groups available for Windows 98: **TCP/IP (Transmission Control Protocol/Internet Protocol)**, **IPX/SPX (Internetwork Packet Exchange/Sequenced Packet Exchange)**, and **NetBEUI (NetBIOS Extended User Interface)**. **DLC (Data Link Control)** is a fourth protocol group, focused on communication with network printers and IBM AS/400 computers. You can also set up Windows 98 to accommodate the **Fast Infrared** protocol for wireless connections. When you connect to a network such as the Internet, data is transmitted in groups of **packets**. The protocol set that you use determines, among other things, the size of each packet as well as the route your data takes over the network. Packets are discussed in more detail in *A Guide to Networking Essentials,* published by Course Technology.

 Many books talk about TCP/IP as if it were one protocol. It is actually a set, or suite, of several different protocols, organized in what is known as a **stack**. Thus you may often hear the term "TCP/IP protocol stack." The stack defines how the different protocols work together as well as their division of responsibility.

Because Windows 98 is designed with the assumption that its users will connect to the Internet, its default protocol is TCP/IP. The remainder of this chapter, as well as Chapters 6 and 7, assumes that all Internet connections are based on TCP/IP. The other protocols, IPX/SPX, NetBEUI, and Fast Infrared, are primarily used in local area networks (LANs) and will be discussed in more detail in Chapter 13.

Windows 98 is often used in a client-server network centered around a Windows NT server. It can also be configured with the Microsoft version of IPX/SPX, known as the IPX/SPX-compatible protocol, as a client in a Novell NetWare network. NetBEUI is the most efficient of the three major protocols, but because NetBEUI packets cannot be transferred from network to network (i.e., it is not routable), its use is limited to small stand-alone networks. DLC, which will also be discussed in Chapter 13, is generally limited to the support of networked printers.

In the following sections, you will learn the basics of networking and TCP/IP as they relate to the functions of Windows 98. TCP/IP includes a number of different protocols. Some are directly related to the way data actually moves across the Internet. Windows 98 includes a number of configuration options that help you set up shop on the Information Superhighway. A comprehensive discussion of other TCP/IP protocols is beyond the scope of this book. For more information on TCP/IP, see *A Guide to TCP/IP on Microsoft Windows NT 4.0*, published by Course Technology.

BASIC NETWORKING

When you send e-mail over the Internet, your computer has to translate the information in your word-processing program into a language that can be sent over wires, specifically the "1s" and "0s" of binary code. Networking programs work in what are known as layers. The programs in each layer are responsible for different types of functions, such as encryption, checking for errors, and routing from one computer to another.

This division of labor is formally defined in the seven layers of the Open Systems Interconnection (OSI) model. If you study networking any further, you will become quite familiar with the different OSI layers. Although the layers of the TCP/IP **protocol stack** do not correspond precisely to the OSI model, OSI does provide a good rigorous model for classifying TCP/IP protocols. A brief description of the seven OSI layers is provided in the following list:

- **Application**: Protocols at this layer translate between the programs that you see, such as Microsoft Word, and basic categories of network protocols. The TCP/IP Simple Mail Transfer Protocol (SMTP) is essentially an Application-layer protocol that starts the translation process.

- **Presentation**: Protocols at this layer translate normal letters and numbers into computer code such as ASCII. **ASCII** is a set of numbers that represents every number and character typed on an English-language keyboard. Encryption routines also work at the presentation layer.

- **Session**: Protocols at this layer manage your time on a network. Computers at either end of the session can exchange data for the duration of the session.

- **Transport**: Protocols at this layer determine how much effort will be expended to make sure your message gets to its destination. You will learn about the two major Internet transport protocols, TCP and UDP.

- **Network**: Protocols at this layer move data from computer to computer. Depending on the network layer protocols that you use, they can also manage congestion; if one line is busy, these protocols include rules that allow your data to go through a less busy route. When you send data on TCP/IP, you send it to a special address known as an IP address. In the same way that you change routes at a highway junction, the network layer moves data from computer to computer based on IP addresses. The IP address is embedded in a label in each network layer packet. Briefly, an IP address is four numbers between 0 and 255, divided by periods. A comprehensive discussion of IP addressing is beyond the scope of this book.

- **Data Link**: Protocols at this level are primarily concerned with ensuring that data is transmitted reliably. Some protocols will transmit only a certain amount of data at a time, and then wait for acknowledgment from the receiving computer before sending another group of data. Information at the data link level is exchanged between hardware addresses. It's important to keep in mind that, unlike IP addresses, which can change and can be duplicated, each modem and network adapter has a fixed and unique hardware address. When an IP address is assigned to a computer, it is actually assigned to a hardware address. In Chapter 13, you will learn how the Address Resolution Protocol (ARP) allows you to make sure that IP addresses have been assigned to hardware in the right computers.
- **Physical**: Protocols at this level translate data into the 1s and 0s of binary code for transmission over phone lines or other physical media.

Don't worry if you feel a little overwhelmed by the complexity of TCP/IP and other networking topics. As you learn more about networking in other books, you'll become more comfortable with these topics. At this point, it is enough to understand that the process of sending data over a network is made possible by a division of labor. The various networking tasks are assigned to various protocols, which, when working together, are referred to as a protocol stack. In the next section, you will learn about some of the different protocols associated with the TCP/IP stack.

The OSI model was created in part to standardize the way different companies create software and build equipment in a network. If OSI worked perfectly, you could mix and match products from different companies on your network. However, OSI is not a complete success, in part because companies now try to differentiate themselves by creating products that work at more than one OSI layer. If you study networking further, you will find that OSI does not adequately define major network types such as Ethernet and ATM. As you study Windows 98 further, you will learn that Microsoft has created models similar to OSI for communication within the operating system. Microsoft has tried to avoid the problems of OSI by taking full responsibility for the layers between applications and hardware. As you become an expert user of Windows 98, you will become a judge of their success.

INSTALLING MULTIPLE PROTOCOLS

When you install a protocol stack, you **bind** it to a specific modem or network adapter. In other words, before you can use TCP/IP, you need to bind it to your modem. Some computers are configured with additional protocol stacks such as NetBEUI and IPX/SPX, so that they can communicate on different types of networks. When binding multiple protocol stacks, you should bind them in a specific order. As your computer reads data from the network, it sends the data through each protocol stack in order, until it finds a protocol stack that works with the data. This takes time and resources. Therefore, while you could use all four of the protocols described earlier in this chapter, it's wise to load only protocols that you need. Unnecessary protocols eat up system resources and can slow down network communications.

TCP/IP

TCP/IP is actually a group, or suite, of protocols. In this section, you will learn about a few of the major TCP/IP protocols; specifically, you will learn about the tasks assigned to these protocols, and about how these protocols work with Windows 98 to transfer data over a network. Understanding these concepts will help you understand the process of connecting to the Internet. The major TCP/IP protocols are as follows:

- **Transmission Control Protocol (TCP)**: The standard transport protocol of the Internet. If your programs use TCP, this protocol asks receiving computers to send an acknowledgment, to verify that a message was received. Therefore, TCP is often referred to as a **connection-oriented** protocol. Just because you are using TCP/IP, that does not mean that your transport protocol is TCP.

- **User Datagram Protocol (UDP)**: Some networks are considered so reliable that the occasional lost packet of data does not matter. UDP transport layer messages do not request acknowledgment. Therefore, UDP is referred to as a **connectionless protocol**. When you use UDP, you may never know if your message got to the destination. On the other hand, UDP uses fewer system resources than a connection-oriented protocol. Acknowledgment requests can be a problem for a busy system.

- **Internet Protocol (IP)**: Every message over the Internet is sent to an **IP address**, which is a set of four numbers between 0 and 255, separated by periods. To avoid confusion, everyone who uses an IP address on the Internet has to register with an official organization, such as the **InterNIC** registration service at *www.internic.com*. Internet service providers (ISPs) generally lease blocks of IP addresses, known as **subnets**. When you connect to the Internet through your ISP, you are assigned an IP address.

- **Point-to-Point Protocol (PPP)**: The more popular of the TCP/IP data-link protocols. Unlike the **Serial Line Interface Protocol (SLIP)**, it provides error-checking features. Conceptually, the difference between PPP and SLIP is similar to the difference between TCP and UDP. SLIP is mostly used by the UNIX operating system, which is a common system for larger-capacity servers.

- **Address Resolution Protocol (ARP)**: Associates IP addresses with the hardware address on every network card and modem. Because of a convention implemented by the Institute of Electrical and Electronics Engineers (IEEE), every hardware address is unique. In Chapter 13, you will learn that if you are troubleshooting a problem, you can use the "ARP" command to make sure that the IP address to which you are sending messages actually points to the right computer.

- **Packet Internet Groper (PING)**: This may be the most useful troubleshooting utility "protocol" in TCP/IP. (It is not a protocol per se.) You do not need any special network hardware to use PING. You can check all of your connections with PING, a process sometimes referred to as "pinging" a site. You can experiment with PING by pinging a favorite Web site. For example: Connect to your

ISP. Click Start, point to Programs, click MS-DOS Prompt. At the C:\ prompt, PING *www.yahoo.com*, then press Enter. After a pause, a response appears in the MS-DOS window, with the IP address for the Web site you just pinged (in this case, *www.yahoo.com*). If you do not see this response, you may not be properly connected to the Internet, or network congestion may have affected your ping attempt. Wait a minute or two and try again. In Chapter 13, you will learn to use PING and a number of other utilities for troubleshooting.

MODEMS AND NETWORK CARDS

Before you configure TCP/IP, you need to install your network interface—that is, the device that will allow you to connect to the network. Today, many computers are built with modems or network adapters already installed. There are several major types of network adapters available for your computer. The following is simply an introduction to the different kinds of available adapters. Modems, ISDN, and ADSL will be covered in more detail in Chapter 6. Other network adapters will be covered in Chapter 13.

- **Modems**: The term "modem" is a shortened version of "modulator/demodulator." A modem is the major consumer computer interface to the Internet. It works by translating digital network signals into sounds that can be transmitted through the telephone system. Current modems have a transmission speed of up to 56 KB/s.

- **ISDN**: The consumer version of the Integrated Services Digital Network offers a direct digital connection to the Internet. Translation from digital signals to sound is not required. The most common transmission speed is 128 KB/s, which can be divided into two equal channels.

- **Asynchronous Digital Subscriber Line (ADSL)**: A technology that transmits data at speeds much faster than ordinary telephone lines. The telephone companies are starting to bring ADSL technology to market.

- **Cable Modems**: Like telephone companies, cable television companies have an installed base of wire that can be used to connect to the Internet. The coaxial cable used for cable TV is closely related to the coaxial cable used for 10 MB/s networking systems. Despite the "modem" in the name, cable modems communicate digitally, like ISDN and ADSL.

- **Ethernet**: The traditional technology of networks. Although Ethernet adapters are rated to transmit at speeds of 10, 100, and 1000 MB/s, their range is limited.

- **ATM**: Windows 98 includes support for Asynchronous Transfer Mode, a rival to Ethernet at similar speeds. Both Ethernet and ATM will be covered in more detail in Chapter 13.

Generally, installation requirements are different for desktop and laptop computers. Installing any card in a desktop computer involves significant risk. The static electricity that can build up in most human beings is sufficient to damage many of the parts in a computer. Wrist grounding straps are available to make sure that you don't build up a significant static charge. Before opening up your desktop PC and installing a new modem or network card, read your manuals carefully. And turn your computer off before you start.

On the other hand, laptop computers have adapted the PC Card (formerly PCMCIA) standard. The components in a PC Card are sealed in a metal case. You can install a PC Card while your computer is running. As discussed in Chapter 1, USB and FireWire adapters will be even easier to install.

But once you've installed your network card, the Plug and Play feature you learned about in Chapter 1 eases the burden of software installation. If the card is inserted properly, it will configure itself automatically when you turn the computer back on. The operating system then adds the appropriate configuration information to the Registry and makes sure that all necessary files are installed. Windows 98 supports just about every type of Plug and Play network card and driver, as long as they run in protected mode, which means that they cannot interact directly with the CPU. Microsoft has avoided the use of real-mode drivers, which do interact directly with the CPU. Real-mode drivers and applications, such as those built for MS-DOS, work to the exclusion of all other drivers and applications, which is not consistent with a multi-tasking operating system.

CONFIGURING TCP/IP

Now that you've installed your network card, you can start customizing your protocol. TCP/IP is automatically installed along with Windows 98. If for some reason it is not installed on your computer, you can install it by following the steps provided in the Hands-on Projects at the end of this chapter. You'll also have a chance to practice the specific steps involved in configuring TCP/IP in the Hands-on Projects. For now, you can simply familiarize yourself with the available configuration options.

To get to the TCP/IP configuration options, click Start, point to Settings, click Control Panel, double-click the Network icon, and then click the Configuration Tab. Scroll through "The following network components are installed:" list. If you have more than one modem or network adapter, TCP/IP may be listed more than once, as shown in Figure 5-1.

Double-click on one of the TCP/IP components associated with your modem (a.k.a.: dial-up adapter). If you use a dial-up adapter to connect to an Internet Service Provider (ISP), you will then have to click OK in a warning box. (You will learn about ISPs later in this chapter.) This opens the TCP/IP Properties dialog box, as shown in Figure 5-2. This is where you choose the configuration settings appropriate for your system. Table 5-1 describes the settings available on each tab.

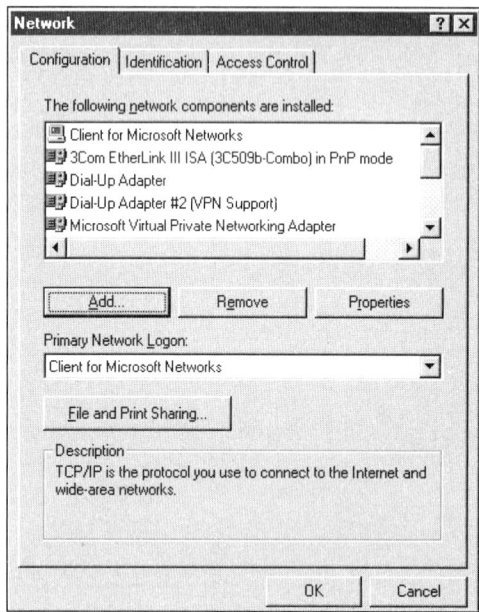

Figure 5-1 Network applet, Configuration tab

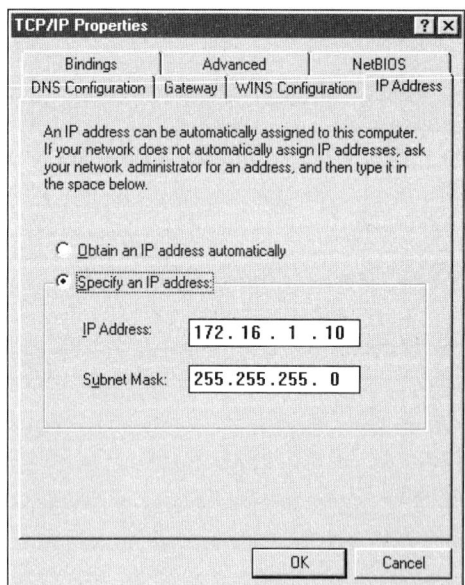

Figure 5-2 TCP/IP Properties dialog box

Table 5-1 Configuring Windows 98 for TCP/IP

Tab	Function
Advanced	Permits you to make TCP/IP the default protocol for all network hardware and software
Bindings	Unless you bind TCP/IP to your modems and other network components, you can't use TCP/IP for your communication. To connect to many ISPs, you need to check the box next to Client for Microsoft Networks. This action "binds" the Client to your modem. If the box is already checked, do not change it.
DNS Configuration	Enables access to a specific DNS Server at a specific IP address. **DNS** servers keep a database of Internet names such as *www.course.com* and their associated IP addresses such as 198.112.168.244
Gateway	Allows you to specify an IP address for a computer on the network that acts as a gateway to the Internet for other computers. If you use TCP/IP on a LAN, you probably have a group of IP addresses assigned to your network. If the IP address to which you are sending data is not on your network, your data is sent to the **gateway**, which then sends it on to the Internet to search for the correct IP address.
IP Address	Although some networks require that you enter an assigned IP address, most networks automatically assign one to you while you are on the Internet. In the latter case, you can use the "Obtain an IP address automatically" option. Note that some ISPs use a Windows NT Server tool (known as the Dynamic Host Configuration Protocol, or **DHCP**) to assign IP addresses automatically.
NetBIOS	The NetBIOS name, which is the official name of your computer, can be found in the Network applet, Identification tab. You would only uncheck the NetBIOS over TCP/IP setting if you do not communicate with the Internet on a Windows 98 system.
WINS Configuration	The Windows Internet Naming Service is a database associating IP addresses and NetBIOS computer names. The database is located on a WINS server, which itself has a certain IP address. As a network administrator, you may instruct your users to identify the IP addresses of the WINS servers on your network.

CONNECTING TO THE INTERNET

Now that you have reviewed the basics of networking, it is time to see how these concepts apply to the process of connecting to the Internet. The remainder of this chapter focuses on translating these concepts into information you can actually use when configuring Internet Explorer, sending e-mail, accessing newsgroups, and transferring files. But first, you should take some time to review the terminology associated with Internet service providers, as described in the following section.

Basic ISP terminology

The average consumer connects to the Internet via an Internet service provider (or ISP). In order to fully understand the process of connecting to an ISP, you should familiarize yourself with the following basic terms.

- **Bandwidth**: The speed of data transfer
- **e-mail account**: The means by which you send and receive e-mail. Some ISPs allow for multiple e-mail accounts with each ISP account; for example, a family with one ISP account can have separate e-mail accounts for each family member. The name assigned to an e-mail account is not necessarily the same as the user's username.
- **Internet service provider (ISP)**: An organization that provides access to the Internet, usually for a fee. Essentially, an ISP leases a line to the Internet and splits the capacity among its subscribers. T3 lines, which can carry the equivalent of 672 telephone lines, are common for even the smallest ISPs. There are literally thousands of ISPs available.
- **ISP account**: The means by which you are identified to your Internet service provider. Each ISP account is associated with a username and a password.
- **Local area network (LAN)**: A group of connected computers in a small area such as an office. Often, all the computers on a LAN will access the Internet through one computer (often a server), which is referred to as the gateway.
- **News account**: The means by which you post and view messages on an Internet newsgroup. Similar to an ISP e-mail account.
- **Newsgroup**: An electronic bulletin board where users share information on common topics. The most common series of newsgroups is known as **Usenet**. When you post a message to a newsgroup, the contents of that message are often accessible through search engines to the entire Internet.
- **Mail server**: The server to which an ISP directs all e-mail. The Internet name of the server often depends on the mail protocol in effect. For example, your ISP's mail server might be named smtp.*yourISP*.com, where *yourISP* stands for the name of your ISP.
- **News server**: Similar in function and address to a mail server. A common Internet name for a news server would be NNTP.*yourISP*.com, where *yourISP* stands for the name of your ISP.
- **Proxy server**: A computer on a local area network that **caches** (that is, stores) information (such as favorite Web pages) that may be accessed repeatedly. If you use a proxy server on a LAN, your browser will look for a Web page on the proxy server first; it is faster for a computer on a LAN to get the data from a cache on the proxy server than from the actual Internet.
- **POP (Post Office Protocol)**: One of the TCP/IP application layer protocols. An ISP usually designates a POP server to receive your e-mail from the Internet.

A common Internet name for your POP server is pop.*yourISP*.com, where *yourISP* stands for the name of your ISP.

- **POP account**: The account used to access the incoming mail server.

- **SMTP (Simple Mail Transfer Protocol)**: One of the TCP/IP protocols, at the application layer. An ISP usually uses an SMTP server to send your e-mail onto the Internet. A common Internet name for an SMTP server is SMTP.*yourISP*.com, where *yourISP* stands for the name of your ISP.

- **UNIX**: An operating system that is commonly used for larger-scale servers. While Microsoft is trying to gain market share through its Windows NT Enterprise operating systems, UNIX is still a popular alternative for those who need more capacity. The operations of some ISPs may be based on UNIX servers, which are usually associated with the SLIP connections discussed earlier in this chapter.

INTERNET CONNECTION OPTIONS

Windows 98 provides a number of configuration wizards for connecting to the Internet. Specific installation methods for network adapters such as modems and ISDN lines are included in Chapter 6. In most cases the actual hardware and software installation is trouble-free. You can configure a connection to the Internet in four different ways:

- **Connecting to an ISP through the Internet Connection Wizard**: To start this wizard, click Start, point to Programs, point to Internet Explorer, and then click Connection Wizard. This opens a series of dialog boxes that lead you through the configuration process. Unless you already have an ISP account or are connecting to the Internet through a LAN, the Internet Connection Wizard leads you to a small and incomplete selection of locally accessible ISPs. You can use the Internet Connection Wizard for connections in a number of different countries.

- **Connecting to a network server through the Internet Connection Wizard**: Using a network adapter, you can connect to a network server that already has a full-time connection to the Internet. The Internet Connection Wizard provides this as an option, and asks you to enter a number of network parameters. Later in this chapter, you will learn how the Internet Connection Wizard helps you connect to an existing ISP account through a local area network (LAN) that is connected to the Internet.

- **Connecting to an ISP using a preconfigured online service**: There are several ISPs with customized connection wizards already set up for Windows 98. Click Start, point to Programs, point to Online Services. This leads you to a choice of five major online services: America Online, AT&T WorldNet Service, CompuServe, Prodigy Internet, and the Microsoft Network.

- **Install TCP/IP and Dial-Up Networking**: There are many more ISPs available than can be set up through the connection wizards. The next section includes the information you need to set up a connection with your ISP.

In the following section you will become familiar with the Internet Connection Wizard. You will have a chance to actually use the Internet Connection Wizard in the Hands-on Projects at the end of this chapter. The specific settings required for creating an Internet connection will vary significantly depending on your choice of ISP. Because of the number of different ISPs, it is not possible to cover all alternatives. Even if you don't use the Internet Connection Wizard, pay close attention to the following instructions, which cover options, such as newsgroups, with which you should be familiar.

INTERNET CONNECTION WIZARD

The Internet Connection Wizard opens automatically the first time you double-click the Internet Explorer icon on the Windows 98 desktop. Alternately, you can click Start, point to Programs, point to Internet Explorer, and then click Connection Wizard. This leads to the three choices shown in Figure 5-3. The first two choices, which involve the Connection Wizard, are described in the following sections.

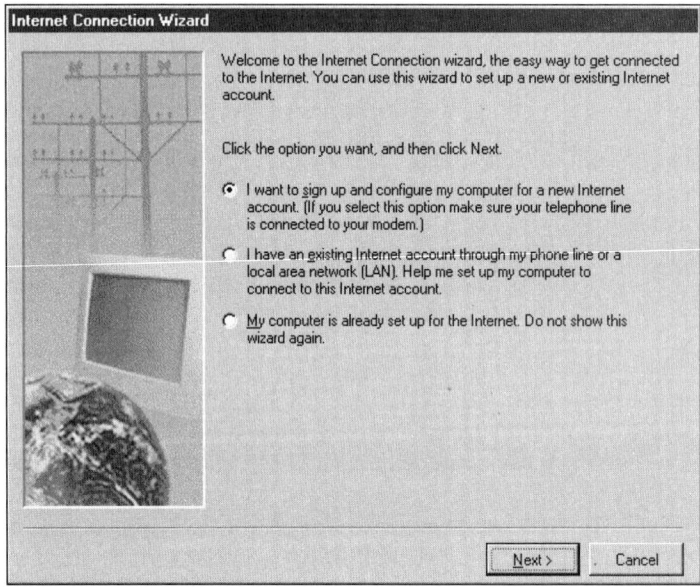

Figure 5-3 Internet Connection Wizard opening page

Signing Up

If you choose to sign up for and configure a new Internet account, the Internet Connection Wizard automatically uses the Microsoft Referral Network to help you locate an appropriate ISP. Be warned that the Referral Network does not cover all ISPs in a local area. When you click Next, the Wizard starts by dialing a national number (an 800 number in the United States) to locate a few ISPs. If you are in the USA and have never set up your dialing properties, as discussed later in this chapter, the wizard prompts you for your area code in order to facilitate the search. Enter your area code and click Next to continue. Assuming your modem is installed and configured properly, the wizard then dials into the Microsoft Referral Service using an 800 number (for U.S.-based callers). If your modem is not configured, Windows 98 attempts to configure it for you; you may be required to participate in this process, for example, by providing manufacturer-supplied driver disks. Once connected, follow the prompts to select a provider.

Connecting to an Existing Account

If you choose the second option in the Internet Connection Wizard, you can connect to an existing ISP account over the telephone or through a local area network (LAN). Connecting through a LAN can be useful if you have an account that can be used on Windows 98 computers on that network. In Chapter 4, you learned about user profiles. The connections that you set up to an ISP from a LAN can move with you from one Windows 98 workstation to another in the form of a roaming profile.

When you select this option and click Next, the wizard leads you to a different set of pages. The first of these pages, shown in Figure 5-4, is primarily for users of America Online and the Microsoft Network. If you are a user of one of these services and choose this option, the wizard tells you to go back to the Online Services menu described earlier in this chapter. Otherwise, you need to choose the first option, as shown in Figure 5-4.

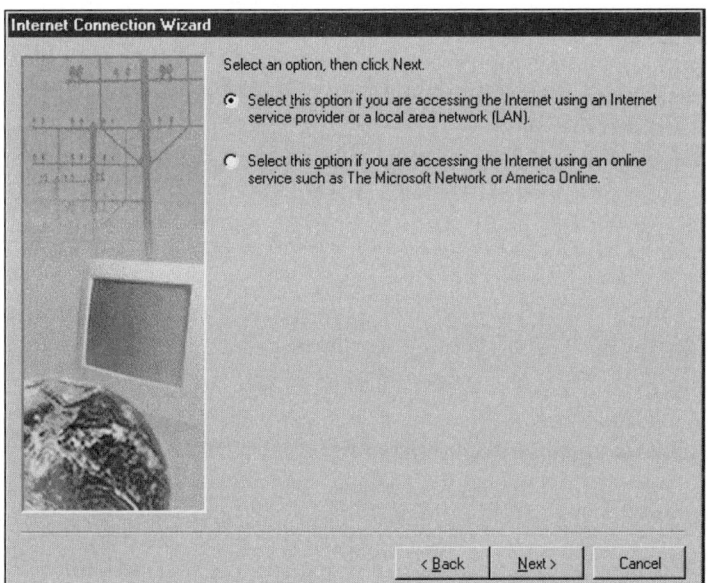

Figure 5-4   Internet Connection Wizard option for AOL or MSN

The next page, shown in Figure 5-5, asks whether you want to connect via a phone line or a LAN that already has a full-time Internet connection. Make your choice, and click Next to continue. The remainder of this section assumes that you are connecting through a phone line. You will learn about connecting to an ISP through a LAN in the next section.

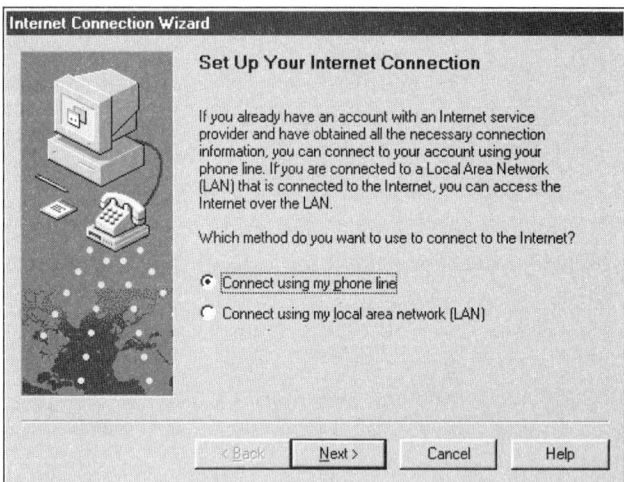

Figure 5-5 Specifying a phone line or a LAN connection

If you are connecting by phone and have not yet installed a modem, the wizard will now ask you to do so. If you are installing a modem on a desktop, quit Windows 98 and turn off your computer. Then follow the precautions explained in your modem and computer manuals before attempting to install the modem. Otherwise, if you have previously configured any Dial-Up Networking connections, the wizard will ask if it should use one of those connections or create a new one. Make your selection and click Next. If you're creating a new connection, the next page prompts you for the area code, phone number, and country of the ISP. Enter this information and click Next. Your ISP will have provided you with a username and password. Enter this information in the appropriate text boxes, and click Next.

If you are connecting by modem through a phone line, the Internet Connection Wizard is capable of handling the rest of the configuration process on its own, using a default group of settings. However, some ISPs do require specific changes to these settings. When you speak with your chosen ISP to open your account, ask about any changes you may need to make here. These changes may involve the following:

- **Connection type**: Determine whether your ISP uses a PPP or SLIP connection. These types of connections were discussed earlier in this chapter. Generally, a PPP connection is a sign of a more user-friendly ISP, while a SLIP connection is associated with ISPs that can handle larger amounts of data through a UNIX server.

- **Logon commands**: Some ISPs require that you use special logon commands or scripts to connect to their service. A script is a special series of commands, similar to a macro. If a script is required, your ISP will probably provide you with a script file to make your connection.

- **IP address**: As discussed earlier in this chapter, IP addresses can be assigned by a DHCP server. If your ISP actually gives you a permanent IP address, you would enter it in the IP Address tab of the TCP/IP Properties dialog box, discussed earlier in this chapter.

- **DNS server address**: As discussed earlier in this chapter, a **DNS server** is a database of Internet domain names such as *www.course.com* with IP addresses such as 198.112.168.244. Some ISPs are configured to automatically reference the appropriate DNS server when you log on. Other ISPs require that you include data for their DNS server in your IP configuration. You enter this information in the DNS Configuration tab of the TCP/IP Properties dialog box.
- **Lightweight Directory Access Protocol (LDAP)**: One of the TCP/IP protocols, which is used for database searches—specifically, for Internet phone and e-mail directories.

Finally, you'll be asked to name your connection; using the name of your ISP is a common choice. After you have configured your Internet connection, the Internet Connection Wizard will offer to configure an ISP e-mail account for you. You're not obligated to complete this process. As with the connection settings, the wizard recognizes any preexisting mail accounts and offers the choice of using an existing account or creating a new one. When creating a new account, you will need to provide the following information:

- **Your name**: This is your real name, not a logon name. When you send e-mail, this is what people who read your e-mail will see.
- **Your e-mail address**: Your ISP will provide you with this information. One common form for your e-mail address is simply your user name, in the form *firstname.middleinitial.lastname@yourISP*.com.
- **E-mail server names and types**: You'll need to know the name of both the incoming and outgoing mail servers. Typical names for the incoming mail server include pop.*yourISP*.com, mail.*yourISP*.com, and postoffice.*yourISP*.com. Your ISP will also need to tell you whether your incoming mail server uses the POP3 or IMAP mail protocol. For the outgoing mail server (SMTP server), a typical name would be SMTP.*yourISP*.com.
- **Mail logon name and password**: Some ISPs require an additional username and/or password for your e-mail box. The name is often referred to as the POP account name. ("POP" is short for Post Office Protocol, which handles e-mail.) **IMAP** is a more fully-featured version of POP. If your ISP requires the use of **Secure Password Authentication (SPA)**, be sure to select that option in the appropriate wizard screen. If you can enable SPA, you'll need to enter your password every time you log on.
- **Mail account name**: Choose an easily recognizable name for this mail account. Applications that integrate e-mail will use this name to help you select which accounts to use when you configure those applications.

Once your mail account is configured, the Internet Connection Wizard will offer to configure an Internet news account. A news account provides access to Usenet newsgroups. Not all ISPs provide access to a news server, so be sure to ask when establishing your account. Should you choose to set up the news account at this time, the wizard scans for existing accounts and offers to use them or to create a new one. When creating a new account, the wizard prompts you for the following information:

- **Your name**: As with e-mail, this name is attached to all messages that you post.
- **Your e-mail address**: When posting a message, you can include your e-mail address, allowing others to contact you via e-mail rather than through the newsgroup.
- **News server name**: Your ISP will provide this information, and it generally takes the form of news.*yourISP*.com.
- **Logon data**: If your ISP requires you to log on to their news server (many do in order to limit usage to only their customers), you'll need your news account name and password. These may be the same as your logon or e-mail account name and password, or your ISP may assign an account name and password specifically for newsgroups. Some ISPs allow or require the use of Secure Password Authentication (SPA). If you can enable SPA, you'll need to enter your password every time you log on.
- **Name your account**: Choose a name for this news account that helps you to identify it easily.

Finally, the wizard offers to set up an **Internet directory service**. A directory service provides you with access to a "white pages" type address book. Popular services include Four11, WhoWhere, SwitchBoard, and Yahoo! People Search. These services may require an LDAP account and specific connection information from your ISP, including:

- **Directory server name**: The address of the server you wish to use.
- **Account name**: Any account name or password that may be required.
- **Check e-mail address**: Instructions to verify the e-mail addresses of your correspondents before you send out an e-mail message. Using this service can greatly slow the speed of your e-mail program; it's best not to use it unless the security of your messages is a significant concern.
- **Name for the service**: An easily recognizable name that you can use to identify this connection.

Connecting to an ISP by LAN

As you saw in Figure 5-5, the Internet Connection Wizard offers you the option of connecting to your ISP though a local area network (LAN). This can be a terrific convenience, if it is allowed by the written and system policies of your organization or school. (Some organizations may not like the idea of an employee or student accessing personal e-mail on company time or facilities.) In the previous section, you learned about connecting to an existing account over a telephone line. The discussion in this section is closely associated with the TCP/IP protocols covered earlier in this chapter.

After choosing the "Connect using my local area network" option in the wizard page shown in Figure 5-5, click Next. The next screen asks you if you are using a proxy server. Most

LANs do include one or several proxy servers. The name of each proxy server is generally unique to your LAN. When you answer yes to the proxy server question and click Next, you are given the chance to enter the names of several servers. Each server is associated with a different TCP/IP protocol. Consult your network administrator or instructor for the actual names of the servers associated with each protocol. The different options for the servers are as follows:

- **Port**: In TCP/IP, there are different port numbers for a number of different application layer protocols. The standard port numbers range from 0 to 1023. Your network administrator may configure some of these servers on a port number above 1023 to improve security.
- **Hypertext Transfer Protocol (HTTP)**: HTTP is the language of the World Wide Web; therefore, an HTTP proxy server contains Web pages that have been recently downloaded.
- **Secure**: For confidential information such as billing and grades, different Web sites use secure servers. Access to these servers should be limited to authorized users.
- **File Transfer Protocol (FTP)**: Since it is more efficient than HTTP, FTP servers are commonly used to transfer large files. However, FTP is less popular than HTTP, because, unlike HTTP, it is text-based and it cannot be used to browse the Internet.
- **Gopher**: Generally obsolete. Use is generally limited to text-only search engines.
- **Socks**: Short for sockets. Programs on clients such as Windows 98 use sockets to plug in to programs on a server. In this way, the client and the server work together to run a program.

Once you have entered all applicable proxy servers, click Next. The following wizard page, entitled "Proxy Server Exceptions," allows you to list Web sites for which you do not want your browser to go first to a proxy server. For example, you might include Web sites with time-sensitive information such as Stock Market quotes. By directing your browser to go directly to such sites (rather than to a stored version on a proxy server) you can ensure that you will always be getting the most up-to-date information possible. Enter Web sites in this list in the Internet address format, e.g., *www.course.com*.

Once you have entered all proxy servers and exceptions, click Next. The next steps allow you to set up an existing Internet e-mail account with the mail manager features of Outlook Express. When you answer yes to the question of setting up an e-mail account, click Next. This leads to the same steps as described in the previous section for setting up an existing ISP account over a phone line.

There are a large number of settings that can be associated with an ISP account. The Internet Connection Wizard provides a format that makes it easier to input the required settings. If you don't have all of the required information, you can always consult your ISP and come back to the wizard later. Some ISPs actually work with their users as if they were on a LAN connected through a telephone line. These ISPs will even have their own proxy servers to speed access to commonly accessed Web pages on the Internet.

If you choose an ISP that is already in the Online Services menu discussed earlier, you can use the wizard associated with the ISP to create the required settings. The following section briefly addresses what you need to do to set up an ISP, before moving on to the Internet Connection Wizard.

OTHER ISPs

There are thousands of ISPs worldwide. Only a few can be set up through the Internet Connection Wizard. Even if you cannot connect to your ISP through the wizard, make sure that you have read the previous sections. Most ISPs require the same information as the Internet Connection Wizard. In the Hands-on Projects at the end of this chapter you will learn how to configure a TCP/IP connection. On the basis of that experience, you should be able to get enough information from any ISP to configure TCP/IP properly.

Once you have installed TCP/IP, you can start configuring the TCP/IP connection. Click Start, point to Programs, point to Accessories, point to Communications, click Dial-Up Networking, and then double-click the Make New Connection icon. This will lead you to a short wizard that will help you set up a connection to the ISP of your choice. When prompted, enter the connection phone number given by your ISP. When you complete the wizard, you will see a new icon in your Dial-Up Networking window. Double-click on this icon to connect to your ISP. If the settings are not complete, complete the Internet Connection Wizard discussed in the last section for additional information.

Except for the discussion on modems and other network adapters in Chapter 6, you are now ready to connect to the Internet. Once you have installed and configured your network connections, Windows 98 is ready to become fully integrated with the Internet. In the local area network client-server model, client computers that run Windows 98 are ready to communicate and cooperate with servers on the network. Windows 98 and Internet Explorer 4.0 have the same functionality. In the next section, you will learn about Internet Explorer as a tool, how it can be set up for security, how it can be its own proxy server, and how you can use the associated Outlook Express tool for mail and newsgroup access and management. But the first step is a brief introduction to the development of the Internet, and Internet Explorer.

THE INTERNET

When the U.S. Government created the ancestors of the Internet back in the 1960s, the intent was to build a communications system that could survive a nuclear war. Backup routes would be required to replace those that might be destroyed. The Internet backbones were built with redundancies everywhere. It is these backups that make the Internet as reliable as it is.

Until the early 1990s, the Internet was used primarily by academics, using text-based communication. Some documents were stored and accessible online. Professors discussed and exchanged research by electronic mail. Text-based search engines related to the TCP/IP Gopher protocol were developed to help users search through the available data. The File Transfer Protocol (FTP) was developed to send files. In those early days, sending pictures over the Internet was considered a waste of bandwidth.

All of this changed with the development of Mosaic. This was the first real "browser," something that could actually send and receive more than just text. One of the developers of Mosaic, Marc Andressen, left the University of Illinois in quest of a user-friendly browser. His project was code-named Mozilla, short for Mosaic Godzilla. Mosaic eventually became Netscape Navigator, which is now one of the most popular browsers in use. Growth of the Internet exploded from there. To compete, Microsoft developed its own browser, Internet Explorer.

To the end user, the current generation of browsers are beginning to look like operating systems. Companies are relying more and more on browsers connected to an internal Internet (known as an **intranet**) for critical communications. Programming languages such as **Java** hold the promise of running programs such as Microsoft Word and Excel over an intranet, through browsers like Internet Explorer and Netscape Navigator. Internet Explorer is becoming a more integrated part of the operating system.

Because Internet Explorer 4.0 is fully integrated into the operating system, you do not have to install it. However, you can install individual components and features at any time, using files available on the Windows 98 installation CD. If you want to use another browser, you can install and run it like any other program.

Internet Explorer 4.0

The Internet Explorer Web browser offers several features that make it easy for you to find the information you need on the Web. The Explorer bars give you quick access to the information you need. For example, the **Active Channels** Explorer bar gives you access to Web sites that are configured to deliver information on a regular basis. The **Favorites** Explorer bar allows you to build and maintain a database of your favorite Web sites. The four Explorer bars are explained in more detail in the following list:

- **History**: Internet Explorer maintains a database of Web sites that you have explored. The number of days that a site is kept in the database can be adjusted via the Internet Options command on the Internet Explorer View menu.

- **Search**: Provides access to search engines and Web guides. Lycos is installed as the primary search engine by default, although a link is provided to allow you to choose any search provider. The Search Explorer bar is available only if you are online, because it accesses content from the Microsoft Web site.

- **Favorites**: Includes a default selection of active channels and a list of Web site addresses that you may have saved.

- **Channels**: A selection of active channels and a link to the full Microsoft Channel Guide.

Internet Explorer Security

The amount of business being done over the Internet is exploding. Credit card numbers and other confidential information are being sent over the network constantly. In a world where people are always trying to break into computer systems, security is a significant concern.

Internet Explorer 4.0 incorporates several new features that can help you manage security when browsing the Web.

For security purposes, Internet Explorer divides Web sites into four types, or "zones": local intranet, trusted sites, Internet, and restricted sites. For each zone, you can assign a specific security level. To assign a security level, click Start, point to Settings, click Control Panel, and then double-click the Internet icon. Click the Security tab in the Internet Properties dialog box, to display the options shown in Figure 5-6. To use this tab, click the Zone list arrow and select the type of Internet site whose security level you want to adjust. Then select from one of the following security options, by clicking the appropriate option button:

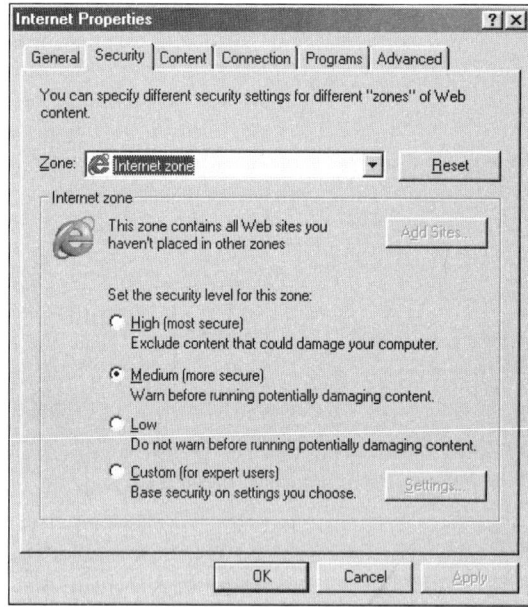

Figure 5-6 Internet Properties dialog box

- **High**: The most secure setting. Content that could damage your computer will automatically be excluded from display or execution.
- **Medium**: A setting that gives you the chance to accept content from a site that you may not trust. Internet Explorer will warn you about potentially damaging Web site content. You must choose whether to accept or reject the content.
- **Low**: No warnings are issued under this security level. Entire Web pages are automatically displayed.
- **Custom**: Expert users or system administrators can use this level to make customized choices regarding various content types.

After you have specified the security for each zone, you can begin adding specific Web sites to each of the four zones. For example, suppose you have young children in your household, and that, by reviewing the History Explorer bar, you notice that they've been to sites you find inappropriate. To restrict access to these sites, open the Security tab, change the entry in the Zones box to the Restricted Sites Zone, then click Add Sites. This opens the Restricted Sites Zone dialog box, where you can enter the Web address of one or more sites. Alternately, you could set all but the Trusted Sites zone to High Security. Then you can add your favorite Web sites to your list of Trusted Sites in the same way.

In addition to security zones, Internet Explorer offers another important security tool known as Authenticode technology. **Authenticode** is similar to a "Good Housekeeping" seal of approval for Web sites. If someone has tampered with *www.microsoft.com*, Internet Explorer will be able to warn you because the Authenticode will not work. If the Authenticode of a Web site is valid, Internet Explorer displays a verification certificate and asks you to accept the contents of the Web site. Internet Explorer has many other built-in security and privacy protection features, including:

- **Secure channel services**: If you have explored the Internet, you may have noticed that the full name of a Web site address starts with "http:", which conforms to the rules of the Hypertext Transfer Protocol, discussed earlier in this chapter. Some Web site addresses start with "https:", indicating that your browser has established a secure connection to the Internet. The data that you send and receive to a secure channel service is encrypted in the presentation layer of the OSI model. Encryption scrambles your signal to make it more difficult for those who might want to tap into the wires to read your messages. This presentation layer protocol is also known as the Secure Sockets Layer (SSL). Most commerce sites on the Internet make use of SSL to protect consumer identity and credit card data.

- **Cookie control**: Cookies are a tool used by some Web sites to store information on the user's computer. Cookies are used to keep track of the Web pages that the user visits on a particular site. For example, the fact that you constantly search for computer books on a Web site bookstore can be stored as a cookie, which the proprietors of the Web site can then retrieve when you visit the site again. With this knowledge in hand, the proprietors of the Web site can then target you for specific forms of marketing. To some, this is an invasion of privacy. Internet Explorer allows you to set preferences for cookie handling. To modify these preferences, click Start, point to Settings, click Control Panel, double-click the Internet icon, and then click the Advanced tab in the Internet Properties dialog box. Near the bottom of the long list on this tab, you can choose to accept, disable, or require your approval before a cookie can be put on your system.

- **Microsoft Wallet**: This feature provides a secure storage area for private information such as credit or debit card data and electronic cash balances. The information can be stored on your hard drive, on 3½-inch disks, or on smart cards, and is protected by a password. Wallet transmits the data securely when needed, using another presentation layer TCP/IP protocol known as Personal Information Exchange (PFX).

- **Platform for Internet Content Selection (PICS) content ratings:** The PICS is a committee that works to define standards for rating Internet content on the basis of language, violence, and sex. Using Internet Explorer, you can control access to sites that have voluntarily rated their content. This can be helpful for parents who want to have some assistance in controlling which sites their children access. In the corporate setting it can help system administrators block access to sites that don't provide content relevant to the company's business ventures.

Earlier in this chapter, you learned to use the Internet Connection Wizard to set up Internet Explorer for specific proxy servers. As networks change, the location of your proxy servers may change as well. To change the proxy server setting for your Windows 98 computer, click the Connection tab in the Internet Properties dialog box. If you have configured Internet Explorer to connect to a LAN, you should see the "Access the Internet using a proxy server" option. Select this option, then click Advanced to view the settings that you entered earlier in the Internet Connection Wizard. Click Configure. In the Automatic Configuration dialog box, enter the location of a Web file that overrides the proxy settings on your computer. Your entry will look something like http://www.theproxyupdater.com/proxy.pac. For details on how to set up such a Web file, consult any guide to the Microsoft Internet Explorer Administration Kit 4.0.

Newsgroup Access

Windows 98 includes Outlook Express, a compact version of Microsoft's Outlook 98 product that provides integrated e-mail and newsgroup access for the Internet Explorer browser. The connection to your news server is configured from the Internet Connection Wizard described earlier in this chapter. If you chose not to set up a news service at that time, the wizard will launch the first time you open Outlook Express. To open Outlook Express, click Start, point to Programs, point to Internet Explorer, and then click Outlook Express.

Upon your first connection to the news server, Outlook Express recognizes that you don't currently download any newsgroups and offers to download the list of available groups. The results are displayed in the Newsgroups dialog box, as shown in Figure 5-7. (Because the list of available newsgroups varies from one ISP to another, your list of news groups will differ from Figure 5-7.)

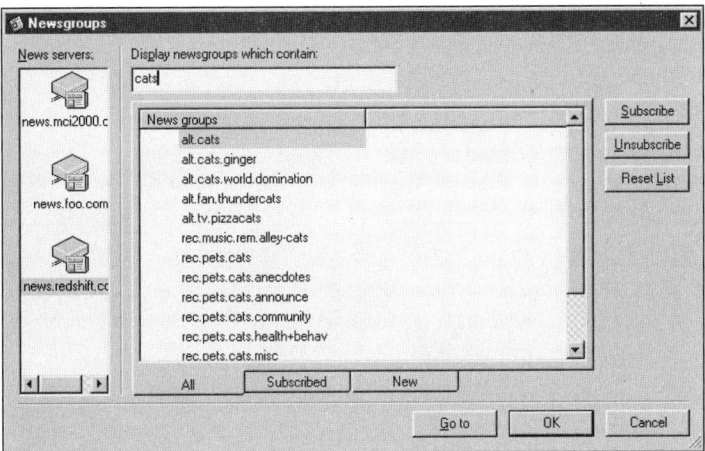

Figure 5-7 The Newsgroups dialog box

Depending on which newsgroups your ISP has chosen to provide, you may be able to choose from thousands of available news groups. To help you wade through all the choices, Outlook Express offers a handy search feature that locates newsgroups containing a specific word or string of characters. For example, if you want to locate newsgroups that deal with cats, you might enter "cats" in the "Display newsgroups which contain" text box. The list is then narrowed down to only those newsgroups containing that word, as shown in Figure 5-7. To view messages from a newsgroup, select the desired group, and then click Go To. To start downloading the messages of a particular newsgroup, select the group, and then click Subscribe. A small newspaper icon then appears to the left of the newsgroup name. The titles of new messages in the newsgroup will then be downloaded periodically. To view only those newsgroups that have been added to your ISP's server since the last time you viewed newsgroups, click the New tab.

Once you have selected your newsgroups, you can review new newsgroup messages whenever you open up Outlook Express. To review newsgroup messages, first select a newsgroup in the left-hand pane, select a message header (title) in the list in the upper-right pane, and then read the message in the pane below. A plus sign to the left of a message header indicates that there are replies to that message. To see the headers associated with those replies, click the plus sign.

FTP Access

File Transfer Protocol (FTP) is one of the most common ways of transferring files between computers over the Internet. Windows 98 is equipped with a very basic FTP utility as a part of the Microsoft TCP/IP protocol. Before you can start FTP, you need to establish a connection to the Internet. A connection to your ISP over a modem is acceptable. To start FTP, click Start, point to Programs, and click MS-DOS prompt. FTP commands can be made only from the MS-DOS prompt. To start the File Transfer Protocol, type "FTP" (without the quotation marks), followed by one of the switches in Table 5-2. For example, to connect to the Microsoft FTP site with anonymous logon, type *ftp -A ftp.microsoft.com*. This starts a session on the Microsoft FTP server.

Table 5-2   Microsoft FTP Syntax switches

Switch	Function
-n	Turns off auto-logon when connected
-i	Disables prompting during multiple file transfers
-d	Displays all commands and responses passed between the client and server. If you have problems downloading from the FTP site of your choice, this can help you find the problem.
-g	Turns off file name globbing (the use of wildcard characters in file or path names)
-A	Enables anonymous logon

Think of these FTP commands as similar to DOS, just less user-friendly. After you type ftp at the C:\ prompt, the prompt changes to "ftp>." Once connected to the server, you can use any of the commands in Table 5-3. For example, you may use the "dir" command to get a list of files in the FTP server. Once you have identified the file that you need, type "get filename.ext" at the FTP prompt.

Table 5-3   Common FTP commands

Command	Function
ascii	Sets the transfer type to ASCII. This option is selected by default.
binary	Sets the transfer type to binary. Examples of binary files include *.exe files and images.
bye	Ends the session and exits FTP
cd	Changes directory (on the server)
close	Ends the session and returns to the FTP interface
delete	Deletes a file on the remote computer
dir	Displays a list of files and folders in the current directory on the remote computer
get	Retrieves a file from the remote computer
lcd	Changes to a different directory on the local computer. Similar to the DOS cd command.
mkdir	Creates a new directory on the remote computer. mkdir newdir creates the directory newdir on the local computer.
put	Places a file onto the server from the local computer
rename	Renames a file on the remote computer
rmdir	Removes a directory (deletes it) on the remote computer
send	Same as put

For anything but the most occasional FTP use, you'll probably want to obtain a graphical FTP client. Many popular ones are available online at the various software repositories, such as *www.download.com*

Chapter Summary

- For computers to communicate, they need to share a set of protocols. With the growth of the Internet, TCP/IP has become the dominant protocol in networking. TCP/IP is actually a series of protocols. One way to classify the TCP/IP protocols is through the seven layers of the Open Systems Interconnect model. Each layer has different functions in the process of translating data from programs such as Microsoft Word to the actual binary code of 1s and 0s that can be delivered over physical media.

- Telephone modems are not the only way to connect to the Internet. There are a number of other options available, from ISDN to Cable Modems to Ethernet. You need to be careful when installing anything like a modem inside a desktop computer. However, PC Cards, USB, and FireWire standard devices hold the promise of allowing you to install peripherals while the computer is on.

- Configuring a Windows 98 computer to access the Internet can be easily accomplished through the Internet Connection Wizard, for the limited number of ISPs that are available in Windows 98. The wizard guides the user through all steps required to set up a dial-up connection, Internet e-mail, news services, and directory services. Internet Explorer 4.0, fully integrated in Windows 98, offers useful features such as Explorer bars, smart favorites, Authenticode, and security zones. Outlook Express, a component of the full Internet Explorer 4.0 suite, offers integrated e-mail and newsgroup access.

- The Internet Connection Wizard allows you to access certain ISPs. It is also possible to connect to an existing Internet account from a Windows 98 computer on a local area network. Both of these options include a number of possible different settings, from e-mail, news, and proxy servers to the IP addresses of WINS, DNS, and gateways.

- This chapter is just an introduction to networking in Windows 98. Chapter 6 will focus on the different available types of communications equipment, as well as on mobile computing. In Chapter 7, you will learn about remote access tools, Web servers, and Web page creation. Chapter 13 will focus on protocols other than TCP/IP related to Microsoft- and NetWare-centered local area networks.

Key Terms

- **active channels** — A term for both the content and the delivery mode for specialized content developed for Internet Explorer.

- **Address Resolution Protocol (ARP)** — A low-level protocol in the TCP/IP suite that maps numeric IP addresses for a computer to physical addresses for that computer. ARP defines a mapping between a numeric IP address and a specific network interface card, and thus, to the computer to which that card is attached. ARP is described in RFC 826.

- **ASCII (American Standard Code for Information Interchange)** — A standard 7- or 8-bit character-encoding scheme still widely used to represent and exchange character data among computers and applications.

- **Authenticode** — A technology that allows digital identification of the publisher of a piece of software and evidence of any tampering.

- **bandwidth** — The speed of data transfer.

- **binding** — The process of installing a protocol for a specific modem or network card.

- **browsing** — In networking terminology, the process initiated by clicking the Browse button within a Windows application, or the Network Neighborhood icon on a Windows desktop, in My Computer, or in Windows Explorer. All of these options launch a request for a local browse list of machines with resources to share, whose entries may in turn be queried to display the resources that each machine offers to the network. More specifically, this is called the Windows browsing service in other definitions here. In Web terminology, "browsing" refers to the process of moving from one Web page to another. The application you use to browse the Web (such as Internet Explorer 4.0) is known as a browser.

- **cache** — The process of storing documents or files that are either commonly requested or recently used. A proxy server can immediately serve back a file that has been cached without having to send a message out onto the Internet to retrieve it.

- **connectionless protocol** — A networking protocol that exchanges individual messages, one at a time, between sender and receiver, whereby no ongoing relationship between the parties to the communication is assumed, and whereby no information from prior messages impinges on sending or receipt of subsequent messages.

- **connection-oriented protocol** — A networking protocol that establishes an ongoing "conversation," usually called a session, between a sender and receiver. Because this creates a connection that persists across multiple message transfers, such protocols are said to be connection-oriented.

- **cookie** — A way to collect data on the habits of a user on a Web site. Stored on the computer of the user.

- **datagram** — A method of sending messages in which sections of a message may be transferred in any order between sender and receiver, and the correct ordering is rebuilt by the receiving computer.

- **DHCP (Dynamic Host Configuration Protocol)** — An IP-based protocol that supports allocation of IP addresses to workstations, for a limited period known as a lease. It is set up as part of a server. A DHCP server has a pool of addresses to lease to workstations. DHCP is defined in RFC 2131.

- **DLC (Data Link Control)** — A nonroutable, connection-oriented protocol used to establish host sessions with IBM mainframe and AS/400 computers, but also to connect print servers to certain network-attached printers (clients need not load the DLC protocol to access such printers, only the print server that manages the printer needs to have DLC installed).

- **DNS (Domain Name Service)** — The address book of the Internet. Contains a database of Internet names such as *www.course.com* and their associated IP addresses such as 198.112.168.244

- **domain name** — A unique symbolic name that identifies a particular IP network host, plus the type of domain to which that host belongs (.edu = education, .gov = government, .com = commercial, and so forth), where course.com, for instance, identifies a host named course in the commercial domain.

- **e-mail account** — The means by which you send and receive e-mail. Some ISPs allow for multiple e-mail accounts with each ISP account; for example, a family with one ISP account can have separate e-mail accounts for each family member. The name assigned to an e-mail account is not necessarily the same as the user's username.

- **Explorer bars** — A tool in Internet Explorer that frames a set of links and their content in two concurrently visible panes.

- **FTP (File Transfer Protocol)** — One of the most common methods of transferring files between local and remote computers via the Internet.

- **gateway** — An IP-based server that handles all IP packets not addressed to any local segment to which the server is attached. If the IP address on your data is not on your network, your data is sent to the gateway, which then sends it on to the Internet.

- **host name** — The portion of a domain name that identifies a specific host within a general domain; for example, the host part of the course.com domain name is course.

- **IMAP (Internet Mail Automation Protocol)** — A more fully-featured mail-handling protocol than POP.

- **Internet Directory Service** — The "white pages" of the Internet. Public or private directories of individuals and their e-mail addresses. Sometimes they also include physical addresses and telephone numbers.

- **Internet Protocol (IP)** — One of the two primary protocols in the TCP/IP suite, the Internet Protocol is responsible for managing network routing and outbound message delivery, handling network addresses, and recognizing inbound messages. IP was initially described in RFC 791, and is the subject of numerous follow-up RFCs.

- **Internet service provider (ISP)** — An organization that provides access to the Internet, usually for a fee. Essentially, an ISP leases a line to the Internet and splits the capacity among its subscribers. T3 lines, which can carry the equivalent of 672 telephone lines, are common for even the smallest ISPs. There are literally thousands of ISPs available.

- **InterNIC (Internet Network Information Center)** — The central Internet domain name and address management facility, located online at *ds.internic.net*
- **IP address** — A unique numeric address for a device on an IP-based network that consists of four numbers between 0 and 255, separated by periods, such as 172.16.1.7
- **IPX/SPX (Internetwork Packet Exchange/Sequenced Packet Exchange)** — IPX is a networking protocol used on Novell networks in the file server portion of the operating system. SPX serves as a transport layer on top of IPX for client/server applications.
- **ISP account** — The means by which you are identified to your Internet service provider. Each ISP account is associated with a username and a password.
- **LDAP (Lightweight Directory Access Protocol)** — A protocol for client applications to query and handle information from an Internet directory service.
- **local area network (LAN)** — A group of connected computers in a small area such as an office. Often, all the computers on a LAN will access the Internet through one computer (often a server), which is referred to as the gateway.
- **mail server** — The server to which an ISP directs all e-mail. The Internet name of the server often depends on the mail protocol in effect. For example, your ISP's mail server might be named smtp.*yourISP*.com
- **NDIS (Network Device Interface Specification)** — The interface for network drivers used in Microsoft Windows operating systems.
- **NetBEUI (NetBIOS Enhanced User Interface)** — A simple, fast, but nonroutable networking protocol included as one of the three major networking protocols in most modern Windows implementations; Microsoft no longer recommends using NetBEUI except for small, single-segment networks.
- **NetBIOS (network basic input/output system)** — A set of simple network services originally defined by IBM in the early 1980s, NetBIOS has become a popular networking API in many environments, and still plays a key role on Microsoft networks, especially for name resolution, browsing, and other important network services.
- **news account** — The means by which you post and view messages on an Internet newsgroup. Similar to an ISP e-mail account.
- **newsgroup** — An electronic bulletin board where users share information on common topics. The most common series of newsgroups is known as Usenet. When you post a message to a newsgroup, the contents of that message are often accessible through search engines to the entire Internet.
- **news server** — Similar in function and address to a mail server. A common Internet name for a news server would be NNTP.*yourISP*.com, where *yourISP* stands for the name of your ISP.
- **packet** — A unit of data of a fixed size separated for transmission.

- **POP (Post Office Protocol)** — One of the TCP/IP application layer protocols. An ISP usually designates a POP server to receive your e-mail from the Internet. A common Internet name for your news server is pop.*yourISP*.com, where *yourISP* stands for the name of your ISP.

- **Point-to-Point Protocol (PPP)** — An industry standard protocol used for dial-up connections.

- **POP account** — Synonymous with e-mail account; the account used to access the mail server.

- **protocol** — A standard, or set of rules, for data communications; among other things, protocols govern how data travels over modems and network adapters.

- **protocol stack** — A group of network protocol layers that work together, such as the seven layers of the Open Systems Interconnect (OSI) model.

- **proxy server** — A server that intercepts requests headed for the Web and tries to fulfill the requests itself, before passing them on to the Internet for completion. Proxies help save bandwidth and can speed up perceived system performance.

- **SLIP (Serial Line Internet Protocol)** — An older and simpler Internet protocol than PPP. From a practical perspective, they're nearly identical.

- **SMTP (Simple Mail Transfer Protocol)** — One of the TCP/IP protocols, at the application layer. An ISP usually uses an SMTP server to send your e-mail on to the Internet. A common Internet name for an SMTP server is SMTP.*yourISP*.com, where *yourISP* stands for the name of your ISP.

- **SPA (Secure Password Authentication)** — An encrypted means of exchanging password information between client and server.

- **subnet** — A network, such as a LAN, that shares part of the same networking address. In most cases, a TCP/IP subnet includes all IP addresses with the same prefix. One example of a TCP/IP subnet might be all addresses that start with 133.133.133.

- **TCP/IP (Transmission Control Protocol/Internet Protocol)** — The standard set of networking protocols used on the Internet, originally developed in the late 1970s and early 1980s, now used on many, if not most, networks all over the world. Installed by default with Windows 98.

- **Usenet** — A newsgroup hierarchy on the Internet. Tens of thousands of topic-related groups are available in the system.

- **User Datagram Protocol (UDP)** — A lightweight, connectionless transport protocol used to provide best-effort, but not guaranteed, delivery services within the TCP/IP protocol suite.

- **WINS (Windows Internet Name Service)** — A Microsoft name resolution service that translates between NetBIOS names and IP addresses.

REVIEW QUESTIONS

1. Which of the following protocols is not used for routine networking on Windows 98?
   a. NetBEUI
   b. TCP/IP
   c. DLC
   d. IPX/SPX-compatible Protocol

2. Which of the following is the primary set of protocols used on the Internet?
   a. NetBEUI
   b. TCP/IP
   c. DLC
   d. IPX/SPX-compatible Protocol

3. Which of the following protocols is used not only for IBM host or AS/400 communications, but also used to communicate with network-attached printers?
   a. NetBEUI
   b. TCP/IP
   c. DLC
   d. IPX/SPX-compatible Protocol

4. Which of the following protocols is used by a NetWare server?
   a. NetBEUI
   b. TCP/IP
   c. DLC
   d. IPX/SPX-compatible Protocol

5. Which of the following services automates client IP address assignment?
   a. DHCP
   b. WINS
   c. DNS
   d. NBT

6. Which of the following services maps IP domain names to numeric IP addresses?
   a. DHCP
   b. WINS
   c. DNS
   d. NBT

7. The Internet Connection Wizard configures:
    a. your dial-up connection
    b. your e-mail account
    c. newsgroup access
    d. directory services
    e. all of the above
8. The Microsoft Referral Network is used to:
    a. select appropriate software for your computer
    b. help you choose interesting newsgroups
    c. help you locate long-lost friends who now have e-mail addresses
    d. select an ISP
9. Some ISPs may require special logon commands or scripts to be run after you enter your username and password. True or False?
10. To configure your e-mail server name and type you need to know:
    a. the name of your incoming mail server
    b. the name of your outgoing mail server
    c. whether the server is a POP3 or IMAP server
    d. your mail logon name and password
    e. all of the above
11. Your mail account username and password will always be the same as your logon username and password. True or False?
12. A news server provides an online version of your local newspaper. True or False?
13. When you use Active Desktop:
    a. Your computer is always connected to the Internet.
    b. Anyone on the network can see all of your files and use your programs.
    c. Internet Explorer is fully integrated into the desktop, allowing for direct delivery of Web content.
    d. none of the above
14. Authenticode can protect you from poorly written software. True or False?
15. The Trusted Sites security zone is a list of sites that Microsoft feels is trustworthy. True or False?
16. Cookies are used by Web developers to: (Choose all correct answers.)
    a. snoop through your computer looking for passwords or other private data
    b. store session or identifying information, such as Web pages that have been browsed
    c. store corporate Web site links in your list of favorites
    d. track your Web site viewing habits

17. Microsoft's FTP utility is only accessible from the command prompt. True or False?
18. If you are using Internet Explorer 4.0, you must use Outlook Express to read and write your e-mail. True or False?
19. A proxy server:
    a. acts as a gateway, handling as many tasks as it can, rather than forwarding requests out onto the Internet
    b. caches frequently used files for faster display on subsequent requests
    c. can block access to sites your boss doesn't want you visiting on company time
    d. all of the above
20. How many layers are there in the Open Systems Interconnect model?
    a. 5
    b. 6
    c. 7
    d. 8

Hands-on Projects

Project 5-1

This project assumes that TCP/IP was installed by default on your computer when you installed Windows 98. In this project you will uninstall TCP/IP. In completing this project, you will write down a variety of settings. Then you will use these settings again in Project 5-2, when you reinstall TCP/IP. For completeness, you should do Projects 5-1 and 5-2 together, to learn to uninstall and then reinstall TCP/IP. To complete this project, you need Windows 98 and TCP/IP installed on a computer that accesses a TCP/IP network such as the Internet. You will also need your Windows 98 Installation CD.

1. If your only network connection is to the Internet, make that connection now. If you do not yet have a connection to a network such as the Internet, skip to Projects 5-3 and 5-4. Return to Projects 5-1 and 5-2 after you have set up your connection.
2. Click **Start**, point to Settings, click Control Panel, and then double-click the Network icon.
3. If necessary, click the **Configuration** tab.
4. In the "The following network components are installed" list box, select **TCP/IP**, and then click **Properties**. If you see more than one instance of TCP/IP, you have more than one adapter to access a network. If available, choose an adapter that your computer uses to access a TCP/IP network; otherwise, choose a dial-up adapter. If you have previously set up an ISP or a Dial-Up Networking connection and chosen

your adapter, you see a warning indicating that the best way to set up TCP/IP is to set up an ISP or similar connection. Otherwise, the TCP/IP Properties dialog box opens.

5. Click **OK** in the warning box, if necessary, to view the TCP/IP Properties dialog box. Next, you will view the tabs in this dialog box, one by one, and write down the settings you see.

6. Click the **Bindings** tab. Make a note of the clients in the list box and whether or not the adjacent box is checked. If it is checked, the client shown is bound, which means it works together with TCP/IP and your modem or network adapter.

7. Click the **Advanced** tab. If there are entries in the Property box, make a note of them. Typically, no settings are specified in the Advanced tab.

8. Click the **NetBIOS** tab. Typically, NetBIOS over TCP/IP is enabled by default. The "I want to enable NetBIOS over TCP/IP" check box is selected but greyed out, indicating that this option cannot be changed. If it can be changed, make a note of whether or not it is selected.

9. Click the **DNS Configuration** tab. Make a note of whether DNS is enabled or disabled. If it is enabled, make a note of the settings in the Host, Domain, DNS Server Search Order, and Domain Suffix Search Order boxes. DNS servers are commonly identified by their IP address, which is four numbers between 0 and 255, divided by periods.

10. Click the **Gateway** tab. Make a note of any settings. Typically, settings are only specified in this tab if you are on a network with multiple gateways. If your computer wants to send data to an IP address outside your network, it sends the data to a gateway, in the order shown. If the computer that is used as the first gateway is not working, multiple gateways give you an alternative.

11. Click the **WINS configuration** tab. The Windows Internet Naming Service (WINS) will be covered in more detail in Chapter 13. Briefly, it is similar to DNS, as it is a database of computer names and IP addresses. Make a note of whether your computer has this function enabled or disabled. If it is enabled, make notes on the search order. When your computer is looking for a WINS server, it searches in the order given here. At the bottom of this tab, there is a setting entitled "Use DHCP for WINS resolution". If this is enabled, there should be a DHCP server on your network that has been set to assign IP addresses to WINS servers. If your computer is looking for a WINS server, it looks at the DHCP database first (unless there are other provisions). This will be covered in more detail in Chapter 13.

12. Click the **IP Address** tab and make a note of any settings. If the "Obtain an IP address automatically" setting is enabled, your network or ISP will give you an IP address when you log on to your network or ISP. This address is used for others when you are not logged on. If you specify an IP address, that means that you have a special IP address, unique worldwide, for your personal use.

13. Click **Cancel**. You return to the Network dialog box, where TCP/IP should still be highlighted.

14. Click **Remove**, and then click **OK** in the Network dialog box. This removes TCP/IP from your computer. You will reinstall it in the next project. Be sure to complete Project 5-2 before you leave your computer, especially if you share your computer with other users.

15. Depending on the setup of your computer, you may see the Insert Disk dialog box, which prompts you to insert your Windows 98 Installation CD into the CD-ROM drive.

16. Restart your computer if prompted.

PROJECT 5-2

In this project, you will install TCP/IP on a Windows 98 computer, using the Network applet. You should not do this Hands-on Project until you complete Project 5-1, preferably on the same computer. TCP/IP is installed on Windows 98 by default. A unique group of settings is associated with TCP/IP as installed on Windows 98. To complete this project, you need a computer with Windows 98 installed. You need the notes that you took for the original TCP/IP settings in Project 5-1. If this is not possible, and you find after Step 2 that TCP/IP has already been installed, you will need to consult your instructor or network administrator for a substantial amount of information.

1. Insert the Windows 98 Installation CD into the CD-ROM drive.
2. Click **Start**, point to **Settings**, click **Control Panel**, then double-click the **Network** icon.
3. If necessary, click the **Configuration** tab.
4. In the "The following network components are installed" list box, look for "TCP/IP." If it is included in the list, do Project 5-1 first. If you have just completed Project 5-1 and TCP/IP for the particular modem or network adapter that you revised is still included in the list, stop and consult with your instructor or network administrator. If TCP/IP is not included in the list, continue to Step 4.
5. Click **Add**. The Select Network Component Type dialog box opens.
6. In the list of network components, click **Protocol** and then click **Add**. The Select Network Protocol dialog box opens.
7. In the Manufacturers list, click **Microsoft**.
8. In the Network Protocols list, scroll down and then click **TCP/IP**.
9. Click **OK**. You return to the Network dialog box. One instance of TCP/IP has been added to the list of installed network components for each network adapter or dial-up adapter you have installed.
10. In the "The following network components are installed" list box, verify that TCP/IP is included.

11. Click **TCP/IP** for the particular modem or network adapter that you changed in Project 5-1, click **Properties,** and then click **OK**, if necessary. The TCP/IP Properties dialog box opens. Next, you will review each tab in this dialog box to adjust settings, using the notes you made in Project 5-1.

12. Click the **Bindings** tab. Verify that the settings in this tab match those you noted in Project 5-1. If this is not the case, then something else may have been installed or removed from your network between the time you did Project 5-1 and now.

13. Click the **Advanced** tab. Typically, no additional settings are required. If there are configurable settings in this tab, check your notes from Project 5-1. If you cannot restore the original configuration, then something else happened to your network settings between the time you did Project 5-1 and now.

14. Click the **NetBIOS** tab. There should only be one choice here, whether or not to enable NetBIOS over TCP/IP. Verify that this setting matches the one you noted in Project 5-1.

15. Click the **DNS Configuration** tab. Check your notes from Project 5-1. If DNS was disabled before, make sure it is disabled here. If it is enabled, use your notes to enter the Host and Domain names in the appropriate boxes. If you originally noted entries in the DNS Server Search Order text box, enter the first one in the appropriate text box, and then click **Add**. The first IP address that you enter will be the first IP address that your computer checks when it needs a DNS server. Repeat the process until you have entered all the DNS IP addresses that you noted in Project 5-1. Repeat this process, if required, for the Domain Suffix Search Order.

16. Click the **Gateway** tab. Check your notes from Project 5-1. Enter the IP address for your gateway in the New gateway text box, and then click **Add**. Repeat this process for any additional gateways. The first gateway that you add will be the first gateway that your computer checks when it wants to send a message outside your network.

17. Click the **WINS Configuration** tab. Check your notes from Project 5-1. If WINS used DHCP was disabled before, just make sure that the right setting is clicked here. If it was enabled before, click the **Enable WINS Resolution** option button, enter an IP address in the "WINS Server Search Order" text box, and then click **Add**. Repeat the process for any additional WINS servers.

18. Click the **IP Address** tab. Check your notes from Project 5-1 and adjust the settings as necessary. Assuming that you followed each of these steps, you have completed your TCP/IP configuration and are now ready to close the TCP/IP Properties dialog box.

19. Click **OK** in the TCP/IP Properties dialog box to close it.

20. Click **OK** in the Network dialog box to close it. Next, you will restart your computer to activate TCP/IP.

21. Follow the prompts to restart your computer. If you do not see any prompts, click **Start**, and then click **Shutdown**. In the Shut Down Windows dialog box, click **Restart**, and then click **OK**.

PROJECT 5-3

In this project, you will completely configure a new Internet connection, including e-mail and newsgroup services. You will need a computer with a modem and Windows 98 installed. You will also need an ISP account and the data required to make a connection to the ISP (phone number, logon username and password, e-mail username and password, and any advanced settings that you must hand-configure.). For the purposes of this exercise, you will assume that you do not have an existing Internet account with either the Microsoft Network or America Online.

1. Click **Start**, point to **Programs**, point to **Internet Explorer**, and click **Connection Wizard**. The Internet Connection Wizard opens.

2. Click the **I have an existing Internet account...** option button (the second one in the list), and then click **Next** to continue.

3. Click the **"Select this option if you are accessing the Internet using an Internet Service Provider or Local Area Network (LAN)"** option button, click **Next** to continue to the Set Up Your Internet Connection page.

4. Click the **Connect using my phone line** option button, and then click **Next** to continue. If you have multiple modems, go to Step 5. If you do not have multiple modems, skip to Step 6.

5. If you have multiple modems, you see a page where you can select the modem of your choice. Select a modem, and then click **Next**.

6. If your computer is already set up with a Dial-Up Networking connection, the Dial-Up Connection page opens. (Otherwise skip to Step 7.) On the Dial-Up Connection page you can choose between existing and new connections. Click the **Create a New dial-up connection** option button, and then click **Next** to continue to the Phone Number page.

7. Enter the area code, telephone number, and country of your ISP, and then click **Next** to continue to the User Name and Password page.

8. Enter your username and password in the appropriate text boxes, and then click **Next** to continue to the Advanced Settings page.

9. If your ISP requires you to specify connection type (PPP or SLIP), logon procedure (automatic, script, or manual logon), your own IP address, and DNS Server IP address, click the **Yes** option button, click **Next**, and then continue with the next step. If your ISP does not require you to make any of these changes, click the **No** option button, click **Next** to continue to the Dial-Up Connection Name page, and then skip to Step 16.

10. Click either the **PPP** (Point-to-Point Protocol) or **SLIP** (Serial Line Internet Protocol) option button, as required by your ISP, and then click **Next** to continue to the Logon Procedure page.

11. Indicate any necessary logon procedures as given by your ISP, and then click **Next** to continue to the IP Address page.

12. If your ISP has assigned you a permanent IP address, click the **Always use the following** option button, and then enter your IP address in the IP address text box. Otherwise, click the **My Internet service provider automatically assigns me one** option button.
13. Click **Next** to continue to the DNS Server page.
14. If required, enter the DNS server information provided by your ISP. If your ISP dynamically configures your address at logon, choose the "My Internet service provider automatically sets this when I sign in" option button.
15. Click **Next** to continue to the Dial-Up Connection Name page.
16. In the Connection name text box, enter a meaningful name for your connection. (The name of the ISP is a good choice.)
17. Click **Next** to continue to the Set Up Your Internet Mail Account page.
18. Click the **Yes** option button to set up an Internet Mail account and then click **Next**. If there is already an Internet Mail account on your computer, the wizard continues to the Internet Mail Account page. Otherwise it skips to the Your Name page, in which case you can skip to Step 20.
19. Click the **Create a new Internet mail account** option button, and then click **Next** to continue to the Your Name page.
20. In the Display name text box, enter the name that you want others to see when you send them e-mail, and then click **Next** to continue to the Internet E-mail Address page.
21. Enter your e-mail address, and then click **Next** to continue to the E-mail Server Names page.
22. Enter your incoming e-mail server type and the names of your incoming and outgoing mail servers, as specified by your ISP. Because every ISP has a different mail server, the name will be unique to your ISP. One example of an incoming mail server name is pop.prodigy.net. One example of an outgoing mail server name is smtp.prodigy.net. These are settings for two more TCP/IP protocols. "POP" stands for Post Office Protocol, a common TCP/IP protocol for collecting mail messages from the Internet. "SMTP" stands for Simple Mail Transfer Protocol, a common TCP/IP protocol for transmitting mail messages over the Internet.
23. Click **Next** to continue to the Internet Mail Logon page.
24. Enter your POP account (e-mail account) name and password, and then click **Next**. For some ISPs, your POP account name could be the same name you use to log on to the system. Ask your ISP about their Secure Password Authentication requirements. If required, select this option instead of entering an account name and password.
25. Click **Next** to continue to the Friendly Name page.
26. Here you can enter a less technical name for your e-mail account. The default is the name of your mail server—for example, pop.prodigy.net. Enter a name for your mail account, and then click **Next** to continue to the Set Up Your Internet News Account page.

27. Click the **Yes** option button, and then click **Next**. If there is already an Internet News account on your computer, this brings up the Internet News account page. Otherwise this brings up the Your Name page, in which case you can skip to Step 29.
28. Click the **Create a new Internet news account** option button, and then click **Next** to continue to the Your Name page.
29. Enter the name that you want others to see when you post newsgroup messages, and then click **Next** to continue to the Internet News E-mail Addresses page.
30. Enter the e-mail address to which you want replies to newgroup messages to be sent, and then click **Next** to continue to the Internet News Server Name page.
31. Here you can enter the name of your news server, such as NNTP.prodigy.net. "NNTP" is short for Network News Transfer Protocol, which is the TCP/IP protocol for transferring bulletin board style messages across the Internet. Enter your news server name, and then click **Next** to continue to the Friendly Name page.
32. In the Internet news account name text box, replace the default name of your news server with something less technical, and then click **Next** to continue to the Set Up Your Internet Directory Service page.
33. Click the **Yes** option button, and then click **Next**. If Internet Directory Services have already been set up as part of an ISP account on this computer, you continue to the Internet Directory Service page. Otherwise you continue to the E-mail Addresses page, in which case you can skip to Step 37.
34. To set up a new directory service, you need to get specific instructions from your provider. For this exercise, click the **Modify an Existing Directory Service** option button, click the service of your choice in the list box, and then click **Next** to continue to the Confirm Settings Import page.
35. If your computer has imported settings before, you will see this line: "The Internet Connection Wizard has detected the following settings." In this case, click **Change Settings**, and click **Next** to continue to the Internet Directory Server Name page. Otherwise, you will have the choice of importing settings from your ISP. In this case, click **Yes**, and then click **Next** to continue to the Internet Directory Server Name page.
36. Unless directed not to do so by your ISP, accept these settings and click **Next** to continue to the Check E-mail Addresses page.
37. Unless you have special reasons to verify e-mail addresses, verify that the Yes option button is selected, and then click **Next** to continue to the Friendly Name page.
38. Here you can enter a less technical name for your directory service. As the default is the advertised name of the service, the default is probably acceptable for most users. Enter a new name if desired, and then click **Next** to continue to the Complete Configuration page.
39. Click **Finish** to accept the default "friendly name" and complete the process of creating an Internet connection.

PROJECT 5-4

In this project, you will create a desktop shortcut for the connection you created in Project 5-3. After creating the shortcut, you will test your new connection. In order to complete this project, you need to have completed Project 5-3.

1. Click **Start**, point to **Programs**, point to **Accessories**, point to **Communications**, and then click **Dial-Up Networking**. The Dial-Up Networking window opens. Here you should see an icon for the connection you created in Project 5-3. The icon should have the name you assigned in Step 16 of Project 5-3.
2. Click and drag the connection icon to the desktop.
3. A new connection icon appears on your desktop. (If necessary, move the Dial-Up Networking window so that you can see the icon.)
4. Double-click the new icon. The Connect To dialog box opens.
5. Enter your password if required, and then click **Connect**. The Connecting To dialog box appears while your computer makes the connection. When the connection is finally complete, you see the Connection Established dialog box.

PROJECT 5-5

In this project, you will locate your computer's name, and then use it along with the PING utility to test your dial-up connection. To complete this project, you need to be connected to the Internet. As Project 5-4 connects you to the Internet, you can start by completing that project first.

1. If you do not know your computer's name, click **Start**, point to **Settings**, click **Control Panel**, double-click the **Network Icon**, then click the **Identification** tab.
2. Write down the name of your computer as it appears in the Computer name text box and then click **Cancel**.
3. While you are connected to the Internet, click **Start**, point to **Programs**, then click **MS-DOS Prompt**.
4. Type **PING <my_computer_name>**, substituting the name of your computer for <my_computer_name>.
5. Press **Enter**.

6. Watch what happens. In a moment, you will see "Pinging <my_computer_name>…" followed by an IP address in brackets. That IP address is yours for as long as you are connected to the Internet during this session. Make a note of the IP address.

7. Disconnect from the Internet, and then reconnect.

8. Repeat Steps 4 through 6. Did you get the same IP address? If you did, that IP address may be permanently assigned for your use. However, in most cases, getting the same IP address twice is just a coincidence.

CASE PROJECTS

1. Your supervisor understands that you will have to bring Internet access to your local area network. Before making any decisions, however, he would like to learn more about protocols. On the basis of what you learned in this chapter, write a concise report on TCP/IP, and how computers use protocols in different situations. What are the different levels of protocols available, and how are they used?

2. Your boss has decided that the time has come to upgrade the network browser to either Internet Explorer 4.0 or Netscape Communicator 4.0. Because security for commercial transactions is a big issue with your business, he is interested in the security features of Internet Explorer 4.0. Write a brief report describing these features.

3. You have volunteered to install Windows 98 on the five desktop computers at your neighborhood community center. Nancy, the director of the center, has asked you to connect each of these computers to the Internet. A local ISP has donated connection services, but the ISP's representative will only speak with Nancy. Write a short report, explaining the Internet Connection Wizard to Nancy. Explain the information she needs to get from the ISP so you can get the computers connected to the Internet.

CHAPTER SIX

WINDOWS 98 COMMUNICATIONS AND MOBILE COMPUTING

A good part of Windows 98 is dedicated to supporting the needs of the mobile user. As a laptop user, you have a different set of needs away from the home or the office than you do when working on your desktop computer. If you use multiple computers, keeping them coordinated is a difficult task. Away from the home or office network, you need to learn how to acquire and manage as much speed as possible.

AFTER READING THIS CHAPTER AND COMPLETING THE EXERCISES YOU WILL BE ABLE TO:

- Install and configure modems and other telecommunications devices
- Implement multilinking and other performance-enhancing techniques
- Use the telephony applications provided within Windows 98
- Configure and manage Dial-Up Networking connections
- Understand the special needs of mobile computing

In this chapter, you will learn how to configure a modem, and how to combine the speed of several modems. You will also learn about some alternatives to modems that provide more speed at greater cost. In addition, you will learn about some tools and alternate utilities that you can use to avoid or troubleshoot problems with data communications.

For laptop computers, Windows 98 provides some useful tools, which, among other things, allow you to manage power to maximize battery life and to switch between multiple hardware configurations. For computers that are not connected via a network, you can take advantage of options designed to make sure you always have the same version of a file stored on each computer.

THE WINDOWS TELEPHONY API

Internal computer networks and the Internet are growing so fast that data requirements will soon take up much more of the worldwide telephone network than voice conversation. Already, practicing network administrators commonly have to deal with telephone and computer wires running side by side through their offices. Not surprisingly, one of the holy grails in networking is integration between computer and telephone networks. The goal is not only to integrate telephones and computers, but also to provide one interface for infrared, cellular, and facsimile communication. The Windows Telephony Application Programming Interface (TAPI) holds the promise of full integration for all forms of voice and data communication. As the networking industry brings these products to market, the development of Windows TAPI allows these products to be managed through Windows 98. Some of these products are discussed later in this chapter.

An **application programming interface (API)** is a common set of protocols, tools, and routines that software engineers can use when building applications. With this common interface, software engineers can build competing products that are consistent with the Windows 98 operating system environment. The APIs discussed in this chapter allow you to configure and control modems and other communications devices. The **Windows TAPI** was designed to standardize the way applications interact with telephone networks. From a user's standpoint, Windows TAPI is the interface to all communications devices, from ISDN to ADSL to regular modems. You will learn about each of these systems and more in this chapter.

MODEMS AND RELATED DEVICES

In Chapter 5, you learned that computers translate messages to binary code (1s and 0s). A modem converts binary code to sound frequencies supported on telephone wires. This process is known as **modulation**. The reverse process is known as **demodulation**. The term "modem" comes from this process: *mo*dulation + *dem*odulation. While some other devices, such as ISDN or cable modem connections, may be known as modems, they are digital and do not modulate or demodulate a signal.

As discussed in the last chapter, Windows can communicate through a wide range of telecommunications devices. Each type of device has been built for a different kind of physical installation; for example, some may be installed inside the computer, while others may be connected via parallel or serial ports to a universal serial bus (USB) or Fire Wire. (The terms "USB" and "firewire" were described in Chapter 1.) If you install multiple communications devices, Windows 98 configures and maintains them all. Once a device is installed and configured, it becomes available to all applications compatible with Windows 98. In some cases, older applications may also be able to access these devices. In the following sections you will learn to install, configure, and manage some of the major telephone-related devices.

INSTALLATION WIZARDS

As you learned in Chapter 3, the Plug and Play feature of Windows 98 allows it to detect hardware installed on a computer automatically. The Plug and Play feature is especially useful with modems. Assuming that your BIOS and modem are completely compatible with Plug and Play, and that the Windows 98 installation CD contains the correct driver, installing a modem is a simple process. You simply need to install it following the manufacturer's directions. Windows 98 will then detect the modem and install the appropriate driver from your Windows 98 installation CD automatically.

If these conditions are not met, the **Add New Hardware Wizard** jumps in to help. If you're simply missing a driver, you will be prompted to insert a 3½-inch disk or CD (supplied by the modem's manufacturer) from which to install the driver. (In some cases, you may be able to acquire the driver you need from the manufacturer's Web site.) If your hardware is not fully Plug-and-Play-compatible, you can choose from a list of modem makes and models known to Windows 98.

You will have a chance to use the Install New Modem Wizard in the Hands-on Projects at the end of this chapter. For now, simply keep in mind that you can activate the installation wizard as follows: click Start, point to Settings, click Control Panel, and then double-click the Modems icon. If you have installed a modem before, click Add. If you have not yet installed a modem on your computer, the Install New Modem Wizard will start automatically.

If the Install New Modem Wizard detects a modem incorrectly, you can change the settings manually, as described in the Hands-on Projects at the end of this chapter. In some cases, you may have to provide the necessary driver from a manufacturer-supplied 3½-inch disk or CD.

After you have installed a modem, you can adjust its properties, as described in the following section.

CONFIGURING GLOBAL MODEM PROPERTIES

Global modem properties are the different defaults and settings that you use for each of your modems. You can adjust global modem properties after installing a modem, as follows: click Start, point to Settings, click Control Panel, and then double-click the Modems icon. This opens the Modems Properties dialog box. Select the modem that you would like to configure, then click Properties. This opens the General tab of a dialog box named after your modem, as shown in Figure 6-1.

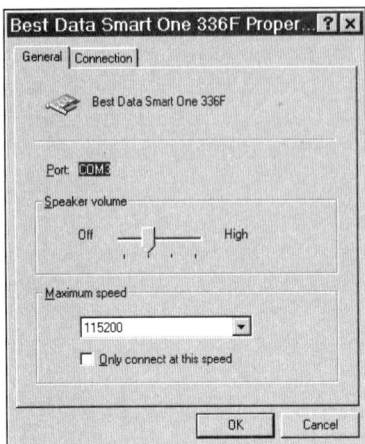

Figure 6-1 General tab of your modem's Properties dialog box

This dialog box always has at least two tabs: General and Connection. Special tabs are available for speakerphone-type modems. You may also see a Distinctive Ring tab, and a Forwarding tab. On the Distinctive Ring tab you can specify whether the line you will be using has Distinctive Ring service. Distinctive Ring service allows a modem to route calls to different telephone lines, such as for data, fax, or voice. On the Forwarding tab, you can indicate whether the line you will be using has Call Forwarding service.

 The Distinctive Ring supported by the Windows TAPI is based on a service provided by the telephone company, in which the telephone company sends the signals for multiple telephone numbers on one set of telephone wires. The modem then routes the call to the appropriate telephone line based on the type of ring. This is different from the more common usage of Distinctive Ring, which allows you to designate different ring patterns based on incoming telephone numbers.

The General tab provides settings for:

- **Port**: Specifies the communications port, or COM port, to which the modem is attached
- **Speaker Volume**: Sets external speaker volume for the modem. This setting is usually separate from your computer sound system. Generally, modem speakers are active when you connect and while the modem is negotiating a speed. The importance of being able to hear your modem connect is explained in the following Note.
- **Maximum Speed**: Defines the maximum speed at which a modem and Windows 98 may communicate with each other. This speed is limited by the hardware in each system. Generally, the maximum speed between Windows 98 and your modem should be higher than the maximum speed of the modem itself. Begin by selecting the highest possible speed. If your connection software

reports data errors, lower this value. Select the "Only connect at this speed" check box only if you want to limit your connection to the selected speed. Most users do not choose this option, because a connection will not be made if that specific rate cannot be obtained.

 By listening to your modem while it connects, you can learn how well it is working. A modem starts by trying to connect at its highest rated speed. If for some reason this does not work, it downshifts to a lower speed. Generally, the longer a modem takes to connect, the more it is downshifting. Of course, different modems take different amounts of time to connect. But if you learn the characteristics of how your modem connects, a change in its behavior can indicate a problem such as trouble with the quality of the line.

Settings pertaining to the connection established by the modem can be adjusted on the Connection tab. These options include:

- **Connection preferences**: Defines how your modem sends and checks data at the physical level. You should only change these settings if specifically instructed to do so when connecting to a private system such as a mainframe or older data terminal. For normal Internet connections, use the default settings. Data bits are the number of bits of data sent in each group. The default is 8. Parity determines how the data is checked. The default is none, for no checking. Checks are made at other levels. Stop bits tell the computer when each group of data stops.

- **Call preferences**: Defines settings related to dial tone and connection time limits. If your modem starts dialing too early, you may need to select the "Wait for a dial tone before dialing" option. This may not work for some dial tones outside the USA. The "Cancel the call if not connected within ___ seconds" option is useful for international connections, which are frequently out of service. If you frequently forget to disconnect at the end of a connection session, use the "Disconnect a call if idle for more than ___ minutes" option to have your connections terminated automatically.

- **Port Settings**: Allows you to specify how your modem uses universal asynchronous receiver-transmitter (UART) first in, first out (FIFO) buffers. The default setting should support all high-speed modems. Choose a lower setting if you are having trouble sending or receiving data at your current modem speed. Most computers and modems sold in the past few years have been built to the 16550 UART standard, which means that they have a 16-byte buffer. To determine whether your modem complies with 16550 UART, return to the Modem Properties dialog box, then click the Diagnostics tab. In the list of active COM ports, select the one your modem uses, then click More Info. Review the UART information in the More Info dialog box.

- **Advanced Connection Settings**: Allows you to specify settings for how your modem transmits and receives data. While not so crucial now, these settings were very important a few years ago, before data transmission settings were standardized. The "Use error" control options address noise issues on telephone lines. They also allow you to enable hardware compression, as explained later in this chapter.

The "Use flow control" options minimize data loss in external modems. The "Modulation type" option allows you to specify special modulation for French Minitel modems and some older U.S. modems. The "Extra settings" option allows you to specify special debugging commands exclusive to each brand of modem. (Consult your modem manual for more information.) The View log option allows you to view data related to data transmission problems.

As a network administrator, you may have to help employees in the field set up their mobile computers to dial into your organization's network. In the next section, you will learn to create the required settings by configuring dialing properties.

CONFIGURING DIALING PROPERTIES

After you have installed (and, if necessary, configured) a new modem, you can specify more detailed settings regarding its geographical location in the Dialing Properties dialog box. In fact, you can establish separate groups of settings for different geographical locations, making it easy for a mobile user to connect from different locations. You will learn more about establishing multiple locations later in this chapter. To open the Dialing Properties dialog box, shown in Figure 6-2, click Start, point to Settings, and then click Control Panel. Double-click the Modems icon, click the General tab if necessary, and then click Dialing Properties.

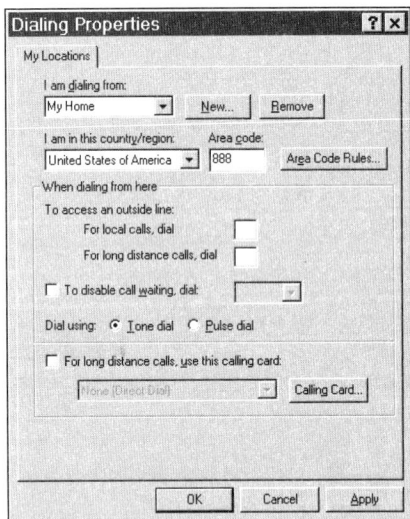

Figure 6-2 Dialing Properties dialog box

The "I am dialing from" list box indicates your current location. You can create as many locations as you need; for example, you might create one location for home, one for your office, and one for a frequent vacation destination. To create a new location, click New, and then click OK. A new location named "New Location" appears in the "I am dialing from" list box. You can type a new name for this location (such as "Home" or "Vacation"), and then specify the settings you need for that location, as explained in the remainder of this section. The next time you need to use this location, you can simply select it in the "I am dialing from" list box.

Once you have created a new location, specify the country or area code. The "Area Code Rules" button makes it easier to negotiate the ever-changing rules regarding area codes in the United States. For example, to make a local call that crosses an area code boundary, you may either have to dial a complete 10-digit number for all calls, or you may simply have to dial a 1 before the 7-digit number. If you need help making sense of this complexity, click the "Area Code Rules" button to open the Area Code Rules dialog box, where you can specify the requirements for different geographical locations. This option is especially useful for mobile computing, when you may have to dial from several locations in a single day.

The settings in the "When dialing from here" box section change depending on which location you selected above, in the "I am dialing from" list box.

The "When dialing from here" settings include:

- Numbers required to obtain an outside line for local calls (often 9)
- Numbers required to obtain an outside line for long-distance calls
- An option to disable call waiting
- A choice of using tone or pulse dialing. Choose pulse dialing if you are dialing from a location with rotary-dial telephones.

At the bottom of the Dialing Properties dialog box, you have the option of using a calling card for long-distance calls. To use a calling card, select the "For long distance calls, use this calling card" check box, and then select your calling card from the list box below. This list box includes 22 preconfigured calling card choices. You can add or remove calling cards from this list by clicking the "Calling Card" button. This opens the Calling Card dialog box, shown in Figure 6-3, where you can click the "New" button to create a new card. Then you can enter any required PIN numbers, long-distance access codes, and international access codes. To specify step-by-step dialing instructions for the new card, click "Long Distance Calls" in the Calling Card dialog box.

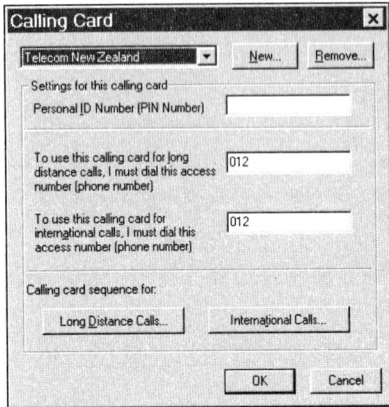

Figure 6-3 The Calling Card dialog box

After you have provided all the relevant information regarding the location from which you will be making a connection, you can specify the information necessary to actually make the connection, using Dial-Up Networking. In the next section, you will learn how to use the Dial-Up Networking Wizard to manage different connections. While the settings that you learned about in this section are all automated, you may occasionally need to configure them manually—for example, when dialing from a hotel, where you have to speak to a real operator before making your modem connection. You will learn how to configure settings manually in the next section.

REMOTE ACCESS WITH DIAL-UP NETWORKING

You connect your computer to the "outside world" of other computer systems by using the Dial-Up Networking (DUN) utility. Using DUN, you can connect to the Internet, to private online services, and to corporate LANs.

In Chapter 5, you learned to use Internet Connection Wizards (which are part of the DUN utility) to set up your interfaces to the Internet. The process of connecting to a computer system other than the Internet is essentially the same as the process for connecting to the Internet: you create a connection with a group of settings, and then you access the connection with its settings via DUN. As when creating an Internet connection, you can take advantage of a special wizard to create your connections to other computer networks. To make a new connection:

1. Click Start, point to Programs, point to Accessories, point to Communications, and then click Dial-Up Networking. The Dial-Up Networking window opens.

2. Double-click the Make New Connection icon. This opens the Make New Connection Wizard, shown in Figure 6-4.

3. In the "Type a name for the computer you are dialing" text box, type the name of your choice, and then click Next.

4. In the "Type a phone number for the computer you want to call" text boxes, enter the phone number and country for your connection, and then click Next.

5. Click Finish. You return to the Dial-Up Networking window. Now that you have specified the phone number you want to call, you need to adjust your modem settings so that your modem can communicate with the modem you want to call.

6. Select the connection that you just created, click File on the menu bar, and then click Properties. This opens a dialog box with the same name as your new connection.

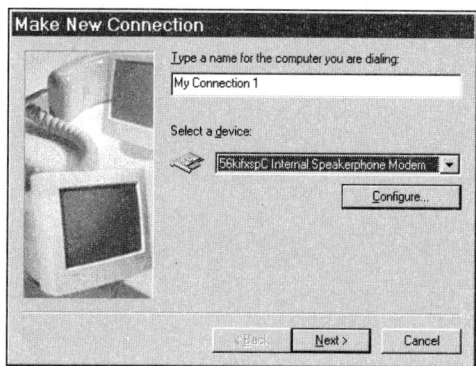

Figure 6-4 Make New Connection Wizard

7. Select the modem you want to use for your new connection in the "Connect using" list box.

8. Click Configure, and then click the Options tab if necessary. The Properties dialog box for the selected modem opens, similar to the one shown in Figure 6-5. This dialog box contains several tabs. You learned about the General and Connection tabs earlier in this chapter. You will examine the Options tab in the next step.

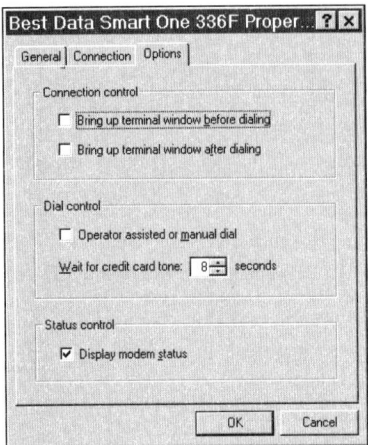

Figure 6-5 Options tab of the Properties dialog box for the selected modem

9. Examine the elements on the Options tab. The Connection Control settings allow you to open up a terminal window for any required special command sequences. The Dial Control settings allow you to specify operator-assisted dialing, manual dialing, and calling card calls. Unlike the dialing properties you learned about earlier in this chapter, these settings allow you to talk to operators and dial phone numbers manually before making your modem connection. The Status Control settings allow you to display the modem's current status. Click OK to close the Properties dialog box.

You can create a shortcut to a Dial-Up Networking connection by dragging the connection's icon from the Dial-Up Networking window onto your desktop. Then, to dial that connection, simply double-click the shortcut on the desktop. You should already be familiar with this process from Chapter 5, where you created a desktop shortcut for an Internet connection.

Earlier in the chapter, you learned how to create multiple locations to dial *from,* by using the Dialing Properties dialog box. Just as you may sometimes need to dial *from* more than one location, you may sometimes need to dial *to* more than one location. For example, freelance consultants may sometimes have to access more than one corporate network. More commonly, you may need to access multiple ISPs. You can create a Dial-Up Networking connection to a second location by following the steps outlined in the previous section. Give the new connection a meaningful name, so that you can distinguish it from your other connections.

Now that you are familiar with the steps involved in installing a modem, creating a location to connect *from,* and specifying settings relating to the location you want to connect *to,* you are ready to learn about some more advanced connection options. In the next section you will learn how to install and configure ISDN devices.

INSTALLING AND CONFIGURING ISDN DEVICES

The difference between regular and Integrated Services Digital Network (ISDN) lines is similar to the difference between cassette tapes and compact discs. Regular phone service transmits voices by translating sound waves into other wave forms, which can sometimes result in distortion. ISDN phone service translates voices into binary code (1s and 0s). Even if a 1 or 0 is distorted, the receiver can translate distortion back into binary code. Thus, the sound over an ISDN phone line is usually as perfect as the sound from a CD played on a stereo.

Before you can use ISDN, you need to install a special hardware device known as an ISDN adapter. ISDN adapters can be installed in the same way as modems.

Each ISDN line is actually two 64 Kbps connections. Each ISDN telephone line can therefore allow for data transfer rates of 128 Kbps, or it can be split into a voice telephone line and a 64 Kbps ISDN data connection.

An ISDN line in the United States actually consists of three channels (two B channels and a D channel), which are collectively known as "2B + D." The two B channels can be used for data or voice lines. Each B line has a capacity of 64 Kbps. The D channel has a capacity of 16 KB/s and is used for signaling—that is for transmitting the phone numbers you dial, busy signals, and commands for your telephone to ring. (In other words, you get 144 Kbps when you use an ISDN line in the USA.)

After you have installed an ISDN adapter, and then configured it using the ISDN Configuration Wizard, using an ISDN connection is the same as using a modem, only faster. Just as with modems, you can create new connections with the Make New Connection Wizard.

In the following steps you will learn how to configure an ISDN adapter. Before you continue with these steps, you need to physically install an ISDN adapter. If you don't have one, follow along as best you can. It is good practice for installing other products. To configure your ISDN adapter:

1. Click Start, point to Settings, click Control Panel, and then double-click the Network icon. This opens the Configuration tab of the Network dialog box, shown in Figure 6-6.

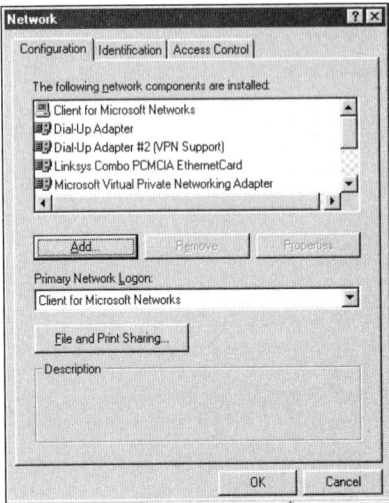

Figure 6-6 The Configuration tab of the Network dialog box

2. Click Add. The Select Network Component Type dialog box opens.

3. In the list of network components, click Adapter, and then click Add. The Select Network Adapters dialog box opens.

4. In the Manufacturers list box, select the device's manufacturer.

5. In the Network Adapters list box, select your adapter's model name or number and then go to Step 6. If your model or manufacturer is not listed, click the Have Disk button and follow the directions on the screen to install the device from a 3½-inch disk or CD supplied by the manufacturer.

6. Click OK. Windows 98 Plug and Play finishes installing the new ISDN adapter.

Once an ISDN device is installed, the ISDN Configuration Wizard opens. Here you'll need to provide three pieces of information that you should be able to obtain from your telephone company or ISDN provider:

- **Switch protocol**: Every phone company uses telephone switches at its central office to forward calls to its main lines. You need to know the protocol, manufacturer, and version of the phone company switches.

- **Telephone number(s)**: The number or numbers assigned to your ISDN line by the phone company. Because ISDN lines can be split into two, you may get two phone numbers.

- **Service Profile Identifier (SPID)**: An electronic name tag for your adapter. Normally consists of the telephone number (or numbers) assigned to your line, with a prefix or a suffix. Generally in the United States, this is a 14-digit number, of which the last four digits identify your adapter.

To configure other ISDN properties, click Start, point to Settings, click Control Panel, and then double-click the Network icon. Once again, this opens the Configuration tab of the Network dialog box, shown earlier in Figure 6-6. In the "The following network components are installed" list box, select the ISDN adapter, and then click Properties. This opens a dialog box named after your adapter, where you can choose from options related to Driver Type, Bindings, Advanced connection behavior, and allocation of resources. You will learn more about these settings in support of other network adapters in Chapter 13. These settings affect ISDN adapters in the same way.

Multilink Connections

To increase the speed of your connections, you can combine modems in a multilink connection. Multilink connections combine modem signals in the same way that ISDN combines B channels. Both processes are governed by the PPP Multilink protocol. As you learned in Chapter 5, the Point-to-Point Protocol (PPP) is more capable than the Serial Line Interface Protocol (SLIP) in part because it supports error checking. Because PPP is involved, you may not be able to use a multilink connection to connect to a UNIX server.

Before you can create a multilink connection, you need to verify that the system that you dial into, such as an ISP, can support it with the appropriate Windows NT system. If you are not able to use modems with identical speeds, the total speed will be the number of modems multiplied by the speed of the *slowest* modem. To configure a multilink connection:

1. Configure at least two Dial-Up Networking devices (i.e., modems). You will learn how to install a modem in the hands-on projects at the end of this chapter.

2. Click Start, point to Programs, point to Accessories, point to Communications, and click Dial-Up Networking.

3. Click the icon for the connection you want to configure as a multilink connection.

4. On the menu bar, click File, and then click Properties. This opens a dialog box named for your connection.

5. Click the Multilink tab, click the Use Additional Devices option button, and then click Add. The Edit Extra Device dialog box opens, where you can choose the additional modems that you want to use for the combined link. Click OK to confirm your selection.

6. Repeat Step 5 for each additional modem that you want to use.

7. Once you have completed this list, click OK. Double-click the connection that you highlighted earlier. Click Connect in the dialog box for this connection. Dial-Up Networking will dial the connections that you have set up, one at a time.

Compression

Hardware compression is a technique that permits communications devices to compress the data they transmit. This effectively creates a higher connection speed. Compression is available on most modern modems and in most digital communications devices. To enable hardware compression on your system:

1. Click Start, point to Settings, click Control Panel, and then double-click the Modems icon.
2. In the General tab, highlight the modem of your choice, and then click Properties. This opens the Properties dialog box for your modem.
3. Click the Connection tab, and then click Advanced. The Advanced Connection Settings dialog box opens.
4. If it is not already selected, select the Use error control check box, and then select the Compress data check box. If these boxes are grayed out, your modem does not accommodate hardware compression.
5. Click OK to close the Advanced Connection Settings dialog box, click OK again to close the Properties dialog box, and then click Close to close the Modem Properties dialog box.

INTERNET ACCESS VIA A LAN GATEWAY

You have just learned to connect to networks such as a LAN through Windows 98 Dial-Up Networking. Once you connect to your LAN in this way, you have all the rights and privileges you would have on any other computer on your LAN. This includes access to other networks through the LAN Gateway. As you learned in Chapter 5, a gateway is the access point from a LAN to another network such as the Internet. To allow your computer to access other networks through your Dial-Up Networking connection:

1. Click Start, point to Programs, point to Accessories, point to Communications, then click Dial-Up Networking.
2. Highlight the icon for your connection to your LAN. On the menu bar, click File, then click Properties.
3. In the dialog box named after your connection, click the Server Types tab.
4. In the Allowed network protocols area of this tab, make sure TCP/IP is checked, then click TCP/IP Settings.
5. In the TCP/IP Settings dialog box, make sure the "Use default gateway on remote network" option is selected, as shown in Figure 6-7.

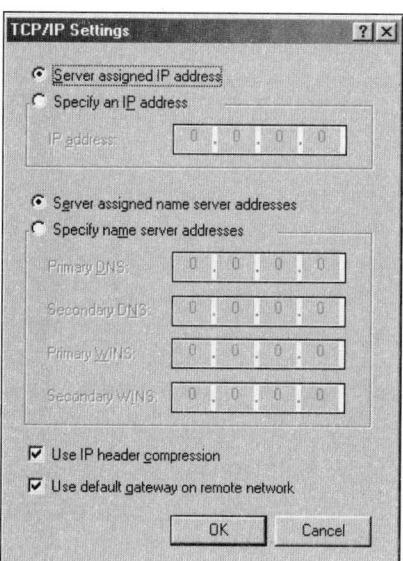

Figure 6-7 TCP/IP Settings for your Dial-Up Networking connection

OVERCOMING PHONE LINE TRANSMISSION PROBLEMS

The structure of your telephone system affects the quality of data traveling to and from your modem. Switches connect ordinary phone lines to the main telephone network. Some switches are located in a **central office (CO)**, while others are located between COs. Thus, the connection between you and your ISP could go through many switches. As you may expect, the quality of the connection to your ISP is inversely related to the number of switches between you and your ISP. Other factors affecting your connection include: the quality of telephone lines, the use of old switching equipment, weather, worn insulation, and the proximity of older unshielded electrical wiring. Such problems can be severe enough that you may need to request a data quality line for your computer. However, not all phone companies can accommodate such a request.

Consult your telephone company's customer service office for assistance regarding problems due to weather or outdated equipment. In some cases, you may be able to obtain line conditioning services that test and guarantee the quality of current lines for modems or digital grade lines.

FASTER CONNECTIONS

The first revolution in networking came in the early 1980s with the development of Ethernet. Before this technology, businesses had to rely on 9600 bps connections for local area networks. Ethernet raised the speed limit to 10 Mbps. The second revolution, which will benefit home users as well as businesses, involves cable modems and asymmetrical digital subscriber lines.

A **cable modem** is not a modulator-demodulator like a regular modem. It takes advantage of the fact that cable TV connection wires are closely related to the wires used for Ethernet. Cable modems have actually been implemented in test markets since early 1997, bringing multimegabit speeds to the home. Actual speeds have varied, but are still significantly greater than the fastest 56 Kbps telephone modems.

Asymmetrical digital subscriber lines (ADSL) allow regular telephone lines to transfer data at a multimegabit per second speed. The potential speed is inversely related to the distance from the central office, where your phone line connects to the telephone switches discussed earlier. A number of telecommunications companies are working furiously to bring ADSL to market. Although Windows 98 has implemented ISDN wizards, it is safe to say that the current consumer ISDN technology is a transitional technology (broadband ISDN is a different and complex topic) that will be phased out when ADSL comes on line.

Large companies and multinational corporations are often equipped with even faster full-time services. The two common introductory corporate lines carry the capacity of 24 and 672 phone lines worth of data. These are also known as T1 and T3 connections, respectively. Given the difference between the two, multilink techniques are important in business. Companies that need an in-between number can also use multilink techniques to achieve a faster connection. At this level, multilink is often known as inverse multiplexing.

TROUBLESHOOTING CONNECTION PROBLEMS

As you try to connect to the Internet or other computer systems, you may encounter trouble at various points along the way. Some basic testing strategies can determine whether or not your connection is working, or can provide clues as to where a failure may be occurring. Generally, if a failure occurs when you are making a connection, Windows 98 will attempt to give you some indication of what went wrong. For example, you may see an alert dialog box indicating that the computer you're dialing isn't answering, that the line is busy, that an invalid username or password may be involved, or a variety of other conditions.

Should Windows 98 fail to provide you with the information you need to correct the problem, consider these other well-known problem areas. If these do not work, you will learn about other network troubleshooting tools such as PING and WinIPCfg in Chapter 13.

- **Bad physical connections**: Most network problems are physical. Check the connections to your modem. Check for a dial tone by plugging in a regular phone. (If you have a digital line, you may not get a dial tone; in this case, you may need to purchase a line tester.)
- **Bad logical connections**: You can check for this by listening to your modem. If the sounds are different than usual, your modem may not be connecting.
- **Bad logon**: Check your username and password. A common mistake is using the wrong (upper or lower) case when you log on. Check with your Internet service provider (ISP) to see if they are still accepting your account.

- **Bad addresses**: In Chapter 5, you learned about the settings for your ISP. Check the ISP settings such as IP and server addresses. Sometimes components of an ISP are under repair. The solution could be as simple as trying again later.
- **Bad applications**: Check the compatibility of your connection software with the server you're connecting to. If you can connect with basic tools such as HyperTerminal (described later in this chapter), then you can verify that there is a problem with the application.

HYPERTERMINAL

HyperTerminal is a basic communications application included with Windows 98 that allows you to connect directly to a text-based system on another computer, to a bulletin board system, or to a private (non-Internet-based) online service. HyperTerminal will not work with graphical connections that are used by browsers such as Internet Explorer. To use HyperTerminal, click Start, point to Programs, point to Accessories, point to Communications, and then click HyperTerminal. In the HyperTerminal window, double-click the Hypertrm.exe icon. In the connection description dialog box, enter a name for your connection, choose an icon, then click OK. In the Connect To dialog box, enter a phone number, choose a modem in the Connect using option box, and click OK. This opens the HyperTerminal window shown in Figure 6-8. In the HyperTerminal window, double-click the Hypertrm icon.

If HyperTerminal is not installed on your computer, you can install it as follows: Insert your Windows 98 Installation CD into your CD-ROM drive. Click Start, point to Settings, click Control Panel, then double-click Add/Remove Programs. Click the Windows Setup tab, highlight Communications in the Components list box, and click Details. In the Communications dialog box, select the HyperTerminal check box, and then click OK. Click OK in the Add/Remove Programs Properties dialog box.

If this is the first time that HyperTerminal has been opened on your computer, this opens a simplified version of the Internet Configuration Wizard. First you will see a Connection Description dialog box. Enter a name in the Name text box, highlight the icon of your choice, and then click OK. In the Connect to dialog box, enter the settings appropriate for you in the Country Code, Area Code, and phone number text boxes. In the Connect Using box, select the modem that you wish to use, then click OK. In the next connect dialog box, you can modify the modem dialing properties that you learned about earlier in this chapter. Then click Dial to connect to the text-based system of your choice. This opens the HyperTerminal window shown in Figure 6-8. When you save this connection, a new icon is saved in the HyperTerminal folder, with the name that you entered in the original Name text box. This icon is associated with all of the settings that you just created.

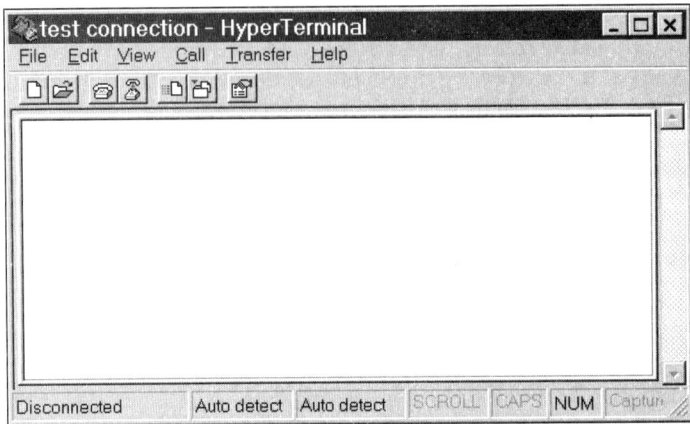

Figure 6-8 HyperTerminal window

HyperTerminal is a simple, no-frills application. It allows you to upload and download files and transmit data. It also allows you to capture the data sent to the HyperTerminal window as text. In addition, HyperTerminal allows you to take advantage of any options the system you are connecting to can provide. Unlike the graphical user interfaces associated with browsers, all HyperTerminal communications use text and commands. A HyperTerminal session can look similar to commands in an MS-DOS screen. The actual commands used in a HyperTerminal session depend on the operating system of the server that you connect to.

PHONE DIALER

The Phone Dialer allows you to place voice calls from your computer. To open the Phone Dialer, click Start, point to Programs, point to Accessories, point to Communications, and then click Phone Dialer. The Phone Dialer window makes use of a familiar telephone touchpad layout. It also includes a text box where you can type a number directly. If you prefer, you can click the list arrow to choose from previously dialed numbers on a drop-down list. The Phone Dialer has eight buttons, similar to speed-dial buttons on a telephone, that can be preset to speed-dial phone numbers on command.

Phone Dialer uses the settings defined in the Dialing Properties dialog box. If necessary, you can change these settings via the Dialing Properties command in the Tools menu.

In the remainder of this chapter, you will learn about some of the ways Windows 98 supports laptop and other portable computers away from the office.

MOBILE COMPUTING AND WINDOWS 98

The term mobile computer is often used to refer to any computer (particularly a laptop) that is not tied to a fixed physical location. Windows 98 includes a variety of mobile computing tools that allow users to retain the capabilities of larger desktop workstations when they switch to portable laptops. For example, the Plug and Play feature allows you to insert PC

Cards into a laptop while the computer is on. You can take advantage of power management systems, which maximize battery life. In addition, you can create multiple hardware configurations so that you can switch quickly between a docked and undocked laptop. You will learn more about these and other mobile computing options in the following sections.

 For smaller hand-held devices known as personal digital assistants (PDA), you can use Microsoft's complementary operating system, Windows CE.

PC Card Support

A PC Card is a peripheral the size of a credit card. Like the cards that you can install in a desktop computer, PC Cards are available for use as modems, sound cards, and even as hard disks. They fit into standard slots, normally in laptop computers. PC Cards, formally known as **PCMCIA (Personal Computer Memory Card International Association)** cards, are vital to mobile computing. In Windows 98, Plug and Play support is automatically enabled within PC Card slots. For best results, each PC Card must contain specific information known as the **card information structure (CIS)** that Windows 98 uses to create a unique identification number for the card. Next, before the PC Card will work, a driver must be supplied in one of the following ways:

- A Plug-and-Play-compatible PC Card includes a CIS that identifies all interface requirements, including required device drivers, as soon as it is plugged into the PC Card socket.

- If there is no specific driver available for the CIS, Windows 98 prompts you to accept installation of a generic driver.

- If no specific or generic driver exists on the Windows 98 CD, the Add New Hardware Wizard prompts you for the location of a specific manufacturer-supplied driver.

Power Management

Properly configured power management tools are critical for mobile computing. The right tools can move a number of PC components automatically to a low-power state after a certain period of time, thereby extending the life of a laptop's batteries. You can choose from two tools for managing power in Windows 98: the Advanced Power Management (APM) BIOS specification and the Advanced Configuration and Power Interface (ACPI).

Windows 98 supports APM version 1.2, which allows the basic input/output system (BIOS) to suspend parts of your system after a certain period of inactivity. It can suspend a battery-powered system such as a laptop when the power reserve reaches a specified level. APM relies on the ability of the BIOS to control access and power to your main computer components. Under APM, if you haven't accessed your hard disk for, say, 20 minutes, then the BIOS will stop the hard disk motor to save power. Since your hard disk is only temporarily suspended, it will restart whenever you look for a file.

APM's dependency on the BIOS results in one major drawback: because every BIOS is different, the effect of APM will vary. Another drawback is that APM does not support power management of the USB and firewire peripherals discussed in Chapter 1. When using APM, you can specify how long a component must be idle before it is powered down. To set specific time limits for your system, click Start, point to Settings, click Control Panel, and then double-click the Power Management icon. This opens the Power Management Properties dialog box, which lists the current settings for your computer.

Windows 98 also supports Advanced Configuration and Power Interface (ACPI) version 1.0 drivers, if your computer's BIOS is compatible. Checking the current status of your BIOS is a two-step process. When you power up your computer, the BIOS type and manufacturer is listed in the opening screen. The Web site of every major BIOS manufacturer should include compatibility and upgrade information for each of their BIOS systems. There are reports that Microsoft will require ACPI for BIOS compatibility with Windows NT 5.0, to be released in 1999, and as a result the BIOS manufacturers are hard at work on upgrades. Many existing BIOS upgrades can be downloaded from the Internet.

An ACPI-compatible BIOS allows applications and peripherals to control the power in your system. With ACPI, program device drivers can make sure that systems such as your monitor are not suspended in the middle of a presentation. Other drivers can activate your hard disk for maintenance in the middle of the night. ACPI can also control power settings for peripherals that APM cannot see, especially those with USB and firewire interfaces.

Older applications may not be fully compatible with APM or ACPI. Such applications often assume that a PC will always be fully powered. The incompatibilities may mean either that APM or ACPI doesn't function, or that your data becomes corrupt when APM or ACPI does work.

To find whether APM or ACPI is installed on your computer, click Start, point to Settings, click Control Panel, double-click the System icon, then click the Device Manager tab. Click View Devices by type, then click the plus sign next to System Devices. Note whether you have APM or ACPI installed on your computer. Click OK to return to the Control Panel. Double-click Power Management to see the current settings for your computer.

HOT DOCKING AND PORT REPLICATION SUPPORT

To save space and weight on laptop computers, the number of connections and expansion cards that can be installed is kept to a minimum. But most laptop users sometimes use their computers at home or at the office. In this situation, port replicators and docking stations can provide the functionality missing from a laptop. A **port replicator** is a device that provides additional connections such as serial and parallel ports. A **docking station** includes the functionality of a port replicator plus additional expansion slots not available on the laptop.

Hot docking refers to the process of docking a device while the computer is up and running. It is a terrific convenience to be able to install and remove a laptop from a docking station without having to power down. With the multiple hardware profiles that you learned to create in Chapter 4, little time is lost when you dock or undock a computer.

When undocking your laptop, you need to consider whether or not your docking station has an auto-eject feature. Auto-ejection acts rather like the eject button on a VCR, in that the device is automatically ejected from the computer. However, before the device is ejected, you are given the opportunity to save files, or close any applications that rely on the device. With manual ejection, the user must manually remove a device from the system. Before manually removing a device, you won't be given any reminders about saving files. Instead, you must remember to save all files, and close any application that relies on the device.

MANAGING FILES WITH THE BRIEFCASE

Anyone who has worked on the same file on both a desktop and a laptop knows how difficult it is to make sure that both computers have the most up-to-date copy of the necessary files. Network users can avoid this problem by always downloading the required files from the same computer. Non-networked users can avoid this problem by using the Windows 98 Briefcase utility.

The Windows 98 **Briefcase** helps ensure that current copies of critical files are available on more than one computer, a process known as synchronizing files. For example, you could use the Briefcase to ensure that both your regular, desktop computer, and your portable laptop contain identical copies of critical files.

A Briefcase is automatically installed and configured under the Portable setup option when you install Windows 98. You can create additional briefcases as follows: click Start, point to Programs, click Windows Explorer, select any directory in the left-hand pane, click File on the menu bar, point to New, then click Briefcase. This creates a briefcase labeled "New Briefcase" in your current Windows Explorer directory in the right-hand pane. For convenience, click and drag your new briefcase to the desktop. Now you are ready to start sharing files between two computers.

If you did not see a Briefcase in the Windows Explorer file menu or folder pane, you need to install the Briefcase, as follows: Insert the Windows 98 Installation CD into your CD-ROM drive. Click Start, point to Settings, click Control Panel, double-click Add/Remove Programs. In the Add/Remove Programs Properties dialog box, click the Windows Setup tab, then double-click Accessories in the Components list box. In the Accessories dialog box, select the Briefcase checkbox, and then click OK to return to the Add/Remove Programs Properties dialog box. Click OK again.

You can transfer the files in a briefcase over a network, via a direct cable connection, or via a 3½-inch disk. As explained earlier, there's no reason to use a briefcase over a network. You will learn how to create a direct cable connection in the next section. The following steps explain how to use a briefcase with a 3½-inch disk. When using a disk, be warned that the files that you synchronize are limited by the capacity of the disk.

1. Using Windows Explorer, copy the files and folders that you are working on into the Briefcase.

2. Put a 3½-inch disk into drive A.

3. Right-click the My Briefcase icon on your desktop, point to Send To on the Shortcut menu, and then click 3½ Floppy (A:). This copies your briefcase to drive A. After the copy process is complete, you should notice that your briefcase is no longer on your desktop.

4. Take the 3½-inch disk and insert it into a different Windows 98 computer.

5. On the desktop, double-click the My Computer icon, and then double-click the 3½ Floppy (A:) icon. The 3½ Floppy window opens, containing your briefcase icon.

6. Double-click the briefcase icon.

7. Open the file that you put in your briefcase, and make any changes that you want. When you save the file, it should automatically save back to your briefcase on the 3½-inch disk.

8. Take the 3½-inch disk and insert it in the original computer.

9. Repeat Steps 5 and 6.

10. In the My Briefcase window, click the Update All button on the toolbar. The Update My Briefcase dialog box opens, indicating which files need to be updated, as shown in Figure 6-9. You can choose to replace the file on the computer with the file on the 3½-inch disk, or vice versa. You can also choose to skip the update process entirely. To choose an update option, right-click a file and then click the option you want.

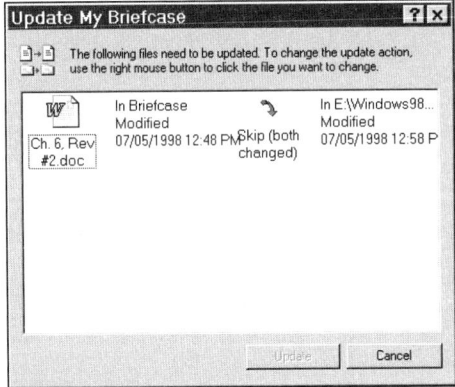

Figure 6-9 Updating a briefcase

DIRECT CABLE CONNECTION

With speeds of up to 115 Kbps, the direct cable connection (DCC) provides a simple network-style interface between two computers. DCCs can be set up in a number of ways. The most common DCC uses what is known as a null-modem cable, which connects to serial or parallel ports on the two computers to be connected. A **null modem** is a cable with two wires crossed to make the cable appear as a modem to each computer. Other options for a DCC include infrared connections, which are primarily used for communication between computers and peripherals such as printers.

DCC does require file and printer sharing, which is covered in Chapter 13. But as you'll see in the Hands-on Projects in this chapter, allowing two computers to share files via a direct cable connection is not difficult. You will need two computers, a host to share files, and a guest to copy files from the host. Once you complete the following steps, you will be ready for the DCC Hands-on Project at the end of this chapter.

1. On your host computer, insert the Windows 98 Installation CD into the CD-ROM drive.
2. On your host computer, click Start, point to Settings, click Control Panel, double-click the Network icon, and then click the Configuration tab, if necessary.
3. Click File and Print Sharing. This opens the File and Print Sharing dialog box.
4. Select the "I want to be able to give others access to my files" check box, and then click OK. You return to the Network dialog box.
5. Click OK to close the Network dialog box. If you haven't enabled file and print sharing before, Windows 98 now copies sharing installation files from your Windows 98 CD. When the process is complete, Windows 98 prompts you to restart your computer.
6. Click Yes to restart your computer.
7. When your computer restarts, you may see a System Security Check dialog box that recommends that you disable file and printer sharing on TCP/IP connections. Since you do want to share files, click No.
8. Click Start, point to Programs, and then click Windows Explorer.
9. In the left-hand pane, select the directory or disk drive of your choice, click File in the menu bar, click Properties, and then click the Sharing tab.
10. Click the Shared As option button.
11. Enter a different share name and password only if desired. (If you see a row of asterisks in the Password text boxes, a password already exists for this share.) Now your host computer is ready to share files with a guest computer.

CHAPTER SUMMARY

- The networking industry is moving towards computer telephony integration, in which data and voice communications are integrated into one system. In response to this shift, Microsoft has developed a Telephone Application Programming Interface (TAPI) for Windows 98. Windows TAPI was designed to provide a common interface to the different types of voice and data communications equipment coming to market today and in the future.

- To support the mobile user, Windows 98 includes a number of communications wizards. These wizards help you install modems, ISDN adapters, and dial-up connections. As the demands for speed increase, Multilink allows you to combine two or more modems together to create a faster interface. Other technologies such as ADSL and cable modems are coming. Suppliers will design drivers to work with Windows 98 through the Windows TAPI.

- With any data connection, there can be problems. To address these problems, you can adjust global modem properties to change the characteristics of data transmission. You can use the HyperTerminal and Phone Dialer to verify the connections. You have learned how the structure of the telephone network can affect the quality of your data transmission, and therefore know more of the right questions to ask when you are setting up your connections.

- Besides communications, Windows 98 provides other features in support of the mobile user. In support of "hot" Plug and Play, PC Cards are set up to allow a user to install and remove them while a computer is running. Hot docking allows laptops to be connected and disconnected from expansion adapters without loss of time. If you use more than one computer, the Windows 98 Briefcase helps you keep files synchronized without the need for a network.

KEY TERMS

- **Advanced Configuration and Power Interface (ACPI)** — A system BIOS feature that allows the operating system to direct power management activities.

- **application programming interface (API)** — A method of communication between application software and the operating system.

- **ADSL (asymmetrical digital subscriber line)** — Technology that allows data to flow over ordinary telephone lines at multimegabit speeds.

- **BIOS (basic input/output system)** — A method of communication between the operating system and the hardware.

- **BRI (Basic Rate Interface)** — The most common ISDN interface. It consists of two B channels (64 Kbps each) and a single D channel (16 Kbps).

- **CIS (card information structure)** — Details about a PC Card's purpose and settings.

- **CO (central office)** — A telephone company facility where switching equipment is located.

- **communications architecture** — The design of system software that controls communications activities.

- **demodulation** — The process of converting waveforms on a telephone line into the binary code (1s and 0s) that can be read by a computer.

- **Dial-Up Networking (DUN)** — A component of the operating system that allows users to connect to remote networks such as the Internet or private services.

- **docking** — Connecting a portable computer to a base station.
- **docking station** — A module that a portable computer can be connected to that may contain drive bays, ports, expansion slots, and a power supply.
- **driver** — Software that controls or emulates a hardware device.
- **hot docking** — Installing or removing a device while the PC is fully powered.
- **infrared** — A means of using light to transmit data between different computers or computer components.
- **Installation Wizard** — A method for Windows 98 to guide the user through the installation process for new components. Simple key questions are asked, and the software performs the rest of the required activities.
- **IP address** — Internet Protocol address. A unique number that identifies a host computer on a network.
- **ISP (Internet service provider)** — A company that provides consumer access to the Internet through dial-up or full-time connections.
- **ISDN (Integrated Services Digital Network)** — A completely digital form of telephone connections that is widely used for data and voice communications in Japan, the U.S., and Europe; ISDN offers higher bandwidth (one or two 64 Kbps channels are typical for most end-user implementations) and better signal quality than conventional analog modems, but is being overtaken by faster digital technologies, such as any of the digital subscriber line (DSL) technologies. Windows 98 includes built-in ISDN support.
- **kernel** — The portion of the operating system that handles the most basic of computing functions, such as managing access to the CPU by the rest of the operating system.
- **LAN (local area network)** — A group of computers connected in a manner that allows communication among all connected devices.
- **legacy** — Hardware or software that wasn't specifically designed to work with the current operating system. In Windows 98, backward compatibility is maintained for most legacy items.
- **modulation** — The process of converting from a digital signal of binary code (1s and 0s) to waveforms that resemble sound on a telephone line.
- **multilink** — A process that enables a dial-up connection using two modems or ISDN connections.
- **null modem** — A parallel or serial cable between two computers. Two of the wires in the cable are crossed, which makes the cable appear to be a modem to each computer.
- **PC card** — A removable device intended to be plugged into a PCMCIA slot. The term PC Card is a trademark of the PCMCIA.
- **PCMCIA (Personal Computer Memory Card International Association)** — The international association that sets the standards for functionality in PC Card devices.

- **PDA (personal digital assistant)** — Small computing devices most often used for contact and task management activities, e-mail, and even Web browsing. Examples include the PalmPilot and Rexx.

- **Plug and Play** — A specification that calls for hardware and peripherals to be installed without any significant technical adjustments. The idea is to simply plug it in, and it will function as designed.

- **port** — A socket used to connect devices such as printers and modems to the PC via a cable.

- **TAPI (Telephony Application Programming Interface)** — A method of communication between application software, the operating system, and telephony hardware (telephones, modems, ISDN adapters, etc.).

- **USB (universal serial bus)** — A serial interface for adding peripheral devices, serial and parallel ports, and input devices onto a single bus.

REVIEW QUESTIONS

1. In a multilink connection involving a 56 Kbps modem and a 33 Kbps modem, what speed will each modem use?

    a. each will use its own top speed

    b. the average of the two (44.5 Kbps)

    c. 33.6 Kbps

    d. the combined speed of both modems

2. The Windows Telephony Application Programming Interface was designed to (choose all correct answers):

    a. control your modems

    b. integrate telephone and data lines

    c. provide a consistent interface for telephone and data communication requirements

    d. address noise issues from telephone company switches

3. If you are connecting to a telephone line while you are traveling and want to use your calling card, which of the following is the best solution?

    a. Pick up the phone and dial all required numbers before connecting your modem to the telephone.

    b. Set up the Phone Dialer to speed dial your required numbers.

    c. Set up your calling card in the Dialing Properties of the Modem Properties dialog box.

    d. Have the network administrator at your office set up the LAN to call you wherever you are.

4. An ISDN connection can be divided into separate channels for voice and data communications. True or False?
5. Which of the following is true about ADSL technology?
    a. ADSL adapters will connect to TV cable.
    b. ADSL requires connections from a T1 or T3 line.
    c. ADSL can use a regular phone line.
    d. ADSL is slower than ISDN.
6. What is a docking station?
    a. an aid for synchronizing files
    b. a bay in a laptop computer that accepts various devices such as a CD-ROM drive, floppy drive, or spare battery
    c. a hardware component that a laptop is connected to, providing additional ports, expansion slots, and a power supply
7. The Multilink feature of Windows 98 allows you to increase the speed of your data transmission by:
    a. connecting two modems through a single phone line
    b. connecting one modem through multiple phone lines
    c. connecting multiple modems through multiple phone lines
    d. connecting multiple computers through a single cable
8. One drawback of Advanced Power Management through the BIOS is:
    a. It cannot manage power to monitors.
    b. It cannot manage USB devices.
    c. It cannot manage power to hard drives.
    d. It cannot suspend power to your laptop when your battery is nearly out of power.
9. A direct cable connection refers to:
    a. a connection between two PCs using a single cable
    b. connecting your cable TV line into your monitor for television viewing
    c. a system that allows you to connect multiple (more than two) computers in a small office network environment
    d. all of the above
10. Using Dial-Up Networking, you can access your company's LAN. True or False?
11. A new Dial-Up Networking connection must be created for each location you want to call from. True or False?
12. Which of the following best describes the purpose of the Windows Briefcase?
    a. file transfer over a network
    b. sets up dialing properties to your Internet service provider

c. synchronizes your files to the network server

d. monitors revisions to key files on multiple computers

13. Which of the following data transfer rates corresponds to a single ISDN B channel?

    a. 56.7 kbps

    b. 33.6 kbps

    c. 128 kpbs

    d. 64 kpbs

14. You can use HyperTerminal for which of the following purposes?

    a. transmitting pictures to a browser such as Internet Explorer

    b. connecting to a text-based bulletin board system

    c. troubleshooting security in your modem setup

    d. supporting hot docking of your laptop computer

15. Which of the following are components of an ISDN line? (Choose all correct answers.)

    a. two voice-only channels

    b. one signaling channel

    c. two data-only channels

    d. two channels that can be used for either data or voice communications

16. Hot docking takes advantage of which of the following features of Windows 98?

    a. hands-free configuration of dialing properties

    b. the Advanced Configuration Power Interface

    c. preconfigured multiple hardware configurations

    d. global modem properties

17. When you have a problem with your modem, what is the first thing you should check?

    a. physical cable connections

    b. correct program interfaces

    c. global modem properties

    d. version level of your modem driver

18. How do you activate the Add New Modem Wizard?

    a. from the Add New Hardware Wizard in Control Panel

    b. from the Add New Modem Wizard in Control Panel

    c. click on the Modems icon in Control Panel. In the Modems dialog box, click Add.

    d. from the driver provided by the modem manufacturer on a 3½-inch disk

19. How do you activate the Dial-Up Networking Wizard?
    a. Click Start, point to Settings, click Dial-Up Networking.
    b. from the Dial-Up Networking icon in Control Panel
    c. from the Dial-Up Networking icon on the default Windows 98 Desktop
    d. Click Start, point to Programs, point to Accessories, click Communication.
20. PC Cards are sometimes known as:
    a. PCMCIA cards
    b. cards that are installed inside a desktop computer
    c. cards that are connected to one of the ports of a desktop computer
    d. USB cards

HANDS-ON PROJECTS

This chapter discusses mobile computing; therefore, the Hands-On Projects concern tasks associated with laptop computers. However, none of these projects absolutely requires a laptop computer.

PROJECT 6-1

In this project, you will install and configure a new modem. You will need a laptop or desktop PC with Windows 98 already installed. If you are using a laptop computer, you will install a PCMCIA modem. (Remember, PCMCIA modems are now known as PC Cards.) If you are using a desktop computer, install the modem using the instructions provided by your modem manufacturer before beginning this project. The first two steps will allow you to delete your modem before restarting the process. You may also need your Windows 98 Installation CD.

The steps in this project relating to laptops are labeled with an "L," while the steps relating to desktops are labeled with a "D". Whether you are using a laptop (L) or a desktop (D) computer, please be careful to follow the steps that apply to you. If you have a desktop computer with a PC Card Modem and adapter, follow the instructions for the laptop computer.

1. (D) If you are using a desktop computer, start Windows 98 after installing your modem. If during startup, Windows 98 detects your modem, follow the prompts to install the modem. Use your Windows 98 Installation CD if required. If you are using a laptop computer, start with Step 2.
2. (D, L) Click **Start**, point to **Settings**, click **Control Panel**, then double-click the **Modems** icon. If no modem is installed, the Install New Modem wizard opens automatically, in which case you can skip to Step 4. If a modem is installed on your computer, the Modem properties dialog box opens, in which case you can proceed to Step 3.

3. (D, L) For either type of computer, highlight your modem in the Modem Properties dialog box and click **Remove**.
4. (D, L) Click **Add**. The Install New Modem wizard opens. If you have a laptop computer, click the **PCMCIA** option button, then click **Next**. (If you do not see a PCMCIA option button, then you are using a computer that does not accommodate PC cards. Skip to Step 10.) The following dialog box prompts you to insert the PC card.
5. (L) Insert the card. PC card slots are typically located in the side of a laptop, usually behind a small access door. The slot is about one inch narrower than a 3½-inch disk. Be careful when you install the card; it should seat easily into the socket. If you force the card, you could damage the connector inside your laptop computer. When the card is fully seated, you should be able to close the access door over the card.
6. (L) If the PC card is Plug and Play compatible and if there is a custom driver for your PC card, the Add New Hardware Wizard opens. It informs you that Windows 98 will now search for drivers for your PC Card. Click **Next**. Otherwise, skip to Step 10.
7. (L) On the next page, choose **Search for the best driver for your device** and click **Next**. On the next page, you can select the locations where Windows 98 should look for drivers.
8. (L) Insert your Windows 98 Installation CD-ROM, select only the **CD-ROM drive** option. Deselect the other boxes and click **Next**. If the wizard finds an appropriate driver, it names it on the next page. If it does not find a driver, Windows 98 will prompt you to enter the manufacturer and name of your modem. In this case, skip to Step 11.
9. (L) Unless you know that there is a problem with this specific driver, approve it by clicking **Next**. On the next page, Windows 98 tells you that it has finished the installation. Click **Finish** to exit the Add New Hardware Wizard. Click **Finish** at the bottom of the Install New Modems dialog box when installation is complete, and then skip to Step 13.
10. (D, L) Select the **Don't detect my modem; I will select it from a list** option and click **Next**.
11. (D, L) You will see a dialog box where you can choose a manufacturer and model for your modem. Scroll the list in the left-hand pane, and select the manufacturer of your modem. A selection of models associated with that manufacturer will appear on the right side.
12. (D, L) If your modem is included in the list of models, select it and click **Next**. If your modem is not listed, insert the 3½-inch disk included with the modem, then click **Have Disk**. (You may then be prompted to select a port to use for your modem from a list. Select a port and click Next.) Windows 98 will now install the modem drivers for you.
13. (D, L) Return to the Modem Properties dialog box. The new modem now appears in the list of installed devices. Next, you can examine the modem's properties to see if you need to change any settings.
14. (D, L) Click **Properties**.
15. (D, L) Review the port, speaker volume, and maximum speed settings.

16. (D, L) Click **OK** to return to the Modem Properties dialog box.
17. (D, L) Click the **Diagnostics** tab. Highlight the port associated with the modem that you just installed and click **More Info**. If your modem is properly connected to your computer, you will see a series of "AT" commands in the More Info dialog box. AT commands are communication commands that check the response of your modem to specific commands. Click **OK** to return to the Modem Properties dialog box.
18. (D, L) Click **Close** to exit the Modem Properties dialog box.

PROJECT 6-2

In this project, you will connect two computers together with a direct cable connection and synchronize files between the two using the Briefcase. Before you can complete this project, you need to complete the steps for enabling file sharing, provided in the chapter. You will need two PCs running Windows 98 and one of the following types of cable:

- A null-modem parallel cable, such as an older LapLink or InterLink cable. ECP parallel cables are acceptable if they are null-modem cables. *Note*: It is not good enough to have a parallel cable with plugs on both ends. It must be a null-modem cable. The wires for 2 of the 25 pins of this cable are crossed for this purpose. If your printer is connected to the only available parallel port, you will have to disconnect your printer cable before proceeding.

- An RS-232 (serial null-modem) cable. This cable will have nine sockets on both ends. If you have a mouse or trackball or similar device connected to this port, you will have to remove it before proceeding.

1. Click **Start**, point to **Settings**, and click **Control Panel**.
2. Double-click the **Add/Remove Programs** icon.
3. Click the **Windows Setup** tab. Windows 98 will take a moment to search for the currently installed features.
4. In the Components list, click **Communications**, and then click **Details**. The Communications dialog box opens.
5. If Direct Cable Connection is not already checked (that is, if the Direct Cable Connection files were not automatically installed along with Windows 98), check it now.
6. Insert the Windows 98 installation CD into the CD-ROM drive, click **OK**, then click **OK** again to exit the Add/Remove Programs dialog box. If required, the Direct Cable Connection files are copied from the Windows 98 installation CD.
7. Next, you will use the Direct Cable Connection Wizard to configure your connection. Click **Start**, point to **Programs**, point to **Accessories**, point to **Communications**, and then click **Direct Cable Connection**. Assuming this is the first time you have configured a DCC, the Direct Cable Connection Wizard opens, specifying options for Host and Guest. Otherwise, click **Change** to get to this dialog box. Here you can

specify whether this computer will be the host computer (the computer you want to access) or the guest computer (the computer you want to use to access resources on the host computer).

8. Click either the **Host** or the **Guest** option button, and then click **Next**. Windows 98 configures the available ports.
9. If there is more than one port available for this operation, you will see a list in which you can select the port you want to use. You will probably have a selection of "COM" and "LPT" ports. If you are using a parallel port, choose LPT1. If you are using a serial port, choose COM1.
10. Plug in the cable, and then click **Next**.
11. If you are configuring the Host and have not yet set up File and Print Sharing, you see a dialog box indicating that File and Print Sharing is required for a guest to use your files or printer. Click **File and Print Sharing** to open the Network dialog box. Click **File and Print Sharing** here as well. In the File and Print Sharing dialog box, enable both file and printer sharing, click **OK**, then click **OK** again to exit the Network dialog box. Then restart your computer when prompted and begin again with Step 7.
12. If the process is successful, Windows 98 will inform you of this, reminding you to set up the other computer as either the host or guest.
13. Repeat Steps 1 through 9 on the second computer, choosing Host if you previously chose Guest, or choosing Guest if you chose Host in Step 7.
14. Click **Finish** on the Host computer, and then click **Finish** on the Guest computer. Windows 98 will attempt to make the connection. If it is successful, you will see a folder on your guest computer named after your host computer.
15. On the Guest computer, copy from the host computer to the Briefcase a file that you want to work on.
16. Make changes to that file either on the original computer or from within the Briefcase.
17. In the Update New Briefcase dialog box, click **Update**.

PROJECT 6-3

In this project, you will set up Dial-Up Networking to contact an existing nationwide ISP from a new location (such as a vacation spot) with your laptop PC. You will need to know your username and password, your local access number, and a local access number for your vacation destination. You need a PC with Windows 98 installed. Although this project is designed for users with a laptop PC, you can do this project with any PC with a modem and Windows 98 installed.

1. Click **Start**, point to **Programs**, point to **Accessories**, point to **Communications**, and then click **Dial-Up Networking**.

2. Double-click the **Make New Connection** icon. The Make New Connection Wizard opens. If you have not installed a modem on your computer, the Install New Modem Wizard is opened. Click Cancel in this dialog box and again in the Make New Connection dialog box. Repeat Project 6-1 to install a modem on your computer.
3. In the "Type a name for the computer you are dialing" text box, enter a name for the connection.
4. In the "Select a device" list box, select the modem of your choice.
5. Click **Next**.
6. Enter the local access area code and telephone number for your ISP, verify that the country code matches your location, and then click **Next**. A dialog box appears indicating that you have successfully created a new Dial-Up Networking connection.
7. Click **Finish**. An icon for your new connection appears in the Dial-Up Networking window.
8. Drag the new icon to the desktop to create a shortcut icon.
9. Double-click the connection shortcut icon on the desktop. The Connect To dialog box opens.
10. Enter your ISP username and password.
11. If you wish to save the password so you don't have to type it every time you use the shortcut, select the **Save password** check box.
12. Click **Dial Properties**. The Dialing Properties dialog box opens.
13. Click **New** to create a dialing location for your vacation location.
14. In the "I am dialing from" box, type a name for your new location, and then enter the applicable data for your vacation location, including country, area code, access codes for local and long distance, and a code to disable call waiting, if required.
15. Click **OK** to return to the Connect To dialog box.
16. Verify that the location you just created is displayed in the Dial from list box. In the future, whenever you open the Connect To dialog box, you can use this list box to select the location you're dialing from.
17. In the Phone number text box, type the local access number for your vacation location. Now you're ready to connect to your ISP from your vacation location.
18. Click **Connect**.

CASE PROJECTS

1. You've recently moved to an old Victorian farmhouse 30 miles from your workplace, and need to set up a home office for telecommuting several times per week. You'll want to be able to connect to the Internet, as well as to your company LAN. You'll regularly be downloading/uploading large documents or new versions of software from your desktop PC at work to/from your desktop PC at home. What information

is important to keep in mind when choosing what type of service to request from the telephone company? Will your file transfer activities affect your decision regarding what type of communications hardware/services to use? Why, or why not? What other considerations might you have?

2. As a California-based employee of an international consulting firm, you've been assigned to help deploy a new rapid development system at several key clients' headquarters in New York, London, and Frankfurt. During your work, you will have your laptop PC with you. You have been given direct dial-in access to your company LAN, as well as access to the private consultants' area on the corporate Web site. You have a database of key information that will remain on your desktop workstation, as well as a suite of documents that you'll be able to take with you to support your installation tasks. Your department's administrative assistant will be updating those documents as final changes are made to the product, which is in the last stages of beta testing as you prepare to leave. What preparations do you need to make before leaving, in order to have access to all the information and most up-to-date documentation while you're gone? Explain any changes that you will make to your laptop before going, and how, through the methods discussed in this chapter, you will be able to access the data without intervention by others.

3. Your boss has recently asked you to purchase two laptop computers. He has heard bad stories about power consumption and the lack of expandability. He has also heard about something called ACPI and how it maximizes the life of a laptop computer battery. Before purchasing the two computers, you need to write a report addressing his concerns.

CHAPTER SEVEN

WINDOWS 98 SERVER SERVICES

This chapter discusses Windows 98 tools for two of the revolutions in corporate communications: small-scale Web sites deployed over intranets, and remote access. An **intranet** is a network that has the TCP/IP characteristics of the Internet, but is usually limited to a single organization. Intranets provide a cost-effective means of communication within organizations, and are being used to standardize the way employees communicate with each other. As explained in this chapter, you can create an intranet Web site on a Windows 98 computer using the many features of the Personal Web Server.

Remote access refers to a situation in which a network user accesses the network from sites away from the office. With the Windows 98 Remote Access Server, employees can work from any location and still remain connected to an internal company network. Until recently, the benefits of remote access were limited to those organizations that could afford Windows NT. (Windows NT Server includes applications such as Internet Information Server and Site Server that you can use to manage and monitor Web sites.) As you will learn, Remote Access Server for Windows NT meets requirements well beyond the capabilities of Windows 98.

AFTER READING THIS CHAPTER AND COMPLETING THE EXERCISES YOU WILL BE ABLE TO:

- Install Personal Web Server
- Create a small-scale Web site using the Web Publishing Wizard
- Manage files and permissions for the Web site
- Configure Remote Access through Remote Access Server
- Share Files and Printers through Remote Access Server

PERSONAL WEB SERVER

Personal Web Server (PWS), which is included on the Windows 98 installation CD, allows you to create and manage a small-scale Web site such as you might find on a company's intranet. A Web site that you create using PWS may consist of only one home page, or it may include a number of pages linked to a home page. You manage the Personal Web Server through a tool known as the Personal Web Manager (PWM). Through the PWM, you can create basic home pages, attach specific files to your Web site, manage access to different parts of your site, and monitor Web traffic. With a limit of 10 simultaneous connections, PWS is not intended for use as a large-scale Web server. It is intended for small business intranet sites or as a test and development platform to be used before a site is moved to a permanent host. In the next section, you will learn about related programs that are intended for larger-scale Web sites.

COMPARATIVE FEATURES

Microsoft has developed Web management tools for a broad range of markets. These tools include Internet Information Server for Windows NT Server, Personal Web Server for Windows NT Workstation, and Personal Web Server for Windows 98. They are all used for sharing files over a network. Personal Web Server 4.0 for Windows 98 is intended to be the entry-level product to the world of creating Web sites. The files you create using these tools can be viewed in browsers such as Internet Explorer 4.0 or Netscape Communicator 4.0.

All three Microsoft Internet tools are disk- and memory-intensive applications. They entail a great deal of file accessing, which in turn requires maximum performance from your hard disks. (As you will learn in Chapter 8, Windows 98 can use a facility known as VCACHE to store frequently accessed files in RAM.) As they entail very little actual processing, a fast CPU is not as important. When you are using any of these tools as a Web server, a dedicated machine is recommended. Table 7-1 lists some of the differences among these three tools:

Table 7-1 Differences Among Web Server Tools

	PWS for Windows 98	PWS for Windows NT Workstation	Internet Information Server
Maximum number of connections	10	10	Not software limited
FTP service	No	Yes	Yes
Publishing sources	Local only	Local and network	Local and network
Authentication	None	Basic or Windows NT Challenge/Response (requires encryption)	Basic or Windows NT Challenge/Response (requires encryption)

In the next section, you will learn how to install Personal Web Server on your Windows 98 Computer. If you have installed another version of Personal Web Server before, you should uninstall that version first. As you complete the installation process, you will learn about the different programs that can be installed along with Personal Web Server for Windows 98.

INSTALLING PERSONAL WEB SERVER

In this section, you will learn how to install Windows 98 PWS. The following steps require access to a Windows 98 computer and a Windows 98 installation CD. You will also need a hard disk with at least 40 MB of free space. It may take some time to complete this section, but when you are finished, you will have a good feel for the possibilities offered by Windows 98 PWS. In the following instructions, do not select a check box unless the step explicitly asks you to do so.

Before proceeding, you should uninstall any previous version of Personal Web Server 4.0, even if it was installed for Windows 95.

If you are working on a Windows 98 dual-boot computer with Windows NT already installed, chances are that Internet Information Server (IIS) is also installed on that computer. Both PWS and IIS publish to the same folders, which could be problematic. Therefore, if you need to use a computer that has both operating systems installed, ask your instructor or network administrator for permission and help for uninstalling Internet Information Server from Windows NT before you continue. If you are the Network Administrator, IIS is the preferred application. You will learn about dual booting your computer with Windows NT and Windows 98 in Chapter 12.

1. Put the Windows 98 installation CD in your CD-ROM drive.
2. Click Start, and then click Run.
3. In the Run text box, type *x*:\add-ons\pws\setup.exe, where *x*: represents the drive letter assigned to your CD-ROM drive, and then click OK. The first Setup Wizard dialog box opens, which describes some of the features of Personal Web Server.
4. Click Next to continue to the next dialog box, where you can specify minimum typical, or custom installation options based on your needs and available disk space.

5. Click Custom to continue to the Select Components page, shown in Figure 7-1. In the next few steps, you will examine the components of PWS by examining the options in the Components list box. Do not actually change any settings relating to these options unless specifically instructed to do so.

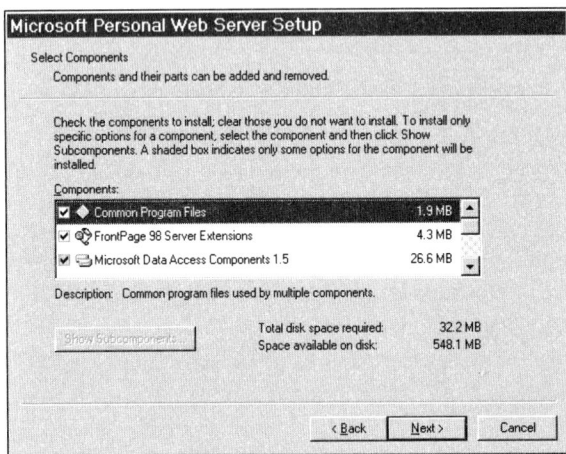

Figure 7-1 Select Components page of the PWS Setup Wizard

6. Click the Common Program Files check box. A Windows Setup dialog box appears with a list of components that you cannot install unless the Common Program Files are installed.

7. Click No. (If you accidentally click Yes, all of the boxes in the Custom Setup dialog box will be unchecked. To restore the original setup, click Back, and then click Custom again.)

8. Click Front Page Server Extensions to select it, and then review the description of this component in the space below the Components list. This particular option links the Web page authoring application, Front Page Express, to PWS.

9. Click Microsoft Data Access Components 1.5 to select it, and then click Show Subcomponents. The Microsoft Data Access Components 1.5 dialog box opens.

10. Verify that Data Sources is selected in the Subcomponents list, and then click Show Subcomponents again. The Data Sources dialog box opens, as shown in Figure 7-2. This dialog box contains a list of some of the databases (such as Oracle, SQL Server, and Microsoft Access) that you can access through PWS.

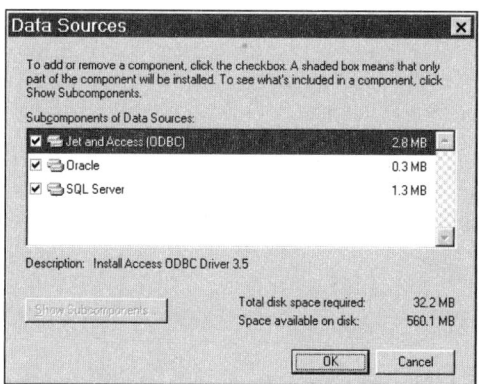

Figure 7-2 Personal Web Server Data Sources

11. Click Cancel, and then click Cancel again to return to the Microsoft Personal Web Server Setup Wizard.

12. Click Microsoft Message Queue (MSMQ) to select it. In Chapter 5, you learned that message delivery in TCP/IP may not be guaranteed. When a message is sent between two machines with MSMQ installed, your computer keeps a copy of the message until the receiving computer acknowledges receipt.

13. Scroll down the Components list if necessary, and then click Personal Web Server (PWS) to select it. The grayed check box indicates that not all of the components of PWS will be installed.

14. Click Show Subcomponents. The Personal Web Server (PWS) dialog box opens.

15. Verify that Documentation is selected in the subcomponents list, and then click Show Subcomponents again. In the Documentation dialog box, you can see that the Active Server Pages documentation will not be installed. **Active Server Pages** are the miniprograms, or applets, that animate Web pages developed on Microsoft systems. If you have room on your hard disk for documentation describing this feature, click the Active Server Pages check box.

16. Click OK to return to the Personal Web Server (PWS) dialog box.

17. In the list of subcomponents, click Personal Web Manager to select it, and verify that a check appears in its check box. Later in this chapter, you will learn to use Personal Web Manager to create and administer a Web site on your computer.

18. Click OK. You return to the Microsoft Personal Web Server Setup Wizard.

19. Click the next component, Microsoft Transaction Server (MTS), to select it. **Microsoft Transaction Server** is similar to the Microsoft Message Queue (MSMQ), but focuses on changes to a database. MTS makes sure that a change to a database is complete before it is written to disk.

20. Click the next component, Visual InterDev RAD (Rapid Application Development) Remote Deployment Support. You can use this tool for creating dynamic Web applications. For example, a search engine may use Visual InterDev to create a Web page of links based on keywords that you may have entered.

21. Now that you have browsed through all of the options available for installing PWS, click Next.

22. In Figure 7-3, you will see entries for three different services. The only one of these three services that can be used on a Windows 98 computer is the WWW Service, which publishes your Web pages on the Internet or on an intranet. The other services are available in the more fully featured application, Internet Information Server for Windows NT. Assuming this directory is satisfactory, click Next.

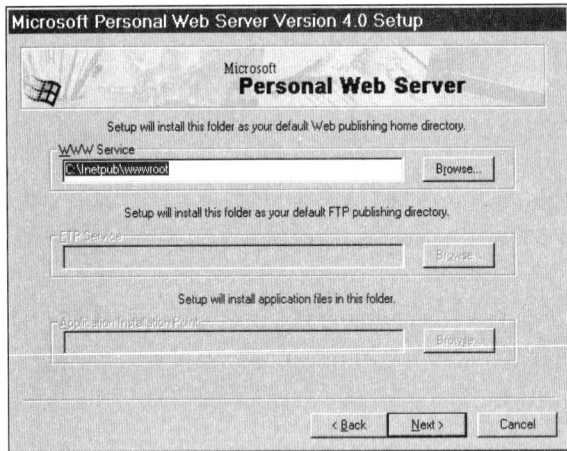

Figure 7-3 Services for Personal Web Server

Microsoft's various Web server applications (which you learned about earlier) are based on the same programming code, which means that the setup process for these applications is similar for all three. When installing the lower-level versions of these applications, you may see useful features. However, you may not be able to use them unless you upgrade to the higher-level program.

23. Next, you see the installation directory for Microsoft Transaction Server. If this is satisfactory, click Next. Setup copies the required files from the Windows 98 Installation CD to your hard drive. This process may take several minutes.

24. When Setup has finished copying files, click Finish.

25. Click Yes to restart your computer.

This section included a lot of steps designed to teach you about the different features that can be installed with Windows 98 Personal Web Server. It is possible that you may have inadvertently selected the wrong components in the process. If, in the remainder of this book, you find that you have a problem with your installation, you can uninstall PWS and then reinstall it. To uninstall PWS, click Start, point to Programs, point to Internet Explorer, point to Personal Web Server, and then click Personal Web Server Setup. In the first Setup Wizard page, click Next; in the next page, click Remove All. To reinstall PWS, repeat Steps 1–4 of this section. At Step 5, click Typical instead of Custom. This will install PWS in a working configuration.

PERSONAL WEB MANAGER

By installing Personal Web Server, you have effectively created a Web site. At this point, however, your Web site doesn't contain any Web pages and cannot be accessed by other users. Now that you have installed Personal Web Server, you are ready to start making it (and your Web site) functional via Personal Web Manager.

Personal Web Manager allows you to manage the Web site that you have just set up on your Windows 98 computer. It is automatically included when you install Personal Web Server. Different features allow you to measure traffic, create a home page, incorporate different files, and set different permissions on different parts of your Web server. To open Personal Web Manager, click Start, point to Programs, point to Internet Explorer, point to Personal Web Server, and then click Personal Web Manager. (If you see a Tip of the Day dialog box, click Close.) This opens the Personal Web Manager window, shown in Figure 7-4.

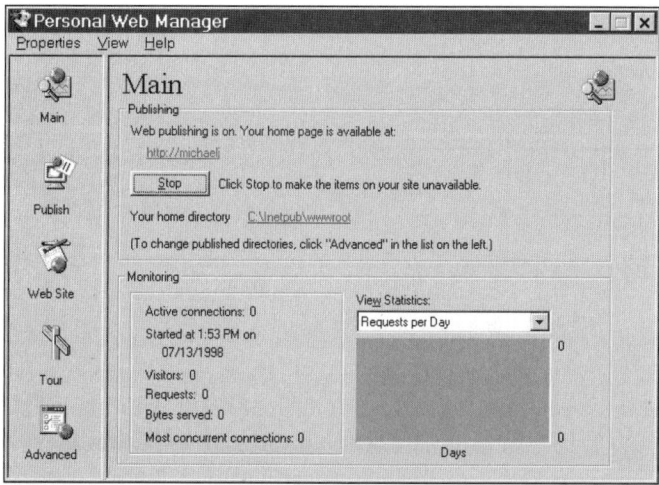

Figure 7-4 Personal Web Manager

In the left-hand pane of Personal Web Manager, click Web Site. If Personal Web Manager is already properly configured, you see the Home Page Wizard in the right-hand pane. If Personal Web Manager is not already properly configured, this will lead to an error caused by the fact that Personal Web Manager is trying to reach your Web site, not realizing that the Web site actually resides on your computer.

To fix this problem, you need to modify your Hosts.sam file in Notepad, as follows: click Start, point to Programs, point to Accessories, click Notepad, and then click File on the menu bar. The Open dialog box appears. In the File name text box, type C:\Windows\Hosts.sam, and then press Enter. As shown in Figure 7-5, insert the following entries: 127.0.0.1 localhost and 127.0.0.1 *your_computer_name,* where *your_computer_name* stands for the name of your computer. (If you don't know the name of your computer, you can find it on the Identification tab of the Network applet.) Then click File on the menu bar, click Save, and close Notepad. Next, you need to change the name of this file from "hosts.sam" to "hosts" in Windows Explorer.

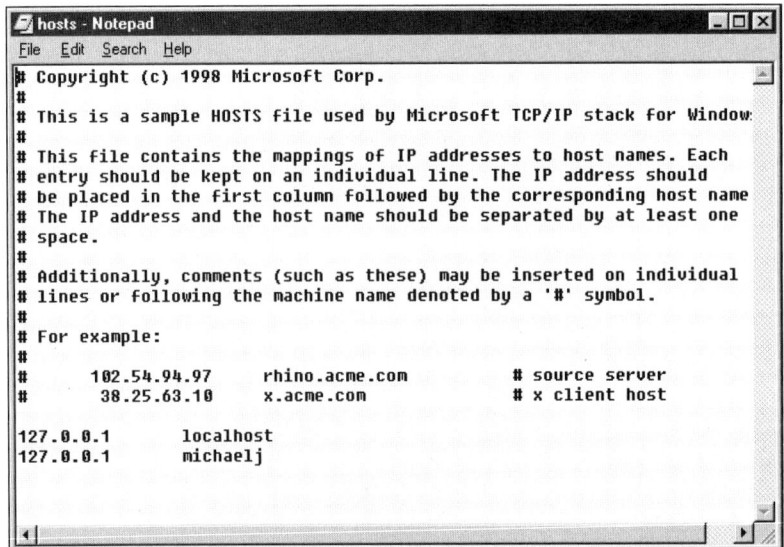

Figure 7-5 Hosts file

 You may recognize the number 127.0.0.1 as an IP address (explained in Chapter 5). In fact, this is a special IP address, known as a loopback address, that specifies resources on the local computer.

In the next sections, you will learn to use Personal Web Manager to help you create a Web site. You will start by creating a home page, then attach the files of your choice, modify permissions on these files, and finally measure the traffic through your Web site.

Creating a Home Page

Now that you have installed Personal Web Server on your local computer, you can start making your Web site operational. The first thing that you need is a home page. In the left-hand pane of Personal Web Manager (PWM), click the Web Site icon. The Home Page Wizard, opens, as shown in Figure 7-6.

Click the wizard or the forward arrow to move to the next page. The first time you do this, you may see a security alert dialog box warning you about the risk of viruses from untrusted sites (which you learned about in Chapter 4). Because you can assume your own computer is a trusted site, click the "In the future do not show the warning for this zone" check box to select it. On some computers, you may then see a dialog box indicating that you cannot connect to your computer in offline mode. Click cancel. You can continue the process of creating a Web page in the Hands-on Projects at the end of the chapter.

After you create your home page, you can view it in the Internet Explorer browser, as follows. In the Address box near the top of the browser, enter *http://<my_computer_name>*, using the name of your computer, which you found earlier in this chapter. Then press Enter. Internet Explorer displays your home page. Even though you didn't include the file name of your home page in the address, Internet Explorer was still able to call up your home page. This is because the home page that you created is saved in two files: Default.htm and Default.asp. By default, PWS calls up these files whenever you go to the *http://<my_computer_name>* address.

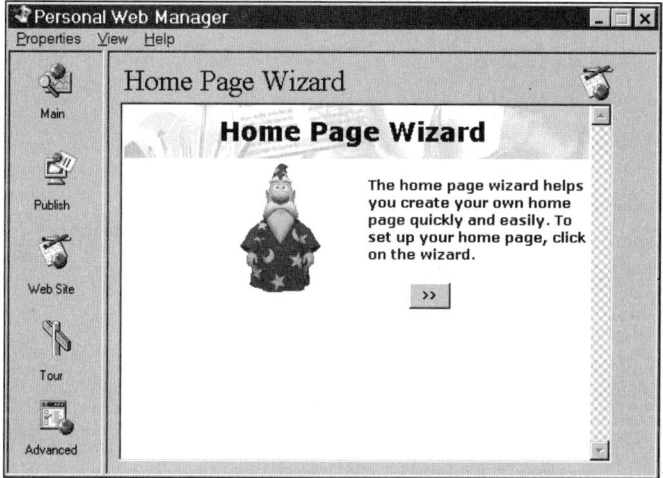

Figure 7-6 Personal Web Manager Home Page Wizard

Most home pages are typically made up of several files. To see the files that contribute to your home page, return to your home page in Internet Explorer. In the menu bar, click View, then click Source. Windows Notepad opens, displaying the Hypertext Markup Language (HTML) code for your home page. (HTML is the language used to create Web pages.) Within the HTML code, you will find at least the following two files: default.asp and layout.css. You created this HTML code using the Personal Web Server Home Page Wizard. In the early days of Web pages, before tools like this wizard existed, Web page authors had to learn HTML code and then type it line by line.

The Personal Web Manager Home Page Wizard is based on the Microsoft Web page authoring application, Front Page 98. Windows 98 provides access to a simplified version of this program, known as Front Page Express. To learn more about creating Web pages with Front Page 98, Front Page Express, or any other Web page authoring application, consult your local bookstore, where you should find numerous books on the topic.

Posting to a Web Site

Now that you have created a home page, you can begin to link it to the files that you want others to see. In the left-hand pane of Personal Web Manager (PWM), click Publish. Despite the name, the Publish option does not put your Web site on a network. It simply allows you to link your home page to other files stored on your computer. PWM will not let you continue unless you have already created a home page. Assuming that your home page is ready, the wizard will allow you to select any file on your computer. The remaining steps for linking files to your home page are provided in the Hands-on Projects at the end of this chapter.

When you installed Personal Web Server, you specified the home directory for your Web site. (The default home directory is C:\Inetpub.) Any files that you post (that is, link to your home page) are copied from their original locations on your hard disk to the C:\Inetpub\webpub directory. Once you are finished with the Publishing Wizard (following the steps provided in the Hands-on Projects), you can open Internet Explorer, and view a new link on your home page entitled "View my published documents," as shown in Figure 7-7.

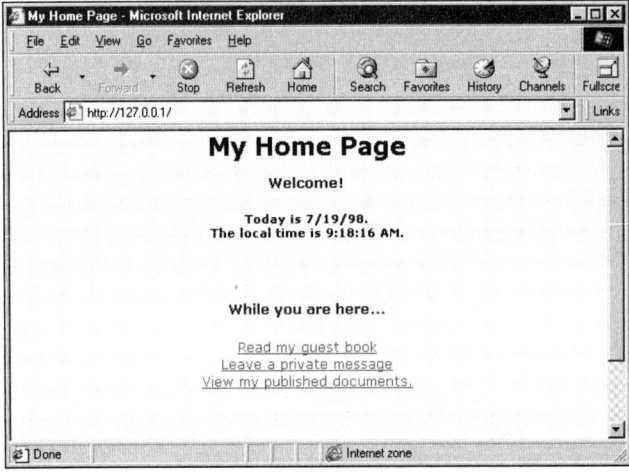

Figure 7-7 Homepage with link to published documents

Note that simply creating this link on your home page does not actually make it functional. If you try to use the link (either by clicking it or by typing *http://<my_computer_name>/webpub* in the Address box), you will see a page entitled "Directory Listing Denied." You see this page because, by default, Personal Web Server does not allow anyone to look through the different files on your hard disk. If you want to give users the right to view the files in your directory, you need to adjust the relevant permissions settings in Personal Web Server, as explained in the next section.

Advanced Settings

In this section, you will learn to control access to the different documents and directories stored on your Web site. You access these settings via the Advanced icon, in the left-hand pane of PWM. When you click this icon, you see a tree of virtual directories in the right-hand pane. A **virtual directory** is a directory of the files associated with your Web site. It does not necessarily correlate with the directories on your hard drive. Currently the Home directory is selected in the virtual directory tree. To see the actual directory on your hard drive that corresponds to this virtual directory, click Edit Properties to open the Edit Directory dialog box, shown in Figure 7-8.

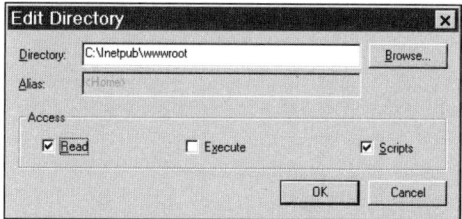

Figure 7-8   Personal Web Server Edit Directory dialog box

The actual directory is shown in the Directory text box. Within the Edit Directory dialog box, you can specify the type of access you want to be associated with this directory. In some cases you will want to specify more than one type of access. You can choose from three different types of access:

- **Read**: Gives any user the right to read or download files from this directory. To keep your Web site secure, you should disable read permission on any directory with programming files, such as .exe, .cgi, and .dll. If outside users can read these files, they can gather clues on how to disable your computer.

- **Execute**: Gives users the right to run a program accessible through the Web page. This is appropriate for a directory with .exe or .dll files.

- **Scripts**: A special version of the Execute permission for applets known as scripts. Typical scripts include **Active Server Pages** (.asp) written to animate Web sites in the ActiveX programming language. You do not need both Execute and Scripts permission on a directory.

 Generally, you don't need any knowledge of programming to manage Windows 98 computers. But it is useful to be able to recognize different types of programs. **Common Gateway Interface** (.cgi) files are similar to the dynamic link library (.dll) files that you learned about in Chapter 3. They help different programs interact with the operating system. While one .dll file in Windows 98 can be loaded to serve multiple programs, one copy of a .cgi program has to be loaded for every program that requires a copy.

At the end of the last section, you saw that simply creating a link to other files does not automatically make that link functional. To configure your Web site so users can actually view the list of files, you need to click the Allow Directory Browsing check box in the lower-left corner of the Advanced Options pane to select it. After you have enabled this option, clicking the "View my published documents" link in your Web page should take you to a page like the one shown in Figure 7-9. To go from this list back to your home page, click [to parent directory].

228 Chapter 7

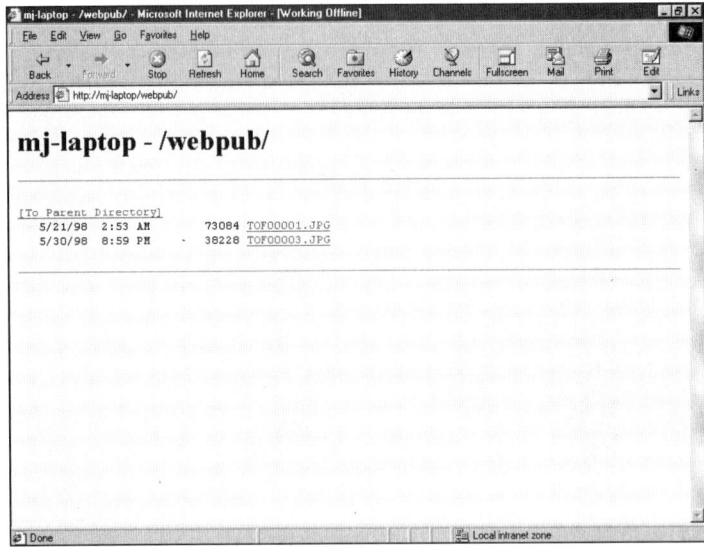

Figure 7-9 Web page displaying published files

You can also use the PWM advanced settings to change the way your home page files are named. By default, PWS names these files Default.htm and Default.asp. But what happens when you turn off this default?

To find out, return to Personal Web Manager. Click Enable Default Document to uncheck this option. Return to Internet Explorer and click Refresh in the toolbar. You should now see a listing of all files and virtual directories to which you have assigned Read permission. Now when users browse your Web site, they can use this list to browse through any files to which you have assigned Read permission.

You have learned to create a home page, link files to that home page, and manage permissions on the various virtual directories in your Web site. In the next section, you will learn to monitor the traffic through your Web site.

Monitoring Web Site Traffic

The Personal Web Manager offers some limited tools to help you monitor traffic through your Web site. The science of monitoring traffic on a Web site involves some very specific definitions:

- **Hits**: Any attempt to retrieve content from a Web site. A Web page with pictures or graphics comes from a number of different files. Thus if a visitor to your site opens up a Web page with nine pictures, this results in 10 hits (one for the Web page itself, and nine for the pictures).

- **Requests**: Any successful attempt to retrieve content. In other words, a successful hit. If you have experience with browsing the Internet, you know that when you go to a Web page, the pictures or graphics may not load every time. A hit becomes a request only when the file is loaded into the user's browser.

- **Visits**: A visit starts when a user goes to a Web site and ends when he or she leaves that site.

- To view the traffic monitoring settings, click Main in the left-hand pane. Near the bottom of the right-hand pane, click the down arrow next to "View Statistics." As you can see in Figure 7-10, you can use this arrow to view traffic statistics based on the number of requests per day, the number of requests per hour, the number of visitors per day, or the number of visitors per hour.

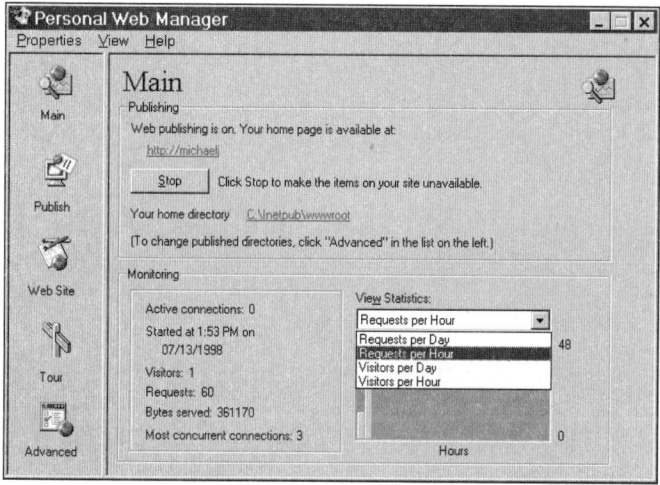

Figure 7-10 Selecting a type of Web site traffic statistic

The traffic monitoring features included with Personal Web Server are based on another Microsoft application known as **Site Server**. There are three versions of Site Server available for Windows NT, known as Site Server Express, Site Server, and Site Server Enterprise Edition. Using Site Server, you can collect data on each visitor's preferred pages within your Web site. In addition you can collect data about your Web site users in a wide variety of categories, from the user's geographic location to the time of the visit. By combining these statistics, you can get a fairly clear picture of your audience.

If the Web site that you develop through Personal Web Server becomes popular, you can upgrade to a more powerful Web server program. One option is to upgrade to Personal Web Server for Windows NT Workstation 4.0. You could also upgrade to a current version of Windows NT Server and the accompanying Web server application, known as Internet Information Server.

You have just set up a Web site, including links to certain files. In the next section, you will learn to share hard disk folders over your network, through the Internet Explorer interface.

WEB SHARING

In Chapter 6, you learned to share folders using File and Print Sharing, the traditional way to share information between computers. As different organizations move towards using intranets, the browser is becoming the new way to share information between computers. Once you set up Personal Web Server, you can set up Web Sharing as follows: Click Start, point to Programs, then click Windows Explorer. In the left-hand pane, highlight a disk or folder that you want to share. On the menu bar, click File, click Properties, then click the Web Sharing tab in the properties dialog box of your folder. Your result should be similar to the interface shown in Figure 7-11.

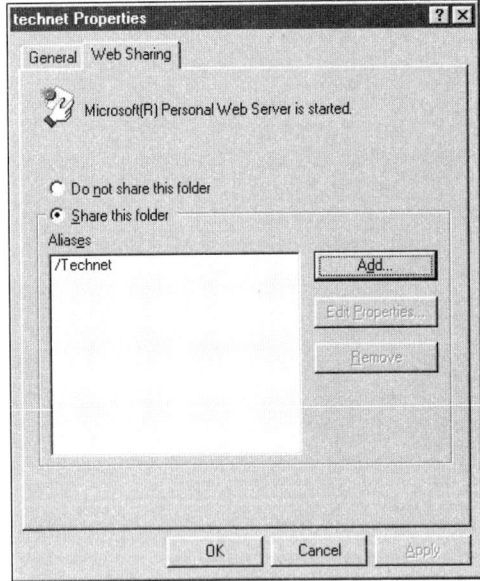

Figure 7-11 Web Sharing

Now click Share this folder. If it is already selected, click Add. The Edit Alias dialog box opens, which includes options identical to those shown in Figure 7-8. Type a name in the Alias dialog box. If Directory Browsing is allowed in Personal Web Server, others can use this alias to look at the folder that you are sharing. Next, you need to open Internet Explorer and type *http:// <my_computer_name>/alias* in the Address text box, where *my_computer_name* stands for the name of your computer. Figure 7-12 includes the list of files in the directory with the alias technet in the computer named mj-laptop.

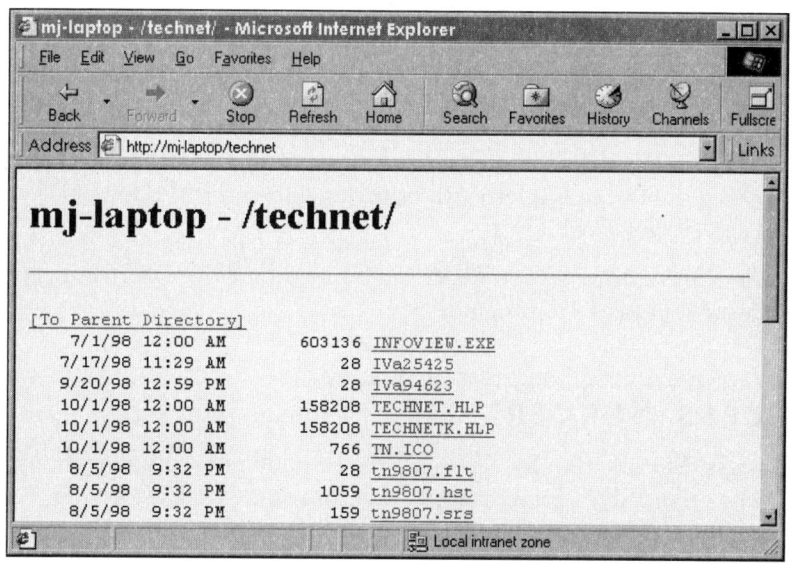

Figure 7-12 Browsing to a Web shared directory

Now that you have created a Web site, you might be tempted to connect it to the Internet immediately. This is possible, but not advisable. In the next section, you will learn why.

CONNECTING YOUR WEB SITE

Personal Web Server 4.0 for Windows 98 is intended for small-scale use. It is useful for testing a Web site on a local area network (LAN) or for intranet communication within a small organization. However, it is generally not a good idea to connect a PWS Web site directly to the Internet. In part, this has to do with the requirements for connecting a Web site to the Internet.

First of all, you need to acquire a fully-qualified Internet domain name (such as *www.thatwaswhatiwanted.com*). You also need a stable IP address, so that Internet domain name servers (discussed in Chapter 5) can properly direct users to your site. If you normally connect to the Internet through a standard consumer ISP, you most likely do not have a stable IP address; instead, you are probably assigned a different IP address every time you connect.

An ISP that specializes in supporting Web sites for business can help you get a domain name and a stable IP address. You can arrange for the ISP to link the Internet to your PWS Web site through this domain name and IP address.

However, even if you go to the trouble of acquiring a domain name and IP address for your PWS Web site, you still have several other hurdles to clear. The first has to do with the number of users who can connect to your site. If your site is on a LAN, PWS allows for 10 simultaneous connections. However, to connect your site to the Internet, you need to use

Windows 98 Remote Access Server (RAS). As you will learn in the next section, Windows 98 RAS allows only one connection at a time. This is not enough.

In order to get the full 10 simultaneous connections for a PWS Web site on the Internet, you need to make your Internet connection through Windows NT Server, rather than through Windows 98 RAS. And if you're going to go to that much trouble, it's just as easy to set up your Web site through Internet Information Server for Windows NT, which offers more features and greater flexibility.

As you will learn in the next section, RAS can be used to allow external users to connect to and access your Windows 98 computer.

REMOTE ACCESS SERVER

Remote Access Server (RAS) allows direct computer-to-computer communication across a modem or an ISDN-based adapter. Also known as Dial-Up Server, RAS is typically used to transfer files between a work and home computer. With the proper security setup, you can use Windows 98 RAS to access your Windows 98 computer remotely. In addition, if your Windows 98 computer is connected to a Windows NT or Novell NetWare network, you can then access your normal network resources, almost as if you were sitting at your desk in the office.

A user who dials into a computer using RAS can access any and all of the resources on the host computer that have been shared, including printers, hard drives, and files. Each resource may require a separate password. You will learn more about sharing resources in Chapter 8. Though they're likely to perform sluggishly, you can even run applications across an RAS link. In the Hands-on Projects, you will have the opportunity to combine Windows 98 RAS with what you learned about Dial-Up Networking in Chapter 6 in order to create your own two-computer network, where you will share files and printers.

Note that you will probably only use Windows 98 RAS on a standalone computer. For a Windows 98 computer connected to a network, you would most likely choose a more powerful option, such as Windows NT RAS.

In Chapter 6, you learned how to use Dial-Up Networking to connect to an ISP or a network server. In this section, you will learn how to use Dial-Up Networking to install RAS on your Windows 98 computer. (Note that within Dial-Up Networking, RAS is referred to by its other name, Dial-Up Server.) Later in this section, you will learn to set up Windows 98 RAS for sharing resources such as files and printers.

In Chapter 6, you learned that a typical ISDN line can be split into two channels for transmitting voice or data. If you use an ISDN adapter for your Windows 98 RAS Server, Windows 98 limits you to only one ISDN channel.

COMPARISONS

Just as Personal Web Server borrows from Internet Information Server for Windows NT, Windows 98 RAS borrows features from Windows NT RAS. Some of the features of RAS for Windows 98 and Windows NT are compared in Table 7-2:

Table 7-2 Comparing RAS for Windows 98 and Windows NT

	RAS for Windows 98	RAS for Windows NT
Maximum number of connections	1	256
PPP support	Yes	Yes
PPTP support	No	Yes
IP routing support	No	Yes

Although Windows 98 RAS cannot function as a PPTP server, you learned in Chapter 6 that it can function as a remote PPTP client, providing secure access to a network through the Internet. Unlike Windows 98, Windows NT can route TCP/IP messages between local area networks (LAN). In other words, when you connect to Windows NT RAS and then try to send a message outside the LAN, Windows NT can route your message to another network. Windows 98 RAS cannot.

Windows NT RAS allows multiple users to make simultaneous remote connections. Windows 98 can only be configured to allow one remote user to connect at a time. If you have many users, Windows NT RAS is the more appropriate tool, but not all organizations can afford a Windows NT system.

INSTALLING RAS FOR WINDOWS 98

Windows 98 RAS is not installed by default along with Windows 98, but the required files are included on the Windows 98 installation CD. You install Windows 98 RAS as follows:

1. Insert the Windows 98 installation CD into your CD-ROM drive.
2. Click Start, point to Settings, click Control Panel, double-click the Add/Remove Programs icon, and then click the Windows Setup tab. A message box appears indicating that Windows 98 is searching for installed components (this could take a few minutes), and then you return to the Windows Setup tab.
3. In the Components list box, highlight Communications, and then click Details. The Communications dialog box opens.
4. In the components list box, click the Dial-Up Server check box to insert a check. (If the box is already checked, Dial-Up Server is already installed on your computer.)
5. Click OK. You return to the Add/Remove Programs Properties dialog box.

6. Click OK. The files for Dial-Up Server are now copied from your Windows 98 installation CD. When the installation is complete, you return to the Control Panel.

CONFIGURING REMOTE ACCESS SERVER FOR WINDOWS 98

Now that you have installed Remote Access Server (RAS) (also known as Dial-Up Server), you need to configure it. As mentioned earlier, you will probably only install Windows 98 RAS on a standalone computer. Thus, the following discussion assumes you employ **share-level security**, which is the only option for a standalone Windows 98 computer. As you'll recall, share-level security requires a password for each resource (such as a folder or printer) that you want to access. The alternative, user-level security, is only possible on a Windows NT or Novell NetWare network. To configure RAS for Windows 98:

1. Click Start, point to Programs, point to Accessories, point to Communications, and then click Dial-Up Networking. The Dial-Up Networking window opens.

2. Click Connections on the menu bar, and then click Dial-Up Server. (If you do not see this option, you need to install Dial-Up Server, as described in the previous section.) The Dial-Up Server dialog box opens. This dialog box includes one tab for each modem and/or ISDN adapter installed in your computer.

3. Click the tab for the modem or ISDN adapter you want to use for your RAS connection.

4. Click the Allow caller access option button.

5. Click the Change Password option button. The Dial-Up Networking Password dialog box opens, as in Figure 7-13. (If the dialog box on your computer does not include a Change Password option button, you are using user-level security. To change to share-level security, click Start, point to Settings, click Control Panel, then double-click the Network icon. In the Network dialog box, click the Access Control tab, click Share-level access control, then click OK. If prompted by the System Settings Change dialog box, click Yes to restart your computer. When your computer restarts, return to Step 1.)

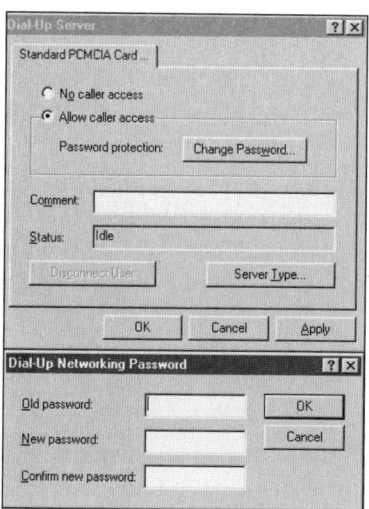

Figure 7-13 Dial-Up Server dialog box

6. If you have never specified a Dial-Up Server password before, leave the old password text box blank. Otherwise, enter your old Dial-Up Server password in the Old password text box.

7. Enter your new password in the New password text box, and then type it again in the Confirm new password text box. If for some reason you do not want to require a password for RAS access, you can leave these boxes blank. But keep in mind that passwords do promote security on your Windows 98 computer.

8. Click OK to close the Dial-Up Networking Password dialog box and return to the Dial-Up Server dialog box.

9. Click Server Type. The Server Types dialog box opens.

10. Click the down arrow to the right of the word "Default" to display a list of possible Dial-Up Server types, as shown in Figure 7-14. In this step you will accept the Default option, but you should familiarize yourself with the different types, as explained in Table 7-3.

Table 7-3 Dial-Up Server Types

PPP: Internet, Windows NT Server, Windows 98	This option supports the TCP/IP, IPX/SPX, and NetBEUI higher-level protocols on a PPP connection. PPP connections to the Internet are explained in Chapter 5.
Windows for Workgroups and Windows NT 3.1	This option supports only the NetBEUI protocol on a legacy RAS connection. If you select this option, the advanced options in Step 11 are not available for your server.
Default	This option begins all connections in PPP mode and switches to another mode only if PPP fails.

11. In the bottom half of the Server Type dialog box, you can see two advanced options: "Require encrypted passwords" and "Enable software compression." The latter is useful when transferring large amounts of data. Verify that both are selected by default.

12. Click OK to return to the Dial-Up Server window.

13. Click OK to return to the Dial-Up Networking window. The server is now ready to accept a dial-in connection.

14. Close the Dial-Up Networking window.

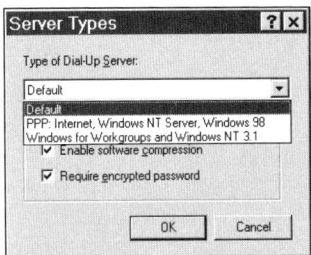

Figure 7-14 Server Types dialog box

Once you configure Dial-Up Server, the modem that you selected in Step 3 is effectively locked into waiting for incoming calls. To make other connections (such as outbound connections to the Internet or connections for sending or receiving faxes), you have two choices. You can use a second modem or ISDN adapter, or you can disable Dial-Up Server by selecting the No Caller Access option in the Dial-Up Server dialog box.

SHARING RESOURCES THROUGH WINDOWS 98 RAS

Before you can begin sharing resources via an RAS connection, you need to enable sharing on your Windows 98 computer.

This is a two-step process. First you enable file and printer sharing generally, that is, you must change your networking settings to allow the files and printers on your computer to be shared. Next, you must choose the specific files and printers you want to share and indicate the type of access you want to make available to remote users.

The following steps explain how to enable file and printer sharing on your computer, and then how to select the specific files and printers you want to share. In the Hands-on Projects, you can use this knowledge to actually gain access to remote files and printers.

To enable file and printer sharing on your computer:

1. Insert the Windows 98 Installation CD into your CD-ROM drive, then open the Configuration tab of the Network applet.

2. Check the setting in the Primary Network Logon list box. If Client for Microsoft Networks is not currently selected, select it now.

If Client for Microsoft Networks is not available, install it as follows: Click Add. In the Select Network Component Type dialog box, click Client, and then click Add. In the Select Network Client dialog box, highlight Microsoft in the list of Manufacturers, and then highlight Client for Microsoft Networks in the list of Network Clients. Click OK. You return to the Network dialog box.

3. Click File and Print Sharing. The File and Print Sharing dialog box opens. This dialog box contains the "I want to be able to give others access to my files" check box, and the "I want to be able to allow others to print to my printer(s)" check box.

4. Click both check boxes to select them, and then click OK. You return to the Network dialog box.

5. Click OK.

6. If prompted, click Yes to restart your computer.

Now Windows 98 will allow you to share your files and printers. The next step is to choose the specific files that you want to share, and to indicate the type of access you want to make available to remote users, as explained in the following steps. Once again, these steps assume that you are using share-level security on your Windows 98 computer.

1. Click Start, point to Programs, and then click Windows Explorer.

2. In the left-hand pane of Windows Explorer, highlight a folder containing the files that you wish to share.

3. Click File on the menu bar, and then click Properties. The Properties dialog box for the selected folder opens.

4. If necessary, click the Sharing tab to display the options shown in Figure 7-15.

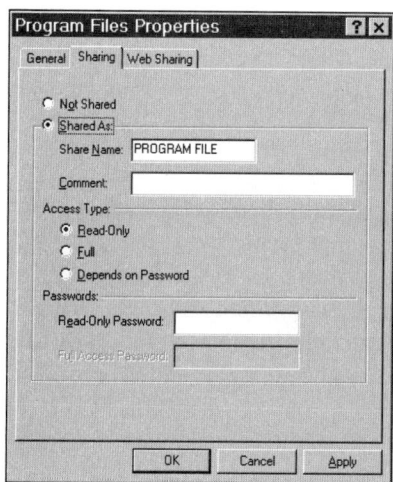

Figure 7-15 Sharing tab of the Properties dialog box

5. Click the Shared As option button.

6. Next, you need to assign a share name to this folder. The share name will be used to identify the folder to the remote user. The Share Name text box displays the folder's original name by default. Accept the default share name or specify a new one. The Share Name can include spaces and can be up to 12 characters long. However, if you use spaces or create a share name longer than 8 characters, client computers with systems such as Windows 3.x may not be able to read this share.

7. In the Access Types section, you can specify the type of access you want remote users to have to this folder. You can choose from three types of access: Read-Only, Full, and Depends on Password. These access types are explained in Table 7-4.

Table 7-4 Possible Types of Access for Shared Files

Access Type	Explanation
Read-Only	Remote users can only read or copy from a folder with read-only permission, if they have the password that you entered in the Read-Only box in Figure 7-13.
Full	Allows remote users to read, modify, or delete the files on your Windows 98 RAS computer, if they have the password that you entered in the Full Access Password box in Figure 7-13.
Depends on Password	Allows you to set two levels of access for your folder. If you choose this option, you need to set two passwords, one in each of the previous two boxes. Users who know the appropriate password can get the associated level of access.

8. Select the access type you want, and then enter the required passwords in the Passwords section.

9. Click OK. If you entered a password in Step 8, the Password Confirmation dialog box opens.

10. Retype your password to confirm it, and then click OK.

11. You return to Windows Explorer.

Now that you have chosen the specific files you want to share, you can choose which printers you want to share. The basic steps are the same, except that you begin in the Printers folder. Click Start, point to Settings, and then click Printers. In the Printers folder, highlight the printer that you wish to share, click File on the menu bar, and then click Properties. In the Properties dialog box for the selected printer, click the Sharing tab, click the Shared As option button, as shown in Figure 7-16, and then enter a share name, comment, and password in the appropriate text boxes.

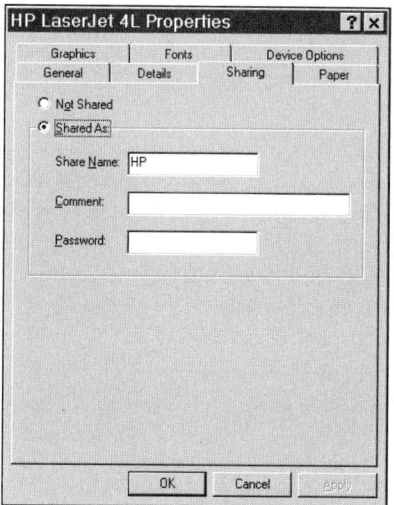

Figure 7-16 Sharing a printer

Now that you know how to share your files and printers, you can learn about what happens when a client computer tries to access a Windows 98 RAS computer. Note that you will learn more about sharing resources on your computer in Chapter 8.

RAS AUTHENTICATION AND ACCESS CONTROLS

As discussed when you learned to set up Windows 98 RAS, you can require passwords for RAS connections. To make your system even more secure, you can use an encrypted password. To use encrypted passwords, you need a Point-to-Point (PPP) capable server. Assuming that you are using Windows 98 RAS, password authentication and encryption is verified via the Link Control Protocol (LCP). Like PPP, LCP is a data-link level protocol. LCP and PPP work together to configure, establish, and test the integrity of a connection. LCP works as a link to the following authentication protocols:

- **Password Authentication Protocol (PAP):** This is the least secure method of authentication. Passwords are sent via clear text soon as a connection is negotiated between the guest and host computers.

- **Challenge Handshake Authentication Protocol (CHAP):** This protocol periodically checks the security clearance of the user while the user is online. The host sends a challenge message, which is a request to verify that the user is still the same user. Every challenge is scrambled with different codes, depending on the type of CHAP used. Windows 98 and Windows NT both use the proprietary Microsoft Challenge Handshake Authentication (MS-CHAP).

- **Shiva Password Authentication Protocol (SPAP):** This protocol encrypts standard PAP passwords for user account information. SPAP is used for Windows 98 computers that are configured for user-level security on a Novell NetWare network.

- **Any method, including clear text**: This choice allows the client and server to negotiate the highest level of security that the two machines share in common. It is recommended when non-Microsoft clients dial in, to permit them to negotiate password security by other means.

Remember that passwords are required when making a dial-up connection to a server with share-level or user-level security enabled. Share-level security is used to access a Windows 98 dial-up server. A special password is assigned to that resource (the dial-up server), and each caller must have the valid password in order to connect. Once your password is accepted, you can make use of the resources assigned to that system.

As described in Chapter 6, you can also use RAS to synchronize Briefcase files.

CHAPTER SUMMARY

- Windows 98 helps even the entry-level user join the revolution in corporate communications. Personal Web Server for Windows 98 allows you to create and manage a small-scale Web site. Through Personal Web Manager, you can create a home page, attach files to your Web site, and manage permissions on your Web site files. Windows 98 Personal Web Server is intended for small-scale use on a small intranet. As the demand on your Web site grows, you can upgrade to Personal Web Server for Windows NT Workstation and Internet Information Server for Windows NT Server.

- You can also access your Windows 98 computer from remote locations. Along with the dial-up networking techniques you learned about in Chapter 6, you can set up Remote Access Server for Windows 98 to share your files and printers. Passwords can be set for each printer and Explorer folder. RAS has different levels of encryption for these passwords. File and printer sharing is a two-step process: first, you set network permissions to allow sharing; then, you choose the printers and Explorer folders that you want to share over your RAS.

- Generally, RAS for Windows 98 will be used for standalone computers. If you are connected to a network, there are more powerful tools available, such as RAS for Windows NT.

KEY TERMS

- **Active Server Pages (ASP)** — A Web server technology developed by Microsoft that allows the dynamic creation of Web pages by the server, at the moment they are requested by the site visitor. For example the output of a search engine uses ASP technology. ASP may be enabled on Personal Web Server, as well as Internet Information Server (IIS) for Windows NT.

- **applet** — A small Web-based program written in Java.

- **Common Gateway Interface (CGI)** — Similar to dynamic link libraries. Programming code that can be used by multiple applications. The disadvantage of CGI in Microsoft operating systems is that separate copies of a .cgi file are open for every separate program. Commonly stored in Web server directories to work with animated or interactive Web pages.

- **FrontPage Server Extensions** — Programs that can be installed with Personal Web Server to facilitate the creation of a Web site home page. Based on the Microsoft Web page creation program FrontPage 98.

- **hit** — Any request for content. For example, when you retrieve a Web page from the Internet, that Web page may include nine pictures. That results in 10 hits: one for the Web page, and one for each of the nine pictures. *See also* Request.

- **HTML (HyperText Markup Language)** — The language used to create basic Web pages.

- **hyperlink** — A bit of text or an image specially marked with HTML to "link" the user to another Web page.

- **Internet Information Server** — Similar to Personal Web Server. The Web server application for the Windows NT Server operating system.

- **intranet** — Similar to the Internet, an intranet is a TCP/IP network limited in scope, usually to a single organization.

- **Link Control Protocol (LCP)** — A TCP/IP protocol that works with PPP at the data-link layer to connect to several different protocols for checking encrypted passwords.

- **Microsoft Data Access Components 1.5** — Programs that can be installed with Personal Web Server that allow access to powerful databases such as Oracle, Microsoft Access, and SQL Server.

- **Microsoft Message Queue (MSMQ)** — Programs that can be installed with Personal Web Server that provide for guaranteed delivery of messages over the TCP/IP protocol.

- **Microsoft Transaction Server (MTS)** — Programs that can be installed with Personal Web Server that provide for guaranteed delivery of database change requests before those changes are written to disk.

- **Personal Web Server** — A desktop Web server included in Windows 98. Intended for personal home page publication on a small intranet, or for testing and development purposes prior to publication.

- **PPP (Point-to-Point Protocol)** — A communications protocol used in modem-based communications.

- **PPTP (Point-to-Point Tunneling Protocol)** — A secure connection, made by tunneling encrypted data through a traditional PPP connection to the Internet or a LAN.

- **remote access** — Used to refer to a connection to a computer from a distant location. Sometimes implemented by Remote Access Server for Windows 98.

- **request** — A hit that successfully retrieves content. Not all hits actually bring a file, such as a picture, into a browser. All requests actually make it into a browser.
- **Site Server** — The Windows NT level program associated with Internet Information Server that collects data such as requests and hits.
- **virtual directories** — The directories in a Web site manager such as Personal Web Server do not necessarily correlate to folders on a physical hard disk. Thus these directories are virtual.
- **visit** — A single session on a Web site. Usually consists of a series of hits and requests.
- **Visual InterDev** — A tool for creating dynamic Web applications.

REVIEW QUESTIONS

1. Which of the following programs is your best choice if you need a Web server that can accommodate many simultaneous connections?
   a. Personal Web Server for Windows NT Workstation
   b. Personal Web Server for Windows 98
   c. Internet Information Server for Windows NT
   d. Remote Access Server for Windows NT

2. Web site programs such as Personal Web Server create the greatest load on which of the following computer components?
   a. CPU
   b. RAM
   c. hard disk
   d. floppy disk drive

3. Which of the following programs can you use to manage a Windows 98 Personal Web Server?
   a. Personal Web Manager
   b. Front Page Express
   c. Remote Access Server for Windows 98
   d. Windows Explorer

4. When you install Personal Web Server from the Windows 98 installation CD, which of the following components can you install? (Choose all correct answers.)
   a. Microsoft Message Queue
   b. Microsoft Transaction Server
   c. Front Page Server Extensions
   d. Remote Access Server for Windows 98

5. When you install Personal Web Server, there is a directory to install FTP files. Which of the following programs can you install to enable FTP for Personal Web Server for Windows 98?

   a. Microsoft Transaction Server

   b. Microsoft Message Queue

   c. Microsoft Data Access Components 1.5

   d. none of the above

6. When you install a file through Personal Web Manager on your Web site, which of the following actions do you need to take to link the file to your home page?

   a. nothing

   b. Edit your home page with Front Page Express.

   c. Edit your home page with a text editor.

   d. Edit your home page through the Personal Web Manager Publish utility.

7. When you create a home page through Personal Web Manager, the Home Page Wizard prompts you to enter which of the following? (Choose all correct answers.)

   a. your name

   b. your spouse's name

   c. links to the Web sites of your choice

   d. There are a number of blank spaces to enter content of your choice.

8. To access the Web site that you create with Personal Web Server, which of the following do you enter in the Address text box in Internet Explorer? *Hint*: your computer name is mycomputer and the computer description is mypc.

   a. *http://mycomputer*

   b. *http://www.default.htm*

   c. *http://www.course.com*

   d. *http://mypc/default.htm*

9. When you edit properties of a directory through Personal Web Server, you can set permissions on each directory. Which of the following best describes what a Script permission allows?

   a. allows all users to read your files

   b. allows all users to execute Active Server Page files

   c. allows all users to execute executable files

   d. allows all users to delete your files

10. What happens when you "Allow Directory Browsing" in the Advanced properties of your Personal Web Server?
    a. You can browse through file lists in the Personal Web Server virtual directories.
    b. You can browse through the different Web sites on your Personal Web Server.
    c. You can browse through the different script files in your Personal Web Server.
    d. You can choose a different home page for your Web site.
11. What is the difference between a hit and a request?
    a. A request is a hit that successfully retrieves content.
    b. A hit is a request that successfully retrieves content.
    c. A request is a hit that does not retrieve content.
    d. A hit is a request that does not retrieve content.
12. Which of the following authentication protocols is used by Personal Web Server for Windows 98?
    a. MS Challenge Authentication Protocol
    b. Password Authentication Protocol
    c. Shiva Authentication Protocol
    d. none of the above
13. How many simultaneous connections are allowed by Remote Access Server for Windows 98?
    a. 10
    b. 256
    c. 1
    d. 5
14. Once you have set up Remote Access Server, what else do you need to do before you can share files? (Choose all correct answers.)
    a. Allow file sharing through the setup for Dial-Up Networking.
    b. Allow file sharing through the Configuration tab in the Network dialog box.
    c. Allow file sharing through the properties of the file folder that you want to share in Windows Explorer.
    d. Allow file sharing through the Configuration wizard in Personal Web Server.
15. When you set up Remote Access Server for Windows 98, which of the following combinations is not allowed?
    a. PPP and password encryption
    b. Windows for Workgroups Dial-Up Server mode and password encryption
    c. software compression and password encryption
    d. password protection and password encryption

16. When you try to set up Remote Access Server through the Dial-Up Networking folder Connections menu, you can't do it because you don't see an entry for Dial-Up Server in this menu. What is the problem?

    a. Windows 98 is defective and needs to be reloaded from the installation CD.

    b. You have not set up the Dial-Up Networking Wizard properly.

    c. Connections is the wrong menu.

    d. You need to install Dial-Up Server from the Windows 98 installation CD first.

17. If your computer is on a Windows NT or Novell NetWare network, your RAS can have security not available on a standalone Windows 98 computer. Which of the following is a feature of this additional security?

    a. share-level security

    b. user-level security

    c. password encryption

    d. Microsoft Challenge Handshake Authentication Protocol

18. Personal Web Server is intended for use as (choose all that apply):

    a. a full-time Web server connected to the Internet

    b. a corporate intranet server for a large company

    c. a small business or low-volume intranet server

    d. a test and development platform for Web professionals

19. When a Windows 98 machine has RAS enabled, the user can make Internet connections or other calls with the modem. True or False?

20. RAS is configured from the computer you are dialing *from*. True or False?

21. Windows 98 RAS can only accept connections made from:

    a. other Windows 98 machines

    b. Windows and Macintosh machines, but not UNIX machines

    c. any computer at all

    d. any machine that can make a PPP connection

22. Which of the following can you accomplish using Windows 98 RAS?

    a. accessing a networked printer across an RAS connection

    b. supporting more than one remote connection

    c. configuration as a PPTP server

    d. configuration as an IP router

Hands-on Projects

Project 7-1

In this project, you will create a home page for your Web site. You will use the Home Page Wizard included in Personal Web Server. To complete this project you need a computer with Windows 98 installed. Unless you have just installed Personal Web Server, you will first need to remove and reinstall Personal Web Server. (This will ensure that you or someone else has not previously adjusted the PWS settings.) If you have just installed Personal Web Server, you can start with Step 8. If your Windows 98 computer is not on a network, you will also need to revise your C:\Windows\Hosts file, as described in the section on Personal Web Manager.

1. Insert your Windows 98 installation CD.
2. Click **Start**, point to **Programs**, point to **Internet Explorer**, point to **Personal Web Server**, and then click **Personal Web Server Setup**. If there is no entry for Personal Web Server in the Internet Explorer Start menu, Personal Web Server is probably not installed; you can skip to Step 6.
3. Click **Next** in the first page of the Personal Web Server Setup Wizard.
4. Click **Remove All**. If required, click **Yes** to confirm. Setup removes Personal Web Server from your computer.
5. When the process is complete, click **Finish**, and then click **Yes** to restart your computer.
6. Click **Start**, and then click **Run**.
7. In the Run text box, type *x:*\add-ons\pws\setup.exe and then press **Enter**. (Substitute the letter representing your CD-ROM drive for *x*.)
8. In the first page of the Personal Web Server Setup Wizard, click **Next**.
9. Click **Typical**.
10. Click **Next**. The Setup Wizard copies the necessary files.
11. When the installation process is complete, click **Finish**, and then click **Yes** to restart your computer. You now have a fresh installation of Personal Web Server. Now you can open PWS and create a home page.
12. Click **Start**, point to **Programs**, point to **Internet Explorer**, point to **Personal Web Server**, and then click **Personal Web Manager**.
13. If you see a Tip of the Day dialog box, click **Close**. If you see a security alert dialog box warning you about the risk of viruses from untrusted sites, click the **In the future do not show the warning for this zone** check box to select it and then click **OK**. If you see a dialog box indicating that you cannot connect to your computer in offline mode, click **Cancel**. The Personal Web Manager window opens.
14. In the left pane, click the **Web Site** icon. The Home Page Wizard opens in the right-hand pane, with a cartoon-like picture of a wizard with a hat.

15. Click the wizard (or the right-facing, forward arrow) to begin creating your home page. If you see the security alert dialog box discussed in Step 13, click the **In the future do not show the warning for this zone** check box to select it, then click **Yes**.
16. On this first page, you can choose one of the three templates for your home page: Looseleaf, Journal, or Gunmetal. These templates provide different wallpaper-type backgrounds for your home page. Click a template in the list, and then click the **forward arrow** button.
17. Next, you are asked if you would like a guest book on your page. A guest book provides a place for visitors to sign in with their e-mail address and a message. Click the **No** option button, and then click the **forward arrow** button to continue.
18. Next, you can choose to include a drop box on your Web page. A drop box allows visitors to leave messages that only you can read. Click the **Yes** option button, and then click the **forward arrow** button to continue.
19. The wizard indicates that it has finished the basic structure of your page. Click the **forward arrow** button to continue.
20. Internet Explorer opens, showing your partially completed home page. It displays the settings that you have just created and provides space for additional information that you may want to enter, as described in the next six steps.
21. Enter a title for your home page in the box provided.
22. Enter your name, e-mail address, phone number, fax number, department name, and physical address in the appropriate spaces.
23. Type a heading for a paragraph that describes yourself, your job, or your hobbies.
24. Enter the details for that paragraph in the large text box.
25. Type additional headings and paragraphs as desired.
26. If you want to add a link to another Web page, such as your department's main page, enter the URL and a description of the link in the spaces provided. To add additional links, click **Add link** and enter the necessary information.
27. Click **enter new changes** to insert the information on your page. Your new Web page is displayed in Internet Explorer.
28. Close Internet Explorer.

PROJECT 7-2

In this project, you will link a file to the home page for the Web site you created in Project 7-1. To complete this project you need a computer with Windows 98 installed. You should also have completed Project 7-1.

1. Unless you still have Personal Web Manager open from project 7-1, click **Start**. Point to **Programs**, point to **Internet Explorer**, point to **Personal Web Server**, and then click **Personal Web Manager**.

2. In the left-hand pane of Personal Web Manager, click on the **Publish** icon. This opens the first page of the Publishing Wizard, which looks similar to the Home Page Wizard described in Project 7-1.
3. Click the wizard (or the forward arrow).
4. In the Path text box, type the location of a file that you want to add. If you can't think of a file, type **C:\Windows\Help\Mts\Html\Vintdev.jpg**. This is a picture file that was copied to your computer when you installed Personal Web Server.
5. In the Description text box, type a description of your file that will be linked to your home page. You can get to a list of these files from your home page by clicking on the "View my published documents" link.
6. Click **Add**.
7. Repeat Steps 4–6 for each file that you want to add.
8. When you have completed adding the files that you want to link to the Web page, click the **forward arrow** button.
9. In the next page, view a list of the files that you have added to your Web site.
10. Now you can test your results by opening up your home page. Click **Start**, point to **Programs**, point to **Internet Explorer**, and then click **Internet Explorer**. If you see the Dial-up Connection dialog box, click **Work Offline**.
11. In the Address text box, enter the location for your computer in the format *http://<my_computer_name>*, and then press **Enter**. You can find your computer name in the Identification tab of the Network applet of Control Panel. (If this does not work, try *http://127.0.0.1*, then press **Enter**.) Your home page is displayed in the browser window.
12. In the left-hand side of your home page, click the **View my published documents** link.
13. A Web page opens with links to the files that you added earlier in this project. To open one of these files with Internet Explorer, click the appropriate link.
14. Close Internet Explorer.

PROJECT 7-3

In this project, you will work with a partner to set up RAS for Windows 98 on one computer that will act as the host, and set up Dial-Up Networking on a second computer to access the host. You will then access and transfer files from one computer to the other. To complete this project you need two computers, each with Windows 98 installed. Each computer should be set up with share-level security. For licensing requirements, you will need a separate installation CD or license from Microsoft to use Windows 98 on each computer. You will also need to install RAS for Windows 98 according to the instructions in that section of the chapter. If RAS has been installed before, you will need the password for the server. You also need a modem and telephone for each computer.

1. On the computer that will act as a host, click **Start**, point to **Programs**, point to **Accessories**, point to **Communications**, and then click **Dial-Up Networking**.
2. In the Dial-Up Networking window, click **Connections** on the menu bar, and then click **Dial-Up Server**. (If you do not see a Dial-Up Server option, you need to install it following the instructions provided earlier in this chapter.) This opens up the Dial-Up Server dialog box, with one tab for every modem or ISDN adapter installed on your computer.
3. Click the tab for the modem or adapter that you will use for the Dial-Up Server connection.
4. Click the **Allow caller access** option button.
5. Click **Change Password**. The Dial-Up Networking Password dialog box opens.
6. Unless you have installed RAS before, leave the Old password text box blank. Enter a password in the New password text box and then again in the Confirm new password text box.
7. Click **OK**. You return to the Dial-Up Server dialog box.
8. Click **Server Type**. The Server Types dialog box opens.
9. Verify that Default is selected in the list box, and that both the "Enable software compression" and the "Require encrypted password" check boxes are selected.
10. Click **OK**. You return to the Dial-Up Server dialog box.
11. Click **Apply** to complete the process of enabling RAS.
12. On the second computer, click **Start**, point to **Programs**, point to **Accessories**, point to **Communication**, and then click **Dial-Up Networking**.
13. Double-click the **Make New Connection** icon.
14. Enter a name for the host computer. ("Dial-Up Server" is a good choice.)
15. If you have more than one modem or device, select the device to be used in the "Select a device" list box.
16. Click **Next**.
17. Enter the area code (if required) and telephone number for the host computer, and then click **Next**. Windows 98 has completed setting up the new connection.
18. Click **Finish**. You return to the Dial-Up Networking window.
19. Double-click the new connection labeled **Dial-Up Server** (or whatever name you chose).
20. Click **Connect** to dial into the host computer.
21. When the connection is made, you should see a message to that effect in each computer. Congratulations, you have succeeded in making a dial-up connection between a Windows 98 client and a Windows 98 remote access server. If you do not plan to do Project 7-4 immediately, return to the Dial-Up Server dialog box on the host computer. Click **No caller access** and then click **OK** to close your Dial-Up Server.

PROJECT 7-4

In this project, you will use the connection that you created in Project 7-3 to access files and printers on a remote Windows 98 RAS computer. You will use the Windows 98 client to access files and a printer on the remote Windows 98 RAS computer. You will need the same equipment that you used to complete Project 7-3. The remote Windows RAS computer should have a local printer. You will also need to complete the steps in the chapter section on sharing files and printers through the Network dialog box. To share files, you then need to complete the steps in the chapter section on sharing files through the properties of the folders that you choose to share in Windows Explorer. Finally, the person on the Windows 98 client computer will need the computer name of the remote Windows 98 RAS computer.

1. On the remote Windows 98 computer, repeat Steps 1 through 4 of Project 7-3 to activate RAS. From the Windows 98 client, repeat Steps 19 through 21 of Project 7-3 to dial into the remote Windows 98 RAS computer.
2. Once the connection is made, click **Start**, point to **Find**, and then click **Computer**.
3. In the Find: Computer dialog box, enter the Computer Name of the remote Windows 98 RAS computer. After a pause, the Find: Computer dialog box lists the RAS computer.
4. Double-click the name of the Windows 98 RAS computer. A dialog box named after the computer opens with a list of the folders and printers that you shared on the RAS computer. (If this does not include the folders and printers that you want, review the instructions in the chapter for sharing resources.)
5. Double-click the folder of your choice.
6. Within the selected folder, double-click the file of your choice, preferably a text or document file. Your computer will now load the file from the Windows 98 RAS computer onto your computer. Assuming that you choose a text or document file, your Windows 98 computer opens up the remote file with a local word-processing program. You have successfully shared a file between computers over a dial-up network. Close your word processing program. You return to the dialog box for the RAS computer.
7. Above the menu bar, click the **Back** button (left-facing arrow) to return to the folder named after your Windows 98 RAS computer.
8. Double-click on the shared printer. Assuming that you haven't installed this remote printer on your remote Windows 98 computer before, this opens an abbreviated version of the Add Printer Wizard. The first dialog box asks you if you want Windows to set up this printer.

9. Click **Yes**. The next dialog box asks if you print from MS-DOS programs.
10. Click **No**, and then click **Next**. The next dialog box asks you for a name for the printer. It also asks if you want to use this printer as the default printer for your computer.
11. Enter the name of your choice, and click **No**, unless you always want to print remotely to the Windows 98 RAS printer.
12. Click **Next**. (If you have installed this printer before, this dialog box asks you if you want to keep the existing installation. Click **Yes**, and then click **Next**.)
13. The final dialog box asks you if you want to print a test page. Click **Yes**, and then click **Next**. If you haven't installed this printer before, your Windows 98 computer will copy the printer files from the remote Windows 98 RAS computer. If you find the test page on the printer connected to the remote Windows 98 RAS computer, you have successfully connected to a remote printer.
14. Now you can close your connection. Right-click the green icon in the system tray (next to the clock). On the shortcut menu, click **Disconnect**. On the Windows 98 RAS computer, return to the Dial-Up Server dialog box. Click **No caller access** and then click **OK** to close the Dial-Up Server dialog box.

CASE PROJECTS

1. Your boss, the vice president of manufacturing, has asked you to create a departmental intranet site. She wants the site to include:
   - A page describing the department, including several photos of the production lines
   - A full page describing her position and accomplishments
   - A page for each employee in the division, that is uniform in appearance and content. The employee pages should include the employee's name, the employee's job title, the employee's job description, an e-mail address, a business mailing address, a list of three hobbies, and a list of three links to other Web sites.

   How will you go about setting up this Web site? Create an instructional memo to be distributed to all employees, teaching them how to set up their own home pages. Include notes on the company's preferred style and content.

2. Now that you have worked with Personal Web Server to create a small-scale internal Web site for your small company, you are ready to grow. Your supervisor is convinced that electronic commerce over the Internet is the wave of the future. He is willing to make some investments to support a public Web site for your company. On the basis of what you have learned in this and previous chapters, tell him about the requirements. Will your Web server require the fastest possible CPU? What software will you need? Whom can you go to for a domain name and IP address?

3. You have successfully lobbied your boss for the ability to telecommute two days per week. Your company has provided a computer system for your home, in addition to the system you have at work. Your network relies on user-level security for access to network resources. Your boss would prefer that you make connections to the network via modem, rather than via the Internet. Describe what steps you will need to take to prepare your workstation at the office the night before your two telecommuting days. What steps will you need to take at home in order to connect to the office workstation? What access will you have to the network once connected? How can you keep your contact management data synchronized between the two computers?

CHAPTER EIGHT

MANAGING WINDOWS 98 SYSTEM RESOURCES

According to Microsoft, the computer of the future will be a kind of electronic appliance. Ideally, a PC would be as easy to use as a toaster, but would also integrate data, voice, and entertainment into a single, simple package. Microsoft has created a model for this vision in the form of the Simply Interactive Personal Computer (SIPC). The SIPC looks to be the driving force for future Microsoft products, and should dictate everything from the structure of Microsoft operating systems to support for USB and FireWire standards, which you learned about in Chapter 1.

While the SIPC is a great idea, it will be a while until this vision is fully realized. In this chapter, you will learn about a number of utilities that you must use to maintain your computer, utilities that would be fully automated in a true SIPC. It still takes significant work to share your files over a network, using share-level and user-level permissions. A true SIPC would have one data connection that integrates voice, fax, and data. A true SIPC would not need disk management utilities that require substantial computer knowledge such as Disk Defragmenter. You wouldn't need to learn about FAT32 or DriveSpace 3 in order to manage the space on your disk. Until the SIPC is fully realized, however, you will have to learn to use the utilities described in this chapter.

AFTER READING THIS CHAPTER AND COMPLETING THE EXERCISES YOU WILL BE ABLE TO:

- Share folders, printers, and fax modems over a network
- Manage, install, and configure printers
- Compress, combine, and partition hard disks to maximize available space
- Discuss the value of the layered multimedia architecture system
- Describe multimedia applications and how they facilitate Microsoft's vision of the PC of the future
- Explain the difference between user-level and share-level security

As an operating system, Windows 98 is responsible for multiple resources, such as files, printers, and disks. To move toward the SIPC, Microsoft has integrated sophisticated multimedia features into Windows 98. These capabilities make it easier than ever to incorporate Internet access, computer telephony, high-fidelity sound systems, and conventional or high-definition television into a PC. Microsoft has devoted considerable energy and effort into making Windows 98 flexible enough to support all these types of media. The key to this flexibility lies in the Windows 98 architecture, which is built around a well-defined, shared driver model called the Win32 Driver Model (WDM). You learned about the advantages of WDM in Chapters 1 and 2. In this chapter you will learn about the many multimedia features that rely on the WDM.

SHARED RESOURCES IN THE WINDOWS 98 ENVIRONMENT

You learned about sharing resources such as files and printers in Chapter 7. In this section you will learn more about the different methods for resource sharing. Chapter 11 will address these topics in even more detail.

As mentioned in Chapter 2, sharing resources on any Windows platform requires share-level or user-level security. While share-level security allows resource access based on passwords, user-level security requires authentication through server software such as Windows NT Server or Novell NetWare. Because NetWare does not support share-level security, the following discussion assumes that resource sharing occurs on a Microsoft network.

Most discussions of networking center around client/server terminology, where a client is a system, such as Windows 98, Windows 95, or some other desktop operating system, attached to a network, and a server is a network operating system such as Windows NT Advanced Server 3.51 or Windows NT 4.0 Server. You can even give specific users permission to access individual files from a Windows NT server. However, this requires a hard disk formatted using the New Technology File System (NTFS). **NTFS**, like FAT, is a system for formatting and organizing a hard disk. Although similar to the FAT16 and FAT32 systems, which you learned about in Chapter 2, it is unique to Windows NT.

A Windows 98 system may be a more appropriate server than Windows NT on a small network of 10 or fewer computers. Windows 98 can share disks, folders (directories), faxes, and printers. This may be enough for a company with relatively small and stable requirements. As you'll learn in the next sections, while you can share folders from a Windows 98 computer, you need a connection to a Windows NT or Novell NetWare computer to specify who has access to specific folders. Remember that NTFS can only be created and read by the Windows NT operating system.

Assigning Access Permissions to Shared Folders

As you learned in Chapter 7, file and print sharing is a two-step process. First you need to enable the ability to share, then you must actually share a particular resource. In a share-level system such as Windows 98, you can specify different levels of password protection for each resource you choose to share. (For more details on sharing resources under share-level security, review the explanation of sharing resources in Chapter 7.)

Assuming you are familiar with the process of sharing resources under share-level security, you are ready to consider the pros and cons of sharing resources under user-level security and share-level security, as explained in the next section.

User-level Versus Share-level Permissions

User-level and share-level permissions each have advantages and disadvantages. User-level permissions allow a network administrator to assign access rights to specific users or groups. In order to access a resource, a user must first be assigned the right to use it (either as an individual or as a member of a group). A group in a Windows NT Server domain contains a list of users, usually people who share a common interest or common job assignments, such as "Engineers" or "Sales." While permissions can be set up on a per user basis, it is more convenient to assign permissions by group, and then to manage user permissions by adding them to (or removing them from) groups with certain types of permissions.

Share-level permissions are easier to configure than user-level permissions. To access a resource under share-level security, you simply need to know the password assigned to that resource. However, user-level permissions provide greater security. For example, under user-level security, when an employee leaves your organization, you can simply delete the user from the Windows NT domain or Novell NetWare server (or NDS tree). Under share-level access, you would have to define a new password, and then inform all affected users of the new password.

Setting Up User-level Security

To employ user-level security, you need a Windows 98 computer connected to a Windows NT or Novell NetWare based network. Creating user-level permissions is a three-part process. First you need to enable your computer to allow user-level access. Second, you must specify the Windows NT domain or Novell NetWare server (or NDS tree) that will govern permissions on your Windows 98 computer. Finally, you need to choose the specific folders and printers you want to share over the network.

The first two requirements are fairly straightforward, as explained in the following set of steps. To complete these steps, you will need the domain name of your Windows NT Server or Novell NetWare network. (If you don't already know the domain name, ask your instructor or network administrator.)

To enable user-level access and name the domain that will govern your permissions:

1. Click Start, point to Settings, point to Control Panel, double-click the Network icon, and then click the Access control tab.

2. Click the "User-level access control" option button.

3. In the "Obtain list of users and groups from:" text box, type the name of the domain. As with share-level permissions, user-level permissions do not become active until you restart your computer.

4. Restart your computer when prompted.

 Keep in mind that you cannot employ share-level and user-level permissions on the same Windows 98 computer simultaneously.

Now that you have enabled user-level access and specified a domain to govern permissions on your Windows 98 computer, you can choose the specific resources you want to share. This process is explained in the next section.

SHARING RESOURCES WITH USER-LEVEL SECURITY

Now that you have enabled user-level security and specified a network domain, you can start sharing folders or printers on your Windows 98 computer. In the process of sharing a resource, you must assign a level of access (to that resource) for each user or group in the domain. You can choose from the following types of access: Read-Only, Full Access, and Custom. You already learned about Read-Only and Full Access in Chapter 7. You can choose from several levels of custom access. On a Windows NT network, you can fine-tune custom access by assigning any combination of the following levels of permissions:

- **Read**: Alone, this is no different from read-only permission.
- **Write**: Allows users to write the file to your disk
- **Create**: Allows users to create new files and folders on your computer
- **Delete**: Allows the networked user to delete all files in the shared folder
- **Change File Attributes**: Allows you to assign four different attributes to every file: Read-only, Hidden, Archive, and System. These are the same attributes that can be assigned to an MS-DOS, Windows 3.x or Windows 95 file.
- **List**: Allows users to search through your Windows Explorer for different files
- **Change Access Control**: Allows users to deny access to your folder to everyone else over a network. If a user were to deny access in this way, it would still be possible to access the folder on the Windows 98 computer that physically contains that folder.

Now that you understand the different types of access, you are ready to share a folder or printer. The following steps explain how to share a folder. The steps for sharing a printer are similar.

To share a folder under user-level security:

1. Click Start, point to Programs, and then click Windows Explorer.
2. In the left-hand pane, highlight the folder that you wish to share, click File in the menu bar, click Properties, and then click the Sharing tab.
3. Click Add. The Add Users dialog box opens, containing a list of users and groups in the left-hand pane. Here you can assign each user or group a level of access to the shared folder.
4. Highlight a user. In the middle of the dialog box, you see three types of access: Read-Only, Full Access, and Custom.
5. Select the type of access you want to assign the highlighted user or group. The right-hand pane then indicates the access level assigned to that user or group. If you select Custom, the Change Access Rights dialog box opens, where you can select the rights you want to assign to the user or group.
6. In the Add Users dialog box, click OK to complete the rights assignment.

   If at some point in the future you want to grant additional users or groups access to the folder, repeat the previous steps.

The previous steps explained how to share a folder under user-level security. To share a printer, begin by selecting the printer you want to share in the Printers folder. You will learn more about sharing and managing printers in the following section.

In addition to sharing printers and folders, you can grant users or groups the right to administer your computer. Users with remote administration rights can, among other things, share files and printers just as you can on your Windows 98 computer. To view a list of administrators who have been granted access to manage the system, click Start, point to Settings, click Control Panel, double-click the Password icon, and then click the Remote Administration tab. If you don't see a list, you are not connected to a Windows NT or Novell NetWare network.

CREATE, SHARE, AND MONITOR NETWORK RESOURCES

In this section, you will learn how to manage and share three different types of network resources: fax modems, telephones, and printers. You're probably already familiar with the concept of sharing fax modems and printers. However, the thought of using a telephone on a computer network may seem strange. But one of the dreams of most network administrators is the ability to combine voice and data into one system. With one system, you wouldn't need all that separate wire, nor would you need separate switches for telephones and computer networks. Huge amounts of resources could be saved. As you will learn in this section, Windows 98 includes new programs that accommodate this dream. In fact, lots of savvy companies are engaged in implementing this kind of powerful convergence between networking and telephony today.

SHARED FAX MODEMS

In this section, you will learn how to share the fax capabilities of a fax modem. The process for sharing a fax is similar to that for sharing a folder. The following steps may look a bit complex, because you can choose from three possible computer setups. Just be sure to read each step carefully and follow the directions to skip steps when necessary.

When you run Windows 98 Setup to install Windows 98 on your computer, it may not install Microsoft Fax unless you upgraded from a Windows 95 computer on which Microsoft Fax was already installed. If required, you can install Microsoft Fax from your Windows 98 Installation CD. Insert the CD into your drive. Click Start, then click Run. In the Open text box, type: *X:*\Tools\Oldwin95\Message\US\wms.exe (where *X:* represents the drive letter for your CD-ROM) and click OK. Follow the prompts to install Windows Messaging. Click Start, then click Run. In the Open text box, type *X:*\Tools\Oldwin95\Message\US\Awfax.exe (where *X:* represents the drive letter for your CD-ROM) and click OK. Follow the prompts to install Microsoft Fax. If you do not want USA settings for Microsoft Fax, substitute Intl for US when you type each command in the Open text box.

1. Click Start, point to Settings, click Control Panel, and then double-click the Mail and Fax icon. (On some computers this icon may simply be labeled "Mail.") This should open the Mail Properties dialog box. If instead you see an MS Exchange Settings Properties dialog box or a Microsoft Outlook Properties dialog box, click the Services tab and skip to Step 4.

2. Highlight a user profile, and then click Properties. This opens a dialog box with three tabs: Services, Delivery, and Addressing.

3. Click the Services tab.

4. In the "The following information services are set up in this profile" list box, look for an entry for Microsoft fax, highlight it, click Properties, and then skip to Step 8. If you don't see Microsoft Fax in this list, click Add to open the Add Service to Profile dialog box.

5. In the "Available information services" list box, click Microsoft Fax, and then click OK. A Microsoft Fax dialog box opens, informing you that you need to specify your name, fax number, and fax modem.

If you upgraded from Windows 95, Windows 98 does incorporate the settings (including the fax settings) from Windows 95.

6. Click Yes. The Microsoft Fax Properties dialog box opens.

7. Click the User tab and enter a phone number in the Fax number text box.

8. Click the Modem tab.

9. Verify that the "Let other people on the network use my modem to send faxes" check box is selected, and then click Properties (the one in the lower half of the dialog box). The Fax Modem Properties dialog box opens.

10. Now you can share your fax modem. What you see in this dialog box is identical to what you see when you share a folder. You have already learned to share folders in this chapter and in Chapter 7. As with folders, the available options depend on whether you are using share-level or user-level security.

11. Depending on whether you have share-level or user-level security, assign passwords or users, as you learned to do in Chapter 7 and in this chapter. When this process is complete, exit all of the dialog boxes that you have opened.

INTEGRATING TELEPHONES INTO A NETWORK

Before 1980, computer networking was relatively simple. All computer network connections required their own dedicated telephone lines. Modem speeds were limited to 110 bps (bits per second). Everything changed with the development of Ethernet, which made it possible to transfer data at 10 megabytes per second, which was about 762,000 times faster than the modems in use at the time. This was a great leap forward in technology, one that eventually enabled the Internet and modern computer networking as we know it today.

Unfortunately, Ethernet didn't work on the phone lines available at that time. Nor could telephones be made to work with Ethernet. Separate lines were therefore necessary for voice, modems, and, eventually, fax machines. Wires proliferated everywhere in modern businesses. Soon, it became apparent that huge savings would be possible if telephones could be integrated into systems like Ethernet. In such a system, your telephone would be connected to your computer, and both telephone and data transmission systems would use the same physical lines. Today, a whole industry has been built around the goal of computer-telephony integration (CTI).

Ethernet is actually a trade name for what is officially known as the 802.3 standard of the Institute of Electrical and Electronics Engineers (IEEE). As with the other IEEE standards, it is based on the OSI model of networking.

Windows 98 supports the Telephony Applications Program Interface (TAPI), version 2.1. TAPI 2.1 is a set of parameters that help develop tools to support CTI. The primary TAPI driver included with Windows 98 is Unimodem V, which provides settings to simplify modem configuration. Unimodem V supports CTI by supporting multiplexed phone lines on a single pair of wires. A **multiplexed** phone line carries more than one phone number on a single set of wires. Other relevant features include:

- **Automated modem settings**: In the past, users had to enter complicated text-based commands known as AT commands. AT commands are cryptic and numerous, and can take a variety of parameters and attributes; perhaps that's why they're also prone to errors, and difficult to troubleshoot. Unimodem V drivers make the requirement for AT commands obsolete.

- **Operator Agent**: This feature enables Unimodem V drivers to handle multiple phone numbers on a single phone line through multiplexing. This technique makes it possible to route voice, fax, and data traffic across a single line. Through the use of distinctive ringing, in which a ring signal is used to identify the type of incoming traffic, Unimodem V can direct incoming calls to the appropriate receiving device.

PRINTING IN THE WINDOWS 98 ENVIRONMENT

Print mechanisms in Windows 98 incorporate a number of important features. The Windows 98 32-bit print subsystem supports two-way communications between computers and printers to help optimize the printing process. Network printing enables Windows 98 systems to print across a variety of networks. Deferred printing allows laptop users to save print jobs until their laptop attached to an available printer. Support for a new Image Color Matching standard (ICM 2.0) takes Windows 98 closer to high-end multimedia applications, and permits colors as shown on the screen to more closely match those that appear on printed output. Finally, Windows 98 also includes Plug and Play enhancements for printers and print drivers, that make it much easier to install and configure printers for everyday use. You will learn about all of these printing features in the following sections.

The 32-Bit Print Subsystem

The 32-bit print subsystem handles communications between Windows 98 and its printer or printers. As well as issuing print jobs, Windows 98 also accepts messages from attached printers, and uses that feedback to support faster, more sophisticated print services. All these communications occur through a Windows 98 system facility known as the "Print Spooler." In the default setting, the Windows 98 Print Spooler defines a temporary file (or files) where output waiting its turn for the printer may be stored. In Windows 98, the Print Spooler supports three important capabilities:

- **Bidirectional communication**: Windows 98 supports two-way communication with printers using an extended capabilities port (ECP). Physically, an ECP-capable printer uses the same parallel port as other printers. Functionally, an ECP permits the printer to send messages back to the computer. These messages can range from a simple "out of paper" to "change the print process to speed printing."

- **Enhanced metafile spooling (EMF)**: In earlier operating systems a file was often sent to the printer in the form of RAW (i.e., uninterpreted) data, in which each character and symbol to be printed was broken down into its component pixels. (**Pixel** is an acronym for "picture element," or a single point in a screen or printout.) The EMF system simplifies the process of sending instructions to a printer. Rather than sending output to the printer pixel by pixel, EMF sends an outline for each character, with additional bits that tell the printer to fill in the outline. This approach delivers the same information much more efficiently, which means that Windows 98 can send print jobs to the printer much more quickly. Once an EMF print job is started, it runs in the background, allowing the user to resume other activities, even as Windows 98 continues to handle the print request behind the scenes.

- **Printer drivers:** Windows 98 printer drivers include two parts: a universal driver, which handles basic communications and interaction with the system, and minidrivers from each printer manufacturer. Before universal drivers, each printer manufacturer created its own driver to interface with the operating system. With universal drivers, a printer manufacturer simply has to create a small "minidriver" to interface with the universal driver. The universal printer driver supports the EMF-compatible TrueType and OpenType font sets. OpenType is the successor to TrueType that is partially compatible with the Adobe PostScript format. OpenType makes it easier for manufacturers to write printer drivers and also provides better support for built-in fonts and character sets.

Network Printing

Windows 98 supports network printing through a variety of print servers. But network printing support is not perfect unless the drivers are identical. If your print server is connected to a Windows 98 computer, you should have the right driver for the printer connected to that computer. Driver compatibility is not assured if the printer is connected to a computer with a different operating system. Example results are as follows:

- **Windows NT:** Windows NT 4.0 (and lower) printer drivers are not always identical to Windows 98 drivers. Windows 98 will not import print drivers from a Windows NT print server. If your printer is connected to a Windows NT 4.0 computer, you may need to adjust various print properties. You will learn to make these adjustments in Chapters 10 and 14.
- **Novell NetWare:** With the right settings, Novell supports point and print capabilities, and can transmit appropriate printer drivers to the proper Windows 98 folder. With **point and print**, you can put an icon for the networked printer on the desktop. Then you can click and drag a document over the icon.
- **DEC PrintServer:** DEC PrintServer supports bidirectional communications between the PC client and a printer during the print process.
- **Hewlett-Packard JetAdmin:** Given the popularity of HP's LaserJet and InkJet printers, it should come as no surprise that the company's printer manager software is bundled with Windows 98. HP permits Windows 95, Windows 98, and Windows NT workstations to share settings from a single JetAdmin server.

On a Microsoft network, you can install remote printers across the network by specifying a valid path to a print server. You will get a chance to do so in the Hands-on Projects at the end of the chapter.

Deferred Printing

For laptops not attached to their docking stations, or for networks where a print server is offline, the ability to defer printing can be useful. When printing is deferred, an application still "prints" the entire print job, but the pending print job remains in the C:\Windows\spool\printers folder. Because the print job is stored on disk, it leaves active memory free to run other programs and services.

To enable deferred printing, click Start, point to Settings, and then click Printers to open the Printers window. Right-click the printer for which you want to enable deferred printing, and then verify that the "Use Printer Offline" check box is selected. If this option is not selected, your computer may send an error message that indicates that it isn't receiving communications from the printer. In some cases the resulting error message is straightforward: "the printer is off-line or otherwise unavailable"; in other cases, the error may be more cryptic (and inaccurate): "the printer is out of paper."

The "Use Printer Offline" option is not available on standalone laptop or desktop computers. Before you can use this option, you need to install a printer over the network.

Image Color Matching

Image color matching (ICM) is a process originally developed by Kodak to accommodate photographic digital equipment. Windows 95 incorporated the ICM 1.0 standard. Unfortunately, ICM 1.0 did not incorporate a more prevalent version of color representation, known as CMYK (a four-color model that uses values for *c*yan, *m*agenta, *y*ellow, and blac*k* to produce highly accurate color values). Consistency across all the Microsoft operating systems also became a problem, because Windows NT 4.0 is not equipped to handle ICM 1.0.

Thus, a multimedia developer working to ICM 1.0 standards on Windows 95 couldn't easily move to Windows NT if she required more power. In response to this situation, Microsoft developed the ICM 2.0 standard. ICM 2.0 is part of Windows 98 and should be incorporated in the planned 1999 release of Windows NT 5.0 as well.

Basically, there are two ways to look at digital color. The traditional method was known as "RGB," which stands for the colors red, green, and blue. Color TV uses red, green, and blue pixels. Many newer multimedia applications use CMYK. The inclusion of black adds significantly to a digital system's ability to accurately represent color information. Apple already incorporates support for CMYK through its Linotype-Hell Color Management engine (Linotype and Hell are two expensive and powerful brands of equipment for high-resolution, high-color imagesetting and scanning). Microsoft has licensed the rights to this engine to form the core of ICM 2.0. ICM's purpose is to keep colors consistent throughout the multimedia production process, which involves the following stages:

- **Input**: There are a number of new ways to put pictures into the computer today. Windows 98 supports three major types of input devices: Scanners, Digital Cameras, and CD-ROM drives. Support for DVD technology is discussed later in this chapter.
- **Editing**: Once a color image has been stored on a computer, you can edit it using a wealth of specialized programming tools.
- **Proofing**: Once an image is final, you must create an initial proof via color printing or digital or film proofing.

- **Distribution**: The proof can be reproduced in numerous ways, including commercial printing or television.

In an effort to simplify the transition from input to editing, Windows 98 APIs have been created to TWAIN standards. TWAIN is a set of software standards for capturing and representing images of all kinds. Until the advent of TWAIN, scanning a page into a word processor required numerous steps. To begin with, each scanner required a special application. You would scan an image to produce a file, and then save that file to disk. Then you might need a second application to convert the scanner's proprietary file format to some more readable format. Only then could you import the file into a graphics application.

With TWAIN, it is possible to integrate scanning of color images directly with desktop publishing applications. This also makes it much easier for vendors to develop scanner drivers, and for such applications to accept scanner input directly. (For further information on the TWAIN working group, and related standards and technology efforts, visit *www.twain.org*.)

Installing and Configuring Printers

As you'll learn in the next section, the Windows 98 Plug and Play feature can automate the process of installing Plug-and-Play-compatible printers. In this section you will learn how to install a printer that is *not* Plug-and-Play-compatible.

You can install non-Plug-and-Play printers using the Add Printer Wizard. To install a local printer:

1. Insert the Windows installation CD into your CD-ROM drive.
2. Click Start, point to Settings, click Printers, and then double-click the Add Printer icon. The first page of the Add Printer Wizard opens.
3. Click Next. In the next page, you need to specify how the printer is attached to your computer.
4. Click the Local printer option button, then click Next.
5. In the Manufacturers list, click the manufacturer of your printer, select your printer model in the Printers list, click Next, and then skip to Step 7. If you don't see your manufacturer or printer in this dialog box, go to Step 6.
6. If you don't see the correct manufacturer or model, you need to obtain the correct driver from the manufacturer. In some cases, this driver may be supplied on a 3½-inch disk or on a CD. You may also be able to download the driver you need from the manufacturer's Web site. After you have acquired the correct driver, click Have Disk and follow the prompts to install the driver.

If you acquire print drivers from the Internet, or from some other source, inspect them to make sure they're in a readable form. Many drivers and ancillary files are delivered in archival or compressed formats, such as ZIP, to speed their delivery across the Internet. In that case, you need to decompress those files and save them to a floppy or a disk directory before you can install them.

7. Next, you need to specify the port you want to use with this printer. If you are printing locally, the standard printer port is LPT1. Click the Configure Port button. On the next page, "Spool MS-DOS print jobs" is usually specified by default. If you print from an MS-DOS application, all you need to do is specify the same printer port in the printer settings for that application.

8. Click OK to exit the Configure LPT Port dialog box. Click Next to go to the next page in the Add Printer Wizard. You can specify a different name for this printer, and set this as your default printer if desired. Accept the defaults and click Next.

9. On the next page, the wizard gives you the option of testing your settings by printing a test page. If your printer is physically connected to your computer, click Yes, then click Finish. Your computer now copies the driver files associated with your new printer from the Windows 98 Installation CD.

10. Now check your settings. In the Printers folder, you should now see a printer icon with the name of the printer that you just created. Right-click the icon for your printer to open the shortcut menu, and then click Properties. This opens a dialog box named after the printer that you just created.

11. Click the General tab if necessary. Every printer includes options for a separator page between print jobs. Click the arrow next to the Separator page text box. You see three options: (none), Full, and Simple. The default is (none), or no separator page between print jobs. Full creates a graphical separator page between jobs. Simple creates a text separator page between jobs.

Plug and Play Support

If a printer complies with Plug and Play requirements, and the driver software is loaded on the Windows 98 CD, all you need to do is plug the printer into an appropriate port and turn on your computer. When it becomes active, the printer sends its device ID to Windows 98. A **device ID** uniquely identifies the make and model of a component such as a printer. Then Windows 98 searches the C:\Windows\inf\msprint.inf and Msprint2.inf files to seek a match to that ID. If a match occurs, Windows 98 proceeds with the installation automatically. If no match occurs, Windows 98 offers three options:

- **Provide an updated Windows 98 driver for your particular printer**: If your printer was manufactured after Windows 98 was released, you may need to provide an updated driver. Choose this option if you already have the driver saved to a disk. As with legacy printers, new PnP printer drivers are usually available on the Internet, or from corporate bulletin boards. But be aware that Windows NT 4.0, Windows 95, and Windows 98 are not always compatible; be sure to pick a driver that specifically mentions support for Windows 98.

- **Install the printer drivers that Windows 98 has found to be the closest match**: Unlike Windows 95, which works with generic printers, Windows 98 does its best to identify a printer driver that is most compatible with whatever printer it finds. This option works well with many current printers. However, in most cases, it's worth looking for an updated driver before accepting any close match that Windows 98 may suggest.

- **Don't install a printer driver at this time**: Choose this option if you want to take some time to look for an updated driver before proceeding further. In most cases, it's worth looking for an updated driver before accepting any close match that Windows 98 may suggest.

All in all, Windows 98 makes it easy to install and use a wide variety of printers, whether attached locally or across the network. In the sections that follow, you will change your focus, and learn about Windows 98 disk management tools and technologies.

MANAGING WINDOWS 98 HARD DISKS

The term **disk management** is used to refer to all the activities necessary to maintain the maximum amount of usable space, to clean up the trash that accumulates over time, and to prevent or repair disk structure problems that can cause system difficulties over time. Because the contents of your hard disks are so critical to a functioning system, and ready access to your disks even more so, good disk management is important. At the same time, space requirements for the latest versions of software continue to grow with no end in sight. Users with smaller hard disks need tools to clean their disks regularly in order to maintain as much free space as possible. Those users fortunate enough to own larger hard disks face a different set of disk management problems, such as appropriate partition size, as discussed in Chapter 2.

Irrespective of disk size, typical disk management tasks include:

- Purge unwanted or unneeded files (this includes deleting obsolete or unwanted files, and purging files retained in the Windows 98 Recycle Bin)
- Compress seldom-used files
- Rearrange files broken across multiple areas on disk, a process known as defragmentation
- Consolidate free space on disk

In the sections that follow, you will learn about five disk management techniques that you can perform using utilities included with Windows 98. These techniques work not only for hard disks, but for many related kinds of Windows 98-compatible removable drives as well, such as Zip, Jaz, and Syquest. These five techniques are:

- Partitioning
- FAT32 format (enabling large disks)
- Compression
- Defragmentation
- Purging the Recycle Bin

Some of the techniques described in this chapter erase the entire contents of the hard disks to which they're applied. As a general rule, this book assumes you are completing the numbered steps on your own PC. However, until you become completely familiar with the techniques described in this section, you should only read the numbered steps. If you do decide to follow along with the numbered steps, make sure you have access to a spare hard disk that contains no critical data. Also, make sure your latest backup is entirely up to date.

DISK PARTITIONING

Before you can use a hard disk, you need to set up disk partitions. A disk partition is a reserved area on a hard disk that is often seen by an operating system as a logical drive such as C:\, D:\, or E:\. You will learn about the four types of disk partitions later in this section. You can use the Fdisk utility to set partition parameters for hard disk drives. The Fdisk.exe program file resides in the C:\Windows\command subdirectory. If you use Fdisk to remove a disk partition, all data in that partition will be permanently erased. If you use Fdisk to repartition or rearrange the partitions on a hard disk, all data on the entire hard disk will be permanently erased. There are four types of partitions, which reflect their roles in a hard disk:

- **Primary DOS partition**: This becomes your boot partition, the part of the disk your BIOS uses to boot your system. As the boot partition, it includes a file allocation table (FAT). There can be up to four primary DOS partitions on every physical hard disk. If you have one hard drive, this means that you can have partitions with drive letters C, D, E, and F.

- **Extended DOS partition**: If you need to divide your hard drive into more than four sections, you can substitute an extended DOS partition for the last primary DOS partition. Although an extended partition does not have a file allocation table, each extended partition gets its own drive letter.

- **Logical DOS partition**: You can divide an extended DOS partition into as many logical DOS partitions as you need. The only limit on the number of logical DOS partitions is the available letters of the English alphabet.

- **Non-MS-DOS partition**: Any partition created by a different operating system such as OS2. Nonprimary partitions created by a utility from a hard disk vendor often appear as non-MS-DOS partitions.

 If your computer uses a third-party utility to get around the partition limitations discussed in Chapter 2, please be careful. Many such utilities substitute their own commands for BIOS functions to get around DOS limits on partition sizes. If you use one of these utilities, you may be able to find it in the startup sequence when you turn on your computer. As the computer starts up, watch for an option to access the built-in BIOS (basic input output system) menu. Allow your computer to continue booting. If you then see an option to access a built-in disk configuration menu, you already have a built-in partition management utility that may not be fully compatible with Fdisk. If you originally used a utility from your hard disk vendor to partition your hard drive, use that utility instead. Fdisk is not customized for the hard disks of different vendors.

Managing Windows 98 System Resources 267

Now that you've been acquainted with its risks, you should also know that Fdisk works in two ways. In the following steps, you will learn how to perform a basic Fdisk procedure for disks with a capacity of less than 512 MB. In the next section, you will perform an Fdisk procedure on a larger hard disk.

 The following steps will destroy whatever is stored on your hard disk. If you plan to perform these steps on your own computer, back up all of your data first.

To run Fdisk on a single physical hard disk smaller than 512 MB:

1. If you're repartitioning drive C, use Windows 98 to create a bootable DOS 3½-inch disk and then copy fdisk.exe to that disk, to avoid losing access to the system while in the midst of this activity. Alternately, you may have already created a bootable DOS disk with fdisk.exe in the Emergency Startup Disk. Since you'll be reformatting the drive where the operating system and this code probably reside, this is well worth doing.

2. Click Start, point to Programs, click MS-DOS Prompt. The Run dialog box opens.

3. In the Run text box, type c:\windows\command\fdisk.exe. An Fdisk options screen appears with the choices described in Table 8-1.

Table 8-1 Basic Fdisk Options

Option	Explanation
Create DOS partition or logical DOS drive.	If you choose this option, you can divide your physical hard disk into primary, extended, or logical DOS partitions.
Set the active partition.	The active partition is the boot partition and must therefore be a primary partition.
Delete a partition or logical drive.	This is a dangerous option. Choose it only if you want to create a larger partition and are confident of restoring all of your files on this drive from backup. If you delete partitions, you need to delete them in the following order: non-MS-DOS, logical, extended, then primary.
Display partition information.	This displays the partitions defined for the current physical hard disk drive.
Change current fixed disk drive.	This option is available only if you have more than one hard disk installed in your computer. If you choose this option, you are sent to a menu to choose another physical hard disk.

If your disk is larger than 512 MB, you are given the option to enable large disk support. This topic is covered in the next section.

ENABLING LARGE DISK SUPPORT

The Fdisk utility included with Windows 98 also includes support for large disks. Large disk support requires that you use the FAT32 file system for your hard disk, instead of the standard FAT16 file system. (In other words, Fdisk can format hard drives using FAT32.) You learned about the differences between the two systems in some detail in Chapter 2. Briefly, while FAT 16 supports drive partitions up to 2 GB in size, FAT32 supports two drives up to 2 TB, or 2048 GB. If you use more than one operating system on your computer, such as MS-DOS 6.x or Windows NT 4.0, in addition to Windows 98, these other systems cannot read a FAT32-formatted disk. (You will learn to set up a "dual boot" between two or more operating systems in Chapter 12.) Instead of formatting a disk as a FAT32 disk, you can start with a FAT16 formatted disk and convert later. You will learn about the FAT32 conversion utility later in the next section.

In the last section, you learned how to use Fdisk with physical disks of less than 512 MB. The Fdisk menu can switch between multiple physical disks. If you run Fdisk with a physical hard disk larger than 512 MB, you will see the screen shown in Figure 8-1.

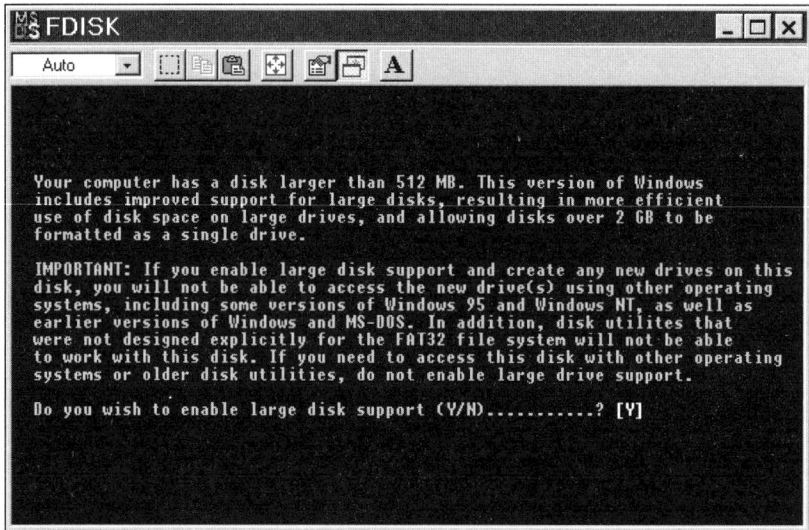

Figure 8-1 Large disk Fdisk screen

If, despite the cautions, you still want to create a FAT32 partition, press the Y key and then press Enter. The Fdisk program will then give you the same options as discussed in the last section. The only difference is that Fdisk will use the FAT32 format on your hard disk.

FAT32 Drive Converter

Instead of creating a FAT32 partition by using Fdisk on a large hard drive, you could start with a FAT16 partition. FAT16 disks can be read by all Microsoft operating systems. But the future of Microsoft operating systems is with FAT32. As you learned in Chapter 2, FAT32 is more efficient. To provide for easier operating system upgrades, Windows NT 5.0 will work with FAT32.

As you learned in Chapter 2, converting a partition from FAT16 to FAT32 format is a one-way process. Windows 98 provides no applications for converting a drive from FAT32 to FAT16 format. The only way to return your hard drive to FAT16 after converting it to FAT32 is to back up the files from the FAT32 partition, reformat that partition as FAT16, and then restore the files from the backup. Be aware that, depending on the size of the drive, the FAT32 Drive Converter could easily take several hours.

To learn about the FAT32 Drive Converter process, review the following steps. Do not proceed with the last step unless you are actually ready to convert a drive, and you do not need your computer for several hours. You can still use your computer while FAT32 is converting a drive that you are not using, but the performance will probably be less than acceptable.

1. Click Start, point to Programs, point to Accessories, point to System Tools, and then click Drive Converter (FAT32). The first page of the Drive Converter (FAT32) Wizard opens.

2. Click Next. This opens the page shown in Figure 8-2.

3. Select the logical drive you wish to convert. You can only select one drive at a time. Unless you are ready to make your conversion to Windows 98 permanent, do not convert your startup "C:\" partition, because Drive Converter would change its boot information. Once the startup partition is converted, you can only boot your computer with Windows 98 (and NT 5.0 when it becomes available).

Drive Converter cannot convert compressed partitions to FAT 32 (even partitions compressed using Windows 98 compression utilities). To continue with the Drive Converter, you must first decompress these partitions.

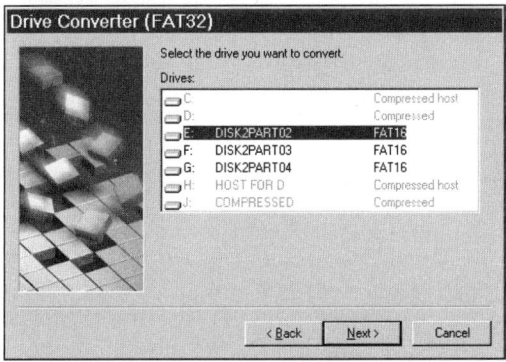

Figure 8-2 Drive Converter choices

4. Click Next. A dialog box appears, warning you about the effects of system hibernation. This refers to the power states related to the Advanced Power Management (APM) and Advanced Configuration and Power Interface (ACPI) drivers, which you learned about in Chapter 6. Laptops that go into a low-power state through APM or ACPI can interfere with and corrupt the conversion process. If you want to convert a laptop to FAT32, consult with your computer's manufacturer first.

5. Click OK. You see a dialog box warning about interactions with antivirus software.

6. Click OK. You see a dialog box explaining how converting can keep you from dual booting with systems such as Windows NT 4.0.

7. Click OK. Drive Converter analyzes the target drive for incompatible programs, especially certain kinds of antivirus software.

8. Click Next. Drive Converter gives you an opportunity to launch the Windows 98 backup program and back up your files. Once the information on your target drive is backed up, Drive Converter is ready to begin converting your drive.

9. Click Next. A final warning dialog box appears, telling you that the process may take several hours.

10. Unless you are actually ready to begin the conversion process, click Cancel. Otherwise, click Next.

Despite potential compatibility issues, FAT32 partitions offer two significant advantages over FAT16 partitions: first, they support much larger drives and partitions; second, FAT32 uses disk space much more efficiently. As you learned in Chapter 2, even though cluster size increases with disk size, the vastly larger number of clusters in a FAT32 partition makes it more efficient than a FAT16 partition. But remember, you can't use FAT32 on all drives; drives smaller than 512 MB may only be formatted with FAT16.

DISK COMPRESSION

Now that you have partitioned your disks, you are ready to manage each disk. One useful disk management technique is compression. Unfortunately, the disk compression utilities included with Windows 98 cannot compress FAT32 drives. Consequently, if you're limited on drive space and want to use the compression utilities available with Windows 98, your partition must be formatted as FAT16. There is one more limitation: once you have compressed a FAT16 drive, you cannot convert it to FAT32 unless you uncompress that drive.

In this section, you will learn to use the Windows 98 utility known as DriveSpace 3. The **DriveSpace 3** utility included in Windows 98 manages the process of compressing files on a hard disk in order to save space. The disk compression process works as follows: first, all the files on a drive are combined into a compressed volume file (**.cvf**). A new drive letter is then created, and the .cvf file is stored on that logical drive as a hidden, read-only file. For example, assume you are using a system with a hard disk, configured with drive C and drive D. If you apply DriveSpace 3 on drive D, it will first create a drive E, with the same space as drive D. The collected contents of the drive D are stored in one .cvf file on drive E. The space that you gain shows up on drive E.

DriveSpace should save your compressed files without any problems. However, no software manufacturer can test its products with every possible combination of computer hardware, disk controllers, hard drives, and third-party disk management software. Thus, it is always a good idea to back up any critical files on any disk you plan to compress. If a Windows boot partition is compressed using DriveSpace3, the Windows 98 uninstall program will be unable to revert to a prior version of Windows.

Windows 98 recognizes drives compressed using either the Windows 95 DriveSpace tool or the Windows 98 DriveSpace 3 tool. DriveSpace 3 works on standard disk storage components (hard disks, 3½-inch disks, and removable drives). To start DriveSpace 3, click Start, point to Programs, point to Accessories, point to System Tools, and then click DriveSpace. This opens the DriveSpace 3 window, where you can choose from several different kinds of compression. To view the compression options, click Advanced on the menu bar, and then click Settings. This opens the Disk Compression Settings dialog box shown in Figure 8-3, which offers the following options:

- **HiPack compression**: Uses the same compression method as standard compression (which is listed next), but applies a different method to determine the order in which files are compressed. This can save 10% more free space than standard compression.

- **Standard compression**: The same method used by Windows 95 DriveSpace.

- **No compression unless drive is at least**: If this option is chosen, you can set DriveSpace to compress only when drive utilization approaches a prespecified percentage of its capacity. The default is 90%.

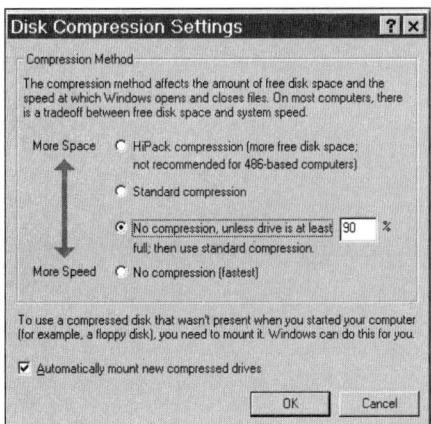

Figure 8-3 Disk Compression Settings dialog box

You can use DriveSpace 3 to save even more space, using what is known as UltraPack mode. To access UltraPack, you first need to run DriveSpace 3 on at least one drive in your system. Then you can click Start, point to Programs, point to Accessories, point to System Tools, and then click Compression Agent. UltraPack delivers the greatest possible compression of hard disk data. However, files compressed with UltraPack are slower to decompress and load onto your system. If your CPU has sufficient power, the speed penalty when you load from your hard disk is less significant.

DISK DEFRAGMENTER

Over time, as space is used and reclaimed on a hard disk, areas of free space become increasingly interspersed with areas occupied by files. Also, the size of these free space areas tends to decrease as more files are written to the disk, and to consume more and more of its surface area. This produces a phenomenon known as disk fragmentation, in which large files must be broken into a series of small chunks, called fragments, because no single area of available free space is large enough to accommodate the entire file. This can cause performance on a system to degrade, because more disk activity is necessary to read a file scattered across several areas on a disk, rather than stored in a single, contiguous area.

Windows 98 includes a built-in defragmenter utility to address this typical disk maintenance chore. To open up this utility, click Start, point to Programs, and then click Windows Explorer. In the left-hand pane select a drive icon, right-click the drive icon, and then click Properties in the shortcut menu. In the Properties dialog box, select the Tools tab, so that your dialog box looks like Figure 8-4. The bottom pane on this Window indicates the selected drive's defragmentation status, and includes a Defragment Now button that you can click to launch Disk Defragmenter. While defragmentation does not take as long as a FAT32 conversion, it still can be a lengthy process, especially with a compressed drive.

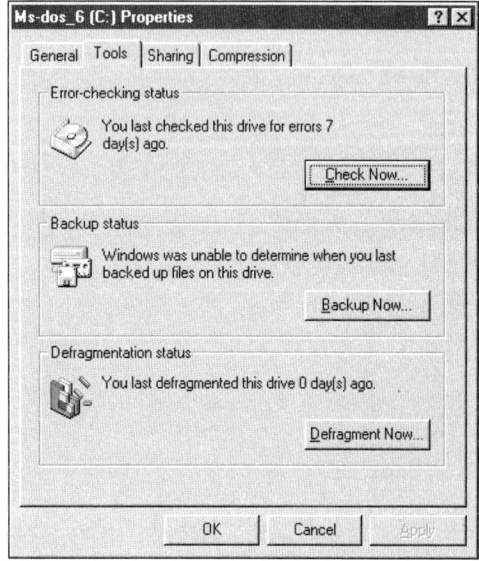

Figure 8-4 Defragment option in the Properties dialog box

On lightly used systems, consider defragmenting your disk monthly; on heavily used systems, weekly intervals are more appropriate. By default, you must run this utility manually. In Chapter 11, you will learn about Task Scheduler, which you can use to make sure that defragmentation and other similar processes are run on a regular, automated basis.

PURGE THE RECYCLE BIN

A quick look at the default Windows 98 desktop shows a wastebasket-like icon called the Recycle Bin. This represents a holding area for deleted files that have not yet been purged from the file system. The Recycle Bin permits users to undelete files after they've been deleted, simply by restoring them from their present location (in the Recycle Bin) to their original locations. Once you have deleted files from the Recycle bin, you cannot recover them using any Windows 98 utilities.

To specify settings related to the Recycle Bin, right-click the Recycle Bin icon on the desktop, and then click Properties on the shortcut menu. This opens the Properties dialog box shown in Figure 8-5. The Global tab appears by default; another tab appears for each drive on the system, identified by its drive letter (C in this case). If you want to specify settings for each drive's Recycle Bin independently, click the "Configure drives independently" option button on the Global tab, and then select settings on the individual tabs. The default is to apply the settings from the Global tab to all drives.

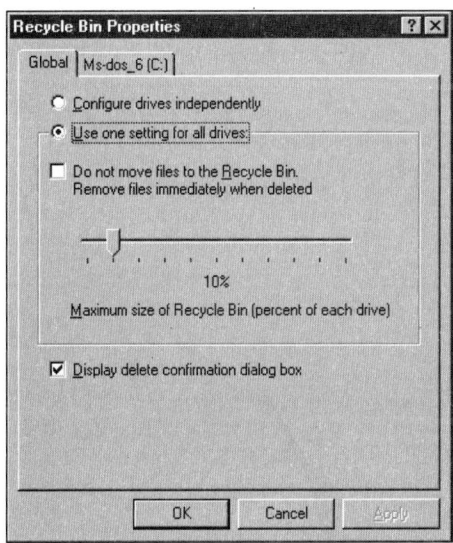

Figure 8-5 Global tab of the Recycle Bin Properties dialog box

The slider control in the middle of the window permits you to allocate the amount of disk space reserved for the Recycle Bin to use. This places a limit on the space that recycled files can consume; once the accumulation of files reaches this limit, the oldest files will be permanently deleted to make room for new files as they're removed from their original locations and placed into the Recycle Bin. If the check box at the bottom of the dialog box is selected, you will see a confirmation dialog box whenever you attempt to empty, or purge, the Recycle Bin.

Emptying the Recycle Bin can release significant amounts of disk space. To empty the Recycle Bin, go to the desktop, right-click the Recycle Bin icon, click Empty Recycle Bin on the shortcut menu, and then, if you see a confirmation dialog box, click Yes.

With the basic techniques for file and disk management under your belt, you can now proceed to an in-depth investigation of the Windows 98 multimedia capabilities, which constitute the rest of this chapter.

MULTIMEDIA AND WINDOWS 98

Microsoft's vision of the PC of the future resembles an appliance for all household electronics. Plug-in outlets will be available on the front of your PC. All you need to do to install a multimedia system is to "plug it in." Drivers will come preinstalled. You will even be able to add items with the PC turned on, without needing to reboot. Microsoft dubs this visionary box the "simply interactive PC" (SIPC). To support multimedia, Microsoft has created the DirectX Application Programming Interfaces (APIs). These APIs now provide a standard interface for multimedia developers. Without a standard interface, developers would have to write different programs for every graphics and sound card on the market.

In the early days of multimedia, just showing a postage-stamp-sized movie screen on a PC was considered quite an accomplishment. Since that time, hardware has improved dramatically; with the multimedia instructions associated with **MMX technology**, PCs have much faster processors with built-in multimedia capabilities. Improvements in all areas of data transfer, from the way graphics are captured, to faster transfer to and from hard drives, have made multimedia commonplace and affordable. The Universal Serial Bus (USB) and FireWire standards have the promise of bringing true multimedia to the home. With the technologies that you learned about in Chapter 6, such as ADSL and cable modems, their multimegabit per second download speeds come close to delivering signals that can even support high-definition television. Until recently, the Windows architecture failed to keep up with such stunning improvements in technology.

One roadblock in the Windows architecture has been the way all Windows operating systems communicate with the CPU. As you will learn in the next section, the Windows operating system required so much interface between different multimedia components that it overloaded the CPU. The new architecture developed for Windows 98 and Windows NT 5.0 addresses this problem in various ways.

RING ARCHITECTURE

Windows 98 is designed to run on computers with Intel CPUs. Intel allows four levels of access from various programs and drivers to the CPU. These levels of access are known as **rings**. In Microsoft operating systems, rings are related to something that you might be more familiar with: real-mode and protected-mode applications. Program commands at Ring 0 communicate directly with the CPU. Any command failure at Ring 0 (also known as the kernel) can cause any operating system to fail. Because most real-mode programs work at Ring 0, real-mode programs such as those based on MS-DOS are not recommended for Windows 98. When you have a Ring 0 problem, all you can do is reboot your computer. Commands at Ring 1, Ring 2, and Ring 3 have progressively lower levels of access to the CPU. Lower levels of CPU access correlate to lower risks of system crashes.

Current Windows operating systems (Windows 98, Windows 95, Windows NT 4.0) use Rings 0 and 3 to represent real-mode and protected-mode applications. Windows 98 protected-mode application programs work mostly at Ring 3 (also known as user level) to minimize the risk of a system crash from a single program fault. This can be a problem for multimedia, which requires frequent access to processors such as the CPU. It takes time to move processing commands between rings, enough time to affect the performance of multimedia applications.

Until Microsoft developed the DirectX/WDM model (described in the next section), multimedia sound and video had to go between rings a number of times before they could be played or displayed. Each instance of communication between rings can result in delayed playback. This may not be important with pay-per-view movies, but it can affect the quality of communication with time-sensitive applications such as video conferencing or computer telephony.

The Windows 98 multimedia features incorporate the new DirectX architecture, which was designed to address this traditional bottleneck. You will learn more about this architecture in the following section.

MULTIMEDIA ARCHITECTURE

Until DirectX, multimedia programmers had to write special programs every time their application had to work with the CPU. Their demands on the CPU exceeded the capacity. The connectors to the CPU (the buses) also have limited communication speed. The DirectX architecture addresses this through a series of layered programming interfaces, similar to the OSI model of networking that you learned about in Chapter 5. The programming within DirectX also minimizes data transfers between multimedia applications (Ring 3) and the CPU (Ring 0), thereby minimizing the load on the buses.

Two approaches to hardware facilitate the design of DirectX. First, PCs can use more than just the CPU for processing; for example, they can use processors on video and sound cards. If the CPU is still busy, DirectX tools can further reduce the processing load through buffers.

The Windows 98 multimedia architecture is illustrated in Figure 8-6. The programs at the top of this figure represent the main applications that you would actually use. They run in the Ring 3 layer of the Intel architecture. The bottom of the figure represents the hardware, in Ring 0 of the Intel architecture. On the left side of the figure are two legacy versions of DirectX. As you can see, these legacy systems, known as Open Graphics Language (OGL) and Graphics Device Interface (GDI), did not incorporate separate layers. The following bullets address some of the components of the DirectX foundation shown in Figure 8-6, also known as the hardware interface layers. The other elements of this architectural diagram are covered in the remainder of this chapter.

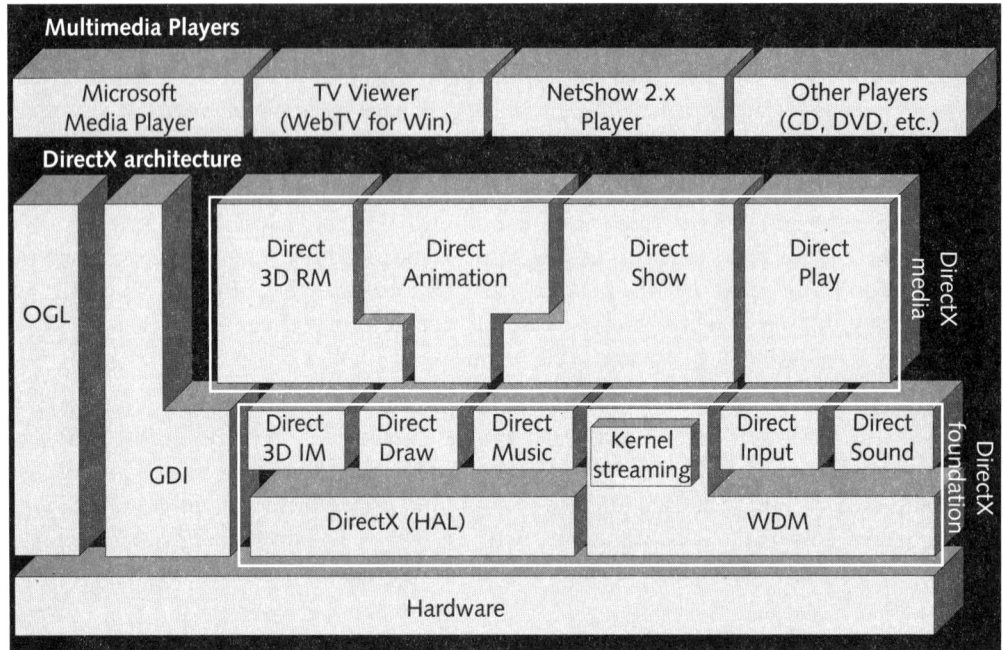

Figure 8-6 DirectX multimedia architecture

- **Win32 Driver Model**: This is represented in the diagram by its acronym, WDM. You learned about the Win32 Driver Model in Chapter 1. For multimedia, the 32-bit support and standardized interface simplify programming requirements. The WDM Connection and Streaming architecture allows most multimedia data to be transferred only once.

- **DirectX Hardware Abstraction Layer (HAL)**: Similar to WDM, in that it too defines a standardized interface to hardware. HAL can actually simulate some of the functions of multimedia hardware such as sound cards, when they are not available. HAL also makes the best use of available hardware acceleration programming for smoother motion.

- **Open Graphics Language (OGL)**: A legacy interface that operates between the application and the hardware. With OGL, a problem with the multimedia application can crash the operating system.

- **Graphics Device Interface (GDI)**: The MS-DOS-based multimedia interface, used to represent graphical images on monitors and printers. Problems with GDI multimedia applications can crash the operating system.

Although Microsoft considers GDI and OGL obsolete, they remain part of the DirectX multimedia architecture. This permits Windows 98 to support legacy applications designed to these standards.

An earlier version of WDM was implemented for the later releases of Windows 95 (known as OSR 2.1). WDM is not even available for Windows NT 4.0, a situation that remains problematic for multimedia developers who must work with both Windows 95 and NT 4.0. In response to this problem, Microsoft plans to incorporate DirectX/WDM architecture into both Windows 98 and Windows NT 5.0.

Plug and Play Support for Multimedia

Multimedia and the SIPC will not work unless Plug and Play works. Two interfaces new to Windows 98 promise to revolutionize Plug and Play. With Windows 95, lots of legacy systems were only intermittently PnP-compliant.

Plug and Play is significantly more reliable in Windows 98. On one side, the industry has had three years to adapt and develop PC hardware and peripherals to this standard. On the other side, Microsoft has improved its drivers for existing systems. The future of PnP depends on two emerging WDM standards for connections: the Universal Serial Bus (USB) and FireWire (IEEE 1394). These standards were introduced in Chapter 1. Here, you'll explore them in more detail.

Universal Serial Bus

The Universal Serial Bus (USB) is a standard that promises to simplify the hardware used in a PC. USB devices include a variety of medium-speed (1.5 to 12 Mbps) components such as keyboards, modems, joysticks, telephones, scanners, printers, and even monitors. You can connect up to 127 USB devices into a single computer. Because computers do not have 127 plug-in outlets, you need the equivalent of a plug with extra outlets. This extra outlet adapter is known as a **USB hub**. The Windows 98 USB driver can determine where you plugged in a USB device. Relevant Plug and Play features include:

- **Hot plug-in capability**: The ability to attach a device to a computer while the computer is on. An example of this is a USB-compliant mouse. You can plug such a mouse into a PC at any time. When you plug the USB device into the PC, the USB driver gives the mouse an ID based on the mouse's serial number. Alternately, the USB driver can identify the mouse by its port address, which specifies where it is plugged in, even identifying which port it is using on a USB hub. But once you connect a USB mouse to a specific USB port, you can only use that port for various kinds of mice. You cannot interchange different kinds of peripherals.

- **Persistent addressing**: Even if 127 USB devices are installed, the Windows 98 USB driver remembers the USB port that every device is connected to.

- **Power management support**: To help conserve power, USB supports three power settings: on, off, and suspend. This is compatible with the Advanced Power Management (APM) and the Advanced Configuration and Power Interface (ACPI) drivers that you learned about in Chapter 6.

There are three different types of USB components. Although these components have different functions, they all have characteristics of a hub. USB hubs are responsible for detecting devices that are connected to them, as well as managing power distribution to each component.

- **Host**: The base hub in the computer. The USB host can either be built into the motherboard or an adapter card connected to the motherboard.
- **Hub**: Hubs are either bus-powered, drawing power from the next hub closer to the computer; or self-powered, having an external source of power. A bus-powered hub can support a maximum of four downstream devices. Bus-powered hubs cannot support other bus-powered hubs.
- **Device**: The peripheral. For example, USB keyboards can have ports to which you could connect a mouse and a joystick. If you make these connections, the keyboard itself also becomes a hub.

IEEE 1394 FireWire

As you learned in Chapter 1, **FireWire** is a standard for devices similar to USB. FireWire standards are designed to accommodate higher-bandwidth devices at higher speeds (98, 196, and 393 Mbps), which makes FireWire especially suited to multimedia equipment. Like USB, FireWire uses a standard plug, and devices may be chained together. Instead of hubs, FireWire uses splitters to add more plugs (ports) for different devices. Since all signals have a range, repeaters literally listen to the signals on both ends and retransmit the signals. This can be used to extend the allowed distance between devices. Because FireWire also supports connections at variable rates, it can be used to accommodate multimedia networking standards, especially those associated with **Asynchronous Transfer Mode (ATM)**. You will learn more about ATM, which is a networking standard like Ethernet, in Chapter 13.

Multiple Monitor Support

With the right hardware, you can set up Windows 98 to work with multiple monitors at the same time. With multiple monitors, you can run different programs in Windows 98 on different monitors. Each monitor that you set up must be connected to its own graphics card. When Windows 98 was released, the number of graphics cards that accommodate multiple monitor support was limited. If you want to use multiple monitors, consult the documentation for your graphics cards as well as the Web site for the manufacturers of your graphics cards.

If you want to enable multiple monitor support, use the following general directions. What you actually do depends on the documentation for your second graphics card.

1. If you have not already done so, set up your first monitor and graphics card. Once complete, turn off your computer.
2. Install your second graphics card. Connect your second monitor to the card.
3. Restart Windows 98. If you do not have a plug and play system or card, you will need to install the card. Click Start, point to Control Panel, double-click Add/Remove Hardware Wizard, and follow the directions within the wizard. Restart Windows 98 once the wizard has copied the necessary files to your computer.

4. When your computer restarts, you should see the following message on your second monitor: "If you can read this message Windows has successfully initialized this display adapter."

5. Once Windows 98 restarts again, click Start, point to Control Panel, double-click Display; then in the Display Properties dialog box, click the Settings tab. You will see a picture of two monitors on this tab. One monitor will be grayed out; click this monitor. When prompted, click Yes to enable your second monitor.

Digital Video Support

Three important components in the DirectX architecture support digital video: WDM kernel streaming, DirectDraw, and Direct3DRM. A fourth component, DirectInput, helps support digital video games. Their functions can be summarized as follows:

- **WDM kernel streaming**: With legacy applications, data has to be transferred between the application and the CPU many times. With this mode, multimedia data is transferred only once.
- **DirectDraw**: Allows mixing between 2-D and 3-D objects. Can use available hardware, or can emulate graphical hardware functions.
- **Direct 3D Intermediate Mode (Direct3DRM)**: In legacy 3-D programs, you had to build a skeleton before you could build a 3-D model. With Direct3DRM, this is no longer required.
- **DirectInput**: Provides APIs that interface directly with graphical hardware, without interfering with the needs of video and sound input to the CPU.

Audio Support

You can choose from a wide variety of sound and MIDI (Musical Instrument Digital Interface) equipment for PCs. With the right hardware, Windows 98 can provide a platform for CD quality sound. With separate controls for channels that include volume and waveform shapers, it is possible to turn a Windows 98 computer into a true high-end audio production machine. To accommodate such requirements, Windows 98 requires at least a 2X CD player (if not an equivalent CD recorder). In the DirectX architecture, audio is supported by the following architectural components:

- **DirectSound**: This is similar to DirectDraw, in that it can either use available hardware or emulate required hardware functions in its programming.
- **DirectMusic**: A DirectX API that supports a customized music palette of different instruments.

DIRECTX MEDIA COMPONENTS

In the DirectX multimedia architecture shown in Figure 8-6, the DirectX media APIs appear just below the application level. These components include Direct3D Retained Mode (RM),

DirectAnimation, DirectShow, and DirectPlay. The major functions of each component are as follows:

- **DirectShow**: Makes use of the WDM streaming architecture to support realistic video playback. DirectShow makes use of compressed and uncompressed video streams.
- **Direct3D Retained Mode**: Supports smoother cartoon animation by creating transition effects between frames. Without transitions, computer videos often look "jerky."
- **DirectAnimation**: Facilitates animation in Web pages. This component is associated with Internet Explorer 4.0.
- **DirectPlay**: A consistent interface for interactive gaming applications, especially over the Internet.

DirectX Multimedia Applications

At the top of the DirectX multimedia architecture are the applications, the programs that you actually run. Microsoft divides its DirectX applications into four categories. More than one program may use the same application interface.

- **Media Player**: Intended to be the one player that you need for all audio and video multimedia. It is designed to play most of the known downloadable audio and video formats. You will learn more about Media Player in the next section.
- **TV Viewer**: Intended to integrate high-definition TV (HDTV) with the Internet browser known as WebTV. Many of the applications associated with this interface are still under development.
- **NetShow**: With compression, NetShow can support real-time multimedia applications such as video conferencing on communications lines with a capacity of around 1–3 Mbps. NetShow functions are now part of the Windows Media Player.
- **Other players**: Other software is available or under development to support CDs and digital video discs (DVDs). With a capacity of up to 18 GB, DVDs will be an important medium in the future of multimedia.

Media Player

Although Microsoft believes that the future of streaming multimedia leads to HDTV, its present incarnation is Media Player. To move multimedia across the Internet, most suppliers use some form of *c*ompression and *dec*ompression, also known as a **codec**. Media Player's advantage is that DirectX enables it to remain relatively independent of the numerous codec schemes developed by different multimedia suppliers, and therefore, to be equally appealing to all potential audiences for streaming multimedia at present.

With the right codec, it is possible to customize multimedia streams for everyone from regular home users with 28.8 kbps modems to business users who want enough bandwidth for video conferences. For home users, most experts assume that some download time is required to get enough data to produce pictures and sound of reasonable quality. For an application like video conferencing, large amounts of bandwidth are required to stream multimedia across the Internet reliably in real time. Estimated requirements for reasonable quality, real-time transmission is on the order of 1 to 3 Mbps, which is the equivalent of 16 to 48 telephone lines.

A codec in the multimedia world differs from codecs in the networking world. In networking, codec is an acronym for a *coder/decoder*. Specifically, a networking codec converts analog data for transmission on digital lines. Networking codecs are common at telephone companies, where they convert analog voice traffic to digital signals for long-distance transmission.

CHAPTER SUMMARY

- You can share folders and printers over the network using share-level or user-level security. Under share-level security, network users can have full or read-only access to a shared resource, assuming they know the correct password. User-level security allows you to assign different users (or groups) different rights to the shared resource, and the user does not have to enter a password in order to access the shared resource. If you no longer want a particular user (or group) to have access to a shared resource, you can change the permissions settings for that resource.

- In addition to folders and printers, you can share and monitor other resources such as fax modems over a network. You can also integrate telephones into a network, so that PCs and telephones share the same cables.

- The Windows 98 print system includes several important features. The 32-bit print subsystem reduces the amount of data that has to be sent from the PC to the printer, thereby returning control of the application to the user more quickly. In addition, you can take advantage of network printing, deferred printing, and image color matching. Installing and configuring printers is almost hassle-free thanks to the Plug and Play feature of Windows 98.

- To manage your Windows 98 hard disks effectively, you should be familiar with several techniques and utilities. For example, you should be able to partition, compress, and defragment your hard disk. You should also be familiar with the various FAT file systems and know how to manage the Recycle Bin.

- Windows 98 includes numerous multimedia features. The DirectX architecture overcomes problems with the way in which the original ring architecture handled multimedia information. It also standardizes the interfaces for hardware and application suppliers, and supports streaming multimedia.

- Microsoft hopes that the "Simply Interactive PC" becomes the home appliance of the future, as easy to use as a toaster, yet a tool that can integrate the Internet, high-definition TV, and interactive video all in one neat package.

Key Terms

- **32-bit print subsystem** — Defines how Windows 98 communicates with printers. Accommodates newer computer to printer communication technologies such as the extended capabilities port and USB.

- **API (Application Programming Interface)** — A set of rules and specifications that permits one computer application to communicate with another, or which allows an application to take advantage of lower-level system services or to gain network access.

- **Asynchronous Transfer Mode (ATM)** — Like Ethernet, ATM is a networking technology for transferring data on a network. As you will learn in Chapter 13, ATM is well-suited to multimedia.

- **CMYK** — Short for cyan, magenta, yellow, and black. Multimedia developers use CMYK to filter out unwanted colors. This is different from the RGB approach used by ICM to add colors as desired.

- **codec** — In the multimedia world, short for the compression required to transmit a multimedia signal over many communications lines. This is different from codecs in the networking world.

- **.cvf** — A compressed volume file. This contains the result when the files in a logical hard disk are compressed.

- **device ID** — Uniquely identifies the make and model of a peripheral such as a printer. When installed on a system for the first time, a Plug and Play peripheral sends its ID to Windows 98. If the ID is found, then the driver is loaded from the appropriate disk or CD.

- **DirectX** — A series of Application Programming Interfaces (APIs) that simplifies the task of multimedia programming. With the DirectX APIs, multimedia programmers no longer need to create programs to handle every make and model of hardware on the market. The DirectX APIs are organized in a series of layers, also known as a multimedia architecture.

- **DirectX hardware abstraction layer (HAL)** — Part of the DirectX multimedia architecture. If multimedia hardware is not available on a computer, the DirectX HAL is able to emulate the functions of that hardware as required.

- **disk partition** — A reserved area on a hard disk that maps to a specific disk structure. Sometimes referred to as a logical drive. In the Windows 98 environment, each recognizable partition will normally be assigned its own drive letter such as C, D, or E.

- **DriveSpace 3** — An enhanced version of Microsoft's built-in disk compression software, originally shipped with the Microsoft Plus! package for Windows 95. Drives compressed with this software cannot be translated from FAT16 to FAT32 formats. They must first be uncompressed before they can be translated. Also, if a Windows boot partition is compressed using DriveSpace 3, the Windows 98 uninstall program will be unable to revert to a prior version of Windows.

- **DVD (digital video disc)** — A new, high-density storage medium similar to a CD-ROM, that offers up to 18 GB of storage.

- **Enhanced Metafile Spooling (EMF)** — The technique used to simplify the data that is sent to the printer. A TrueType font can be sent as an outline and a command to fill that outline with ink, which takes a lot less data than a character that is filled in pixel by pixel.

- **Ethernet** — The popularized trade name for the first major networking topology, jointly developed by Digital, Xerox, and Intel. Ethernet was so much faster than the modems and terminals of the time that it helped to revolutionize how computers are connected.

- **file and print sharing** — In Microsoft terminology, the ability of Microsoft network-attached computers to make file system directories (called file shares) and printers available to other users on the network.

- **GDI (Graphics Device Interface)** — A special set of programming interfaces used in Windows 3.x and Windows 95 to represent graphical images and transfer them to monitors and printers.

- **HiPack compression** — A technique for file distribution that saves about 10% extra space despite being based on the same compression methods as standard Windows 95 style compression.

- **Image Color Management (ICM) 2.0** — A color-matching specification developed by Microsoft to help designers match output colors to digital color values or to other standard color-matching systems.

- **MMX technology** — Multimedia technology, developed originally by Intel to add multimedia processing instructions to the CPU.

- **New Technology File System (NTFS)** — Like FAT, a system for formatting and organizing a hard disk. Can only be done with and read by the Windows NT operating system. NTFS files cannot be read by Windows 98.

- **OGL (Open Graphics Language)** — Legacy graphical system that is included in the DirectX multimedia architecture model. OGL allows a multimedia application to interface directly with the hardware.

- **pixel** — One of the dots that make up the image on a computer monitor. Each pixel requires its own unique address, and depending on your monitor and graphics card, carries anywhere from 1 to 32 bits worth of color information.

- **RGB (red, green, and blue)** — The three primary colors of the television spectrum. Used by ICM 1.0, as supported by Windows 95.

- **Ring architecture** — The type of design incorporated into Intel processors. Intel processors include four rings. Ring 0 (kernel level) interacts directly with the CPU. If there is a problem with something running at Ring 0, the computer may be shut down. Therefore, Microsoft has set up most applications in Windows 98/NT 4.0 to run in Ring 3, as far away from the CPU as possible. Windows systems without the DirectX architecture are forced to bring all multimedia data back and forth from Ring 3 to Ring 0. This causes performance problems with the multimedia.

- **SIPC (Simply Interactive Personal Computer)** — Microsoft's PC of the future. The PC would become the heart of the family entertainment center, almost as easy to use as a toaster.
- **Telephony Application Programming Interface (TAPI)** — A standard devised to help develop integration between computers and telephones.
- **TWAIN** — A set of software standards devised to incorporate image capture directly into applications such as Microsoft Office without the need for intermediate, proprietary programs.
- **UltraPack** — The compression option in DriveSpace 3 that saves the most possible space. Uses a compression method different from Standard or HiPack compression.
- **Unimodem V** — A TAPI protocol that allows the multiplexing of more than one telephone number on one telephone line. Thanks to Unimodem V, Windows 98 can make use of distinctive ringing to determine which number is being called. Windows 98 can then send the phone call to the correct telephone appliance (e.g., modem, fax, or voice telephone).
- **USB (Universal Serial Bus)** — A medium-speed serial bus designed to handle up to 127 peripheral devices through a single port, including mice, keyboards, modems, telephones, scanners, joysticks, and so forth.
- **Win32 Driver Model (WDM)** — Part of the DirectX multimedia architecture. The WDM is a series of APIs designed to minimize the multimedia data that gets transmitted between the application and the CPU.

REVIEW QUESTIONS

1. Which of the following statements best describes Microsoft's vision of the future of the "simply interactive personal computer"?

   a. a computer that works in Ring 0 of the multimedia architecture

   b. a computer that is based on the OGL and GDI graphical interfaces

   c. a computer that will become the central entertainment appliance in the home, one that is easier to use than a VCR

   d. a computer that is based on an advanced version of the MS-DOS operating system

2. When Windows 98 is set up to use user-level security, Windows 98 cannot be used as a (choose all correct answers):

   a. file server

   b. print server

   c. fax server

   d. authenticator for user accounts

3. The Quick Launch folder is located in the C:\Windows\Application Data\Microsoft\Internet Explorer directory. You have just set read-only share-level permissions on the C:\Windows directory. What happens to permissions on the Quick Launch folder and why?
   a. The Quick Launch folder cannot be seen over the network. It is more than two steps down the directory tree from Windows.
   b. The Quick Launch folder is also shared. Because it is a subsidiary of the Windows folder, it is shared with full permissions.
   c. The Quick Launch folder is also shared. Any folder that is shared also results in the sharing of anything within that folder.
   d. The Quick Launch folder can be seen over the network, but nothing in that folder is shared.
4. How can you share a modem over a small local network?
   a. In Control Panel, double-click on the Mail and Fax icon, click Microsoft Fax, click Properties, and then click Modem on the menu bar.
   b. In Windows Explorer, double-click the Dial-Up Networking folder. Right-click the modem you want to use, click Properties on the menu bar, and then click the Sharing tab.
   c. In Windows Explorer, find the Dial-Up Networking folder. Highlight it with a right click, and then go to the Properties menu. Go to the Sharing tab.
   d. With Windows 98, it is not possible to share a modem over a local network, unless you have third-party software.
5. How does the Telephony Applications Program Interface (TAPI 2.1) support computer-telephony integration?
   a. TAPI 2.1 allows computer modems, voice telephones, and Ethernet to share the same cable. The computer routes signals to the correct device using a technique called distinctive ringing.
   b. TAPI 2.1 allows computer modems, fax machines, and voice telephones to work over the same phone line. The computer can route the signal to the correct device by means of a technique called automated modem settings.
   c. TAPI 2.1 allows computer modems, fax machines, and voice telephones to work over the same phone line. The computer can route the signal to the correct device by means of a technique called distinctive ringing.
   d. TAPI 2.1 is not included as a part of Windows 98.
6. In the 32-bit print subsystem, what is the purpose of the extended capabilities port (ECP), and what kind of connector is it based on?
   a. The extended capabilities port is required to support interactive communication with a printer on a remote server on the network. It is based on a bidirectional, serial port connector.
   b. The extended capabilities port is required to support enhanced metafile spooling. Since spooling is done through a port in the network architecture, ECP

enhances the communication to optimize the speed of transmission to the spool file. It is based on a bidirectional, parallel port connector.

c. The extended capabilities port provides a means of bidirectional communication with a local printer. It allows the printer to tell the computer when it is having problems, such as when the printer is out of paper.

d. The extended capabilities port provides a means of bidirectional communication with all external peripherals. When it is incorporated into Universal Serial Bus technology, computer processing can be distributed among different components.

7. How do you specify that only certain users on the local network have permission to read a certain folder?

a. Enable user-level access control in the User Profiles tab of the Passwords applet. Specify a Windows NT security provider for Windows 98 to get a list of users and groups. In Windows Explorer, right-click the folder that you want to be shared. Click Sharing in the shortcut menu, then click the Sharing tab, and specify the users to whom you want to assign permissions.

b. Enable user-level access control in the Access Control tab of the Network Neighborhood Properties dialog box. Specify a Windows NT security provider for Windows 98 to get a list of users and groups. In Windows Explorer, right-click the folder that you want to be shared. Click Sharing in the shortcut menu, then click the Sharing tab, and specify the users to whom you want to assign permissions.

c. Enable share-level access control in the Access Control tab of the Network Neighborhood Properties dialog box. Specify a Windows NT security provider for Windows 98 to get a list of users and groups. In Windows Explorer, right-click the folder that you want to be shared. Click Sharing in the shortcut menu, then click the Sharing tab, and specify the users to whom you want to assign permissions.

d. Enable user-level access control in the Access Control tab of the Network Neighborhood Properties dialog box. Specify a Windows 98 security provider for Windows 98 to get a list of users and groups. In Windows Explorer, right-click the folder that you want to be shared. Click Sharing in the shortcut menu, then click the Sharing tab, and specify the users to whom you want to assign permissions.

8. Which of the following problems does ICM 2.0 address? (Choose all correct answers.)

a. Multimedia developers hesitated to work on applications that complied with the Windows 95 ICM 1.0 standard. If they found that the multimedia that they were working on required workstation-level power, they could not move their files to Windows NT 4.0 Workstation without significant problems with color consistency.

b. ICM 1.0 did not incorporate the RGB standard. Multimedia developers found that the CMYK standard did not meet most of their needs.

c. ICM 1.0 did not incorporate the CMYK standard. Multimedia developers found that the RGB standard did not meet most of their needs.

d. none of the above

9. Suppose you have a new printer (released in 1998) that could not be identified by the Windows 98 Add New Printer Wizard. How could you determine whether or not this printer is Plug-and-Play-compliant? Choose all correct answers.
   a. Check your documentation for the words "Plug and Play." If you find that your printer complies with the Plug and Play 2.0 standard, call Microsoft to complain.
   b. Go to the Internet Web site for your printer manufacturer. If they have a Plug and Play driver on line, choose the one for NT 4.0. Because NT is a more fully featured operating system, the Plug and Play driver for NT is certain to have more features.
   c. Go to the Internet Web site for your printer manufacturer. If they have a Plug and Play driver on line, download the one for Windows 98, or at least the one for Windows 95. Go through the Add New Hardware Wizard again and load this new driver when prompted.
   d. Attempt to install the printer. If your printer isn't recognized by the Windows 98 Plug and Play system, then you must accept the printer drivers that Windows 98 chooses for you as the closest match.
10. Which of the following statements are true about the compatibility of the Windows 98 disk management tools with third-party utilities? Choose all correct answers.
    a. The Windows 98 disk partitioning system is not compatible with third-party utilities.
    b. DriveSpace 3 is like Plug and Play; it recognizes all third-party disk compression and disk management utilities.
    c. The Windows 98 disk partitioning system can create large disks without erasing any data, because no formatting is required.
    d. none of the above
11. Intel developed the Ring architecture to help minimize the risk of a premature computer shutdown due to the failure of an application. Which of the following statements describes how the Ring architecture affected multimedia on the PC?
    a. The Ring architecture does not allow applications to control how multimedia data was processed.
    b. The Ring architecture requires the whole package of multimedia data to go back to the application for every instruction.
    c. Multimedia problems were addressed with the introduction of the Pentium chip with MMX technology.
    d. none of the above
12. For peripherals installed outside of a computer, which of the following interfaces is fastest?
    a. FireWire
    b. Universal Serial Bus
    c. Pentium MMX 200
    d. PCI bus

13. With OGL and GDI, there used to be only one layer between the application and the hardware. Now there are several layers. What is the advantage of using several layers?
    a. The additional layers are required to accommodate Pentium MMX technology.
    b. The additional layers allowed Microsoft to standardize interfaces at the hardware and application levels. With the DirectX architecture, it is no longer necessary to write applications to handle every different kind of multimedia hardware card.
    c. The additional layers allowed Microsoft to standardize interfaces at the hardware and application levels. The DirectX architecture is designed to take advantage of a multimedia application that specifies everything that needs to be done in each processor.
    d. The additional layers were required to accommodate the new technologies required to share modems over a network.
14. You can create a separator page between print jobs:
    a. with the Add Printer Wizard
    b. through the General tab of the Properties dialog box for your printer
    c. by always having an extra blank page at the end of your print jobs
    d. through the Printer icon in Control Panel
15. Which of the following is the preferred disk format, if you also plan to install Windows NT 5.0 when it is released?
    a. FAT16
    b. VFAT
    c. FAT32
    d. NTFS
16. What is the purpose of a DirectX media layer API like DirectPlay?
    a. DirectPlay sets the communication parameters for interactive gaming.
    b. DirectPlay is the tool to animate the source code for HTML to enhance the Internet experience.
    c. DirectPlay takes advantage of legacy applications such as GDI to simulate the most realistic gaming conditions that are possible.
    d. DirectPlay is an application that is installed as part of Internet Explorer 4.0. Interactive games are run in the DirectPlay application.
17. Which of the following best describes the Microsoft vision of TV Viewer?
    a. Microsoft wants to integrate the Internet and interactive TV into the home entertainment experience. The entire system should be as easy to use as a toaster.
    b. Microsoft TV Viewer will be a direct extension of NetShow and DVD.
    c. Microsoft wants to integrate the ability to set up pay-per-view movies with the WebTV component of TV Viewer.
    d. Microsoft wants to sell TVs. Microsoft R&D is hard at work developing a pixel-free picture tube to support HDTV.

18. A USB bus-powered hub can draw power from which of the following devices?
    a. another USB device
    b. another USB bus-powered hub
    c. the USB Host
    d. none of the above
19. Which of the following DirectX applications now incorporates the features of the other? (Choose two answers.)
    a. NetShow
    b. MediaPlayer
    c. WebTV
    d. HDTV
20. When you are printing over a network, what happens to your print job when your computer is not connected to the network?
    a. Even if you only have a local printer, print jobs are deferred. You will not see an error message.
    b. If you have only a network printer, your print job will not be accepted. You need to install a new local printer from the Printers folder.
    c. Even if you only have a network printer, print jobs are deferred. You will not see an error message.
    d. The information for your print job is stored in the fax spool.

HANDS-ON PROJECTS

PROJECT 8-1

In this project, you will share a folder on your computer over a network. To complete this project, you will need two computers, preferably both with Windows 98 installed. However, your second computer can have Windows 95, 98, or NT installed. You need both computers configured with share-level security. You will also need your Windows 98 Installation CD. Before you start this project, you need to connect the two computers. You can use two Windows 98 computers that are already connected by a network, as long as they are set up for share-level security. Alternately, you can refer to Chapter 7, Hands-on Project 7-3 for instructions on how to connect two computers over a telephone line with two modems.

1. Insert your Windows 98 Installation CD into the CD-ROM drive.
2. On the Windows 98 computer, right-click the **Network Neighborhood** icon on the desktop, and then click **Properties** on the shortcut menu. The Network dialog box opens.

3. Click the **Configuration** tab if necessary.
4. Click **File** and **Print.** This opens the File and Print Sharing dialog box.
5. If it isn't already checked, select the **I want to be able to give others access to my files** check box, and then click **OK**. You return to the Configuration tab of the Network dialog box.
6. Review the list in the "The following network components are installed:" list box. Because you just enabled sharing, you should find File and Printer Sharing for Microsoft Networks. (Since you are using share-level security, File and Printer sharing for NetWare networks is not applicable.)
7. Click the **Identification** tab and make a note of the computer name.
8. Click **OK** and restart your computer when prompted.
9. Click **Start**, point to **Programs**, and then click **Windows Explorer**.
10. In the left-hand pane, find the C:\Windows folder.
11. Right-click on the **C:\Windows** folder, and then click **Sharing** in the shortcut menu. The folder's Properties dialog box opens, with the Sharing tab selected.
12. Click **Shared as**.
13. In the Access Type list, click **Full**.
14. In the Full Access Password text box, type a password, and then click **OK**.
15. Type the password again to confirm it, then click **OK**.
16. Close **Windows Explorer**.
17. Go to the second computer and open **Windows Explorer**. Click **Start**, point to **Programs**, and then click **Windows Explorer**. (If you are using a Windows NT computer, open **NT Explorer**.)
18. In the Network Neighborhood folder, double-click the name of your computer, which you noted in Step 9.
19. The share appears beneath the name of your computer.

PROJECT 8-2

In this project, you will try out the features of one of the components of the DirectX architecture model, Microsoft Media Player. In the first part of this project, you will download and install the Microsoft Media Player. Therefore, to complete the tasks in this project, you will need a computer with Windows 98 and Internet Explorer 4.0 installed, and at least a 28.8 kbps modem connection to the Internet.

1. Click **Start**, point to **Programs**, point to **Internet Explorer**, and then click **Internet Explorer**.

2. Connect to the Internet. If you have already set up an Internet connection on your computer in Chapter 5, Project 5-3, the Dial-Up Connection box opens. Enter your user name and password if required and then click **Connect**.

3. Go to the Microsoft Web site (*www.microsoft.com*). On the top of the Microsoft Home Page, click **Search**. This opens the search engine for the Microsoft Web site. In the open text box, type **Media Player** and press **Enter**. Examine some of the Web pages that appear in response to your search request.

4. If you haven't already done so, go to the Microsoft Web site for Media Player (try *www.microsoft.com/windows/mediaplayer*). Look for a link to download this application. Follow the instructions to save the file to your computer. Once you save the file, run it and follow the prompts to install Windows Media Player.

5. Now that you have installed it, you can open Media Player. Click **Start**, point to **Programs**, point to **Accessories**, point to **Entertainment**, and then click **Windows Media Player**. On the Windows Media Player menu bar, click **Favorites**, and choose one of the shows in the list. It opens a Web page.

6. On the Web page that you open, find and then activate a show or program to play. You will see a show either on the Web page or the Windows Media Player.

7. When the Player starts, right-click the active picture. It does not matter whether the picture is playing on the Web page or the Windows Media Player. On the shortcut menu, click **Options**.

8. In the Options dialog box, click the **Playback** tab if required. Experiment with the Audio, Playback, and Video options. Click **Apply** after each change, and watch what happens.

9. Click the **Advanced** tab. In the Advanced options text box, highlight **Windows Media** and click **Change**. In the Windows Media dialog box, try a different number of seconds for buffering. Click **OK** to return to the Options dialog box, then click **OK** to return to your show and see if the performance changes.

10. Other commands of interest are Properties and Statistics. Right-click the picture again to get to each command. You can find the frames or packets transmitted in the Statistics dialog box. You can find the current Codec routines under the Advanced tab in the Properties dialog box.

PROJECT 8-3

This project builds on Project 7-4. You will need the same computers that you used in that project. You also need to show all files, including hidden files. Before you start this project, review the steps in Project 7-4, to make sure you are familiar with them.

1. To check whether your Windows 98 computer currently shows hidden files, click **Start**, point to **Programs**, and then click **Windows Explorer**.

2. Click **View** in the menu bar, and then click **Folder Options**. The Folder Options dialog box opens.

3. Click the **View** tab. In the Advanced settings box you should see three entries under Hidden files. Click the **Show all files** button to select it, then click **OK**.

4. Click **Start**, point to **Settings**, and then click **Printers** to open up the Printers folder.

5. Select the network printer that you set up in Hands-on Project 7-4. (You can identify a network printer by the horizontal cable located directly beneath the icon.)

6. If there is a check mark above that printer, then it already is the default printer. Skip to Step 8.

7. Right-click the networked printer, and then click **Set as Default** on the shortcut menu.

8. Open a word-processing application, open a file, and print it.

9. If an error message appears indicating that the network printer is no longer available, click **OK**. In any case, you should now see a printer icon in your System Tray (adjacent to your clock). Your print job is saved in the local print queue. You will examine your print queue next.

10. Click **Start,** point to **Programs,** point to **Accessories,** and then click **Notepad.**

11. Click **File** on the menu bar, then click **Open**. Then use the Look in list box to navigate to the C:\Windows\Spool\Printer directory.

12. In the bottom of the Open dialog box, click the **Files of type** list arrow and select **All Files (*.*)**. You see two files in the file list area.

13. Open and view each file. You will note that the file with the .shd extension includes the name of your printout. The other file, with the .spl extension, contains links to files in your C:\Windows\Temp folder. When you reconnect to the Windows 98 RAS computer with the printer, it will first look to your spool. The file in the spool then refers to your C:\Windows\Temp directory for the actual printout. If you are printing to a printer capable of enhanced metafile spooling (EMF), these files will start with Emf. Next you will connect to your Windows 98 RAS.

14. Click **Start**, point to **Programs**, point to **Accessories**, point to **Communications**, and then click **Dial-Up Networking**.

15. Double-click the icon you created in Project 7-4. (If you followed the recommendation in Project 7-4, the icon will be labeled Dial-Up Server.)

16. Enter a password if necessary, and then click **Connect**. After your computer connects to the remote server, you should be able to observe the process of printing the file.

CASE PROJECTS

1. As a network administrator, you need to determine which of the disk management strategies you should implement. You have asked your company to begin using identical software and hardware in all departments, but have found that differing requirements

among various departments in your organization mean that such standardization is not possible. You have created a standard software list, with a minimum space requirement of 600 MB and a typical space requirement of 1.2 GB. You also know that software requirements increase every year. You have three basic systems, depending on which department is involved:

   a. Desktop computers with 500 MB hard disks. The budget will not allow hard disk upgrades today, but will permit new computers to be purchased in a year.
   b. Laptops with 800 MB hard disks. You can replace these in two years.
   c. Desktop computers with 4 GB hard disks. You are not presently concerned about their disk capacity requirements.

   Given these requirements and capacities, which of the disk management tools from this chapter is most appropriate? The first two groups presently use Windows 95, and the third group uses Windows NT 4.0 Workstation. Is it worth upgrading to Windows 98 (the accountants are open to spending some money here) for its improved disk compression technologies? What can you do as software space requirements increase? At what point should you become concerned with disk space for the third group of machines?

2. Your supervisor has just read about DirectX and what it can do for multimedia software. He has asked you to investigate these technologies further. He has read that DirectX does allow more independence between hardware and applications. He believes that if that is true, DirectX could reduce the total cost of ownership for computers in the department. These computers presently run Windows 95.

   Do your own investigation of the DirectX architecture. Go to the Microsoft Web site at *www.microsoft.com*. Do a search based on the topics shown in Figure 8-6. You should be able to find a wealth of information on each of these applications and APIs.

   Do your research with the following questions in mind. Which of these technologies are included in which operating systems? What can you incorporate today by means of downloads from the Microsoft site? Will a series of downloads over the Windows 95 operating system provide a sufficiently stable platform for the multimedia that you're looking for? What would be the advantage of upgrading to Windows 98 in terms of multimedia?

3. Your boss has heard of a number of disk management tools. He has heard that DriveSpace 3 and FAT32 are two great ways to optimize available space on your hard disk. He wants you to implement both on all computers in your organization. You need to explain to him that both tools cannot be used simultaneously on the same hard disk. Given what you learned in this chapter, and the plans of your organization to upgrade to Windows NT 5.0 when it is released, what would you recommend, and why?

CHAPTER NINE

Managing Windows 98 Applications

Windows 98 is a 32-bit operating system, but has the ability to run 16-bit DOS and Windows applications. This is possible, in part, because Windows 98 is built on a modular design. Some important features of this design are: A 32-bit kernel that manages memory and CPU time allocation, a 32-bit file system that eliminates the need to rely on DOS for file management, 32-bit file system drivers that support a variety of file formats, and mechanisms for cleanup after an application or driver fails.

In this chapter, you will learn how to use these features to manage applications in Windows 98. In particular, you will learn how the Windows 98 architecture is able to support both 32-bit and 16-bit applications. You will also learn how to run MS-DOS programs in Windows 98. Finally, you will learn how the Installable File System Manager works.

> **AFTER READING THIS CHAPTER AND COMPLETING THE EXERCISES, YOU WILL BE ABLE TO:**
>
> - Describe the 32-bit system and memory architecture
> - Explain how Windows 32-bit, and Windows 16-bit applications share memory and CPU access
> - Configure MS-DOS applications to run in Windows 98
> - Describe the Windows 98 file systems and the Win32 Driver Model

32-BIT SYSTEM AND MEMORY ARCHITECTURE

As you know, Windows 98 is a multitasking operating system. In other words, it allows multiple programs to run simultaneously. Note, however, that not all programs can run concurrently with others. Specifically, MS-DOS-based programs require exclusive access to system resources such as disk drives and printers while being run. In addition, the 16-bit programs common to Windows 3.1 cannot truly be run at the same time as other programs. However, Windows 98 is designed to accommodate the special needs of these programs, while at the same time taking advantage of 32-bit memory.

Windows 98 is able to accommodate both types of programs, in part because it runs all applications in protected mode, which means that they run in Ring 3 of the Intel protection architecture. (You learned about the Intel ring architecture in Chapter 8.) Because programs run in protected mode, the failure of any one program should not compromise the integrity of the operating system. In order to understand exactly how the operating system is protected from problems with its applications, you need to understand the terms and concepts explained in the following sections.

DEFINITIONS

This section summarizes some key terms related to the way Windows 98 manages applications. Don't worry if you don't completely understand these definitions after reading this section. These concepts will be explained more fully throughout this chapter.

- **Address**: A particular location in memory where data is stored. When used as a verb (as in "32-bit programs can address its memory") this term means to use, or reference, a particular data storage location.

- **Virtual machine (VM)**: A separate, self-contained part of Windows 98 in which programs run. Each virtual machine looks like a separate PC to the programs running inside it. Windows 16-bit and 32-bit programs run in one VM known as the System Virtual Machine, which allows them to share resources such as printers. Windows 98 can manage multiple virtual machines at one time.

- **Virtual memory**: The memory allocated to an active program or group of programs. Virtual memory can exceed the amount of available physical memory.

- **Virtual memory address space**: The specific portion of virtual memory allocated to an active program or group of programs. 32-bit programs can use, or address, 2^{32} (4 GB) bits of information. Thus, Windows 98 allocates one 32-bit virtual memory address space to each 32-bit program, as well as to each MS-DOS program. All 16-bit Windows programs together share the same 32-bit virtual memory address space.

- **Paging**: The process of transferring, or swapping, memory between RAM and the hard disk. Windows 98 pages memory in 4 KB chunks. Paging allows your programs to store inactive data on your hard drive, and to retrieve that data when required. The storage location is known as a swap file. This process is sometimes known as demand paging.

- **Mapping**: The process by which paged memory is associated with a specific location in virtual memory.

- **Flat address space**: A single, complete memory address space. Because Windows 98 32-bit programs can use, or point to, 4 GB of information, they require only one flat address space. Compare to "segmented address space."

- **Segmented address space**: A memory address space divided into separate pieces, known as segments. 16-bit programs can point directly to only 64 KB of memory. Since your Windows 98 computer has a lot more than 64 KB of memory, a flat address space is not possible. To address the additional memory, you need to specify a segment (64 KB) and an offset (64 KB). With the segment/offset model you can address 64 KB $\times$ 64 KB = 4 GB of memory.

- **Process**: Any program or part of a program that is currently running. In Windows 98, every application is a process. One 4 GB virtual memory address space is assigned to each 32-bit and MS-DOS process. All 16-bit processes run together in the same 4 GB virtual memory address space.

- **Thread**: A subcomponent of a process. Every process has at least one thread. 32-bit processes (which make up the majority of applications in Windows 98) can include multiple threads. For example, a 32-bit process might contain one thread for keyboard input, one for data transfer, and one for program execution. Individual threads must share access to system resources such as the CPU time and the printer. This access can take the form of preemptive multitasking or cooperative multitasking.

- **Kernel**: The heart of the Windows 98 operating system. You learned about some kernel functions in earlier chapters. To support different applications, the kernel includes schedulers devoted to dividing system resources among threads. The primary kernel scheduler gives each thread a priority between 0 (lowest) and 31 (highest). Input/output operations such as keyboard tasks typically get a higher priority than printing or spreadsheet operations. The secondary kernel scheduler adjusts priorities by up to two levels (up or down) to help ensure that all threads have a chance to use system resources.

- **Preemptive multitasking**: A technique for controlling how threads are granted access to system resources, in which threads are allotted a predetermined amount of time to access each resource. After the predetermined amount of time is up, the operating system makes the resource available to other threads. Windows 98 uses preemptive multitasking to manage threads from 32-bit and MS-DOS applications.

- **Cooperative multitasking**: A technique for controlling how threads are granted access to system resources, in which threads periodically cede system resources to other threads. Windows 98 manages threads from 16-bit programs through cooperative multitasking, relying on the cooperation of each thread in giving up access to system resources after a certain amount of time. Poorly written 16-bit programs can "hog" the processor to the exclusion of other programs.

- **Win32 application**: Shorthand for a Windows 32-bit program that runs in Windows 98. Each Win32 application runs in its own virtual memory address space.

- **Win16 application**: Shorthand for a Windows 16-bit program that runs in Windows 98. Note that a Win16 application is different from an MS-DOS program. While an MS-DOS program is also 16-bit, it can run in an MS-DOS prompt window.

- **MS-DOS application**: Shorthand for a 16-bit program that runs in its own 4 GB virtual memory address space through the MS-DOS prompt window.

- **Virtual DOS machine (VDM)**: The 4 GB virtual memory address space assigned to an MS-DOS application that is running in Windows 98.

- **High memory area**: For MS-DOS applications, the area in RAM between 640 KB and 1 MB.

VIRTUAL MACHINES

Programs written for Windows, whether they are 16-bit or 32-bit, are written to share system resources such as disks and printers. However, programs written for MS-DOS require the exclusive use of system resources. To accommodate this need, Windows 98 creates special software constructs, known as virtual machines. Practically speaking, a virtual machine functions like a separate computer within Windows 98. Because they can share resources, all Windows programs operate within the same virtual machine, known as the **System Virtual Machine**. No matter how many Windows programs you may have running, you only need one System Virtual Machine. However, Windows 98 creates a new virtual machine for every MS-DOS program that you open within Windows 98. Thus, the failure of an MS-DOS program only directly affects the virtual machine in which the program runs. Theoretically, the failure of an MS-DOS program should not affect any other Windows application running at the same time. Figure 9-1 illustrates the allocation of virtual machines.

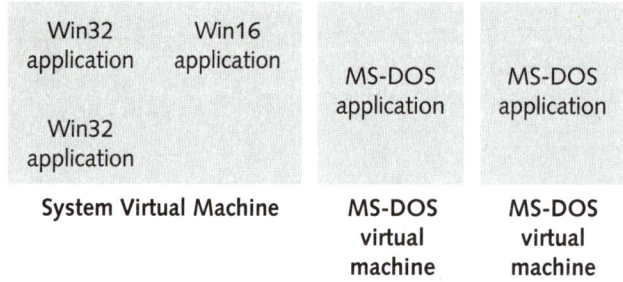

Figure 9-1 Allocation of virtual machines

VIRTUAL MEMORY

The term **virtual memory** refers to the memory allocated to a program or group of programs. The specific virtual memory assigned to a particular application is known as the application's **virtual memory address space.** Each 32-bit address space includes 2^{32} bits, or 4 GB of memory. In most cases, the total amount of virtual memory allocated to applications is not only larger than the amount of RAM installed on the computer, but, in fact, larger than the computer's total hard drive capacity. For example, as illustrated in Figure 9-2, every 32-bit Windows program, as well as every program run in MS-DOS, is allocated a single virtual memory address space of 4 GB. In addition, all 16-bit Windows programs together are allocated another address space of 4 GB.

Because the type of memory in question is "virtual," the physical limits of the computer are not necessarily an issue. Windows 98 uses a number of techniques to simulate the memory that applications need. In the next sections, you will learn how the 4 GB of each virtual memory address space are actually made up of resources drawn from the computer's various memory and storage devices. Then you will learn how, through the process of paging, information in RAM can be temporarily stored on the hard disk while RAM is used for another operation.

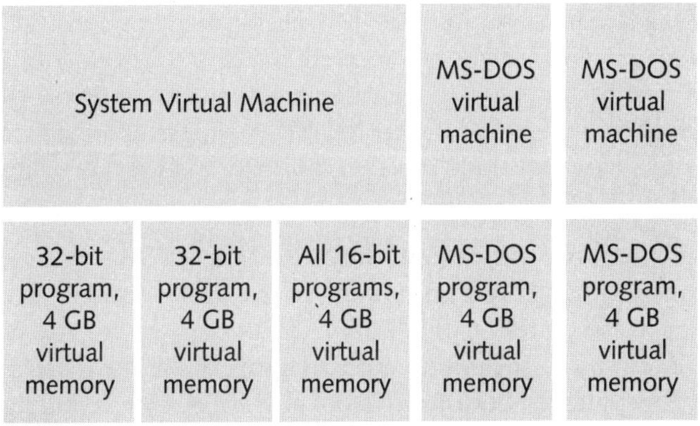

System Virtual Machine			MS-DOS virtual machine	MS-DOS virtual machine
32-bit program, 4 GB virtual memory	32-bit program, 4 GB virtual memory	All 16-bit programs, 4 GB virtual memory	MS-DOS program, 4 GB virtual memory	MS-DOS program, 4 GB virtual memory

Figure 9-2 Allocation of virtual memory

As shown in Figure 9-3, both an application and components of the operating system run in each 4 GB virtual memory address space. The top 2 GB belong to components of the Windows 98 operating system. The very top 1 GB is allocated to the following Ring 0 components, which communicate directly with the hardware: FAT16, FAT32, the CD-ROM File System (CDFS), and the various Windows 98 virtual device drivers. (You will learn about the CDFS in Chapter 10. You will learn more about the virtual device drivers later in this chapter.) The next GB is allocated to other system-wide processes, including some kernel processes and the processes of the dynamic-link libraries (which as you learned in Chapter 3 provide programming steps or code that can be used by more than one application at a time).

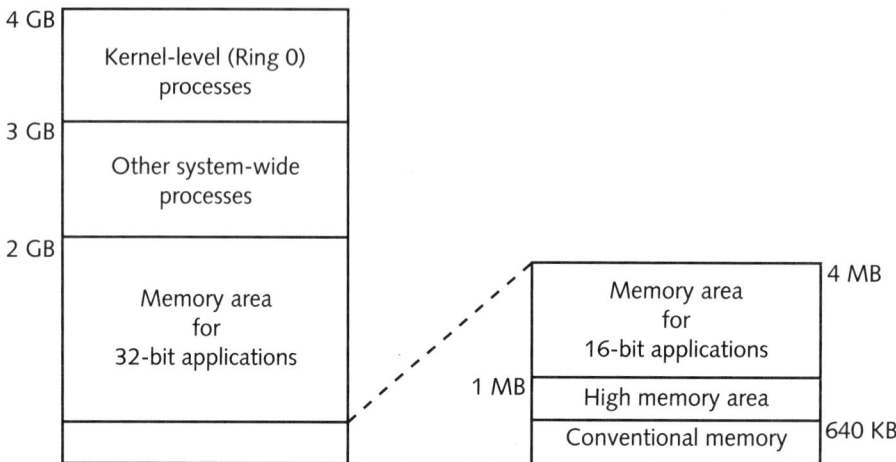

Figure 9-3 Functional division of virtual memory

Only the bottom 2 GB of memory space are actually used by the 32-bit and 16-bit programs. To be precise, the 32-bit programs can use all of the bottom 2 GB *except* for a small 4 MB layer at the bottom of the memory stack. The area between 1 MB and 4 MB is rarely used, and then only by 16-bit Windows programs. MS-DOS programs and real-mode drivers run in the very bottom 1 MB of the memory address space. The lowest 640 KB of memory are known as conventional memory. Everything between the first 640 KB and the first 1 MB is known as high, or upper, memory. In MS-DOS, programs are generally run in conventional memory. MS-DOS real-mode drivers often run and are stored in the upper memory area.

Some MS-DOS programs are **terminate-and-stay-resident (TSR)** programs, which means that once they are opened, they remain running in the background at all times. TSR programs load components in the bottom 640 KB of RAM. Because of the way Windows 98 creates virtual memory address spaces, the position of TSR programs in the memory stack can be problematic. Windows 98 copies the bottom 1 MB of physical RAM (including any active TSR programs) to the bottom 1 MB of each MS-DOS virtual machine. If any MS-DOS program adversely affects a TSR, the TSR then affects the 1 MB that is copied to all virtual memory address spaces, which can lead to a crash of your Windows 98 system.

To get a sense of how much memory your TSRs take up, click Start, point to Programs, then click the MS-DOS prompt. At the C:\Windows prompt, type mem and then press Enter. This displays information about how RAM is allocated, as shown in Figure 9-4. You will learn about the relationship between RAM and the virtual memory address space in the next section.

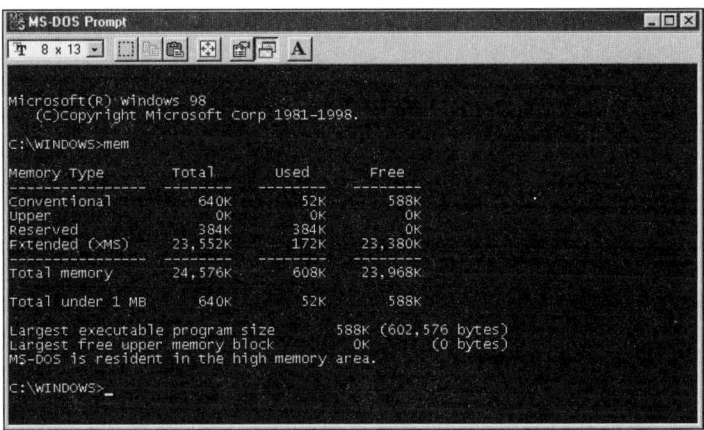

Figure 9-4 Memory allocations in RAM

As you can see in Figure 9-4, the total amount of conventional memory is 640 KB. Some part of this is always used by some TSR(s), which leaves less than 640 KB of conventional memory for MS-DOS programs. In Figure 9-4, 52 KB of conventional memory is already in use (by TSRs), leaving only 588 KB free for other uses.

MEMORY MANAGEMENT

As explained in the previous section, the top 2 GB of each virtual memory address space are reserved for the use of the operating system, while the bottom 2 GB are reserved for the actual programs. Each of these 2 GB sections is divided into smaller 4 KB portions called **pages**. Application and user data are loaded into the virtual address space in page-sized chunks.

One way Windows 98 is able to provide more virtual memory than the actual amount of RAM installed on the computer is by moving memory back and forth between your RAM and the hard disk. Memory is moved (or swapped) in 4 KB pages, which is why the process is usually referred to as paging.

By definition, a 32-bit application can address up to 2^{32} bits, or 4 GB, of memory with one address, which is why each virtual memory address space is 4 GB. This single, complete address is known as a **flat address space**. In contrast, a 16-bit application can address only 2^{16} bits, or a 64 KB segment of memory with one address. To address more than 64 KB, 16-bit applications use the segment/offset model of memory addressing. In this model, a program stores data in a group of small, distinct memory segments; however, these segments actually appear to the program as one contiguous area of memory.

In addition to paging, Windows 98 also manages its virtual memory through the use of processes and threads. Every program is its own process. Each process is made up of at least one thread, which is devoted to performing a specific task. A **thread** is the smallest unit of a program that can be run (or executed) in an operating system. 32-bit programs can run more than one thread simultaneously. A process running multiple threads is said to be **multithreaded**. As you will learn in the next section, the kernel schedulers actually allocate CPU time to individual threads.

In managing memory, Windows 98 also makes use of memory protection, which makes it difficult for applications running in different virtual memory address spaces to crash each other. In order to protect memory, Windows 98 works with the memory requirements of only one thread at a time. Memory protection between virtual memory address spaces is designed to prevent processes from inadvertently sharing information. However, it's still possible for threads in different processes to share information when required.

In any multitasking system, CPU time is shared among all active threads. Any time a thread from a new process takes over the CPU, the system must perform a **context switch**—that is, it must load the contents of that process's virtual address space into RAM (physical memory). Even though different processes can point to (be mapped to) the same locations in RAM, only one memory map is visible to Windows 98 at any given time. Context switches take a little time, so the more processes running on a system, the less responsive the system.

CPU ACCESS

In order to understand how different types of programs function under Windows 98, you need to understand how processes and threads work. Each thread is devoted to a specific task, such as mouse input or word-processor spell checking. CPU time is divided among active threads. Windows 98 allocates priority to different threads via schedulers that are part of the Windows 98 kernel.

Generally, Windows 98 manages threads by **preemptive multitasking**, in which threads run for a predetermined period of time called a **timeslice** and then give up the processor. The only exception to this rule lies with 16-bit Windows applications, which are managed through the Windows 3.x method of determining CPU access known as **cooperative multitasking**. In cooperative multitasking, threads are supposed to "listen" for other threads that need the processor and give it up at intervals. It is possible for a poorly written application to monopolize the processor. DOS applications can use preemptive multitasking because each of them is assigned its own virtual memory address space.

The kernel's schedulers give every thread a priority between 0 (lowest) and 31 (highest). Threads with the same priority are given their share of the CPU one at a time. The Task Scheduler includes primary and secondary components. The kernel gives a task priority based on the importance to the system. Critical system tasks such as I/O (input/output) from the keyboard have higher priority than general application programs. The kernel can increase the priority of threads that have been waiting by up to two levels, on the basis of :

- **User input needs**: Active applications are given higher priority. For example, if Microsoft Word is the active application on your system, the threads for user input into Word get a priority increase.

- **Just for being there**: All threads that have waited get a temporary priority boost to make sure that their parts of their programs are run periodically.

- **Computational requirements**: Programs that require heavy mathematical support, such as spreadsheets, actually get a priority decrease to avoid interfering with other active programs.

As you will learn in Chapter 10, you can monitor some of these components through the System Monitor tool. For now, you can find the number of threads and virtual machines currently running on your system, as well as the current percentage of processor usage:

1. Click Start, point to Programs, point to Accessories, point to System Tools, and then click System Monitor. This opens the System Monitor window.

2. Click View on the menu bar, then click Line Charts, to verify that the information about active threads will be displayed in a line chart. System Monitor may currently be measuring items on your system. In the next three steps, you can stop System Monitor from gathering data on any other items. If you prefer, you can skip Steps 3, 4, and 5.

3. Click Edit on the Menu bar, and then click Remove Item. This opens the Remove Item dialog box.

4. Make a note of any items currently included in the list box, in case you want to return System Monitor to its original state later.

5. Select any item in the list box, and then click OK. If you want, repeat Step 3 and select another item to remove. Repeat this as many times as required or desired. You return to the System Monitor window, where the display area should now be blank. Next, you can indicate that you want to gather information regarding the number of active threads.

6. Click Edit on the Menu bar, and then click Add Item. This opens the Add Item dialog box.

7. In the Category list box, click Kernel, click Processor Usage (%) in the Item list box, and then click OK.

8. Repeat Steps 6 and 7 twice to select Threads and Virtual Machines in the Add Item dialog box. Watch the results on your screen, which should look something like Figure 9-5.

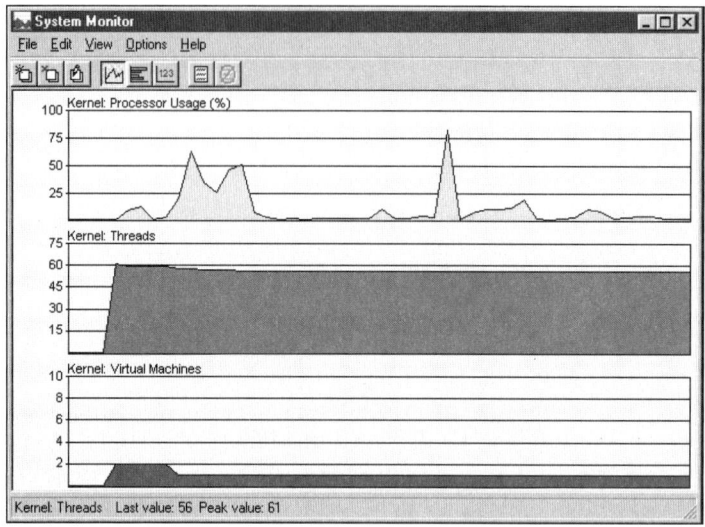

Figure 9-5 Viewing System Monitor

The charts in Figure 9-5 show one virtual machine. As you learned earlier, that means that only Windows-based programs (which all run together in one system virtual machine) are running. The charts also show around 50 active threads. Even if you close all of your currently running programs, you may still have 40 or more active threads. A number of threads are created by the Windows 98 operating system itself. Other active threads come from whatever might be in your System Tray, the icons located usually in the lower-right corner of your desktop, adjacent to the clock. In the Hands-on Projects, you will learn how these measures change in the System Monitor as you open up new and different kinds of programs.

INSIDE THE SYSTEM VIRTUAL MACHINE

As you learned earlier in this chapter, all Windows 98 applications, whether 16-bit or 32-bit, run in the System Virtual Machine. They can share the System Virtual Machine because they can share the hardware in your computer. The 32-bit characteristics of Windows 98 make 16-bit Windows programs run more smoothly than they otherwise would. The Windows 98 Registry incorporates many of the settings of system and initialization programs that were required to support 16-bit programs in earlier versions of Windows. In this section, you will learn how the 16-bit and 32-bit components of Windows 98 work together within the System Virtual Machine to share memory and CPU access.

WINDOWS 98 AND WIN16 APPLICATIONS

A Win16 application designed for Windows 3.x runs the same in Windows 98 as it does in Windows 3.x, except that the toolbar buttons look somewhat different. These applications actually run better in Windows 98, thanks to the improvements in device drivers and memory handling. If you have upgraded from Windows 3.x to Windows 98, you have probably noticed that your applications run faster in Windows 98, and that you can keep more applications active simultaneously with fewer system crashes.

Although they perform better in a 32-bit operating system than in the 16-bit one they were designed for, Win16 applications cannot take full advantage of the features of the Windows 98 operating system. This limitation springs from the fact that all Win16 applications run in a single 4 GB address virtual memory space. In the following sections, you will learn more about exactly how Win16 applications run in Windows 98.

Windows 98 Compatibility with Win16 Applications

As you know, most Windows 98 programs obtain the hardware and software settings they need from the Registry. However, programs originally written for MS-DOS and early versions of Windows obtained this information from a number of 16-bit configuration files. As explained in Chapter 3, when you upgrade to Windows 98, some of these settings are actually incorporated into the Registry. The most important 16-bit configuration files are:

- **Autoexec.bat**: Besides its role as the boot file for 16-bit operating systems such as MS-DOS and Windows 3.x, it also calls up the 16-bit programs that support hardware such as CD-ROM drives and sound cards. It does not load drivers. Windows 98 does not rely directly on this file, but refers to it to configure operating settings for MS-DOS applications.

- **Config.sys**: After Autoexec.bat calls the setup files for hardware, Config.sys loads the associated real-mode drivers. Config.sys cannot be run by itself. Windows 98 does not rely directly on this file, but refers to it to configure real-mode drivers for MS-DOS applications.

- **System.ini**: This file, known as the system initialization file, loads general virtual device drivers into Windows, which are then modified by the Win.ini file. Most of the functions of System.ini are now part of the Registry.

- **Win.ini**: Most of the functions of this Windows customization settings file have also been taken over by the Registry.

- **Other .ini files**: Many Win16 applications had their own .ini files for their own specialized settings under Windows 3.1.

Initialization files, also known as **.ini** files, are used by 16-bit applications and operating systems to store settings. Although Windows 98 stores this kind of information in the centralized database called the Registry, .ini files are maintained under Windows 98 to allow for backward compatibility with Win16 applications, which can't retrieve information from the Registry.

Note that Windows 98 does not directly support MS-DOS. Unlike Windows 3.x, Windows 98 does not need MS-DOS to run and doesn't use it, which allows just about everything in the Windows 98 environment to run in protected mode. As you learned in Chapter 8, protected mode programs run at Ring 3, three rings away from Ring 0, where direct interaction with the CPU occurs.

Protecting Win16 Applications

The fact that all Win16 applications run in the same virtual address space affects the stability of these applications. Because they share virtual memory, any failure in a single Win16 application can potentially bring down all running Win16 applications. One erring Win16 application can overwrite the information that another Win16 application has stored in memory. That is why application protection is the thorniest problem for Win16 applications under Windows 98.

If you have a problem with a Win16 application, you might be able to prevent such a crash by pressing Ctrl+Alt+Del to open the Close Application dialog box. If you succeed in opening this dialog box, you can then close individual Win16 applications without affecting others. But any Win16 application that crashes can affect memory in the common 4 GB virtual address space. If one Win16 application crashes and others start acting oddly or begin to crash, you should at least close all currently running Win16 applications.

RUNNING WIN32 APPLICATIONS IN WINDOWS 98

In contrast to running Win16 or MS-DOS applications, running Win32 applications in Windows 98 is a simple process. You don't have to configure any MS-DOS-type environmental settings, you can use the Add/Remove Programs applet in the Control Panel to install and uninstall them, and they're not likely to crash each other unless they really crash and take down the operating system with them.

The only big problem with running Win32 applications is that they use lots of memory. DOS and Windows 3.x applications were built with memory constraints in mind, and thus realized an immediate performance improvement when run on a faster operating system. Not so for Win32 applications, because their programmers usually assume that such applications have access to as much memory as they need. Thus, they tend to be feature-rich (that is, they include many features that you don't necessarily need), sloppy about memory handling, and lavish with unnecessary animations that eat up CPU cycles without doing anything useful. Other than that, though, the applications themselves work fine. They're just built more for fun than economy.

32-BIT COMPONENTS VS. 16-BIT COMPONENTS

You might wonder why Windows 98 uses a combination of 16-bit and 32-bit components, if 32-bit components are supposedly superior (except for their extreme memory needs). Just about everything in computing represents a compromise between speed (the new components) and compatibility (the old components that won't go away). However, not all operating systems make this compromise in the same way—Windows NT, for example, sacrifices some backward compatibility in order to take advantage of new technology.

But Windows 98, which is targeted toward both business and personal use, has to satisfy users who are not prepared to give up older applications. This means that, unlike Windows NT, Windows 98 must remain compatible with these older applications. Thus, Windows 98 is designed so that the 32-bit components take care of the main operations, while the 16-bit components fill in when an application can't work with the 32-bit components—such as when a Win16 application needs to access configuration information, or when a DOS environment needs to be configured.

THUNKING

Communication between 16-bit and 32-bit programs takes place at the Windows core (described in Chapter 1) user layer via a process known as **thunking**. As you learned earlier in this chapter, while a 32-bit application can use 4 GB of virtual memory, a 16-bit application works with 64 KB memory segments and 64 KB offsets. Remember, since 64 KB × 64 KB = 4 GB, the 4 GB virtual memory address space can be translated to the 64 KB × 64 KB of the segment/offset model. Essentially, the term "thunking" refers to the translation between these different memory systems. The alternative to thunking is to have two parallel operating systems, 16-bit and 32-bit, working side by side. (You will learn how to run two operating systems at once, a process known as dual booting, in Chapter 12.)

SEPARATE MESSAGE QUEUES

One advantage of Win32 applications over Win16 applications is the way that messages are passed to the applications. In the discussion of processes earlier in this chapter, you learned that the 4 GB virtual memory address space provides an operating environment for the threads of each application. All operations send their threads to wait in a message queue. Each thread waits in its own message queue.

LONG FILENAME SUPPORT

One of the best features of Windows 95 was its support for long filenames, of up to 255 characters. Long filenames make it possible to name files descriptively (such as The 1998 Engineering Budget.xls) instead of using cryptic abbreviations (such as Engbud.xls). Only Win32 applications will support long filenames directly. Although Win16 and DOS applications will not overwrite long filenames, they must refer to files by aliases—that is, by abbreviated versions of the long filenames.

Aliases are based on the first letters of the long filename. A typical alias starts with the first six alphanumeric characters in the filename, followed by the tilde character (~), followed by the number 1. Any spaces in the long filename are deleted. The alias ends with a period followed by the standard three-letter file extension. For example, a filename such as Annual Fall Report.doc would be abbreviated as annual~1.doc. If more than one filename in a particular folder begins with the same first six alphanumeric characters, the second filename would include the next consecutive number (annual~2.doc, annual~3.doc, and so on). If you have more than nine of these files, the remaining aliases consist of the first 5 characters of the long filename, followed by the tilde character (~), followed by the appropriate number (for example, annua~10.doc).

SUPPORT FOR MS-DOS APPLICATIONS IN WINDOWS 98

Just about any DOS application will run under Windows 98. Some will run better than others, and some will have different requirements. Most MS-DOS applications can run in a partial or full-screen window. Other graphics-intensive MS-DOS applications, such as some games, can be set up to run in MS-DOS mode. In **MS-DOS mode**, most of Windows 98 is shut down. In the following sections, you will learn about fine-tuning MS-DOS applications to run in a 32-bit multitasking operating system.

BENEFITS OF WINDOWS 98 FOR MS-DOS APPLICATIONS

Because MS-DOS applications run in their own virtual memory address space, they have capabilities and resources available to them under Windows 98 that were impossible in MS-DOS. These features include:

- **Improved graphical support**: Although graphical MS-DOS applications can be run in a window, extremely graphics-intensive applications may appear "jerky" because of the demands of other programs running in Windows 98. You can improve performance further by running the MS-DOS application in MS-DOS mode, which turns off the demands of other applications.

- **Support for multitasking**: Although MS-DOS applications were not originally designed to multitask, each MS-DOS application has its own thread in a 32-bit virtual memory address space. These threads can therefore share access to the CPU with other threads.

- **Improved memory protection**: Because each MS-DOS application runs in its own virtual machine, errant MS-DOS applications can only crash themselves, not the operating system or even their MS-DOS window.

- **A different approach to memory**: As you learned earlier in this chapter, MS-DOS programs include TSRs that occupy conventional memory. Windows 98 32-bit protected-mode drivers substitute for many TSRs in the 4 GB virtual memory area to increase available conventional memory.

- **Improved printing performance and font support**: MS-DOS applications can print faster and more efficiently in Windows 98, and have access to a greater variety of fonts, including the scalable TrueType and OpenType fonts.

- **Local settings for virtual DOS machines (VDMs)**: Each DOS application can run in the environment that it needs without forcing you to reboot and maintain a boot library of configuration settings.

It's important to keep in mind that MS-DOS applications running under Windows 98 behave as if they're running in an MS-DOS environment. That is, they access information in Config.sys and Autoexec.bat, they attempt to directly manipulate hardware, and they perform other functions characteristic of MS-DOS programs. The Windows 98 operating system simply intercepts this MS-DOS-like behavior and executes it as it would for a 32-bit application.

MS-DOS MODE

Most DOS applications can run under Windows 98 and multitask with the operating system and other applications. However, some applications, particularly graphics-intensive applications, demand a lot of CPU time to run smoothly. These applications work better if they can have the system to themselves. You can run such applications in MS-DOS mode, thus shutting down most of Windows 98 and all other applications. When you're finished with your DOS application, you'll need to restart the system to return to the familiar Windows 98 screen.

To configure a DOS application to run in MS-DOS mode: open Windows Explorer, right-click the application's icon, click Properties on the shortcut menu, click the Program tab, and then click the Advanced button. This opens the Advanced Program Settings dialog box, shown in Figure 9-6.

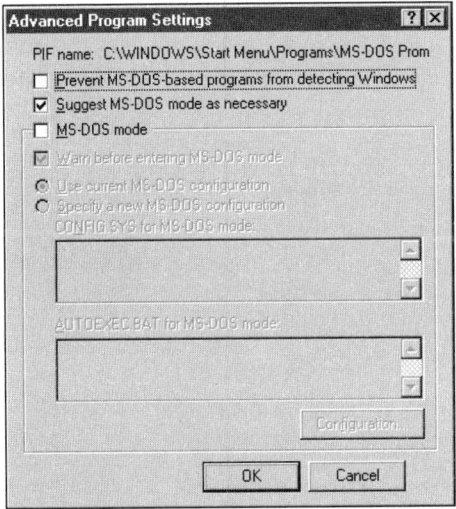

Figure 9-6 Advanced Program Settings dialog box

Click the check box for MS-DOS mode. If you want to review the Config.sys and Autoexec.bat information that will be used for this VDM, select the Specify a Configuration button to view the current settings. You will learn how to change these settings in the Hands-on Projects at the end of the chapter.

MEMORY PROTECTION

As explained earlier, all MS-DOS applications run in their own virtual MS-DOS machine (VDM) and are therefore prevented from accessing each other's memory. You also have the option of protecting MS-DOS system programs such as TSRs in each VDM from being overwritten by MS-DOS applications. To do so, open Windows Explorer, right-click the application's icon, click Properties on the shortcut menu, click the Memory tab, and then click the Protected check box to select it. As a result, the application may run more slowly, but it won't crash the MS-DOS VDM session.

OPERATIONAL DEFAULTS

The operational defaults for each MS-DOS program can be found in its Property dialog box (or properties sheet), which is accessible via Windows Explorer. For example, to access the properties sheet for the MS-DOS Command.com startup utility, click Start, point to Programs, and then click Windows Explorer. In the left-hand pane, highlight your Windows directory. In the right-hand pane, scroll down, right-click the MS-DOS application file named Command or Command.com, and then click Properties in the shortcut menu. This opens up the program's Properties dialog box. By default, all MS-DOS applications share the following settings:

- They run in a window just like any other application, neither minimized nor maximized.
- When you exit the application, the MS-DOS session itself does not end.
- They can detect Windows if necessary and multitask with other running applications.
- They can use extended memory.
- They use the \Temp directory in the Windows folder to store temporary files.
- They do not support the MS-DOS utilities known as SmartDrive and DOSKEY. SmartDrive is a real-mode hard disk access controller. You will learn about DOSKEY in the Hands-on Projects at the end of this chapter.
- They do not require direct real-mode access to disk data structures.
- The font size in the MS-DOS window is based on the size of the program window.
- The amounts of conventional, extended, expanded and MS-DOS Protected Mode Interface (DPMI) memory are dynamically optimized on the basis of available physical memory.
- If you attempt to close a DOS session while a program is still running, you'll be warned of the possibility of losing data.

To change any of these default settings, you need to click the relevant Properties tab. In the next sections, you will learn about the other available settings for MS-DOS applications in each Properties tab. The different options available in each tab are exclusive to the properties of that specific MS-DOS program.

General Tab

This tab lists the general properties associated with a specific MS-DOS application. It includes basic statistics for the file, such as when the file was created and modified, the file's size, and the location of the file. The four attributes at the bottom of the dialog box may be familiar to you if you have worked with MS-DOS before:

- **Read-only**: Files with this attribute cannot be modified or deleted in MS-DOS mode. They can be deleted through Windows Explorer.

- **Hidden**: Files with this attribute are not visible in MS-DOS mode. You can see hidden files if you change the default settings in Windows Explorer. In the Explorer menu bar, click View, and then click Folder Options. Click the View tab, then under Hidden files, select Show all files. Click Apply to activate your new setting.

- **Archive**: Some MS-DOS programs use this attribute to mark the files that are to be backed up.

- **System**: Reserved for files required to run the Windows operating system

Program Tab

If you have worked with MS-DOS applications, you know that you do not always run programs directly. For example, your computer may run batch programs—a series of MS-DOS commands consolidated into one program so that they run in sequence (similar to a macro in Microsoft Word). You can set up these parameters under the Program Tab, as shown in Figure 9-7. It's important to note that these tabs are only available if the application is set to run in a window. If the application is configured to run in MS-DOS mode, you will not be able to adjust MS-DOS window-related properties.

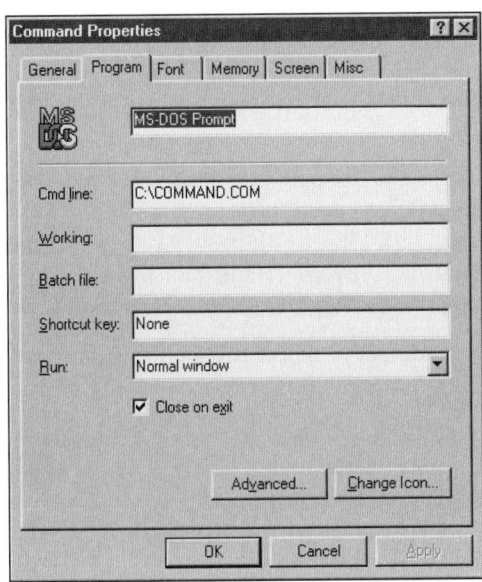

Figure 9-7 Programs tab for a DOS program

Most of the options in the Program tab are self-explanatory. In the first text box at the top of the tab, you can rename the program. The other options are explained in the following list:

- **Cmd line**: Allows you to change the MS-DOS command line that you use to run the program

- **Working**: Allows you to change the working directory, which is the default location from which files are loaded and to which files are saved

- **Batch file**: Allows you to provide the name of a batch file to be run every time you start this program

- **Shortcut key**: Allows you to define a shortcut key with which you can switch back and forth (toggle) between this program and Windows 98. The toggle key must be an Alt-key or Ctrl-key combination, and cannot include the Backspace, PrintScreen, Escape, Tab, Spacebar, or Enter keys.

- **Run**: Allows you to specify whether the application should run in a normal application window like any other Windows 98 program. You can also set a minimized window, which shows up only in the desktop toolbar, or a maximized window, which fills your whole screen but still has the Windows 98 MS-DOS prompt menu bar.

- **Close on Exit**: Allows you to specify whether the DOS window should close when you exit the program

- **Change Icon**: Allows you to change the icon that represents this program in Windows Explorer. You have a library of icons to choose from.

The Advanced button on the Program tab provides access to the Advanced Program settings shown in Figure 9-8. You have already learned how to use this dialog box to specify that you want a program to run only in MS-DOS mode. The following list summarizes the settings related to the MS-DOS environment:

- **Prevent MS-DOS-based programs from detecting Windows**: Select this check box if you want the MS-DOS application to be unaware of Windows. Ordinarily, this isn't necessary, and checking this box won't disable the Windows Clipboard for that MS-DOS session. Only check this box if you know that the presence of Windows could affect your MS-DOS application.

- **Suggest MS-DOS mode as necessary**: Select this option if you want Windows 98 to suggest running a program exclusively in MS-DOS mode to improve performance for MS-DOS graphics-intensive applications such as games.

- **MS-DOS mode**: Select this option to shut down all other applications and most of Windows 98 itself when you run the application. If you activate this option, you'll have to restart the system after quitting your MS-DOS application.

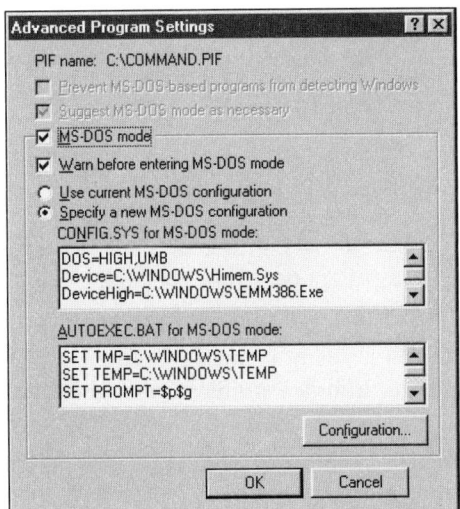

Figure 9-8 Advanced Program Settings dialog box

To configure the operating environment for MS-DOS mode, click the "Specify a new MS-DOS configuration" option button. This displays the application's Config.sys and Autoexec.bat settings. If you are comfortable with MS-DOS, you can simply type the commands you want to run in each configuration file. Otherwise, you can click Configuration to access some predefined options. You will get a chance to see how this works in the Hands-on Projects at the end of the chapter.

Font Tab

This is the simplest MS-DOS properties program tab. You can access this tab by clicking it in the Properties dialog box, or via the MS-DOS prompt window, as follows: click Start, point to Programs, click the MS-DOS prompt, and then, in the toolbar, click the Font button (the button with an "A" on it). There are two types of fonts available for the MS-DOS screen: bitmap only (where each letter is defined pixel by pixel) and TrueType (Windows standard scalable fonts). Once you choose a font type, you can select a font size for the MS-DOS screen in the Font Size list box. Click Apply to see the effect on the screen immediately, assuming the program is currently running.

Memory Tab

The settings in this dialog box affect the way your MS-DOS application uses memory. As memory types are dynamically allocated according to the needs of the application, you probably won't have to adjust these settings. Some older MS-DOS applications expect only a certain amount of memory to be available, and balk if more is offered. The settings in this dialog box are as follows:

- **Conventional memory**: Specifies the amount of RAM to dedicate to the MS-DOS program. By definition, this comes from the first 640 KB of RAM.

- **Initial environment**: Specifies the number of bytes (not kilobytes) available to the MS-DOS command interpreter, Command.com. This is also the memory available for MS-DOS batch files.

- **Expanded memory**: The RAM between 640 KB and 1 MB, also known as the MS-DOS high memory area. Usually, this takes settings from third-party utilities.

- **Extended memory**: The RAM above 1 MB. Windows 98 manages the use of extended memory for MS-DOS applications. Up to 16 MB of extended memory is available for use by some MS-DOS programs.

- **MS-DOS protected-mode interface (DPMI) memory**: Based on DOS Protected Mode Interface memory. Like memory used by Win32 applications, protected-mode memory does not communicate directly with the CPU and therefore is less likely to crash the system.

Screen Tab

With the Screen tab, you can manage the look and feel of MS-DOS in Windows 98. You can change type of display, use of toolbars, and relative memory allocation between your MS-DOS application and other programs, as follows:

- **Usage**: Although full-screen mode runs your MS-DOS program in your entire screen, this is different from running a program in MS-DOS mode. The initial size setting allows you to set the number of lines that you display when you run an MS-DOS program. Other Windows programs are still available when you run an MS-DOS program in full-screen mode.

If you have more than one program running in Windows 98, you can switch between programs by pressing the Alt and Tab keys simultaneously. If you have more than two programs running, keep the Alt key depressed while you hit the Tab key again and again. Watch what happens. This even works in MS-DOS full-screen mode.

- **Window**: Allows you to specify whether the toolbar (which you will learn about shortly) is opened when you start an MS-DOS program in window mode.

- **Performance**: Fast ROM emulation is used by Video Display Drivers (VDDs) for increasing the speed of video display by emulating some of the functions included in video ROM. Dynamic memory allocation changes the amount of memory given to a DOS program that runs in both textual and graphics modes. When the program switches to text mode, some of its memory is allocated elsewhere, to be returned when it switches back into graphics mode. Most applications can handle these options, but if you're having display problems, or if the program isn't getting all the memory it needs due to heavy demands on the system, you might try disabling one or both options.

Misc Tab

The Misc (miscellaneous) tab provides a grab bag of options. Some, such as the "Allow screen saver" option are self-explanatory. The Background option determines whether the DOS application will continue to run in the background when you're working on something else. To save system resources, check this option only if you need it—perhaps to calculate a spreadsheet while you're using another program. The mouse options determine whether you can use the mouse to copy text just as with any other Windows program, and whether the mouse should be exclusive to the DOS application and unavailable to other programs or to Windows 98. When selected, the "Warn if still active" option gives you the chance to change your mind before ending an MS-DOS session. The Fast Paste option speeds up the process of pasting to documents. You can disable the shortcut keys at the bottom of the Misc tab, but you cannot then assign any of these combinations as MS-DOS application shortcuts.

RUNNING MS-DOS APPLICATIONS IN WINDOWS 98

As you can see, running MS-DOS applications under Windows 98 can be almost like running Win32 applications, allowing for the difference in interface. MS-DOS applications can take advantage of preemptive multitasking, because they run as threads in Win32 processes, and they can use the memory enhancements and better disk access, just like Win32 processes.

The main challenge of running MS-DOS applications under Windows 98 lies in configuring their myriad options. If you are familiar enough with MS-DOS to *want* to run an MS-DOS application, then you should be able to negotiate your way through the options fairly easily. Most settings shouldn't require adjustment. However, if you're running applications in MS-DOS mode, you may need to adjust some of the advanced options.

FILE SYSTEMS AND THE WIN32 DRIVER MODEL

As with most other features of Windows 98, file systems also work through the Win32 Driver Model (WDM) that you learned about in Chapter 1. The layered architecture allows those who design applications and peripherals to work independently, without excessive concern for direct interface. Regarding file systems, the only thing programmers and drive manufacturers need to worry about is the interface to the Win32 Driver Model.

You have already learned about some of the major Windows 98 drivers in previous chapters. In the following sections, you will learn some basics about drivers and how the different classes of drivers are structured in the WDM. When you understand the structure, you can understand how the WDM brings physical drives and file systems such as FAT together through a system known as the Block I/O Subsystem.

VIRTUAL DEVICE DRIVERS

As you learned in previous chapters, device drivers are software used to manage a particular resource, usually a piece of hardware. A **virtual device driver** is a 32-bit driver that manages a resource so that more than one application can use the resource at a time. When a new application asks for access, the virtual device driver remembers the state in which the first application left it, so that when the first application regains control of the device it will be in the expected state. Virtual device drivers under Windows 98 are collectively known as VxDs, with the "x" standing for the type of device. For example, a virtual display driver is a VDD and a printer driver a VPD. Each hardware component has its own VxD.

VxDs were first implemented in Windows 3.x (with the .386 extension). The new VxDs are better designed than those earlier versions. First, VxDs are now dynamically loaded and unloaded by the programs that use them, so they only take up memory while in use. Modern VxDs can store part of their data on the hard disk. With paging, VxDs can access this data as required. This leaves more RAM available for higher-priority applications.

THE WINDOWS 32-BIT DRIVER MODEL

As you learned in Chapter 1, Microsoft includes a Windows NT device driver in the Windows 32-bit Driver Model (WDM) for driver compatibility with Windows NT 5.0 (and above). Even though these Windows 98 VxDs are 32-bit Windows NT components, they don't work under the more established Microsoft 32-bit operating system, Windows NT 4.0. The design of WDM drivers is illustrated in Figure 9-9. The layered architecture of this diagram should look familiar to you because it resembles the Registry architecture that you learned about in Chapter 3, the OSI model of networking that you learned about in Chapter 5, the printer driver architecture that you learned about in Chapter 6, and the multimedia architecture that you learned about in Chapter 8. The basic components are as follows:

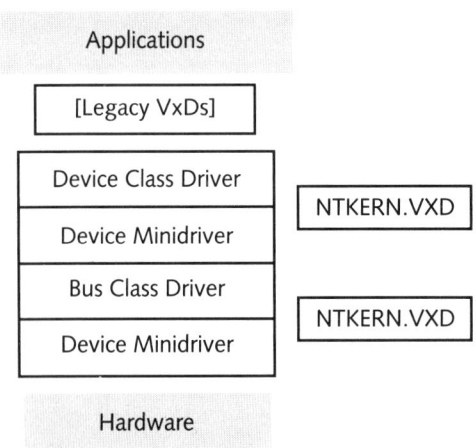

Figure 9-9 The Windows Driver Model

- **Applications**: This component initiates a request to use a piece of hardware. Such a request could come from any program you might run in Windows 98.

- **Legacy VxDs**: This component supports compatibility with most drivers designed for previous Microsoft Operating Systems. Legacy VxDs generally bypass the Device and Bus class drivers and minidrivers shown here.

- **Device class driver**: This component provides a generic driver that translates input for use by an application or a program. One example would be a single driver that handles input from a keyboard, game controller, or mouse. Another example would be a single driver that handles audio and video.

- **Device class minidrivers**: This component translates device driver input so that it can be understood by the appropriate buses. For example, a device minidriver would coordinate inputs from a keyboard, game controller, or a mouse to the bus that controls the appropriate type of hardware. They can also contain more than one type of interface, such as audio and video. Minidrivers are created by hardware manufacturers to WDM specifications provided by Microsoft.

- **Bus class driver**: Facilitates communication among Device Class minidrivers, Bus class minidrivers, and actual hardware.

- **Bus class minidrivers**: Written by hardware manufacturers to Microsoft WDM specifications to translate inputs for use by the appropriate Bus Class driver.

- **Ntkern.vxd**: Allows hardware and software designers to work with the same interfaces for both Windows 98 and Windows NT 5.0. When Ntkern.vxd is used over the Windows 98 WDM, the driver interface looks identical to that planned for Windows NT 5.0.

When an application makes a request to use a particular piece of hardware, this request is passed either to the device class driver or to the bus class driver (depending on which device the application requested), which then passes it to the specific minidriver for that device or bus. That minidriver then communicates with the hardware in question. The legacy VxDs (at the top of the WDM) are only used when necessary to transfer hardware requests from an application, such as an MS-DOS program, that can't talk to WDM drivers.

THE INSTALLABLE FILE SYSTEM MANAGER

Fundamental to any operating system is file access. Windows 98 maintains several file systems: one for FAT16 and FAT 32, another for CD-ROMs, another for DVD devices, and another for networks. Each of these various file systems requires its own device driver. Rather than trying to make all applications figure out which file system driver to use, the Windows 98 kernel includes the **Installable File System (IFS) Manager**. The IFS Manager intercepts requests to file system drivers and sends them to the appropriate location, such as a hard disk or a server on a network. This manager also makes it easier for Windows 98 to support new or updated file systems such as DVDs. Instead of changing all software associated with all applications, you can accommodate a new file system by modifying the IFS Manager.

The basic structure of the IFS Manager and its components is illustrated in Figure 9-10. The elements of Figure 9-10 are explained in the following sections.

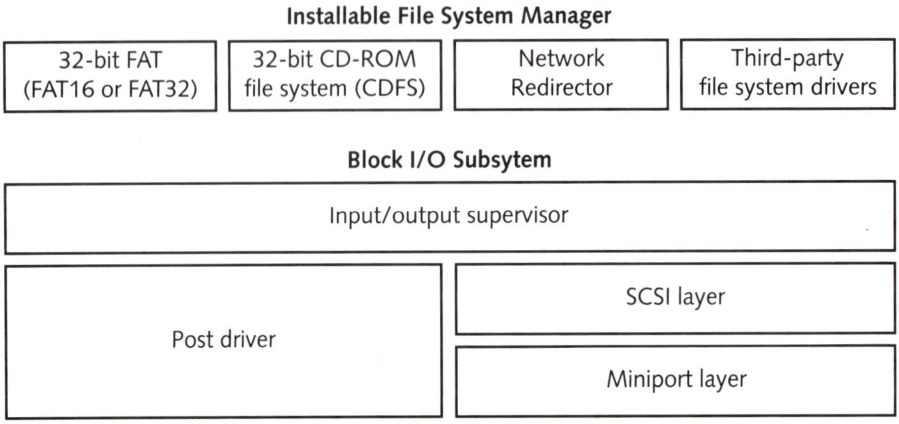

Installable File System Manager

32-bit FAT (FAT16 or FAT32)	32-bit CD-ROM file system (CDFS)	Network Redirector	Third-party file system drivers

Block I/O Subsytem

Input/output supervisor	
Post driver	SCSI layer
	Miniport layer

Figure 9-10   Installable File System Manager structure

File System Drivers

Windows 3.x used DOS to support its file system drivers. Under Windows 98, the file system drivers are part of the operating system itself, so there's no need to switch from protected mode to real mode in order to access the disk structure. These file system drivers maintain a record of which clusters on the disk are used and which files—or parts of files—are stored in each one.

As shown in Figure 9-10, the IFS Manager is responsible for four different systems. Depending on where the file is located, IFS automatically calls up the file from the appropriate system. You learned about some of these systems in previous chapters.

- **32-bit FAT**: Refers to Windows 32-bit access to either file system, FAT16 or FAT 32.

- **32-bit CD-ROM**: As you will learn in Chapter 10, there are two different file systems available for CD-ROMs: the real-mode MSCDEX system used with MS-DOS, and the Windows 98 system known as CDFS (CD-ROM File System).

- **Network Redirector**: 32-bit file finders used by Windows 98 computers on a network. When you are on a network, you may want access to a file or program on another computer. A request for a file or program is sent through IFS to the redirector for routing to the appropriate server on the network. These requests do not go any lower in the architecture, as shown in Figure 9-10. Redirectors correspond to the application and presentation layers of the OSI model that you learned about in Chapter 5.

- **Third-party file system drivers**: The third-party supplier is responsible for creating an interface compatible with IFS.

Block I/O Subsystem

Although the file system drivers manage read and write access to the various file systems supported by Windows 98, they have no direct access to the physical disks. That aspect of file reads and writes is handled by the Block I/O Subsystem. The input/output supervisor accepts the file requests sent to it by the file system drivers, and the IDE or Ultra ATA port driver or SCSI miniport driver does the actual reading and writing. For IDE or Ultra ATA drives, the port drivers provide the same functionality as the combination of the SCSI layer and the miniport drivers The components of the Block I/O Subsystem include:

- **Input/output supervisor**: Handles requests from the file systems. It queues these requests and routes them to the appropriate file system driver, and notifies the drivers of file system events such as reads, writes, and file programs that are run.

- **Port driver**: Communicates with a specific disk device, such as a hard disk controller. In Windows 98, all communication with IDE and ESDI drivers is handled with a port driver.

- **SCSI layer**: Communicates with the SCSI host adapter and provides a general interface for communicating with SCSI devices. The specifics are handled by the miniport driver.

- **Miniport driver**: Handles SCSI functionality for a specific device

CHAPTER SUMMARY

- Windows 98 is a 32-bit operating system that maintains some 16-bit components to ensure backward compatibility with DOS and Win16 applications. Although all Windows applications are run together in the System Virtual Machine, each MS-DOS application has its own virtual machine. While each Win32 and MS-DOS application is given its own 4GB virtual memory address space, all Win16 applications share one 4 GB address space. Each application is a process. A process, in turn, is made up of threads, each of which is devoted to an individual task. Win32 applications can run multiple threads simultaneously. Win32 threads share CPU time through preemptive multitasking; Win16 applications compete for their share of their virtual memory address space time through cooperative multitasking.

- Most MS-DOS applications actually run better in Windows 98 than they do in the MS-DOS operating system. Because they run in their own 4 GB virtual memory address space, they have access to improved memory, graphics, and printing features. Through MS-DOS mode, Windows 98 can accommodate other applications with a group of settings that allow an MS-DOS program to have direct access to your computer hardware. The available settings are extensive, and can fully define the operational parameters for your MS-DOS programs. With the appropriate settings, running an MS-DOS program in Windows 98 is generally the same as or better than running it in the MS-DOS operating system.

- This hybrid approach permits support for Win32, Win16, and DOS applications. Regardless of their type, all applications run in the context of a Win32 process, but some implementation details are different due to the varying requirements of the different kinds of applications. For example, Win32 applications use preemptive multitasking, in which all threads of a particular priority get access to the CPU in turn; however, Win16 applications—even when running under Windows 98—must use cooperative multitasking, in which threads get the CPU until they realize that another thread needs it, at which point they release it.
- Each class of applications can access the file structure through the Installable File System (IFS) Manager. Like other parts of Windows 98, the layered architecture of the IFS Manager allows application programmers and hardware manufacturers to work relatively independently of each other. The IFS Manager can translate from several current file systems such as FAT and CDFS to a form that can be translated by the Block I/O Subsystem to port drivers for IDE drives or to SCSI drivers for SCSI hard drives.

KEY TERMS

- **Autoexec.bat** — The boot file for 16-bit operating systems such as MS-DOS and Windows 3.x. It also calls up the 16-bit programs that support hardware such as CD-ROM drives and sound cards. It does not load drivers. Windows 98 does not rely directly on this file, but refers to it to configure operating settings for MS-DOS applications.
- **Block I/O Subsystem** — Handles read and write access to storage disks. One part of it takes the requests sent to it by the file system drivers and interprets these requests, and another does the actual reading and writing.
- **Config.sys** — The configuration file for 16-bit operating systems such as MS-DOS and Windows 3.x. Before Autoexec.bat calls the setup files for hardware, Config.sys loads the associated real-mode drivers. Config.sys cannot be run by itself. Windows 98 does not rely directly on this file, but refers to it to configure real-mode drivers for MS-DOS applications.
- **Context switch** — When a CPU is allocated to a thread from a process in a new 4 GB virtual memory address space, memory must be switched around. That is known as a context switch.
- **cooperative multitasking** — A method for sharing CPU time, in which Win16 threads listen for other threads and voluntarily give up CPU access after a fixed period of time. Poorly written applications can take over the CPU, which can lead to problems in the Win16 virtual memory address space.
- **Flat address space** — A single, complete memory address space. Because Windows 98 32-bit programs can use, or point to, 4 GB of information, they require only one, flat address space. *Compare to* Segmented address space.

- **.ini files** — Initialization files used by 16-bit applications and operating systems to store settings. Although Windows 98 stores this kind of information in a centralized database called the Registry, .ini files are maintained under Windows 98 for backward compatibility with Win16 applications, which can't retrieve information from the Registry.

- **Installable File System (IFS) Manager** — The part of Windows 98 that intercepts requests to file system drivers and sends them to the appropriate location such as a hard disk or a server on a network.

- **long filenames** — Filenames that can be up to 255 characters long, rather than following the 8.3 format required by 16-bit applications based on MS-DOS or Windows 3.x.

- **minidrivers** —Dynamically loaded drivers that usually take data only from hardware-specific functions. Windows 98 minidrivers are designed to work with Windows NT 5.0. They can also contain more than one type of interface, such as audio and video.

- **MS-DOS mode** — A Windows 98 environment that simulates the MS-DOS operating system, and in which most of Windows 98 is shut down.

- **multithreaded** — A term used to describe 32-bit programs, which can run multiple threads simultaneously, in competition for CPU time.

- **page** — A 4 KB area of user data. Memory can be swapped from the virtual memory address space to RAM (and vice versa) in pages.

- **port driver** — A component of the Installable File System Manager that communicates with a specific disk device, such as a hard disk controller. In Windows 98, all communication with IDE and ESDI drivers is handled with a port driver.

- **preemptive multitasking** — A method of multitasking in which all threads have a preset time to run before ceding control of the CPU to another thread. DOS and Win32 applications use preemptive multitasking under Windows 98.

- **Redirector** — Part of the Installable File System Manager. A 32-bit system that directs file requests over a network as required.

- **SCSI layer** — The portion of the Block I/O Subsystem that communicates with SCSI devices. It's a general interface for dealing with all SCSI devices—the specifics for a particular device are handled by a miniport driver.

- **segmented address space** — A memory address space divided into separate pieces, known as segments. 16-bit programs can point directly to only 64 KB of memory. To address all of a virtual memory address space, you need to specify a segment (64 KB) and an offset (64 KB) for a total of 64 KB × 64 KB = 4 GB of memory.

- **System Virtual Machine** — The one virtual machine in which all Windows programs run together. Since Windows programs can share resources, they only need the one System Virtual Machine.

- **Terminate-and-stay-resident (TSR)** — MS-DOS-based programs that are run to load real-mode components in the first MB of RAM.

- **thread** — One part of a process devoted to performing a single task. CPU time is allocated to individual threads.

- **thunking** — The communications process between 16-bit and 32-bit programs at the Windows core user layer.
- **Timeslice** — In multitasking, a predetermined period of CPU time allotted to a thread, after which the thread has to cede the CPU to another thread.
- **virtual device driver** — A 32-bit device driver that manages a resource such as hardware so that more than one application can use the resource at a time. Virtual device drivers (VxDs) are 32-bit and operate in protected mode. The VxDs used with Windows 95 and Windows 98 are dynamically loaded and unloaded, requiring less memory.
- **virtual memory address space** — The specific portion of virtual memory allocated to an active program or group of programs. 32-bit programs can use, or address, 2^{32} (4 GB) bits of information. Thus, Windows 98 allocates one 32-bit virtual memory address space to each 32-bit program, as well as to each MS-DOS program. All 16-bit Windows programs together share the same 32-bit virtual memory address space.
- **VxD** — *See* Virtual device driver.
- **Win16 applications** — Applications originally written to operate in the 16-bit Windows 3.x environment. They are supported under Windows 98 and will look like Win32 applications, although they don't run quite as Win32 applications do.
- **Win32 applications** — Applications originally written to operate in a 32-bit environment, whether Windows 95, Windows NT, or Windows 98. Win32 applications are those most able to take advantage of all the internal and external advances of Windows 98.

REVIEW QUESTIONS

1. Which of the following operating systems include(s) 32-bit components? Choose all correct answers.
    a. Windows 98
    b. Windows NT 5.0
    c. Windows NT 4.0
    d. MS-DOS 6.0
2. A 32-bit device driver that manages a resource so that more than one application can use the resource at once is called a(n):
    a. Installable File System device driver
    b. virtual device driver
    c. universal device driver
    d. minidriver

3. Which of the following file extensions is a generic term for any Windows 98 virtual device driver?
   a. .386
   (b.) .VxD
   c. .VPD
   d. .VDD
4. Which of the following (is/are) not an advantage of .VxDs over .386s? Choose all that apply.
   a. They are 32-bit.
   b. They are compatible with both Windows 3.x and Windows 98.
   c. They are compatible with Windows NT 4.0 VxDs.
   d. They are statically loaded for faster reaction to application requests.
5. Which of the following best describes the purpose of Ntkern.vxd?
   a. It makes Windows NT 4.0 look like Windows 98 to a device driver.
   b. It makes Windows 98 look like Windows NT 4.0 to a device driver.
   c. It makes Windows 98 look like Windows NT 5.0 to a device driver.
   d. It makes Windows NT 5.0 look like Windows 98 to a device driver.
6. Which of the following operating systems support WDM device drivers? Choose all that apply.
   a. Windows NT 4.0
   b. Windows NT 5.0
   c. Windows 98
   d. MS-DOS 5.0
7. The WDM eliminates the need for virtual device drivers. True or False?
8. What is the smallest unit of execution in Windows 98?
   a. a thread
   b. a process
   c. application code
   d. none of the above
9. How large is a page in memory?
   a. 2 KB
   b. 4 KB
   c. 64 KB
   d. none of the above

10. Which of the following statements accurately describes the characteristics of a virtual memory address space?
    a. You need 4 GB of RAM to take full advantage of the 4 GB of virtual memory.
    b. No application in one virtual memory address space can read the data from another memory address space.
    c. You need at least 4 GB free on your hard drive to take full advantage of the 4 GB of virtual memory.
    d. none of the above
11. What is the unit by which CPU time is allocated?
    a. the application
    b. the process
    c. the thread
    d. the code
12. Which of the following are associated with 16-bit Windows applications?
    a. cooperative multitasking
    b. preemptive multitasking
    c. Installable File System Management
    d. thread management
13. Which of the following application types use cooperative multitasking under Windows 98?
    a. Win32
    b. Win16
    c. DOS
    d. none of the above
14. Graphics-heavy Win16 applications are more likely to run out of virtual memory addresses than are graphics-heavy Win32 applications. True or False?
15. Which of the following are characteristics of Win16 applications when one of them fails?
    a. If you shut one down, they all go down.
    b. If you shut one down, you need to reboot Windows 98.
    c. You can shut one down, because their threads can be shut down independently of each other.
    d. If you shut one down, you need to shut down all MS-DOS applications that you are running.
16. If you want to give a DOS application full control of the machine, what do you do?
    a. Run the application in MS-DOS mode.
    b. Run the application in full-screen mode.

c. Set the application up to use all available memory.

d. Prevent the application from running in the background.

17. Which of the following actions would keep a DOS application from crashing its virtual machine?

   a. Running it in MS-DOS mode

   b. Running it as a full-screen application

   c. Setting up memory protection from the Memory tab

   d. none of the above

18. How many virtual machines are running in your Windows 98 system if you are running the following programs: WordPerfect 5.1 for MS-DOS, two Win16-based games, Microsoft Excel for Windows 95, and Freecell (a Win32-based game program)?

   a. 2

   b. 4

   c. 5

   d. 6

19. How many virtual address spaces are running in your Windows 98 system if you are running the following programs: WordPerfect 5.1 for MS-DOS, two Win16-based games, Microsoft Excel for Windows 95, and Freecell (a Win32-based game program)?

   a. 2

   b. 4

   c. 5

   d. 6

20. Which part of the Installable File System Manager will send a file request to another computer on a network?

   a. the miniport driver

   b. the compact disc file system

   c. the port driver

   d. The network redirector

21. The IFS Manager is responsible for managing disk reads and writes. True or False?

22. Suppose Company X were to come up with a different file system to manage access from Windows 98 to high-definition television signals. Which part of the Installable File System would Microsoft have to change to accommodate the new file system?

   a. the Installable File System Manager

   b. the port drivers and the minidrivers under the SCSI layer

   c. just the SCSI layer

   d. FAT 32

23. What part of the Block I/O Subsystem handles requests from the file system? Choose all correct answers.

    a. the port driver

    b. the miniport driver

    c. the SCSI layer

    d. none of the above

24. Which of the following terms refers to the situation in which applications have to give up access to the CPU at predefined intervals?

    a. cooperative multitasking

    b. preemptive multitasking

    c. Installable File System Management

    d. thread management

Hands-on Projects

Project 9-1

MS-DOS applications normally run in a Windows 98 window and share processor time and RAM with the rest of the operating system and other running applications. This arrangement works fine for many MS-DOS applications, but some work better if they don't have to share at all. In this exercise, you will configure an application to run in MS-DOS mode, thereby giving it exclusive access to the system, reducing even Windows 98 to a minimal operating system. The program used here is Command.com, the MS-DOS utility used to start the MS-DOS command line. This was chosen because some Windows 98 machines will not have any other MS-DOS programs installed. In the process, you will create a new MS-DOS mode configuration for that application by adding a terminate-and-stay-resident program (TSR) called DOSKEY. To complete this project you will need any computer running Windows 98.

When you run an application in MS-DOS mode, you must shut down all other applications. You cannot reuse them until you restart the computer.

1. Click **Start**, point to **Programs**, and click **Windows Explorer**.

2. In the left-hand pane, highlight the **Windows** folder.

3. In the right-hand pane, scroll down, right-click the MS-DOS application file named **Command**, and then click **Properties** in the shortcut menu. This opens the Properties dialog box. (Be sure to select the file adjacent to the MS-DOS icon, not command.com.)

Managing Windows 98 Applications

4. Click the **Program** tab, and then click **Advanced**.
5. Click the **MS-DOS mode** check box to select it. The MS-DOS mode settings, in the bottom half of the dialog box, are now available.
6. Click the **Specify a new MS-DOS configuration** option button, click **Configuration**, and then, if necessary, click **Yes** in the Warning dialog box. This opens the Select MS-DOS Configuration Options dialog box, as shown in Figure 9-11. The settings you specify here will only apply to the MS-DOS program whose properties you are currently editing.

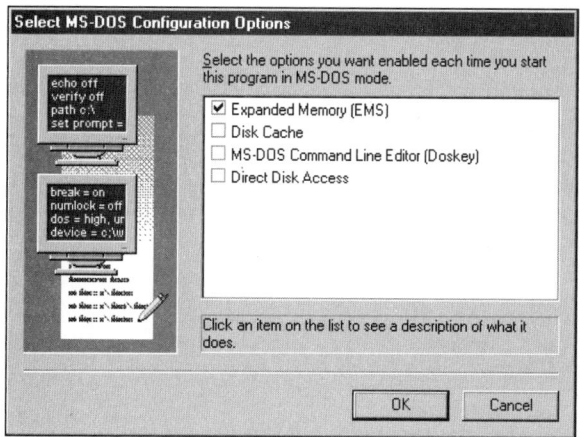

Figure 9-11 Select MS-DOS Configuration Options dialog box

7. Click the **MS-DOS Command Line Editor (Doskey)** check box to select it. This activates the MS-DOS utility known as DOSKEY.
8. Click **OK** to close the Select MS-DOS Configuration Options dialog box, click **OK** to close the Advanced Program Settings dialog box, and then click **OK** again to close the Command Properties dialog box.
9. Close any programs that are currently running, except for Windows Explorer.
10. In Windows Explorer, double-click the MS-DOS application file named **Command**.
11. If prompted, click **Yes**. Your computer restarts in MS-DOS mode. In the next step, you will try a few commands to check that DOSKEY is working. It does not matter whether or not you enter valid MS-DOS commands.
12. Type **Testing**, and then press **Enter**. You see the message "Bad command or file name," indicating that you did not enter a real MS-DOS command.
13. Repeat Step 12 several times, each time replacing "Testing" with the command of your choice. Now that you have typed a few commands, you can use DOSKEY to view a reminder of the commands you just typed. This can be very useful in a real-life situation, when you may have lost track of the commands you just entered.

14. Press the **up arrow key** on your keyboard. The last command you typed appears at the DOS prompt.
15. Continue pressing the **up arrow** until you see the first command you typed, Testing, and then press the **down arrow** to return to the last command you typed.
16. Reboot your computer. If Windows Explorer does not open automatically when you reboot, click **Start**, point to **Programs**, then click **Windows Explorer**. Repeat Steps 2, 3, and 4.
17. In the Advanced Program Settings dialog box, click **MS-DOS** mode to deselect it. Click **OK** to close the Advanced Program Settings dialog box, and then click **OK** again to exit the Command Properties dialog box.

Regarding the different options in Figure 9-11, expanded memory is useful for some older DOS applications created before extended memory was available, as well as for some games. The Disk Cache option loads SmartDrive for improved disk access from within DOS applications. As you see in this Hands-on Project, DOSKEY is a very useful tool. Direct Disk Access allows DOS applications to bypass the IFS Manager and directly modify disk structures.

PROJECT 9-2

In this project, you will use the System Monitor to measure the number of threads and virtual machines running on your computer. No special equipment is required for this project; all you need is a computer with Windows 98 installed.

1. Close all open programs.
2. Click **Start**, point to **Programs**, point to **Accessories**, point to **System Tools**, and then click **System Monitor**. This opens the System Monitor window.
3. Click **View** on the menu bar, and then click **Line Charts**, to verify that the information about active threads will be displayed in a line chart. System Monitor may currently be measuring items on your system. In the next three steps, you can stop System Monitor from gathering data on any other items. If you prefer, you can skip Steps 4, 5, and 6.
4. Click **Edit** on the menu bar, and then click **Remove Item**. This opens the Remove Item dialog box.
5. Make a note of any items currently included in the list box, in case you want to return System Monitor to its original state later.
6. Select the items in the list box, and then click **OK**. Repeat Steps 4 and 5 and this part of Step 6 as many times as required to delete any other currently running items in System Monitor. You return to the System Monitor window, where the display area should now be blank. Next, you can indicate that you want to gather information regarding the number of active threads.

7. Click **Edit** on the menu bar, and then click Add Item. This opens the Add Item dialog box.

8. In the Category list box, click **Kernel**, click **Threads** in the Item list box, and then click **OK**.

9. Repeat Steps 6 and 7 to select Virtual Machines in the Add Item dialog box. (Remember, you need to select Kernel under category before you see and can select Virtual Machines in the Item text box.) After a few seconds, you should see data illustrated on the two line charts, one for threads, and one for virtual machines. If you don't see any data on the chart, click **Options** on the menu bar, and then click **Chart**. This opens the Options dialog box. Drag the slider to the left, towards "Faster," and then click **OK** and view the charts again.

   Assuming you have no other programs running, the Virtual Machines chart should indicate that there is currently only one virtual machine. The Threads chart probably indicates that you have somewhere above 40 active threads. (If you have fewer than 40 active threads, you have set up Windows 98 on your computer to run quite efficiently. Congratulations.) Next, you will open a program and view the effects on both charts.

10. Open a Windows program of your choice, and then return to the System Monitor window and view the chart again. The number of threads increases, while the number of virtual machines remains the same.

11. Repeat Step 10 for a few more programs. Next, you will see what happens when you open an MS-DOS program.

12. Click **Start**, point to **Programs**, click **MS-DOS prompt**, and then return to the System Monitor window and view the chart again. The number of threads increases, as well as the number of virtual machines. As you'll recall, Windows 98 creates a new virtual machine for every MS-DOS prompt that you open. If this action rebooted your computer, you forgot to complete the final steps in Project 9-1.

13. Repeat Step 12 for other MS-DOS programs, if desired.

14. Close System Monitor and every MS-DOS window or program that you opened in this project.

PROJECT 9-3

The simplest way to start an MS-DOS application is not to put it on the Desktop or Start menu, but to assign it a key combination that will immediately invoke it. In this exercise, you'll create a shortcut for an MS-DOS application. No special equipment is required for this project; all you need is a computer with Windows 98 installed.

1. Find the icon for the application you wish to configure. You can find it in Windows Explorer, My Computer, or even in the settings for the Start menu.

2. When you've found it, right-click on it to open its pop-up menu. (If you don't know what application to choose, select the command file from Project 9-1.) Choose **Properties** from the menu to open the Properties dialog box.
3. Click on the **Program** tab.
4. In the Shortcut key box, press the **Alt** or **Ctrl** keys plus a letter, assigning a combination not in use elsewhere on the system, and not including the Esc, Enter, Tab, PrntScreen, Spacebar, or Backspace keys.
5. Click **OK**.
6. Now try it out. Open the MS-DOS program that you set up by pressing the **Alt** or **Crtl** key plus the letter that you assigned in Step 4.

CASE PROJECTS

1. Your company runs a lot of applications such as spreadsheets that require significant computing power. Most employees generally run several of these applications at a time on their Windows 98 computers. Would it make more sense to get 16-bit or 32-bit versions of those applications? Would this decision have any effect on system performance?

2. Your boss is confused about the difference between virtual machines, virtual memory address spaces, processes, and threads. Your organization has a variety of Win32, Win16, and MS-DOS applications. She is concerned about the number of virtual machines that employees open up on each computer, because she has heard about memory conflicts between different virtual machines. Write a short report on how virtual machines and virtual memory address spaces work with respect to the three different types of applications that you can run. Explain the conditions that result in memory conflicts.

3. You are working at a software company that is putting together a new game system for Windows 98. Unfortunately, it will require a new file system on the same level as FAT or CDFS. Your marketing people are telling you that it will be a bestseller, so it is worth paying Microsoft a significant amount of money to revise Windows 98 to accommodate your new file system. You are concerned that Microsoft will use your money to finance changes to different systems. Write a note to your negotiating team explaining what you need Microsoft to change, and which drivers related to it do not need to be changed in the Windows 98 operating system.

CHAPTER TEN

Monitoring, Tuning, and Optimizing Windows 98

In this chapter, you will learn to monitor and optimize the performance of your Windows 98 system. Three other chapters in this book address various maintenance issues in a Windows 98 system. In Chapter 8, you learned to configure resources such as hard disks and printers. In Chapter 11, you will learn to protect your system with backups and regular maintenance. In Chapter 14, you will get a chance to troubleshoot various problems that might arise within your system.

Before you can measure the performance of any system, inside or outside the world of computing, you must first establish a baseline, which is a collection of information that describes how your system functions under normal, stable circumstances. Any changes to your system's performance are then measured relative to the baseline. You can gather baseline data using the tools and techniques described in this chapter. Be sure to establish your baseline at a time when your system is functioning normally. Do not attempt to establish a baseline immediately after installing new software or hardware. Instead, it makes more sense to establish the baseline first, so that you can measure the effects of any new software or hardware on your system. Of course, in order for baseline data to be useful, you must have it carefully documented and readily accessible.

AFTER READING THIS CHAPTER AND COMPLETING THE EXERCISES, YOU WILL BE ABLE TO:

- Take an inventory of your system's components
- Use MSInfo to monitor and maintain the status of hardware, software, and their associated drivers
- Establish a performance baseline for your Windows 98 system
- Find the right System Monitor tool to monitor your PC components
- Use various disk and configuration utilities to optimize system performance

In this chapter, you will learn the techniques necessary for establishing your system's baseline, and for generally monitoring and optimizing your system. This chapter starts by covering the Microsoft System Information (MSInfo) tool, which provides a broad overview of the status of hardware components, drivers, and dynamic-link libraries. It moves on to examine performance parameters for each major hardware driver, device driver, and software component.

TAKING STOCK: SYSTEM INVENTORY AND OVERVIEW

The first step in establishing any PC baseline is taking an inventory of your computer's hardware, software, and associated drivers. The combination of software and drivers creates a load on the system, which drives performance. Before you can gather useful baseline statistics, you need to understand your computer's individual components. The Microsoft System Information tools were developed to address this need. Prior to Windows 98, third-party tools were commonly used to take a system inventory. You'll learn about Microsoft System Information tools and third-party tools in the following sections.

MICROSOFT SYSTEM INFORMATION

The Microsoft System Information utility (commonly called **MSInfo**) provides a profile of the system. To start MSInfo, click Start, point to Programs, point to Accessories, point to System Tools, and then click System Information. As shown in Figure 10-1, the Microsoft System Information window provides information on basic system components. Like Windows Explorer, this window is divided into two panes. The information you see in the right-hand pane depends on what you have selected in the left-hand pane. The left pane lists three categories of information: Resources, Components, and Software Environment. When System Information is selected in the left pane (as in Figure 10-1), the right pane displays basic configuration information for the PC. Although most of the details in MSInfo can be found in other utilities throughout Windows 98, MSInfo is the only program that collects all of this information in one place. In addition, MSInfo keeps a history of configuration changes. In Chapter 14 you will learn how to use the MSInfo History feature as an aid in troubleshooting.

Monitoring, Tuning, and Optimizing Windows 98   333

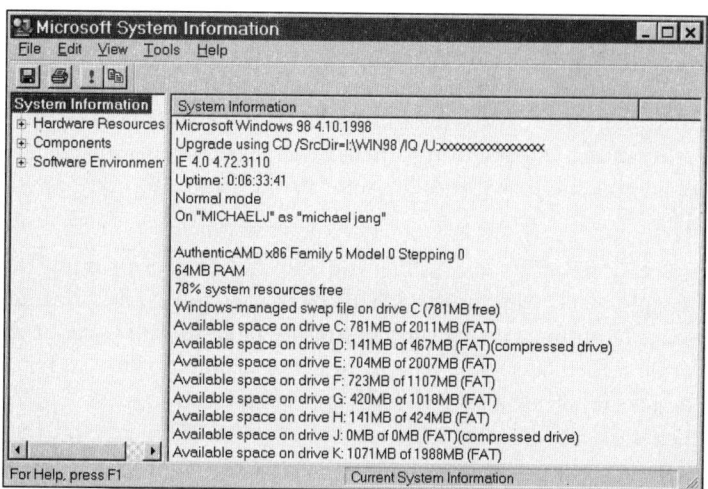

Figure 10-1 Microsoft System Information window

MSInfo provides a level of information somewhere between the Control Panel System Properties utility and the Registry. To display more detailed information in subcategories, click the plus sign next to one of the main categories in the left-hand pane. Figure 10-2 shows a number of subcategories.

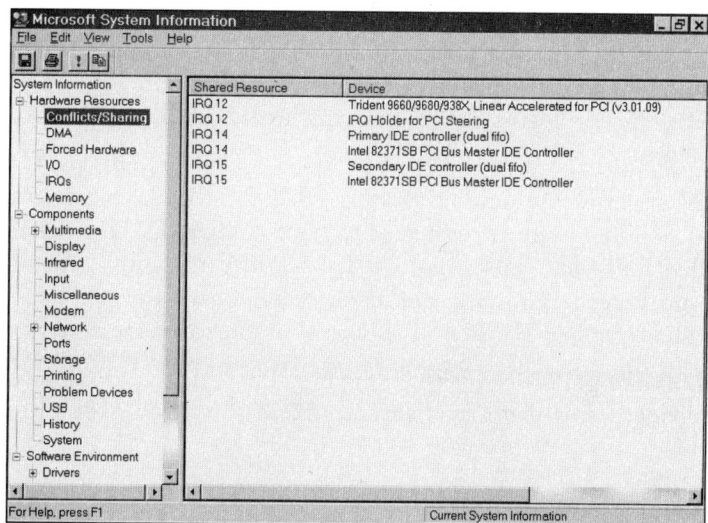

Figure 10-2 Subcategories in the Microsoft System Information window

You can save your baseline configuration from MSInfo in a file. Then if you ever have a problem with your system, you can check the relevant MSInfo data from when your system functioned normally. To save the information displayed in the right-hand pane of the MSInfo window, click File, click Save, type a filename in the File name text box, and then click Save. MSInfo checks the information to make sure it is current, and then saves it to a file. You can then open this file in MSInfo anytime in the future to compare the baseline data with current data.

To make your data as easy to access as possible, you should consider printing the information displayed in the right-hand pane of the MSInfo window. You could print directly from MSInfo, but because an MSInfo printout can commonly take 50-100 pages, it makes more sense to simply copy the information you want to preserve to a text editor, and then print the information from the text editor. To copy everything displayed in the right-hand pane of the MSInfo window, click Edit on the menu bar, click Select All, click Edit on the menu bar again, and then click Copy. Then open a text editor (such as WordPad), paste the information from the clipboard, and print it. Then be sure to store your printed documentation in an organized way, and in a safe place, where you can reach it when you need it.

In the following sections, you will learn more about the three major categories of information provided by MSInfo.

Hardware Resources

In earlier versions of Windows, before MSInfo existed, you could only get hardware resource information by clicking the "View Devices by Type" option button in the Device Manager tab of the System applet. As you'll learn later in this chapter, you will still want to use the Device Manager tab to obtain certain information. However, in most cases, you will want to use the Hardware Resources category in MSInfo, which provides more complete hardware information.

While the Device Manager focuses on the hardware itself, the MSInfo Hardware Resource category focuses on how hardware is connected to your computer. These connections are documented in the following subcategories: I/O, DMA, Memory, and IRQ. The Conflicts/Sharing and Forced Hardware subcategories document any problems related to these connections. The complete Hardware Resources subcategories are as follows:

- **Conflicts/Sharing**: Lists conflicts among non-Plug-and-Play PCI devices, such as multiple video cards, that may share the same hardware channels or memory addresses
- **DMA**: Lists the devices that are currently using a direct memory access (DMA) channel, which is a path for communication between hardware components that bypasses the CPU. One component that uses DMA is a sound card with its own sound-processing routines. Through DMA, the sound card can access and process a .wav sound file directly from the hard drive.
- **Forced Hardware**: Not all hardware is Plug and Play. Sometimes a user may choose to disable Plug and Play by changing jumpers on a hardware card. This category lists all devices that have been forced into a particular channel.

- **I/O**: Lists the input/output port address for every component. Some components, such as a video adapter, require a large number of I/O ports. For most systems, this is a very long list.

- **IRQs**: Lists each of the standard 16 interrupt request ports and the drivers using each port. To access the CPU, every hardware component requires an interrupt request port. If you use multiple modems or monitors, each modem or monitor gets its own IRQ. If more than one device wants CPU access simultaneously, they get access depending on their IRQ port number, in the following order: 0, 1, 8, 9, 10, 11, 12, 13, 14, 15, 3, 4, 5, 6, 7. (IRQ 2 is used by IRQs 8–15, which is why 2 is not included in this list.)

- **Memory**: Lists the range of memory addresses in RAM or ROM used by various hardware devices.

Components

The Components category provides information about each type of hardware. For components that use device drivers, the right-hand pane offers an Advanced Information option that you can use to list additional driver and resource information, and the location of device settings within the Registry. By comparison, the Device Manager tab provides a more limited degree of information. (You will learn more about Device Manager later in this section.) The following list describes each Components subcategory. You will learn more about these components in Chapter 14.

- **Multimedia**: A list of sound and game card information. Multimedia subcategories include audio and video CODECs (data compressors/decompressors). If you select the CD-ROM subcategory, your system automatically performs a speed test, also known as a data transfer test, and then (in the right-hand pane) lists the read rates, which indicate how fast your computer actually reads from your CD-ROM.

- **Display**: Lists video card and monitor information

- **Infrared**: Lists infrared communications devices, if available and connected. This category does not recognize an infrared port that is only searching for a connection. Only those devices with an actual active connection are listed here.

- **Input**: Lists all input devices, such as keyboards, mice, joysticks, and game pads

- **Miscellaneous**: Lists installed printers

- **Modems**: Lists all ports (i.e., COM) that have been set up for communication. PC cards are listed separately.

- **Network**: Includes information on all network adapters and protocols. The Network Winsock subcategory lists Winsock version information as well as limits on sockets and UDP datagrams. You learned about sockets and UDP in Chapter 5. Winsocks are sockets between programs enabled for Windows.

- **Ports**: Lists available and active COM and LPT ports
- **Storage**: Lists all installed storage devices, including floppy and hard disk drives, CD-ROM drives, and DVD drives, as well as removable storage media
- **Printing**: Lists all local print options, including printers, fax subsystems, and rendering subsystems
- **Problem Devices**: Lists all devices that may not be operating properly
- **USB**: Lists all installed Universal Serial Bus drivers and controllers
- **History**: Lists all hardware and driver changes in the past seven days
- **System**: Lists basic hardware information, including BIOS, motherboards, buses, and ports

Software Environment

The term "software environment" refers to all the software components required to run programs on your system. As described in earlier chapters, drivers provide a common link from different applications to Windows 98. While most programs store file configuration information in the Registry, some still require .ini files. MSInfo provides all types of configuration information in the following Software Environment subsections.

- **Drivers**: Lists information on three types of drivers: real-mode MS-DOS drivers, protected-mode kernel drivers, and user-mode device drivers. You learned about the kernel and user layers in Chapters 1 and 9.
- **16-bit Modules Loaded**: Lists all modules, also known as DLLs (dynamic-link libraries) associated with 16-bit programs. As you learned in Chapter 3, DLLs are programming functions that can be used by more than one application at the same time. The version level can be used to verify whether the applicable DLL is up to date.
- **32-bit Modules Loaded**: Similar to the 16-bit Modules Loaded category. Also provides information about the memory address or addresses used by each module.
- **Running Tasks**: Lists all tasks (also known as programs and utilities) currently running in Windows 98. Similar to the Windows NT 4.0 Task Manager.
- **Startup Programs**: Lists all programs that run automatically when Windows 98 is started. It can include defaults from the Win.ini file.
- **System Hooks**: Lists Windows 98 programs resident in memory and system hooks. An example of a program resident in memory is the MS-DOS terminate-and-stay-resident (TSR) programs that you learned about in Chapter 9. An example of a system hook is the F1 key in many applications, which displays Help information for that particular application. Many systems may not have any TSRs or system hooks currently running.
- **OLE Registration**: Lists the file types associated with the various applications. As you learned in Chapter 3, **OLE** is short for object linking and embedding, a

feature that allows you to insert files from one program into another. If you click on the plus sign adjacent to OLE Registration, you can see that applications controlled by .ini files and applications controlled by the Registry are divided into separate subcategories: INI File and Registry. Highlight one of these categories to display the relevant information in the right-hand pane. The leftmost column of information describes the object to be embedded. The third column from the left indicates the program file for the program you would use to edit the object.

DEVICE MANAGER

You can use the Device Manager to display a list of the hardware installed on your computer. Click Start, point to Settings, click Control Panel, double-click the System icon, click the Device Manager tab, and click the "View Devices by type" option button to select it.

Figure 10-3 shows a typical device manager. The devices that you see under "View Devices by type" should correspond to the hardware present on your computer. You will learn more about the Device Manager in the Hands-on Projects at the end of the chapter.

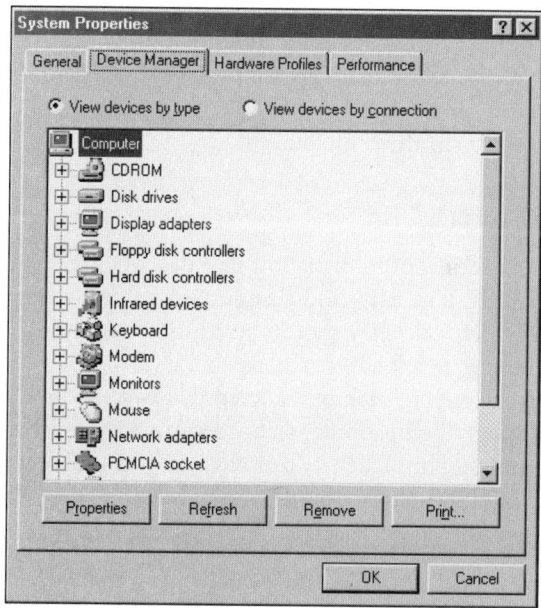

Figure 10-3 Typical Device Manager tab

THIRD-PARTY ALTERNATIVES

Before Microsoft System Information was introduced, the only way to collect information about your system's components in one place was through third-party utilities, such as Norton's System Information (which is part of Norton Utilities) and Ziff-Davis's WinBench. A number of new third-party alternatives for monitoring system performance have appeared with the release of Windows 98.

Understanding Windows 98 Performance

Now that you know how to use MSInfo to become familiar with all the elements of your computer, you are ready to evaluate its performance.

Each PC system could involve any of an incredible number of hardware and software combinations. Each possible combination will provide an at least slightly different level of performance. Even a business that uses similar hardware and software systems company-wide will experience variable levels of performance.

Given the number of variables, it's important to proceed systematically when evaluating your system's performance. Once you have established a baseline, you can concretely measure the effects of the performance-tuning measures available within Windows 98.

Establishing a Baseline

Every component in a PC is rated to perform at a certain level. For example, some CPUs can run at 200 MHz. Ultra ATA-3 disk drives can be read at 33 Mb/s. Network cards can transfer data at so many Mb/s. But such performance is possible only under ideal conditions. Within any system, a bottleneck always exists that causes some or most of the components to run more slowly than the maximum rated speed. This section examines desirable baseline measurements for each major system component. Later in this chapter, you will learn how to use the System Monitor utility to obtain these measurements.

Baselines and Bottlenecks

As discussed earlier, a baseline is a collection of information that describes the stable performance level of a system or component. You may find that some of these components are always operating at full capacity, in which case they should be considered bottlenecks. Other components may never seem to reach their full advertised capabilities. The following sections describe the basic performance characteristics of each of the major hardware, device, and system components. Once you have read through the upcoming sections, you will have a better understanding of what to expect from your system. Later in this chapter, you will learn to adjust and/or monitor the performance of these characteristics through either the Windows 98 System Monitor utility or trial-and-error observation.

CPU

The central processing unit (CPU) always processes information at its constant, rated speed. As you learned in Chapter 9, threads of programming instructions compete for CPU time. If a multimedia presentation appears "jerky," this could be due to too many threads competing for too little CPU time. For example, if the CPU is operating 100% of the time for relatively long periods, other PC components generally have to wait until the CPU is free. In this case, the CPU is a bottleneck, which means that performance will suffer in all components that depend on the CPU. In the section on System Monitor, you will learn to determine if the CPU is a bottleneck in your system.

Memory

Although static and dynamic memory (also known as ROM and RAM, respectively) are used for all kinds of hardware and peripherals, you should be primarily concerned with random access memory (RAM) when evaluating your system's performance. Windows 98 demands a certain amount of memory, based on the number and type of programs that you have open. If the amount of RAM is not sufficient, Windows 98 uses **swap files** (as you learned in Chapter 2) stored on the hard disk. From the point of view of an application, swap files look like RAM. But data transfer to your swap file is actually much slower than data transfer between RAM and your CPU.

Later in this chapter you will determine whether you need more RAM, on the basis of the number of times data has to be transferred between RAM and your hard disk. This measure is also known as page-ins and page-outs. As you learned in Chapter 9, **paging** is the process by which data is transferred between RAM and other locations such as a swap file on your hard disk.

Hard Disk

If you have programs that require more RAM than you have available, some of these programs are stored in a swap file. Those unlucky programs will work more slowly than those stored in RAM. Even the fastest hard drives (and their SCSI or IDE controller cards attached to your computer motherboard) are slower than the slowest RAM. If the swap file is even slightly fragmented, a program's response time will be even slower. As you will learn later in this chapter, you can organize your hard disks using techniques designed to optimize data transfer, making for a faster effective rate of data transfer.

CD-ROM and DVD Drives

Given the speed limits in the hardware of many computers, a CD-ROM that is rated at 40x can transfer data to the CPU no more quickly than a CD-ROM that is rated at 20x. No matter how fast a device you install, the maximum speed is always governed by bottlenecks such as the system bus, which is the set of hardware data transfer connections on your computer motherboard. By default, Windows 98 sets up a memory cache, which is a dedicated amount of space in the RAM of your computer. Data from your CD-ROM is first transferred to the cache. The effectiveness of memory caching varies with the kind of file transferred. For example, multimedia files that can support larger screens are huge (hundreds of MB). The approximately 1 MB Windows 98 CD-ROM cache is not big enough to smooth out this amount of data transfer. Without a sufficient cache, multimedia presentations can begin to appear "jerky."

Digital video discs (DVD) have around 30 times the capacity of CD-ROMs. Physically, a DVD looks like a CD-ROM, and DVDs can be physically placed in a CD-ROM reader. Unfortunately, as you will learn later in this chapter, they cannot use the same file systems. The size of DVD files presents the same problems as the size of multimedia files; in fact, DVDs were developed, in part, to support more extensive multimedia such as movies.

Printing

Windows 98 can take advantage of enhanced metafile (EMF) spooling, which simplifies data in the print job. (This topic is explained in more detail in Chapter 8.) As printers have relatively little available memory, EMF can help speed the print job. EMF data can be spooled—in other words, moved to a file on the hard disk to wait for the printer memory to process the job that is in progress. This also allows the printing subsystem to return processing power to the system more quickly.

Network

Generally, networks do not perform at their advertised rate of speed. Different network cards run at different speeds. The actual rate for a file transfer over a 33.6 kbps modem is in fact closer to 3 kbps. The actual data transfer rate for a 10 Mb/s standard Ethernet system in a multiuser network is closer to 3 Mb/s. The baseline for network speed is not what the high-level specifications may lead us to believe. Later in this chapter, you will learn to use System Monitor to monitor some performance measurements on a network.

Drivers

As you learned in earlier chapters, **DLLs (dynamic-link libraries)** provide multiple programs with commonly used programming commands. Hardware manufacturers use these **DLLs** and create minidrivers to interface with Windows 98 unidrivers. There are so many drivers and DLLs operating simultaneously in Windows 98 that it is a wonder that problems do not occur more often. Later in this chapter, you will learn to use System File Checker to manage the different versions of DLLs that may be stored on your system.

CACHE MANAGEMENT

To understand the requirements for a number of the components mentioned in the previous section, it is important to have a solid understanding of VCACHE. **VCACHE** is the 32-bit, protected-mode driver introduced with Windows 95. Windows 98 dynamically manages the amount of RAM allocated to VCACHE. It can reduce the load on the following components within your PC:

- **Hard disks**: Because RAM access is much faster than hard disk access, it would be convenient if the most frequently accessed files could be stored in RAM. VCACHE fulfills this function by dynamically allocating pages (blocks of memory) in RAM to store some data from the hard disk. What is stored in VCACHE depends on the frequency and timing with which files were previously accessed.

- **Digital video discs (DVD)**: Physically, digital video discs look like CD-ROMs. Unfortunately, the **CD-ROM File System (CDFS)** is not good enough for DVDs. The typical CD-ROM cache of around 1 MB is not nearly enough to support DVD caching. Microsoft has set up a new file system for DVDs, known as the Universal Disk File (UDF) System. You learned in Chapter 9 that FAT and CDFS work with the Installable File System (IFS) Manager. Microsoft has revised IFS to work with UDF. DVD files contain a large amount of data. The dynamically allocable VCACHE system has the flexibility to help DVD multimedia files run as smoothly as possible.

- **Network Redirector**: This is a file system driver associated with network clients that access files over networks. When commonly used network files are found in the local VCACHE, the load on the network is reduced.

VCACHE is the successor to **SMARTDrive**, a 16-bit, real-mode disk-caching system associated with Windows 3.x and DOS. SMARTDrive has two limitations that VCACHE was designed to address. First, real-mode drivers have a higher risk of crashing the operating system when there are problems. Second, SMARTDrive cache sizes are fixed; they need to be reset when drive needs change. As discussed, the 32-bit, protected-mode, dynamically allocable VCACHE driver does not have these problems.

MEASURING PERFORMANCE

One of the problems with the Windows 98 performance-measuring tools is that they do not directly measure what you might consider useful information. For example, there is no measure that directly states that you need more RAM. Nothing in Windows 98 directly tells you that the free space on your hard disk is too small for an appropriate disk cache. Instead, you need to use the two basic means of measuring performance in a Windows 98 PC—the System Monitor utility and trial-and-error observation—and then extrapolate the information you need from the results these two methods provide.

DIAGNOSING PROBLEMS

Solutions to PC problems are not always obvious. For example, if it takes longer and longer to load a program, that does not necessarily mean that a faster hard disk will help. Instead, the solution may be to reorganize the files on the disk so that the hardware can find the desired program more quickly. Some common performance problems are addressed in the following list:

- **Slower performance over time**: Often the result of "memory leaks." All applications are run through threads, which are sets of tasks. (You learned about threads in Chapter 9.) Each thread is allocated a certain amount of memory. 32-bit applications are often multithreaded. When closed, applications are supposed to release their threads back to the main system. However, this does not always happen. Threads can accumulate, blocking access to sections of memory (thus creating a memory leak), which can affect performance.

- **Slow performance with an active hard disk**: If RAM is not sufficient for all required tasks, Windows 98 will page the memory requirements from the hard disk. This can slow performance, because hard disk access is slower than RAM access.

Performance Monitoring in Windows 98

The main tool for measuring performance in Windows 98 is **System Monitor**. You can use it to monitor local as well as remote computers over the network. You will learn about System Monitor in the coming sections. You will have a chance to use System Monitor to check the performance of your system in the Hands-on Projects at the end of this chapter.

System Monitor Features

You first previewed System Monitor in Chapter 9. Although the Windows 98 System Monitor does not offer as many features as the Windows NT 4.0 Performance Monitor, it is a sophisticated tool that you can use to monitor the state of system hardware, software services, and applications. To open System Monitor, click Start, point to Programs, point to Accessories, point to System Tools, and then click System Monitor. To view the list of the items you can monitor using System Monitor, click Edit on the menu bar, and then click Add Item. This opens the Add Item dialog box, as shown in Figure 10-4. The Category list box shows different types of items you can monitor. The Item list box shows the various items in the selected category. These items are sometimes referred to as counters, or measures. The various categories are explained in the following sections.

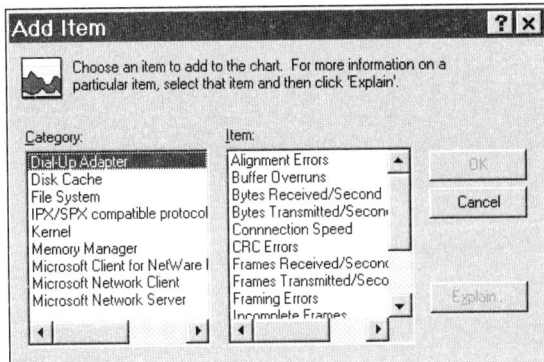

Figure 10-4   Add Item dialog box

Dial-Up Adapter

The items in the Dial-Up Adapter category are related to modem functionality. Modem performance is measured by data transmission in bytes, packets, and frames. Modems have their own memory storage areas, known as buffers. Buffers are similar to memory caches. If the system encounters problems in buffering, there may be problems with data timeouts and overruns. The Dial-Up Adapter measurement items are the same as the Windows NT Performance Monitor measurements for the Windows NT Remote Access Service. Within the Dial-Up Adapter category, you can monitor your system for the following items:

- **Alignment Errors**: An **alignment error** occurs when a computer receives a packet of a size different than expected.

- **Buffer Overruns:** This is a potential problem with external modems at higher transmission speeds. The buffer in the modem controller is also known as the universal asynchronous receiver-transmitter (UART). UART standards allow for 8 or 16 byte buffers. The UART 8250 (8 byte) buffer works for modems up to 9600 bps. For speeds above 9600 bps, data can overflow the capacity of the buffer, leading to lost packets. Any UART that is not up to the latest 16550 standard for most current modems is at risk of a buffer overrun.

- **Bytes Received/Second:** Actual inbound transmission from the connection over the Dial-Up Adapter on your Windows 98 computer

- **Bytes Transmitted/Second:** Actual outbound transmission through the Dial-Up Adapter on your Windows 98 computer

- **Connection Speed:** Indicates the maximum speed of data transfer between the computer and the modem. You specify this speed using the Properties tab of the Modems applet.

- **CRC Errors:** Provides results of a **CRC (cyclic redundancy check).** To understand a CRC, you need to keep in mind that data is transferred in bytes, which are a series of 1's and 0's. The cyclic redundancy check looks for fixed combinations of certain bytes. CRC numbers are calculated at both ends of the transmission. A CRC error (also known as a checksum error) occurs when these two numbers do not match.

- **Frames Received/Second:** Even though the number of bytes in a frame is variable, the Frames Received/Second should be nearly proportional to the Bytes Received/Second.

- **Frames Transmitted/Second:** Similar to Frames Received/Second

- **Framing Errors:** Occur when frames are not sent in their intended sequential order. This is usually the result of a "noisy" line.

- **Incomplete Frames:** A complete frame includes specific kinds of data for a header and a trailer. In the event that a frame is received without one or both of these components, it is considered an incomplete frame and recorded here.

- **Overrun Errors:** Frames are transmitted in sequence. When a frame is not processed through the CPU interrupt (IRQ) before the next frame is received, an overrun error occurs.

- **Timeout Errors:** Occur when a transmission ends unexpectedly.

- **Total Bytes Received:** Indicates bytes received in a single session

- **Total Bytes Transmitted:** Indicates bytes sent by your computer in a single session.

Disk Cache

As mentioned earlier in this chapter, reading from a hard disk is much slower than reading from RAM. VCACHE provides a solution to this potential problem, because it dynamically adjusts the size of the disk cache in RAM. If more data can be read from a larger cache, less data has to be read from the physical hard disk.

In addition to VCACHE, you can choose from a number of other older and third-party systems that can also manage disk cache. Some of these other systems also use a hardware cache that is physically installed on some hard disks. Microsoft recommends that you disable all other disk caching systems (including the Windows 3.x/DOS SMARTDrive system) to avoid conflict with VCACHE. The reason for this is that disk and hardware caching systems all read from the hard disk. If these other systems are not disabled, your system may end up storing different versions of the same file in different caches. There is no guarantee that the combination of VCACHE and another system would write the correct version of your file to your hard disk.

The System Monitor Disk Cache category measures how the RAM on your computer works with the disk cache on your hard drive. The disk cache counters are similar to those in the Cache Object category in the Windows NT Performance Monitor. The System Monitor Disk Cache category allows you to measure the following items:

- **Cache Buffers**: A cache buffer serves a function similar to that of a hard disk file allocation table. This item provides a count of the number of files available in the RAM VCACHE buffer.

- **Cache Hits**: The number of times that data requested from the hard disk is successfully retrieved from the RAM cache

- **Cache Misses**: Occur when data cannot be retrieved from the cache, thereby requiring access to the hard disk. If cache misses happen often enough, Windows 98 will adjust the size of the RAM buffer.

- **Cache Pages**: As you learned in Chapter 9, any Windows 98 system contains a number of 4 GB virtual memory address spaces. Data is transferred between RAM and your hard disk in 4 KB blocks of memory called "pages." The Cache Pages item measures the number of available pages.

- **Failed Cache Recycles**: When disk caches are filled, cache pages need to be recycled. Generally, the **LRU (least recently used)** cache pages are recycled first. This item lists the number of times recycling has failed. Failed cache recycles are an indicator of a lack of virtual memory on your hard disk.

- **LRU Cache Recycles**: The number of times the hard disk cache is recycled

- **Maximum Cache Pages**: The maximum possible number of cache pages in the RAM cache

- **Minimum Cache Pages**: The minimum possible number of cache pages in the RAM cache

- **Random Cache Recycles**: When the RAM disk buffer has been unused for a while, VCACHE will attempt to recover pages at random. This item measures the number of times VCACHE searches for old data to recycle.

File System

The File System items in System Monitor provide data on the reads and writes, to and from disks, whether direct or through VCACHE. If there is no activity to or from the disks, the file system counters will indicate this. The File System category includes five items:

- **Bytes Read/Second**: The amount of data read from hard disk, 3½-inch disk, compact disc, or VCACHE

- **Bytes Written/Second**: The amount of data written to the hard disk, floppy disk, or VCACHE

- **Dirty Data**: The amount of data stored in VCACHE that needs to be written to disk. Writing to the hard disk requires access to the CPU and disk controllers. When either of these components is busy, dirty data waits. It is then written to disk when these components are less busy, moderating the overall load on the system.

- **Reads/Second**: The number of read operations received by the file system per second

- **Writes/Second**: The number of write operations received by the file system per second

Kernel

The kernel includes the processor-level commands that directly interface with the CPU. Microsoft has designed Windows 98 to protect the kernel from the demands of different applications. In a multitasking system, the priority is to protect the system from a failure in any single application. If the kernel continues to run, all other programs can continue to run as well.

There are three System Monitor measures for the kernel:

- **Processor Usage**: The approximate percentage of time that the processor is in use

- **Threads**: The number of active threads. Every running program includes at least one thread. Multitasking programs open up multiple threads. Threads run concurrently. A thread is a program or an applet that can get an allocation of RAM and processing power from Windows 98. Sometimes programs do not release their threads when they are complete, leading to "memory leaks," as explained earlier in this chapter.

- **Virtual Machines**: A virtual machine (VM) looks like a separate computer to each program. As you learned in Chapter 9, every DOS program runs in a separate VM. All 16-bit and 32-bit Windows programs run together in one special VM known as the System VM. If your system is slow, use System Monitor to measure the number of VMs in your system. Using what you learned in Chapter 9, count the number of VMs that should exist. If these numbers do not match, a significant memory leak may exist.

Memory Manager

For your system memory to function properly, it must be able to coordinate RAM, VCACHE, and memory swap files. VCACHE is dynamically allocated. The default swap file is also dynamically allocated. As conditions change, memory faults may occur. For example, the disk may get too full for an optimal swap file, or RAM may not be sufficient for an optimal VCACHE. You can monitor numerous kinds of memory faults using the options available in the Memory Manager category:

For discussion purposes, the 18 items in the Memory Manager category have been divided into five areas: memory allocation, faults, swap files, pages, and disk cache.

Memory Allocation.   With the different possible combinations of RAM, VCACHE, and swap files, you sometimes need to be able to determine which type of memory is serving what function. Five items within the Memory Manager category can provide helpful clues in this regard. Unfortunately, none of them precisely addresses which part of the RAM and the hard disk is dedicated to each of the various caches:

- **Allocated Memory**: A combination of Other Memory and Swappable Memory, as described below. Changes in disk cache size, especially when requirements change, show up as changes in this measure.

- **Locked Memory**: Indicates the amount of memory exclusively dedicated to one function (and therefore "locked" to other programs). Locked memory may be necessary for some programs that require that a dedicated amount of RAM always be available. In order to provide hard disk access, the disk cache is also "locked" from use by other programs. A high amount of locked memory relative to total RAM reduces the effectiveness of swap files.

- **Other Memory**: Provides information on a variety of elements assigned within RAM, including 32-bit executable files, 32-bit DLLs, swappable (in RAM) memory-mapped files, nonpageable memory, and disk cache pages.

- **Swappable Memory**: Provides information on a specific allocation from the total swap file. This number includes the disk cache (described later in this chapter) and 16-bit executable files along with their DLLs. However, it also includes memory locked in RAM (i.e., memory that can't be swapped to disk) by certain applications.

- **Unused Physical Memory**: Indicates the amount of free RAM, in bytes. If this value is zero, memory can still be allocated from what is or can be made available on the disk swap file. But a low value of available physical memory can indicate a need for more RAM.

Faults. Within Windows 98, the term "memory fault" refers to a situation in which data required by an application or by the operating system does not exist in RAM, but instead must be retrieved from a swap file on the hard disk. A memory fault is not a type of error, or failure, but instead is something that occurs by design in order to save RAM for the most pressing needs. Memory is swapped between RAM and the hard disk on a regular basis. System Monitor includes two counters that you can use to track memory faults:

- **Instance Faults**: Indicates when data unique to a VM is not found in RAM
- **Page Faults**: Tracks page faults, which occur every time memory swapping to the hard disk swap file is required

Swap Files. In Windows 98, swap file size depends on the needs of loaded applications and the limits on available RAM and hard disk memory. System Monitor provides five counters to help you assess the performance of the swap file:

- **Discards**: Sometimes, the paging of memory to the swap file is not necessary, because the data that is being transferred from RAM is already in the swap file. In this case, the duplicate data is discarded. This counter indicates the number of memory pages between the RAM and swap file that are discarded per second.
- **Swap File Defective**: Lists defects in the swap file, in bytes. Swap files are paged in 4 KB units. If one byte out of any 4 KB swap file page is defective, this counter will be 4 KB.
- **Swap File In Use**: In Windows 98, the default swap file is variable, depending on memory requirements and available hard disk space. This counter indicates the size of the swap file that contains current virtual memory data, in bytes.
- **Swap File Size**: Indicates the total size of the current swap file. Under the default settings, it can grow if the size of the swap file in use grows.

Pages. The 32-bit architecture of Windows 98 makes virtual memory far more efficient than in Windows 95. For example, paging to a swap file is now accomplished via the flat address space that you learned about in Chapter 9, which allows hard disk sectors to be allocated to addressable virtual memory. The 16-bit segment/offset model used by Windows 3.x required a hierarchy of addresses. Because finding memory in the segment/offset model requires an additional step, this model requires additional time. When coupled with the slower speed of hard disk access, the performance penalty is significant. Paging to a swap file on a hard disk is different from paging to VCACHE in RAM, although the techniques are the same. The following counters are System Monitor measures for paging:

- **Page-ins**: Indicates the number of memory pages swapped into RAM every second
- **Page-outs**: Indicates the number of memory pages swapped to a disk every second
- **Pages Mapped From Cache**: Measures the effect of the WinAlign utility, which reorganizes executable files into 4 KB segments. Because Intel chips page in 4 KB units, the alignment can increase the efficiency of application memory caching. However, WinAlign is not compatible with all applications and should be monitored regularly using this counter.

Disk Cache. As discussed earlier in this chapter, VCACHE is a section of RAM used to minimize the number of reads to the hard disk. The Memory Manager counters relating to the disk cache help you monitor the effectiveness of VCACHE. In particular, these counters allow you to measure the actual memory that is and can be allocated to the disk cache:

- **Disk Cache Size**: Indicates the current size of the cache allocated to disk management, in bytes
- **Maximum Disk Cache Size**: Indicates the largest possible disk cache size, as determined at system startup. By definition, this should never be larger than total available RAM.
- **Minimum Disk Cache Size**: Indicates the smallest possible disk cache size, as determined at system startup

Microsoft Network Client

To understand the counters included in the Microsoft Network Client category, you need to understand the concept of a redirector. The **redirector** is a software service that moves user file requests over a network or to local resources, as appropriate. Windows 98 includes network redirectors for both Client for Microsoft Networks (Vredir.vxd) and Microsoft Client for NetWare Networks (Nwredir.vxd). In the Open Systems Interconnect (OSI) model of networking, the redirector operates at the interface between the presentation and application layers.

- **Bytes Read/Second**: Indicates the amount of data that Windows 98 reads through the redirector per second
- **Bytes Written/Second**: Indicates the amount of data that Windows 98 sends through the redirector per second
- **Number of Nets**: Indicates the number of networks to which your Windows 98 computer is connected. It is possible to be connected to multiple networks simultaneously. For example, a direct dial-up connection to an Internet service provider and a local connection to an Ethernet network would each count as a network connection. If you notice that your system is connected to multiple networks, you should check for delays due to multiple protocols being used for the different networks. If more than one protocol is running on your machine, data has to be checked through each protocol service, in the order that the protocols are bound to their network adapters, before being read. This can cause delays.
- **Open Files**: Indicates the number of files that have been opened over the network
- **Resources**: Indicates the number of resources in use, with a resource being anything that can be shared over the network
- **Sessions**: Lists the number of current sessions. Any logon counts as a session.
- **Transactions/Sec**: NetBIOS is the IBM standard for network communication adapted by Microsoft. NetBIOS transmissions consist of **SMBs (server message blocks)**. Every network transaction involves the sending of an SMB over the network. Transactions/Second measures the number of SMBs sent by the local PC over the network per second.

Microsoft Network Server

As you've learned, Windows 98 can operate as both a client and a server. For this reason, Microsoft has provided separate monitoring categories for each function.

- **Buffers**: Indicates the number of working buffers on the server. Just as a local machine has a disk cache to minimize reads from the hard disk, a server has buffers in RAM that hold the data most commonly requested over the system. This explains why it is useful to install as much RAM as possible in a server.

- **Bytes Read/Sec**: Indicates the rate at which the server reads from disk per second

- **Bytes Written/Sec**: Indicates the rate at which the server writes to disk per second

- **Bytes/Second**: Combines the server read and write rates from the hard disk

- **Memory**: Indicates the amount of memory required for server functions. This counter is useful if you have configured your computer to function as both a server and a client.

- **NBs**: Server network buffers. While this probably indicates the buffers dedicated to server communication on the network, the Microsoft documentation is unclear on this point.

- **Server Threads**: Indicates the number of threads being used by the server processes in Windows 98.

USING SYSTEM MONITOR

Once you are familiar with what System Monitor allows you to measure, you can begin tracking (or logging) specific items. The information compiled by System Monitor can be saved in a log file. To begin logging in System Monitor, click File on the menu bar, and then click Start Logging. In the Save As dialog box, choose a name and location for your log file. The default log file name is Sysmon.log, saved in the root C:\ directory. The log of the items that you have selected in your System Monitor will be saved to this file.

It is useful to examine a sample log file. In Hands-on Project 9-2, you used System Monitor to take measurements related to the kernel. You will now examine the log file that results from taking such measurements.

1. If you have not done so already, complete Hands-on Project 9-2, to become familiar with the process of taking kernel measurements.

2. In the System Monitor menu bar, click File, and then click Start Logging.

3. In the Save As dialog box, enter the name of your choice for a new log file, select the folder of your choice using the Save in list box, and then click Save. System Monitor begins logging data from kernel counters.

4. Click Options, and then click Chart. In the Options dialog box, move the pointer as far left as possible (towards "Faster"). The update interval should now read "1 second."

5. Click OK to close the Options dialog box.

6. Wait at least 1 minute to be assured of getting sufficient data.

7. In the menu bar, click File, and then click Stop Logging. Now you can open the log file you just created.

8. Click Start, point to Programs, and then click Windows Explorer. Find the file that you saved in Step 3.

9. Double-click the log file.

10. If you see an "Open With" dialog box, scroll down the "Choose the program you want to use" list box, click Notepad, and then click OK.

11. You can now examine the log file that you just created.

Figure 10-5 shows a sample log file, similar to the one you just created. As you can see, it can be difficult to translate the information saved in a log file. However, System Monitor log files are set up in comma-delimited format, which means you can easily import them into a spreadsheet program such as Microsoft Excel.

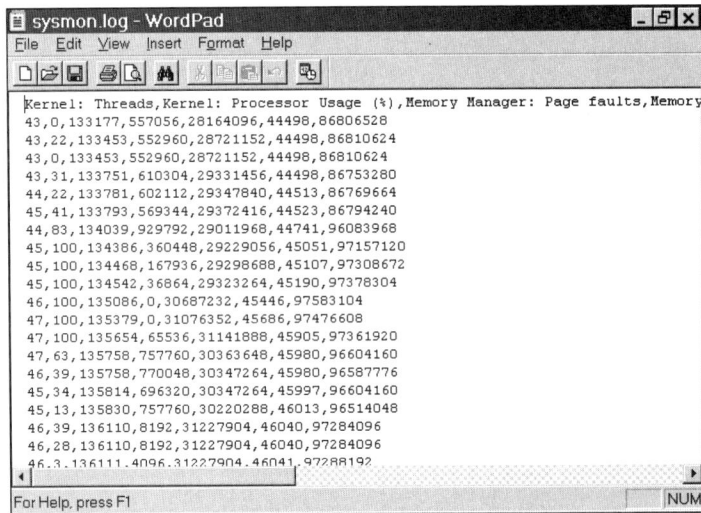

Figure 10-5 Sample log file

If the Windows 98 computer that you use is run continuously, you may wish to create log files on a periodic basis. You can also simply observe the behavior of your computer as you work by running System Monitor continuously. In the System Monitor menu bar, click View, and then click Always on Top. System Monitor will run on top of any programs that you currently have running, which can help you observe the performance of your system over time.

USING TRIAL AND ERROR

Unfortunately, System Monitor is not a complete tool. It does not measure things like the performance of a printer or graphics on a monitor. Thus, in some cases, the preferred way to determine what works best on your system is to use trial and error: make a change to your system, and then make notes on how the change affects the system. In other words, you simply have to make some adjustments and see how your system reacts. Trial and error works as long as you carefully document every change and the corresponding effects of each change.

There are no special tricks involved in trial and error. A proper use of trial and error is based on the traditional scientific method: observe, theorize, and attempt to prove your theory. This means that when optimizing your Windows 98 system, you need to watch the behavior of your system by using System Monitor and any other objective performance measures, such as the time it takes to print a page. Using the settings that you will learn about in the following sections, you use the trial and error method to make changes and observe the results. Only in this way, through trial and error, can you really optimize the performance of your Windows 98 system.

Printing

As you learned in Chapter 8, Windows 98 can send data to a printer in one of two formats. The **RAW** format sends the control of creating the print job back to the program. This means that the printing of every character is processed pixel by pixel. The default EMF (enhanced metafile) format simplifies the data sent to the printer, and allows the application to resume its work more quickly. Optimal print settings depend on the balance of memory and graphical power in the system. Determining the best printing option for your environment is a good example of the trial and error method of optimization at work. Later in this chapter, you will learn to adjust the different settings for memory and graphical power.

Monitor

For most hardware components, the best way to enhance performance is to add RAM. The one exception to this rule relates to the video systems. To improve video performance, you need to add memory and processing power to the graphics card itself. Windows 98 provides a series of settings that allow you to experiment with different graphics cards.

MICROSOFT SYSTEM INFORMATION TOOLS

You already learned how to use MSInfo to learn about the components installed on your system. In this section you will learn how to use its diverse tools to monitor the status of your system. Not all of the MSInfo tools are used for monitoring, tuning, or optimizing Windows 98. However, all of these tools are useful in troubleshooting.

To access any of the Microsoft System Information tools, click Tools on the menu bar, and then click the tool you want to use. The following sections describe some of these tools. You will learn about the Update Wizard Uninstall tool and ScanDisk later in this chapter. You will learn about the tools not addressed here in Chapter 14.

System File Checker

One important tool in the MSInfo Tools menu is System File Checker. The main function of System File Checker (SFC) is to verify the integrity of the Windows 98 operating system files by scanning for problem files. Problem files are defined as those that may be missing, changed, or corrupted. As you learned in previous chapters, Windows 98 is built on a layered architecture. Without the layered architecture, software and hardware manufacturers have to build configuration files (such as the .ini files) with interfaces all the way from the program to the hardware. The layered architecture has reduced the requirements on each system file. But the increasing number of layers increases the number of system files required for each application. As shown in Figure 10-6, SFC can scan files for errors and also extract compressed files to replace corrupt system files from the relevant installation disk.

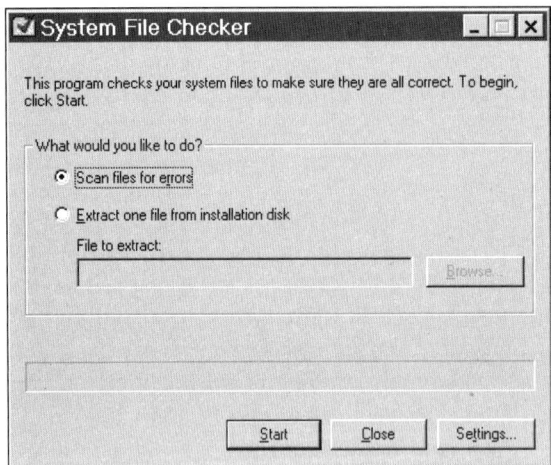

Figure 10-6 System File Checker dialog box

System File Checker verifies Windows 98 system files by performing cyclic redundancy checks (CRCs) to verify the integrity of binary file data. (As you learned earlier in this chapter, you can use System Monitor to check for CRC errors when transmitting data.) When you install Windows 98, a file containing the preferred CRC results for your system is copied to C:\Windows\default.sfc. Then, when you use SFC to calculate CRC data for each Windows 98 system file, SFC compares this new CRC data to the original data stored in the Default.sfc file. If the new CRC data does not match the original CRC data, your system contains a corrupt system file that should be reloaded. You will learn more about SFC in Chapter 14.

Signature Verification Tool

You can use the Microsoft Signature Verification tool to check whether or not you are using an authorized copy of your software. From the MSInfo menu bar, click Tools, and then click Signature Verification Tool. The Signature Verification Tool dialog box, as shown in Figure 10-7, is similar to the Find File dialog box. In the Look for text box, you can specify a search for signed or unsigned files. Make sure this is set to signed files. In the Named text box, you can specify the types of files that you are looking for. In the Look in text box, you can specify the directory to search. Enter C:\Windows in this text box, and then click Find Now. When the search is complete, highlight a file in the list of files, and then click Details to display current information on the validity of the certificate associated with the program.

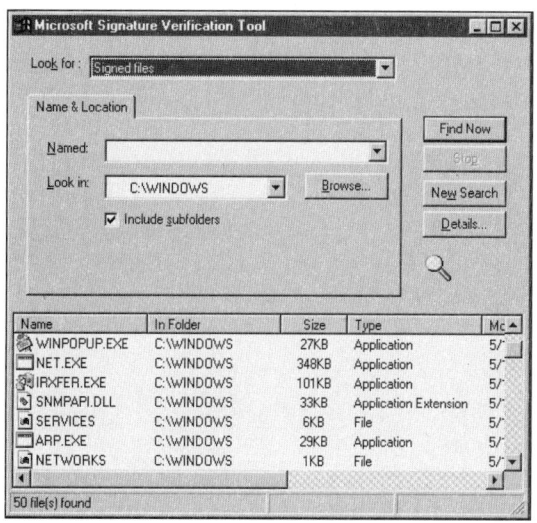

Figure 10-7 Signature Verification Tool

Registry Checker

The next tool in the MSInfo Tools menu is the Registry Checker. As discussed in Chapter 3, the Registry Checker scans the Registry every time you start Windows 98. Two tools associated with the Registry Checker, ScanReg and ScanRegW, check for inconsistent file structures and corruption. If these tools locate a problem, you can correct the problem by restoring a previous version of the Registry, assuming you've made a backup of your Registry, as described in Chapter 3. If you manually open the Registry Checker from within the MSInfo window, it automatically scans the Registry for errors, and then, assuming it finds no errors, it gives you the option of backing up the Registry. See Chapter 3 for a full discussion of the Registry Checker.

Dr. Watson

Dr. Watson is yet another tool in the MSInfo Tools menu. You can use Dr. Watson to diagnose and log software-related problems. You can also use it to compile information on currently running applications and system files. Once you click the Dr. Watson command on the MSInfo Tools menu, the Dr. Watson utility becomes resident on your system for as long as you are logged on to your current session of Windows 98. In other words, it starts recording in the background, examining your running applications for software faults. The only indication that Dr. Watson is running is an icon in the system tray (the set of icons adjacent to the clock in the taskbar). To actually view the Dr. Watson window, double-click the icon in the system tray.

If you're not sure which icon is the Dr. Watson icon, place the pointer over each system tray icon to display its label.

Once you have displayed the Dr. Watson window, you can examine the information compiled by Dr. Watson. Click View on the menu bar, and then click Advanced View. This displays a number of tabs. For the performance monitoring purposes of this chapter, the System and Tasks tabs are of the greatest interest. As shown in Figure 10-8, the System tab gives information similar to the opening screen of MSInfo. Like the NT 4.0 Task Manager, the Tasks tab lists all programs currently running in your Windows 98 system.

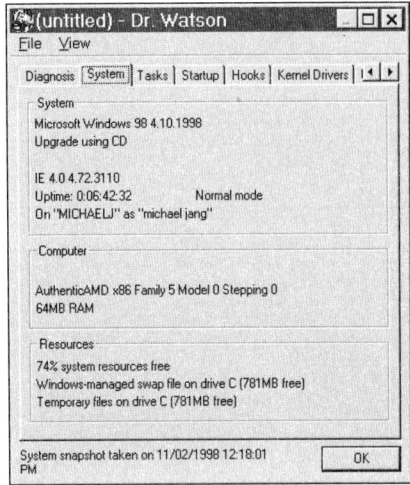

Figure 10-8 System tab of Dr. Watson

System Configuration Utility

The next tool in the MSInfo Tools menu is the System Configuration utility. This utility provides a relatively user-friendly method for editing several critical startup configuration files: Config.sys, Autoexec.bat, System.ini, and Win.ini. You can edit sections in each of these files on an experimental basis to check the effects on the system before actually implementing changes. This utility will be discussed in more detail later in this chapter, in the section on optimization.

Version Conflict Manager

The final tool in the MSInfo Tools menu is the Version Conflict Manager (VCM). Because of the layered structure of the Windows driver architecture, the same drivers are often used for different applications. However, when installing new software, you automatically install new drivers. This can result in conflicts, in which drivers installed for new software may be of a different version than drivers required for previously installed software. If you have a problem with an older program due to the driver installed for a newer program, you should first contact the company that made the older program and ask for an updated version of the program, which will work with the current driver. If that does not work, click Tools in the MSInfo menu bar, and then click Version Conflict Manager.

As shown in Figure 10-9, the VCM creates a list of existing and backed-up driver files with conflicting version levels. If you have a problem with a specific driver, highlight a previous version of the driver listed here, and then click Restore Selected Files. Try your old and new programs again. It is possible that the program that you just installed won't work with the older driver, in which case you may have to decide which program is more important to you on this particular computer. If the version level that you chose does not work with the new program, you can use the VCM to restore the previous version of the relevant driver. To view a history of such revisions, open the VCM log file, C:\Windows\verback.log in Notepad. As shown in Figure 10-10, the Verback.log file lists the system files that have been changed, the date of the change, and the location in which the operational system file, related to the relevant program, is stored.

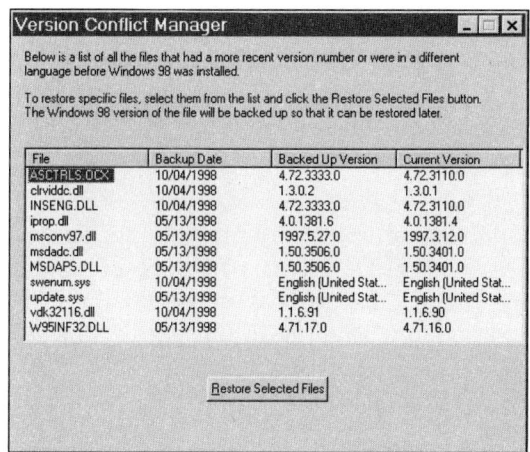

Figure 10-9 Version Conflict Manager window

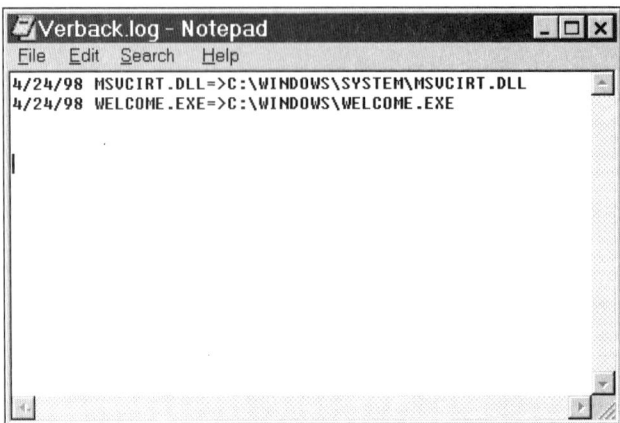

Figure 10-10 Verback.log file displayed in Notepad

OPTIMIZING WINDOWS 98

Now that you are familiar with the various monitoring tools available in Windows 98, you can learn how to use them to optimize the performance of your computer's components. In Chapter 14, you will learn how to use some of these same tools to locate and correct system problems.

OPTIMIZING THE CPU

In any multitasking system, it is important to protect the smooth operation of the CPU from faults in any one program. That way, if one program fails, the others can still run. Microsoft has dedicated substantial effort to this goal in Windows 98, through the use of the Intel ring architecture. As you learned in Chapter 8, an Intel CPU is made up of four **rings**: 0, 1, 2, and 3. Windows 98 functions in Rings 0 and 3. Ring 0 is dedicated to the kernel operations that interface directly with the CPU, while Ring 3 is dedicated to applications run in a 32-bit protected-mode environment. Any failure in a Ring 3 operation need not affect any Ring 0 operation, thereby protecting the CPU.

However, in order to provide compatibility with legacy DOS and Windows 3.x applications, Windows 98 has to accommodate some 16-bit real-mode operations. When real-mode operations occur, the ring architecture can no longer protect the CPU.

To help avoid this problem, Microsoft has created several 32-bit protected-mode substitutes for real-mode drivers. These special drivers are actually substituted for the 16-bit drivers from the list below, when you start Windows 98. Limiting your use of real-mode applications to the drivers in the following list will help your CPU operate more smoothly:

- MS-DOS version 5.0 (or higher) drivers
- Drivers that access the CPU via the BIOS, also known as drivers that access INT 13
- ASPI (the DOS Advanced SCSI Programming Interface) Manager

A number of real-mode drivers are considered unsafe in Windows 98. To optimize CPU performance, you should avoid them whenever possible. Although equivalent 32-bit protected-mode applications are available, they are not automatically substituted as required. The dangerous drivers are associated with the following applications and utilities:

- Data compression (unless DriveSpace-compatible)
- Data encryption
- Disk mirroring
- Bad sector mapping (also a ScanDisk function)
- Fault tolerance

MEMORY MANAGEMENT

Good memory management is probably the most important factor governing the performance of Windows 98. No PC today can have sufficient RAM to cover the memory requirements of a single Windows 98 virtual machine (VM). A single Windows 98 VM requires 4 GB of addressable memory, and each PC can have multiple VMs. Windows 98 overcomes the lack of RAM by using portions of the hard disk as if it were RAM, through the use of swap files.

However, swap files are not the perfect solution to this problem. As mentioned earlier in this chapter, it takes longer to access data stored in a swap file than it does to access data stored directly in RAM. In addition, like other hard disk files, a swap file can become fragmented, thus slowing the data access process even more. Furthermore, a swap file that is used frequently can grow so large that it becomes hard to manage; as a result, application performance will suffer. You can check for swap file problems using two System Monitor items. The following list first indicates the appropriate category in the System Monitor's Add Item dialog box, and then indicates the relevant item within that category:

- **Kernel, Processor Usage (%)**: If this counter indicates a high rate of processor usage accompanied by constant accesses to the hard disk (a situation known as "disk thrashing"), a good part of the processor time is being spent moving memory back and forth between RAM and the swap file. As a result, less processor time is available to run applications. In other words, if your processor (CPU) is in use 100% of the time for more than a few seconds at a time, you may need more RAM.

- **Memory Manager, Swap file in use**: Ideally, this counter should indicate that the swap file in use is smaller than available RAM. If it is larger, this means that Windows 98 requires an excessive amount of hard disk space to simulate RAM functions. This is also a performance problem that can be addressed by additional RAM.

If your Windows 98 system is short on memory, you can take advantage of a few memory optimization techniques. Some of these techniques make use of Windows 98 protected-mode applications, while others can be a general drain on memory.

The first step in optimizing your system's memory is to use the Windows 98 autotuning features, which allow you to allocate memory to meet the specific needs of your computer.

As discussed in the next paragraph, you do this by adjusting the caches for directory paths and filenames. If the cache is big enough, your processor only has to look in the cache for a file path or name. This saves access time to the hard disk FAT.

To activate the Windows 98 autotuning features, click Start, point to Settings, click Control Panel, double-click the System icon, click the Performance tab, and then click File System. This opens the File System Properties dialog box. Here you can choose from three possible roles for your computer, as shown in Figure 10-11. These options are:

- **Desktop computer**: This assumes that the desktop computer has more than sufficient RAM and access to regular (not battery) power.
- **Mobile or docking system**: This assumes that the computer has a limited amount of RAM and limited power from batteries. The RAM dedicated to disk file caching is also limited.
- **Network server**: This assumes a generous amount of RAM as well as frequent access to the hard disk(s). File caching in RAM is maximized.

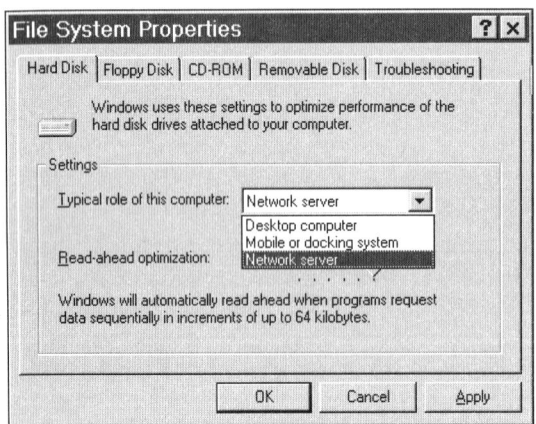

Figure 10-11 Selecting a role for your computer

HARD DISK MANAGEMENT

A good hard disk is important to memory performance. By itself, hard disk management is also vital to keeping access time as low as possible, to minimizing drive errors, and to maximizing available room for elements such as memory swap files. You should be familiar with the three basic hard disk management tools: ScanDisk, Disk Defragmenter, and DriveSpace 3.

ScanDisk

ScanDisk is the Windows 98 disk analysis and repair program. It works with FAT32 as well as with FAT16-formatted drives. It is also designed to work with DriveSpace 3 or DoubleSpace compressed drives. Unlike some other disk utilities, it does not damage long filenames. You can use it on all PC storage media. ScanDisk is designed to check and fix disk problems in the following areas:

- **Bad sectors**: Physical surface problems. A hard disk consists of a device that reads the data, and the actual hard disk platen, which spins at thousands of revolutions per minute. Because the reader makes physical contact with the platen, a hard disk will eventually wear out. As a hard disk wears, some sectors become unusable.

- **File System Structure**: ScanDisk looks for lost or cross-linked file clusters. Hard disks are divided up into clusters. Many files are large enough that they require more than one cluster of storage space. Cluster locations are kept in the disk **file allocation table (FAT)**. If the location data is damaged, the file allocation table may point to the wrong cluster as the remainder of a file. If nothing is stored in that cluster, it is considered to be lost. If the FAT assigns more than one file to the same cluster, that cluster is said to be **cross-linked**. It is possible to recover data lost to this kind of failure, but the recovery techniques depend on a close reading of recovered clusters and are rarely successful with anything but text files. Problems with lost or cross-linked files can usually be traced to an excessively fragmented hard disk. As you'll learn in the next section, you can use Disk Defragmenter utility to address this problem.

To keep your system in top condition, you should run ScanDisk regularly. In general, you can use ScanDisk to detect, and, in some cases, recover lost files and folders. You can use Disk Defragmenter to prevent files and folders from becoming lost in the first place. You can configure ScanDisk to run automatically, as described later in this chapter. To open ScanDisk manually, click Start, point to Programs, point to Accessories, point to System Tools, and then click ScanDisk. This opens the ScanDisk dialog box. As shown in Figure 10-12, ScanDisk offers two basic options: a standard and a thorough scan.

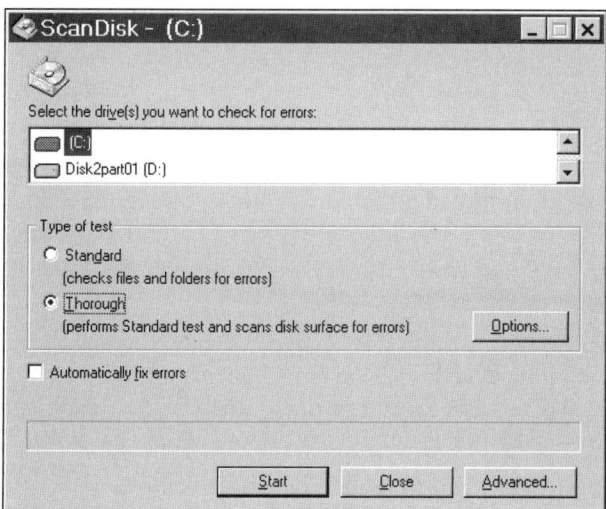

Figure 10-12 ScanDisk dialog box

A standard scan checks files and folders for errors. If you choose the thorough scan, you can choose from several options for scanning the physical hard disk. To view these options, click

Options in the ScanDisk dialog box. This opens the Surface Scan Options dialog box, shown in Figure 10-13. Here, you first need to specify what part or parts of the disk you want to scan. Next, you can disable the write-testing feature, which tests whether or not your computer can read from and write to your hard disk. Finally, you can choose whether you want to repair bad sectors in system and hidden files. The write-testing and repair options should only be disabled if time is limited. Disable the repair option if you prefer to reinstall system files from the relevant installation media.

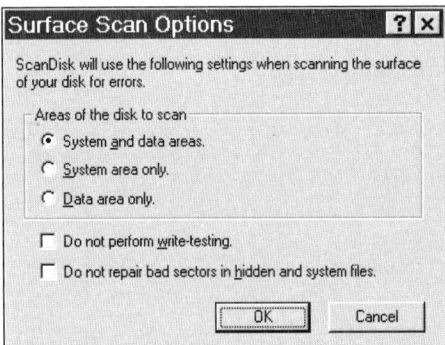

Figure 10-13   Surface Scan Options dialog box

Now click OK to return to the main ScanDisk dialog box. You can specify even more disk-scanning options by clicking the Advanced button. This opens the ScanDisk Advanced Options dialog box, shown in Figure 10-14. The following list describes the various Advanced options:

- **Display summary**: Allows you to display a summary of ScanDisk activity, which includes information on the disks that have been searched, errors that have been found, and what has been done to recover lost or cross-linked clusters

- **Log file**: The results of the disk scan, based on the options that you choose in this and the Surface Scan Options dialog box, are written to a log file. The ScanDisk log file is stored in C:\Scandisk.log. You can replace (i.e., overwrite) any existing log, add the results to the end of any existing ScanDisk log, or choose not to log the results at all.

- **Cross-linked files**: Allows you to specify what to do with cross-linked files—that is, two different files with links pointing to the same information on the hard disk. If two files are cross-linked, the data for at least one of the files is corrupt. The "make copies" option allows for the potential full recovery of at least one of the files.

- **Lost file fragments**: Allows you to specify what you want to do with lost file fragments, as explained earlier. You can choose to convert lost file fragments to files that will be stored in the root directory. However, keep in mind that it's not easy to recover usable data from such a file.

- **Check files for**: Allows you to check for specific problems that can affect the ability of applications to access data

- **Check host drive first**: When checking a compressed drive, it makes sense to first check the drive where the compressed CVF file is stored. Errors in the host drive can affect the compressed drive.

- **Report MS-DOS mode name length errors**: Use this option only if your files do not need the long filename format.

Figure 10-14 ScanDisk Advanced Options dialog box

Operational parameters for ScanDisk will be addressed in Chapter 14.

Disk Defragmenter

The main purpose of Disk Defragmenter is to organize all files and folders on a hard disk so they are contiguous, that is, they can be found in consecutive clusters to minimize read time. Previous versions of Disk Defragmenter focused on making each file contiguous. But there is a faster way to organize files for Windows 98.

As you learned in previous chapters, applications are associated with a number of dynamic-link libraries (DLLs). When you call up an application such as Microsoft Word, Windows 98 reads part of the executable file, then it reads a .dll file, and then it returns to the executable file. The Windows 98 Disk Defragmenter organizes files the way that they are read, which speeds the loading of your applications.

The key to this is an internal Windows 98 utility called Task Monitor. Task Monitor watches how executable and .dll files are opened. These files are located in specific places on your hard disk. The disk access patterns and frequencies are recorded in log files, stored in the C:\Windows\applog directory.

To open Disk Defragmenter, click Start on the menu bar, point to Programs, point to Accessories, point to System Tools, and then click Disk Defragmenter. This opens the Select Drive dialog box, where you can specify which logical drive you want to defragment. If you have two or more logical drives on your hard disk (e.g., C and D), you can choose to defragment them all at once. You can specify additional settings by clicking the Settings button. This opens the Disk Defragmenter Settings dialog box, shown in Figure 10-15, which offers two basic options: "Rearrange program files so my programs run faster" and "Check the drive for errors." The first option uses Task Monitor to optimize program and .dll file organization on the hard drive. The second option checks for drive errors, as discussed in the section on ScanDisk. If drive errors are found, Disk Defragmenter stops and requests that you first run the ScanDisk utility.

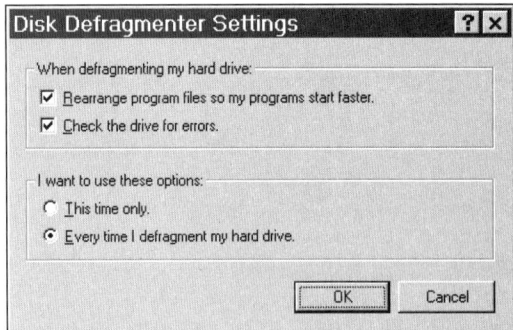

Figure 10-15 Disk Defragmenter Settings dialog box

DriveSpace 3

As you learned in Chapter 8, you can use **DriveSpace 3** to compress the space taken by the files on your hard disk. The Windows 98 version of DriveSpace 3 is fully compatible with DoubleSpace from Windows 95 and with DriveSpace 3 from the Windows 95 Plus! pack. DriveSpace 3 has been updated to recognize, but not to compress, FAT32 formatted drives. Consider using DriveSpace 3 if you need more room on your hard disk for a swap file. For details on the mechanics of DriveSpace 3, see Chapter 8.

Disk Space Cleanup Manager

You can use the Disk Cleanup utility to find and remove files with obsolete information. To open Disk Cleanup, click Start on the menu bar, point to Programs, point to Accessories, point to System Tools, and then click Disk Cleanup. This opens the Select Drive dialog box, where you can specify the drive you want to clean up. After you select a drive and click OK, you see the Disk Cleanup dialog box for the selected drive. In the Disk Cleanup tab, shown in Figure 10-16, you can choose to remove files such as the following:

- **Temporary Internet Files**: Files downloaded from the Internet on Internet Explorer. If you return to a Web page while a file is still in this folder, depending on your browser settings, Internet Explorer retrieves the page from this folder.

- **Downloaded Program Files**: Programs downloaded from the Internet. These usually take the form of ZIP files that can be safely deleted after the contents of the ZIP file has been installed on the computer.

- **Recycle Bin**: All files deleted via Windows Explorer or other file management applications. You should empty the Recycle Bin regularly.
- **Old ScanDisk Files in the root folder**: As you learned earlier in this chapter, when ScanDisk finds a lost file cluster, it can save the file in the root (C:\) folder. If you do not have any old ScanDisk files, this option does not appear in the dialog box.
- **Temporary file**: Any file that is saved to the C:\Temp folder by an application. These files can be safely deleted after the application that created them has closed. By default, the Disk Cleanup utility waits until a temp file has been in the temp folder for one week, before marking the file as nonessential.
- **Delete Windows 98 uninstall information**: All files required for uninstalling Windows 98. When you install Windows 98, you have the option of saving all essential Windows 95 files. Saving these files allows you to uninstall Windows 98 later, by restoring all the saved Windows 95 files. If the decision to upgrade to Windows 98 is permanent, you can delete these files. If these files have already been deleted, this option will not be included in the list of files to delete.

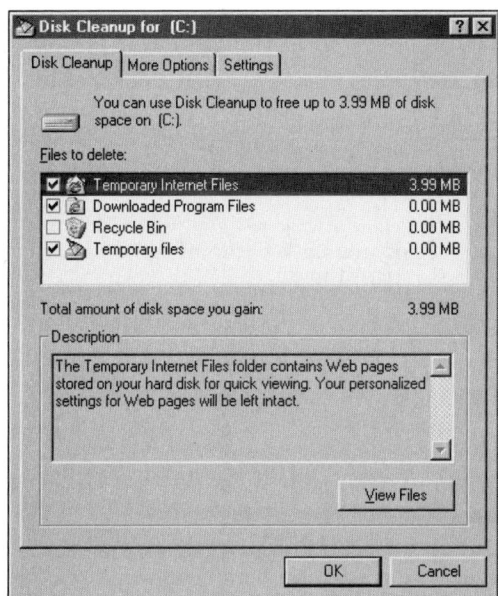

Figure 10-16   Disk Cleanup tab

In the More Options tab, shown in Figure 10-17, there are three options. The first two Clean up buttons bring you to the Windows Setup and Installed Programs tabs of the Add/Remove Programs dialog box, which you can use to reduce the number of Windows 98 utilities and other installed programs on your computer. (You could also access these tabs via the Add/Remove Programs applet.) The Convert button opens the FAT32 drive converter that you learned about in Chapter 2. Remember, converting your drive from FAT16 to FAT32 is a one-way process. To convert back, you would have to back up your files on a separate disk, and then reformat your drive.

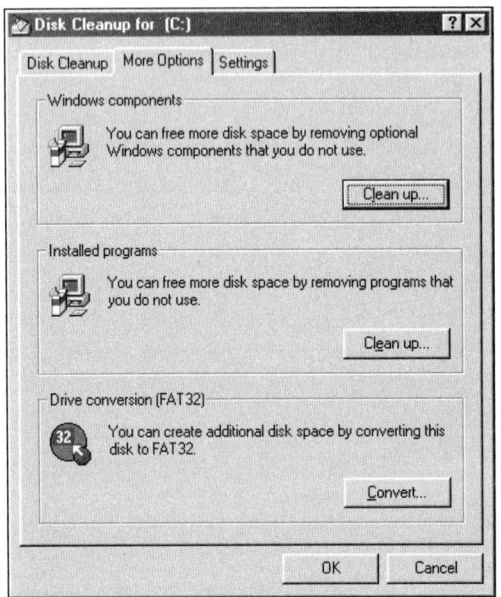

Figure 10-17   More Options tab

In the Settings tab, you can indicate whether or not Disk Cleanup should start automatically when you are nearly out of disk space. The threshold is when your disk has 25-65 MB of free space, depending on the size of your drive (larger drives have larger thresholds).

OPTIMIZING CD-ROM AND DIGITAL VIDEO DISC DRIVES

Earlier in this chapter, you learned about optimizing the file system properties of a hard disk. Managing CD-ROMs and Digital Video Discs (DVDs) requires some different techniques. This is due to the fact that, as you learned in Chapters 2 and 9, CD-ROMs use a different file system than the FAT and NTFS file systems used on hard disks.

Although access from a hard disk is much slower than access from RAM, access from a CD is even slower. While CD-ROM data is being read into a system, its cache is placed in RAM, separate from VCACHE. To specify a size for the CD-ROM cache, open the System applet via the Control Panel, click the Performance tab, and then click File System. This opens the File System Properties dialog box. The CD-ROM tab, shown in Figure 10-18, contains the relevant settings. The "Optimize access pattern for" list box provides five settings for the CD-ROM cache, which correspond to the different speeds available for a

CD-ROM. At this time, the highest setting is for CD-ROMs that run at "Quad-speed or higher." You can also adjust the supplemental cache size between 214 and 1238 kilobytes.

DVDs were developed in part to handle multimedia; they are much faster and larger than CD-ROMs. This speed and capacity require significantly larger caches than are required for CD-ROMs. To accommodate this need, DVDs are generally configured to employ the UDF file system. UDF can make use of the VCACHE, which is much larger than the CD-ROM cache.

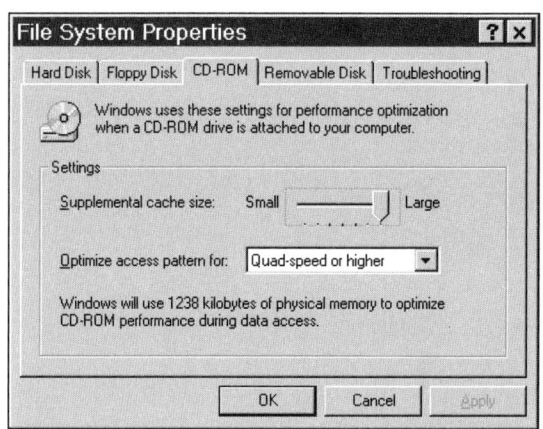

Figure 10-18   File System Properties dialog box CD-ROM tab

REMOVABLE MEDIA

As discussed in Chapter 2, you can choose from a large variety of removable media (also known as removable disks), including Tape Drives, Zip Drives, and rewritable CDs. You can specify settings for removable media using the File System Properties dialog box described in the previous section. In this case, however, you need to use the Removable Disk tab. In this tab you can enable the use of a special cache for removable media. Note that this cache is different from that used for CD-ROMs or VCACHE.

GRAPHICS

Despite all the technological advances in recent years, displaying graphics on computers is still somewhat problematic. Animated graphics often appear "jerky" on your monitor. To help avoid this problem, the video cards attached to monitors are usually programmed with acceleration functions that reduce the "jerkiness" of a picture. Sometimes, the graphics acceleration functions on the video card are incompatible with Windows 98, as configured with the hardware on your computer. You can adjust how Windows 98 uses the video card via the Performance tab of the System applet. Within the Performance tab, click the Graphics button to open the Advanced Graphics Settings dialog box. Here you can choose from four settings for hardware-based graphics acceleration. The default is full acceleration. The other settings are useful for troubleshooting graphics-related problems. Try out the different settings. The dialog box explains each setting when you move the Hardware Acceleration slider.

PRINTING

Windows 98 provides a number of options that can optimize the way your computer works with your printer. To optimize printing, click Start, point to Settings, click Printers, right-click the printer you want to optimize, and then click Properties in the shortcut menu. This opens the Properties dialog box for the selected printer. In the following sections, you will learn how to use three tabs in this dialog box to optimize printing: the Details tab, the Graphics tab, and the Device Options tab.

Printing Format

As you learned in Chapter 8, programs in Windows 98 print by default to a spool, a set of files that is then transmitted to the printer. As you know, you can choose to send data to the printer in either EMF or RAW format. Which option is best depends on the application. If your Windows 98 computer is connected to a network, the best option depends on the privileges given to your computer through server software such as Windows NT. You can use the Spool Settings button on the Details tab to specify options related to EMF and RAW format printing. Clicking the Spool Settings button opens the Spool Settings dialog box, shown in Figure 10-19.

First, you can choose between printing to the spool and printing directly to the printer. The best choice depends on where free memory is located. If the printer has a significant amount of resident memory, then there is no need for spooling, and you choose the "Print directly to the printer" option. In most cases, however, printers have much less free memory than the hard disk, in which case control is returned to your application more quickly.

You also need to consider issues related to printing over a network, such as the nature of the print server. If the print server is a Windows 98 machine, it does the translation from EMF to a language that your printer understands, a process known as rendering. You can also use the memory on the Windows 98 print server by using the "Print directly to the printer" option, thereby bypassing the spool on the local computer. However, if the printer is on a NetWare or Windows NT server, these options are not available. You need to have your Windows 98 machine translate your printer output from EMF to your printer language, in other words, do the rendering before the print job is sent over the network.

If you select the "Spool print jobs so program finishes printing faster" option, you can then specify whether you want to start printing after the first or last page is spooled. Starting printing after the first page is spooled minimizes print time. Starting after the last page is spooled minimizes the return-to-application time.

Next, you need to specify the format you want to use for spooled data. As you learned in Chapter 8, RAW format specifies each pixel of every character that has to be printed. EMF format, on the other hand, sends an outline of each character to the printer, along with information telling the printer how to complete each printed character. EMF is preferred when it is supported, because print jobs in EMF format are smaller and therefore print faster. (Note that EMF is not supported on PostScript-type printers.) The final choice is whether or not to enable bidirectional support for the printer. If the printer supports bidirectional communication, the feedback can help speed the print process.

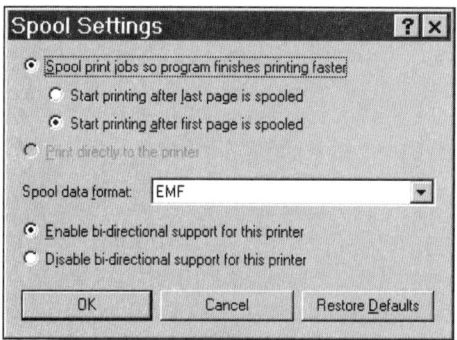

Figure 10-19 Spool Settings dialog box

Printer Memory Tracking

The Device Options tab in the printer's Properties dialog box provides a printer memory tracking option, which allows you to specify how fast Windows 98 sends data to your printer. You can choose from settings between "Conservative" and "Aggressive," with the default lying in the middle. Aggressive memory tracking tends to speed printing by allowing larger units of data into the printer. However, this advantage carries with it the risk of overloading printer memory, which can result in the loss of your print job.

Printer Graphics

You can specify settings related to printing higher-level shapes (such as polygons) through the Graphics tab of the printer's Properties dialog box. You can choose to use vector or raster graphics. Raster graphics are similar to RAW format, in that pictures and shapes are defined pixel by pixel. Vector graphics define shapes in the same way that EMF format defines TrueType letters—that is by specifying only an outline, and then providing additional information that tells the printer how to complete the shape. However, since TrueType fonts do not exist for all different shapes, it is not always possible for vector graphics to send an outline of the desired shape to the printer, resulting in errors on the printed page. Thus, raster graphics is the more reliable option when you need to print graphics of any sort. The best way to determine your precise needs is to try printing a variety of items using both raster graphics and vector graphics, and decide for yourself which option produces the best results.

NETWORK OPTIMIZATION

In order to make your workstation function most efficiently on the network, you can do two things. First, minimize the number of protocols. Every packet your workstation receives must be read by every protocol service, in the order in which the protocols are bound to the network adapter, until a protocol matching the parameters of the packet is found. Naturally, this takes time, but the fewer protocols installed on your computer, the faster the process. Second, you should make sure you are using the right kind of network adapter. Many brands of network adapters with the same advertised functionality exist in the marketplace. However, they are not identical. Interactions between network components from different companies can cause problems. Minimizing the number of brands maximizes the degree of network compatibility.

SYSTEM CONFIGURATION UTILITY

The System Configuration utility (which you can access from within MSInfo) provides a structured method for managing each step in the startup of Windows 98. To open the System Configuration utility, click Start, point to Programs, point to Accessories, point to System Tools, click System Information, click Tools on the MSInfo menu bar, and then click System Configuration Utility. As shown in Figure 10-20, the System Configuration Utility includes six different tabs, one for each step of the startup process:

- **General**: Allows you to specify whether you want to run the specified startup configuration files when you start Windows 98

- **Config.sys**: Allows for editing of the Config.sys commands. Useful for a step-by-step transition from real-mode to protected-mode drivers

- **Autoexec.bat**: Allows you to modify the commands executed from the Autoexec.bat file when you start Windows 98. As you have learned in various chapters, Windows 98 includes **drivers** that substitute for a number of functions in this file and in the Config.sys file. You can see under these tabs that some of these functions have a "REM" in front of them. "REM" is a BASIC programming command that tells your computer to ignore that line. It is a good idea to retain these files to enable comparisons with the corresponding real-mode drivers.

- **System.ini**: Allows you to modify the commands executed from this file when you start Windows 98. System drivers are organized into groups. You can specify whether to execute each driver or group of drivers by checking the appropriate check boxes.

- **Win.ini**: Includes options that are similar to those in the System.ini tab

- **Startup**: Allows you to modify the programs that start when you start Windows 98. The items listed in this tab start along with the operating system. You can uncheck those items that you do not want opened during the startup of your Windows 98 system.

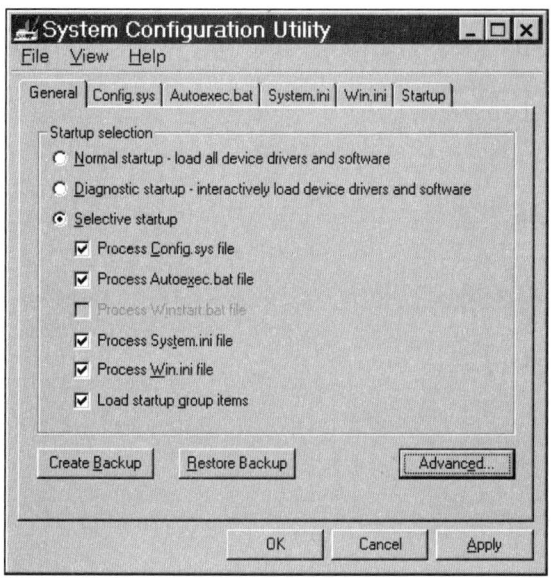

Figure 10-20 System Configuration Utility dialog box

By first documenting every original setting in every tab, and then systematically adjusting these settings, you can conduct a structured trial-and-error analysis of the startup environment. In Chapter 14 you will learn how to use this utility to troubleshoot the startup process.

OPTIMIZATION UTILITIES

Three utilities in Windows 98 help you automate the optimization process: Task Scheduler, Maintenance Wizard, and Windows System Update Manager. The first two tools will be explained in Chapter 11. You learned to use the Windows System Update Manager in the Hands-on Projects in Chapter 1.

CHAPTER SUMMARY

- Windows 98 includes a set of improved tools and utilities to monitor, maintain, and optimize the workings of applications. The MSInfo tool details, in one place, basic settings for the system, hardware, software, and devices. Although System Monitor does not necessarily include measures to directly check the performance of all hardware and software components, it is a sophisticated tool that can be used to record baseline performance measures.

- By first establishing a baseline, you can measure the effects of changes to your system. Windows 98 provides a number of adjustable settings for memory, graphics, printing, and other components. You can also monitor operating and application system files for changes and corruption. The effects of changes can be monitored through System Monitor measures, as well as by trial-and-error observation.

- You can take advantage of a number of utilities that are designed to improve system performance. You can use disk utilities to reorganize files on a hard disk for faster access, and to eliminate obsolete files. You can automate these tools through the Task Scheduler and Maintenance Wizard. Finally, you can keep Windows 98 up to date over the Internet through the Windows System Update Manager.

KEY TERMS

- **alignment error** — A transmission error in which a data packet of incorrect size is received.

- **CRC (cyclic redundancy check)** — A method to check for proper transmission of data packets. CRC numbers are calculated on both sides of a transmission. If they do not match, there is a problem with the transmission, and the data is corrupt.

- **cross-linked** — Term used to refer to files that have become corrupted, causing the FAT to point to the same cluster as other files.

- **DLL (dynamic-link library)** — A group of executable programming commands that can be used by one or more Windows applications.

- **DMA (direct memory access)** — A channel between hardware components that does not require routing through the CPU.

- **driver** — Programming instructions that interface directly with the CPU. Drivers regulate the functions of hardware devices.

- **DriveSpace 3** — An enhanced version of Microsoft's built-in disk compression software, DriveSpace 3 originally shipped with the Microsoft Plus! package for Windows 95. While it is included in the Windows 98 package, drives compressed with this software cannot be translated from FAT to FAT32 formats. They must first be uncompressed before they can be translated. Also, if the Windows boot partition is compressed using DriveSpace 3, the Windows 98 uninstall program will be unable to revert to a prior version of Windows.

- **DVD (digital video disc)** — A new, high-density storage medium that uses the same form as a CD-ROM, but that offers up to 18 GB of storage on a two-sided platter, and support for high-resolution digital video data delivery (which gives this technology its name).

- **Enhanced Metafile (EMF) Spooling** — The technique used to simplify the data that is sent to the printer. A TrueType font can be sent as an outline and a command to fill that outline with ink, which requires a lot less data than a letter that is filled in pixel by pixel.

- **FAT (file allocation table)** — A table used by the operating system to locate files on a disk. Windows 98 can use the FAT16 and FAT32 systems. MS-DOS and previous versions of Windows use FAT16. FAT32 will be common only to Windows 98 and Windows NT 5.0.

- **IRQ** — An IRQ is an interrupt request to a CPU through a dedicated channel. There are 16 common IRQs allocated by Windows 98.

- **locked memory** — Some programs require a certain amount of dedicated RAM. This area is known as locked memory, because the information within cannot be moved out to a swap file on a hard disk.

- **LRU (least recently used)** — A means of identifying blocks in VCACHE that are used least often. LRUs are the first blocks that are recycled when new candidates for VCACHE are identified.

- **MSInfo** — A Microsoft utility that consolidates current driver, hardware, and device information about the current configuration in one place.

- **OLE (object linking and embedding)** — The method by which file types are associated with certain programs.

- **paging** — The process by which data is transferred between RAM and virtual memory, or between RAM and the swap file.

- **RAW** — Printer data that has not been processed by the Windows 98 system.

- **Redirector** — Network software that directs requests to the proper network service or local resource. Works at the interface between the application and presentation layers of the OSI model.

- **Ring** — A feature of the Intel ring architecture associated with protection levels for Intel CPUs. Windows 98 uses Ring 0 for communication with the CPU and Ring 3 for execution of standard programs.

- **SMB (Server Message Block)** — The basic unit of transmission on NetBIOS networks.

- **SMARTDrive** — The 16-bit hard disk caching system on the local RAM. Windows 98 uses the successor to SMARTDrive, known as VCACHE.

- **swap file** — A hidden file used by Windows 98 to extend the amount of data that can be stored in RAM. Data is exchanged between RAM and the swap file as the data is required.

- **System Monitor** — The Windows 98 utility used to monitor various performance characteristics in an operating PC.

- **USB (Universal Serial Bus)** — A medium-speed serial bus designed to handle up to 127 peripheral devices through a single port, including mice, keyboards, modems, telephones, scanners, joysticks, and so forth.

- **VCACHE** — The Windows 98 32-bit protected-mode driver for hard disk caching in RAM.

REVIEW QUESTIONS

1. Which of the following categories are included in the MSInfo utility? (Choose all correct answers.)
   a. Resources
   b. Software Environment
   c. Hardware
   d. Components

2. Which of the following are true?
   a. MSInfo summarizes basic system information in one place.
   b. Device Manager includes easy references to the Registry.
   c. MSInfo includes user-friendly icons for different hardware components.
   d. Device Manager lists all device drivers.

3. For what kinds of hardware devices does MSInfo provide information?
   a. printers
   b. monitors
   c. infrared connections
   d. all of the above

4. Before doing anything to optimize a system, it is important to:
   a. defragment the hard drive
   b. establish a baseline
   c. execute the Disk Cleanup utility
   d. record the Kernel, Processor usage

5. Which of the following statements about VCACHE and the swap file are true?
   a. VCACHE is a storehouse for hard disk information, while the swap file is stored in VCACHE.
   b. The swap file is stored on the hard drive; VCACHE exists in RAM.
   c. VCACHE exists on the hard drive; the swap file is stored in RAM.
   d. There is no difference between the two concepts.

6. When you store frequently accessed files in dynamic memory such as RAM, you can speed access to these files. Which of the following is the best way to do this in Windows 98?
   a. VCACHE
   b. SMARTDrive
   c. third-party disk caching utilities that use dynamic memory on the hard drive
   d. all of the above

7. Which of the following categories is part of System Monitor? (Choose all correct answers.)
   a. Disk Cache
   b. Hard disk seek time
   c. Dial-Up Adapter
   d. Kernel
8. Which of the following file systems is used for digital video discs?
   a. DVD
   b. FAT
   c. CDFS
   d. UDF
9. Which of the following statements about logging in System Monitor are true?
   a. Logging is activated by default.
   b. System Monitor log files are formatted to be read into Microsoft Excel for analysis.
   c. There are limits on the number of System Monitor items that can be logged.
   d. Logging has no effect on the system baseline.
10. Which of the following best describes the process of paging?
    a. occurs when a CPU accesses VCACHE in 4 KB units
    b. occurs when a CPU goes through the FAT for a file location on the hard disk
    c. occurs when virtual memory that is mapped to a hard disk is sent back to RAM
    d. occurs when RAM is mapped to the CPU
11. Suppose you have a problem with data that is not arriving at your computer from across the network. Which of the following items should you measure through System Monitor?
    a. Page faults
    b. Locked Memory
    c. Incomplete Frames
    d. Bytes Written/Second
12. If you are printing to a printer over a network, and the print server is on a Windows NT computer, which of the following options can you choose?
    a. print directly to the printer
    b. print using the memory on the printer server
    c. enable rendering on the printer server
    d. none of the above

13. What is the purpose of a cyclic redundancy check?
    a. to make sure that data is retrieved from a hard disk if the attempt fails the first time
    b. to verify that the file sent is the same as the file that is received
    c. to ensure compatibility with a layered networking architecture
    d. to work with all numbers in a Dial-Up Adapter
14. Which of the following files are addressable in the System Configuration utility? (Choose all correct answers.)
    a. Config.sys
    b. System.ini
    c. Autoexec.bat
    d. Win.ini
15. What kind of drive can you compress with DriveSpace 3?
    a. FAT16
    b. FAT32
    c. Any kind of disk partition
    d. Any kind of logical drive
16. If you have a desktop computer with slightly more than the minimum required amount of RAM, which of the following settings from the Control Panel System utility would result in the most optimized system?
    a. Desktop Computer
    b. Network Server
    c. Mobile or docking system
    d. Maximum read-ahead caching
17. Disk Defragmenter cannot work on removable media. True or False?
18. Which of the following can you detect with the Version Conflict Manager?
    a. Conflicts between .exe program revision levels
    b. Conflicts between Dynamic Link Library (.dll) drivers
    c. Conflicts in help files when you upgrade from Windows 95 to Windows 98
    d. Conflicts between Client for Microsoft networks and Client for NetWare networks
19. When you use ScanDisk, you can:
    a. Always restore usable data from lost file fragments
    b. Unlink cross-linked files
    c. Check the physical integrity of each sector of your hard disk
    d. Rearrange the files on your hard disk so they load faster

20. When you use Disk Defragmenter, you can:
    a. Rearrange the files on your hard disk so they load faster
    b. Check the physical integrity of each sector of your hard drive
    c. Adjust the size of VCACHE on your hard disk
    d. Record the speed of your hard disk
21. Which of the following can you check with Device Manager?
    a. Hardware installed on your computer
    b. Format of your hard drive (FAT16 or FAT32)
    c. The amount of space that can be freed by Disk Cleanup
    d. The speed of data transfer to your CD-ROM

HANDS-ON PROJECTS

PROJECT 10-1

In this project, you will use MSInfo to do two different things: measure the speed of data retrieval from your CD-ROM and identify the Registry keys associated with your video monitor. To complete this project, you need a Windows 98 computer with a monitor and CD-ROM installed. You will also need a CD in your CD-ROM drive.

1. Click **Start** on the menu bar, point to **Programs**, point to **Accessories**, point to **System Tools,** and click **System Information**. The Microsoft System Information window opens.
2. In the left-hand pane, click the **plus** sign next to Components. You see the Components subcategories displayed in the left-hand pane.
3. Click the **plus** sign next to Multimedia to display the Multimedia subcategories.
4. Under Multimedia, click **CD-ROM**. Your CD-ROM drive starts running, while Microsoft System Information tests its data transfer speed. As soon as your CD-ROM stops spinning, data on your CD-ROM's performance appears in the right-hand pane.
5. In the left-hand pane of the MSInfo window, click **Display**. After a pause, information about your monitor is displayed in the right-hand pane.
6. Click the **Advanced Information** option button in the top of the right-hand pane. The information displayed in the right-hand pane is arranged in two columns. Near the top of the left-hand column you should see the label "Registry Key".
7. Make a note of the cited Registry key. It should read something like: "HKEY_LOCAL_MACHINE\enum\PCI\..." Now you will actually examine that key in the Registry.
8. Click **Start**, and then click **Run** to open the Run dialog box.
9. In the Run text box, type **regedit**. The Registry Editor opens.

Be very careful when using the Registry Editor. Do not save any changes. The slightest change to the Registry can disable Windows 98 entirely, in which case you would have to reinstall the operating system.

10. In the left-hand pane click the **plus** sign next to HKEY_LOCAL_MACHINE. Continue going deeper into the Registry, clicking on each subcategory. When you get to the last subcategory, highlight the item. It should be entitled something like "BUS_00&..."
11. The right-hand pane displays basic configuration information about your monitor. You would most likely not have been able to find this information in the Registry, without first finding the relevant key information in Microsoft System Information.
12. Close the Registry Editor, *without saving any changes*.
13. If you have not already done so, close the MSInfo window.

PROJECT 10-2

In this project, you will use System Monitor to determine whether you have enough RAM on your computer. To complete this project, you need a computer with Windows 98 installed.

1. Click **Start**, point to **Programs**, point to **Accessories**, point to **System Tools**, and then click **System Monitor**. Next, you can delete any currently running counters, as described in Step 2. Or, if you prefer, you can skip Step 2 and go directly to Step 3.
2. In the System Monitor menu bar, click **Edit**, then click **Remove Item**. In the Remove Item dialog box, highlight the item that you wish to remove, and then click **OK**. Repeat this step as many times as desired.
3. Now you will add some System Monitor Kernel counters. On the menu bar, click **Edit**, and then click **Add Item**.
4. In the left-hand pane of the Add Item dialog box, under Category, highlight **Kernel**.
5. In the right-hand pane, click **Processor Usage (%)**, and then click **OK**.
6. Repeat Steps 3 through 5, but highlight **Threads** instead of Processor Usage (%).
7. Now you will add some System Monitor File System counters. On the menu bar, click **Edit**, and then click **Add Item**.
8. In the left-hand pane of the Add Item dialog box, under Category, highlight **File System**.
9. In the right-hand pane, click **Reads/Second**, and then click **OK**.
10. Repeat Steps 7 through 9, but highlight **Writes/Second** instead.
11. Now you will add some Memory Manager counters. On the menu bar, click **Edit**, and then click **Add Item**.
12. In the left-hand pane of the Add Item dialog box, under Category, highlight **Memory Manager**.
13. In the right-hand pane, click **Swapfile Size**, and then click **OK**.

14. Repeat Steps 11 through 13, but highlight **Swapfile in Use**. Next, for convenience, you will arrange for System Monitor to be always on top.
15. In the System Monitor menu bar, click **View**, and then click **Always on Top**.
16. Now that you've configured the necessary counters in System Monitor, open up at least 10 programs of your choice. After activating each program, watch the effect on each of the measures that you selected. Observe the effect of different programs on the processor and the swap file.
17. As discussed in this chapter, consistently high levels of processor usage usually indicate a high level of use of virtual memory. You can repeat the previous step to open up the maximum number of programs that you usually run in Windows 98. The results in System Monitor indicate whether you have sufficient memory for optimum performance.

PROJECT 10-3

In this project, you will evaluate the hardware (and associated drivers) that you currently have installed on your computer. If you need a new driver, you will be able to install it. For this project, you need a computer with Windows 98 installed, as well as access to your Windows 98 CD.

1. Click **Start**, point to **Settings**, click **Control Panel**, double-click the **System** icon, and then click the **Device Manager** tab. Next, you will find the IRQ connections set up on your computer.
2. In the list box, click **Computer** to select it, and then click **Properties**.
3. In the Computer Properties dialog box, click the **View Resources** tab, and then click the **Interrupt Request (IRQ)** option button. The list box shows the hardware item associated with each IRQ channel on your computer.
4. Click **OK** to return to Device Manager, and scan the settings under Computer. A yellow question mark in this list indicates a hardware device that is not working.
5. Highlight your nonworking device. If all of your devices are working properly, click the **plus** sign to the left of Display Adapters, and then highlight your display adapter under this listing.
6. Click **Properties**. In the dialog box for your device, click the **Driver** tab.
7. In the Driver tab, click **Driver File Details**. The Driver File Details dialog box opens, where you should see the location for the drivers associated with your hardware device. If the Driver File Details box is unavailable (grayed out), select a different device.
8. Click **OK** to return to the Driver tab.
9. Click **Update Driver**. This opens the Update Driver Device Wizard dialog box. Click **Next**.
10. In the next screen of the Update Driver Device Wizard dialog box, make sure the option to search for a better driver is selected, and then click **Next**.

11. In the next screen of the Update Driver Device Wizard dialog box, you choose where to search for updated drivers. Make sure that only the CD-ROM drive check box is checked, and then click **Next**.

12. If the next screen tells you that the best driver is already installed, or that Windows was unable to locate a driver, click **Cancel**. If you are searching for a driver for a device that you know has a problem (as indicated by the question mark next to it in the Device Manager tab), you will need to get an updated driver from the manufacturer of your hardware device. In this case, this is the end of this project for your particular computer. Otherwise, the wizard finds an updated driver, and you are given the option of installing the updated driver from your Windows 98 CD.

13. To install the new driver from the Windows installation CD, click **Next**, and then click **Next** again.

14. When your updated driver is installed, click **Finish** to exit the Update Driver Device Wizard.

15. Restart your computer when prompted.

CASE PROJECTS

1. Your supervisor has heard of System Monitor, but does not know what it can do. Your organization has a number of computers with variable amounts of memory. The computers are networked, and he has heard that there are problems with the data received by your Windows 98 computers. Write a short report explaining how you can use System Monitor to address these issues.

2. You work for a software manufacturer that is considering creating a third-party alternative to System Monitor. Your boss has asked you to look at the Windows 98 System Monitor, to evaluate what can be improved. You know that System Monitor does not precisely measure hardware peripherals on a component-by-component basis. An improved System Monitor would have measures that could be automated to flag problems as they occur.

    If you were setting up a new version of System Monitor, what measures would you choose for each of the following peripherals, and why? Is there any way to adapt existing measures to obtain these measurements?
    - CPU
    - Hard disk
    - Printer
    - Network access
    - Monitor
    - CD-ROM

3. You work as a consultant for a company that wants to know some of the advantages of upgrading to Windows 98. In particular, your employers would like to know more about how MSInfo compares to Device Manager. Write a short report evaluating the differences between these two utilities.

CHAPTER ELEVEN

SECURITY, ACCESS CONTROLS, AND FAULT TOLERANCE

In this chapter, you will review and extend your knowledge of a number of concepts—such as user-level and share-level security—and Windows 98 features—such as the Registry, the System Policy Editor, and maintenance tools such as Maintenance Wizard and Task Scheduler. This chapter focuses on these topics as they relate to the job of a systems administrator, who is responsible for configuring and maintaining standalone and networked computer systems.

As a network manager, you will be responsible for maintaining the security of data stored on your network. You will also be responsible for ensuring the reliability of your system's hardware and software. In this chapter, you will learn how to keep your network secure by controlling the access that network users have to data. You will also learn about the fault-tolerance capabilities of Windows 98, which encompass its abilities to withstand system and software failures. More importantly, you will learn how to incorporate your understanding of these processes and practices into your daily work as a network manager.

AFTER READING THIS CHAPTER AND COMPLETING THE EXERCISES YOU WILL BE ABLE TO:

- Describe the security options available on a Windows 98 computer
- Describe user-level and share-level security, as they apply to a Windows 98 computer
- Create a security plan for your system
- Compare the fault-tolerance mechanisms available in the various versions of Windows
- Perform and schedule routine system maintenance
- Back up and restore files using Microsoft Backup

An Overview of Windows 98 Security

As you learned in previous chapters, you can manage security on a Windows 98 computer either over a network, or directly on the local computer. In general, managing security is a matter of controlling access to resources, such as printers, fax modems, files, and folders. On a local Windows 98 computer, you can control security through the use of user profiles and system policies. On a network, you have a choice of two kinds of security: share-level and user-level.

Under **share-level security**, you must manage access to each individual resource (or share). You do this by assigning a password to a share, and then revealing the password only to those users who need to access that resource. You must do the same for every resource on the network.

You can assign two different levels of access to a share-level resource: read-only or full access. It is sometimes useful to assign both types of access to one resource, as long as you specify a different password for each level of access. A user who knows the read-only password will only be able to read or copy from the resource. But a user who knows the full access password will be able to overwrite, replace, or even delete files in the resource.

The advantage of share-level security is that it is easy to set up on a small network. It's also inexpensive, because it does not require the use of a Windows NT server. Instead, you can administer it locally, on the Windows 98 computer where the resource is located. The disadvantage of share-level security is that it is not as secure as user-level security, because anyone who finds the right password can access the resource. Also, on a large network, the management of an ever-expanding number of passwords can become extremely difficult.

In order to implement **user-level security**, you need a connection to a network with a Windows NT or Novell NetWare server. You use the server to create accounts for every user on the network. You can organize user accounts (often just called users) into groups, such as Students or Sales. Then you assign each user or group of users permissions (or rights) to the various resources on the network. You can assign different rights to different users or groups. For example, you might choose to give the Marketing group rights to a color printer and a laser printer; at the same time, you might give the Support Staff group rights to only the laser printer. You can assign different levels of permissions to different resources. For example, you can assign the right to:

- Read a particular file or query a database
- Delete or edit files
- Grant other users access to resources
- Configure a computer's desktop
- Install programs
- Edit user profiles

User-level security is more secure than share-level security. However, it is more expensive to implement and maintain because of the need for a server such as Windows NT.

In the following sections, you will review the security controls available on a Windows 98 computer.

Pass-through Security and Windows 98

User-level security requires Windows 98 to pass your logon and password information through to the Windows NT or NetWare server that can verify your rights to network resources. This mechanism is known as **pass-through security**. On a user-level security network, users can log on to the network from multiple physical locations and be granted the same level of access to network resources. No matter which computer the user utilizes to access the network, the logon request will be "passed through" to the appropriate server for verification. Pass-through security is realized when you implement user-level security on your Windows 98 computer. It allows you to assign privileges to users on a Windows 98 computer, as discussed earlier. Because you are connected to your Windows NT or Novell NetWare server, you can then share your folders with specific users on the network.

Creating and Documenting Your Security Plan

As you learned in Chapter 10, to understand the behavior of your system, it is important to document every setting. Documentation is equally important when planning and implementing your system security. Assigning access rights to resources can be a complex task. At least one administrator should be responsible for creating and managing a master access plan that fully describes the kinds of access granted to various groups and individuals. Security may be compromised if all such access is not fully documented and fully understood.

Any master access plan should organize computers by department or other functional group. And keep in mind that in most organizations, it is necessary to assign different levels of access to regular users, managers, and network administrators.

The way you organize your network depends on the way your company does business. If you are working in a standard, hierarchical organization in which coworkers occupy the same physical area, you might choose to create a simple local area network (LAN) with share-level security. On the other hand, if you are working within a matrix organization where people constantly work in different areas, you will want to implement user-level security, which allows you to manage user permissions, independent of the computer that they are using on your network.

Administering User-level Security from a Windows 98 Computer

As you know, user-level security on a Windows 98 computer requires cooperation between a server and the local Windows 98 client. You can manage user-level security from the server itself, or remotely, from a Windows 98 computer on the network, using Windows 98 Remote Administration tools. To use your Windows 98 computer to remotely manage user-level security, the Remote Administration tools must be loaded on the Windows 98 system and remote administration rights must be assigned on the server. Remote management rights on the server allow you to do the following:

- Assign, distribute and maintain user passwords
- Create and modify system policies for individual users, groups, or specific computers
- Manage user profiles to control desktop appearance and functionality

In addition, users with remote administration rights can manage these resources on a local Windows 98 machine:

- Dial-up network access
- Backup capabilities
- The Registry
- **NetWatcher** access (As you will learn in Chapter 13, NetWatcher allows remote administration of shared resources such as files and directories.) Unlike the other resources, all you need to use NetWatcher is share-level security.
- Performance-monitoring utilities such as System Monitor

Before you begin using Remote Administration on your Windows 98 computer, you must be assigned remote administration rights through the network Windows NT or Novell NetWare server. You also need to configure your Windows 98 computer for remote administration. Once you have been assigned Remote Administration privileges, these rights apply to any computer within the domain that has been configured to be managed remotely. In a Windows NT based domain, users in the Domain Admins group have administration rights to the Windows 98 computer by default. In a Novell NetWare based domain, these rights are assigned to users with Supervisor, NWAdmin, or Admin accounts.

To configure Remote Administration of a Windows 98 computer:

1. Click Start, point to Settings, click Control Panel, double-click the Passwords icon, and then click the Remote Administration tab.
2. Click the "Enable remote administration of this server" check box to select it.
3. If the computer is already configured for share-level security, you must next specify a remote administration password. If user-level security is in force, a list of potential administrators is retrieved from the domain controller. You may add or remove administrators using the appropriate buttons.

Configuring Remote Administration on the Windows 98 computer is the first step. The next step is to install Microsoft's Remote Registry Services on a local Windows 98 computer. Then, if you are a member of the Windows NT Domain Admins or Novell NetWare Supervisor group, you can control the Registry on a remote Windows 98 computer. Remote Registry control allows an administrator to incorporate scripting functionality, to make use of system management tools, to use setup scripts to configure new machines, and to control an entire enterprise remotely.

For Remote Registry Services to work properly, both computers (remote and local) must share at least one of the following networking protocols: Microsoft **NetBEUI**, Microsoft **TCP/IP**, or the **IPX/SPX**-compatible protocol known as NWLink. You learned about these protocols in Chapter 5, and will learn more about them in Chapter 13.

To install Remote Registry Services on a Windows 98 computer:

1. Insert your Windows 98 installation CD into the CD-ROM drive.
2. Click Start, point to Settings, click Control Panel, double-click the Network icon, and then click the Configuration tab.
3. Click Add. The Select Network Component Type dialog box opens.
4. In the list of network components, click Service, and then click Add. The Select Network Service dialog box opens.
5. Click Have Disk. The Install From Disk dialog box opens.
6. Click Browse. The Open dialog box appears.
7. Use the Drives list arrow to switch to your CD-ROM drive.
8. In the Folders box, navigate to the Tools\Reskit\Netadmin\Remotreg directory, verify that the file name "regsrv.inf" appears in the File Name text box, and then click OK.
9. Back in the Install From Disk dialog box, click OK. Another Select Network Dialog box appears.
10. Verify that Microsoft Remote Registry is selected in the Models box, and then click OK. You return to the Network dialog box.
11. Click OK.
12. Restart your computer when prompted to do so.

To edit registries on remote Windows 98 computers, you must first install the Remote Registry Service, and then use one of several system management tools, such as the **System Policy Editor**, on the local computer. (You learned how to install the System Policy Editor in Chapter 4.) To use the System Policy Editor to administer a computer remotely over a network from a Windows 98 machine: click Start, point to Programs, point to Accessories, point to System Tools, and then click System Policy Editor. In the menu bar, click File, and then click Connect. In the Connect dialog box, type the name of the computer that you want to administer, and then click OK. (These steps assume that your Windows 98 computer is connected to a network.) Once you are connected to a remote computer, you can use the System Policy Editor to perform the same tasks described in Chapter 4:

- Create default computer and user policy entries that activate when a user logs on
- Establish policies for individual users, individual computers, or groups of users and computers. If a special policy does not exist for such constituencies, default policies will apply.

- Define where each system's associated policy will reside: whether on a centralized server or at another location on the network. (System policies may even be stored locally, but most security experts recommend that policy files reside on network servers that can enforce user-level access controls.)

THIRD-PARTY AUTHENTICATION AND SECURITY TOOLS

A whole range of third-party software solutions is on the market today. Such tools can enhance, expand, and double-check those security features native to Windows 98 and related network server environments. Such tools can assess your current security setup, and even recommend areas for improvement. Others can assist in the creation of enterprise-wide rules and setup scripts to ensure security and policy compliance across all desktops.

In some cases, you can use third-party software to track access permissions, manage resource passwords, and oversee the authentication process. For example, you can use biometric controls to scan fingerprints, voice prints, or even retinal images. In addition, you can take advantage of key card systems, or other hardware, that force users to insert some kind of special object, such as an ID card, to gain access to the local computer or to a computer on a network. Many such systems are used in highly secure environments, including government agencies that handle classified information, and banking or securities trading environments where financial exposure is an issue. Providing details on these products is beyond the scope of this text; however, considerable information is available from other sources, including the Internet and many texts on networking.

FAULT TOLERANCE IN WINDOWS 98

The term **fault tolerance** refers to a system's ability to respond to a catastrophic event without loss of data, and without disrupting work currently in progress. The principles of fault tolerance are the same from industry to industry. For example, commercial airplanes are designed so that the failure of any single system cannot compromise the safety of any part of the airplane. Risks are further minimized through regular maintenance. Fault-tolerance in computer systems and networks follows the same principles.

The first step in ensuring the fault tolerance of your system is to back up essential data. As a network administrator, you also need to know that your backed-up data is secure in case of fire, floods, or earthquakes; often this means storing your backups off-site, at a secure location. If your backup data is not secure, your company may not be able to recover from a major failure. You also need to maintain your system in a condition that minimizes your risks.

Windows 98 was designed to be more fault-tolerant than previous desktop versions of Windows. Thus, a Windows 98 computer is less likely to fail unexpectedly, or to corrupt or lose data. In this section, you will learn about some ways to make your system as fault-tolerant as possible.

FAT32 Boot Sector Backups

Any hard disk eventually wears out, sector by sector. If a sector of the hard disk fails, you may lose the data on that sector. But if the sector that contains the file allocation table or the root directory structures is corrupted, you lose your connection to all data on the hard disk. To prevent such a failure, you should consider using the FAT32 file system, which backs up the boot sector on your hard disk. These backup copies will allow access to data, should the original copies of those essential sectors on the drive ever become damaged or lost.

Preventative Maintenance Utilities

Another way to make your Windows 98 system more fault-tolerant is to perform routine preventative maintenance on your hard disks, using the disk maintenance utilities included with Windows 98. In some cases, Windows 98 performs maintenance automatically. For instance, when Windows 98 is shut down improperly (owing to a user error, a power failure, or perhaps a system crash or lockup), it runs ScanDisk in MS-DOS-mode when you restart your computer to detect and correct any disk errors before they have a chance to compound themselves. Likewise, the system performs a Registry integrity scan each time the system boots, for similar reasons.

It is good practice to schedule several preventative maintenance tasks regularly. You can automate these tasks using the **Maintenance Wizard**, which schedules and automatically runs the tasks of your choice. With the Maintenance Wizard, you can schedule any of the following utilities to run automatically: ScanDisk, Disk Defragmenter, Disk Cleanup, and Compression Agent. You learned about the first three tools in Chapter 10. You learned about the Compression Agent in Chapter 8.

To use the Maintenance Wizard:

1. Click Start, point to Programs, point to Accessories, point to System Tools, and then click Maintenance Wizard.

2. If Maintenance Wizard has been used before on your computer, you see a dialog box that allows you to choose between performing maintenance now or changing your schedule. Click the "Change my maintenance settings or schedule" option button to select it, and then click OK.

3. The Maintenance Wizard page shown in Figure 11-1 opens. Here you can choose from two setup options: Express, which enables the most common maintenance settings, or Custom, which allows you to choose your own approach. Make sure Express is selected, and then click Next. (You will learn how to use the Custom option in the Hands-on Projects at the end of this chapter.)

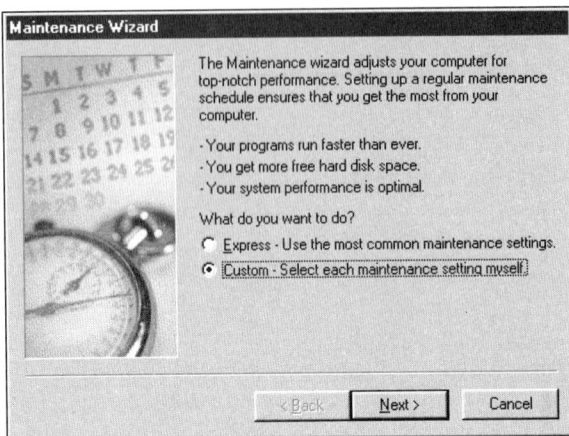

Figure 11-1 Maintenance Wizard

4. Next, you are asked to choose a time frame for maintenance tasks. Express setup gives three choices: Nights between midnight and 3:00 AM, Days between noon and 3:00 PM, or Evenings between 8:00 PM and 11:00 PM. Select one and click Next.

5. Next, you see a list of the following tasks that will be performed by the Maintenance Wizard:

   - Speed up your most frequently used programs (using Disk Defragmenter)
   - Check hard disk for errors (using ScanDisk)
   - Delete unnecessary files from the hard disk (using Disk Cleanup)

The relevant utilities are run in the following order: Disk Cleanup, ScanDisk, and then Disk Defragmenter. This is the most efficient sequence. First, Disk Cleanup removes files from your hard drive. Having fewer files means that there is less for ScanDisk to do. As you learned in Chapter 10, ScanDisk can address lost or cross-linked file clusters. Since Disk Defragmenter stops every time it locates a lost or cross-linked cluster on your disk, it is better to run ScanDisk before you run Disk Defragmenter.

6. Click Finish to close the Maintenance Wizard. (If your hard disk is FAT16-formatted, you may see another Maintenance Wizard dialog box suggesting that you convert your drive to FAT32. Click No.) Next, you will review the schedule that Windows 98 has created for you.

7. Click Start, point to Programs, point to Accessories, point to System Tools, and then click Scheduled Tasks. In the Scheduled Tasks folder, click View on the menu bar, and then click Details. This displays a list of tasks and their scheduled completion times, as shown in Figure 11-2. Of course these tasks will be completed only if Windows 98 is running on your computer at the scheduled time.

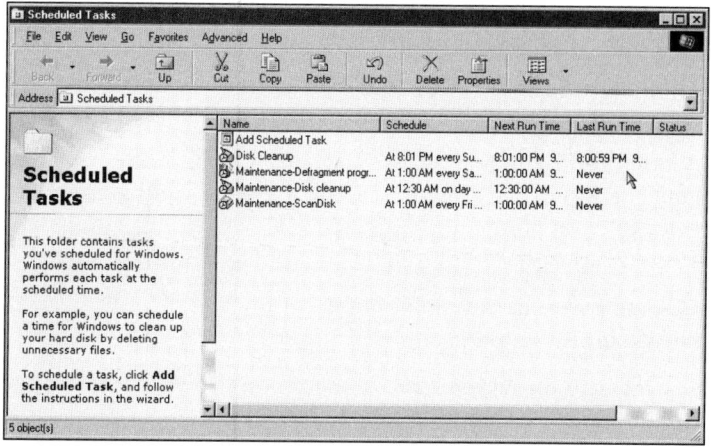

Figure 11-2 Scheduled Tasks

 Be sure to run maintenance at a time when you know the computer will be on, but not in use. If the computer is turned off during scheduled maintenance, the utility can't run. Likewise, you don't want to schedule disk defragmentation for 2:30 on Friday afternoons, for example, if you are using your computer for some critical business task at that time.

BACKUP

No computer system can be considered fault-tolerant unless a complete backup copy of all data and programs exists. At the very least, you need to back up the data on your system, particularly data stored on shared servers. (You can always reinstall software, assuming you have carefully documented the settings required on your system; however, the process of reinstalling and reconfiguring software can be time-consuming, and therefore expensive.)

You can use the backup options included in Windows 98, or you can use a third-party backup program. In this chapter you will learn how to use Microsoft Backup. For information on third-party backup options, search for relevant Web sites, using key terms that you will learn about in the following sections.

You can use Microsoft Backup to back up every bit of data on your system, or just certain selected files or directories. Backup is automatically installed along with a typical installation of Windows 98. If you do not have it installed, follow these steps to add it to your system:

1. Insert the Windows 98 installation CD into the CD-ROM drive.
2. Click Start, point to Settings, click Control Panel, double-click the Add/Remove Programs icon, and then click the Windows Setup tab.
3. In the Components list, double-click System Tools. This opens the System Tools dialog box.
4. Click the Backup check box to select it, and then click OK.
5. Click Apply, and then click OK to complete the update installation process.

The first time you run Microsoft Backup, Windows 98 should detect and configure your backup device. If it doesn't, use the Add New Hardware Wizard to install the required drivers, using a manufacturer-supplied disk or CD-ROM. Once the software is installed, follow these steps to perform a backup:

1. Click Start, point to Programs, point to Accessories, point to System Tools, and then click Backup. The Microsoft Backup window opens. (If you have not installed a backup device on your computer, you may see a message suggesting that you need to run the Add Hardware Wizard to install one. Click No to continue.)
2. Click the Create a new backup job option button, and then click OK. This starts the Backup Wizard.

The Backup Wizard walks you through the rest of the process. You will need to specify information such as:

- Whether you want to back up the entire system or only selected files and folders
- Whether the process should back up all of the files selected or only those that have changed since the last time this job was run
- The destination for the backup (where the resulting files should reside)
- Whether you want to check backed-up data for integrity after backup
- Whether you want to compress backup data to save space
- A name for the backup job

Once you've reviewed the Backup Wizard, return to the Backup window. Make sure the Backup tab is active, and then click Options in the lower-right corner. This opens the Backup Job Options dialog box, which contains six tabs:

- **General**: Allows you to verify the quality of the backup, configure data compression requirements, and specify what to do if your backup medium already contains data
- **Password**: Allows you to protect your backup with a password
- **Type**: Allows you to specify whether to back up all files, or only files that are new or have been changed. For new and changed files, you can choose between differential and incremental backups. The Differential Backup option backs up all files that have changed since the last full backup. Files that have changed are not marked as backed up. The Incremental Backup option backs up all files changed since the last incremental or full backup. Files that have changed are marked as backed up, to allow Windows 98 Backup to know what to record.
- **Exclude**: Allows you to add or remove file types from the **Do not backup files of this type** list. This is most often used to exclude operating system files, such as .exe or .dll, from the backup.
- **Report**: Used to specify items for the backup report, as well as bypassing all prompts during an unattended backup.

- **Advanced**: Allows you to determine whether the Registry will be backed up during the operation. By default, the Registry is backed up each time the Windows folder is selected for backup.

You will practice creating a backup in the Hands-on Projects at the end of this chapter.

Backup Formats

The Windows 98 Backup utility supports a wide range of hardware devices, including parallel port units, IDE/ATAPI drives, and SCSI backup devices. Hardware options for this program include the following:

- **QIC-80 and 80 Wide, QIC-3010 and 3010 Wide, and QIC-3020 and 3020 Wide**: QIC stands for "quarter-inch cartridge," which is a standard form of magnetic tape used for backup purposes. Drives that use QIC format tapes generally use the floppy controller for system connectivity.

- **TR1, 2, 3, and 4**: TR refers to the **Travan** technology developed by the 3M corporation. Like QIC technology, it makes use of magnetic tapes, but it allows for a significantly higher data density. Devices that use Travan tapes are backward-compatible with QIC tapes. Travan media can hold from 400 MB of uncompressed data all the way up to 4 GB.

- **DAT (DDS1, 2, and 3)**: DAT tapes are digital audio tapes, which may seem like a misnomer since they can store more than audio data. DAT offers greater per tape storage capacity than Travan tapes, from 2 to 24 GB. **DDS** stands for digital data storage, a form of DAT tape. The newest version, DDS3, supports the highest capacities.

- **DC 6000**: A 5.25-inch cartridge for quarter-inch tape, originally developed by 3M Corporation, with a capacity of up to 4 GB of data

- **8 mm**: 8 mm refers to the width of the tape used in these cartridges (rather like 8 mm video film). Capacity ranges from 2.5 GB to 40 GB.

- **DLT**: Digital linear tape, developed by Digital Equipment Corporation (DEC), and now produced by several companies. Cartridges have capacities of 20 to 40 GB.

- **Removable media**: This category includes floppy disks, Zip and Jaz disks (or compatibles), and Syquest cartridges.

Which format is best for you will depend on many factors. These factors include: system capacity (how many gigabytes of data your drives can hold), available expansion slots (e.g., whether you have room for a SCSI hardware card inside your computer), the need to use multiple tapes for your backup, and whether the process can proceed unattended. The following sections discuss important issues related to the most commonly used backup devices.

Tape Drives

Tape drives generally offer the most hardware configuration options of currently available storage devices. Drives can be connected by parallel port or via a floppy drive controller cable, an IDE interface, or a SCSI connection. Both internal and external models are available. Tape cartridges are considered cheap when judged in terms of their costs per megabyte of storage. Tape drives do have a drawback, in that, by their nature, they store data sequentially on a linear tape. In contrast, your computer can easily access a file in different parts or sectors of a hard disk. The sequential nature of a tape drive can lead to significant delays while the tape advances and rewinds to find the files you request.

Other Removable Media

Syquest and Iomega **Zip** and **Jaz** drives are popular backup options. Although the parallel port versions can be slow, disk access to a SCSI Zip drive is nearly as fast as hard disk access. The Zip drive suffers from its relatively small format—100 MB per disk vs. the average hard drive of over 4 GB—but it is a convenient way to store groups of files or to transfer larger files or programs. For full system backups, consider multi-GB devices such as the Jaz or Syquest products.

The drawback to removable media products is the high cost of the media. As of this writing, Zip disks retail for $10–$16 per disk, depending on the number purchased, and the larger Jaz and Syquest media often cost more than $100 per disk or tape. Clearly, the cost per megabyte quickly adds up over the life of a system, and may be as much as 5 to 10 times more than tape options.

Floppy-based Backup

Floppy disk drives are still standard equipment for every PC, although with the advent of CD-ROMs they are used less and less; 3½-inch disks are very inexpensive, and MS Backup readily recognizes them. However, with a storage capacity of 1.44 MB, it would take over a thousand 3½-disks to back up a multigigabyte hard drive. Floppies are best used to create copies of only the most critical files, since backing up an entire system with 3½-inch disks requires considerable time, attention, and manual labor, owing to the constant swapping of disks involved.

SYSTEM RECOVERY STRATEGIES AND TECHNIQUES

As a network administrator, you should be prepared in advance for a complete system failure. First and foremost, this means you should always have access to a current backup of all critical files. At minimum, your backup jobs should include the following:

- A current copy of the Registry and files located in the \Windows directory, updated after each new application or service pack is installed, or any other Registry changes occur
- Weekly backups of the entire system
- Daily backups of files changed since the previous day

A common practice for backups is to rotate a fixed number of tapes or disks. For example, you might keep a daily backup of new files for the last seven days, a weekly backup of all data, and a monthly backup of your entire hard disk.

Many system administrators advocate storing copies of current full-system backups at an off-site facility such as a data storage facility or a bank safe-deposit box. Should system outages occur owing to fire or some natural disaster, backup media kept on the premises where the computer resides are likely to be lost. For this reason, some ISPs (and other communication vendors) now offer services in which backups can be transmitted across the Internet or a private network for automatic storage off-site.

Immediately after a system failure, you should first focus on the health of your hard disk. Begin by attempting to reboot the system. If the failure resulted in an improper shutdown of the system, ScanDisk will automatically run in MS-DOS mode to check files and folders for errors. Once Windows 98 is running, you should run the full ScanDisk utility with surface checking enabled. A surface check looks for and marks bad sectors. Windows 98 does not store files on hard disk sectors that are marked as bad. If you do not do a surface check, you may end up storing files on bad sectors. Storing files on bad sectors is a recipe for additional failures.

Even worse, some system failures can render hard drives inoperable. It is at best difficult to retrieve data from a broken hard drive. Replacement is often the more cost-effective option. After replacing the hard drive, you will have to reinstall the operating system.

In some cases, even though the hard disk is functional, the system will fail to boot, in which case you need an **Emergency Startup Disk (ESD)**. As you learned in Chapter 2, you can create an ESD when installing Windows 98. To create a new ESD, click Start, point to Settings, and then click Control Panel. Double-click the Add/Remove Programs icon. Click the Startup Disk tab, and then click Create Disk. Insert a 3½-inch disk in your computer when prompted, and click OK.

If you have a problem booting your Windows 98 computer, insert the Emergency Startup Disk into the 3½-inch disk drive, and reboot your system. The ESD installs a number of utilities in your RAM. If you boot with your ESD, you will see the following message: "The diagnostic tools were successfully loaded to drive X," where X represents the actual drive letter on your computer. By default, it also installs real-mode CD-ROM drivers. You can use it to run basic recovery utilities, such as ScanDisk and ScanReg, which you learned about in previous chapters.

Once you have restored your operating system, you can then start restoring data. If you have reinstalled the operating system, you'll also need to reinstall the backup agent (such as Microsoft Backup) before you can restore any data from your backup media. When you restore data from tape or other media, files are placed in their original directory structures unless you choose to restore all files to another location. The following steps assume that you have previously used Microsoft Backup to create a backup.

To restore data previously backed up using Microsoft Backup:

1. Click Start, point to Programs, point to Accessories, point to System Tools, and then click Backup.

2. Click the Restore Wizard button on the Microsoft backup toolbar and follow the prompts.

3. The restore process is successful if an Operation Completed dialog box appears. Click OK to exit the utility.

FAULT TOLERANCE IN EARLIER VERSIONS OF WINDOWS

Fault tolerance in Windows 98 is considerably improved compared to that of earlier versions of Windows. The virtual memory address spaces that you learned about in Chapter 9 will generally prevent a problem with a single program from affecting other programs or the operating system. Operating systems without virtual memory address spaces, such as Windows 3.x, react badly to problems. If a program fails, the operating system can fail due to either a lockup (sometimes called a hang or a system freeze) or a **General Protection Fault** (**GPF**). Both scenarios require a warm reboot of the system (that is, use of the CTRL-ALT-DEL key combination to restart the system), or sometimes even a cold reboot (that is, turning the power switch off and then on again). As a result, it was easy to lose data in Windows 3.x.

Windows 95 improved things by allowing users to terminate nonresponsive tasks or programs. Should any process fail under Windows 95, the CTRL-ALT-DEL keyboard combination doesn't immediately attempt a warm reboot of the system; instead, it produces a list of currently operating processes and indicates any processes that are not responding. Users may choose to terminate such nonresponsive tasks, and attempt to continue working within the current session, or they may shut down their systems to begin a new session.

FAULT TOLERANCE IN WINDOWS NT

Windows NT provides fault-tolerance mechanisms beyond those available in Windows 98. Windows NT requires a more aggressive approach to fault tolerance, because it is used as an enterprise-level network operating system, where data and system integrity is more critical than for most consumer-oriented desktop PCs. For one thing, as discussed in Chapter 9, the protective isolation between virtual memory address spaces in Windows NT is superior to that in Windows 98. In addition, Windows NT provides support for tape backup support, disk mirroring, disk duplexing, and disk striping with parity.

Disk mirroring, disk duplexing, and disk striping with parity are variations of a form of fault tolerance known as **RAID (redundant array of independent disks)**. Although Windows 98 does not support RAID, you need to understand how it can play a part in a network fault-tolerance plan. RAID requires a minimum of two or three hard disks. Windows NT supports three levels of RAID, as follows:

- **RAID 0**: Also known as **disk striping without parity**. RAID 0 allows different parts of a file to be stored on different hard disks. With RAID 0, it takes less time for your computer to get parts of your file from different hard disks simultaneously, rather then getting the whole file from one disk. RAID 0 works with up to 32 different hard disks on one computer.

- **RAID 1**: Also known as disk mirroring and disk duplexing. Using this technique, you maintain identical copies of data on two different hard disks. **Disk mirroring** connects two hard drives to one hardware controller. (The hardware controller is the means by which a hard drive is connected to a computer's motherboard. The time it takes to retrieve a file from a hard disk is limited by the hardware controller.) **Disk duplexing** connects each hard drive to a different hardware controller. The latter is more fault-tolerant, because the failure of one controller will not bring down your entire system.

- **RAID 5**: Also known as **disk striping with parity**. Requires a minimum of three and a maximum of 32 hard disks. As with RAID 0, each file is distributed among the disks. Parity information allows your computer to recreate data on any one disk in the event of a failure. For example, if your RAID 5 set includes six hard disks and one fails, the parity information contained on the remaining five disks is used to rebuild the information on the sixth disk when it is replaced.

For more information on RAID, see *A Guide to Microsoft Windows NT Server 4.0*, published by Course Technology.

INTELLIMIRROR

Intellimirror provides users and network administrators with a set of management tools for managing Windows 98 and Windows NT 5.0 Workstation computers from a Windows NT server. When Microsoft releases Windows NT 5.0, it will probably release an upgrade for Windows 98 to accommodate Intellimirror. Once released, it should simplify backups and maintenance of Windows 98 computers. In addition, Intellimirror should allow you to remotely manage the software of each computer on your network. The planned features include:

- **PC mirroring**: Allows network administrators to rebuild the data and user profiles for every user, even if individual Windows 98 computers are destroyed

- **Simplified policy support**: Allows network administrators to use policies (rather than rights or permissions) to manage user profiles and access to applications

- **"No touch" maintenance**: Allows network administrators to remotely install or update programs on all Windows 98 computers

In general, Intellimirror can "intelligently mirror" (or replicate) a user's data, applications, system files, and settings across the network onto appropriately equipped Windows NT 5.0 servers. Businesses and organizations can implement all of Intellimirror's many capabilities, or only a few key components.

CHAPTER SUMMARY

- Managing the physical security of computing devices and the user-access security of data is a complex issue, especially in a networked environment. Windows 98 includes native support for share-level access control to system resources, and can cooperatively support user-level security with Windows NT and Novell NetWare network operating systems. System behavior and end user functionality may be controlled remotely using Remote Administration tools, the Remote Registry Services, and the System Policy Editor.

- Care and maintenance of the physical system is an integral part of Windows 98 fault tolerance. Tools are available to monitor the status of files, folders, and the surface of each hard disk, and also to defragment the file system, and to clean up unnecessary files. Backup agents are available to routinely save data to separate backup media, which makes it possible to restore that data should data corruption, physical failure, or other catastrophic losses occur.

KEY TERMS

- **8 mm** — 8 millimeter tape media, used for data backup.
- **DAT (digital audio tape)** — High-capacity sequential tape storage media.
- **DC 6000** — A 5.25-inch cartridge for quarter-inch tape, originally developed by 3M Corporation, able to accommodate as much as 4 GB of data on a single cartridge.
- **DDS (digital data storage)** — A form of DAT tape. DDS comes in three versions, DDS1, 2, and 3, each capable of increased storage capacities.
- **differential Backup** — A backup of all files that have changed since the last full, complete backup.
- **disk duplexing** — Similar to disk mirroring, except that each physical drive is connected to your computer through a different hardware controller connection to your motherboard. One of the options with RAID 1.
- **disk mirroring** — The process of creating a mirror image of a disk on a second physical drive. One of the options of RAID 1.
- **disk striping without parity** — A technique for putting different parts of the same file on different hard disks. File retrieval speed is often limited by the hardware controller. Placing portions of files on separate disks means that all the disks can be writing or reading at the same time, speeding up access. Sometimes known as RAID 0.
- **disk striping with parity** — Requires three or more hard disks. With parity data, this is a fault-tolerant storage technique; even if you lose one of your hard disks, you still have access to your data. Sometimes known as RAID 5.
- **DLT (digital linear tape)** — A magnetic tape medium used for high-capacity data storage.
- **Emergency Startup Disk (ESD)** — A disk containing a small set of files required for a minimal boot of the PC after a catastrophic operating system failure or corruption. An option to create this disk is provided during initial Windows 98 installation.

- **fault tolerance** — A computer system's ability to withstand element or component failures. This term also refers to a design and deployment strategy for computer systems that systematically seeks to eliminate any single-factor causes of failure that could lead to system downtime or losses of data.

- **GPF (General Protection Fault)** — A response in Windows 3.x and 95 to an unrecoverable error (generally followed by a reboot).

- **incremental backup** — A backup of all files that have changed since the last full, or incremental backup.

- **Intellimirror** — A real-time backup technology that supports Windows 98 and Windows NT 5.0 clients, in which client-side file system changes are automatically mirrored on a designated network server; when Microsoft releases Windows NT 5.0, it will probably also release an update to Windows 98 to add Intellimirror.

- **Jaz** — A storage media format developed by Iomega Corporation. Disks have capacities of 1 to 2 GB, and are read by proprietary hardware devices.

- **Maintenance Wizard** — A Windows 98 utility that schedules and runs maintenance tasks.

- **NetWatcher** — A system administration tool that allows administrators to monitor and control usage of and access to the Internet.

- **pass-through security** — The process of passing responsibility for authentication from a local operating system to a server elsewhere on the network.

- **QIC** — See TR1

- **RAID (redundant array of independent disks)** — A series of different techniques for using multiple hard disks on a single computer. Some versions of RAID emphasize speed, while others emphasize fault tolerance. Windows NT supports RAID levels 0, 1, and 5.

- **Remote Registry Services** — A Windows 98 utility that allows a system administrator to make use of system management tools, to use setup scripts to configure new machines, and to control an entire enterprise remotely.

- **share-level security** — A security model that uses passwords assigned to individual resources that may be shared on the network.

- **System Policy Editor** — A system management tool in Windows 98, used to edit registries on remote computers.

- **TR-1 through TR-4** — A family of tape format designations normally associated with Travan tapes that are backward compatible with QIC tape cartridges. TR1 is used with QIC-80, TR2 with QIC-3010, and TR3 with QIC-3020. TR4 is Travan only.

- **Travan (TR)** — An extended-capacity magnetic tape format developed by 3M Corporation.

- **user-level security** — A security model that assigns a username and password to each individual person who will be accessing the network. Access to individual resources is then assigned to specific users.

- **Zip** — A medium developed by Iomega Corporation. A Zip disk capable of storing up to 100 MB of data. Requires a special drive unit.

REVIEW QUESTIONS

1. Because share-level security requires more passwords, it requires logon requests to be "passed through" to a network server. True or False?
2. A share is:
   a. a peripheral device that can be accessed by more than one user
   b. a program that resides on the server, but will run on any computer on the network
   c. a utility that you can try out before purchasing
   d. a defined set of directories, files, or resources treated as a single object that can have access control properties assigned to it
3. The Remote Administration utility allows (choose all correct answers):
   a. an administrator to implement changes in a user's Registry, system policies, and security settings from another PC over a network
   b. a user to access his or her computer from another location, via Dial-Up Networking
   c. a supervisor to restrict Internet access completely, to allow access only to individually approved sites or to restrict access to individually disapproved sites
   d. an administrator to remotely monitor system performance
4. You can use the Remote Registry Service to edit a user's Registry. True or False?
5. Which of the following are known requirements of Intellimirror?
   a. administration from a Windows NT 4.0 Workstation computer
   b. administration from a Windows NT 5.0 Server computer
   c. It can be run on a network with only Windows 98 computers.
   d. It can be run on a mixed network that contains only Windows 98 and Windows 95 computers.
6. The Maintenance Wizard is responsible for:
   a. remotely managing software updates over a LAN
   b. internally checking the status of the computer's connection to the network
   c. periodically reminding users of the need to defragment their hard drives
   d. the scheduling and running of disk management tools

7. Tape drives are connected to the PC through:
   a. a SCSI controller
   b. a parallel port
   c. the IDE controller
   d. any of the above
8. Which of the following media requires the largest amount of time for backups?
   a. another hard disk
   b. tape drives
   c. Jaz drives
   d. floppy disks
9. The Windows 98 Emergency Startup Disk is:
   a. used to restore all system settings in the event of a failure
   b. a table of contents for your computer that is reinstalled first after data loss
   c. a utility that allows the user to escape from a locked system or program
   d. a set of files that can boot your PC if Windows 98 is not loading
10. The term Pass-through security refers to the process by which:
    a. the logon password is automatically assigned to shared resources on the local Windows 98 machine
    b. Windows 98 passes the authentication information to a Windows NT or Novell NetWare server
    c. a user logs on twice
    d. none of the above
11. Which of the following utilities can you use to schedule ScanDisk and Disk Defragmenter? (Choose all correct answers.)
    a. Maintenance Wizard
    b. ScanDisk
    c. Task Scheduler
    d. Disk Defragmenter
12. Which of the following methods correspond to a version of RAID? (Choose all correct answers.)
    a. Microsoft Backup
    b. disk duplexing
    c. disk mirroring
    d. user-level security

13. When you are planning the security of your data, which of the following considerations are important? (Choose all correct answers.)

    a. protection from flood or fire

    b. size of backup media

    c. passwords

    d. regular maintenance

14. Which of the following are indicators of a fault-tolerant system? (Choose all correct answers.)

    a. a hard disk formatted to FAT32

    b. separate connections between your hard disks and your motherboard through separate hardware controllers

    c. a copy of your Windows 98 CD, ready to load if your system loses data

    d. backups made on a regular basis

15. What are your options for scheduling ScanDisk through the Maintenance Wizard? (Choose all correct answers.)

    a. to run whenever you start Windows 98

    b. to run only on one schedule

    c. to run on different dates every month

    d. to run once, then stop

16. Which of the following are required before you can do remote administration of another computer on the network from your Windows 98 computer? (Choose all correct answers.)

    a. You must enable Remote Administration through the Users applet of your Windows 98 computer.

    b. You must be a member of the Domain Administrators group on a Windows NT Server based network.

    c. You must be a member of the Supervisors group on a Novell NetWare Server based network.

    d. You must enable Remote Administration through the Passwords applet of the remote Windows 98 computers.

17. Which of the following balances efficiency and fault tolerance in backing up the data on a mission-critical Windows 98 computer?

    a. create a full backup once a day

    b. create a full backup once a week, with daily incremental backups

    c. create only incremental backups

    d. create only differential backups

18. Which of the following statements best describe differential and incremental backups? (Choose the two correct answers.)
    a. Differential backs up all files since the last full backup.
    b. Incremental always backs up files since the last full backup.
    c. Incremental backs up files since the last incremental backup.
    d. Differential backs up all files since the last differential backup.
19. Which of the following is the most efficient way to run Disk Defragmenter, Disk Cleanup, and ScanDisk, and is therefore the order used by the Maintenance Wizard?
    a. Disk Defragmenter, Disk Cleanup, ScanDisk
    b. ScanDisk, Disk Cleanup, Disk Defragmenter
    c. Disk Cleanup, ScanDisk, Disk Defragmenter
    d. ScanDisk, Disk Defragmenter, Disk Cleanup
20. Which of the following requires you to put different users in your organization in different groups?
    a. share-level security on a Windows NT based network
    b. user-level security
    c. user profiles on a Windows 98 computer
    d. Remote Domain Administrator tools
21. Which of the following privileges do you have with Remote Administration? (Choose all correct answers.)
    a. assign, distribute, and maintain user passwords
    b. create and modify system policies for individual users, groups, and/or specific computers
    c. manage user profiles to control desktop appearance and functionality
    d. find all the passwords on the computer of a remote user
22. Which of the following is required before you can remotely administer a computer?
    a. a common networking protocol, such as TCP/IP
    b. Remote Administration can only be done on Windows NT based networks.
    c. Remote Administration can only be done on Novell NetWare based networks.
    d. the cooperation of your Internet service provider

Hands-on Projects

Project 11-1

In this chapter, you learned how to use the Maintenance Wizard's Express setting. In this project, you will use the Custom setting. For this project, you will need a computer with Windows 98 installed.

1. To start the Maintenance Wizard, click **Start**, point to **Programs**, point to **Accessories**, point to **System Tools**, and then click **Maintenance Wizard**.
2. If the Maintenance Wizard has been used before on your computer, you will see a dialog box with the following two options: Perform Maintenance Now, and Change my maintenance settings or schedule. Choose the latter option, and then click **OK**. If you don't see this dialog box, skip to Step 3.
3. On the next page, choose **Custom – Select each maintenance setting myself**, and then click **Next**.
4. On the next page, you can select a maintenance schedule. Click the **Custom – Use Current Settings** option button, and then click **Next**.
5. The next page lists programs that open automatically when you start Windows 98. If you have fewer programs starting automatically, Windows 98 will start faster on your computer. When you uncheck these programs, you remove them from the startup sequence for your Windows 98 computer. If desired, uncheck the programs that you do not want started automatically, and then click **Next**.
6. The next page, "Speed Up Programs," provides settings for Disk Defragmenter. Click **Reschedule**.
7. In the Reschedule dialog box, click the **Schedule Task** down arrow. You see a list of options for scheduling the Disk Defragmenter: Daily, Weekly, Monthly, Once, At System Startup, At Logon, and When Idle.
8. Click **Monthly**, and then click **Advanced**. The Advanced Schedule Options dialog box opens.
9. In the Start Date text box, you see a start date with the current date. Click the **down arrow** adjacent to that date to open a calendar for the current month. The currently scheduled date is highlighted, while today's date is circled. In the next step you will change the date on which Disk Defragmenter will run.
10. Click a new date. You return to the Advanced Schedule Options dialog box.
11. Observe the new date in the Start Date text box.
12. Click the **Repeat Task** check box and note your options for repeating Disk Defragmenter. Click it again to deactivate it.
13. Click **OK** to return to the Reschedule dialog box.

14. Click the **Show multiple schedules** check box to select it. A list box and two buttons appear at the top of the Reschedule dialog box. You can use the list box to display a list of schedules for Disk Defragmenter. You can use the New and Delete buttons to create new schedules and delete existing schedules.
15. Click **OK** to return to the Maintenance Wizard dialog box.
16. Click **Settings**. The Scheduled Settings for Disk Defragmenter dialog box opens. If you remember the settings for Disk Defragmenter in Chapter 10, you may note that this dialog box offers slightly different options from those you see when you run Disk Defragmenter directly, via the Start menu. However, note that you can select the disks you want defragmented through the Maintenance Wizard in the same way that you did in Chapter 10.
17. Click **OK** to return to the Maintenance Wizard.
18. Click **Next** to view the settings for scheduling ScanDisk.
19. Click **Reschedule**. The Reschedule dialog box opens. Note that the scheduling options for ScanDisk are identical to those for Disk Defragmenter.
20. Click **Cancel** to return to the Maintenance Wizard, and then click **Settings**. This opens up the Scheduled Settings for ScanDisk dialog box, which is similar to the ScanDisk window you saw in Chapter 10. You can do everything in this dialog box that you can do in the ScanDisk utility, except actually run the utility. If you have multiple drives to scan, you can select the drives of your choice, just as in the regular ScanDisk utility.
21. Click **OK** to return to the Maintenance Wizard, and then click **Next** to view the settings for Disk Cleanup.
22. Click **Reschedule** to open the Rescheduling dialog box. Note that the scheduling options for Disk Cleanup are identical to those for Disk Defragmenter and ScanDisk.
23. Click **OK** to return to the Maintenance Wizard.
24. Click **Settings** to open the Disk Cleanup Settings dialog box. Next, you will compare the options offered here to those available via the Disk Cleanup utility (accessed from the Start menu).
25. Click **Start**, point to **Programs**, point to **Accessories**, point to **System Tools**, and then click **Disk Cleanup**. In the Select Drive dialog box, select the **C:** drive, and then click **OK**. The Disk Cleanup for (C:) dialog box opens.
26. Arrange the two dialog boxes, **Disk Cleanup for (C:)** and **Disk Cleanup Settings**, side by side, as shown in Figure 11-3.

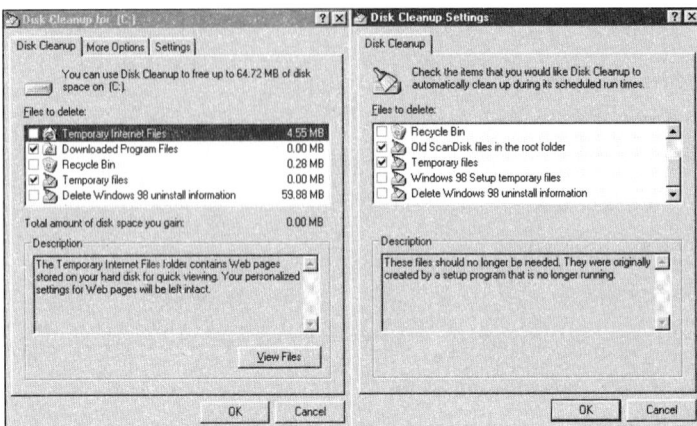

Figure 11-3 Disk Cleanup dialog boxes

27. Compare the lists in the two "Files to Delete" list boxes. Chances are that the list in the Disk Cleanup Settings dialog box contains more categories. The reason that some of these categories may not show up in the Disk Cleanup for (C:) dialog box is that no files of that type currently exist on your hard drive. Note that even if you have multiple hard drives, you cannot limit the scheduled Disk Cleanup to a single drive.

28. Click **Cancel** in the Disk Cleanup for (C:) dialog box to close it.

29. Click **OK** in the Disk Cleanup Settings dialog box to return to the Maintenance Wizard, and then click **Next**.

30. The next Maintenance Wizard page summarizes the settings that you just created for the three disk maintenance utilities. Select the **When I click Finish...** check box if you want Windows 98 to execute each of these utilities immediately, in sequence. If you have the time to allow Windows 98 to execute these utilities now, check this box. (Keep in mind that running these utilities could take a while.)

31. Click **Finish**.

32. If you checked "When I click Finish..." in Step 30, watch as Disk Cleanup, ScanDisk, and Disk Defragmenter run on your Windows 98 computer. Otherwise, these utilities will run when scheduled.

33. If your hard drive is FAT16-formatted, you may get another page stating that you may be able to convert FAT32. If you click Yes, Windows 98 brings you to the FAT32 Drive Converter. Click **No**.

PROJECT 11-2

In the last project, you used the Maintenance Wizard to automate the start of Windows 98 maintenance utilities on your computer. In this project, you will learn to use the Task Scheduler to automate the start of several other programs. This is useful if you are using third-party maintenance tools that can be set up to run automatically.

1. Click **Start**, point to **Programs**, point to **Accessories**, point to **System Tools**, and then click **Scheduled Tasks**.
2. This opens the Scheduled Tasks folder. Double-click the **Add Scheduled Task** icon to open the Scheduled Task Wizard.
3. On the first Scheduled Task Wizard page, click **Next**.
4. On the next Scheduled Task Wizard page, you see a list of most of the applications that have been installed on your computer since you installed Windows 98. Highlight the program you want to automate, and then click **Next**.
5. On the next Scheduled Task Wizard page, you can first type a different name for the program in the text box. In the "Perform this task" options, click the **Monthly** option button, and then click **Next**.
6. On the next Scheduled Task Wizard page, you can choose the Time, day of the Month, day of the Week, and Month to run your program. Click **Back**.
7. On the Previous Scheduled Task Wizard page, choose the **One time only** option button, and then click **Next**.
8. On the next Scheduled Task Wizard page, choose a time 10 minutes from the current time, and click **Next**. (You can set a different time depending on how long you think it will take to complete the next few steps.)
9. On the next Scheduled Task Wizard page, select the **Open Advanced Properties for this task when I click finish** check box, and then click **Finish**.
10. This opens a dialog box named after the program you selected earlier. By default, you see the Task tab, which lists the location for your program. You can change this if it is not correct. If you deselect the Enabled check box, your task will not run as scheduled.
11. Click the **Schedule** tab. This opens scheduling options similar to those that you used in the Maintenance Wizard. You can reschedule your task in the same way.
12. Click the **Settings** tab. This opens other options related to how your program is run. In the Scheduled Task completed area, you can stop the task after a specified period of time, or delete the task after it is complete, from the Scheduled Tasks folder. In the Idle Time area, you can keep the program from running if other programs are currently in use. In the Power Management area, you can allow the program to run or not, depending on the power status of your computer.
13. Click **OK** to return to the Scheduled Tasks folder.
14. Now review your selection. Highlight the task that you just created, and view the scheduling information in the left-hand portion of the Scheduled Tasks folder. Note that you can reopen the dialog box for the selected task by clicking File on the menu bar, and then clicking Properties.
15. Close the Scheduled Tasks folder.
16. Verify that your scheduled task occurs as scheduled.

PROJECT 11-3

In this project you will install and use Microsoft Backup to back up a single file to a 3½-inch disk. You will need a blank formatted 3½-inch disk and your Windows 98 setup CD-ROM. You will also need a computer with Windows 98 already installed. This project assumes Backup is installed on your computer (either by default, in a Typical installation of Windows 98, or according to the steps provided in this chapter).

1. Click **Start**, point to **Programs**, point to **Accessories**, point to **System Tools**, and then click **Backup**.
2. Select the **Create a new backup job** option button, and then click **OK**. The first page of the Backup Wizard opens.
3. Click the **Backup selected files, folders, and drives** option button, and then click **Next**.
4. In the left-hand pane, click the **drive C** icon (the icon, not the check box).
5. In the right-hand pane, double-click any folder, locate any file, and then click it to insert a check mark in the box next to that file.
6. Click **Next**.
7. Verify that the All Selected Files option button is selected, and then click **Next**.
8. Verify that File appears in the "Where to Back up" list box. This means that you are saving your backup as a file.
9. Click the folder icon. The Where to back up dialog box opens.
10. Insert a 3½-inch disk into your disk drive, and then navigate to the 3½-inch disk drive for your computer.
11. Next, you need to specify a filename for your backup. In the File name text box, type **testback**, and then click **Open**. (Don't be confused by the name of the "Open" button; you're not really opening a file when you click it.) You return to the Backup Wizard.
12. Click **Next**.
13. Select both check boxes to indicate that you want to compare data to verify it, and that you want to compress data.
14. Click **Next**.
15. Enter a name for this backup job. You can enter any word or series of words of your choice, up to 52 characters (including spaces).
16. Click **Start**.
17. When the process finishes, click **OK** in the alert box.
18. Click **OK** again in the Backup Progress dialog box.
19. Exit Microsoft Backup.

CASE PROJECTS

1. As a network administrator, you've been asked to select a backup system (including both the required hardware and media). You will need to implement a full system and incremental backup schedule for your network. The system has a total capacity of 25 GB of data. Discuss what hardware options you would choose for this task, and what scheduling concerns should be addressed. Detail how your choices might differ if you only needed to deal with up to 2 GB of data vs. 25 GB.

2. As a network administrator, you need to devise a security plan for your network. You have a workgroup with nine Windows 98 computers running on a peer-to-peer network, and a client-server network consisting of 20 Windows NT workstations and 15 Windows 98 machines using Windows NT Server 4.0 for networking. Describe which security models you would implement on each system, detailing any limitations imposed by the machines present. Point out any potential security holes or limitations inherent in your choices.

3. You are working in a company that makes cockpit seats for commercial airplanes. Your network is in a factory that runs 24 hours per day, 7 days per week. Production proceeds in batches, i.e., not in an assembly line. As a network administrator, you would like to automate the basic disk maintenance tools for your system. How do you use the Maintenance Wizard and/or the Task Scheduler to automate this process? Outline how you would document this process, especially with respect to how it fits into the production schedule.

CHAPTER TWELVE

ADVANCED WINDOWS 98 INSTALLATION OPTIONS

In Chapter 2, you learned to install Windows 98 on your computer. In this chapter, you will learn more about the Windows 98 installation process. As a network administrator, you probably will spend considerable time figuring out the right configuration for your Windows 98 computer. Once you have created settings on your computer, the Windows 98 CD provides a batch script utility to help you install Windows 98 in the same way on the computers of all of your users. A batch script is a file that acts as a substitute for user input. Of course, you may not want all of your users to share all of your settings. In this chapter, you will learn to customize the batch script file in considerable detail.

Once you have created a batch script file, you can install Windows 98 on every computer with one command line. That is good enough in a small network, where you can easily go to each computer to start the installation process. But for larger networks, this can be more difficult. You will also learn various methods to automate this process over the network, so you never have to physically visit the computers where you are installing Windows 98.

Sometimes, you want more than one operating system on the same computer. In this chapter, you will also learn how Windows 98 can work side by side with other operating systems such as Windows NT.

AFTER READING THIS CHAPTER AND COMPLETING THE EXERCISES YOU WILL BE ABLE TO:

- Discuss the Windows 98 setup process in detail
- Customize a batch script file for automated Windows 98 installation
- Install Windows 98 over a network
- Understand how Windows 98 can work on the same computer with other operating systems

Windows 98 Setup in Detail

In Chapter 2, you learned to install Windows 98. Now you can step back and learn how the Windows 98 installation process actually works. The Windows 98 installation process can be divided into four parts: preparing the Setup wizard, accepting user input, copying Windows 98 files, and detecting hardware. As you will learn later in this section and in Chapter 14, the progress of the Windows 98 installation is documented in several files that are created during the Windows 98 installation process.

Preparing the Setup Wizard

Before installing anything, Windows 98 prepares the computer. When you launch the installation program, it runs a real-mode version of ScanDisk to check the integrity of your hard drive. If Windows 95 is already installed on your computer, ScanReg then checks the integrity of your Registry. (ScanReg is the real-mode Registry Checker that you learned about in Chapter 3.) Next, the files required to run the Setup wizard (often simply referred to as "Setup") are temporarily installed in a new directory, C:\Wininst0.400. Related groups of setup files are combined into special types of files known as cabinet files. A **cabinet file** contains a number of other files in compressed format. The Setup wizard files are stored in three cabinet files (Mini.cab, Precopy1.cab, and Precopy2.cab). In this stage of the installation process these cabinet files are decompressed and transferred to the C:\Wininst0.400 directory.

User Input and Copying Files

Next, you actually begin interacting with the Setup wizard by entering a number of parameters. Then the wizard rechecks the state of your computer by running the ScanDisk utility, for a second time, this time in protected mode. If you are upgrading from Windows 95, it runs the Windows Registry Checker (ScanRegW), in part to record settings for non–Plug-and-Play devices. After that, you are given the opportunity to specify which Windows 98 features you want to install. In response to your choices, the Setup wizard creates the necessary directories in which to install Windows 98 files, and in which to save your old Windows 95 files. Then you are guided through the process of creating an Emergency Startup Disk (ESD) to use in case you have trouble booting Windows 98 in the future. Finally, once your computer is prepared and the Setup wizard has all the settings it needs, the Windows 98 Setup wizard begins to copy files to your computer. This includes any drivers required to access the CD-ROM or network drive from which you are installing Windows 98.

The Setup Smart Recovery feature (described later in this chapter) can help you recover from most installation failures, unless Setup is interrupted while copying Windows 98 files to the hard disk. If this happens, try running Setup from the installation CD-ROM again. If the Setup wizard does not restart, you will need to use either your Emergency Startup Disk or the boot disk (that you will learn to create later in this section) to reboot your computer. Then you can restart Setup from the beginning.

Detecting Hardware

Once the Windows 98 files are copied to your computer, Setup resumes running, and prepares to start Windows 98 for the first time. In order to start Windows 98, the Setup wizard installs a driver database. Using this database, Setup detects and installs the drivers for all installed Plug and Play devices that are compatible with Windows 98. If you are upgrading from Windows 95, Setup can also install any non-Plug-and-Play (legacy) devices, using information in the Windows 95 Registry.

Because of constant updates in software and hardware, hardware manufacturers update their drivers regularly to keep them compatible with the latest systems. Microsoft has built an extensive library of these drivers into the Windows 98 installation CD. Unfortunately, if your computer has drivers that are older than those in the Windows 98 CD, the Setup wizard may not always update them. One driver that is commonly not updated when you install Windows 98 is that for your video card (a.k.a. display adapter). You will learn how to check the status of your drivers, and update them as required, in the Hands-on Projects at the end of the chapter.

The key to hardware detection is a process known as Bus Enumeration. As you learned in Chapter 3, the Windows 98 Bus Enumerator checks all the connections to your computer. When it finds hardware such as a printer, it adds the device type, hardware ID, manufacturer, and drivers for each piece of hardware to your Windows 98 Registry.

Smart Recovery

During the setup process, Windows 98 creates several log files, documenting which processes have been attempted or completed. These files, which you can open and read from your C:\ directory, are named Setuplog.txt, Detlog.txt, and Netlog.txt. If installation should fail, Setup also generates a Detcrash.log file, in a format that only the Setup wizard can read. When you try to restart the Setup wizard, it will search these log files for clues as to which process failed, and where it needs to pick up again in order to complete the installation. You can find these files in your C:\ directory. Because the only time that you need to look at these files is when you are troubleshooting, you will learn about these files in Chapter 14.

Setup Options

Windows 98 Setup comes with a multitude of command-line switch options that you can invoke during the setup process. For example, you can use setup switches to avoid running ScanDisk, skip the license agreement, or even accommodate Windows 98 installation on computers with settings customized for Japan. Experienced system administrators may wish to utilize these switches. See Appendix B details on several of the more commonly used options.

Boot Disks

As discussed in Chapter 2, the cleanest way to install Windows 98 is from a 3½-inch boot disk. By definition, a boot disk contains system files. In this section, you will learn to create a boot disk containing system files based on previous Microsoft operating systems. If you are installing

Windows 98 from a CD-ROM or a network, you will also need the corresponding real-mode drivers. Before you install Windows 98 from a boot disk, you should test it on your current operating system, as described later in this chapter. If you are currently using a non-Microsoft operating system, you will still need an MS-DOS boot disk, based on version 5.0 or higher.

It is extremely important to test a boot disk before putting yourself in a situation where you have to rely on it. If you plan to install Windows 98 on a freshly formatted hard disk, test your 3½-inch boot disk. Make sure you can access your CD-ROM drive or network after you start your computer with your boot disk. If you are installing from a network drive, make sure that you can actually connect to the server where the Windows 98 Installation files are installed.

Ideally, once you start your system with a boot disk, then you can access your CD-ROM driver files. As you will learn in this chapter, the Windows 98 ESD includes real-mode CD-ROM drivers good for many (not all) CD-ROM drives. If you do not have a Windows 98 ESD, or it does not work with your CD-ROM drive, you may have to do one of several things. It is not possible to give precise instructions here. On some systems, you will need to install the CD-ROM drivers on your hard disk. On others, you may already have a separate CD-ROM boot disk. Unfortunately, with the number of different CD-ROMs on the market today, your best bet is to refer to the manual for your CD-ROM drive.

The following sections explain how to create a variety of boot disks. To test a boot disk after you have created it:

1. Insert the boot disk into the 3½-inch floppy drive.
2. Reboot your computer.
3. Verify that the MS-DOS prompt appears on the screen.
4. If you plan to install Windows 98 from a CD-ROM, make sure you can access your CD-ROM drive. Unless you are using a Windows 98 ESD, you need to install and activate CD-ROM drivers per the documentation that came with your CD-ROM drive.
5. If you plan to install Windows 98 from a network, make sure you can access your network. You will need to install and activate real-mode network drivers per the documentation of your real-mode network clients. You will learn to use some of these clients later in this chapter.
6. Now that you have verified that your boot disk works, you can return to your current operating system. Remove the 3½-inch disk from your computer and reboot your computer.

Windows 95

The Windows 95 Emergency Startup Disk can serve as a boot disk. You can create an Emergency Startup Disk in Windows 95. Assuming you installed Windows 95 from a CD, you will need to insert your Windows 95 installation CD into your CD-ROM drive, as well as a 3½-inch disk into drive A. In Windows 95, click Start, point to Settings, and then click Control Panel. Double-click Add/Remove Programs, click the Startup Disk tab, and then click Create Disk.

Windows 3.x

You can create a boot disk in Windows 3.x from the File Manager, which you can usually access via Program Manager. (Normally, Program Manager opens when you start Windows 3.x.) Since every user can configure Windows 3.x differently, File Manager may be located in different places on different computers. Insert a 3½-inch disk in drive A. In the menu bar of File Manager, click Disk, and then click Make System Disk. In the Disk dialog box, click the Make System Disk check box to select it, and then click OK. This actually transfers MS-DOS system files to your 3½-inch disk. Unlike creating the Windows 98 or Windows 95 ESD, creating the Windows 3.x boot disk does not require you to have your installation CD.

MS-DOS

As you learned in Chapter 2, if MS-DOS is your operating system, you can't install Windows 98 until you've already installed MS-DOS 5.0 or higher. Alternately, you can start with an MS-DOS 5.0 or higher boot disk. To create an MS-DOS boot disk, go to the MS-DOS command prompt. Insert a 3½-inch disk in your disk drive. At the MS-DOS prompt, type "sys a:" and then press Enter to transfer system files to your 3½-inch disk. You can also type "format a: /s" but this erases everything currently on your 3½-inch disk.

CD-ROM DRIVERS

There are a number of ways to access the real-mode CD-ROM drivers that you need to access your Windows 98 CD-ROM installation disc. If you already have Windows 98 installed on another computer, you can use the real-mode CD-ROM drivers from the Emergency Startup Disk (ESD) of that computer. You can create an ESD as follows:

1. In the Windows 98 computer, insert a 3½-inch disk into drive A.

2. Insert the Windows 98 CD into the CD-ROM drive on that computer.

3. Click Start, point to Settings, click Control Panel, double-click the Add/Remove Programs icon, click the Startup Disk tab, and then click Create Disk. (If you have Windows 98 installed but can only get to the MS-DOS prompt, you can begin creating an ESD as follows: Type C: and press Enter. Type CD\Windows\Command\ and press Enter again. Type Bootdisk.bat, press Enter, and then follow the instructions on your screen. *Hint*: If you use the Bootdisk.bat utility, you do not need your Windows 98 Installation CD.)

4. Follow the prompts to create the Emergency Startup Disk. Now in the next step, you can test this disk in the computer on which you want to install Windows 98.

5. Insert the Emergency Startup Disk that you just created into drive A of the computer on which you want to install Windows 98.

6. Restart the computer. If you can access your CD-ROM drive, then you can use this disk for a clean boot installation. You will see if this is possible in the next step.

7. After your computer restarts, you will see a Microsoft Windows 98 Startup Menu with three choices. Select Choice 1, "Start computer with CD-ROM Support." (If you wait 30 seconds, Windows 98 will automatically make this choice for you.)

8. If the real-mode CD-ROM driver works with your CD-ROM drive, you will see something like the following lines before the A:\> MS-DOS prompt (the driver and the drive letter may be different):

```
MSCDEX Version 2.25

Copyright (c) Microsoft Corp. 1986-1995. All rights
reserved.

Drive E: = Driver MSCD001 unit 0
```

9. If it is not already there, insert your Windows 98 Installation CD-ROM in the CD-ROM drive. At the A:\> prompt, type E: and press Enter. (The drive letter assigned to the CD-ROM on your computer may be different from E. If it is, substitute accordingly.)

10. At the prompt for your CD-ROM drive, type setup and press Enter. If you see the Windows 98 Setup screen, you have verified that your Windows 98 Emergency Setup Disk can be used to boot a fresh hard drive and set up a new installation of Windows 98.

11. Click Exit Setup.

If the previous steps do not work, or if you do not have access to a computer running Windows 98, you can use the 3½-inch installation disk provided by the manufacturer of your CD-ROM. Consult your CD-ROM documentation for how to use this disk to install real-mode drivers on your computer; in many cases, directions are stored in a file on the disk itself. Another alternative is to consult the Web site for the manufacturer of your CD-ROM drive. Search for instructions on how to download and install real-mode or MS-DOS drivers for your CD-ROM into your computer. Pay particular attention to the instructions regarding what to add to your system files, known as Autoexec.bat and Config.sys. These files are the startup files for MS-DOS that can be copied to your boot disk.

USING THE BOOT DISK

There are three cases in which your boot disk is essential. You need a good boot disk when you want to install Windows 98 on a freshly formatted hard disk. You need a good boot disk if the Windows 98 Setup wizard is interrupted in a way that results in the failure of the Smart Recovery feature. Finally, you need a good boot disk if you cannot start Windows 98 because of a corrupted or damaged hard drive. In any of these cases, you need to rely on the operating system that you included on your 3½-inch boot disk. There are several features that you may want to add to your 3½-inch boot disk. If you have a computer where Windows 98 is already installed, you can find these files in your C:\Windows\Command directory:

- **Sys.com**: Allows you to transfer the system files from your 3½-inch boot disk to your hard drive. If you have a freshly formatted hard drive, you can make it bootable from the A:\> prompt by typing sys c: and pressing Enter.
- **Scandisk.exe**: Allows you to fix problems on your hard disk that may be keeping you from installing Windows 98
- **Format.com**: Allows you to reformat your hard disk, if all else fails
- **Fdisk.com**: Allows you to repartition your hard disk. Especially useful when you need to accommodate different operating systems, as discussed in Chapter 8.

Be sure that you copy these files from a computer with at least MS-DOS 5.0 or higher (Windows 95 or 98 versions of these files are preferred). Other versions of these files, available on other operating systems, may not work for you. Once you have copied these files to your boot disk, you can use it to install Windows 98 on a freshly formatted hard disk. The actual steps will vary depending on the size of your hard disk, on whether you have a Windows 98 ESD, and on your Windows 98 installation media.

If you use the format command on a hard disk, all data on that disk will be lost. If you use a utility provided by your hard disk manufacturer to format and partition your hard disk, do not use the format and fdisk commands to format and partition your hard disks separately.

UNINSTALLING WINDOWS 98

As you learned in Chapter 2, if you are upgrading from Windows 3.x or 95, you can choose to save the files from your current operating system. This allows you to restore your previous operating system, should you ever decide to uninstall Windows 98. As long as you do not delete these files, and you do not convert your file system to FAT32, you can uninstall Windows 98. To uninstall Windows 98, click Start, point to Settings, and then click Control Panel. Double-click the Add/Remove Programs icon. Click the Install/Uninstall Tab. In the lower text box, highlight Uninstall Windows 98. Click Add/Remove. In the Windows 98 Uninstall dialog box, if you really want to uninstall Windows 98, click Yes.

Be very careful when uninstalling Windows 98. If you highlight a program other than Uninstall Windows 98 and then click Add/Remove, Windows 98 will probably remove your program without warning. If you highlight Uninstall Windows 98, click Add/Remove, and click Yes, Windows 98 will uninstall itself. You would then need to reinstall Windows 98 (and all programs that you installed since installing Windows 98).

You can also uninstall Windows 98 from the command prompt. To do so, reboot your computer with a boot disk or ESD. Type C: and press Enter. Type CD \Windows\Command and press Enter. Type Uninstal.exe and press Enter. Follow the instructions on your screen. If you previously converted to FAT32, Windows 98 removed the Uninstall utility as part of the conversion process.

BATCH MODE INSTALLATION

A script is a collection of commands that run automatically, similar to a macro. There are several types of scripts used in Windows 98. A **logon script** is a series of commands used when you log on to a network. It is similar to the autoexec.bat file that is run when you start your computer in MS-DOS or Windows 3.x. You can create a batch script file to automate the setup of Windows 98 on other computers. The Common Gateway Interface script that you learned about in Chapter 7 supports Web-based communication.

The main focus of the following sections is creating batch scripts to automate the installation of Windows 98. You can use batch scripts when you are satisfied with the Windows 98 configuration on one computer, and want to re-create that configuration on other computers. (For the purposes of this chapter, these other computers are referred to as target computers.) You will also learn how to use logon scripts for logging on to special accounts on a network with a Windows NT or Novell NetWare Server.

You can take advantage of a number of different settings in order to customize a batch script for your target computers, so that the Windows 98 installation is not necessarily identical from one computer to the next. Using batch scripts allows you to install Windows 98 quickly on the target computers, by automating the process. You create batch scripts using Microsoft Batch 98, as described in the following section.

INSTALLING MICROSOFT BATCH 98

You can install the batch mode tool on your Windows 98 computer. To install Microsoft Batch 98:

1. Insert the Windows 98 installation CD into your CD-ROM drive.

2. Remove any disks from your 3½-inch disk drive.

3. If a Windows 98 CD-ROM window appears, click Add/Remove Software. Otherwise click Start, point to Settings, click Control Panel, and double-click the Add/Remove Programs icon. Click the Install/Uninstall Tab, and then click Install.

4. In the "Install Program From Floppy Disk or CD-ROM" dialog box, click Next.

5. In the Run Installation Program dialog box, click Browse.

6. The Browse dialog box shows the drive and the Windows 98 Installation Setup program on your CD-ROM. Keep the current drive letter. Change setup.exe to \Tools\Reskit\Batch\setup.exe, and then click Finish.

7. In the Run Installation Program dialog box, click Open.

8. In the Microsoft Batch 98 Setup dialog box, click OK.

9. The next Microsoft Batch 98 Setup dialog box shows the intended installation directory. If the default directory is satisfactory, click the picture of the computer to start the installation. (Otherwise, use the Change Directory button to specify a new directory.)

10. When the process is complete, you see a dialog box telling you that Microsoft Batch 98 installation was completed successfully. Click OK.

Now you can start the Batch tool. Click Start, point to Programs, and then click Microsoft Batch 98. This opens the Untitled – Microsoft Batch 98 window, shown in Figure 12-1.

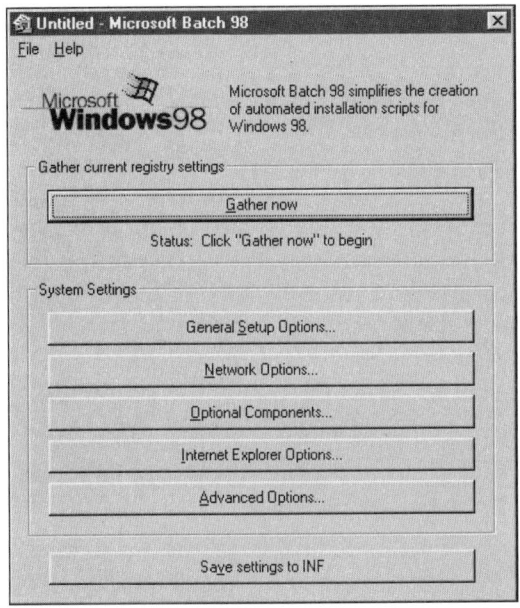

Figure 12-1 Untitled – Microsoft Batch 98 window

In the next sections, you will explore the various options in this tool.

COLLECTING REGISTRY SETTINGS

As you learned in Chapter 3, Windows 98 saves thousands of settings in the Registry. If you want others to use the settings on your computer, you need Microsoft Batch 98 to collect as many settings from the Registry as possible, via the "Gather Now" option.

In the Untitled – Microsoft Batch 98 dialog box, click "Gather Now" to collect Registry settings from your computer. This enters a number of parameters into your batch script. Microsoft Batch 98 does not collect the whole Registry, nor does it collect data related to 16-bit programs or drivers. Note also that Microsoft Batch 98 does not include all of the choices that you made when you first installed Windows 98. Microsoft Batch 98 collects the following categories of data from your computer:

- User/computer name
- Directory where Windows 98 is installed
- Installed optional utilities, such as those found in Accessories or System Tools
- Installed printers

- Installed time zone
- Microsoft 32-bit networking settings
- **Most Recently Used (MRU)** locations for folders on local and remote computers
- User-level security configuration data

As you will learn later in this chapter, you can use the Advanced Options in Batch 98 to incorporate portions of the Registry into the batch script that are not included with the Gather Now option.

GENERAL SETUP OPTIONS

After collecting your Registry settings, you can use the General Setup Options button to open the Batch 98 – General Setup Options dialog box. Here, you can specify all the settings (such as the Product Key) that you would normally have to provide during the user input portion of the installation process.. By entering the proper settings here, you can create a truly automated setup for your target computers. In the following sections, you will learn about the settings that you can use in each of the General Setup Options tabs.

Install Info

On the Install Info tab, shown in Figure 12-2, you enter basic installation information about the target computer:

- **Product ID**: The code on the back of your Windows 98 installation CD container. If you are installing Windows 98 on multiple computers from one installation CD, it is your responsibility to purchase the appropriate quantity of licenses. Each license includes its own Product ID.

- **Installation Directory**: Where Windows 98 will be installed. If you leave this text box blank, an upgrade installation will use the current Windows 95 or 3.x directory. If you are installing from MS-DOS, the automated setup will stop and prompt you to enter a directory. If you are installing Windows 98 on computers with different operating systems, you will need different setup scripts for each situation.

- **Do not show installation directory warning**: Not everyone has installed Windows in the C:\Windows directory. When a different directory is used, Setup normally will stop and warn you that it will be installing Windows 98 in that directory. If this box is checked, your automated setup will not display this warning.

- **Uninstall Options**: By selecting the "Automatically create uninstall information" option button, you can ensure that your previous Windows 95 and/or MS-DOS files are saved. That way, if you ever choose to uninstall Windows 98 (as described later in this chapter), your previous operating system will be restored automatically.

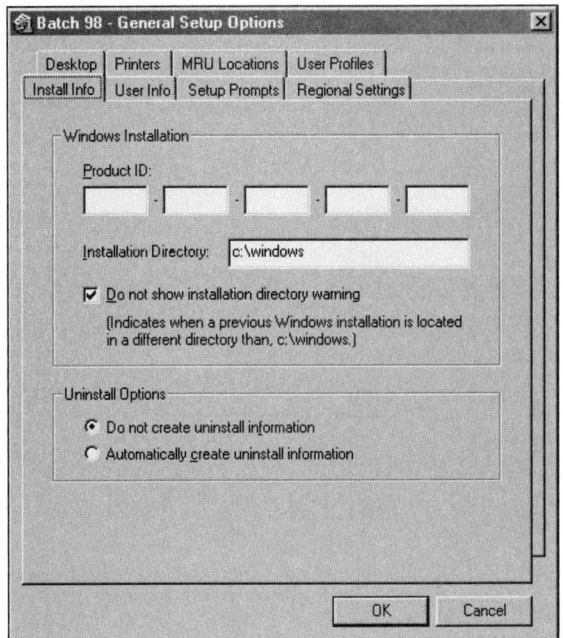

Figure 12-2 Batch 98 – General Setup Options dialog box, Install Info tab

User Info

The User Info tab, shown in Figure 12-3, contains user and network information for your setup script. You will probably leave all fields in this tab blank. If you are upgrading from a previous version of Windows (3.x or 95), blank entries here will tell the batch script to take this information from the previous version of Windows.

If you are using the batch script to set up Windows 98 on multiple computers, you can enter a generic username such as the name of the organization. You can use the same workgroup name and description for all computers in the department. Since every computer name is different, Microsoft Batch 98 allows you to create a Multiple Machine Name file to use with your script, which will provide the correct computer name for each target computer during the installation process. You will learn about this technique later in this chapter.

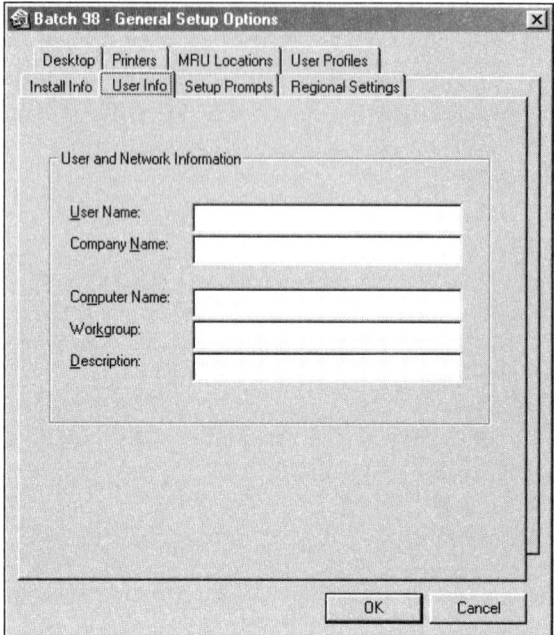

Figure 12-3 Batch 98 – General Setup Options dialog box, User Info tab

Setup Prompts

The Setup Prompts tab, shown in Figure 12-4, provides a number of options that you can select in order to automate the installation process. For example, you can choose to accept the license agreement automatically, rather than forcing a user to accept the agreement manually before the installation can proceed. However, the advice given at the bottom of the Setup Prompts tab ("For unattended installation, check all boxes.") may not be appropriate for all systems. The boxes that you need to check for an unattended installation depend on the configuration of your target computer.

- **Auto-accept end user license agreement**: If this option is checked, Windows 98 Setup will not display the Windows 98 license agreement.

- **Do not prompt for emergency startup disk**: If this option is checked, Windows 98 Setup will assume that you choose not to create an Emergency Startup Disk for this installation. You will not need a separate Emergency Startup Disk for every computer. If you have already created a Windows 98 Emergency Startup Disk, it will work in all computers where Windows 98 is installed.

- **Automatically reboot PCI and PnP machines during setup**: If you have Plug and Play components or PCI hardware cards, Windows 98 Setup normally warns you before rebooting your computer. If this is checked, Windows 98 Setup skips the warning.

- **Do not search source folder for new devices**: The source folder is the location of the Windows 98 installation files, whether on the Windows 98 CD, on 3½-inch disks, or in a directory on a network server. To speed the installation process, Windows 98 Setup normally searches for current drivers for your hardware. If this box is not selected, Windows 98 will search the source folder for other drivers. Keep in mind that if this box is unchecked, the Windows 98 Setup wizard may replace your current drivers, even if your drivers are more up to date.
- **Skip the PC Card (PCMCIA) wizard**: Checking this box skips the PC Card Installation Wizard. If you have PC Card slots with real-mode drivers installed, and you check this box, Windows 98 Setup will fail. In this case, you need to keep this box unchecked. Then you will just have to go through the PC Card Installation Wizard after Windows 98 is installed, as discussed in Chapter 6.

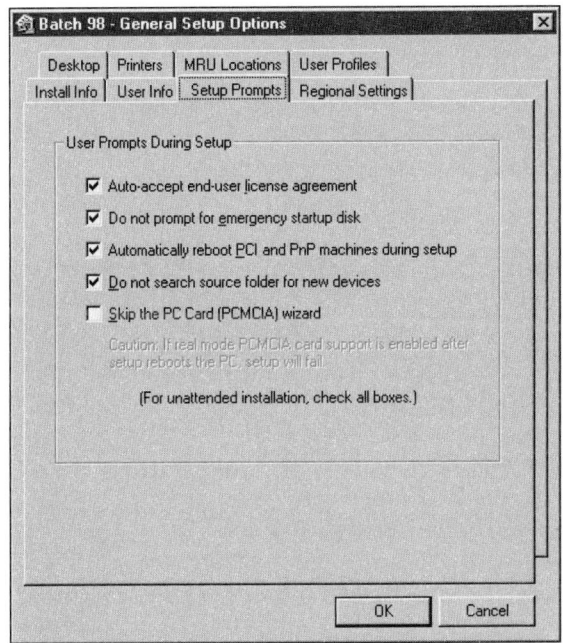

Figure 12-4 Batch 98 – General Setup Options dialog box, Setup Prompts tab

Regional Settings

As long as you are working locally, you should not have to change any of the settings in the Regional Settings tab. These settings relate to Time Zone, Keyboard Layout, and Language criteria used for Windows 98.

User Profiles

In Chapter 3, you learned how to allow users to create their own desktop layout and settings. These settings are recorded in the User.dat part of the Registry. The options in the User Profiles tab are identical to those in the User Profiles tab of the Passwords applet.

MRU Locations

For purposes of the setup script, the phrase "MRU (Most Recently Used) Locations" refers to local directories or the directories from a server that a user may have shared on the network. Windows 98 Setup will use these MRUs (as specified in the MRU Locations tab, shown in Figure 12-5) to search for drivers during installation.

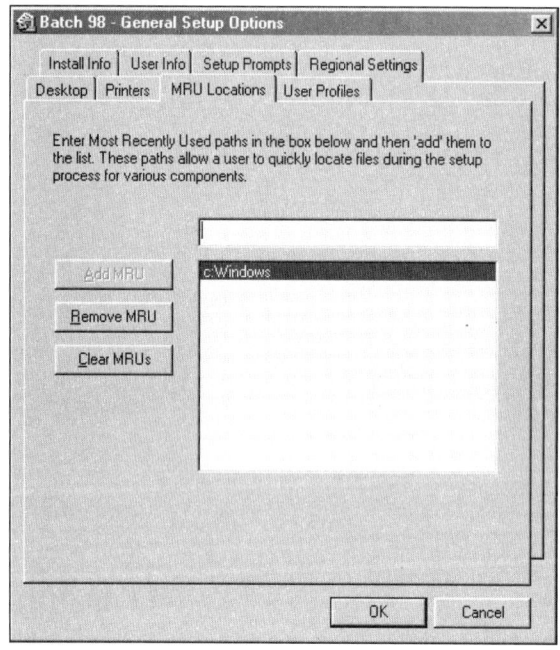

Figure 12-5 Batch 98 – General Setup Options dialog box, MRU Locations tab

You can enter an MRU in the upper, unlabeled text box, in the format *Server_name**share_name*. The *Server_name* is the computer name of the server, while the *share_name* is the share name of the directory. As you learned in previous chapters, you can locate the share name in the Sharing tab of the Properties dialog box for each disk or directory. By default, the share name corresponds to the name of the disk or folder, but it can be changed.

You may want to enter MRUs to help the users on your target computers find certain directories or folders on the network. To enter an MRU, type it in the upper, unlabeled text box, then click Add MRU. You can add up to 26 different MRUs. You can remove MRUs from the list, one at a time, by highlighting an MRU and clicking Remove MRU. You can remove all MRUs from the list by clicking Clear MRUs.

Printers

You use the Printers tab, shown in Figure 12-6, to configure printer installation.

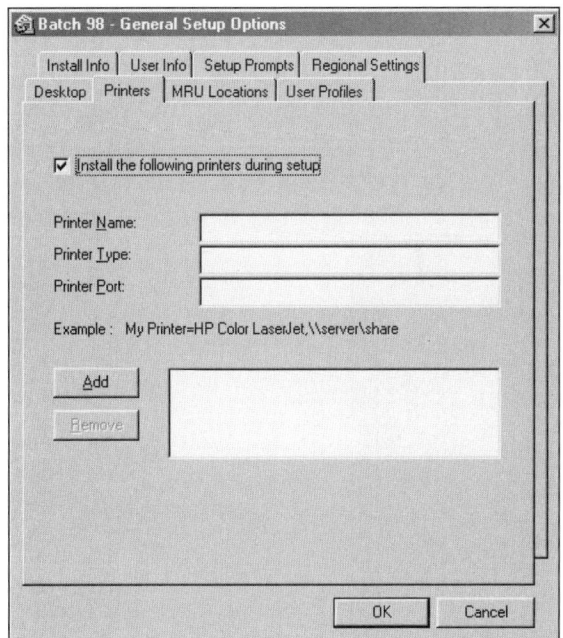

Figure 12-6 Batch 98 – General Setup Options dialog box, Printers tab

There are two basic printing scenarios. In the first, each Windows 98 computer is connected locally to identical printers. In the second, all Windows 98 computers are connected to a common network printer. If you want to install a printer during Windows 98 setup, select the "Install the following printers during setup" check box.

If you specify a printer name in the Printer Name text box, this becomes the reference name for the printer in the Windows 98 computer. You need to specify the Printer Type exactly. For example, if you are installing an HP LaserJet version 6 printer, you should check for the exact name expected by Windows.

If you don't know the exact name, you can find it using the Printer Setup Wizard, as follows: click Start, point to Settings, click Printers, and double-click the Add Printer icon. In the Add Printer Wizard dialog box, click Next. The next dialog box gives you a choice between installing a local or a network printer. Even if you will be installing a printer over the network, click Local Printer, then click Next. In the Manufacturers list, select your printer's manufacturer. In the Printers list, look for the exact name of your printer. Make a note of the printer's name, exactly as shown in this list and then click Cancel. Back in the Batch 98 General Setup Options Printers tab, type the printer name correctly in the Printer Type text box.

What you enter in the Printer Port text box depends on whether the printer is local to the target computer. If it is local, enter the appropriate port, usually LPT1 or LPT2. If it is a network printer, enter the appropriate *Server_name**share_name*. The rules for a server name and share name are the same as that for a shared folder, as you learned in the previous section.

Desktop

In a sense, the options in the Desktop tab, shown in Figure 12-7, are window dressing. Your choices here do not change the content of the programs installed or stored on the computers where you are installing Windows 98. They just affect the "look and feel" of the desktop.

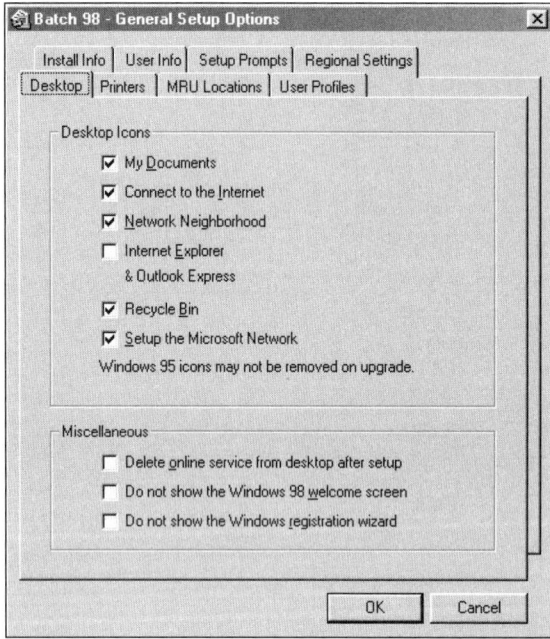

Figure 12-7 Batch 98 – General Setup Options dialog box, Desktop tab

The options are as follows:

- **My Documents**: If this box is checked, this folder is installed on the desktop. If it is not checked, the folder is still installed as a folder on your C:\ drive.
- **Connect to the Internet**: If this box is checked, this icon is installed on the desktop. This icon starts the Internet Connection Wizard, which is also accessible through the Start menu. (Click Start, point to Programs, point to Internet Explorer, and then click Connection Wizard.) If you are setting up Windows 98 on a group of networked computers, you may not want to check this box. For greater network security, it's a good idea to discourage your users from setting up independent connections to the Internet.

- **Network Neighborhood**: If this box is checked, this icon is installed on the desktop. If you do not install Network Neighborhood on the desktop, you can still get to Network Neighborhood through Windows Explorer. Click Start, point to Programs, and then click Windows Explorer. You can find Network Neighborhood near the bottom of the left-hand pane.

- **Internet Explorer & Outlook Express**: If this box is checked, icons for both of these programs are installed on the desktop. If the box is not checked, both programs are still installed through Windows 98 Setup.

- **Recycle Bin**: If this box is checked, the Recycle Bin is installed on the desktop.

- **Setup the Microsoft Network**: This allows your users to set up their own connections via Microsoft's Internet service provider division known as the Microsoft Network.

NETWORK OPTIONS

After you have used Batch 98 to collect your Registry settings, and to specify general setup options, you can use the Network Options button to specify the protocols and services required to connect your computers to Microsoft Windows NT Server or Novell NetWare networks. The Network Options button opens the Batch 98 – Network Options dialog box.

You learned to configure a number of network settings in previous chapters. When you enter these settings here, you allow your users to do what they need to connect to the network without learning the language of networking. You will learn more about some of these settings in Chapter 13.

A number of these options relate to different clients. In Chapter 5, you learned that a client accesses resources such as files and printers from a server in a client-server network. You have learned how to install Microsoft and NetWare clients. In addition, you'll notice other clients mentioned in the tabs of the Batch 98 – Network Options dialog box, which are essentially programs installed with Windows 98. All of these tabs are described in the following sections.

Protocols

You specify settings related to protocols in the Protocols tab, shown in Figure 12-8. Protocol settings are required only if the target computers will be connected to a network (including the Internet). If you do not make any changes, Windows 98 Setup will install the default network components, namely TCP/IP. Otherwise, you can install any or all of the protocols shown under this tab, which you first learned about in Chapter 5, by selecting the appropriate check boxes. Ideally, you should install as few of these protocols as possible.

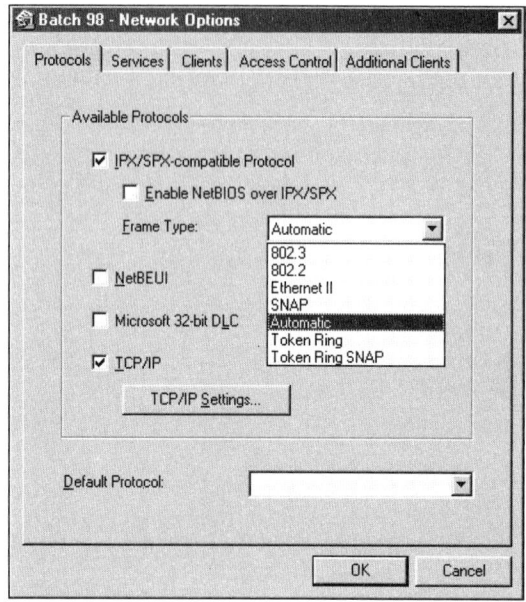

Figure 12-8 Batch 98 – Network Options dialog box, Protocols Tab

The following list describes the options on the Protocols tab:

- **IPX/SPX-compatible Protocol**: Primarily used when your Windows 98 computer is connected to a Novell NetWare network. If you "Enable NetBIOS over IPX/SPX," you allow your network computer names to be sent over the network. As long as you follow the criteria for a computer name as discussed in Chapter 2, the computer name is also used as a NetBIOS name. If you are using IPX/SPX, be sure that you know the frame type used on your network. The **frame type** is the type of data transmitted at the data-link layer of the OSI model from Chapter 5. The wrong frame type is a common IPX/SPX network problem.

- **NetBEUI**: Short for NetBIOS Extended User Interface. This is the simplest protocol, common for Microsoft- and IBM-based networks. It is considered simplest because it requires the least amount of additional information. It is not **routable**; in other words, you cannot use NetBEUI to communicate between networks.

- **Microsoft 32-bit DLC**: Used primarily to link Windows 98 computers to HP print servers and IBM AS400 mainframe servers

- **TCP/IP**: The protocol of the Internet. When you click TCP/IP settings, you open the Batch 98 – TCP/IP Options dialog box. You first learned about these settings in Chapter 5. These settings are important enough to review later in this section.

- **Default Protocol**: You can set any of these protocols to be the default. If you have a network that uses more than one protocol, Windows 98 checks each of these protocols in sequence. If you know which of these protocols is most commonly used, you can optimize the connection of your computer to the network because the default protocol is checked first.

Advanced Windows 98 Installation Options 425

There are a number of additional settings related to TCP/IP. To view these settings, click TCP/IP Settings in the Protocols tab. This opens the Batch 98 – TCP/IP Options dialog box, shown in Figure 12-9, where you can configure a number of settings, similar to those you learned about in Chapter 5.

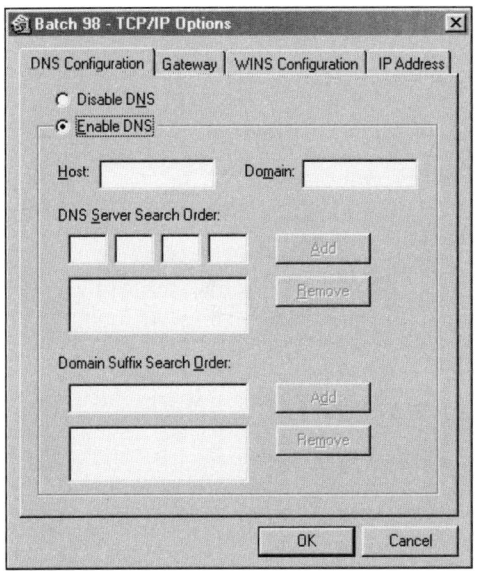

Figure 12-9 Batch 98 – TCP/IP Options dialog box

A few of these settings differ from those discussed in Chapter 5, as described in the following list:

- **DNS Configuration**: As you learned in Chapter 5, a Domain Name Service (DNS) server associates domain names such as *course.com* with IP addresses such as 198.112.168.244. If you are working within a local area network, you may want to click Enable DNS to allow you to add settings within this tab. As you will learn in Chapter 13, these settings determine the DNS servers that your Windows 98 computers will search, and the way your computer searches for a domain name.

- **Gateway**: When you want to send a message outside your local area network, your computer sends the message to the computer that is serving as a gateway between the two networks.

- **WINS Configuration**: The Windows Internet Naming Service (WINS) is similar to DNS. It is a server-based database for computer names (a.k.a. NetBIOS names) and IP addresses. Before checking the server, your Windows 98 computer can check the **LMHOSTS file**, which is a local database of NetBIOS names to IP addresses. You can also use the Dynamic Host Configuration Protocol (DHCP) to assign IP addresses to your WINS servers. With this setting, DHCP tells your Windows 98 computer where to look for a WINS server. Otherwise, you can Enable WINS resolution by adding the IP addresses of your WINS servers.

- **IP Address**: If you have an active DHCP server, you can obtain an IP address automatically. Later in this chapter, you will learn to specify IP addresses with a machine name file. **Autonet** is a new way of assigning IP addresses under development for Windows NT Server 5.0.

Services

Within the context of Microsoft Batch 98, a **service** is an operating system function that provides the ability to share resources such as files and printers. In the Services tab, you can configure your Windows 98 computers for file and printer Sharing, just as you have done in previous chapters. As you can see in Figure 12-10, there are different settings for Microsoft NT and Novell NetWare networks. You can only enable services for one type of network on your target Windows 98 computers. The other settings relate to the way in which Windows 98 communicates its existence to other computers on the network. You can only enable one or the other type of networking in the batch script. If you choose file and printer sharing for Microsoft networks, your available settings include:

- **LM Announce**: LM is short for **LAN Manager**, a Microsoft client originally developed for MS-DOS and Windows 3.x. If you are sharing files or printers from your Windows 98 computer with LAN Manager clients, you want to check this box to announce the presence of your computer on the network.

- **Browse Master Options**: A **browse list** is a listing of computers on a Microsoft network. The browse list is maintained by a computer known as the **browse master**. ("Browse master" and "master browser" are often used interchangeably in Microsoft documentation.) You can use the enable or disable options to indicate whether or not you want your Windows 98 computer to be the browse master. Only one computer on a network can be a browse master. Windows NT Server or NT Workstation computers on the same network take priority as browse master. If you set this option to automatic, your Windows 98 computer can maintain the browse list if necessary.

If you choose file and printer sharing for NetWare networks, your available settings include:

- **SAP Advertising**: The **Service Advertising Protocol (SAP)** is the means by which a Windows 98 computer announces its presence to Novell NetWare clients. If you are sharing files and/or printers with NetWare clients, select this box so the NetWare clients will be aware of your computer.

- **Workgroup Advertising**: Unlike Microsoft clients, NetWare client computers are not organized into workgroups. If you enable workgroup advertising on a Windows 98 computer, it will look like a member of a workgroup to other Microsoft computers. The master computer maintains the browse list. The options here help determine the hierarchy of computers in a network that can be the browse master.

Remember, you cannot activate sharing for both Microsoft and NetWare networks on any single Windows 98 computer.

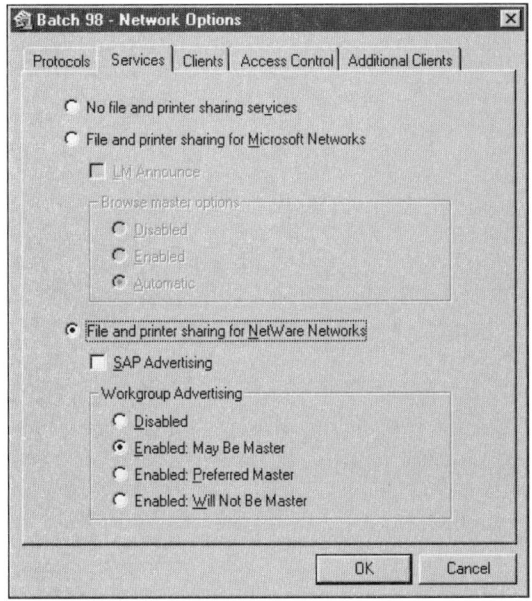

Figure 12-10 Batch 98 – Network Options dialog box, Services tab

Clients

In the Clients tab, shown in Figure 12-11, you can set up your Windows 98 computers to be clients on Microsoft NT or Novell NetWare networks. To join a network, you need to enable at least one of these network clients. The settings here determine how you log on to each or both networks.

- **Client for Microsoft Networks**: If your Windows 98 computer is to be part of a Windows NT network, check this box. Validating a logon to a Windows NT domain is a prerequisite for user-level security on a Windows NT network. If you want to log on to a Windows NT domain, you need to enter the name of the domain or the name of the Windows NT server in the Logon Domain text box.

- **Client for NetWare 3.x/4.x Networks**: If the target computer is to be part of a Novell NetWare network, check this box. You can enable logon script processing when logging onto different NetWare servers. A logon script is a series of commands that are run when you log on to a network. Your logon is sent to the preferred server; any of the user profiles or system policies that you learned about in Chapters 3 and 4 should be stored on that server. The first net drive specifies the first drive letter that your Windows 98 computer uses for the first directory that you access from a remote server.

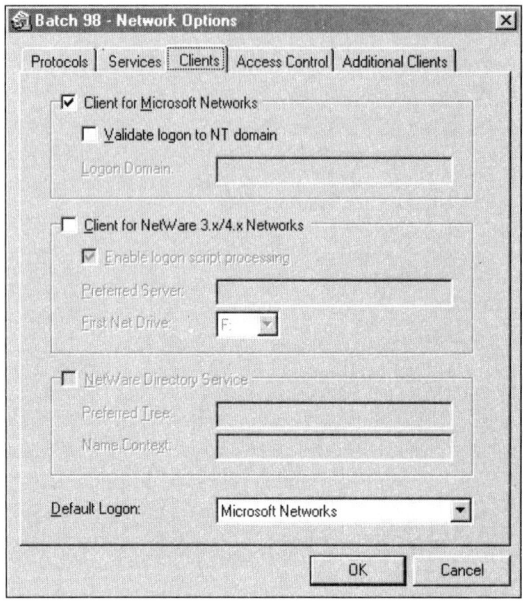

Figure 12-11 Batch 98 – Network Options dialog box, Clients tab

- **NetWare Directory Service**: Novell NetWare versions 4 and 5 keep a list of the resources you can access on a network through the NetWare Directory Service (NDS). An NDS tree includes a group of NetWare servers. When you have a preferred tree, you get access to all servers within that tree. The name context is the first folder or directory you see in your preferred tree.

- **Default Logon**: There are three possible ways to log on as a user: to a Microsoft Network, to a NetWare Network, and to the local Windows 98 computer, which is shown as "Windows Logon."

Access Control

The options in the Access Control tab, shown in Figure 12-12, may look familiar. They are the same access control options that you can find in the Access Control tab of the Network applet.

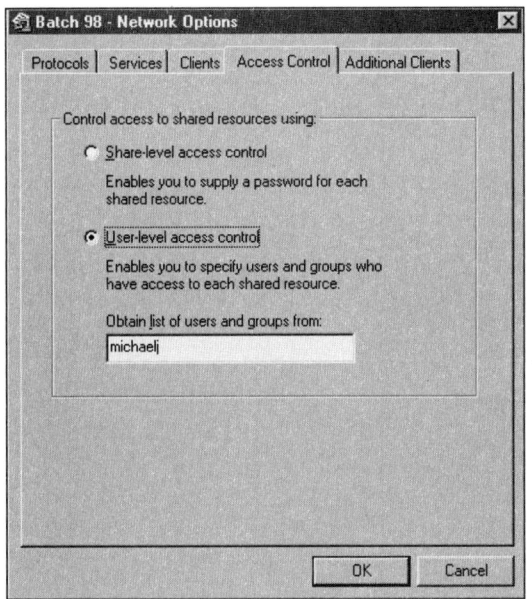

Figure 12-12 Batch 98 – Network Options dialog box, Access Control tab

If you did not enable File and Print Sharing for Microsoft or NetWare networks in the Services tab, the options here are grayed out. In other words, if you do not plan to share the resources of the target computer, you do not need to control the access others have to the target computer. You learned about these options in previous chapters. Share-level access control allows you to set a password for everything that you share. User-level access control allows you to specify the users who are allowed access to the resources on your Windows 98 computer.

Additional Clients

Microsoft and Novell are not the only companies that make network clients or servers. The Additional Clients tab shown in Figure 12-13 includes settings for real-mode Novell clients, specifically **NETX** and **VLM**.

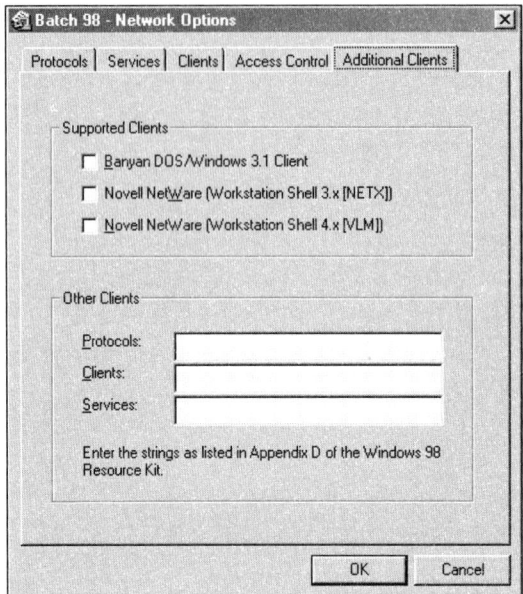

Figure 12-13 Batch 98 – Network Options dialog box, Additional Clients tab

If you are using either the NETX or the VLM real-mode client, you can't get to it from within Windows 98; you need to set up your computer to go into MS-DOS first, log on, and then start Windows 98. This is set up when you install your real-mode Novell client. For more information, see *Hands-On NetWare: A Guide to NetWare 4.1 and IntranetWare 4.11 with Projects*, published by Course Technology. Additional Clients options include:

- **Banyan DOS/Windows 3.1 Client**: You can check this box to configure your Windows 98 computer for use with the real-mode Banyan VINES client, on a Banyan VINES network. Windows 98 only supports version 7.1 or higher of the real-mode Banyan client. Although Banyan has a protected-mode 32-bit client, you cannot install it through the batch setup. If you choose to use the 32-bit client, install it after installing Windows 98.

- **Novell NetWare (Workstation Shell 3.x [NETX])**: If you don't want this replaced with Microsoft Client for NetWare networks, you need to check this option.

- **Novell NetWare (Workstation Shell 4.x [VLM])**: If you don't want this replaced with Microsoft Client for NetWare networks, you need to check this option.

- **Other Clients**: You can set up Novell Client for Windows 95/98 by typing "NovellIPX32" in the Services text box and "Novell32" in the Clients text box. You can also set up the Remote Registry service by typing "Remotereg" in the Services text box. These and other clients require an .inf file and associated drivers.

Advanced Windows 98 Installation Options

 If you want to install one of these other clients on your Windows 98 computer, you should get a copy from the client supplier, possibly over the Internet. Then you can include the instructions from the supplier .inf file with the Windows 98 setup files through the Inf Installer tool. To access the Inf Installer, insert your Windows 98 installation CD into your CD-ROM drive. Click Start, then click Run. Type in *X*:\Tools\Reskit\Infinst\Infinst.exe and click OK. (Substitute the drive letter of your CD-ROM for *X*:.) In the "Inf to add to Windows 98 Setup" text box, type the directory containing your .inf and driver files. In the "Windows 98 Setup.exe" text box, type the directory of the server where the Windows 98 CD files are stored, and then click Add Inf. When you install Windows 98 from this server directory, the appropriate client will be installed as well.

OPTIONAL COMPONENTS

The Optional Components button in the Microsoft Batch 98 window allows you to specify settings for the utilities and programs that you do not absolutely need to install with Windows 98. It opens the Batch 98 – Optional Components dialog box, which contains a list of utilities that you may recognize if you did a custom setup in Chapter 2. You may also recognize this list if you added programs such as Dial-Up Server in Chapter 7. The choices provided in the Batch 98 – Optional Components dialog box are almost identical to those provided in the Windows Setup tab of the Add/Remove Programs applet. Note that you can also use the Optional Components option to install certain screen savers.

INTERNET EXPLORER OPTIONS

The Internet Explorer Options button in the Microsoft Batch 98 window allows you to determine the settings for Internet Explorer 4.0 (IE) on the target computers. It opens the Batch 98 – Internet Explorer Options dialog box, which contains six tabs of options. If you have or are setting up an intranet, these options are important; you need to choose settings that allow you to promote communication without greatly compromising security during Internet access. Using these settings, you can set up Internet-Explorer-related icons on the target computer's desktop, change the look and feel of IE, modify security settings for different types of Web sites, and add proxy server information. You learned about a number of these settings in Chapter 5. The following sections explain the tabs in the Batch 98 – Internet Explorer Options dialog box.

Desktop

You can use the Desktop tab, shown in Figure 12-14, to insert the icons you want to include in the Quick Launch toolbar.

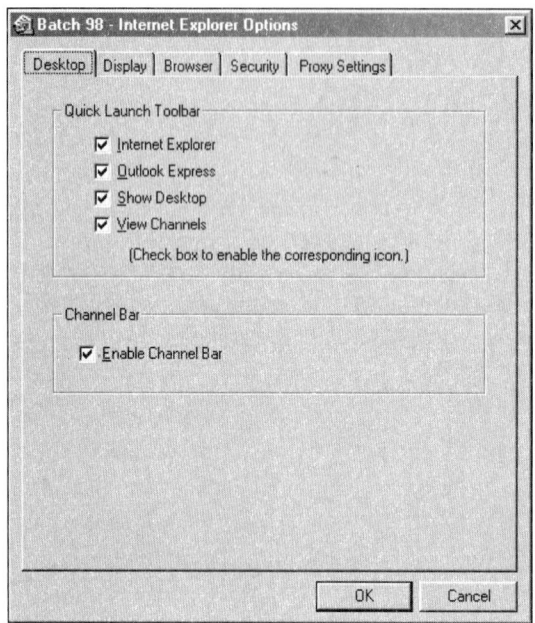

Figure 12-14 Batch 98 – Internet Explorer Options dialog box, Desktop tab

 The Quick Launch toolbar, located in the taskbar, contains a set of icons you can use for quick access to commonly used programs such as Internet Explorer. To verify that the Quick Launch toolbar is currently displayed on your computer, right-click a blank portion of the taskbar, point to Toolbars in the shortcut menu, and then verify that a check mark appears beside "Quick Launch."

Using the Desktop tab, you can include the following icons on the target computer's Quick Launch toolbar: Internet Explorer, Outlook Express, Show Desktop, and View Channels. You can also enable the Channel Bar, which provides preformatted shortcuts to certain commercial Web sites.

Display

In the Display tab, shown in Figure 12-15, you can choose from three different settings for the Internet Explorer display. The choices that you make here do not directly affect anything that you use outside of Internet Explorer. They relate to how Internet Explorer responds to your actions.

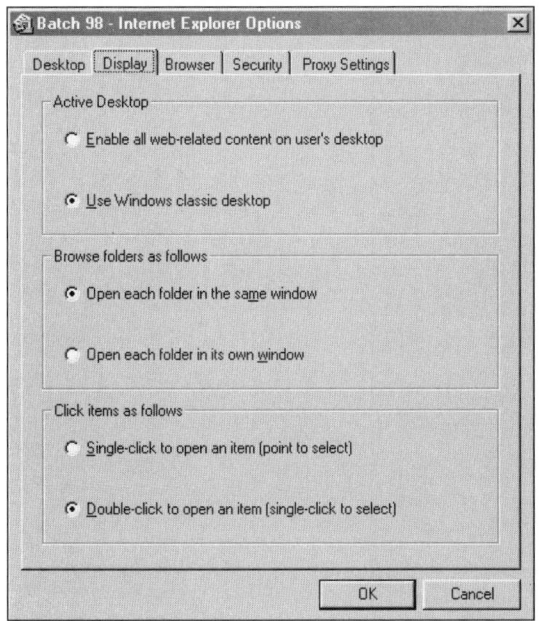

Figure 12-15   Batch 98 – Internet Explorer Options dialog box, Display tab

- **Active Desktop**: Choose the "Enable all web-related content on user's desktop" option if you want your users to display Web-related content on the desktop.
- **Browse folders as follows**: Remember that Internet Explorer 4.0 is designed to access all information, both files and Web sites, in the same manner. When you browse through the World Wide Web, you most likely go from Web site to Web site by clicking links. Each new Web page can appear either in the same or in a new browser window. If you choose to open each page or directory in a new Internet Explorer window, it will not be too long before you are running more copies of Internet Explorer than is optimal on your system. Thus, it's wise to keep the default "Open each folder in the same window" setting.
- **Click items as follows**: You can choose whether to open new Web pages, directories, or files via single- or double-click. If you choose double-click, you will open up Web pages just as you open up programs by double-clicking items on the desktop.

Browser

You can use the Browser tab, shown in Figure 12-16, to specify default pages for the target computers.

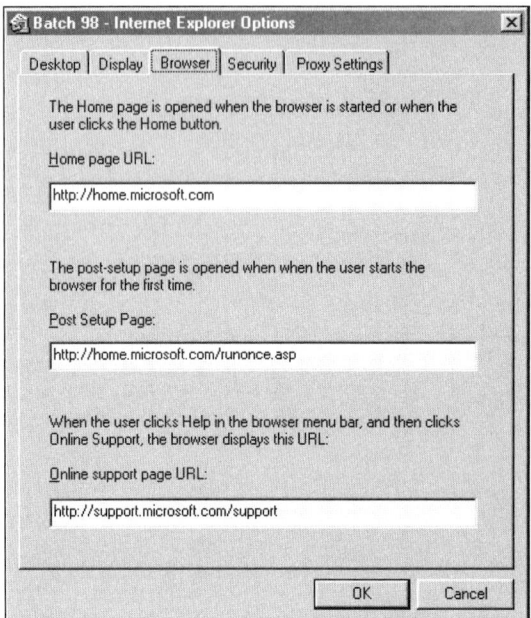

Figure 12-16 Batch 98 – Internet Explorer Options dialog box, Browser tab

If you want to control the access of your users to the Internet, you may wish to use these settings to point your users to Web pages internal to your organization or company. In other words, you can specify the following:

- **Home page URL**: Defines the first Web site that opens when the user starts Internet Explorer. This setting can be changed after Windows 98 is installed, as follows: in the Internet Explorer menu bar, click View, and then click Internet Options. In the General tab (opened by default), change the home page setting. You may wish to set this to the home page for your company.

- **Post Setup Page**: Defines the first Web site that appears when the user starts Internet Explorer for the very first time after starting Windows 98. The default Web page in this category is *http://home.microsoft.com/runonce.asp*. This is the Microsoft introduction for new users to the Internet. This may be a good place for a Web site listing the Internet access policy for your company or organization.

- **Online support page URL**: Defines the online help database that you use. You navigate to it from Internet Explorer. The user can access this database as follows: in the Internet Explorer menu bar, click Help, and then click Online support. The default Web site, *http://support.microsoft.com/support*, is very good.

Security

The Security tab provides a simplified version of the Web site security settings that you learned about in Chapter 5. Briefly, there are three different security settings available (High, Medium, and Low) for different zones of Web content. The different zones are the Local

Intranet Zone, Trusted Sites Zone, Internet Zone, and Restricted Sites Zone. As you learned in Chapter 5, you can set different levels of security for each zone. Unlike the settings in Chapter 5, these settings have no options to add specific sites to a zone or to customize the settings for each level of security.

Proxy Settings

You can use the settings in the Proxy Settings tab to determine the proxy server settings that will be installed on your Windows 98 computers. These settings are similar to the proxy server settings discussed in Chapter 5. These settings are important when you are setting up Windows 98 on multiple computers; you can use them to make sure the computers in your organization provide the most efficient and secure Internet settings possible. As you learned in Chapter 5, you can set up different proxy servers for each of several different TCP/IP-related protocols.

You may wish to bypass Proxy Servers for sites when users request time-sensitive information, such as stock market quotes, as well as for intranet Web sites, where speed and security are less important issues.

ADVANCED OPTIONS

The Advanced Options button in the Microsoft Batch 98 window opens the Batch 98 – Advanced Options dialog box, which contains two tabs: Additional Files and Windows Update. You can use the Additional Files tab (shown in Figure 12-17) to set up Registry or policy files for the target computers.

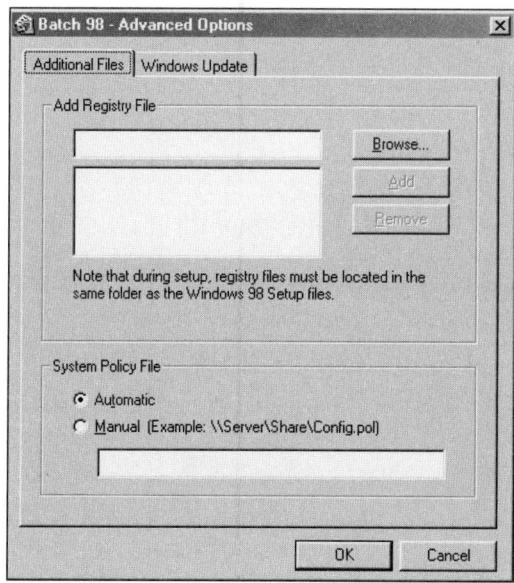

Figure 12-17 Batch 98 – Advanced Options dialog box, Additional Files tab

The following list describes the options on the Additional Files tabs:

- **Add Registry File**: As you learned earlier in this chapter, the Gather Now feature collects some, but not all, Registry settings for inclusion in the batch script. You can use the Add Registry File settings to include additional parts of the Registry saved in .reg format. You learned to save parts of the Registry in this format in Chapter 3. Before you include .reg files in a batch script, you need to save them to the same folder in which you have stored the Windows 98 setup and installation files (probably on a network server). Click Browse to specify the .reg files in the Windows 98 setup folder that you will use.
- **System Policy File**: If you choose Automatic, Windows 98 looks for policy files in default directories, which are different on Windows NT and Novell NetWare servers. Alternately, you can set your Windows 98 computers to look for your policy file in a customized directory.

You can use the Windows Update tab, shown in Figure 12-18, to enable the update of drivers and software through the Windows Update tool that you learned about in Chapter 1. You can get to this tool by clicking Start, then clicking Windows Update. On this tab, you can also specify which Web page Windows Update accesses automatically. If limiting the Internet access of your users is important, you may want to change the settings under this tab. (The default settings direct Windows Update to the Microsoft Web site. Once there, users may be able to navigate to the rest of the Internet.) You may also wish to limit driver updates on Windows 98 configurations that already work well.

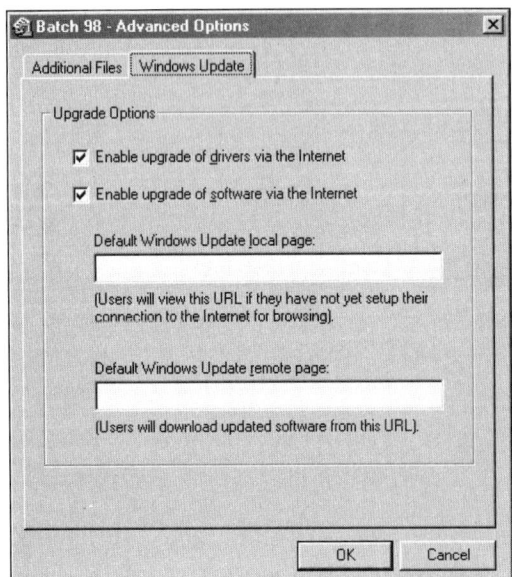

Figure 12-18 Batch 98 – Advanced Options dialog box, Windows Update tab

The following are the options on the Windows Update tab:

- **Enable upgrade of drivers via the Internet**: If this is checked, your users will be sent to the Internet for updated drivers. Unless you specify a Web site in the Default Windows Update remote page text box, your Windows 98 computers will look for updates at *http://windowsupdate.microsoft.com*.

- **Enable upgrade of software via the Internet**: If this is checked, your Windows 98 computers will search for updated Windows 98 related software on the Internet. Unless you specify a Web site in the Default Windows Update remote page text box, your Windows 98 computers will look for updates at *http://windowsupdate.microsoft.com*.

- **Default Windows Update local page**: Enter a URL accessible on your network. Users who have never run the Internet Connection Wizard (or otherwise connected to the Internet) will be sent here.

- **Default Windows Update remote page**: If you leave this blank, your users will be sent to *http://windowsupdate.microsoft.com*. Otherwise, you can enter a URL or Web site address different from that listed above. If you have specialized software that you want to keep up to date, you may want to direct users to a Web page that you develop for this purpose.

MULTIPLE MACHINE-NAME FILES

You can use a multiple machine-name file to set up different batch files for different computers. You can create this file, which simply contains a list of computer names and available IP addresses, with a text editor such as Windows Notepad. An example file might contain the following entries:

```
Mechanic
Manager
Lead, 193.194.195.196
Engineer, 193.194.195.197
Drafter, 193.194.195.198
Intern, 193.194.195.199
```

If you create a multiple machine-name file, you can accommodate the default settings in Microsoft Batch 98 by saving it as C:\Program Files\Microsoft Batch 98\machine.txt. There are some specific things that you need to watch out for when creating a multiple machine-name file:

- Avoid blank lines between computer names. The batch program considers a blank line to be the end of a file.

- Make sure that the computer names that you use are correct. Incorrect data can cause the automated installation to stop to prompt you for the correct information.

Note that you need to create your multiple machine-name file before saving your batch settings, as described in the next section.

SAVING YOUR BATCH SETTINGS

After compiling all the necessary Batch 98 settings, you need to save them by clicking the Save Settings to INF button. By default, this saves your settings as C:\Program Files\Microsoft Batch 98\Msbatch.inf. Next, if you created a machine.txt file (as described in the last section), you need to make the machine names available to Batch 98. You do this by creating a different script file for each computer that you specify, as follows:.

1. On the Microsoft Batch 98 menu bar, click File, and then click Multiple Machine-Name Save. This opens the Batch 98 – Multiple Machine-Name Save dialog box, shown in Figure 12-19, which lists the four steps involved in completing a multiple machine-name save.

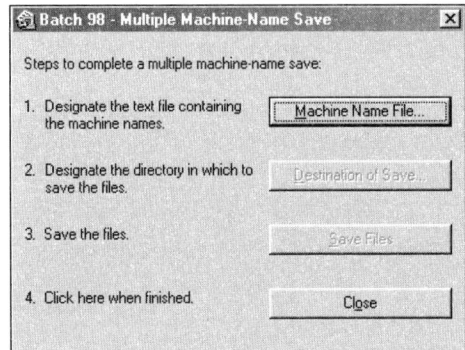

Figure 12-19 Batch 98 – Multiple Machine-Name Save dialog box

2. Click Machine Name File. The Open File dialog box defaults to the C:\Program Files\Microsoft Batch 98 directory. The default file name is machine.txt.

3. If you did not use the name and directory as discussed in the previous section, navigate to your machine name file.

4. Click Open. This loads your current machine name file into Microsoft Batch 98. Then you see a confirmation dialog box, entitled Microsoft Batch 98, which lists the number of entries in your machine name file.

5. Click OK. Now you can proceed to the second step in the Batch 98 – Multiple Machine-Name Save dialog box.

6. Click Destination of Save. This opens a dialog box entitled Select a Target Directory.

7. As long as you use the .txt extension, the name of the file does not matter. For the purposes of this exercise, save the file in the default C:\Program Files\Microsoft Batch 98 directory, and then click Open. Now you can proceed to the third step in the Batch 98 – Multiple Machine-Name Save dialog box.

8. Click Save Files. This step creates one .inf setup file for each computer name that you typed into the machine.txt file.

9. Click OK to acknowledge the saving of the files. Back in the Batch 98 – Multiple Machine-Name Save dialog box, click Close.

You will get a chance to practice this in the Hands-on Projects at the end of the chapter.

THE BATCH FILE

Once you have gone to the trouble of creating a batch file, you should take some time to find out what you created. When you clicked "Save Settings to INF" your settings were saved by default as a Msbatch.inf file in the C:\Program Files\Microsoft Batch 98 folder. To review this file, open it in the text editor of your choice. It is not practical to review all of the approximately 200 settings or 40 categories in this file. A few of the major categories are listed here:

- **[Setup]**: Includes General Setup parameters such as creating a boot disk and showing the license agreement
- **[NameandOrg]**: Specifies the name and organization to which Windows 98 will be registered
- **[Network]**: Specifies computer name, clients, and servers to be connected. If you used a multiple machine-name file, check the various .inf files and note the different settings in this section.
- **[NWLink]**: Specifies IPX/SPX-compatible protocol settings. In Microsoft documentation, IPX/SPX is sometimes known as NWLink.
- **[MSTCP]**: Settings related to TCP/IP networking
- **[Optional Components]**: Utilities to be installed with Windows 98
- **[Proxy Settings]**: Proxy server setup

Now that you have gone through the process of creating a batch file, you might actually want to use it. You will learn to set up a batch file and use it to install Windows 98 on a single computer in the Hands-on Projects at the end of the chapter. But the real benefit of a batch file comes when you can use it on multiple computers. In the next sections, you will learn about using a batch file to install Windows 98 on multiple computers on the network.

INSTALLING WINDOWS 98 ACROSS A NETWORK

Life would be easier if you, as a network administrator, could rely on your users to set up their own upgrades to Windows 98. All you would need to do is copy the files from the Windows 98 installation CD to a network drive. Users would connect to the drive and set up Windows 98 on their own computers, at their own convenience. Unfortunately, this is rarely possible.

Instead, you need to do much of the work yourself, by configuring either push installations or pull installations. The term **push installation** refers to a situation in which the installation of a program, in this case Windows 98, happens automatically with a minimum of user input. The term **pull installation** refers to a situation in which the user initiates the steps to install the program. The user may also be allowed to input some of the program settings.

The choice of using a push or pull installation should be based on the amount of experience you expect your users to have. In some organizations, every user has studied Windows 98 books in great detail, and would therefore be comfortable with a pull installation. However, in most cases users will need some help installing Windows 98, in which case a push installation is probably the best choice, so that you can automate the process as much as possible.

In the following sections, you will learn to use script files to "push" the installation of Windows 98 on inexperienced users. Then you will learn how to allow experienced users to "pull" Windows 98 from the network.

BASIC NETWORK INSTALLATION

When implementing a network installation of Windows 98, your objective is to get your users to run the "setup msbatch.inf" command in the appropriate directories. The Setup.exe and Msbatch.inf files may be located on different directories, even on remote servers connected by a network. You already learned how to create the Msbatch.inf file using Microsoft Batch 98.

The techniques that you will learn in the following sections are all designed to allow users with different Microsoft operating systems to install or upgrade to Windows 98 in a controlled fashion. For push installations, you can determine when and how your users install Windows 98 on their systems. Depending on the system, you may set up your network to push Windows 98 installation onto the computers when users log on and/or connect to the network. For pull installations, you can distribute the tools required to perform the upgrade. You can provide disks with the appropriate boot, batch, and script files, and the drivers for the user to start the process. Alternately, you can even set it up in an attachment to an e-mail message that allows the user to control when he or she wants to upgrade to Windows 98.

Keep in mind that installing Windows 98 over a network involves sending lots of files across the network. Thus, if your network is heavily used, it would not make sense to have all your users upgrade simultaneously.

In the following sections, you will learn about the different methods for installing Windows 98 over a network.

WINDOWS NT PUSH INSTALLATION

You set up a "push" installation via a **logon script**. When your user logs on to the network, his or her computer automatically runs the logon script—which, like a Microsoft Word macro, is a series of commands. Different scripts are required for upgrading from MS-DOS, Windows 3.1, and Windows 95. You will learn about these requirements in the coming sections.

You could attach a logon script to every user account. But in some networks, this may seem as labor-intensive as going to every computer to install Windows 98. When you are upgrading computers to Windows 98 via a Windows NT server, Microsoft suggests creating an upgrade account, which can be used by every user on the network. Since only one user at a time can use this account, you can control the traffic on the network caused by the upgrade. If you have enough capacity, you can set up multiple upgrade accounts.

To learn how to set up an account on a Windows NT network, refer to *A Guide to Microsoft Windows NT Server 4.0*, published by Course Technology.

Upgrading from Windows 95

When you are ready to have your users upgrade to Windows 98 from Windows 95, you need to tell them to log on as the upgrade user that you have previously created on the Windows NT server. You can configure the login script to automatically run the upgrade script as soon as the user connects to an upgrade account. The following is an example of an upgrade script:

```
Net use G: \\upgrade_server\w98_instfiles
G:\setup.exe G:\msbatch.inf
```

These commands can be broken down and explained as follows:

- **net use**: Links your computer to the resource or share on a connected network
- **G**: The drive that you will use to represent the shared folder on your computer. When this command is accepted, you will be able to access this folder through Windows Explorer by highlighting the (G:) drive. You do not have to use "G" as a drive letter. If the C:\Config.sys file on your computer includes a line "lastdrive=Z", you can use any free drive letter between A and Z.
- **upgrade_server**: The computer name of the server where you have stored Msbatch.inf as well as the files from the Windows 98 installation CD. You will probably have a different name for this server.
- **w98_instfiles**: The name of the folder where you have stored the required files. You will probably have a different name for this folder.
- **G:\setup.exe**: Now that you have linked your computer to the remote folder as drive G, you can use it just like any other drive. This calls up the Windows 98 installation setup command that you have stored on the server folder.
- **G:\msbatch.inf**: The script file that you customized with the Microsoft Batch 98 utility should be in the same folder as the Windows 98 installation files.

Windows for Workgroups

Windows for Workgroups is the network-ready version of Windows 3.x. The directions for upgrading from Windows for Workgroups in this section assume that you use a protected-mode network client. If your Windows for Workgroups computers use real-mode network clients, the next section is applicable.

Before you can upgrade Windows for Workgroups computers to Windows 98, you need to create a Startup group. When you start Windows for Workgroups, the operating system automatically runs all programs and commands that you have placed in the Startup group. Note that this Startup group will be transferred into Windows 98 and should be removed once Windows 98 is installed to prevent the startup script from running each time Windows 98 is initialized.

The Startup group should include an upgrade option such as:

```
G:\setup.exe G:\msbatch.inf
```

As you learned in the previous section, you can substitute the drive letter of your choice. For details on how to create a Startup group, see any book on Windows for Workgroups or Windows 3.x. Once you create the Startup group with the upgrade option, copy it to the installation directory on the Windows NT Server.

As you learned earlier, you can control the traffic from upgrades by creating an upgrade account on your Windows NT server. The logon script file that you include with the account will be somewhat different from the script used for other operating systems. One example is as follows:

```
Net use G: \\upgrade_server\w98_instfiles

Rename C:\Windows\startup.grp *.sav

Copy G:\Winnt\system32\repl\import\scripts\startup.grp C:\Windows\startup.grp
```

You learned about the first command in the last section. The second command backs up any existing Windows for Workgroups Startup group. The final command takes the Startup group that you created to the Windows for Workgroups computer that you are upgrading. The next set of commands, which you can add to the Msbatch.inf file, restores the original Startup group:

```
[install]
renfiles=replace.startup.grp

[replace.startup.grp]
startup.grp, startup.sav

[destinationdirs]
replace.startup.grp=10
```

MS-DOS

Generally, users of the MS-DOS and Windows 3.x operating systems use real-mode network clients. Unlike Windows 95 and Windows for Workgroups, these operating systems are generally not set up to automatically connect to the network. Therefore, a proper logon script will look something like:

```
Net start full

Net use G: \\upgrade_server\w98_instfiles

G:setup G:msbatch.inf
```

This set of commands is almost identical to those used in upgrading from Windows 95. The "Net start full" command is required on real-mode MS-DOS clients to connect your target computers to the network. If you are upgrading from Windows 3.x with a real-mode client, you need to change your System.ini file to include the line lmlogon=1 under [Network]. This ensures that you have complete access to the network for the Windows 98 installation files.

In the next section, you will learn how to configure push installations when the installation files are stored on a Novell NetWare server.

NOVELL NETWARE PUSH INSTALLATION

The basic techniques for installing Windows 98 using installation files on a Novell NetWare server are similar to those that you learned for installing from a Windows NT server. The directions in this section assume you have a real-mode and a protected-mode Novell network client on your computers. This is similar to the different types of installations on a Windows NT server; real-mode clients are generally associated with MS-DOS and Windows 3.x, while protected-mode clients are generally associated with Windows for Workgroups and Windows 95.

As with NT Server, you need to set up a special upgrade account on the NetWare server. Also, you need to copy the Windows 98 installation files and your Msbatch.inf script file to the same folder on that server.

Protected-mode Client

There are two main protected-mode Novell NetWare clients: Microsoft Client for NetWare Networks and Novell Client for Windows 95/98. As you learned with Windows NT, you need to create logon scripts to start the installation process. Interestingly enough, you do not need to link the Windows 98 installation directory on the server to a specific drive letter. An example of a protected-mode Novell client script is as follows:

```
#start \\upgradeserver\install\windows\setup
\\upgradeserver\windows\msbatch.inf
```

Now to translate this command:

- **#**: Indicates that this command is not part of the logon script processor
- **\\upgradeserver\install\windows\setup**: Calls up the Windows 98 setup command in the directory where you copy the Windows 98 installation files
- **\\upgradeserver\windows\msbatch.inf**: Calls up the script file from the appropriate server folder

Real-mode Client

As you learned earlier in this chapter, there are two major NetWare real-mode network clients, known as NETX (3.x) and VLM (4.x). Although real-mode clients are associated with operating systems such as MS-DOS and Windows 3.x, many are still in use with Windows 95 systems. A typical logon script for a real-mode Novell client might look like:

```
Map G:=upgradeserver\install\windows
#G:setup G:msbatch.inf
```

This is similar to the logon scripts used to connect and use a Windows NT server. A Novell client uses the "map" command in place of "net use." As you can see from the use of # and =, the syntax is slightly different as well.

Pull Installations

If you have confidence in the expertise of your users, you can create a pull installation of Windows 98. When configuring a pull installation, you can set up the Msbatch.inf script file to allow your users to do things such as enter their own computer name, select optional components, and create their own network settings after installation. You can send the batch script file by e-mail or by 3½-inch disk. You need to schedule your users for their upgrades, to avoid overburdening your network with extra traffic.

You've just learned the mechanics of automated Windows 98 installations. But not everyone will want to use Windows 98 as his or her only operating system. In the next sections, you will learn the mechanics of dual-boot installations. In particular, you will learn about dual booting a computer with Windows 98 and Windows NT.

Managing Dual or Multiboot Machines

There are times when a single operating system just isn't good enough. Users may want the power of a Windows NT workstation, yet want to have the support for legacy applications that comes with Windows 98. Businesses that depend on software created for MS-DOS or Windows 3.x may not wish to upgrade, so backward support for those operating systems will be a requirement. To that end, Windows 98 supports dual-boot and multiboot setups. The Windows 98 function that enables dual-boot and multiboot configurations is called the boot manager. **Dual-boot** refers to two operating systems coexisting on the same computer. **Multiboot** refers to two or more operating systems on one computer.

Windows 98 can dual boot with a number of different operating systems, including Windows 3.x, MS-DOS (version 5.0 or higher), and Windows NT. However, Windows 98 cannot dual boot with Windows 95 or the IBM OS/2 operating systems. (If you are upgrading from OS/2, you will need to deactivate or delete your OS/2 autoexec.bat and config.sys files before installing Windows 98.)

Setting up Partitions

Microsoft's operating systems use a variety of file systems. MS-DOS and Windows 3.x are designed to use FAT16. Windows 98 is designed to use FAT32. Windows NT 4.0 is designed to use NTFS. Although all of these operating systems can use FAT16, you cannot take full advantage of the features of Windows 98 or Windows NT unless you use their file systems. You can accommodate different file systems on one computer by partitioning its hard drive.

As you learned in Chapter 8, you can set up partitions with the Fdisk utility. You can divide a hard disk into primary, extended, and logical partitions. Once you have created the different partitions, you can install different operating systems on the different partitions.

Dual Booting with MS-DOS

Before you can create a dual-boot configuration, you need to verify that the dual-boot capabilities of Windows 98 are enabled. You do this by verifying that the C:\Msdos.sys file contains the following line: BootMulti=1. This ensures you can make changes when you see "Starting

Windows 98" during the boot-up of your computer. Pressing F4 at this time starts the version of MS-DOS that you installed before you installed Windows 95 or Windows 98. Pressing F8 takes you to the Windows Startup menu, shown in Figure 12-20, from where you can also start MS-DOS. These function keys work only if you have a previous Microsoft operating system such as MS-DOS or Windows 3.x installed in your computer. They do not work if you have a computer where Windows 98 is the only operating system installed, or where you installed Windows 98 as an upgrade to a system with only Windows 95 installed.

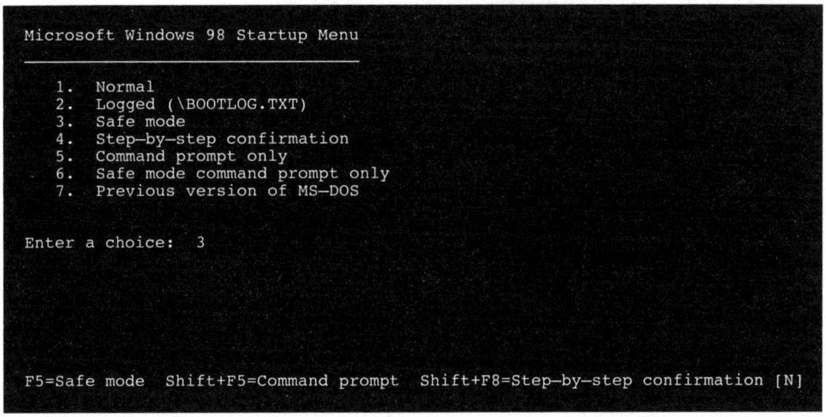

```
Microsoft Windows 98 Startup Menu

    1. Normal
    2. Logged (\BOOTLOG.TXT)
    3. Safe mode
    4. Step-by-step confirmation
    5. Command prompt only
    6. Safe mode command prompt only
    7. Previous version of MS-DOS

Enter a choice:  3




F5=Safe mode   Shift+F5=Command prompt   Shift+F8=Step-by-step confirmation [N]
```

Figure 12-20 Windows 98 Startup Menu

Dual Booting with Windows NT

If you plan to dual boot with Windows NT, the NTFS and FAT32 file systems are problematic, because Windows NT 4.0 cannot read FAT32 files, while Windows 98 cannot read NTFS files. If you also plan to use MS-DOS and Windows 3.x, the situation is further complicated by the fact that these operating systems cannot read NTFS or FAT32 files. The only common file system today for these operating systems is the traditional FAT16 system.

If you are installing Windows 98 on a system that was set up only for Windows NT 4.0, special parameters are required, related to the location of each operating system on your physical disks. For more information, refer to *A Guide to Microsoft Windows NT Server 4.0,* published by Course Technology, which also details the problems related to dual booting.

THIRD-PARTY BOOT MANAGERS

Third-party products are available that can manage multiple operating systems, including Windows 98. Some go beyond a simple dual-boot system, and can allow half a dozen or more operating systems to peacefully coexist on the same system, provided sufficient compatible file formats and partitions exist on the drives. Popular products that can assist in this process include System Commander, published by V Communications *(http://www.v-com.com)*. The latest version of this product, System Commander Special Edition for Windows 98, does preserve your Windows 95 installation while fully installing Windows 98. Each time you boot, you can choose which operating system you wish to use. Additional operating systems supported include OS/2, other Windows products, and any PC-compatible UNIX environment such as Linux.

Chapter Summary

- The Windows 98 setup process can be divided into four basic steps: preparing the Setup wizard, user input, copying Windows 98 files, and hardware detection. Once Windows 98 has run ScanDisk on your computer, it sets up the Setup wizard in temporary files on your computer. User input includes everything that you typed into the wizard when you first installed Windows 98. Once user input is complete, the Setup wizard starts copying the actual installation files to your computer. Some of these files include an extensive driver database, which is used when the Setup wizard detects hardware on your computer. Progress in the Windows 98 installation is documented in the Setuplog.txt, Detcrash.log, Detlog.txt, and Netlog.txt files. You can set up special boot disks to make Windows 98 the first thing that you install on a new hard disk. If you saved your previous operating system during Windows 98 Setup, and you keep your hard disk formatted to FAT16, you can uninstall Windows 98 through the Control Panel Add/Remove Programs applet, or through the Uninstal.exe utility in the C:\Windows\Command folder.

- Installation can be customized and automated through the use of batch files and setup scripts, and may be performed at each individual machine or over a network. Microsoft Batch 98 can take the settings from your computer to create a batch script file to help you set up automated installations. You can customize a batch script file in the following ways:

  - The Gather Now option takes identification and 32-bit settings from your computer.
  - The General Setup Options allow you to keep your users from having to input anything during the installation of Windows 98.
  - The Network Options allow you to set up Windows 98 on many different types of networks.
  - Optional Components allow you to choose the utilities that are installed with Windows 98.
  - Internet Explorer Options allow you to customize the browsers for different types of networks.
  - Advanced Options allow you to import specialized Registry settings, customize access to policy files, and customize access to Windows 98 software and driver upgrades.

- Once you set up one batch script file, you can turn it into multiple customized scripts with a multiple machine-name file. With these files, you can have a standard setup with different computer names and IP addresses.

- With batch script files, you can install Windows 98 over a network. Although this is a great help when you are installing Windows 98 on numerous computers, you have to consider the resulting additional network traffic. To avoid this problem, you can copy the Windows 98 Installation files to a Windows NT server. You can then set up special upgrade accounts for all users to automate their installations. Since only one user at a time can log on to an upgrade account, this helps control the additional traffic. You will need to create different logon scripts for users upgrading from Windows 95, Windows for Workgroups, Windows 3.x, and MS-DOS. Similar provisions can be made on networks centered around a Novell NetWare server. However, if you have a good level of trust with your users, you can also allow them a greater degree of control of their own installations by implementing pull installations.

- Windows 98 can successfully coexist with many other operating systems using either Microsoft's boot manager or third-party applications. Each Microsoft operating system works best with a different file system. You can set up different file systems on different partitions. If one of the multiple operating systems on your computer is Windows NT, there is a specific set of instructions that direct the boot-up of your computer to the appropriate partition on the correct physical disk. If you are dual booting Windows 98 and Windows 3.1 and/or MS-DOS, you can use the boot manager, which you can access by hitting the F8 key while Windows 98 is starting.

KEY TERMS

- **Autonet** — The Windows NT 5.0 method for assigning IP addresses, similar to the Dynamic Host Configuration Protocol (DHCP).
- **Banyan DOS/Windows 3.1 Client** — The real-mode client software created for the Banyan VINES network.
- **batch script** — A file that can substitute for user input. In the context of the Windows 98 Installation Wizard, it can help you automate the installation with a group of customized settings.
- **BIOS translation** — A technique you can use to overcome size limits on hard disks.
- **browse list** — A listing of computers on a Microsoft network. Microsoft clients are added to the browse list when you have activated LM Announce on those computers.
- **browse master** — The computer that maintains the browse list. Computers refer to the browse master to find other computers on a Microsoft network.
- **cabinet file** — A file that contains a number of other files in a compressed format. A number of cabinet files are used to store Windows 98 Setup wizard and installation files.
- **Default Logon** — The network to which you log on when you start your computer.
- **dual boot** — The ability of a computer to boot into two different operating systems.
- **frame type** — The type of data transmitted at the OSI Data Link layer. One example is Ethernet.
- **LAN Manager (LM)** — Microsoft client software originally used on MS-DOS and Windows 3.x systems.

- **LM Announce** — The technique by which Microsoft clients announce their presence to other computers with LAN Manager.
- **LMHOSTS file** — A database that associates NetBIOS names with IP addresses.
- **logon script** — A series of commands that runs automatically when a user logs on to a network.
- **Most Recently Used (MRU)** — Term used to refer to the most recently accessed folders on local and networked computers.
- **multiboot** — The ability of a computer to boot into multiple operating systems.
- **Net use** — A command to link a Microsoft client to a folder on a server connected through a network.
- **NetWare Directory Service (NDS)** — NetWare 4 and 5 database that is used to manage network resources on a Novell NetWare network.
- **NETX** — The real-mode Novell Workstation Shell client, version 3.x.
- **NWLink** — A Microsoft designation for the IPX/SPX-compatible network protocol.
- **pull installation** — An installation technique in which a user initiates the steps required to install a program such as Windows 98. The user may be allowed to input some of the program settings.
- **push installation** — An installation technique in which the installation of a program such as Windows 98 happens automatically with a minimum of user input.
- **routable** — Term used to describe a protocol that can be used to communicate between different networks.
- **SAP (Service Advertising Protocol)** — A protocol used by a Windows 98 computer to announce its presence to Novell NetWare client computers.
- **service** — An operating system process that provides the ability to share resources such as files and printers. When you enable File and Printer Sharing, you are providing a service to the computers that are connected through a network.
- **VLM** — The real-mode Novell Workstation client, version 4.x.

REVIEW QUESTIONS

1. If the Windows 98 installation setup is interrupted, which of the following files can you review to try to figure out what went wrong? (Choose all correct answers.)

    a. Detcrash.log

    b. Detlog.txt

    c. Setuplog.txt

    d. Netlog.txt

Advanced Windows 98 Installation Options

2. If you are upgrading from Windows 95, the Windows 98 Installation Wizard installs drivers for Plug and Play devices by which of the following methods?
   a. by copying the appropriate settings from the Registry
   b. by using a database from the Windows 98 installation CD-ROM
   c. by calling the drivers from the Web site of each hardware manufacturer
   d. by detecting the drivers through the Msbatch.inf script

3. If you are installing Windows 98 from the installation CD-ROM on a freshly formatted hard disk, you need to create a boot disk. Which of the following should you include on the boot disk(s)? (Choose two answers.)
   a. boot files from Windows 95
   b. system files from MS-DOS 5.0 or higher
   c. real-mode drivers for your CD-ROM
   d. protected-mode drivers for your CD-ROM

4. Which of the following commands can you use to create a bootable 3½-inch system disk on your A: drive? (Choose all correct answers.)
   a. Format a: /s
   b. Click Start, then click Run. Type sysdisk in the text box and click OK.
   c. In the Windows 95 Add/Remove Programs applet from Control Panel, go to the Startup Disk tab. Click Create Disk.
   d. In Windows 3.1 Program Manager, click File, and then click Run. Type sysdisk in the text box and press Enter.

5. What does the Gather Now option do in Microsoft Batch 98?
   a. It collects all data currently in your Windows 95 Registry.
   b. It collects all data currently in your Windows 98 Registry.
   c. It collects only the data related to 16-bit programs and drivers.
   d. It collects data such as computer name, printers, and 32-bit networking settings.

6. When setting the General Setup Options in Microsoft Batch 98, it is a good idea to:
   a. force each installation to create a 3½-inch Emergency Startup Disk
   b. force each user to type in the Product Key to ensure security and compliance with Microsoft requirements
   c. always install Windows 98 to a different directory than Windows 95, because Microsoft has set it up so that you can use both operating systems on the same computer
   d. select options to minimize user involvement in the upgrade process

7. When you are setting up the installation of a printer through Microsoft Batch 98, you need to consider the following (choose all correct answers):
   a. If you have a local printer installed on your computer, make sure that your target computers have an identical printer installed.
   b. If your printer is on the network, you need to modify settings if your target computers will be on another network.
   c. If you need to install a new printer, you need to use the Add Printer Wizard that is linked to Microsoft Batch 98.
   d. If you need to install a new printer, you need to use the syntax shown for your printer shown in the Add Printer Wizard.
8. If you do not install any of the optional items (My Documents, Network Neighborhood, Internet Explorer, Recycle Bin) on the desktop, which of the following will happen to your target computers:
   a. You cannot connect the target computer to the network.
   b. You will need to load Internet Explorer separately.
   c. You cannot use the Recycle Bin; everything that you delete cannot be recovered.
   d. You will not see any icons for the optional items on your desktop.
9. Which of the following protocols can you set up on the target computer using the Network Options settings in Microsoft Batch 98? (Choose all correct answers.)
   a. TCP/IP
   b. NetBEUI
   c. NetWare
   d. IPX/SPX-compatible
10. Which of the following do you have to do to allow others to see the computer that you are setting up on a NetWare Network?
    a. enable LM Announce
    b. allow your Windows 98 computers to be the browse master
    c. enable SAP Advertising
    d. enable Workgroup Advertising
11. Which of the following real-mode clients can you configure through Microsoft Batch 98? (Choose all correct answers.)
    a. Novell NetWare VLM Client
    b. Novell NetWare NETX Client
    c. Novell Client for Windows 95/98
    d. Banyan VINES DOS/Windows 3.1 Client

12. When setting up Internet Explorer through Microsoft Batch 98, which of the following modifications to the settings can help you minimize, but not eliminate, the interaction of your users with the Internet? (Choose all correct answers.)
    a. modify the Home page URL to reflect a Web site internal to your company
    b. modify the Online support page URL to reflect a Web site internal to your company
    c. modify your Internet Options to keep your users from accessing the Internet
    d. set the security settings for all zones to high
13. Under which of the following circumstances might you want to allow your users to bypass a proxy server? (Choose all correct answers.)
    a. when you want to allow your users to access Web sites related to library information
    b. when you want to allow your users to access Web sites related to time-sensitive information
    c. when you want to allow your users to access Web sites on your internal corporate network
    d. when you want to allow your users to access Web sites such as *www.microsoft.com* to update drivers
14. Why would you want to add a Registry file to a script created through Microsoft Batch 98? (Choose all correct answers.)
    a. It is not required; the Gather Now command collects all necessary Registry settings.
    b. Adding the Registry to your script minimizes the setup required on your target computer.
    c. to import the settings associated with 16-bit real-mode clients
    d. to import the settings associated with 32-bit protected-mode clients
15. Why would you keep users on your target computers from using the Windows Update feature?
    a. The drivers and programs that you download from Microsoft are not reliable.
    b. Windows Update is harmful to Novell NetWare clients.
    c. You are trying to keep the users on your network off the Internet, and Windows Update provides a back door for those users.
    d. It is less time-consuming to set up your own Web page to keep a library of updated drivers and programs.

16. If you want to create individual batch scripts for different users, which of the following techniques would provide the most reliable results?
    a. After installing Windows 98 on your target computers, ask your users to change the computer names on their computers.
    b. You cannot create individual batch scripts for different users.
    c. Use a multiple machine-name file with a list of computer names and IP addresses to make copies of a batch script customized for multiple users.
    d. Use a multiple machine-name file with a list of NetBIOS names and network clients.

17. Which of the following network clients can you use to access folders on remote computers without using a command such as "attach," "map," or "net use"?
    a. Client for Microsoft Networks
    b. Client for NetWare Networks
    c. NetWare Workstation Shell 3.x [NETX]
    d. Banyan DOS/Windows 3.1 Client

18. Which of the following methods for controlling Windows 98 upgrades is the most reliable way to minimize additional traffic on the network?
    a. Create one or two special upgrade accounts on the Windows NT or Novell NetWare server.
    b. Give everyone upgrade startup disks and a specific time to access the Windows 98 installation files from the network.
    c. Create a fixed number of startup disks. Have users pass them along to others when they have finished their installations of Windows 98.
    d. Create a separate logon script for every existing account to automatically upgrade users to Windows 98.

19. Associate the operating systems in the left-hand column with their most advanced file systems in the right-hand column:
    a. MS-DOS   1. FAT16
    b. Windows 3.x   2. FAT32
    c. Windows 95   3. NTFS
    d. Windows 98
    e. Windows NT 4.0
    f. Windows NT 5.0

20. Which of the following combinations of operating systems require different partitions to use their most advanced file systems? (Choose all correct answers.)
    a. Windows 98 and Windows NT 4.0
    b. MS-DOS and Windows 3.x
    c. Windows 98 and Windows NT 5.0
    d. MS-DOS and Windows NT 4.0

21. Which pair of operating systems can you install and use on the same computer only with a third-party boot manager?
    a. Windows 98 and Windows 3.1
    b. Windows 98 and Windows 95
    c. Windows 98 and Windows NT 4.0
    d. Windows 98 and Windows NT 5.0

HANDS-ON PROJECTS

PROJECT 12-1

In this project you will create a batch file to automate installation of Windows 98 and save it to a floppy disk. For this project, you will need a computer with Windows 98 installed. You also need the Microsoft Batch 98 utility installed (following the steps described in this chapter), as well as a Windows 98 CD with the product key. You can find the product key on the back of the Windows 98 CD cover, or on the Microsoft license that you purchased to install Windows 98 from a single installation CD on a different computer. If you plan to use your target computer on a TCP/IP network and do not have a Dynamic Host Configuration Protocol server (described in Chapter 5) to assign IP addresses, consult your instructor or network administrator for an appropriate IP address.

In Project 12-2, you will use the script file that you create in this project with a multiple machine-name file to create different script files for different computers. In Project 12-3, you will also use this script file to install Windows 98 on a second computer.

1. Click **Start**, point to **Programs**, and then click **Microsoft Batch 98**. The Untitled – Microsoft Batch 98 window opens. First, you will collect the basic 32-bit settings on your computer.
2. Click **Gather Now**. When this step is successful, the text "Status: Complete" appears below the Gather now button.
3. Click **General Setup Options**. The Batch 98 – General Setup Options dialog box opens with a choice of eight tabs. The Install Info tab is open by default.
4. In the Install Info tab, enter the product key from the back cover of your Windows 98 Installation CD.
5. In the Uninstall Options section, click **Automatically create uninstall information**.
6. Click the **User Info** tab. When you clicked Gather Now, Batch 98 collected the information that you see here. If for some reason you choose not to do project 12-2 before project 12-3, you need to change at least the name listed in the Computer Name text box. You learned about the rules for computer names in Chapter 2.

7. Click the **Setup Prompts** tab. Verify that all but the last option ("Skip the PC Card…") are checked. If you plan to use this batch script to install Windows 98 on a computer with a PC Card slot with no real-mode drivers, check this last box as well.

8. Click the **Regional Settings** tab. Unless you plan to do project 12-3 in a different time zone, there is no need to change the time zone setting. Click the arrow adjacent to the Keyboard Layout text box. There is a wide range of keyboards available. The "United States 101" keyboard is good for almost all keyboards used in the USA. Exceptions are shown in this list. Unless you plan to do project 12-3 in a different nation-state or on a computer set up in a different language, there is no need to change the Regional Settings text box.

9. Click the **User Profiles** tab. If your target computer will be on a network, select the "**Users can customize…**" option. Enter a check mark next to both options under User Profile Settings.

10. Click the **MRU Locations** tab. Review the Most Recently Used paths under this tab. This lists the directories, local and network, that you have recently searched. If you do not want your target Windows 98 directories copied to your target computer, click **Clear MRUs**.

11. Click the **Printers** tab. Select the **Install the following printers during setup** check box. A list of any printers installed on your current computer appears in the lower text box. These printers will be installed on the target computer.

12. Click the **Desktop** tab and review the settings. If you want to make changes regarding the desktop on your target computer, make the changes here.

13. Click **OK**.

14. Click **Network Options**. The Batch 98 – Network Options dialog box opens, with five different tabs. By default, the Protocols tab is displayed.

15. Review the selected protocols. If TCP/IP is not selected, select it now. It is the default protocol in many cases and should generally be enabled.

16. Click **TCP/IP Settings**. The Batch 98 – TCP/IP Options dialog box opens.

17. If TCP/IP will be used on the network, click the **IP Address** tab. If an IP address is specified, note that this is the IP address of the computer on which you are currently working. You will need to change it to the IP address of the target computer. If the target computer will ever actually be used on a network, consult your instructor or network administrator for an appropriate address. Otherwise, for the purposes of this project, the settings imported from your current computer will work. (You can find out more about IP addresses in *A Guide to TCP/IP on Microsoft Windows NT 4.0,* published by Course Technology.)

18. Click **OK**. You return to the Batch 98 – Network Options dialog box.

19. Click the **Services** tab. The settings here should match the settings on your current computer. Unless you plan to install your target computer on a different network, no changes are required. Remember, you cannot install file and printer sharing for both NT and NetWare networks on the same computer.

20. Click the **Clients** tab. If you plan to install your target computer on a Windows NT or Novell NetWare network, review the logon domain or preferred server. If you are connecting to a Windows NT domain, select the **Validate logon to NT domain** check box.

21. Click the **Access Control** tab. No change should be required here. The information here determines whether you use share-level or user-level security to protect any resources that you may be sharing on your target computer.

22. Click the **Additional Clients** tab. Unless you plan to install one of these real-mode network clients on your target computer, no information is required here. Click **OK**. You return to the Untitled – Microsoft Batch 98 window.

23. Click **Optional Components**. The Batch 98 – Optional Components dialog box opens, displaying a list of components that is almost identical to the list of components currently installed on your computer. Compare this to the actual list; click **Start**, point to **Settings**, and then click **Control Panel**. Double-click **Add/Remove Programs**, and then click the **Windows Setup** tab. In the next step, you will compare the components that you have on your computer with the components currently selected in Microsoft Batch 98.

24. Return to the Batch 98 – Optional Components dialog box. In the Available Areas text box, highlight **Accessories**, and then view the Available Components in the right-hand pane. Note that Briefcase is included in this list. Even if Briefcase is currently installed on your computer, it will not be selected here. In the Add/Remove Programs dialog box, highlight **Accessories** and click **Details**. Compare the two lists. Compare other components as desired. Assuming the list is acceptable, click **OK**. You return to the Untitled – Microsoft Batch 98 window.

25. Click **Internet Explorer Options**. The Desktop tab of the Batch 98 – Internet Explorer Options dialog box opens.

26. Click the **Proxy Settings** tab. If your target computer will be installed on a network, you will probably have one or more proxy servers controlling your access to the Internet. If your computer is already set up with the correct proxy servers, the data should be reflected here, which means you don't need to make any changes.

27. Click the **Browser** tab. If your target computer will be installed on a network, you may wish to specify Web sites internal to your organization or company for each of the settings here.

28. Review the information in the other tabs, which are related to the display and behavior of Internet Explorer. When you have finished your review of these tabs, click **OK** to return to the Untitled – Microsoft Batch 98 window.

29. Click **Advanced Options** to open the Additional Files tab of the Batch 98 – Advanced Options dialog box. As you learned earlier in this chapter, you can add any complete or partial Registry files that you saved. If you have any 16-bit information, Microsoft Batch 98 did not collect the relevant settings when you clicked Gather Now back in Step 2. If you store a System Policy file in a nonstandard location, click **Manual** and enter the path to that file in the bottom text box. If it is on a remote server, you can enter the path as *Server_name**folder_name*\config.pol. (You learned about system policy files in Chapter 4.)

30. Click the **Windows Update** tab. If you are setting up your target computer on a network, this is another opportunity to control how much your users access the Internet. If you wish, uncheck both boxes to disable access to the Microsoft Update Web site.

31. Click **OK**. You return to the Untitled – Microsoft Batch 98 window.

32. Click **Save Settings to INF**. Accept the suggested filename of Msbatch.inf. However, save the file to a 3½-inch disk rather than the suggested directory folder. After you save the file, note how the name of the dialog box changes to "msbatch.inf – Microsoft Batch 98."

33. Click **File**, and then click **Exit**. You have now created a customized script file. You should be able to use it to install Windows 98 on another computer by typing only one command.

PROJECT 12-2

In this project, you will create a multiple machine-name file. Then you will use it with the Msbatch.inf file that you created in the first project to generate a different script file for each computer in your machine name file. The first step is to create a text file with settings for multiple computers. You can do this in Windows Notepad or with the text editor of your choice. For this project, you will need a PC with Windows 98 and Microsoft Batch 98 installed. You will also need the 3½-inch disk (where you saved the Msbatch.inf file in project 12-1) in drive A.

1. Click **Start**, point to **Programs**, point to **Accessories**, and then click **Notepad**.

2. Type the following lines:

   Supervisor, 221.221.221.65

   Lead, 221.221.221.66

   Engineer, 221.221.221.67

   Drafter, 221.221.221.68

3. Click **File** on the menu bar, and then click **Save** to save the file as machine.txt to the 3½-inch disk with your msbatch.inf file.

4. Click **File**, and then click **Exit**. Next, you need to open Microsoft Batch 98.

5. Click **Start**, point to **Programs**, and then click **Microsoft Batch 98**.

6. Click **File** on the menu bar, click **Open**, and then open the file **msbatch.inf** that you just saved to your 3½-inch disk. Now you're ready to create multiple scripts.

7. Click **File**, and then click **Multiple Machine-Name Save**. This opens the Batch 98 – Multiple Machine-Name Save dialog box.

8. Click **Machine Name File**. The Open file dialog box opens.

9. In the File name text box, type **A:\machine.txt** (the name of the machine file that you just created), and then click **Open**.

10. You then see a Microsoft Batch 98 dialog box displaying the message "4 entries processed." This indicates the number of entries that you entered into the machine.txt file.
11. Click **OK**. You return to the Batch 98 – Multiple Machine-Name Save dialog box.
12. Click **Destination of Save**. The Select a Target Directory dialog box opens, where you can designate the location where your multiple script files will be saved.
13. Verify that the "Look in" text box still points to drive A, enter any name in the File Name text box, and then click **Open**. (The name of the file that you choose does not matter. No file is saved with the name that you choose. The batch files that are generated are listed when you perform Step 18.) You return to the Batch 98 – Multiple Machine-Name Save dialog box.
14. Click **Save Files**. Batch 98 now takes your msbatch.inf file and processes it with the names in your machine.txt file. The resulting files are saved to your 3½-inch disk. When the process is complete, a Microsoft Batch 98 dialog box appears with the message "Done saving 4 files to the directory A:\" .
15. Click **OK**.
16. Click **Close** to return to the msbatch.inf – Microsoft Batch 98 dialog box.
17. Click **File**, and then click **Exit**. Now you can review what you just created.
18. Click **Start**, point to **Programs**, and then click **Windows Explorer**. In the left-hand pane, click **3½ Floppy (A:)**. You should find four files, Bstp0001.inf through Bstp0004.inf.
19. Double-click the file **Bstp0001.inf** to open it in Notepad.
20. Scroll down to display the heading [Network]. Under this heading, confirm that you see an entry: ComputerName="Supervisor". Under the [MSTCP] heading, next to a line starting with IP address, confirm that you see the Supervisor IP address you typed earlier, in Step 2.
21. You have now created four script files that your users can employ to install Windows 98 on their own computers.

Project 12-3

In this project, you will take the batch file you created in project 12-1 and use it to install Windows 98 on a second computer (the target computer). For this project, you will need a computer that does not have Windows 98 installed. It should have Windows 3.x or Windows 95 installed. It should not be a PC with a real-mode PC Card driver. If other users will be working with the same computer, you will uninstall Windows 98 after the main part of this exercise is complete.

1. Insert the floppy disk created in Project 12-1 into the floppy drive of the target computer.
2. Insert the Windows 98 distribution CD-ROM into the CD-ROM drive on the target computer.

3. From the command prompt, enter **X:\setup A:\msbatch.inf** to launch Setup using your batch file. (Replace *X* with the drive letter for your Windows 98 installation CD.)

4. Monitor Setup's progress, and only intervene to resolve unexpected trouble.

5. If others will be using the same computer to install Windows 98, you next need to uninstall Windows 98. Click **Start**, point to **Settings**, and then click **Control Panel**. Double-click the **Add/Remove Programs** icon. Click the **Install/Uninstall** tab. In the lower text box, highlight **Uninstall Windows 98**.

6. If you are really uninstalling Windows 98 from this computer, click **Add/Remove**. Then in the Windows 98 Uninstall text box, click **Yes**.

Do not click Yes unless you are absolutely certain you want to uninstall Windows 98. After you click Yes, you cannot change your mind, and will be forced to continue with the process of uninstalling Windows 98.

PROJECT 12-4

In this project, you will check the state of your drivers after installing Windows 98 on your computer. You will then update your drivers from the Windows 98 CD, as appropriate. In many cases, installing Windows 98 does not necessarily update all of the hardware drivers on your system. In this project, you will focus on one of these cases, the driver for your graphics card (a.k.a. display adapter). To complete this project, you will need a computer with Windows 98 installed.

1. First, you will check the date on your drivers by opening Device Manager. Click **Start**, point to **Settings**, click **Control Panel**, and then double-click the **System** icon. This opens the System Properties dialog box.

2. Click the **Device Manager** tab.

3. Click **View devices by type**. You see a view of all devices on your computer, categorized by hardware component.

4. Click the **plus** sign adjacent to Display Adapters. Highlight your display adapter under this heading, and then click **Properties**.

5. In the dialog box named after your display adapter, click the **Driver** tab. Note the date for your current driver, if available.

6. Click **Update Driver**. This opens the Update Driver Device Wizard.

7. Click **Next**.

8. In the next page, click **Search for a better driver...**, and then click **Next**.

9. In the next page, verify that only the box next to the CD-ROM drive is selected, and then click **Next**.

10. Windows 98 begins searching the Windows 98 Installation CD for a list of updated drivers for your display adapter. If it locates a more up-to-date adapter, you will see the recommendation in the next dialog box. Otherwise, you will see a recommendation to stay with the current adapter in the next dialog box. Click **Next**.

11. Whether or not you are updating your driver, the next dialog box will list the appropriate action, to install a new adapter, or to keep the current adapter. Click **Next**.
12. The next dialog box states either that Windows 98 will keep your current driver or that it has updated your system with a new driver. Click **Finish**. If you did choose to update a driver, skip to Step 14. Otherwise, continue with Step 13.
13. Back in the dialog box named after your display adapter, click **Close**, and then click **Close** again in the System Properties dialog box. If you did not choose to update a driver, you are now finished with this project.
14. If you have installed a new driver, click **Yes** to restart your computer.

CASE PROJECTS

1. You are the part-time network administrator for your firm. Your business is small and growing. You have 10 computers with Windows 3.1 installed. You have just installed Windows 98 on your computer, and your supervisor likes what he sees. Write a brief report explaining what you need to do to install Windows 98 in the same way on the nine other computers. How can you do this without spending excessive time at each computer? Can you let each employee install Windows 98 on his or her own computer? Each computer has a different computer name. How would you set this up?

2. As a system administrator, you need to upgrade the 36 computers in the Marketing Department to Windows 98. Currently, some of these computers are running MS-DOS 5.0, others have Windows for Workgroups, and still others have Windows 95 installed. Network traffic is already quite heavy. Your users are not expert by any means. Your boss has asked you to create settings in the upgrade that will minimize access to the Internet. Write a plan for upgrading these systems. Include details on how you will set up the upgrades, how you will address the different operating systems, and how you will ensure that all users will end up with the same settings.

3. You are the system administrator for a medium-sized Web development firm. Two of your multimedia developers have asked you for additional computers so that they may use different operating systems (MS-DOS, Windows 98, Windows NT) to test that their creations work consistently on the different systems. Your budget will not allow you to provide them with the extra machines. Describe in detail how you can meet their needs with the current computers.

CHAPTER THIRTEEN

Advanced Windows 98 Networking Topics

Throughout this book you have already learned a great deal about networking with Windows 98. In Chapter 5, you learned enough about networking to connect your Windows 98 computer to an Internet service provider. In Chapter 6, you learned the techniques required to manage dial-up networking on a portable computer. In Chapter 7, you learned to use your Windows 98 computer as a dial-up server, to accept connections from other computers.

In Chapter 8, you learned to share resources such as files, folders, printers, and fax modems from your Windows 98 computer with user-level and share-level security. In Chapter 9, you learned how the Installable File System Manager integrates the sharing of files on the network into Windows 98. In Chapter 10, you learned to monitor the performance of Windows 98 on a network. In Chapter 11, you learned how Windows 98 networking can be integrated with a security plan for your network. You also learned to set up control of the Registry from remote computers. In Chapter 12, you learned to set up networking parameters for automated installations of Windows 98.

This chapter covers some more advanced networking topics. You will start by tracking the life of a network request, step by step. Then you will learn more about the role of network clients, or redirectors. Next, you will learn some basics about configuring the five major network protocols available to Windows 98.

> **AFTER READING THIS CHAPTER AND COMPLETING THE EXERCISES YOU WILL BE ABLE TO:**
>
> - Describe what happens to a request for a file from the network
> - Understand the role of the Installable File System Manager and Redirector
> - Set up and configure the major protocols
> - Manage the binding of protocols to adapters and redirectors (clients)
> - Describe the hardware required on the network
> - Work with different TCP/IP troubleshooting utilities

The Installable File System Manager and File Requests

A file request is generated whenever you use an application (such as Microsoft Word) to open a file. Windows 98 handles requests for files via the Installable File System (IFS) Manager. You can think of the IFS Manager as a traffic cop positioned at a fork in a road. It directs requests for files stored on the local computer in one direction, and requests for files stored on the network in another direction. As you learned in Chapter 9, the IFS Manager can send file requests to hard disks, to CD-ROMs, or to the network. If the file is located on a local hard disk, it sends the request to a FAT32 or FAT16 driver, to match the file format of your hard disk. If the file is located on a CD-ROM, it sends the request to the CDFS driver.

If the file is on the network, a simplified version of the process is as follows:

1. You start a program such as Microsoft Word.
2. You request a copy of a Word document stored on a network server.
3. The Installable File System (IFS) Manager intercepts the request.
4. The IFS Manager sends the request to a **redirector** (also known as a network client, such as Client for Microsoft Networks or Client for NetWare Networks) on your computer.
5. The redirector prepares the request for the network. Microsoft Windows NT networks prepare messages using the Server Message Blocks (SMB) protocol. Novell NetWare networks use the NetWare Control Protocol (NCP). You will learn more about these protocols later in this chapter.
6. Depending on the type of network, the request is then translated to a protocol stack. You learned about the TCP/IP protocol stack in Chapter 5. Later in this chapter, you will learn more about TCP/IP as well as IPX/SPX, NetBEUI, and DLC, and Fast Infrared.
7. The request is sent to a specific address. In NetBEUI, you send your request to a NetBIOS address, sometimes known as a computer name. In TCP/IP, you send your message to an IP address. In IPX/SPX, you send your message to an IPX address. In any case, all of these types of addresses are translated to the hardware address of the network adapter on a server.
8. The request is sent through the network adapters that you learned about in Chapter 5. Client for Microsoft Networks uses adapters configured to the **Network Device Interface Specification** (NDIS), developed by Microsoft and 3Com. Client for NetWare Networks primarily uses adapters configured to the **Open Datalink Interface** (ODI), developed by Novell and Apple. You will learn more about these standards later in this chapter.
9. The request is then sent over the network in binary form (1s and 0s). Network requests are translated to binary data in different ways. You learned about Ethernet in Chapter 5. You will also learn about Token Ring and Asynchronous Transfer Mode later in this chapter.

10. The request is delivered to the hardware address of a network adapter on the server.
11. The server translates this data back into a request for a Microsoft Word file. If your server is running Windows NT, it has an IFS Manager that can give the request to the appropriate file system (FAT16, FAT32, NTFS, CDFS, etc.).
12. The server prepares the file to send back to your computer, in the same way that your computer originally prepared the request to send to the server.
13. The Microsoft Word file is sent back to your computer.

Note that in a real-mode operating system such as MS-DOS, the file is first sent to a redirector. The MS-DOS-based redirector determines whether the file is local or on the network. If the file is local, then a file system such as FAT16 takes over.

The remainder of this chapter explains how to configure the various network clients (especially Client for Microsoft Networks and Client for NetWare Networks), which work in the context of SMBs and NCPs. You will also learn more details about using protocols such as TCP/IP, IPX/SPX-compatible protocol, DLC, and NetBEUI to communicate with a network. Finally, you will learn about hardware and the use of NDIS and ODI standards.

Afterwards, you will learn about how you can set up your Windows 98 computer as a server, from which you can share files and printers. You will also learn more of the basics of domains and domain permissions. But first, you need to become familiar with the concept of binding, as it applies to redirectors and network protocols.

BINDING

As you learned in Chapter 5, binding is a process of association. You can bind a protocol such as TCP/IP to a network adapter such as your modem. You can also bind a redirector such as Client for Microsoft Networks to a protocol such as TCP/IP. In Windows 98, the default is to bind every protocol you install to every network adapter on your computer. By default, every redirector that you install is bound to every protocol. Once bound, the protocols, adapters, and redirectors act as one unit.

As you learned in Chapter 5, when you bind multiple protocols to an adapter, the adapter checks each incoming message against each protocol, in the order in which the protocols are bound. The adapter then uses the first protocol that matches the incoming message.

NETWORK CLIENTS AS REDIRECTORS

As you learned in Chapter 9, redirectors and file systems (FAT16, FAT32, and CDFS), are part of the Windows 98 Installable File System (IFS). Within the IFS, the IFS Manager determines where to send a file request. You have learned in earlier chapters to install and use specialized protected-mode redirectors known as Client for Microsoft Networks and Client for NetWare Networks. In Chapter 12, you learned about some of the real-mode clients that can be installed on Windows 98, such as Banyan VINES, NETX, and VLM. The right redirector for your system is compatible with both the operating system on the server (typically Windows NT or Novell NetWare) and the protocol on your network (such as TCP/IP). On Windows 98, you may install one real-mode 16-bit redirector, and as many 32-bit protected-mode redirectors as you need.

PREPARING THE MESSAGE

Once the IFS Manager knows that the file or object that you need is on the network it sends the request to the redirector. The redirector then prepares the message. Network messages are organized into **network control blocks** (NCB). Windows 98 works with two major types of NCBs: Server Message Blocks (SMB) and NetWare Core Protocol (NCP) blocks.

Server Message Blocks is a protocol developed by Microsoft, Intel, and IBM. Redirectors process SMBs into NCBs for transmission on a network. The data is then translated into a protocol such as TCP/IP. (You do not need to know how this works to understand how to network Windows 98.)

The NetWare Core Protocol (NCP) is a proprietary Novell system that supports file and print services. NetWare clients such as NETX, VLM, and Novell Client for Windows 95/98 use NCP to communicate with NetWare servers. Since Novell owns the rights to NCP, Microsoft has adapted SMBs for use on Microsoft Client for NetWare Networks.

CLIENT FOR MICROSOFT NETWORKS

The 32-bit redirector for Microsoft networks is also known as Client for Microsoft Networks, which you learned to install in Chapter 7. If you upgraded to Windows 98 from MS-DOS or Windows for Workgroups, a real-mode network client may already have been installed on your computer. In that case, Windows 98 Setup automatically replaces the real-mode client with Client for Microsoft Networks. This may be a problem if you used a real-mode DLC client to connect to a network printer or IBM AS400 server, because Client for Microsoft Networks does not work with many networked printers or with the IBM AS400 server. Later in this chapter, you will learn about the Windows 98 protected-mode version of the DLC client to help you restore your connectivity to these systems. If you did not upgrade from an operating system with a real-mode Microsoft client, you can install Client for Microsoft Networks as described in Chapter 7.

Because Client for Microsoft Networks uses Server Message Blocks (SMBs), it also supports limited communication with other SMB-based networks, such as Samba, LAN Server, Pathworks, and LAN Manager.

Once Client for Microsoft Networks is installed, you can configure it for use with a Windows NT network. The following instructions assume that you are connecting your computer to log on to a Microsoft network through a Windows NT server. To configure Client for Microsoft Networks:

1. Click Start, point to Settings, click Control Panel, and then double-click the Network icon.

2. In the list of network components, click Client for Microsoft Networks, and then click Properties. The Client for Microsoft Networks Properties dialog box opens, as in Figure 13-1.

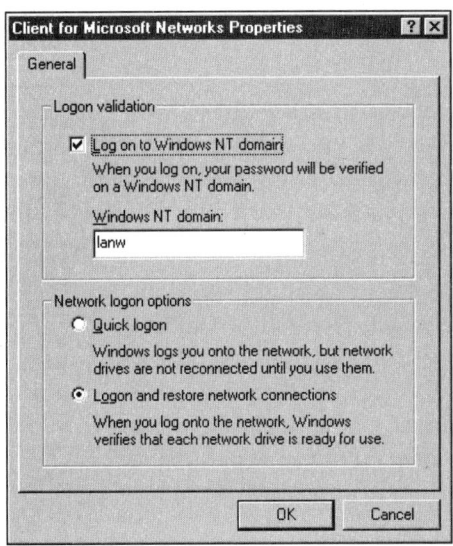

Figure 13-1 Client for Microsoft Networks Properties dialog box

3. To configure your computer to log on to a Windows NT network, select the "Log on to Windows NT domain" check box.

4. Type the name of the domain in the Windows NT domain text box. If you plan to log on to a Windows NT server or workstation instead of a domain, type the computer name in this box.

5. Every time you log on to a network, you can reconnect to your shares—that is, to any folders and printers to which you had previously connected. (As you learned in Chapter 12, information about the most recently used shares is stored in the MRU list.) The options under the "Network logon options" heading determine whether you reconnect to these shares when you log on. If you choose quick logon, the connection is made after you log on, only when required. Choose the option you want, and then click OK. You return to the Network dialog box.

6. Change the setting in the Primary Network Logon text box to Client for Microsoft Networks, if required.

7. Click OK to close the Network dialog box.

8. Click Yes to restart your computer.

CLIENT FOR NETWARE NETWORKS

Instead of a Microsoft network, your Windows 98 computer could be part of a Novell NetWare network, in which case you can use Microsoft's 32-bit redirector for NetWare networks, known as Client for NetWare Networks. You will learn to install Client for NetWare Networks later in this section. If you upgraded to Windows 98, your original operating system may have used a real-mode NetWare client such as NETX or VLM. By default, Windows 98 Setup automatically replaces such real-mode clients with Client for NetWare Networks. In Chapter 12, you learned how to create a batch script file to keep NetWare clients such as NETX or VLM when you upgrade. Windows 98 Setup does not replace some real-mode clients such as Btrieve, LAN Workplace, and Novell NetBIOS TSR.

You can use the Windows 98 Installation CD to install Client for NetWare Networks, NETX, and VLM. If you need the Novell NetWare Client for Windows 95/98, you need to get the appropriate files from Novell. You learned in Chapter 4 that Windows 98 looks for system policies (the Config.pol or Config.man files) on the Sys/Public directory of the NetWare server. However, this is really only true for Microsoft Client for NetWare Networks. If you are using another client created by Novell on your Windows 98 computer, you need to set up your logon script to look for system policies in the appropriate directory.

To install Microsoft Client for NetWare Networks:

1. Insert the Windows 98 Installation CD into your CD-ROM drive.
2. Click Start, point to Settings, click Control Panel, and then double-click the Network icon. The Network dialog box opens.
3. If necessary, click the Configuration tab.
4. Click Add. The Select Network Component Type dialog box opens.
5. In the list of network components, click Client, and then click Add. The Select Network Client dialog box opens.
6. In the Manufacturers list box, click Microsoft.
7. In the Network Clients list box, click Client for NetWare Networks, and then click OK.
8. Click OK in the Network dialog box.
9. Click Yes to restart your computer.

Configuring Client for NetWare Networks

After the client is installed, you should configure it. Some changes may be required to get Client for NetWare Networks working with your network. Click Start, point to Settings, click Control Panel, and then double-click the Network icon to open the Network dialog box. In "The following network components are installed" text box highlight Client for NetWare Networks, and then click Properties. This opens the Client for NetWare Networks Properties dialog box, which contains two tabs, as explained in the following sections.

General Tab. You can specify three settings in the General tab. If your computer is on a NetWare 3.x network, enter the name for your preferred server in the Preferred Server text box. If you are on a NetWare 4.x or higher network, enter the name of a NetWare Directory Services (NDS) server. As you learned in Chapter 12, NDS is a directory of NetWare resources such as files and printers.

The First Network Drive list box indicates the first drive letter to use for shared folders from a server on the network. This letter is F or greater. If you have only one logical drive, the first network drive is F. If you have three logical drives and a CD-ROM, the first network drive is G. You can change this value to accommodate removable drives. The Enable logon script processing check box allows you to set up logon scripts on the NetWare server, as discussed in Chapter 12. Among other things, a logon script can direct a computer to required system policies.

By design, the drive letter is supposed to change if you have more than four drives. For example, if you have a C drive, a D drive, and an E drive on your hard disk, as well as an F drive for your CD-ROM, your first network drive should be G. Unfortunately, this does not work with the first release of Windows 98. In this case, if you connect to a network drive, you will not be able to connect to your CD-ROM from within Windows 98.

Advanced Tab. Except for passwords, text that you type on Microsoft networks is generally not case-sensitive. In contrast, the files and commands that you type in NetWare (and also UNIX) networks are generally case-sensitive. On the Advanced tab, you can indicate whether you want the server to preserve case in the filenames stored on NetWare folders.

Other Client for NetWare Configuration Options

There are other choices that you can make for your Windows 98 computer on a NetWare network. First, you can set up your computer to log on to a NetWare network. You can configure access to NetWare Directory Services (NDS) to allow you to browse the files and printers on a NetWare network. You can also set up the NetWare server to accommodate long filenames.

To configure your computer to log on to a NetWare network:

1. Click Start, point to Settings, click Control Panel, double-click the Network icon, and then click the Configuration tab.

2. Click the "Primary Network Logon" list arrow, and then click "Client for NetWare Networks."

3. Click the Access Control tab, and then click the "User-level access control" option button.

4. Enter the name of your NetWare server in the "Obtain list of groups and users from" text box, and then click OK.

5. Click Yes to restart your computer.

To set up access to NetWare Directory Services, you need to install Service for NetWare Directory Services (NDS). To install Service for NetWare Directory Services:

1. Insert the Windows 98 Installation CD into the CD-ROM drive.
2. Click Start, point to Settings, click Control panel, double-click the Network icon, and then click the Configuration tab.
3. Look for any of the following in the list of network components: NETX Client, VLM Client, or IPXODI Protocol. If you see any of these, highlight them in the list box, and then click Remove. (The real-mode NETX and VLM clients are not compatible with NDS. You learned about these clients in Chapter 12. IPXODI is the NetWare IPX/SPX protocol that is used with these incompatible clients.)
4. Click Add. The Select Network Component Type dialog box opens.
5. In the list of network components, click Service and then click Add. The Select Network Service dialog box opens.
6. In the Manufacturers list box, click Microsoft.
7. In the Network Services list box, click Service for NetWare Directory Services, and then click OK.
8. Click OK again to close the Network dialog box.
9. Click Yes to restart your computer.

If your NetWare server is below version 4.11, you need to add settings from the IBM OS2 operating system to allow for long filenames. You learned about long filenames in Chapter 9. To learn how to enable long filenames, please refer to *Network Administrator: NetWare 4.1*, published by Course Technology.

DUAL-PROTOCOL CLIENTS

You may encounter a Novell network that has both NetWare 3.x and 4.x generation servers. Different protocols can be set up to communicate with the different generations of NetWare servers. In order for a Windows 98 server to successfully communicate with both generations of servers, you need a dual-protocol client on your Windows 98 computer. You can obtain the files for installing these clients from Novell.

WORKING WITH NOVELL CLIENT SOFTWARE AND WINDOWS 98

With Client for NetWare Networks you can use the 32-bit protected-mode tools such as Net Watcher (described later in this chapter). With NetWare Supervisor permissions, you can also manage and administer NetWare servers with NetWare 16-bit command-line utilities. The **bindery** is the NetWare database of users, groups, passwords, and rights. From Windows 98, you can run NetWare 3.x and most NetWare 4.0 bindery management utilities on the server. Once you have set up NDS, you can manage the NetWare bindery with the following NetWare commands: SYSCON (NetWare 3.x), NETADMIN (NetWare 4.x command-line utility), or NWADMIN (NetWare 4.x GUI utility).

Configuring a Windows 98 NetWare Client

You can use Windows 98 purely as a NetWare client, or as a server for other NetWare clients. In this section, you will learn how to decide which NetWare redirector to use, as well as how to provide file- and printer-sharing services to NetWare clients.

Windows 98 can be configured to support five different NetWare clients:

- Microsoft Client for NetWare Networks (32 bit, protected mode)
- Novell Client for Windows 95/98 (32 bit, protected mode)
- NetWare 32-bit Client for NetWare 5.0 (32 bit, protected mode, compatible with Microsoft TCP/IP)
- NETX, Novell's NetWare 3.x real-mode networking client
- VLM, Novell's NetWare 4.x real-mode networking client

Generally, 32-bit protected-mode clients have the advantage in increased speed, greater stability, increased flexibility, and minimal conventional memory overhead. Although you can only run one real-mode client under Windows 98, a client such as NETX or VLM may be more appropriate for interaction with mainframe computers.

You may also need a real-mode client to connect to the network before starting Windows 98. For example, you need a real-mode client to allow a network computer to connect to the network, so that it can then access Windows 98 from a server. To help you choose, Table 13-1 explains the features supported by different NetWare clients.

Table 13-1 Features Supported by Different NetWare Clients

Feature	Supported by
3270 emulation (IBM mainframe terminal)	NETX or VLM
Centralized user profiles	Microsoft Client for NetWare Networks or NetWare Client for Windows 95/98
Custom VLM components	VLM
IPX/SPX-compatible protocol	Microsoft Client for NetWare Networks, NetWare Client for Windows 95/98, NETX, or VLM
NCP Packet signature (security from unauthorized access)	NetWare Client for Windows 95/98, Microsoft Client for NetWare Networks, or VLM
NetWare IP (For Internet access; not compatible with Microsoft TCP/IP)	NetWare Client for Windows 95/98, NETX, or VLM
Novell Directory Services (NDS)	NetWare Client for Windows 95/98, VLM, or Microsoft Client for NetWare Networks with Microsoft Service for NetWare Directory Services

Table 13-1 Features Supported by Different NetWare Clients (continued)

Feature	Supported by
Network management tools for Windows 98	Microsoft Client for NetWare Networks
Novell utilities such as Application Launcher, IP Gateway, Remote Access Dialer, and Distributed Print Services	NetWare Client for Windows 95/98
Programs that use application programming interfaces (APIs)	NetWare Client for Windows 95/98, NETX, or VLM
Windows 98 peer resource-sharing without running another client	Microsoft Client for NetWare Networks

CONFIGURING AND MANAGING WINDOWS 98 PROTOCOLS

For two networked computers to communicate, they must share a common form of communication, called a protocol. Windows 98 supports five built-in, general-purpose networking protocols:

- **Transmission Control Protocol/Internet Protocol (TCP/IP)**: This suite of protocols is used for general LAN and WAN communication, especially on the Internet. You learned about some of the different protocols in the TCP/IP suite in Chapter 5.

- **IPX/SPX-compatible protocol**: Used most commonly on NetWare networks, and required for communication from a Windows 98 computer to a NetWare server (below version 5.0).

- **Data Link Control (DLC)**: Used to allow PCs to work as, or "emulate," a terminal on networks centered around IBM AS400 and mainframe computers, as well as with printers connected to a network.

- **NetBEUI (the NetBIOS Extended User Interface)**: Includes networking extensions of the NetBIOS command set, the original protocol for Microsoft networks. Since NetBEUI is not routable, this can only be used on small networks.

- **Fast Infrared**: Windows 98 is set up to the Infrared Data Association (IrDA) standard 1.1, which accommodates data transfer of up to 4 MBps.

Several other protocols are available to Windows 98, but are only used for specialized functions. This chapter focuses on the five general-purpose network protocols.

While you could install all five of the major Windows 98 protocols, it makes more sense to install only the protocols that you need. Unnecessary protocols eat up system resources and can slow network communications. Your computer attempts to use protocols in the order in which they are associated, or bound, with a particular network component. Once a protocol is bound to a client or an adapter (as described in Chapter 5), the two components act as one software unit. For example, you might bind protocols to a dial-up adapter as shown in Figure 13-2. Note that the adapter will try to match each packet of data arriving over the network to each protocol, in the order in which the protocols are bound. After every attempt, a "timeout" period must expire before the adapter can try the next protocol. This slows the speed of data transfer to and from your computer.

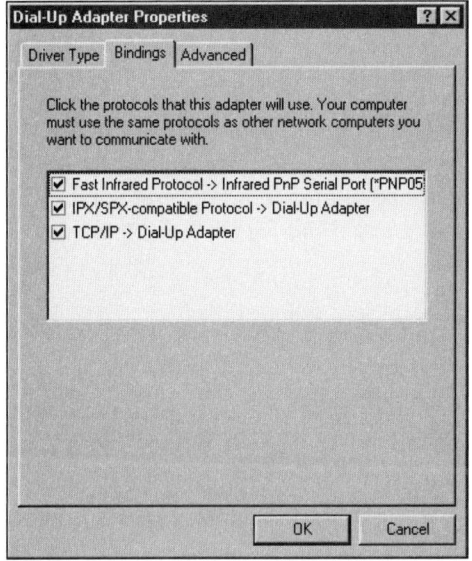

Figure 13-2 Bindings on a dial-up adapter

Protocols should only be bound to those network components that use them. For example, if you know you will never use the IPX/SPX-compatible protocol to communicate with a Microsoft network, don't bind that protocol to the Client for Microsoft Networks. By default, all protocols are bound to all compatible network components when installed. After installation, you can unbind unneeded protocols to improve performance.

The following sections explain the five general-purpose protocols in more detail.

TCP/IP

In Chapter 5, you learned about a number of the protocols in the TCP/IP protocol suite and how they prepare information for the network. In that chapter, you learned to set up TCP/IP gateways from a local area network (LAN) to an external network. A gateway is a path from a LAN to another network. For the purposes of this book, you can assume that gateways and routers are identical; in reality, they serve different functions. While gateways can work at all seven layers of the OSI model that you learned about in Chapter 5, routers work at the lower three layers (physical, data-link, and network).

Windows NT provides three TCP/IP services that may be useful to Windows 98 clients. You learned the basics of what you can do with these services in Chapter 5.

- **Dynamic Host Configuration Protocol (DHCP)**: A server with DHCP installed automatically assigns IP addresses to those Windows 98 computers that request them.
- **Windows Internet Name Service (WINS)**: A database of computer names and IP addresses
- **Domain Name System (DNS)**: A database of host names and IP addresses

As you learned in Chapter 5, TCP/IP is automatically installed along with Windows 98. If for some reason it is not installed on your computer, you can install it by following the steps provided in the Hands-on Projects in Chapter 5. Note that the steps for installing other protocols are more or less identical to those for installing TCP/IP. Chapter 5 familiarized you with the various TCP/IP services. In the coming sections, you will learn a bit more about IP addresses and the workings of DHCP, WINS, and DNS. For a more comprehensive explanation of each service, refer to *A Guide to TCP/IP on Microsoft Windows NT 4.0*, published by Course Technology.

IP Addressing

As you learned in Chapter 5, an IP address takes the form of four numbers, separated by periods. IP addresses are generally assigned in blocks known as subnets. They can be assigned directly from the authority for assigning IP addresses (such as InterNIC), or subassigned by your ISP.

Some network addresses are reserved for special purposes. For example, all IP addresses that begin with 127 (i.e., 127.x.x.x) are reserved for loopback testing. A loopback address refers back to the computer that originally sent the message. As you will learn later in this chapter, you can use the PING utility with a loopback address to test whether your computer is properly set up and connected to the network. All IP addresses that begin with 10 are reserved for use on private networks.

Dynamic Host Configuration Protocol (DHCP)

On Microsoft Windows NT 4.0 networks, you can configure the Windows NT server to be a Dynamic Host Configuration Protocol (DHCP) server. As a network administrator, you typically have a limited number of IP addresses at your disposal. If your Windows NT network includes a DHCP server, you can list these addresses on your DHCP server. That server then manages the allocation of your IP addresses to the Windows 98 (and other) computers on your network. DHCP addresses are assigned to computers for a specific period of time. To configure your Windows 98 computer to get an IP address automatically from a DHCP server:

1. Click Start, point to Settings, click Control Panel, and then double-click the Network icon.

Advanced Windows 98 Networking Topics

2. Click the Configuration tab if necessary.
3. In the list of network components, click the TCP/IP protocol setting associated with your network adapter, and then click Properties.
4. If you selected TCP/IP associated with a Dial-Up Adapter, click OK. The TCP/IP Properties dialog box opens.
5. Click the IP Address tab and select the "Obtain an IP address automatically" option button.
6. Click OK to close the TCP/IP Properties dialog box, and then click OK again to close the Network dialog box.

As a general rule, you configure a protocol by opening the Configuration tab of the Network applet, selecting the version of the protocol associated with your network adapter, and then clicking Properties. You will use these general steps throughout this chapter to configure the various network protocols.

Windows Internet Name Service (WINS)

The Windows Internet Name Service (WINS) is an automated database of computer names and their associated IP addresses (such as 198.155.132.201) set up on a Windows NT server. If you do not want to rely on WINS, you can maintain your own database of computer names and IP addresses in a local file, C:\Windows\Lmhosts. A sample LMHOSTS file, C:\Windows\Lmhosts.sam, is installed with TCP/IP.

The best way to begin learning about WINS is to look at your Lmhosts.sam file in Notepad. The comments that are included with the Windows 98 version of this file provide basic instructions on how to set up this database. The process by which a WINS server matches a computer name to an IP address is known as WINS resolution, or sometimes simply name resolution. This process is also known as mapping—that is, a computer name is mapped to its associated IP address. For a more comprehensive explanation of Lmhosts, see *A Guide to TCP/IP on Microsoft Windows NT 4.0*, published by Course Technology.

If you cannot find the Lmhosts.sam file on your computer, you can extract it from your Windows 98 Installation CD as follows: Insert your Windows 98 Installation CD into your CD-ROM drive. Click Start, point to Programs, then click Windows Explorer. In the left-hand pane, click the plus sign adjacent to your CD-ROM drive letter. Highlight the Win98 folder. In the right-hand pane, double-click on the Net8.cab file. This opens up a window with a compressed section of your Windows 98 installation files. Double-click the Lmhosts.sam file. This opens the Browse for Folder dialog box. Here, you can choose where you want to save the Lmhosts.sam file.

The advantage of WINS is that it is updated every time a user logs on to the network. The user's computer tells the WINS server its computer name and IP address. If you are only using a LMHOSTS file, you need to update this file manually.

To take advantage of WINS, you need to configure your Windows 98 computer as a WINS client. You do this via the WINS Configuration tab of the TCP/IP Properties dialog box that you used in the previous section.

The following list explains the available options in the WINS Configuration tab, as shown in Figure 13-3. Note that the Disable WINS Resolution, Enable WINS Resolution, and Use DHCP for WINS Resolution options are mutually exclusive; you can only enable one of these three.

- **Disable WINS Resolution**: Click to disable the use of any WINS server on your network.

- **Enable WINS Resolution**: Click to enable the use of the WINS server on your network.

- **WINS Server Search Order text box**: If you have more than one WINS server on your network, you can specify the IP address of each server here. Type an IP address for the first WINS server, and then click Add. Repeat for each WINS server. Your Windows 98 computer will check WINS servers in the order that you entered their IP addresses here.

- **Scope ID text box**: You can set up a group of Windows 98 and other computers on your network with a common Scope ID. Computers with a Scope ID can only communicate with other computers with the same Scope ID. This can be dangerous; if you set up your Windows 98 computer with a different Scope ID from that of the Windows NT server that allows you to log on to the network, you will no longer be able to log on to your network.

- **Use DHCP for WINS Resolution**: Click if you use DHCP on your network. This enables WINS resolution and uses DHCP to help your computer identify the IP address of each WINS server.

Domain Name System (DNS)

The Domain Name System (DNS) is one of the core services in TCP/IP and is used to map domain names, such as *microsoft.com*, to IP addresses, such as 198.112.168.244. DNS is used by all operating systems that can use TCP/IP.

In other words, like WINS, the Domain Name System (DNS) is used for name resolution. While WINS maps NetBIOS names to IP addresses, DNS maps host names to IP addresses. DNS is most commonly used to identify and locate Internet-accessible resources such as FTP servers or Web servers so that users do not need to remember numeric IP addresses.

DNS names consist of two parts: a domain name and a host name. For example, a typical DNS name might be something like: jones.advertising.microsoft.com. The domain name typically represents the name of a company or organization(advertising.microsoft.com), and a host name (jones) represents the name of some particular computer within the domain. For Windows 98 computers, the computer name is the default host name. However, you can specify a different host name via the DNS Configuration tab of the TCP/IP Properties dialog box, shown in Figure 13-4.

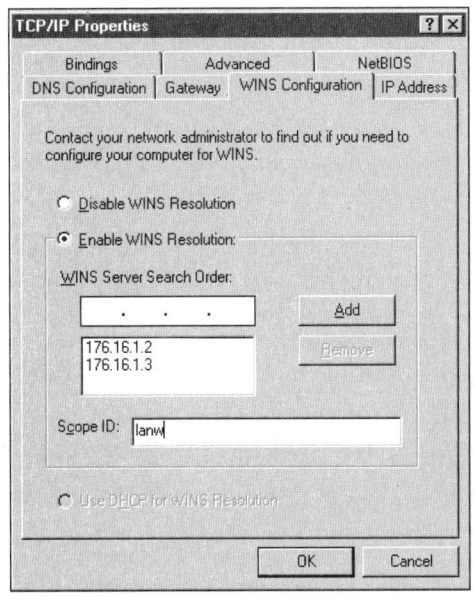

Figure 13-3 WINS Configuration tab of the TCP/IP Properties dialog box

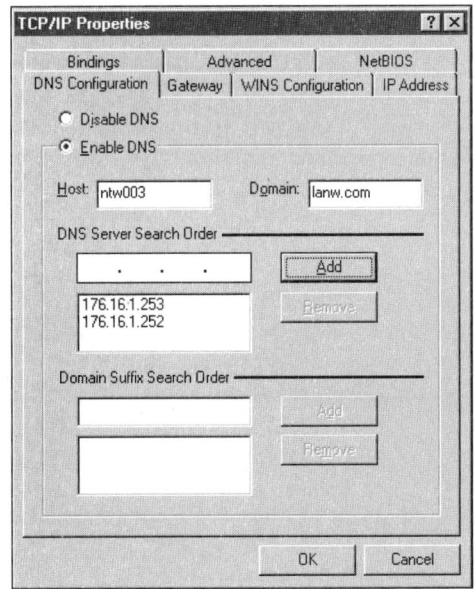

Figure 13-4 DNS Configuration tab of the TCP/IP Properties dialog box

The following list explains the options in the DNS Configuration tab. If your computer is on a network that is connected to the Internet, a number of these settings identify your computer on the Internet.

- **Disable DNS**: Click if you do not want your Windows 98 computer to use a DNS server on your local network. If you disable DNS, you can still use a DNS server while you are connected to an ISP.
- **Enable DNS**: Click to allow your computer to use a DNS server on your network.
- **Host**: Your default host name is your computer name. You learned about the rules for Windows 98 computer names in Chapter 2. Unlike computer names, host names cannot include an underscore character. If your computer name has an underscore character, or if you want a different host name, type a host name for your computer.
- **Domain**: Type your domain name. If your computer is connected to the Internet, you should enter the domain name assigned to your organization. One example is microsoft.com.
- **DNS Server Search Order**: Enter the address for the DNS server that you want to use, and then click Add. Repeat for all available DNS servers. Your Windows 98 computer will check these servers in the same order that you entered them on this tab. Windows 98 checks the second DNS server only if the first DNS server does not answer. It does not check the second server if the first DNS server simply doesn't know the IP address that you are looking for.
- **Domain Suffix Search Order**: By default, the domain name is added to the end of your host name to define how your Windows 98 computer looks through the DNS server database. For example, suppose the domain is advertising.microsoft.com. If your computer name is "jones", your Windows 98 computer will look through the DNS server for the IP address of jones.advertising.microsoft.com. You could type in advertising.microsoft.com and then click Add. If you did, your Windows 98 computer would look through the DNS server for the IP address of jones.advertising.microsoft.com.

After the next sections on troubleshooting TCP/IP, you will learn to configure the Microsoft IPX/SPX-compatible protocol following steps similar to those you used for TCP/IP. Unlike TCP/IP, the Microsoft version of IPX/SPX does not offer services similar to WINS and DHCP. Yet the Microsoft IPX/SPX-compatible protocol is still routable, which means that it allows you to communicate with computers on different networks. Even Microsoft acknowledges that IPX/SPX is more efficient than the Microsoft version of TCP/IP.

Troubleshooting TCP/IP Connections

You will learn about troubleshooting in general in Chapter 14. In this section, you will learn about Windows 98 TCP/IP utilities that can help you troubleshoot your connection on a network. You can use the Address Resolution Protocol (ARP) to help you determine the hardware address associated with a particular IP address. WinIPCfg lists your basic settings on a TCP/IP network. With PING, you can troubleshoot your connection to the network. You can use Tracert to look at the path your messages take, one IP address at a time.

Address Resolution Protocol (ARP). The Address Resolution Protocol (ARP) is a TCP/IP utility. There are two main purposes for ARP. One is to identify the physical or hardware address (used interchangeably) of a computer on the basis of the known IP address. The other is to keep a cache of such addresses on your Windows 98 computer connected to the network. The following are examples of ARP commands:

- **arp –a**: specifies current entries in your ARP cache, associating IP and physical addresses

- **arp –a 198.156.123.111**: Looks for the physical address of the computer with an IP address of 198.156.123.111

- **arp –s 198.156.123.111 6F5BD7**: Specifies a physical address to associate with an IP address in your ARP cache. The second alphanumeric value is based on hexadecimal notation, which you learned about in Chapter 5. It is sometimes also known as base 16, where the digits are 0, 1, 2, 3, 4, 5, 6, 7, 8, 9, A, B, C, D, E, F.

- **arp –d 198.156.123.111**: Deletes the entry for that particular IP address from your cache

Winipcfg. Winipcfg is the Windows 98 version of the TCP/IP utility known as Ipconfig. Winipcfg identifies the current configuration of TCP/IP on your Windows 98 computer. You will have a chance to experiment with Winipcfg in the Hands-on Projects at the end of this chapter. Figure 13-5 shows an example of the kind of TCP/IP configuration information you can access via Winipcfg.

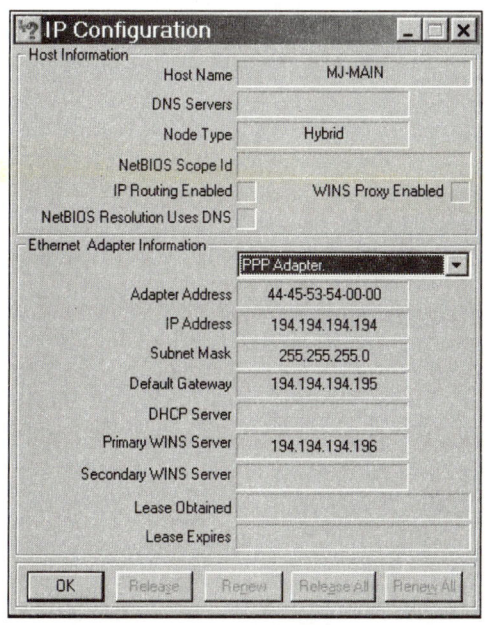

Figure 13-5 TCP/IP configuration information displayed by Winipcfg

PING. As you learned in Chapter 5, you can check your connections on the Internet with the Packet Internet Groper (PING). If you are having problems connecting to your network, the first thing to check, as always, is your physical connections. After that, you can try using PING. Testing a connection via PING is sometimes referred to as "pinging." When using PING, you should use the following commands in this order:

- **PING 127.0.0.1**: This works on every computer. The IP address 127.0.0.1 is known as the **loopback address**. If you can ping your loopback address successfully, you have verified that TCP/IP is installed and configured correctly on your computer. The ping is successful if you get a response that starts with "Reply from...".

- **PING** *your_ip_address*: The IP address that you enter here is your own IP address. You can find your current IP address through the Winipcfg utility that you learned about in the last section. This works even if your IP address is assigned by a DHCP server.

- **PING** *your_computer_name*: This should work identically to PING your_ip_address. If it does not, you may have a problem with your Lmhosts file or your WINS server.

- **PING** *default_gateway_ip_address*: You can also find your current default gateway IP address through the Winipcfg utility. This command verifies that your computer can send messages through your gateway to other networks.

- **PING** *someone_else's_ip_address*: While you are connected to the Internet, try PING on some valid IP address. As you learned in Chapter 5, IP addresses are four consecutive numbers between 0 and 255, separated by decimal points. By convention, the first number in a valid IP address cannot contain the numbers 0, 10, 127, or 225–255.

Tracert. As you have learned, there is more than one network on the Internet. Messages traveling between networks travel through routers according to gateway IP addresses. With Tracert, you can determine the route your data takes over the Internet. Tracert is most useful when your messages cannot reach their intended destination. It tracks your data from IP address to IP address. If there is a problem in the network, the output from Tracert will stop at the gateway or router that may not be working. It also stops if your data does not reach its destination by an arbitrary maximum number of hops. In this context, a **hop** is the movement of a request from one IP address to another, usually on different routers.

If you cannot access a Web site, you can use Tracert to find out if there is a problem on the Internet somewhere between your computer and the Web site. For example, assume you are having a problem reaching *www.microsoft.com*. While connected to the Internet, click Start, point to Programs, and then click MS-DOS Prompt. In the MS-DOS command line, type Tracert *www.microsoft.com* and press Enter. Even if you are not having a problem reaching a particular Web site, try it out for yourself. The results may be rather interesting, as it shows you the path that your request to retrieve the Web page took to get to the Web site.

THE IPX/SPX-COMPATIBLE PROTOCOL

If you want to set up your Windows 98 computer to communicate with NetWare servers (below version 5.0) on a network, you need to install the IPX/SPX-compatible protocol that comes with Windows 98. The official IPX/SPX protocol is only available from Novell. However, Windows 98 includes an IPX/SPX-compatible protocol, sometimes known as NWLink.

 Novell provides software, known as Novell IP, that supports TCP/IP. However, only Novell IP for NetWare 5.0 is compatible with the Microsoft version of TCP/IP.

Next to NetBEUI, IPX/SPX is the most efficient protocol available to a Microsoft Windows NT based network. Because NetBEUI is not routable, it can only be used on standalone networks. Because the IPX/SPX-compatible protocol is routable, it is the most efficient protocol available to a Microsoft network connected to another network.

Installing IPX/SPX-compatible Protocol

If you have already installed Client for NetWare Networks or File and Printer Sharing for NetWare networks, you have already installed the Microsoft IPX/SPX-compatible protocol. However, if you have not installed these services, you can install the Microsoft IPX/SPX-compatible protocol as follows:

1. Insert the Windows 98 installation CD into the CD-ROM drive.
2. Click Start, point to Settings, click Control Panel, and double-click the Network icon.
3. If necessary, click the Configuration tab, and then click Add. This opens the Select Network Component Type dialog box.
4. In the list of network components, click Protocol and click Add.
5. In the list of Manufacturers, click Microsoft, and in the list of Network Protocols, click IPX/SPX-compatible Protocol.
6. Click OK to close the Select Network Component Type dialog box, and then click OK to close the Network dialog box.
7. Click Yes to restart your computer.

The previous steps install one copy of the IPX/SPX-compatible protocol for each network adapter or dial-up adapter on your computer.

Configuring the IPX/SPX-compatible Protocol

When you install the IPX/SPX-compatible protocol, Windows 98 automatically configures IPX/SPX using a number of default settings. You can adjust three groups of settings. First, you can enable or disable bindings. As you learned earlier in this chapter, you can associate the IPX/SPX-compatible protocol with different adapters or clients. Finally, you can set up NWLink to use your NetBIOS names to identify your computers.

To do this, open the Configuration tab of the Network applet, as you did when configuring TCP/IP. In the list of network components, click the IPX/SPX-compatible protocol associated with your network adapter, and then click Properties. In the IPX/SPX-compatible Properties dialog box, click the Bindings tab to display a list of Client software that Windows 98 has bound to this protocol. One example of this tab is shown in Figure 13-6. If you do not share files and printers with other Microsoft computers on your network through IPX/SPX, you should deselect the "File and printer sharing for Microsoft Networks" check box.

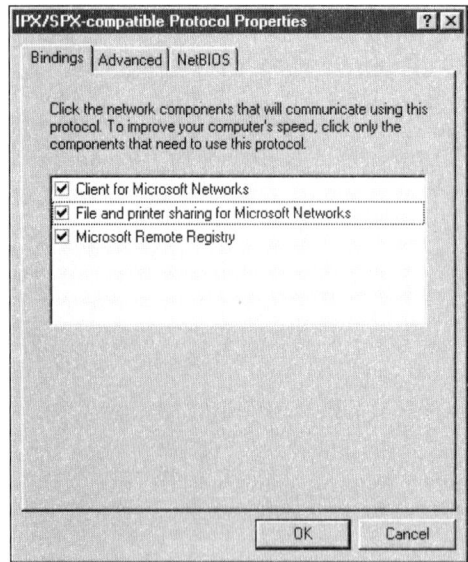

Figure 13-6   IPX/SPX-compatible Protocol Properties dialog box, Bindings tab

The NetBIOS tab contains only one setting, which is related to the use of NetBIOS commands. Some applications, such as Lotus Notes, require NetBIOS commands. In order to use NetBIOS commands on an IPX/SPX-compatible network, you need to select the "I want to enable NetBIOS over IPX/SPX" check box.

You can adjust a number of settings on the Advanced tab, shown in Figure 13-7.

If the "Set this protocol to be the default protocol" check box is available, you can choose to make the IPX/SPX-compatible protocol the default protocol. If it is grayed out, another protocol has already been set as the default.

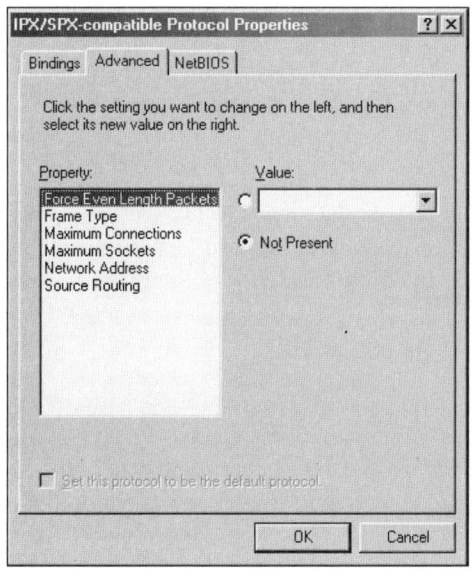

Figure 13-7   IPX/SPX-compatible Protocol Properties dialog box, Advanced tab

You adjust the Property settings on the Advanced tab by selecting an item in the Property list box, and then specifying the relevant setting in the Value list box. When the Not Present option button is available, you can choose it to avoid selecting a value for this property. The various Property settings are described in the following list:

- **Force Even Length Packets**: By definition, an Ethernet packet includes 64 to 1518 bytes of data. Some Ethernet networks cannot manage this variation of data and require packets of even (consistent) length.

- **Frame Type**: There is more than one type of Ethernet and token ring network, and each type of network packages data in one of five different frame types. If you know the frame type required by your network, you should set it here. Choosing a setting here that does not match the frame type on your network will result in a frame mismatch, which will in turn prevent you from connecting to other computers.

- **Maximum Connections**: This setting specifies the number of connections you can establish with IPX. The default is 16 connections. If you wish to specify a number, keep in mind that the number must be greater than 16 to avoid problems loading the IPX/SPX-compatible protocol to connect to the network.

- **Maximum Sockets**: This setting specifies the maximum number of IPX sockets that IPX will assign. The default is 32 sockets. If you wish to specify a number, keep in mind that the number must be greater than 32 to avoid problems loading the IPX/SPX-compatible protocol to connect to the network.

- **Network Address**: The network address in IPX/SPX serves the same function as an IP address in TCP/IP.
- **Source Routing**: Applicable to token ring networks. As you will learn later in this chapter, a source routing cache lists computers on other token ring networks on the other side of a bridge.

In the next section, you will learn about the Data Link Control (DLC) protocol. DLC was originally developed by IBM for communication with its mainframe computers. As you will see, DLC is a specialized protocol not generally in common use for full network communication.

DLC

The third of the major network protocols, Data Link Control (DLC), is used for communication between Windows 98 computers and mainframes, networked printers, and IBM AS400 computers. (A networked printer is connected directly to the network. Note that a networked printer is not the same thing as a printer that is connected to the network through a print server computer.) You can install DLC by following steps similar to those for installing IPX/SPX-compatible protocol, as described earlier in this chapter. In the list of Manufacturers, click Microsoft, and in the list of Network Protocols, click Microsoft 32-bit DLC. (You can also install the real-mode version, Microsoft DLC, if required.) Installing DLC creates one copy of Microsoft 32-bit DLC which can be bound to each network adapter or dial-up adapter on your computer.

There are two groups of settings available for DLC. To view them, open the Configuration tab of the Network applet, highlight the version of DLC associated with your network adapter, and then click Properties. In the Microsoft 32-bit DLC Properties dialog box, click the Bindings tab. Unless you have a protected-mode client for AS400 computers, this box may be empty. Click Advanced. As you can see in the Property list box, there are a substantial number of adjustable parameters. A discussion of these parameters is beyond the scope of this book.

NetBEUI

NetBIOS Extended User Interface (NetBEUI) is the fourth and simplest of the five major network protocols. Since it is not routable, it does not need information regarding gateways or IP addresses. Because it does not include a lot of information, it is the most efficient of the protocol stacks.

Since NetBEUI is based on NETBIOS, it allows you to use commands such as "net use," which you learned about in Chapter 12 as a way to connect to a shared drive on a network. Compatible with any Microsoft network, this high-speed protocol is useful for small local area networks and LAN segments. You can install NetBEUI by following steps similar to those for installing IPX/SPX-compatible protocol, as described earlier in this chapter. In the list of Manufacturers, click Microsoft, and in the list of Network Protocols, click NetBEUI.

As with other protocols, you can configure NetBEUI via the Configuration tab of the Network applet. In the list of network components, click NetBEUI and then click

Properties. This opens the NetBEUI Properties dialog box. The options on the Bindings tab are identical to those for the IPX/SPX-compatible protocol. The Advanced tab provides the following settings:

- **Maximum Sessions**: A session is a connection to another computer. The default value is 10 sessions, which is consistent with a typical small network.
- **NCBS**: Network control blocks. This setting controls the number of NetBIOS commands that can be used. You learned about one example of a NetBIOS command, net use, in Chapter 12, to connect your computer to a network share.
- **Set this protocol to be the default protocol**: If you are using your Windows 98 computer primarily on a NetBEUI network, select this check box.

FAST INFRARED

The final major network protocol is Fast Infrared, which you can use to configure a Fast Infrared adapter to the Infared Data Association (IrDA 1.1) standard. You can install Fast Infrared by following steps similar for installing IPX/SPX-compatible protocol, as described earlier in this chapter. In the list of Manufacturers, click Microsoft, and in the list of Network Protocols, click Fast Infrared Protocol.

As with other protocols, you configure Fast Infrared by selecting it in the Configuration tab of the Network applet, and then clicking Properties. The Fast Infrared Protocol Properties dialog box includes only one tab, the Bindings tab. You won't see any settings on this tab until you install a Fast Infrared capable network adapter on your computer. As you have learned in previous chapters, you need a driver to connect your hardware to Windows 98. To connect a Windows 98 computer on a Fast Infrared network, you need an infrared miniport driver compatible with NDIS 4.0 or higher.

Now that you have learned how to set up some of the different available protocols on your Windows 98 computer, you will review the standards related to network driver interfaces. Windows 98 accommodates two of the major network driver standard types, known as NDIS and ODI.

NETWORK DRIVER INTERFACE SPECIFICATION (NDIS)

Some network types use a monolithic protocol stack, which combines a network adapter driver such as NDIS and one or more network protocol suites such as TCP/IP. They can only run in real-mode. These arrangements have drawbacks. For example, a change to one component requires a change in all components in the protocol stack.

Windows 98 supports NDIS version 5, which incorporates the following features:

- **Functionality**: NDIS 5 includes support for ARCNET, FDDI, and ATM. These protocols are alternatives to token ring and Ethernet.
- **Support for Plug and Play**: With NDIS version 5, Windows 98 automatically determines which protocols to bind to each adapter.

- **Compatibility with Windows NT 5.0**: Accommodates the Windows Driver Model (WDM) that you learned about in previous chapters
- **Support for legacy NDIS drivers**: NDIS 5 supports the use of legacy NDIS network driver versions 2, 3, and 4.
- **Support for broadcast media**: NDIS 5 also supports broadcast media such as Intercast and DirecTV broadcasts.

OPEN DATALINK INTERFACE (ODI)

The **Open Datalink Interface (ODI)** specification is Novell's standard network interface driver. It is also designed to make it easy for vendors to write device drivers for their hardware without having to address network protocol or network adapter issues. ODI includes **Link Support Layer (LSL)**, which is a Novell-specific Data Link layer protocol. LSL allows more than one protocol stack (e.g., TCP/IP and IPX/SPX-compatible) to be bound to the same network card. Although Windows 98 does not support ODI as well as it supports NDIS, ODI is required to accommodate connections to Novell NetWare networks. For more information on ODI, please refer to *Network Administrator NetWare 4.1,* published by Course Technology.

A FOCUS ON HARDWARE

In this brief section, you will learn and review the different hardware components involved in networking. The material relating to networking hardware and software is extensive. Although Windows 98 computers are network clients, they generally play only a small role in the management of a network.

One of your options is to create a network of Windows 98 computers. In Chapter 8, you've learned to set up your Windows 98 computers as servers with share-level security. But in general, share-level security is good only for networks of up to 10 computers. A network that size can be attached to a single hub. You will learn about hubs, routers, and gateways in the following sections.

NETWORK CARDS

The Plug and Play feature you learned about in previous chapters makes it easy to install a network card, sometimes known as a **network interface card (NIC)**, as follows:

1. Turn off your computer.
2. Install a Plug and Play NIC in your computer.
3. Turn your computer back on. If the card is inserted properly, it should configure itself automatically. Windows 98 adds configuration data to the Registry.

Windows 98 supports Plug and Play network cards for different bus types such as IDE, PCI, and PC Cards. However, this only works if your Windows 98 computer is running protected-mode networking components, including protocols, clients, and drivers.

Hardware on the Network

This section briefly describes some common types of networking hardware. (You may already be familiar with some of these definitions from other chapters.) Note that the following definitions only tell you as much as you need to know in order to understand the other concepts in this chapter.

- **Repeater**: Takes a digital signal of "1s" and "0s," and reproduces it. Repeaters can extend the allowable distance in a network. They work at the physical layer of the OSI model, which you learned about in Chapter 5. A **hub** is a repeater that can connect to several computers, just as a wheel axle is connected to numerous spokes.

- **Bridge**: Sometimes known as a switch. Bridges are often used to split a network into different logical networks known as **segments**. Works at the data-link layer of the OSI model. Source routing allows a Windows 98 computer on a token ring network to save a cache of directions to other computers. You will learn about token ring networks later in this chapter.

- **Router**: Creates a connection between different networks. When you use TCP/IP, each connection to the router has an IP address. When you configure a TCP/IP gateway, you specify the IP address of your network connection to the router. With this information, a router can look for that IP address on all networks connected to it. Works at the network layer of the OSI model.

- **Gateway**: In Windows 98 documentation, the terms routers and gateways are often used interchangeably. However, this is not strictly accurate. While routers work at the network layer of the OSI model, gateways work at the application layer. Routers take binary data (1s and 0s) at the physical layer and translate them to the network layer. Gateways translate between different applications such as different e-mail programs. Nevertheless, for the purposes of this book, you can assume that a gateway is the same thing as a router.

Types of Networks

The following sections provide some basics about Ethernet, token ring, and Asynchronous Transfer Mode (ATM). These descriptions, which are by no means comprehensive, include a number of simplifications and are therefore not strictly precise. The goal of these sections is to help you understand how to install Windows 98 on these types of networks. By reading these sections, you will not actually learn how to create such networks.

Ethernet

As you learned in Chapter 8, Ethernet was the first modern network architecture, more formally known as the IEEE 802.3 standard. Access to an Ethernet network is governed by a method known as Carrier Sense Multiple Access/Collision Detection (CSMA/CD). According to this method, your Windows 98 computer checks to make sure that the network is free before transmitting data. If the network is free, it starts transmitting.

One potential drawback to Ethernet is that more than one Windows 98 computer may decide to transmit data at almost the same time. That is, the network may *appear* to be free to a Windows 98 computer, although in reality another computer on the same network may just be initiating the process of sending a packet. Data packets from two computers can "collide" in the middle of the network, and as a result neither message gets through to its destination. Note that all computers that are trying to send data detect such collisions (thus the term "Collision Detection" in the official description of Ethernet).

In order to avoid these collisions, each computer that wants to send data waits a different period of time before sending a packet. Unless a lot of computers try to send data simultaneously on an Ethernet network, this random element eventually allows your Windows 98 computer to send your data without getting into a collision. For more information on how Ethernet packets may collide, refer to one of the many books dedicated to Ethernet.

Token Ring

Unlike Ethernet, a token ring network allows only one computer to talk at a time. The active computer is the computer with the "token." Physically, token ring networks are set up in a circular fashion. Token ring networks can be configured to a capacity of 4 MBps or 16 MBps. The corresponding size of token ring packets, 4096 and 17,952 bytes, is not a problem because computers on a token ring network take turns sending packets. Since they take turns, their packets do not collide. Since no time is wasted in Ethernet-style collisions, token ring networks can handle much more traffic relative to their rated capacity.

Token ring networks are often segmented by bridges. If you want to send a message to a computer on another segment, for example, on the other side of the bridge, you cannot simply send the message to the address of the target computer. That's because the only computers that will see the address are the computers on your segment—that is, the computers on your side of the bridge. The target computer, which is on the other side of the bridge, will not see the message.

A source-routing cache can help. Each entry in a source-routing cache tells your Windows 98 computer how to send a message to a computer outside your network segment. That is, the cache tells your computer which bridge the message has to cross. As you learned earlier in this chapter, you can set up a source-routing cache with the IPX/SPX-compatible protocol.

Asynchronous Transfer Mode (ATM)

Packets on an ATM network are different from those on an Ethernet or token ring network. An ATM packet (53 bytes) is so much smaller than an Ethernet (1518 bytes) or a token ring packet (4096 bytes) that it is more often known as a cell. The small size of an ATM packet improves overall reliability; depending on the network, you may have problems with one in a trillion packets.

The following is a very simplified explanation of what is meant by a reliability level of one in a trillion. Say you are transferring a megabyte of information. This megabyte is split into around 20,000 packets—that is, 1,000,000/48 bytes per packet. (It is 48 and not 53 bytes, because ATM allocates at least 5 bytes per packet for other information such as addressing.)

A one in a trillion reliability level means that, when transferring a megabyte of data, you will experience problems only 1 in 50 million times (1 trillion divided by 20,000 packets). Chances are that something else in your network will fail first.

As mentioned earlier, TCP/IP is automatically installed along with Windows 98. The one exception is if the only network adapter on your computer is an ATM card, in which case you need to install TCP/IP yourself, following the steps provided in the Hands-on Projects in Chapter 5. To set up TCP/IP or IPX/SPX to work on an ATM network, you need to configure **LAN emulation**, which allows you to simulate the characteristics of a local area network while using TCP/IP or IPX/SPX (or both). To set up LAN emulation:

1. Insert the Windows 98 installation CD into your CD-ROM drive, and then open the Configuration tab of the Network applet.
2. Click Add.
3. In the Select Network Component Type dialog box, click Protocol, and then click Add.
4. In the Select Network Protocol dialog box, click Microsoft in the Manufacturers list.
5. In the Network Protocols list, click ATM Call Manager, and then click OK.
6. Repeat Steps 2 through 4.
7. In the Network Protocols list, click ATM LAN Emulation Client, and then click OK.
8. Repeat Steps 2 through 4.
9. In the Network Protocols list, click ATM Emulated LAN, and then click OK.
10. In the Network dialog box, click OK.
11. Click Yes to restart your computer.

Virtual Private Networking

In this section, you will learn to create a virtual private networking (VPN) connection to a LAN through a dial-up connection to your Internet service provider (ISP). VPN makes use of the Point-to-Point Tunneling Protocol (PPTP), which you learned about in Chapter 1. When properly configured, VPN provides two separate connections over your network adapter: your regular network connection and the PPTP connection. To implement VPN, you first need to create a dial-up connection, as you learned in Chapter 5. Then you install a VPN adapter. Finally, you can connect to your ISP, and then connect to your VPN network through your second "dial-up" connection.

If you need instructions on how to create a dial-up connection, please review Chapter 5. After you create a dial-up connection, you can install a VPN adapter as follows:

1. Insert the Windows 98 installation CD into your CD-ROM drive, and then open the Configuration tab of the Network applet.

2. Click Add. In the list of network components, click Adapter, and then click Add to open the Select Network Adapters dialog box.

3. In the list of Manufacturers, click Microsoft. Then in the Network Adapters list, click Microsoft Virtual Private Networking Adapter.

4. Click OK to return to the Network dialog box, and then click OK again to close the Network dialog box.

5. Click Yes to restart your computer.

6. Now you can set up your VPN connection, using a procedure similar to setting up a dial-up connection. Click Start, point to Programs, point to Accessories, point to Communications, click Dial-up Networking, and then double-click the Make New Connection icon.

7. In the Make New Connection dialog box, enter a name for your VPN connection in the Type a name for the computer you are dialing text box.

8. In the select a device text box, select Microsoft VPN Adapter.

9. The next Make New Connection dialog box prompts you for the host name or IP address of your VPN server. Enter this information and click Finish.

Now that you have set up your connections, you can use them. First, connect to your ISP. Generally, you can do this through the Dial-up Networking folder. Click Start, point to Programs, point to Accessories, point to Communications, click Dial-up Networking, and then double-click the icon that you created in Chapter 5 to connect to your ISP. In the Connect to dialog box, enter your username and password (if they are not already there), and then click Connect. In most cases, this will give you a direct connection to the Internet. If you are using an ISP that cannot use a dial-up networking icon, such as America Online, you need to connect to that ISP and then to the Internet using whatever directions you may have from your ISP.

Once connected to the Internet, you can start your "dial-up" VPN connection. Click Start, point to Programs, point to Accessories, point to Communications, click Dial-up Networking, and then double-click the name of the connection that you created earlier in this section. In the Connect To dialog box, enter your username and password for your LAN, and then click Connect.

If you are successful, you will see two "Connected to" dialog boxes: one for your ISP, the other for your PPTP connection.

In the next section, you will take the other point of view regarding Windows 98. Instead of using Windows 98 as a client, you will set up Windows 98 as a server. When you shared files from your computer in Chapters 7 and 8, you set up Windows 98 as a server on a Windows network. In the next section, you will also set up your Windows 98 computer as a server on a Novell NetWare network.

Configuring Windows 98 as a Server—Using File and Printer Sharing

Networks are generally built on the client/server model. Software such as File and Printer Sharing for Microsoft Networks allows Windows 98 to share files and printers in the same way as a Windows NT server. File and Printer Sharing for NetWare Networks allows Windows 98 to share files and printers in the same way as a Novell NetWare server. You already learned how to enable file and printer sharing for Microsoft networks in Chapter 8. In addition, in Chapter 12, you learned to create a Windows 98 batch script in order to set up file and printer sharing on multiple computers. In this section, you will learn how to enable file and printer sharing for Windows 98 computers on NetWare networks. (Note that a Windows 98 computer cannot function as a server on both types of networks simultaneously.) In the Hands-on Projects at the end of the chapter, you will learn to set up Microsoft-style browsing and Novell-style advertising with file and printer sharing.

Configuring a Windows 98 Computer as a Browser

Users need to know what resources are available on a network. In Microsoft networks, the user can find this information in the browse list—a list of all accessible network resources. The browse list is maintained by a browse master. (You learned about the browse list and browse master in Chapter 12.) A computer with resources to share sends messages to the browse master whenever the computer joins the network, and thereafter on a periodic basis. In every workgroup, there is one browse master and up to three backup browsers. For details on how this works, refer to *A Guide to Windows NT 4.0 in the Enterprise,* published by Course Technology.

When you set up file and printer sharing, you need to decide whether you want your Windows 98 computer to maintain the browse list. If your Windows 98 computer is part of a Windows NT network, this question usually does not matter, because Windows NT servers and workstations will always be chosen as browse masters and backup browsers before any other computers on the network.

However, it is possible to configure a Windows 98 machine as a browse master or a backup browser. Note that you should only consider doing so if your Windows 98 computer has extra RAM and a network connection with extra capacity. Otherwise, a slow Windows 98 computer would in turn slow other computers in their search for resources on your network. To set up your Windows 98 computer as a browser, open the Configuration tab of the Network applet, and then verify that "File and Printer Sharing for Microsoft Networks" appears in the list of network components. If it does not, you need to enable file and printer sharing as described in Hands-on Project 8-1.

Next, click File and Printer Sharing for Microsoft Networks, and then click Properties. This opens the File and Printer Sharing for Microsoft Networks Properties dialog box. In the

Advanced tab, highlight Browse Master in the Property list box. In the Value list box, you can choose from three values:

- **Automatic**: Your Windows 98 computer can become a backup browser.
- **Disabled**: Your Windows 98 computer will not maintain the browse list on your network.
- **Enabled**: Your Windows 98 computer will try to become the browse master. If there are higher-ranked computers (i.e., NT Server or NT Workstation), your Windows 98 computer may not get to maintain the browse list.

You may also want to set up your computer to announce the files and printers that it is sharing to the network. In the File and Printer Sharing for Microsoft Network Properties dialog box, highlight LM Announce in the Property list box. As you learned in Chapter 12, the LM Announce setting is based on the way LAN Manager clients announced their presence on a network. Under Value, you can see two choices: No and Yes. Select the Yes setting if you want your Windows 98 computer to announce its resources to the rest of its network.

FILE AND PRINTER SHARING FOR NETWARE

If you want to share files and printers with a NetWare network, you need to install the Microsoft Service named File and Printer Sharing for NetWare Networks on your Windows 98 computer. File and printer sharing with NetWare requires user-level security. Since you can't keep NetWare passwords on a Windows 98 computer, you need a Windows_Passthru account on a NetWare server. A **Windows_Passthru account**, which has no password, links your Windows 98 computer to the NetWare bindery on a NetWare Server.

As mentioned earlier, you cannot set up a Windows 98 computer to share files and printers on a Microsoft and a Novell NetWare network simultaneously. So before you can install File and Printer Sharing for NetWare Networks, you first need to disable File and Printer Sharing for Microsoft Networks. To do so, open the Configuration tab of the Network applet. In the list of network components, click File and Printer Sharing for Microsoft Networks, and then click Remove.

Now you can install File and Printer Sharing for NetWare Networks. You will learn to install this service in the Hands-on Projects at the end of this chapter.

NET WATCHER

Once you have set up file and printer sharing on your Windows 98 computer, you can manage it remotely using the Net Watcher utility. This assumes that you have Remote Administration set up on both Windows 98 computers, as you learned in Chapter 8. The Windows 98 computer on which you start Net Watcher and the remote Windows 98 computer that is sharing files and printers must be compatible. In other words, if your remote Windows 98 computer is enabled for File and Printer Sharing for NetWare Networks, you need to set up Client for NetWare Networks on the computer where you set up Net Watcher.

Advanced Windows 98 Networking Topics

You can use Net Watcher to share and monitor connections to file and printer resources. It allows you to identify the user connected to your Windows 98 computer and to identify the files the user opens. You can use Net Watcher to disconnect users who are currently sharing your Windows 98 computer on a Microsoft or a NetWare network. If you are managing a Windows 98 computer with File and Printer Sharing for Microsoft Networks, you can close files that others have open on that Windows 98 computer.

You can install Net Watcher as follows:

1. Insert the Windows 98 installation CD into your CD-ROM drive.
2. Click Start, point to Settings, click Control Panel, and double-click Add/Remove Programs. This opens the Add/Remove Programs Properties dialog box.
3. Click the Windows Setup tab. In the Components text box, click System Tools, and then click Details. This opens the System Tools dialog box.
4. In the Components list box, scroll down until you see Net Watcher. If there is a check mark next to this item, it is already installed on your computer. Otherwise, click to insert a check mark and click OK.
5. Click OK again in the Add/Remove Programs Properties dialog box.
6. Even though you are not prompted to do so, restart your computer to activate the settings associated with Net Watcher.

Assuming that you have already set up file and printer sharing services per Chapter 7, you can now start monitoring other, remote, Windows 98 computers as they share files and printers. Remember, before you start, you need to know the names of the remote Windows 98 computers that have already been configured for file and printer sharing. If you are using share-level security, you need to know the Remote Administration share-level password you entered on the remote Windows 98 computer. If you are using user-level security, you need the appropriate Windows NT Administrator or Novell NetWare Supervisor account and password.

To monitor remote computers using Net Watcher:

1. Click Start, point to Programs, point to Accessories, point to System Tools, and then click Net Watcher.
2. In the menu bar, click Administer, and then click Select Server. This opens the Select Server dialog box.
3. Type the computer name of the server that you want to administer.
4. In the next dialog box, type the password required for remote administration.

The Administer menu in the Net Watcher window provides a complete list of all the functions available to you via Net Watcher. This menu contains commands for disconnecting users, closing files, adding shared folders, or stopping the sharing of folders on remote Windows 98 computers.

Workgroups and Domains

Computers in a network can be organized into workgroups and domains. A workgroup is a set of computers that share file and printer resources. Unlike with a domain, workgroup resources are not centralized around a server. Since workgroups are not centralized around a server, they are associated with share-level security. You can group any small collection of computers together under a common workgroup name. You can find the name of your workgroup in the Identification tab of the Network applet.

As you learned in previous chapters, computers can also be organized into domains, which require user-level security. Users in a domain are typically organized into groups. Groups can be either global or local. Unlike local groups, global groups can link resources across different domains. When you set up a user account, you can assign it to be a part of either a global or a local group. You can even assign a global group to be a part of a local group, but you cannot include a local group in a global group.

Don't worry if this seems confusing. For the purposes of understanding Windows 98, you simply need to remember that it is more flexible to organize your users into global (instead of local) groups. In addition, you should be familiar with two particular global groups: Domain Users and Domain Admins (Administrators).

If you assign a user to the Domain Admins group, that user gets all the privileges and rights of an administrator. When you set up user accounts in a Windows NT network, each user is also included in the Domain Users group. By default, each Domain Users group is included in the local Users group.

This section barely scratches the surface of the subject of domains. If you would like more information on domains, users, groups, and permissions, refer to *A Guide to Windows NT 4.0 in the Enterprise*.

Chapter Summary

- When you issue a request for a file, the Installable File System Manager has to decide whether the file is local or on the network. If it is on the network, the IFS Manager sends your request to a redirector such as Client for Microsoft Networks.

- There are a number of different real-mode and protected-mode clients that you can use with Windows 98. The client that you choose prepares the message for the network with SMBs for Microsoft networks or with NCPs for Novell NetWare networks. If you upgrade from another Microsoft operating system that had a real-mode client, Windows 98 Setup replaces this with the protected-mode Client for Microsoft Networks. In addition, it replaces most real-mode NetWare clients with the protected-mode Client for NetWare Networks. The Client for NetWare Networks includes a number of configuration options, including the Service for NetWare Directory Services. With Novell

Client software and supervisor-level permissions, you can manage the NetWare bindery of users. You can choose between different Novell clients and specify how they are bound to your network adapters.

- The TCP/IP suite allows you to use DHCP, WINS, and DNS services to help with your IP addressing needs. You need the IPX/SPX-compatible protocol if you want your Windows 98 computer to communicate with NetWare servers (below version 5.0). DLC is a specialized protocol to connect to mainframes and printers connected directly to a network. NetBEUI is the simplest of these protocols, because it does not carry the overhead required for routing to different networks. Fast Infrared allows you to connect to a network without wires, using hardware that is at least NDIS 4.0 compliant. Each of these protocols are stacked with either the Network Driver Interface Specification or the Open Datalink Interface.

- You can use a number of TCP/IP network troubleshooting utilities to check your network connections. With ARP, you can keep a database of IP to hardware addresses. Winipcfg lists a number of your TCP/IP parameters when you are connected to a TCP/IP network such as the Internet. You can test your connections to various points on the network with PING to help determine where you might be having trouble on your network. If the problem is not close to home, Tracert tracks the life of your request on the Internet to identify where your requests get stopped.

- Network communication requires the use of several types of hardware, including repeaters, hubs, bridges, routers, and gateways. These can be set up in several different types of networks: Ethernet, token ring, and ATM. You can set up virtual private networking over a dial-up connection to provide a degree of security over the Internet.

- Windows 98 computers can be configured with some of the characteristics of a server, specifically to share files and printers. A Windows 98 computer can share files and printers on either a Windows or a Novell NetWare network, but not on both simultaneously. Once you have enabled file and printer sharing on the Windows 98 computers on your network, you can use the Net Watcher utility to monitor who looks at what on remote Windows 98 computers.

- The process of setting up users on a network is fairly complex. Domains require user-level security to accommodate the organization of users into groups. The most prominent groups are Domain Admins and Domain Users.

KEY TERMS

- **bindery** — The NetWare database of users, groups, passwords, and rights.

- **binding** — An association between network components, such as between an adapter and a protocol, or a protocol and a client. Allows the two components to act as one unit.

- **bridge** — Sometimes known as a switch. Bridges are often used to split, or segment, a network into different logical networks. Works at the data-link layer of the OSI model.

- **Fast Infrared** — A protocol for network communication, in the same category as Ethernet and token ring. Windows 98 is set up to the Infrared Data Association (IrDA) standard 1.1, which accommodates data transfer of up to 4 MBps.
- **hop** — The movement of data from one IP address to another, usually from router to router.
- **hub** — A repeater that can connect to several computers.
- **LAN emulation** — A process commonly used to allow an ATM network to simulate the characteristics of a local area network.
- **loopback address** — Used in reference to a specific TCP/IP address, 127.0.0.1. If you can contact your loopback address with the PING utility, you have confirmed that you are properly connected to a network.
- **Network control blocks (NCB)** — The generic term for the means by which a redirector prepares data for a network. In Windows 98, Client for Microsoft Networks uses the server message block (SMB) type of NCB, while Client for NetWare Networks uses the NetWare Core Protocol (NCP) type of NCB.
- **Network Device Interface Specification (NDIS)** — The Microsoft standard for network driver interfaces.
- **Network interface card (NIC)** — The hardware card that connects your computer to the network.
- **Open Datalink Interface (ODI)** — The Novell version of NDIS, for network driver interfaces.
- **Redirector** — Also known as a client, such as Client for Microsoft Networks or Client for NetWare Networks. Software that prepares your message in your computer for the network.
- **repeater** — A device that regenerates a network signal. As signals travel over distance, they degenerate. An amplifier turns up the volume on a signal, but a repeater actually interprets what it receives and regenerates the binary code of 1s and 0s that make up the signal. Works at the physical layer of the OSI model of networking.
- **router** — A device that divides networks into segments. Although the term "router" is often used interchangeably with "gateway," they are not the same. While a router works at the network layer of the OSI model, a gateway works at the application layer of the OSI model.
- **segments** — Distinctly different local area networks. Different network segments can be joined with a router, or a bridge.
- **Windows_Passthru account** — An account on a NetWare server that allows a Windows 98 computer to use the username and password data on that server. A Windows 98 computer that is set up for File and Print Sharing for NetWare Networks uses a Windows_Passthru account on a NetWare server with a bindery.

REVIEW QUESTIONS

1. Microsoft Client for NetWare Networks is:
   a. a software application installed on a NetWare server that allows Windows machines to make network connections
   b. a software client installed on the Windows 98 machine that allows access to Novell NetWare 3.x or 4.0 generation servers
   c. a network adapter card
   d. none of the above

2. Which protocol can you use to access file and printer sharing on Microsoft systems? (Choose all correct answers.)
   a. TCP/IP
   b. IPX/SPX-compatible protocol
   c. Novell IP
   d. NetBEUI

3. A dual-protocol client is:
   a. a software program that can run under both Windows 98 and Windows 95 or NT
   b. a software program that can run on NetWare 3.x or NetWare 4.0
   c. a client that allows Windows 98 machines to access Novell NetWare servers that have multiple clients such as NWLink and Novell IP for NetWare 5.0
   d. software that enables both TCP/IP and NetBIOS

4. When you install Microsoft Client for NetWare Directory Services, which of the following is automatically installed?
   a. NetWare Client for Windows 95/98
   b. Microsoft Client for Windows 95/98
   c. Client for Microsoft Networks
   d. Microsoft Client for NetWare Networks

5. Of the following Windows 98 components, which are involved in assisting network access? (Choose all correct answers.)
   a. Installable File System Manager
   b. Redirector
   c. Local file system
   d. SMB or NCP
   e. Transport protocol
   f. NDIS or ODI

6. Which of the following groups of users can use Net Watcher to manage shared folders on a remote Windows 98 computer?

   a. Power Users

   b. Power Administrators

   c. Domain Users

   d. Domain Administrators

7. Which is the highest version of NDIS supported by Windows 98?

   a. NDIS 2

   b. NDIS 3

   c. NDIS 3.1

   d. NDIS 5

8. Which of the following cannot be installed at the same time on the same Windows 98 computer?

   a. file and print sharing for Microsoft and NetWare networks

   b. Client for Microsoft and NetWare networks

   c. TCP/IP and NWLink

   d. NetBEUI and NetBIOS

9. Which of the following is another name for a client?

   a. Novell NetWare

   b. DLC

   c. redirector

   d. server

10. Which of the following can Windows 98 support? (Choose all correct answers.)

    a. multiple 32-bit redirectors

    b. multiple 16-bit redirectors

    c. a maximum of one 32-bit redirector

    d. a maximum of one 16-bit redirector

11. Which of the following files can you use if you do not want to connect to the Windows Internet Naming Service?

    a. Hosts

    b. Lmhosts

    c. NetBIOS.nam

    d. Long.nam

12. When you use the Net Watcher utility on a NetWare network, which of the following can you do on a remote Windows 98 computer? (Choose all correct answers.)

    a. disconnect users

    b. share folders

    c. disconnect access to a file

    d. watch the packet traffic between users and the remote Windows 98 computer

13. Which of the following clients can provide access to a NetWare server on Windows 98? (Choose all correct answers.)

    a. Client for Microsoft Networks

    b. Client for NetWare Networks

    c. NETX

    d. VLM

14. Which of the following SMB networks work with the Client for Microsoft Networks? (Choose all correct answers.)

    a. NetWare

    b. Samba

    c. DEC LAN Server

    d. LAN Manager

15. If you upgrade to Windows 98 from Windows 3.1 and you have a real-mode MS-DOS Client for Microsoft Networks installed on your computer, Windows 98 Setup installs which of the following clients on your computer?

    a. File and Printer Sharing for MS-DOS Networks

    b. File and Printer Sharing for NetWare Networks

    c. File and Printer Sharing for NetBIOS Networks

    d. File and Printer Sharing for Microsoft Networks

16. Which of the following types of computers are at the bottom of the priority list when a browse master and backup browsers are selected on a network?

    a. Windows 98

    b. Windows NT Workstation 4.0

    c. Windows NT Server 4.0

    d. Windows NT Workstation 5.0

17. If a Windows 98 client needs access to NetWare Directory Services, the Service for NetWare Directory Services is required. True or False?

18. Which of the following NetWare versions supports LFNs by default?
    a. NetWare 2.*x* and newer versions
    b. NetWare 3.*x* and newer versions
    c. NetWare 4.*x* and newer versions
    d. NetWare 5.0 only

19. Which of the following can you do to make a Novell NetWare client (other than Microsoft Client for NetWare Networks) work with the TCP/IP protocol that you can install from your Windows 98 CD? (Choose all correct answers.)
    a. Install the Novell IP protocol with Novell Client for Windows 95/98.
    b. Install Microsoft TCP/IP on your Novell Client for Windows 95/98.
    c. Install the Novell IP protocol with the NETX real-mode client.
    d. Install Novell NetWare version 5.0.

20. Which of the following Novell NetWare clients automatically checks the Sys/Public directory on the NetWare server for a policy file?
    a. Novell Client for Windows 95/98
    b. Microsoft Client for NetWare Networks
    c. Novell NETX Workstation
    d. Novell VLM Workstation

21. Which of the following types of information can you get about your computer using the Winipcfg utility while you are connected to the Internet? (Choose all correct answers.)
    a. IP address of your computer
    b. IP address of your default gateway
    c. IP address of your DNS server
    d. hardware address of the remote connection on your ISP

22. Which of the following addresses and names can you PING while you are connected to the Internet? (Choose all correct answers.)
    a. IP address of your computer
    b. IP address of *www.yahoo.com*
    c. 122.256.0.1
    d. 127.0.0.1

23. Which of the following best describes what you can see with the Tracert utility?
    a. IP address of your computer
    b. IP address of *www.yahoo.com*
    c. full path of IP addresses to a Web site that you cannot connect to
    d. full path of IP addresses until your search for a Web site gets to the maximum number of hops

Hands-on Projects

Project 13-1

In this project, you will learn to set up your Windows 98 computer as a browse master on a Microsoft network. For this project, you will need a Windows 98 computer with File and Printer Sharing for Microsoft Networks installed. If it is not already installed, complete the first six steps, which are taken directly from Chapter 7, where you learned to set up File and Printer Sharing for Microsoft Networks. If you have recently installed and enabled File and Printer Sharing for Microsoft Networks, you can start with Step 7.

1. Insert the Windows 98 Installation CD into your CD-ROM drive, and then open the **Configuration** tab of the Network applet.
2. Verify that "Client for Microsoft Networks" appears in the Primary Network Logon list box.

If Client for Microsoft Networks is not available, install it as follows: Click Add. In the Select Network Component Type dialog box, click Client, and then click Add. In the Select Network Client dialog box, highlight Microsoft in the list of Manufacturers, and then highlight Client for Microsoft Networks in the list of Network Clients. Click OK to return to the Network dialog box, then click OK again. When prompted, click Yes to restart your computer.

3. Click the **File and Printer Sharing** button. The File and Printer Sharing dialog box opens. This dialog box contains the "I want to be able to give others access to my files" check box, and the "I want to be able to allow others to print to my printer(s)" check box.
4. Click both check boxes to select them, and then click **OK**. You return to the Network dialog box.
5. Click **OK**.
6. Click **Yes**.

If you have already set up file and printer sharing on your Windows 98 computer, you should have skipped the previous steps. Start with Step 7, where you will configure browsing to allow others to see your computer on the network.

7. Open the **Configuration** tab of the Network applet.
8. In the list of network components, click **File and Printer Sharing for Microsoft Networks**, and click **Properties**. This opens the Advanced tab of the File and Printer Sharing for Microsoft Networks Properties dialog box.

9. In the Property list box, Browse Master is highlighted. Click the **Value** list arrow, view the options with respect to setting up your Windows 98 computer as a browse master, and then click **Enabled**. Remember, just because you enable your computer to be the browse master does not mean that it will become the browse master. Windows NT Server and Workstation computers have browse master priority.
10. Next, you need to change the LM Announce setting so that other computers on your network can find the resources that you are sharing. Click **LM Announce** in the Property list box, click the **Value** list arrow, click **Yes**, and then click **OK** to return to the Network dialog box.
11. Click **OK** to close the Network dialog box.
12. Click **Yes** to restart your computer.

PROJECT 13-2

In this project, you will learn to set up SAP and Workgroup Advertising to share files and/or printers from your Windows 98 computer on a Novell NetWare network. As you learned in Chapter 12, if you enable SAP advertising, you are announcing that you are sharing files and printers to other Novell clients on a Novell NetWare network. Enabling Workgroup Advertising configures your Novell clients in Microsoft-network-style workgroups. This project assumes you have just completed Project 13-1, in which you configured File and Printer Sharing for Microsoft Networks. Because you cannot enable file and printer sharing for both Microsoft and NetWare networks simultaneously, you begin this project by disabling File and Printer Sharing for Microsoft Networks.

1. Insert the Windows 98 Installation CD into the CD-ROM drive, and then open the **Configuration** tab of the Network applet.
2. In the list of network components, click **File and Printer Sharing for Microsoft Networks**, and then click **Remove**.
3. Click **Add**. The Select Network Component Type dialog box opens.
4. In the list of network components, click **Service**, and then click **Add**. The Select Network Service dialog box opens.
5. Click **Microsoft** in the Manufacturers list, click **File and Printer Sharing for NetWare Networks** in the Network Services list, and then click **OK** to return to the Network dialog box.
6. Click **OK**.
7. Click **Yes** to restart your computer.
8. Now that you have installed File and Printer Sharing for NetWare Networks, you can configure it. Open the **Configuration** tab of the Network applet.

9. Click **File and Printer Sharing for NetWare Networks** in the list of network components, and then click **Properties**. This opens the Advanced tab of the File and Printer Sharing for NetWare Networks Properties dialog box.
10. Verify that SAP Advertising is highlighted in the Properties list box, click the **Value** list arrow, and then click **Enabled**.
11. Click **Workgroup Advertising** in the Property list box, and then click the **Value** list arrow. Note that the different values in this list determine the position of your computers in the hierarchy of potential browsers. You need to allow at least one computer to be the browse master.
12. Click **Enabled: May Be Master**, and then click **OK** to return to the Network dialog box.
13. Click the **Access Control** tab. Note that you can no longer enable share-level access to your computer. NetWare networks work only with user-level access. Type the name of your NetWare network server in the "Obtain list of users and groups from:" text box.
14. Click **OK**.
15. Click **Yes** to restart your computer.

PROJECT 13-3

In Chapter 5, you already learned to use PING to test your connection to the Internet. In this project, you will take advantage of some of the more advanced capabilities of PING. To complete this project, you need a computer with Windows 98 installed and a connection to the Internet. A connection to the Internet through an ISP is acceptable. Before completing this project, you may want to review Project 5-5.

1. Activate your connection to the Internet through your ISP. If you need instructions on how to do this, refer to Chapter 5.
2. Click **Start**, point to **Programs**, and then click **MS-DOS prompt**.
3. At the MS-DOS prompt, type **PING 127.0.0.1** and press **Enter**. Watch the results. If you see lines starting with "Reply from...", TCP/IP is set up correctly on your computer. If not, either you are not connected to an ISP or you are connected to a network that is using a protocol other than TCP/IP. In this case, connect to a different network that is using TCP/IP such as your ISP and repeat Steps 1 and 2.
4. Next, you will use the Winipcfg utility to find your IP address. Click **Start**, and then click **Run**. In the Run dialog box, type **Winipcfg** in the Open text box, and then click **OK**.

5. This opens the IP Configuration dialog box. Write down the number in the IP Autoconfiguration address text box, which should consist of four numbers separated by decimal points. (If you see "0.0.0.0" in this text box, you are probably not connected to the Internet.)

6. Click **More Info**. This opens an expanded version of the IP Configuration dialog box.

7. Write down the IP Address listed in the DNS Servers text box.

8. Click **OK**.

9. Open the MS-DOS prompt window again.

10. At the MS-DOS prompt, type **PING** *your_ip_address* and then press **Enter**. (Be sure to substitute the IP address that you found with the Winipcfg utility for "*your_ip_address*".) Look for a response beginning with "Reply from…", indicating that the PING test was successful. If the test is not successful, check your physical connections, reboot your computer, and try again.

11. At the MS-DOS prompt, type **PING** *your_dns_server_address* and then press **Enter**. (Be sure to substitute the IP address that you found with the Winipcfg utility for "*your_dns_server_address*".) Even if you are connected to an ISP, you should have access to a DNS server. Until Windows NT 5.0 is released, there is no other practical way to navigate to the Internet. If this works, then your connection to your ISP is solid. Look for a response beginning with "Reply from…", indicating that the PING test was successful.

12. At the MS-DOS prompt, type **PING** *www.microsoft.com* and then press **Enter**. If you receive a successful reply, you are properly connected to the Internet. Look for a response beginning with "Reply from…", indicating that the PING test was successful.

PROJECT 13-4

In this project, you will trace the route taken by your connection to the Internet, using the Tracert utility. To complete this project, you need a computer with Windows 98 installed and a connection to the Internet. A connection to the Internet through an ISP is acceptable.

1. Activate your connection to the Internet through your ISP. If you need instructions on how to do this, refer to Chapter 5.

2. Click **Start**, point to **Programs**, and then click **MS-DOS prompt**.

3. Type **Tracert 10.0.0.1** and press **Enter**. As you learned in this chapter, the 10.0.0.1 IP address is reserved for private use, so you will receive a reply as shown in Figure 13-8.

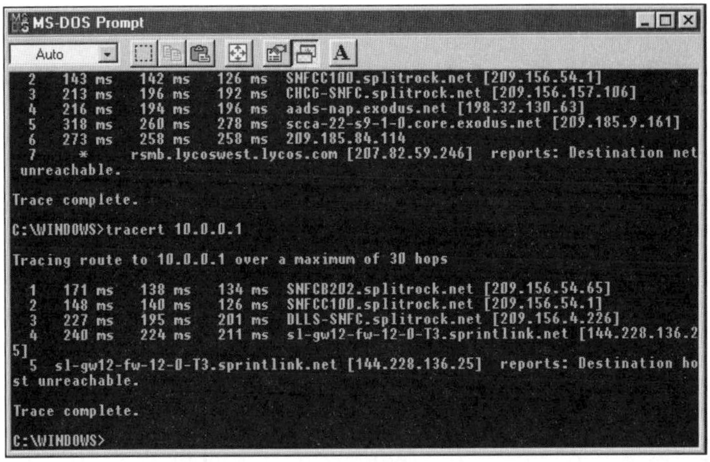

Advanced Windows 98 Networking Topics 503

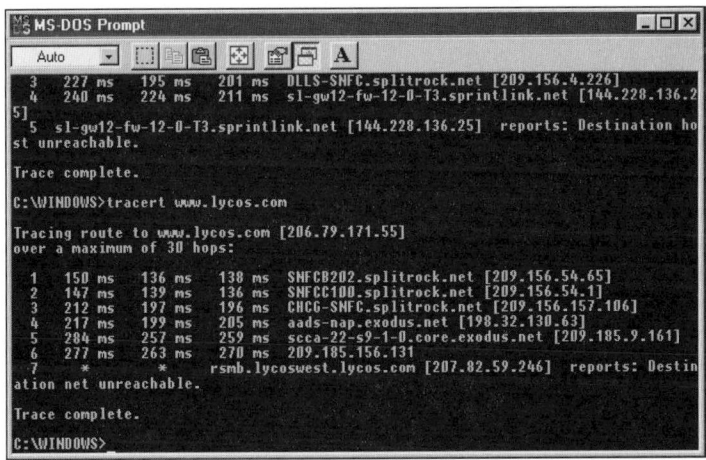

Figure 13-8 Tracing the route to an unusable address

4. Use your Web browser to visit various Web sites, in search of one that is unreachable. If you find one, return to your MS-DOS prompt. Type **Tracert** *www.unreachable.hij* and then press **Enter**. (Be sure to substitute the URL for the Web site that you could not reach for *unreachable.hij*.) If you cannot find an unreachable Web site, you can still see a sample of the result of this type of Tracert test in Figure 13-9.

Figure 13-9 Tracing the route through a broken connection

5. Look at number 7 in Figure 13-9. The message indicates that the destination net, in this case *www.lycos.com*, is not reachable. If this IP address referred to a location on your own network, you would have isolated the problem. You would simply have to check your records to find the computer, gateway, or router to which that particular IP address was assigned.

CASE PROJECTS

1. You've been asked to connect several existing Windows 98 machines (that were previously using LAN Workplace) to an existing Novell NetWare network. The Novell network has both 3.x and 4.0 generation servers. Write a report explaining which client components you would need to install, and any other steps required to integrate these machines into their new network environment.

2. New Generation, Inc. has 10 NetWare servers, plus two Windows NT servers in use, along with 220 client machines running a variety of Windows desktops. Management only wants to use one protocol. Which protocol makes the most sense in this environment? Explain why.

3. Because the developers at New Generation, Inc. require all network users to download files when they start their computers, the company's Windows 98 computers must access the network before Windows 98 (and its networking support) is fully loaded. How can you do this in the Windows 98 environment? What kind of software components are required in order to meet these requirements?

CHAPTER FOURTEEN

TROUBLESHOOTING

The term "troubleshooting" refers to the process of identifying and solving system problems. Before you can consider yourself an expert at troubleshooting Windows 98, you need to master a wide body of knowledge. This chapter is simply intended as a starting point. It by no means attempts to address troubleshooting methods for everything that can possibly go wrong with your system. If you understand the following material, you will be able to diagnose problems that are fundamental to your system—and you will know where to go for more information. This chapter starts with a basic discussion of the philosophy of troubleshooting. It continues with an introduction to troubleshooting the Windows 98 installation process, and then provides a discussion of the Windows 98 troubleshooting wizards. It then goes on to cover common Windows 98 problems, and concludes with a discussion of resources you can consult for help with some of the more difficult problems in Windows 98.

> **AFTER READING THIS CHAPTER AND COMPLETING THE EXERCISES YOU WILL BE ABLE TO:**
>
> - Discuss the elements of a systematic approach to troubleshooting
> - Perform regular maintenance on your Windows 98 system
> - Troubleshoot the installation process, and the startup and shutdown processes
> - Discuss the importance of checking cables and connections
> - Solve problems related to printers, disks, file systems, the network, and other components
> - Use the troubleshooting tools of MSInfo
> - Discuss other sources for troubleshooting information

Troubleshooting 101: Basic Skills and Approaches

There is more than one way to analyze a problem. Even with a system as complex as Windows 98, some people can identify a problem and its solution more or less simultaneously. However, as someone new to the field, you need to take a rigorous, step-by-step approach. First, you need to identify the problem. Then you can deduce the cause. Finally, you can begin to formulate a solution. In most cases, you will be troubleshooting network problems as a team, working with the other administrators in your department. Thus, it is important to document your every step, so your coworkers can easily understand the approach you've taken to identifying and solving a particular problem. When dealing with complex systems, it's especially important for the members of the troubleshooting team to use a consistent approach to all problems.

The standard approach to any serious technical problem is to use the basic scientific method, which involves three steps: observe, theorize, and test. As you will learn in the following sections, Windows 98 includes tools designed to facilitate all three steps. Note, however, that there are no clear dividing lines between these tools. For example, while ScanDisk can help you identify a problem, the logfile included with ScanDisk can also help you form a theory as to the cause of the problem.

Identifying the Problem

Identifying the cause of a problem is not as easy as you might at first think. For example, suppose a printer attached to a Windows 98 computer stops printing in the middle of a document. A user might e-mail you (the network administrator) to ask for your help. From the user's perspective, the problem is that the printer is not working. However, being more familiar with Windows 98, you can see that the real problem might have to do with incompatible protocols or drivers. Then again, the problem could simply be that the printer is out of paper.

When attempting to identify a problem, keep in mind that almost every system problem will manifest itself as a deviation from the baseline measurements discussed in Chapter 10. As you learned in Chapter 10, every time you make adjustments to your system, you should verify that the adjustments work as expected. Then you should establish a new baseline. Once you have established a working configuration, you can consider any deviation from that baseline a potential problem.

If you have good records of your baseline hardware and software configurations, you are well on your way towards finding the solution to just about any problem. As discussed in Chapter 10, one of the most important tools for establishing a baseline in Windows 98 is MSInfo, which allows you to identify the resources currently in use. It is also important to know the drivers associated with each one of your hardware components.

Once you have compared the current system measurements with the baseline, you can use System Monitor (also discussed in Chapter 10) to further define the symptoms of the problem. MSInfo also includes several tools to help determine what went wrong. For example, System File Checker can help you verify the integrity of your Windows 98 system files. Dr. Watson collects error information and makes recommendations about the configuration of your software. The Automatic Skip Driver agent tells you if there is a problem with the way that Windows 98 loaded on your system.

FORMING A THEORY

From your study of the rest of this book, you should have solid knowledge of Windows 98 and its systems. You know something about how the hardware and software use unidrivers and minidrivers in the Windows 98 architecture. If you have completed the case studies, you understand the interactions among the Windows 98 tools, utilities, and wizards. Combining this knowledge with your documented configuration and baseline, you have a basis for theorizing about the cause of any problem. Your formal theory should suggest a possible cause of a problem, as well as a potential solution.

Windows 98 includes several tools to help you formulate such a theory. The logfile included in ScanDisk can help you locate errors in your storage media. The Version Conflict Manager can help you identify drivers and libraries that may create conflicts between different programs. The Windows 98 Startup Menu can help you examine the reaction of your system to each startup command (line by line, if necessary). As you will learn later in this chapter, you can activate the Windows 98 Startup Menu in several different ways, including by pressing the F8 or Ctrl key when the "Starting Windows 98" picture appears on your screen. (As you will learn, this does not work for all configurations.)

The Resource Meter is yet another tool that you can use to formulate a theory. To open the Resource Meter, click Start, point to Programs, point to Accessories, point to System Tools, and then click Resource Meter. (See the Note below if you do not see Resource Meter on your System Tools menu.) If you see a message explaining the general purpose of the Resource Meter, click OK. A new icon, which looks like a cup with one or more stoplight colors, is added to your System Tray (adjacent to the desktop clock). Double-click this icon to open the Resource Meter window. The Resource Meter shows three gauges that look like the gauges on some automobiles:

- **User Resources**: Measures the resources available to maintain the windows in your display and manage input by mouse or keyboard.
- **GDI Resources**: Measures GDI resources. As you learned in Chapter 8, GDI manages monitor and printer graphics.
- **System Resources**: Measures the composite of User and GDI Resources.

The level of each resource is color coded: green means that resources are adequate, yellow indicates a problem, red means that the situation is critical. Different programs consume different amounts of resources. In this chapter, you will learn how to manage resources for things like your display and printers. If nothing else works, you may have to figure out which programs are consuming the most resources. Then you can use what you learned about System Monitor in Chapter 10 to decide whether you need more CPU speed or memory.

If the Resource Meter is not on the System Tools menu, you can install it from your Windows 98 Installation CD as follows: Insert the installation CD into your CD-ROM drive. Click Start, point to Settings, click Control Panel, and then double-click Add/Remove Programs. In the Add/Remove Programs Properties dialog box, click the Windows Setup tab, highlight System Tools, and then click Details. In the System Tools dialog box, select System Resource Meter, click OK, then click OK again back in the Add/Remove Programs Properties dialog box.

TESTING YOUR SOLUTION

The final step in the scientific method is testing your hypothesis. In other words, you need to test your proposed solution before implementing it throughout your system. Windows 98 includes several tools to help you test your hypothesis and solution. The System Configuration Utility can help you test changes to your startup files. Tools such as Version Conflict Manager and System File Checker allow you to create a backup, in case your solution does not work. However, Windows 98 does not keep records of every change you make to the system. Thus, before you test a solution, you should verify that you have carefully documented every system setting. That way, if your solution accidentally makes things worse, you can at least restore your original configuration.

When you have identified your problem, you may be faced with a series of possible solutions. For example, if the gas mileage in your car suddenly goes down, you can try a different grade of gasoline, clean your fuel injectors, or replace your engine. The smart thing to do is to start with the simplest (and cheapest) possible solution, and work your way up from there. However, you need to keep in mind that the simple and cheap solutions may not be effective. On the other hand, some solutions may be so expensive that you may, in the end, decide it's better simply to live with the problem. For example, trying a different grade of gasoline is easy, but may not work. Cleaning your fuel injectors regularly can help you maintain good gas mileage. Replacing your engine should be a last resort. Lower mileage might be less expensive than a new engine.

REGULAR MAINTENANCE

As discussed in Chapter 10, you can take advantage of a number of tools designed to help you perform regular maintenance on your system. For starters, you should run utilities such as ScanDisk, Disk Defragmenter, and Disk Cleanup on a regular basis.

You can also use MSInfo to analyze hardware, software, and drivers for conflicts. You should get in the habit of running some of the MSInfo tools, especially System File Checker, the Signature Verification tool, and Version Conflict Manager, whenever you install a new program. System File Checker ensures the integrity of your operating system files. The Signature Verification tool checks for valid copies of your software. Version Conflict Manager identifies those drivers that differ from the drivers that were installed originally. As you will learn in this chapter, all of these tools (which were introduced in Chapter 10) can also be used for troubleshooting. Once you're satisfied with your new configuration, these tools can help you set a new baseline.

Windows 98 also performs some preventive maintenance automatically. For example, whenever you install a new program that requires Registry settings, Registry Checker ensures that your program has modified the Registry in a workable fashion. If you are satisfied with the installation, it also allows you to create a backup for your new baseline Registry.

TROUBLESHOOTING THE WINDOWS 98 INSTALLATION

The Windows 98 installation includes self-correcting mechanisms for most foreseeable problems. As a result, the Setup wizard is able to detour around most roadblocks.

However, the Setup wizard does not address every possible combination of systems, drivers, and hardware in use today. Some combinations may cause the Setup wizard to stop. For example, a lack of conventional memory can stop the Windows 98 installation before it really has a chance to get started. In addition, the Setup wizard may stop if it finds hardware that it does not recognize. Also, keep in mind that hard disks with certain types of compression schemes can also create problems for the Setup wizard.

With the exception of the situation described in Chapter 12, if your Windows 98 installation stops, you simply need to restart the process and choose the Safe Recovery option. If you encounter multiple problems, the best approach generally is to restart the process as many times as it takes to get Windows 98 installed. The goal is to be able to open up the tools you need to fix your configuration.

Each time you restart the process, the Setup wizard will skip over areas where it previously ran into problems. The end result will be a flawed installation of Windows 98, but at least the software will have been installed. You can then attempt to correct the flaws by consulting the installation documentation created by the Setup wizard. You can use the documentation files to figure out how you need to change your system, in order to get Windows 98 running in a workable configuration. If you plan to install Windows 98 on more than one system, you can use the Safe Recovery option along with the documentation files to put together a working configuration on one machine. Then you can reproduce this configuration on other computers, using the batch script technique described in Chapter 12.

In the following sections you will learn about the documentation the Setup wizard creates when installing Windows 98. Then you will learn about some other issues to consider when installing Windows 98.

AUTOMATED SETUP DOCUMENTATION

Microsoft divides the operations of the Windows 98 Setup wizard into three sections: before, during, and after hardware detection. The Setup wizard documents the process in three files: Setuplog.txt, Detcrash.log, and Bootlog.txt. There is a fourth file if you are setting up a network configuration on your computer: Netlog.txt, which is created before the Bootlog.txt file. The Setup wizard uses these files to facilitate automated recovery whenever the Setup wizard is forced to stop. These files can be found in your root directory once they are created by the Setup wizard. The Setup wizard uses these files to document which components it has successfully installed and, more importantly, which components it was not able to install. These four files are described in the following sections.

Setuplog.txt

As the Windows 98 installation makes progress, but before it starts to detect hardware, it adds setup information to the Setuplog.txt file in a readable text format. Every step of the installation process, before hardware detection, is recorded in this file in a way that indicates whether the step was a success or a failure. If you have to restart the installation, the Setup wizard uses this file to ensure that the setup does not stop again for the same reason.

The Setuplog.txt file is long and complicated. You can analyze it in two different ways. First, you can search for the keywords "fail" and "error," which are associated with the components that could not be installed. Second, you can look at the end of the **Setuplog.txt** file when the Windows 98 Setup wizard stalls. Once you have restarted the Setup wizard as many times as is required to get to a working copy of Windows 98, you will be able to look through this file in a text editor, such as Windows 98 WordPad. Alternately, you can use the editor included with the Windows 98 ESD. (The Setuplog.txt file is typically too big for the Windows 98 Notepad text editor.) You should find an explanation for the stalled installation there.

If you are working on a computer where Windows 98 has been installed more than once, you may need to refer to the Setuplog.old file for the full setup.

Detlog.txt

As discussed earlier in this chapter, if the Setup wizard has a problem during the hardware detection phase of the Windows 98 installation, it creates the Detcrash.log file. However this file is not written in any human language. To learn about the hardware detection phase, you actually need to consult the **Detlog.txt** file.

If Setup has to recover from a failure during hardware detection, it checks the Detcrash.log file for installation status to make sure that it does not crash again for the same reason. Once the Windows 98 Setup wizard has completed the hardware installation, it creates the Detlog.txt file, which contains information based on the binary data in the Detcrash.log file.

Every time you use the Add New Hardware Wizard to detect non-plug and play hardware, you create a new Detlog.txt file. If you have problems installing new equipment after installing Windows 98, the Detlog.txt file can help you identify the reasons. Like the Setuplog.txt file, the Detlog.txt file can be quite long. To learn about the hardware that was and was not detected during any installation, you can search for the following terms:

- **Detected**: Search for this term to find the Plug and Play hardware devices that have been detected. Each detected device is listed, along with a number in brackets indicating the order in which it was detected, e.g. [1].
- **VerifyHW**: Search for this term to find hardware components that were configured when the Windows 98 Setup wizard analyzed a previous version of the Registry, for example components from an installation of Windows 95.

- **Error**: Search for this term to find errors that were logged by the Setup wizard.

Netlog.txt

After hardware detection, the Setup wizard stores documentation regarding your network configuration in the Netlog.txt file. The Windows 98 Setup wizard divides the network detection process into four categories: adapters, protocols, clients, and services. The Setup wizard starts documenting your hardware configuration in the Netlog.txt file with lines such as "Examining class net" and "Examining class nettrans." You can search the **Netlog.txt** file for the following, which describe the network components installed by the Windows 98 Setup wizard:

- **NET**: Detected network adapters. The Setup wizard looks for and detects existing installed network adapters.
- **NETTRANS**: Detected network protocols, such as NetBEUI and TCP/IP
- **NETCLIENT**: Detected network clients, such as Client for Microsoft Networks, or other redirectors from your previous operating system
- **NETSERVICES**: Detected network services, such as File and Printer Sharing

As you learned in Chapters 12 and 13, the Setup wizard may replace some real-mode network components with the corresponding 32-bit components. If the components are already suitable to a Windows 98 configuration, the Setup wizard imports the necessary data from your previous configuration.

Bootlog.txt

Once the Windows 98 Setup wizard has copied files, detected hardware, and set up network components, it starts your Windows 98 system for the first time. If you run into problems during this phase, you can examine the **Bootlog.txt** file to see if your drivers have loaded successfully.

You can also have problems with your drivers after installing Windows 98. To check for this type of problem, you can create a new Bootlog.txt file after installing Windows 98, as follows: When you reboot your system, press F8 when you see the line "Starting Windows 98." For most installations, this brings you to the Windows 98 Startup Menu. Alternately, you can use MSInfo to configure your boot process to always open the Startup Menu when you reboot, as follows:

1. Click Start, point to Programs, point to Accessories, point to System Tools, and then click System Information.
2. On the menu bar, click Tools, and then click System Configuration Utility.
3. In the General tab of the System Configuration Utility dialog box, click Advanced.
4. In the Advanced Troubleshooting Settings dialog box, select the "Enable Startup Menu" check box.

5. Click OK, and then click OK in the System Configuration Utility dialog box.

6. Click Yes to restart your computer.

7. When you see the Startup Menu, type 2 and press Enter to reload Windows 98 while creating a Bootlog.txt file. You will learn more about the Startup Menu later in this chapter.

It is worth taking some time to examine the long C:\Bootlog.txt file to understand what Windows 98 does in the startup sequence. Once you have set up Windows 98 to create this file, open a text editor such as Windows WordPad (click Start, point to Programs, point to Accessories, and then click WordPad) and use the Find command on the Tools menu to search for files containing the word "fail." This will display a list of drivers that did not load properly. Fortunately, not all drivers need to load successfully. The list of drivers that are not strictly necessary includes:

- **DSOUND**: Most up-to-date sound drivers can support the DirectX DirectSound driver. DirectSound was created in support of DirectX-based games. If you do not have any DirectX-based multimedia games, this driver will not load.

- **EBIOS**: This driver will not load if you do not have an extended BIOS. One example of an extended BIOS supports some auxiliary hard disk drivers.

- **Ndis2sup.vxd**: If you have no NDIS 2 network drivers, this will list as a load failure. Because NDIS 3.1 and above is the standard today, this is usually not a concern.

It is important to look for drivers that failed to load in the C:\Bootlog.txt file. However, if you do find a driver that failed to load, this may not necessarily be a problem. Try to determine the function of the driver by consulting Windows 98 Help files, Microsoft TechNet (which you will learn about later in this chapter), or the Internet, and then try to decide for yourself whether the driver affects a system that you're using in Windows 98.

INCOMPATIBLE COMPRESSION REGIMES

You will run into problems installing Windows 98 if you do not have a generous amount of free hard disk space. One solution to a lack of hard disk space is to install a larger, or an additional, hard disk. However, even though the price of a hard disk on a per megabyte basis is going down, the installation of a new hard disk is a significant investment of money and time. As an alternative, you can install Windows 98 on drives compressed through the **DriveSpace** and **DoubleSpace** utilities. However, Microsoft does not recommend this approach.

If your hard drive has been compressed with third-party tools such as SuperStor or XtraDrive, the Setup wizard won't be able to proceed. To avoid such problems, Microsoft recommends that you deactivate any of these, as well as any other compression tools that are not fully compatible with DriveSpace or DoubleSpace. Instead of compressing your hard drive when space is tight, consider moving nonessential files to a removable drive. Or consider installing a new hard drive.

CONVENTIONAL MEMORY REQUIREMENTS

The Windows 98 Setup wizard includes two real-mode programs, Setup.exe and Scandisk.exe. These programs require a minimum of 432 KB of free conventional memory. This may not sound like a lot for a computer that meets the minimum Windows 98 RAM requirement of 16 MB. However, as you learned in Chapter 9, conventional memory includes only the first 640 KB of RAM.

Part of this first 640 KB of RAM may be occupied by TSRs, or programs that terminate and stay resident. As described in Chapter 9, you can check your level of free conventional memory by running the "mem" utility at the DOS prompt. The conventional memory limit only applies to the Windows 98 Setup wizard. You can choose from a number of options for your TSRs while the Setup wizard is active. The simplest approach is to deactivate or uninstall any TSRs, but especially those that are considered unsafe in Windows 98. (In Chapter 10, you learned about the different categories of unsafe TSRs.) If you still need your TSRs after Windows 98 is installed, you can restore them to your startup files later.

You could also choose to move any TSRs to the high memory area. The high memory area is the RAM between conventional memory (the first 640 KB) and extended memory (above 1 MB). To use your high memory area for TSRs, add the following command to your computer's Config.sys file: device = himem.sys.

If your MS-DOS system is 5.0 or higher (the DOS drivers included with Windows 95 are considered equivalent to MS-DOS 7.0), you can also add these commands to your Config.sys file:

- device = emm386.exe noems
- dos = high, umb

In some configurations, one of the last two commands can lead to a "Standard Mode: Fault in MS-DOS Extender" error message. Some trial and error may be required.

Other memory requirements can also affect the Windows 98 installation. If you are installing Windows 98 as an upgrade from Windows 95 or Windows 3.x, make sure that you have closed all currently running programs. If you receive the error message "Cannot Open File *.inf," you may need to disable the SMARTDrive system. Check your Autoexec.bat file. If you see a statement such as: "C:\DOS\smartdrv.exe," you can disable SMARTDrive by adding "REM" in front of this statement so it reads "REM C:\DOS\smartdrv.exe."

TROUBLESHOOTING THE STARTUP AND SHUTDOWN PROCESSES

Problems starting and ending Windows 98 can be the most frustrating problems that you can have on your Windows 98 computer. To help troubleshoot such problems, Microsoft includes a number of tools specially suited to the task. For starters, you can choose from a series of special wizards known as troubleshooters. As you will see, a troubleshooter walks you through the process of solving a problem. Along the way, a troubleshooter helps you use many of the Windows 98 troubleshooting tools.

In the following sections, you will learn to use a troubleshooter devoted to startup and shutdown problems. Then you will take a look at some of the tools at work behind the troubleshooters.

STARTUP AND SHUTDOWN TROUBLESHOOTER

To look at the variety of troubleshooters, click Start, then click Help. In the Windows Help dialog box, click the Contents tab, click Troubleshooting, and then click Windows 98 Troubleshooters. You can see the list of troubleshooters in Figure 14-1.

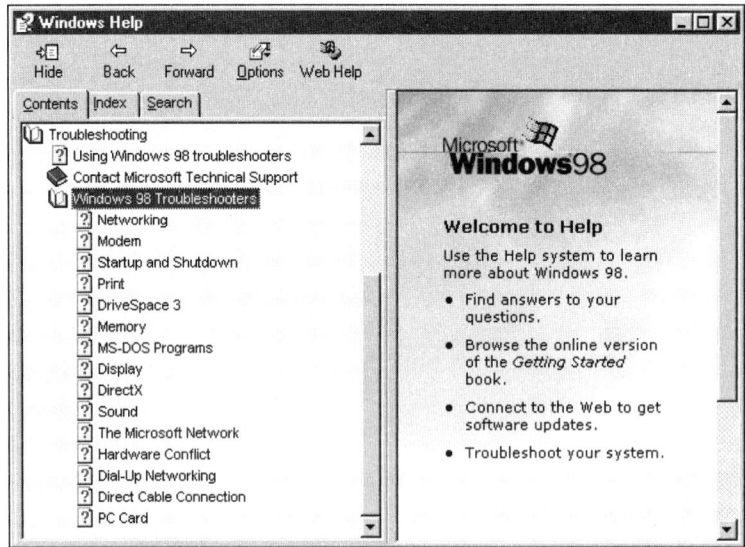

Figure 14-1 Windows 98 Help Menu troubleshooters

To examine the Startup and Shutdown troubleshooter:

1. Click Startup and Shutdown in the left-hand pane of the Windows Help dialog box. In the right-hand pane, you see three options, as shown in Figure 14-2. For this exercise, assume that the "My computer stops responding when I try to start Windows 98" option is the correct choice.

2. Click the "My computer stops responding when I try to start Windows 98" box, and then click Next.

3. You are asked if it's possible to restart your computer in safe mode. The troubleshooter also provides directions for starting your computer in safe mode. Note that Windows 98 corrects many of its own problems when you go into Safe Mode. If necessary, you can install or revise a number of different components in Safe Mode. Click No, and then click Next.

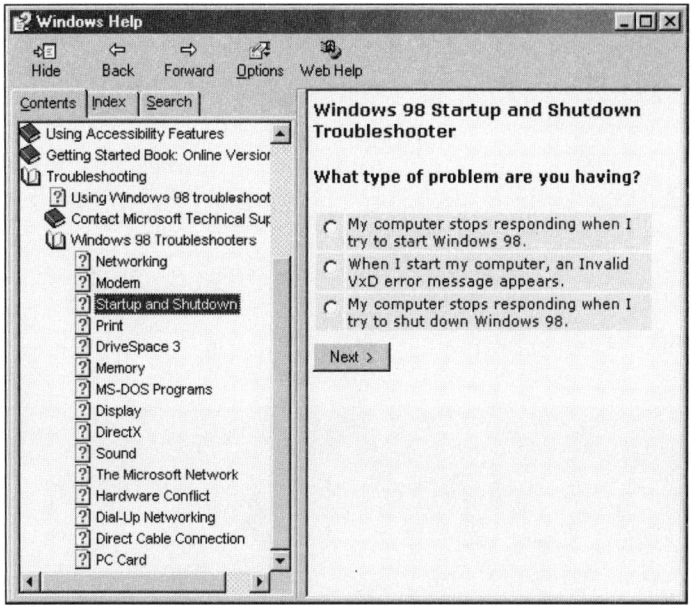

Figure 14-2 Startup and Shutdown troubleshooter

4. You are given directions for trying to restart your computer with the safe mode command prompt option. This brings you to the C:\ prompt, from which you can run a number of troubleshooting utilities in the C:\Windows\Command folder. Click No, and then click Next.

5. You are given instructions on how to check whether your primary hard disk is working, using your Windows 98 Startup Disk, also known as your ESD. Click I don't know and then click Next.

6. You are given instructions on how to overlay software or third-party disk compression software. Click No, and then click Next.

7. You are asked to check your computer for viruses. Click No, and then click Next.

8. You are asked to check the status of your hard disk with the ScanDisk utility. Click No, and then click Next.

9. You are asked to verify the CMOS settings within your computer. Your CMOS settings determine how your computer keeps time, and configures your disk before starting Windows 98. Click No, and then click Next.

10. You are asked to restart your computer with your ESD, then to transfer system files to your hard disk. Click No, and then click Next.

11. You are given instructions on how to check your file system for damage. Click No, and then click Next.

12. The troubleshooter states that it is unable to solve your problem. Each of the other troubleshooters are just as or even more detailed. Click Start Over to return to the original options in this Troubleshooter.

The Startup and Shutdown troubleshooter that you just examined referred to several troubleshooting tools, including safe mode, the Emergency Startup Disk, and the System Configuration Utility. You will learn more about these and other tools in the following sections.

STARTUP MENU AND SAFE MODE

You can use the Startup Menu (shown in Figure 14-3) to troubleshoot the boot process.

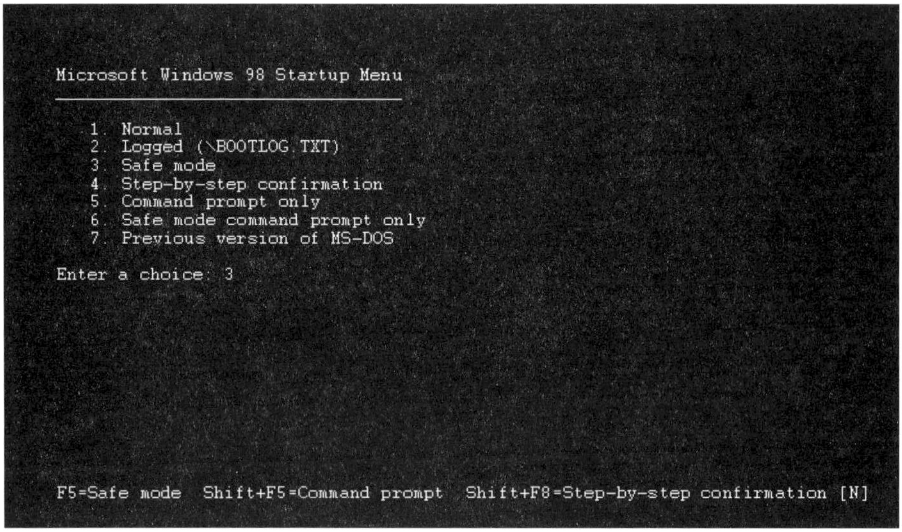

```
Microsoft Windows 98 Startup Menu

  1. Normal
  2. Logged (\BOOTLOG.TXT)
  3. Safe mode
  4. Step-by-step confirmation
  5. Command prompt only
  6. Safe mode command prompt only
  7. Previous version of MS-DOS

Enter a choice: 3

F5=Safe mode  Shift+F5=Command prompt  Shift+F8=Step-by-step confirmation [N]
```

Figure 14-3   Windows 98 Startup Menu

If Windows 98 has problems booting, it automatically displays the Startup Menu. In addition, configuration problems can cause Windows 98 to display the Startup Menu. Otherwise, you can display the Startup Menu in three different ways:

- **Press the F8 key when the "Starting Windows 98" message appears**: This may not work if you have not installed MS-DOS and/or Windows 3.x on your computer previously.
- **Press the Ctrl (Control) key while your system is booting**: This may not work if the Ctrl key is used for some other purpose, such as your hard-disk initialization software.
- **Use MSInfo to configure your boot process so that the Startup Menu always opens**: You'll find the relevant steps earlier in this chapter, in the discussion on the Bootlog.txt file.

If the Startup Menu should display automatically (when you haven't taken any steps to display it), you should select Option 3 or 6, to go into Safe Mode. Option 3, Safe Mode, brings you to the graphical Windows 98 screen. Option 6, Safe Mode Command Prompt Only, brings you to the MS-DOS style C:\command prompt. The Safe Mode options load the minimum number of drivers required to allow you to troubleshoot the parameters of your Windows 98 system. One example of a safe mode driver is the VGA driver that substitutes for the video driver you have installed. If the hard disk is compressed, safe mode loads DoubleSpace or DriveSpace drivers as appropriate.

The remaining five options on the Startup Menu are detailed in the following list:

- **Normal**: If you are confident that nothing is wrong, use this option to open up Windows with all normal startup and Registry defaults.

- **Logged**: This option creates a new Bootlog.txt file, which you learned about earlier in this chapter.

- **Step-By-Step Confirmation**: This allows you to confirm every line in every startup file, one at a time. If you know you have a failure in your startup sequence, this can help you isolate the command that is causing the problem.

- **Previous version of MS-DOS**: This option starts the previous version of MS-DOS. This assumes that a previous version of MS-DOS is installed and that the C:\Msdos.sys file contains the following line: BootMulti=1 as described in Chapter 12. If your system dual boots with Windows 3.x, use this option, and then start Windows 3.x from DOS.

- **Command Prompt Only**: This option brings you to the MS-DOS command prompt, with a full set of real-mode drivers.

EMERGENCY STARTUP DISK

As you first learned in Chapter 2, when you install Windows 98 on your computer, the Setup wizard prompts you to create an Emergency Startup Disk (ESD). The ESD can be used to boot up your computer and access system files even when Windows 98 will not start. The ESD actually includes more than 1.44 MB of files. This is more than can normally fit on a 3½-inch disk. Some of the utilities are compressed in a cabinet file on your ESD. They are uncompressed onto your RAM, in an area known as a **RAMDrive**, which is set up to look like a small hard drive on your computer. The RAMDrive has its own drive letter, and contains the following real-mode files:

- **Attrib.exe**: Adds or removes file characteristics such as whether a file is read-only, system, or hidden

- **Chkdsk.exe**: A simpler version of ScanDisk

- **Debug.exe**: For program debugging

- **Edit.com**: Text editor

- **Ext.exe**: File extraction program

- **Format.com**: For formatting disks
- **Mscdex.exe**: Microsoft real-mode CD-ROM driver installer
- **Scandisk.exe**: The real-mode ScanDisk utility that you have used throughout this book
- **Scandisk.ini**: Settings to allow you to customize what ScanDisk checks
- **Sys.com**: Transfers system files
- **Uninstal.exe**: Uninstalls Windows 98

Although you can boot your system with a Windows 95 ESD, the Windows 98 ESD includes a number of unique capabilities that can save your system.

When you boot your computer with the ESD, you see a number of lines relating to the various stages of the boot process. It is important to watch the boot process for the location of the RAMDrive, so that you know where to access the unloaded system files. When you restart your computer with the ESD in your 3½-inch disk drive, you will see the following line: Microsoft RAMDrive Virtual Drive X (where X stands for the drive letter for your RAMDrive).

The following list describes some ways in which the ESD tools can be useful:

- **Restoring system files**: If the system files somehow get deleted or corrupted in your configuration, you will probably need the ESD to boot your system. You can then use the ESD to restore the system files to your hard disk. Booting from your ESD will create a RAMDrive. Change your prompt to that RAMDrive letter, probably D, E, or F. Type that letter followed by a ":" and press Enter. Then enter the "SYS C:" command to transfer the basic system files to your root drive.

- **Restoring Command.com**: If the operating system file Command.com is not available, you can copy it from your ESD. Normally, you need to change the attributes of this file. As you learned earlier in this section, the attributes of a file indicate whether that file is hidden, read-only, or a system file. Go to your RAMDrive as discussed earlier. From your RAMDrive, type "attrib –r –s –h A:\command.com" and press Enter. This file should now be readable. You can now copy this file to your root directory.

- **Checking TEMP directory parameters**: One essential requirement for a number of programs and utilities is a temporary directory on a disk with sufficient room to handle the needs of each program. If some programs are stopping prematurely, run a SET command from the DOS prompt. The output on your screen is a series of variables, including the location of your TEMP directory. You can check the disk partition that contains the TEMP directory for adequate space. The amount of room required depends on the program. If you are having memory problems with a particular program, consult the documentation for that program.

- **Verifying the integrity of your hard disk**: You can run several disk maintenance utilities from the RAMDrive; for example, you can format disks, and use Chkdsk and ScanDisk to verify the basic integrity of each disk drive.

- **Restoring the Registry**: If you ever install something on your computer that revises the Registry in a way that keeps your computer from booting, you can run the ScanReg /restore command. ScanReg and ScanRegW were discussed in more detail in Chapter 3. The ScanReg command is located in your C:\Windows\command directory.

CONFLICTS

A number of conflicts can keep you from being able to start or shut down Windows 98 properly. You could have problems before Windows 98 begins to load. You might have a driver that conflicts with the startup or shutdown of Windows 98. In addition, while deleting a program, you may have deleted a driver that you need for some other program.

When you turn it on, your computer reads from the basic input/output system (BIOS) before starting Windows 98. Every computer has some configuration settings based on its BIOS, where you can at least set basic parameters for your system clock, CD-ROM, and hard disk. If the settings in your BIOS are wrong, your computer will not be able to read your hard disk. The correct settings depend on your hard disk. If you have reached this point in the Windows 98 Troubleshooting Wizard, consult the documentation for your hard disk for the correct settings for your BIOS. How you get to this menu (sometimes called BIOS Setup) depends on your BIOS. Typically, the startup sequence on your display will tell you to press a certain key to get to this menu, such as F2, Del, or Ctrl. Consult the documentation for your BIOS or motherboard for guidance on this menu.

A number of third-party disk- and file-related programs may conflict with Windows 98 disk and file management software. As you learned in Chapter 8, utilities provided by your hard disk manufacturer may conflict with your BIOS or with Windows 98. What's more, viruses can make it difficult or impossible for your computer to read part or all of your hard disk. If none of these turns out to be the problem, you can examine the current state of the partitions on your hard disk as follows: click Start, point to Programs, and then click MS-DOS Prompt. At the C:\ prompt, type Fdisk /status.

Perhaps the biggest problems during the startup and shutdown processes have to do with drivers. As you learned in earlier chapters, drivers are commonly used to support multiple programs. When you remove a program, you should not haphazardly delete everything associated with that program. The Windows 98 Install/Uninstall utility is designed to remove only those drivers solely associated with a particular application. To get to this utility, click Start, point to Settings, click Control Panel, double-click the Add/Remove Programs icon, and then click the Install/Uninstall tab, if required. Sometimes when you install different programs, you install different versions of the same driver. Later in this chapter, you will learn to use Version Conflict Manager to find conflicting drivers.

System Configuration Utility

In previous sections, you learned about a number of different issues that could make it difficult for you to start or shut down Windows 98. Another potential problem can occur with the drivers that you load with basic system configuration files such as Autoexec.bat, Config.sys, System.ini, and Win.ini. You can use the System Configuration Utility (SCU) to audit and experiment with these files. In fact, the SCU is one utility from which you can edit each of the system configuration files. (It is similar to the Windows 3.x Sysedit utility.) You can open SCU through MSInfo, as follows: Click Start, point to Programs, point to Accessories, point to System Tools, and then click System Information. On the MSInfo menu bar, click Tools, then click System Configuration Utility.

The following sections describe the six tabs in the System Configuration Utility.

General tab

As shown in Figure 14-4, the General tab in the System Configuration Utility provides three optional startup sequences that you can use when starting your Windows 98 system. The default is Normal startup, whereby all devices and drivers are loaded automatically. The second option is Diagnostic startup, in which the Startup Menu appears when Windows 98 is first launched. The third option, Selective startup, controls the use of the files shown in the other five tabs of the SCU.

When you choose Selective startup, you can choose to omit any of these startup files in the Windows 98 startup cycle by deselecting the appropriate check box. The third file in the list, Winstart.bat, is active only if you have real-mode Windows terminate-and-stay-resident (TSR) programs installed on your system. On occasion, the Windows 98 Setup wizard moves some specialized TSRs from Autoexec.bat to Winstart.bat. In most cases, the Winstart.bat option will be inactive and unchecked.

The Advanced button in the General tab opens the Advanced Troubleshooting Settings dialog box, shown in Figure 14-5. Several options in this dialog box relate to the use of hard disk drivers, while others relate to settings for the startup and shutdown sequences. There are also settings to force the use of a VGA driver, to set memory addresses for adapters, and to test Windows 98 behavior if you suspect a problem with your RAM. The following list describes these options in detail:

- **Disable System ROM Breakpoint**: Most computers include some read-only memory (ROM) to at least store critical startup information, such as information from your BIOS. When you start your computer, it reads the BIOS from your ROM. The breakpoint occurs when the system converts from real-mode to protected-mode. If there is a problem with the ROM space that contains your BIOS, this option changes the conversion point, which can keep Windows 98 from stalling during system startup. You can also specify this option when starting Windows 98 from a DOS prompt with the command: "C:\win.com /d:s."

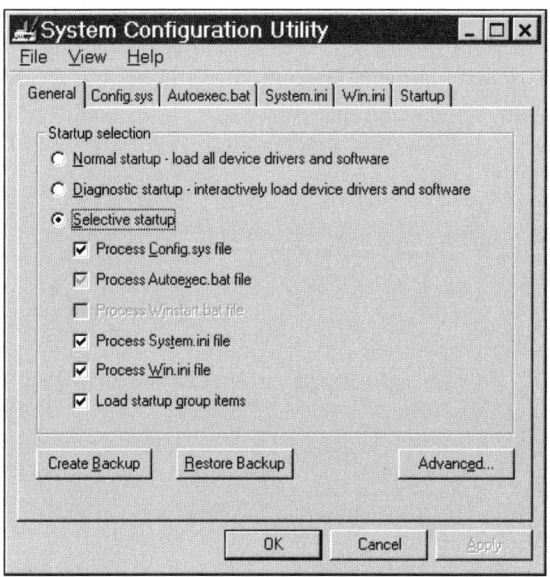

Figure 14-4 System Configuration Utility, General tab

- **Disable Virtual HD IRQ**: Some hard disks, by default, attempt to send hard disk interrupt requests (HD IRQ) to the CPU via the controller. As you learned in Chapter 10, every hardware component requires an interrupt (IRQ) channel to communicate with the CPU. This IRQ can conflict with the Windows 98 protected-mode hard disk IRQ. For computers with a hard disk with its own IRQ, this option can keep Windows 98 from stalling during system startup.

- **EMM Exclude A000-FFFF**: A000 through FFFF are memory addresses. When some hardware cards (e.g., sound, video, modems, etc.) use these addresses, Windows 98 cannot find these cards in computer memory. Therefore, to allow these cards to work, you may need to exclude these memory addresses.

- **Force Compatibility mode disk access**: This option forces your computer to access the hard disk through a real-mode hard disk driver. This is appropriate for those hard disks that are not compatible with 32-bit protected-mode drivers.

- **VGA 640 x 480 x 16**: This option loads the standard Windows 98 VGA-mode driver in place of any graphics driver that might be causing some sort of video problem. You do not need to go into safe mode to load this driver.

- **Use SCSI Double-buffering**: Some SCSI drives require two buffers for their data. This option inserts the line DoubleBuffer=2 in the C:\Msdos.sys file, thereby enabling double-buffering for all SCSI drives, whether or not it is required.

- **Enable Startup Menu**: This option configures Windows 98 to display the Startup Menu automatically when the operating system starts.

- **Disable ScanDisk after bad shutdown**: This option keeps ScanDisk from running whenever Windows 98 is shut down improperly. Because a premature shutdown can easily corrupt system files, you should be wary of using this option. However, if you are in the middle of troubleshooting a shutdown issue and you know that corruption on your hard disk is not causing the problem, this option can save time by speeding up the boot process.
- **Limit memory to __ MB**: This option limits the amount of memory used by Windows 98. It can be useful if you suspect a problem with your physical RAM. However, Windows 98 may not start normally if this is set at anything less than the recommended minimum of 16 MB of RAM.
- **Disable fast shutdown**: When you shut down Windows 98, the default is a fast shutdown, which is supposed to be faster than the shutdown of Windows 95. Microsoft claims that this faster shutdown is possible because of the way Windows 98 is cached. For some systems, the Windows 98 fast shutdown technique seems to make little difference in actual shutdown time. If you need to troubleshoot the shutdown sequence, you should disable fast shutdown.
- **Disable UDF file system**: As you learned in previous chapters, the UDF file system is the Windows 98 file system that supports digital video disk (DVD) players. Consult the documentation for your player. If it is not compatible with UDF, check this option.
- **Enable Pentium F0 (Lock CmpXchg) workaround**: If you have a computer with an older Intel Pentium CPU, it may be susceptible to a flaw in which a certain sequence of binary digits will stop your computer. The literature on this topic suggests that this sequence would only be input with malicious intent. If you have this type of Pentium CPU, you may wish to check this option.

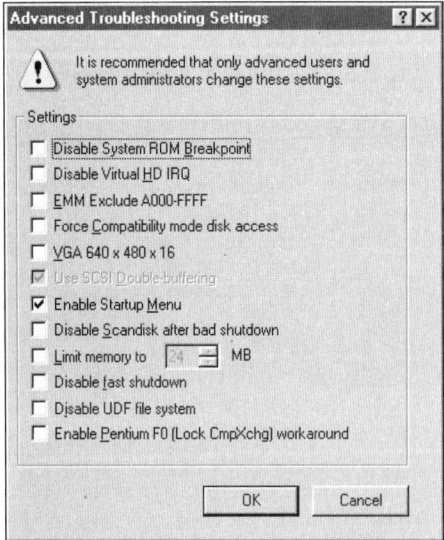

Figure 14-5 System Configuration Utility, Advanced Troubleshooting Settings

Config.sys Tab

As shown in Figure 14-6, the Config.sys tab in the System Configuration Utility displays the contents of your Config.sys file. Using the Config.sys tab, you can disable or edit every line in this file. Click the Config.sys tab. If you have upgraded your system from Windows 3.x, you may notice a REM at the beginning of some lines. These lines are not executed, only retained for possible future use. If you have a system that does not require the use of real-mode drivers, you do not need the Config.sys or Autoexec.bat files. If you ever need to boot into DOS or Windows 3.x, you should keep these files.

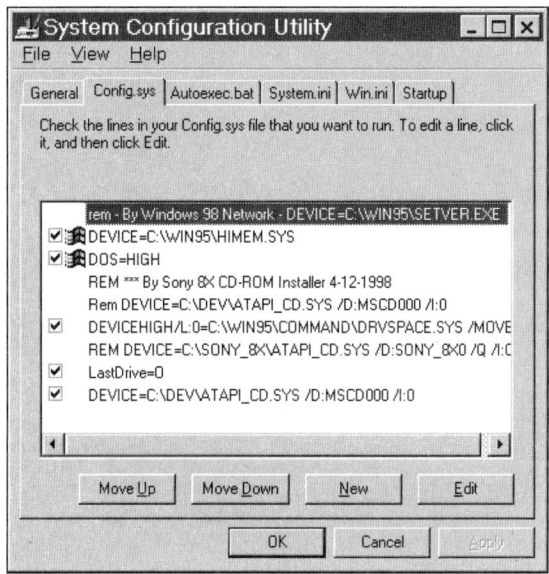

Figure 14-6 System Configuration Utility, Config.sys tab

In the Config.sys file you can disable any line next to a check mark. Suppose, for instance, that your CD-ROM is not running in Windows 98, and that you suspect a conflict with the real-mode driver loaded through Config.sys. By deselecting the "DEVICE=C:\DEV\ATAPI_CD.SYS/D:MCSD000 /l:0" check box, you could prevent your computer from loading the real-mode CD-ROM driver. (This is definitely *not* something you should try now.)

Autoexec.bat Tab

The Autoexec.bat tab in the System Configuration Utility displays the content of your Autoexec.bat file. You can use the Autoexec.bat tab to edit or disable every line in this file. If you want Windows 98 to disable a line in your Autoexec.bat file, uncheck the box next to that line.

The next two tabs in the System Configuration Utility, System.ini and Win.ini, give you access to configuration files originally designed for the first versions of Windows (1.x, 2.x, and 3.x). While the System.ini file contains hardware information, the Win.ini file contains user-specific information. They roughly correspond to the System.dat and User.dat files from your Registry.

System.ini

The System.ini tab of the System Configuration Utility, shown in Figure 14-7, allows you to edit or disable the contents of the System.ini file.

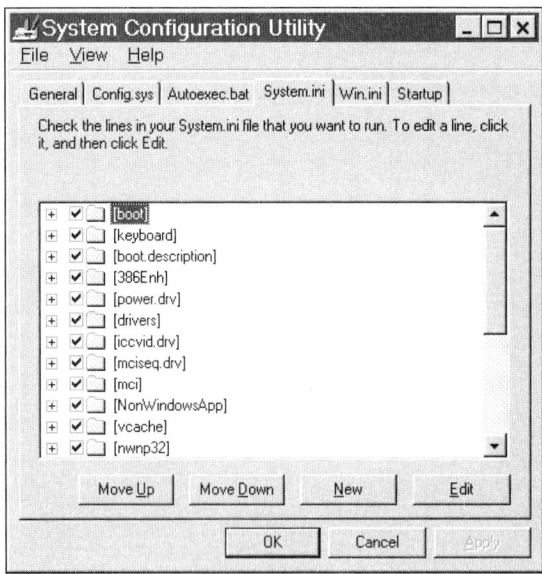

Figure 14-7 System Configuration Utility, System.ini tab

Note that the organization of the System.ini file on this tab is little different from that of the actual file itself. You can see this for yourself by comparing the System.ini tab with the actual file displayed in Notepad. To compare these two, first click the System.ini tab. Now open your own C:\Windows\System.ini file in Windows Notepad. Arrange the System Configuration Utility dialog box and your Notepad with the System.ini file side by side.

The categories as listed in the System.ini brackets correspond to the folder structures in the System.ini tab. The advantage of the System.ini tab is that it allows you to try out changes to the System.ini file without modifying the file itself. If you make an error, it is easy to restore the full functionality of the original System.ini file by rechecking whatever you unchecked.

Win.ini

The Win.ini tab of the System Configuration Utility, shown in Figure 14-8, organizes the Win.ini file in the same way the System.ini tab organizes the System.ini file. Like the System.ini tab, the Win.ini tab allows you to experiment with a minimum of risk.

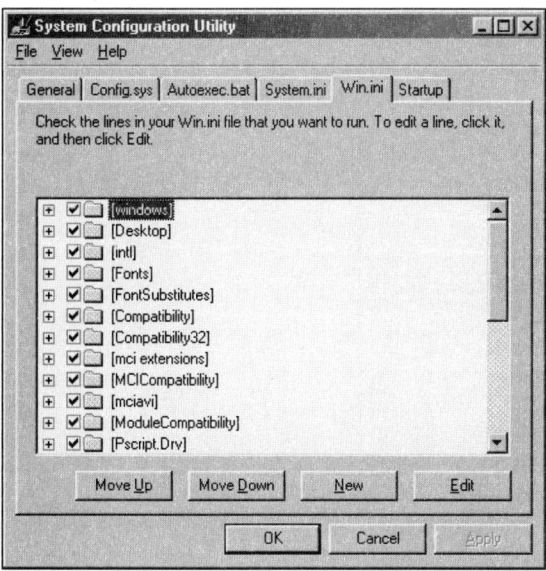

Figure 14-8 System Configuration Utility, Win.ini tab

Startup tab

The Startup tab of the System Configuration Utility, shown in Figure 14-9, allows you to modify the list of programs that start when you start Windows 98. This list takes two different forms within Windows 98. First, there is the Startup tab in the System Configuration Utility. Second, there is the StartUp menu that you access by clicking Start, pointing to Programs, and then pointing to StartUp. (Although the Startup tab is related to the StartUp folder, they are two different things.) The items on the StartUp menu correspond to the items you include in the StartUp folder. The Startup tab lists the programs that start along with Windows 98, and includes programs over and above those in the StartUp folder. If you do not want programs in your StartUp folder to run when you start Windows 98, you need to disable each program in both this tab and the StartUp folder.

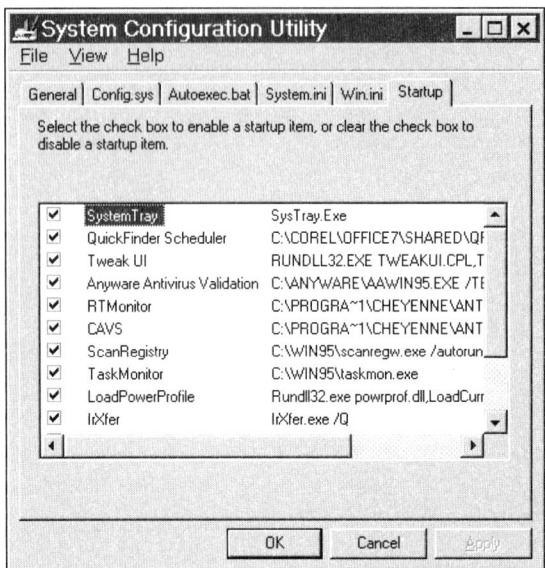

Figure 14-9 System Configuration Utility, Startup tab

You can disable programs in the System Configuration Utility Startup tab by unchecking them. To disable programs in your StartUp folder, click Start, point to Programs, and then click Windows Explorer. In the left-hand pane, click the plus sign next to Windows. Click the plus sign next to Start Menu, then the plus sign next to Programs, and then highlight the StartUp folder. In the right-hand pane, you can see the current list in your StartUp folder. Highlight the items you want to disable, and then press the Delete key. In the Confirm File Delete dialog box, click OK.

SYSTEM FILE CHECKER

The final tool you can use when troubleshooting the startup and shutdown processes is the System File Checker utility. Generally, you should use System File Checker if another tool such as Dr. Watson points to some problem with a system file. As described in Chapter 10, System File Checker (SFC) performs a cyclic redundancy check (CRC) on the Windows 98 system files. As you learned in Chapter 10, if the CRC numbers from your files and the original Windows 98 installation do not match, Windows 98 assumes that the system file is corrupt and should be restored from the original medium. (See the upcoming note for a description of how the CRC works.) You can restore files from your installation medium (e.g., CD-ROM, 3½-inch disk) with the "Extract one file from installation disk" option.

The Settings button in System File Checker opens the System File Checker Settings dialog box, where you can configure specific settings. This dialog box contains three tabs: Settings, Search Criteria, and Advanced. The Advanced tab was discussed in Chapter 10. The remaining two are described in the following list:

- **Settings tab**: If SFC finds a corrupt file, you can restore it from your installation medium. In the Settings tab, shown in Figure 14-10, you can indicate what to do with the "corrupt" file. The "Back up file before restoring" settings will help you back up your current configuration. That way, if restoring files from the original medium somehow makes things worse, you can easily return to your current configuration. What SFC finds is shown in the log file unless you choose the "No log" option. If you want to see your results, click View Log to open the log file, named Sfclog.txt, in Notepad.
- **Search Criteria tab**: Perhaps you do not want SFC to inspect all of your system files. You can use this tab, shown in Figure 14-11, to limit your search. The default for system file searches goes through a substantial number of folders and file types. You can use Add Folder or Remove to widen or narrow your search.

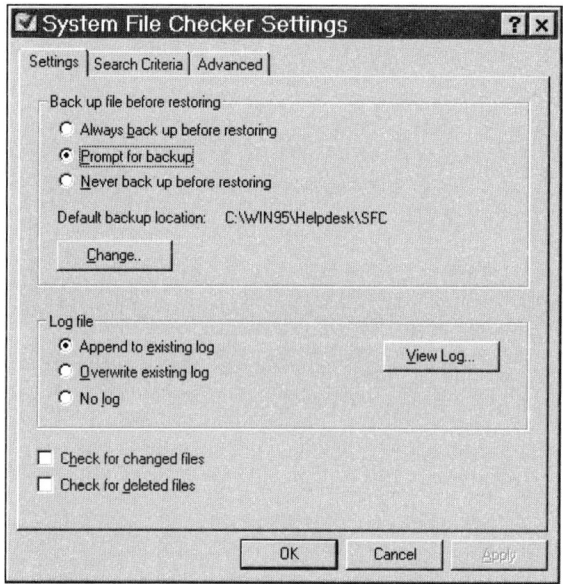

Figure 14-10   System File Checker, Settings tab

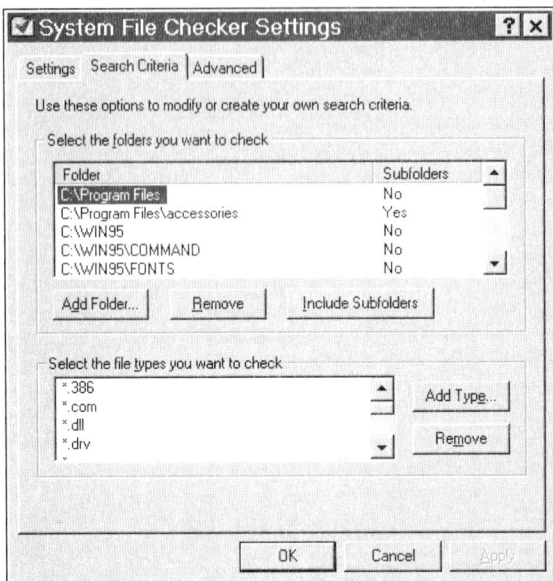

Figure 14-11   System File Checker, Search Criteria tab

 A cyclic redundancy check is a common way of verifying that a file was transferred without problems, especially over a network. The Windows 98 Setup wizard loads a set of CRC numbers for each system file. The System File Check utility calculates the CRC number for each Windows 98 system file on the local machine. If the numbers match, the system files are almost certainly in good condition.

CABLES AND CONNECTIONS

Many books on computer networking will tell you that a substantial number of network problems are the result of problems with physical cables or connections. In fact, a substantial number of problems with printers, disks, and other peripherals are also the result of problems with physical cables or connections. Thus, one of your first steps in troubleshooting any system is to verify that all devices are properly connected and that all cables are functioning properly. For example, a peripheral such as a printer could very well be at the end of a parallel cable "daisy chain" that also includes a tape drive and a scanner. That particular system would have six possible loose connections and three potentially faulty cables.

Infrared ports require additional checks. Not only do you need to check for a clear line of sight between infrared transmitters and receivers, but you also need to check that the angle of transmission is within the limits set for both transmitter and receiver.

Printer Troubleshooting

Printing can be a problematic process, whether it takes place locally or over a network. For example, in the physical configuration, wires can become loose, and the port settings of different peripherals can come into conflict. In addition, for various reasons, the printer spool can lose its ability to communicate with the printer. You may also experience any number of problems involving the basic software and driver setup.

One good starting point for printer problems is the Print Troubleshooter in the Help menu. To get to it, click Start, click Help, click the Contents tab, click Troubleshooting, click Windows 98 Troubleshooters below Troubleshooting, and then click Print. Although it is comprehensive, the order of steps in this particular troubleshooter is not always appropriate. For example, if your document is not printing at all, the Troubleshooter does not suggest that you check whether your printer is on and connected, until about the sixth step. Nevertheless, this troubleshooter can help direct you towards different kinds of solutions.

Once you have completed your physical check of cables and connections to the printer, you can begin troubleshooting print problems by checking the Properties tab of the printer, and the available resources in MSInfo. In the following sections you will learn how to adjust different printer properties to address different problems.

MSInfo and Print Problems

The Hardware Resources category in MSInfo can sometimes provide useful information regarding print problems. Two key items under Hardware Resources are "Conflicts/Sharing" and "IRQ." The Conflicts/Sharing category can indicate any interference with another device. (If there is no interference, this category will be blank.) The IRQ (interrupt request) category can indicate if a printer port is active. As you can see in Figure 4-12, the standard printer port LPT1 corresponds to IRQ 7, which confirms that a printer is active on that IRQ.

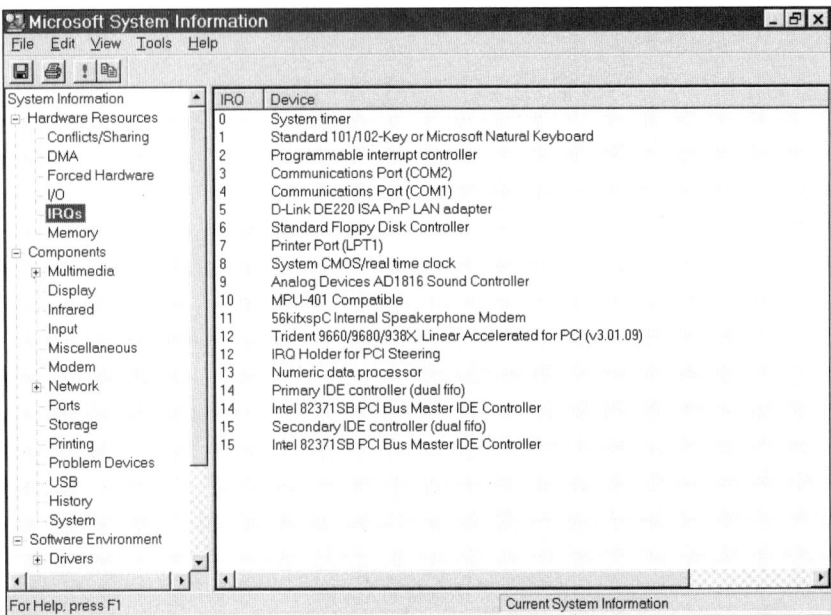

Figure 14-12 MSInfo, view of IRQ conflicts

PRINTER SPOOL

As discussed in Chapter 8, the printer spool is part of the Windows 98 32-bit print subsystem. Through enhanced metafile (EMF) printing, Windows 98 sends the print job to a temporary file known as the spool, and returns control back to the system. The print job continues in the background, while messages are sent back and forth between the printer and spool according to the IEEE 1284 ECP bidirectional print standard. You learned about the extended capabilities port back in Chapter 8. (Do not confuse the IEEE 1284 printer cable standard with the IEEE 1394 standard for FireWire peripherals. These are two numbers worth remembering to help you more quickly understand the subject when you read more about Windows 98.)

The IEEE 1284 bidirectional standard allows the printer to send messages back to the computer, about the status of the printer and the print job. If you have an IEEE 1284-enabled printer, you should be able to monitor items (such as the number of pages that have been printed) by double-clicking your printer in the printers folder, as shown in Figure 14-13.

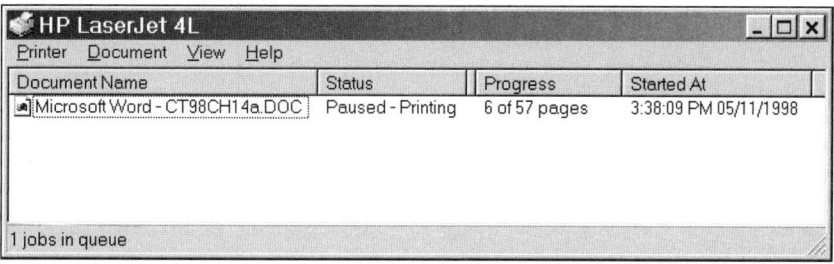

Figure 14-13 Status of a print job

Sometimes a print job gets stuck in the printer spool, possibly because the printer is not working properly. To make sure that the printer is *not* the problem, try printing directly to the printer. To print directly to a network printer, first make sure you know the print server name and printer sharename. Then click Start, point to Programs, click MS-DOS Prompt, and then type the following command: net use lpt1: *servername**sharename*. This connects your computer to the network printer. The port "lpt1:" now represents the printer. For either network or local printing, you can try printing to the local port by typing this command: copy /b *filename.txt* lpt1: (where *filename.txt* stands for the file you want to print). If your printer works with these commands, your spool is the problem.

To check your print spool: Click Start, point to Programs, and then click Windows Explorer. Navigate to the C:\Windows\Spool\Printers folder. If you see a filename with a .spl extension, there is an open print job in your spool, which is either a print job that is stuck or a print job on a laptop computer that is waiting for a connection to a remote printer. See the upcoming discussion on printer properties for possible solutions.

 The IEEE 1284 standard actually addresses all basic modes of data transfer over a parallel port. Although ECP is a subset of IEEE 1284, parallel cables that are labeled with "IEEE 1284" conform to the IEEE 1284 ECP mode. All printers work with some IEEE 1284 standard. A printer is not enabled for bidirectional communication unless it conforms to the IEEE 1284 standard for extended capability ports.

PRINTER MEMORY

There are two types of printer memory problems. Either the printer does not have sufficient memory, or the print job is lost in the printer memory. Generally, once you have a printer memory problem, at least part of your current print job is lost. Until you address this problem, you probably will not be able to print anything else.

If your printer does not have enough memory, your print job could get stuck in the printer or the spool. Some printers have several megabytes of memory available, which is sufficient to hold a number of text jobs. In the last section, you learned how to find out if your print job is stuck in the spool. If your print job has already passed through the spool, the printer could be jammed, out of paper, or out of toner. Or, it could be waiting for special paper such as an envelope to be manually fed. After you have ruled out these problems, the last resort is to clear the printer memory. Generally when you clear the printer memory, any job waiting in memory is lost. To clear the memory in your printer, consult the documentation for your printer.

Printer Properties

The Properties dialog box of your printer can be useful in troubleshooting. To get to your printer's Properties dialog box, click Start, point to Settings, and then click Printers. In the right-hand pane of the Printers window, right-click the icon for your printer, and then click Properties in the shortcut menu. Different printers have different sets of properties tabs. You will learn about the tabs common to most printers in the following sections.

General Tab

In Chapter 8, you learned to set up separator pages between your print jobs. As you learned there, you can set up separator pages as full (with graphics) or simple (text only). You can also add a comment to the printer. If your printer is on a network, you can identify the printer, perhaps by location, in the comments. The comment is part of what a network user sees when browsing for a printer through Network Neighborhood. But like printer drivers, comments are not automatically updated in Network Neighborhood, unless you reinstall the network printer on your remote computers.

Details Tab

You can address a number of different printing problems in the Details tab of your printer's Properties dialog box, as shown in Figure 14-14. You can manage your printer spool, printer ports, and printer drivers here. It is useful when solving problems such as:

- **Printer port problems**: Earlier in this chapter, you learned to check print spool problems by printing directly to a printer port. Check the setting in the "Print to the following port" text box. If it is different from the one that you tried earlier, try printing to this particular port. Assuming that you have checked your physical connections, the next step would be to try a new printer cable, or even a new physical printer port on your computer.

- **Network printer port problems**: Click "Capture Printer Port." In the Capture Printer Port dialog box, check the location associated with your printer port (probably LPT1 or LPT2) in the Path text box. If this matches the location that you see in your Network Neighborhood, then the network is probably *not* the problem.

- **Driver problems**: If your output is garbled, on a local or a network printer, one possible cause is an incompatible driver. If you suspect a problem with your printer driver, you can test your theory by using a generic text or laser printer driver. To do so, click New Driver, and then click Yes in the Printers dialog box. This opens the Select Device dialog box. In the list of manufacturers, click Generic. Then select a generic driver on the models list. Click OK to accept the change, and then test the new driver by trying to print. If the generic driver makes a previously malfunctioning printer work properly, then your printer driver is the problem. One possible solution is to get an updated or replacement printer driver from your printer manufacturer. Many printer manufacturers make updated drivers available over the Internet.

- **Spool problems**: You learned about the printer spool earlier in the chapter. If you know that the print job is not stuck in the printer, i.e. is stuck in memory, the spool may be the problem. To adjust some spool-related settings, click Spool Settings. This opens the dialog box shown in Figure 14-15. Because some printers cannot take EMF data, you might want to consider changing the spool data format from EMF to RAW. Other printers cannot work with a spool. To test this possibility, try selecting the "Print directly to the printer" option button.

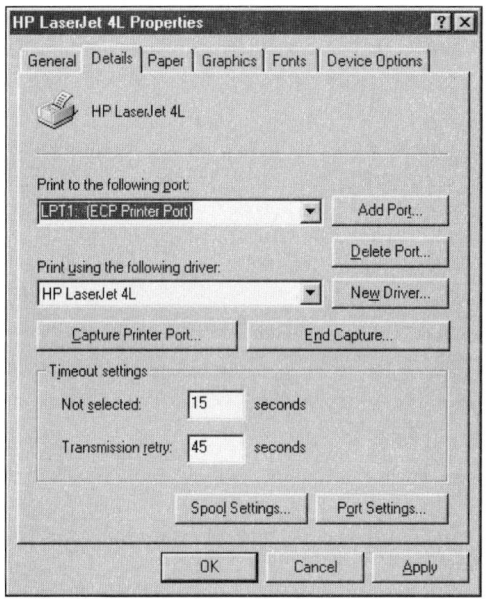

Figure 14-14 Printer Properties dialog box, Details tab

Paper Tab

On the Paper tab, shown in Figure 14-16, it's important to check the Paper source setting. If the Paper source setting is listed as manual feed, your print job is waiting for you to insert paper into the manual feed slot of your printer. If you are printing over the network, anyone else who has printed to the same printer is also waiting for you to manually feed the paper.

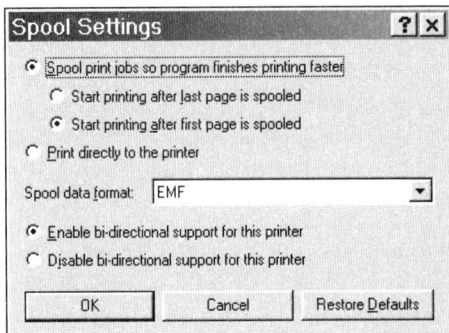

Figure 14-15 Spool Settings dialog box

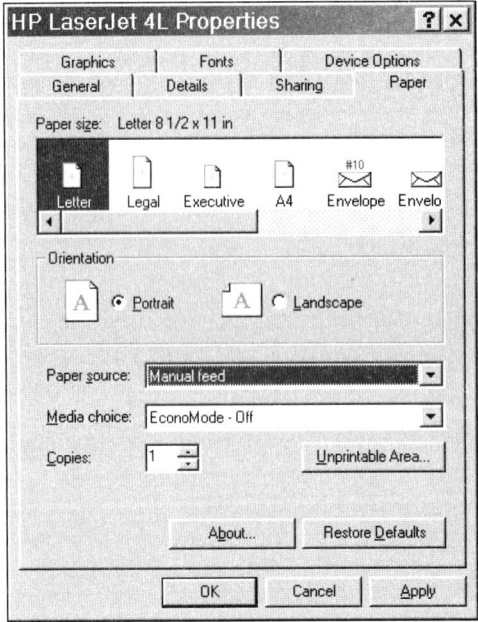

Figure 14-16 Printer Properties, Paper tab

Device Options Tab

For those printers that do not conform to the IEEE 1284 ECP bidirectional printer communication standard, the printer memory has to be manually set. There is a certain amount of memory that is physically installed in your printer. Consult your printer documentation if you do not know how much memory you have in your printer. The Printer Memory text box, shown in Figure 14-17, allows you to set memory levels up to the maximum amount of memory that you can install in your printer. If you have overstated the available memory in the printer, your print spool will send data faster than the printer can handle it, resulting in an out-of-memory condition.

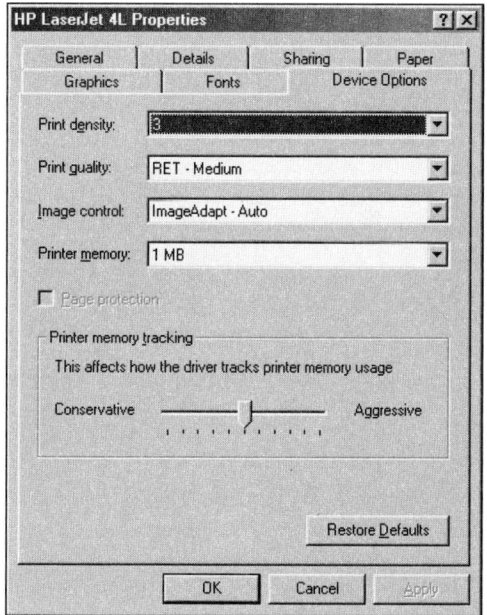

Figure 14-17 Printer Properties, Device Options tab

Graphics Tab

You first learned about some of the settings on the Graphics tab (specifically the difference between vector and raster graphics) in Chapter 10. When printing a drawing with geometric shapes, the default is generally set to use vector graphics, as shown in Figure 14-18. This is much more compact than raster graphics, which represent each pixel individually. Some printers that do not recognize TrueType fonts also do not recognize vector graphics. If you are having problems with printing shapes, raster graphics may be worth a try.

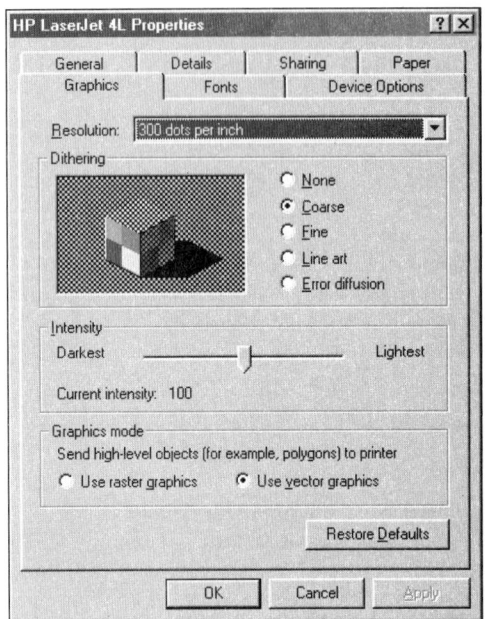

Figure 14-18   Printer Properties, Graphics tab

TROUBLESHOOTING DISK AND FILE SYSTEM PROBLEMS

When troubleshooting disks and file systems, you may encounter any number of problems. For starters, disks can become fragmented, fill up with unneeded data, or get compressed in a way that is not compatible with Windows 98. Some programs have trouble with the long filenames used in Windows 98 VFAT. In addition, some types of files are incompatible with certain protected-mode disk drivers. The tools discussed in this section can help you identify and resolve these and other problems.

HARD DISKS

When troubleshooting a hard disk, you should start with the same tools you use to optimize hard disks, as explained in Chapter 10. Specifically, you should use ScanDisk, Disk Defragmenter, and Disk Cleanup. The exact steps you take depend on whether (and how) your disk is compressed. The following list explains some troubleshooting issues related to the three optimization tools and disk compression utilities:

- **ScanDisk**: You learned about cross-linked files in Chapter 10. A program with a cross-linked file may not work. ScanDisk addresses this type of problem.
- **Disk Defragmenter**: If it is taking longer to get to your files, you may need to defragment your hard drive.

- **Disk Cleanup**: Memory problems may relate to an overly crowded hard disk. Disk Cleanup can help solve this problem by deleting unneeded files from your hard disk. A hard disk with more room is a hard disk that can accommodate a larger swap file. As you may remember from Chapter 2, the swap file uses free space on your hard drive to augment the RAM on your computer. If you still have memory problems, then you can use System Monitor, as discussed in Chapter 10, to determine if you need more RAM.

- **Compression**: Incompatibility in compression regimens can cause all sorts of problems, as discussed earlier in the troubleshooting section on loading Windows 98. Dual-booting with an operating system such as Windows NT 4.0 makes it possible to use three different file systems (FAT16, FAT32, and NTFS) on one computer. However, you need to keep in mind that the methods available for compressing each of these file systems are not compatible.

FILE SYSTEMS

The Systems applet provides several options for troubleshooting file systems in Windows 98. Click Start, point to Settings, click Control Panel, double-click the System icon, then click the Performance tab. In the Performance tab, click File System, and then click the Troubleshooting tab to display the options shown in Figure 14-19. These options can help you identify a problem. However, because they can degrade system performance, it is not a good idea to make any of them permanent. These options are described in the following list:

- **Disable new file sharing and locking semantics**: Generally, two different applications in Windows 98 cannot open the same file at the same time. If you have problems with how an MS-DOS application saves and shares a file, check this box. If this solves the problem, an upgrade of your MS-DOS application may be appropriate, since Microsoft did not incorporate the sharing features of these MS-DOS programs in Windows 98.

- **Disable long name preservation for old programs**: You learned about long filename aliases in Chapter 9. Windows 98 associates long filenames with aliases in a process known as "tunneling." (This is different from the tunneling process for PPTP that you learned about in Chapter 13.) Some older real-mode programs cannot open files with tunneling.

- **Disable protected-mode hard disk interrupt handling**: As you learned earlier in this chapter, an interrupt is a request from the hardware to the CPU for information. Some hard disks can only make interrupt requests (IRQs) in real-mode. The Windows 98 protected-mode drivers do not have the capability to simulate these real-mode interrupts. When this option is selected, the real-mode interrupts are processed through a routine, or program, embedded in the read-only memory (ROM) in the hard disk controller. According to Microsoft, this process is slower than the normal protected-mode interrupt handling, and it is not recommended.

- **Disable synchronous buffer commits**: As you learned in Chapter 10, VCACHE is the Windows 98 RAM buffer that stores data to be read to disk. After storing data, VCACHE writes complete files to disk when more resources are available. Disabling synchronous buffer commits speeds the process of writing to disk, but may result in VCACHE writing unreadable files to your hard disk.
- **Disable all 32-bit protected-mode disk drivers**: If your computer does not start because of a requirement for real-mode disk drivers, this is a viable troubleshooting option. Windows 98 does not work very well with real-mode drivers. If you need to use this option, you should install a protected-mode disk drive as soon as possible.
- **Disable write-behind caching for all drives**: This option disables VCACHE. If you choose it, all data from any program or utility is then written immediately to the hard disk. This may be appropriate when the reliability of your power supply is questionable.

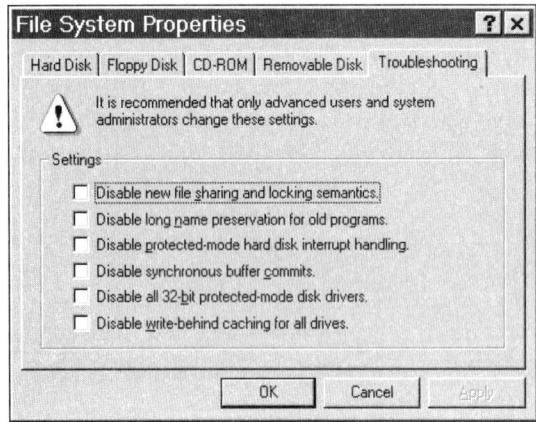

Figure 14-19   File System Properties dialog box, Troubleshooting tab

MICROSOFT SYSTEM INFORMATION (MSINFO)

As discussed in Chapter 10, Microsoft System Information (MSInfo) is a powerful tool for monitoring and maintaining a system. It collects hardware, software, and driver settings all in one place, making it an excellent tool for developing a system baseline. In the realm of troubleshooting, MSInfo provides a number of settings that help you understand installed hardware and associated drivers, as well as any potential or actual conflicts among drivers. As described earlier in this chapter, you can consult the Conflicts/Sharing and IRQ subcategories in the Resources category for information regarding conflicts in sharing IRQs. The two MSInfo tools most directly related to troubleshooting—Windows Report Tool and the Automatic Skip Driver agent—are described in the following sections.

AUTOMATIC SKIP DRIVER AGENT

You can use the **Automatic Skip Driver (ASD) agent** to troubleshoot devices or drivers that do not load properly in the Windows 98 startup sequence. To use the ASD agent, open MSInfo, click Tools on the menu bar, and then click Automatic Skip Driver Agent. If a critical system failure has occurred, the ASD agent will list failed operations in the Hardware Troubleshooting Agent dialog box. Click an operation in the list to display details and recommendations, usually for updating the driver.

WINDOWS REPORT TOOL

As a network administrator, you may want to train your users to present their problems via Windows Report Tool. It provides a format for users to describe their problem. The report is saved in a cabinet file along with the basic parameters for their computer system. You can also have your users save various system and other files, as you desire.

To open Windows Report Tool: click Start, point to Programs, point to Accessories, point to System Tools, and then click System Information. In the menu bar, click Tools, and then click Windows Report Tool. This opens the window shown in Figure 14-20.

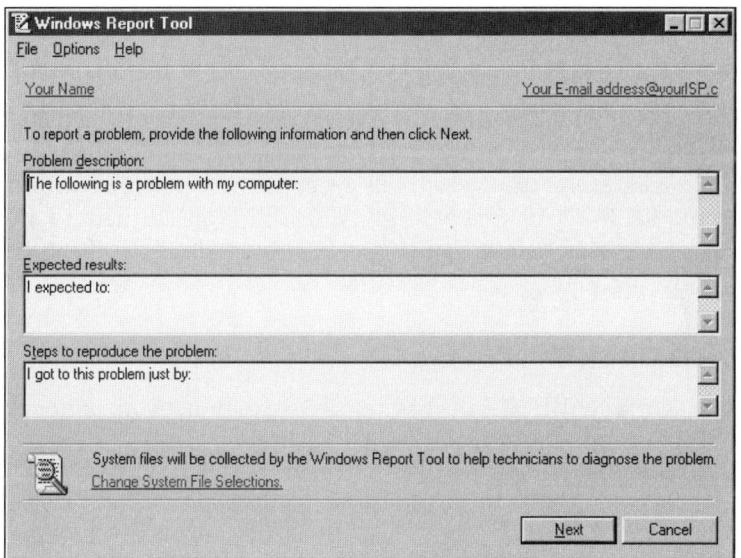

Figure 14-20 Windows Report Tool

Within this window, you can specify which system files Windows Report Tool will collect by clicking "Change System File Selections" near the very bottom. This opens the Collected Information dialog box, which is a selection of System files and settings to be copied from your computer. In the Files to copy text box, you see a list of most of the system and log files available on your computer that can be read by human beings. Select the check box for each file you want to include. To add additional files, click Add. To choose all files in this box, click Select All. When you are finished choosing the files you want to include in a report, click OK.

Windows Report Tool makes it easy for users to provide information about themselves. Simply click on the line corresponding to "your name" in the upper left of the Windows Report Tool window to open the User Information dialog box. You can instruct your users to fill in this dialog box as required, to identify themselves to you.

To save a report, click Next in the Windows Report Tool window. This opens the Save As dialog box. Reports are saved in a cabinet file format to save space.

The user can send the saved file over a network, perhaps as an attachment to e-mail. When you receive such a file from a user, you can easily open it in Windows Report Tool via the Open command on the File menu. To view information about the user, click Options on the menu bar, and then click User Information. After reviewing the information provided by the user, you can turn your attention to the more important information provided in the form of the system files. To view these files, open Windows Explorer and double-click the cabinet file sent to you by the user. This opens a window that contains all files exported by the user. As a network administrator, you can highlight the files that you are interested in, then click File in the menu bar, then click Extract.

TROUBLESHOOTING THE NETWORK CONFIGURATION

The details of networking with Windows 98 were discussed in Chapter 4 and Chapter 13. This section explains how to solve problems related to connecting on the network. When troubleshooting network connections, you will generally be concerned with the following three protocols: TCP/IP, IPX/SPX, and NetBEUI. You learned to troubleshoot TCP/IP in Chapter 13. This section is focused on troubleshooting the NetBEUI and IPX/SPX-compatible protocols.

TROUBLESHOOTING NetBEUI

As discussed in Chapter 5, NetBEUI is the traditional Microsoft network protocol. However, because NetBEUI is not routable, its use is limited.

There are 15 NetBIOS commands that you can use in Windows 98. Although you need a command line for these NetBIOS commands, some of these commands do not work in the MS-DOS Prompt window; to use them, you need to restart your computer in MS-DOS mode with a real-mode network redirector. If you know that physical cables and connections are not the problem, the following are three commands that you can use to troubleshoot your NetBEUI connection from the MS-DOS Prompt window:

- **Net View**: If you are connected to and are a part of a network workgroup, the response will be a list of computers on your network.
- **Net Use**: As you learned previously, as long as you know the computer and share names, you can use this command to connect to a folder or printer on the network.

- **Net Ver**: The response on your screen is the type and version of your current network redirector (client).

You can try these commands while you are connected to a network, as follows: click Start, point to Programs, and then click MS-DOS Prompt. Type either Net View or Net Ver, and press Enter. If you want to use the Net Use command, type Net Use X: *Servername**sharename*, where you know the name of the server and the sharename of the folder that you want to connect to. For a list of and instructions on how to use any of the other commands, type Net /? and press Enter.

Alternately, you can use System Monitor, as you learned in Chapter 10, to monitor the status and performance of your NetBEUI network. You need to be connected to a NetBEUI network for any of these readings to be effective.

TROUBLESHOOTING THE IPX/SPX-COMPATIBLE PROTOCOL

Given the large installed base of Novell networks, installation of Windows 98 computers in mixed networks is inevitable. You can use System Monitor to measure the performance of your system on a Novell NetWare IPX/SPX network, as follows: click Start, point to Programs, point to Accessories, point to System Tools, and then click System Monitor. Click Edit on the menu bar, and then click Add Item. This opens the Add Item dialog box, which provides a number of counters for the IPX/SPX-compatible protocol and Microsoft Client for NetWare Networks.

You will not see these measures on your System Monitor unless you install the IPX/SPX-compatible protocol and Microsoft Client for NetWare Networks on your computer.

First you will look at the different measures available in the System Monitor IPX/SPX-compatible protocol category. Keep in mind that while IPX loosely corresponds to IP in the TCP/IP protocol stack, SPX corresponds to TCP. The speed at which SPX and IPX packets are sent should be roughly proportional; if they are not, parts of your messages are not getting through.

The following are the counters in the Add Item dialog box:

- **IPX Packets Lost/Second**: As you may remember from previous chapters, data is sent over networks in units known as packets. This measure indicates IPX packets received, but not used by your computer. If your computer cannot read many packets, then you may need to change your frame type, as shown later in this section.
- **IPX Packets Received/Second**: IPX packets received by your computer
- **IPX Packets Sent/Second**: IPX packets sent by your computer anywhere on the network
- **Open Sockets**: The number of available connections between applications on your computer and the network. If this value is 0, you cannot start any more applications that depend on a network with the IPX/SPX-compatible protocol.

- **Routing Table Entries**: The number of computers to which you have directions on the network. Similar to source routing, which you learned about in Chapter 13, except that routing table entries work at the network layer of the OSI model.

- **SAP Table Entries**: As you learned in Chapters 12 and 13, the Service Advertising Protocol (SAP) lets other computers know that your computer has resources to share on a NetWare network. The number of SAP table entries is the number of NetWare servers that have used SAP to let you know that they are ready to share resources.

- **SPX Packets Received/Second**: The number of SPX packets received by your computer each second

- **SPX Packets Sent/Second**: The number of SPX packets sent from your computer each second

As you may remember, the IPX/SPX-compatible protocol operates at the lower layers of the OSI model, whereas redirectors, such as Microsoft Client for NetWare Networks, are at the higher layers of the OSI model. This means your data must travel through the intervening layers each time your application needs to send or receive data through the network. If you have installed Microsoft Client for NetWare Networks on your computer, the Add Item dialog box also includes the following measures:

- **Burst Packets Dropped**: Number of packets from your computer that are lost

- **Burst Receive Gap Time**: Time between incoming packets, in microseconds (10^{-6}s)

- **Burst Send Gap Time**: Time between outgoing packets, in microseconds (10^{-6}s)

- **Bytes in Cache**: Number of bytes in the cache of your NetWare network client

- **Bytes read/second**: Bytes read by your applications from the network (via the client) per second

- **Bytes written/second**: Bytes sent by your applications to the network (via the client) per second

- **Dirty Bytes in cache**: Amount of data in the cache of your NetWare network client waiting to be written to your applications. Similar to dirty data in your RAM waiting to be written to your hard drive.

- **NCP Packets dropped**: The number of NCP packets dropped. In Chapter 13, you learned that NetWare clients communicate in packets known as NCPs.

- **Requests Pending**: Number of requests that you have sent to a server that are waiting for answers

You should be aware of several common problems relating to Windows 98 computers on a Novell IPX/SPX network. You can find useful information regarding these problems via the Configuration tab of the Network applet. In the list of installed network components, click IPX/SPX-compatible protocol, and then click the Properties button. In the

IPX/SPX-Compatible Protocol dialog box, click the Advanced tab, as shown in Figure 14-21. The settings under this tab address a number of common problems.

- **Frame Type**: The most common problem in a Novell network is a frame type mismatch. Although it is not recommended, some networks include multiple frame types. The default frame type setting is "auto," which tells Windows 98 to match the first frame type that comes across the network. However, this may not necessarily be the frame type that you need to communicate with the computer you want to access over the network. If you cannot standardize frame types on your network, you at least need to match the frame type on your computer with the computers you are working with.

- **Source Routing**: To keep networks at a manageable size, it often makes sense to split them into subnetworks, connected by bridges, switches, or routers. As discussed in Chapter 13, source routing allows a Windows 98 workstation to send data across a bridge or a switch. If the Source Routing setting is not active, your workstation may not know where to send data. You learned how to modify your Source Routing setting in Chapter 13.

- **Force Even Length Packets**: Older Novell NetWare servers require packets of even length. If you are on a system with an older NetWare server, make sure to set the "Force Even Length Packets" property. You learned how to modify your Force Even Length Packets property in Chapter 13.

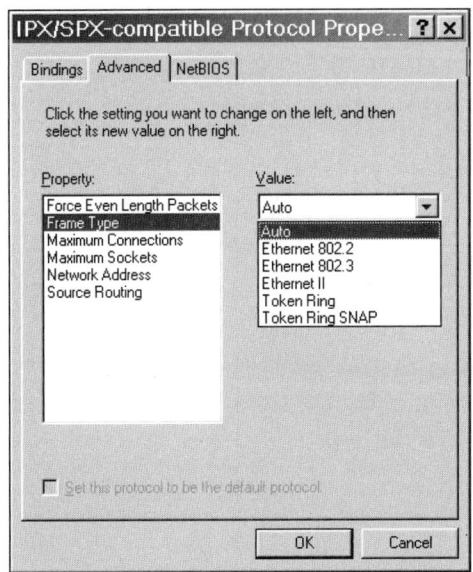

Figure 14-21 IPX/SPX-Compatible Protocol dialog box, Advanced tab

TROUBLESHOOTING OTHER DEVICES

This section addresses problems associated with monitors, SCSI devices, and input devices such as a mouse and the keyboard. You can take advantage of a substantial number of adjustment options, especially for monitors. The different settings for each of these devices can help you determine whether you need updated drivers or hardware.

Display

Windows 98 drivers are not compatible with all combinations of graphics cards and monitors. If it can't find the exact driver required by a piece of display hardware, the Windows 98 Setup wizard will use the closest possible match. If the attempted match does not work, you can end up with display settings that are not fully compatible with your monitor or graphics card. A number of display problems can be addressed in the Settings tab of the Display applet, shown in Figure 14-22.

As you learned in Chapter 10, one typical display problem has to do with "jerky" motion on your screen. As you learned, there are three basic causes for this problem: competition for CPU time, insufficient CD-ROM cache, and a video graphics card without enough memory. It's important to keep in mind that smooth on-screen motion requires lots of processing power, as does the generation of 32-bit color and 1280 x 1024 pixels. What's more, using the wrong display driver can eat up even more processing power. You will learn to adjust the related options on the Settings tab in the Hands-on Projects at the end of this chapter.

Windows 98 does not work well with many older display drivers. After reading through this section, if you conclude that you need a new display driver, you can probably find the driver you need on your manufacturer's Web site.

The following settings illustrate some important options available via this Settings tab:

- **Colors**: Sometimes the display driver or card does not support the maximum color capabilities offered by Windows 98. You may end up with anything from incorrect colors to a black and white screen. You can adjust the number of displayed colors in the Colors text box. If you are having problems, try changing this setting to 16 or 256 colors, and then click OK. If required, restart your computer. If this works, maintain this setting until you are able to update your driver or graphics card.

- **Screen area**: Sometimes what you see on your screen does not coincide with what is actually being displayed. For example, the display may only fill a portion of your monitor, or your monitor may show only a part of your Windows 98 desktop. In either case, look to the lower-right corner of the Settings tab, where you can adjust the total screen area or the number of pixels depicted on your screen. To understand what is possible, try changing this setting to 640 x 480 pixels, then click OK. If required, restart your computer. If this addresses your problem, maintain this setting until you are able to update your driver or graphics card.

- **Display adapter**: One way to determine if you need a new display adapter (also known as a driver for your hardware graphics card) is to try switching to a standard VGA adapter. If performance actually improves with the standard VGA adapter, you need an updated driver. You can switch to a VGA adapter from your Settings tab as follows: click the Advanced button to open the Properties dialog box for your display driver, and then click the Adapter tab. Then click Change to start the Update Device Driver Wizard. Click Next, then select the "Display a list of all the drivers…" option button, and click Next again. Click the "Show all hardware" option button. In the Manufacturers list, click "(standard display types)." In the Models list, select "Standard Display Adapter (VGA)," and then click Next. Click Yes in the Update Driver Warning dialog box. Back in the Update Driver Device Wizard, click Next. In the next page of this dialog box, click Finish. Click Close in the Properties box for your display adapter, and then click OK in the Display Properties dialog box. Restart your computer if prompted.

- **Version**: Windows-98-capable display driver files should be version 4.00 or higher. You can access information regarding your driver version from the Settings tab as follows: Click Advanced, and then click the Adapter tab. Review the information in the Adapter/Driver information box. You can verify driver version information in MSInfo, as follows: click Start, point to Programs, point to Accessories, point to System Tools, and then click System Information. In the left-hand pane of MSInfo, click the plus sign next to Components, then click Display. The driver version should be prominently shown somewhere in the right-hand pane.

- **Location of your driver**: To verify that the display driver is compatible with Windows 98, check the C:\Windows\system.ini file. In the [boot] section, look for the following statement: "display.drv=pnpdrvr.drv". When you boot Windows 98, it reads the System.ini file. This statement directs Windows 98 to the display settings in the Registry, which conform to the requirements of a Windows 98 version of a driver. If you cannot find your driver in the System.ini file, you can add it with a text editor.

When you change settings in the Settings tab, you may not have to restart your computer to activate your new settings. To find out whether this is the case on your computer, click Advanced in the Settings tab. In the General tab of the Properties dialog box named after your adapter, look at the Compatibility box. Your results depend on the option you choose, your graphics card, and degree of change you want to make.

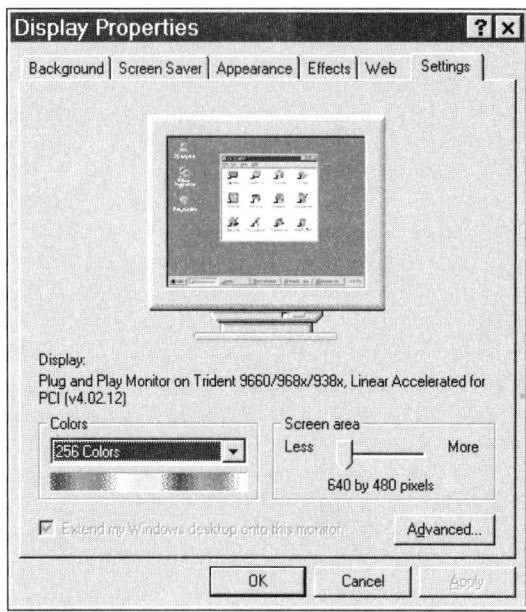

Figure 14-22 Display Properties, Settings tab

SCSI/CD-ROM

Windows 98 supports up to 15 internal or external SCSI devices connected in daisy-chain fashion. If you have SCSI removable media of the types you learned about in Chapter 11, you need to install them before installing Windows 98. When troubleshooting SCSI devices, you should first verify that the chain is terminated properly. In addition, certain types of SCSI devices require installation at certain points in the daisy chain. Refer to the manual for each SCSI device for details.

A terminator is a loopback connector that is installed at the end of a SCSI daisy chain. A loopback connector sends the SCSI signal back along the cable. When properly connected, it tells your system that there are no more devices installed beyond the terminator.

Input Devices

Input devices include keyboards, mice, joysticks, and game pads. Troubleshooting an input device is similar to troubleshooting a printer. The first step, as always, is to check the physical connections. Then you can use MSInfo to check for conflicts, as explained earlier in this chapter. Any conflicts will show up under Hardware Resources, in the Conflicts/Sharing subcategory.

The next step is to check the applicable driver. Any drive problems will show up in the Device Manager tab of the System applet. Some input devices are connected to COM ports. Figure 14-23 shows a problem with a COM port. The yellow exclamation point in this figure indicates a device that is not working. You will learn to address a similar problem in the Hands-on Projects at the end of the chapter.

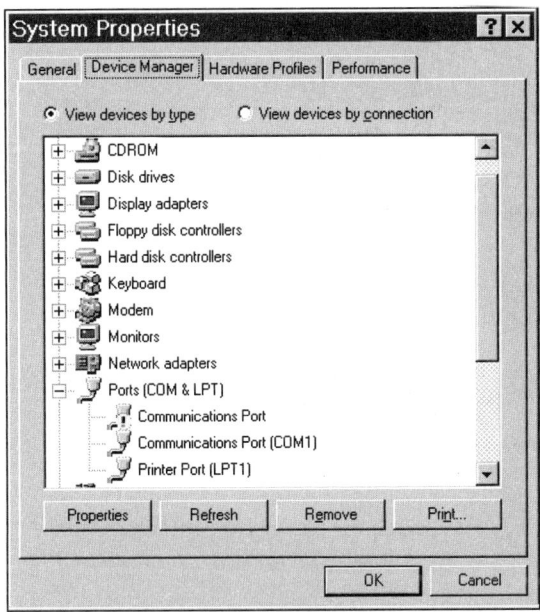

Figure 14-23 Device Manager tab, indicating a COM port conflict

When troubleshooting a mouse or touchpad, you can use the Mouse applet, shown in Figure 14-24, which includes diagnostic tests and adjustments for your mouse. Sometimes an adjustment here is all that is required. If you have more tabs than are shown in this figure, you have a more fully featured mouse.

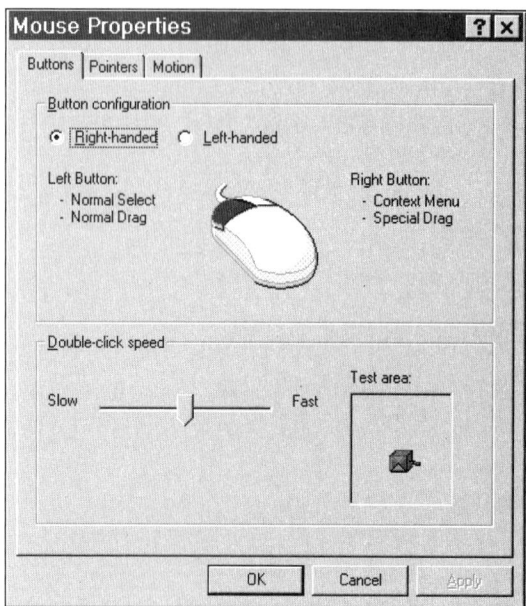

Figure 14-24 Mouse applet

OTHER SOURCES FOR TROUBLESHOOTING INFORMATION

In addition to the utilities discussed earlier in this chapter, you can take advantage of a number of other sources for troubleshooting information, such as the Dr. Watson utility and Microsoft Technet.

You learned about some of the features of Dr. Watson in Chapter 10. It is also a program error debugger that captures application faults in a log file for analysis. Whenever you see a dialog box similar to the illegal operation error dialog box shown in Figure 14-25, start the Dr. Watson utility, which is accessible through the Tools menu of MSInfo. After you have started Dr. Watson, repeat the steps that generated the error in the first place. After you generate the error again, you can reopen Dr. Watson by clicking on its icon in the System Tray, as you learned to do in Chapter 10. Then you can click the Diagnosis tab shown in Figure 14-26 to tell you how to address the problem. If you are interested in what went wrong from a programming perspective, take a look at the Details tab.

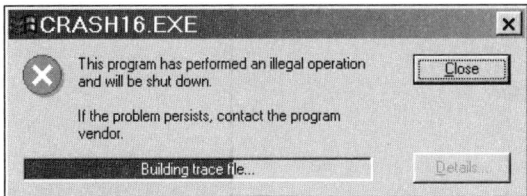

Figure 14-25   Illegal operation

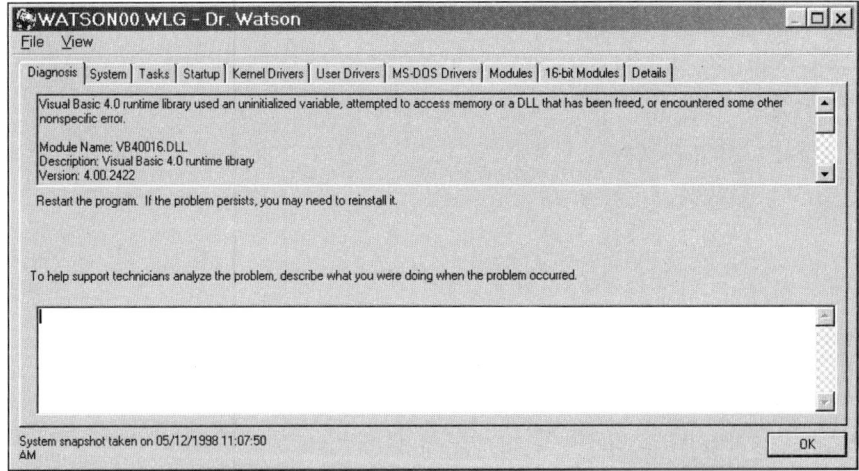

Figure 14-26   Diagnosis tab of the Dr. Watson utility

Microsoft TechNet is a comprehensive list of articles, manuals, and resources on all major Microsoft operating systems. It is available on compact disks and is updated monthly. One significant feature of TechNet is that it is accessible offline, and not subject to Internet speed and connection problems. The amount of information available about Windows 98 on TechNet is growing monthly. At present, a yearly subscription to TechNet is $299 for a single user. More information is available at *http://www.microsoft.com/technet*.

Yet another source of troubleshooting information, the Microsoft Knowledge Base, is a collection of technical articles available on the Microsoft Web site. Knowledge Base articles are regularly cited in TechNet and provide more detailed information on a particular topic. The Microsoft Knowledge Base is now included as a separate CD with a TechNet subscription. Alternately, to access the Microsoft Knowledge Base, connect your computer to the Internet, then navigate to *http://support.microsoft.com*.

Finally, you can find useful information in many of the numerous Web sites devoted to Windows 98. Organizations that maintain Web sites with good Windows 98 resources include:

- **Microsoft**: As you would expect, Microsoft maintains the official Windows 98 Web site, located at *http://www.microsoft.com/windows/windows98*.

- *Windows* **online magazine**: This organization provides an extensive resource of Windows 98 information, including reviews that discuss the pros and cons of many of the new Windows 98 features. You can find this site at *http: // www.winmag.com/win98.*

- **Ziff-Davis**: This major computer publishing house maintains a "Windows 98 Help" site at *http: //www.zdnet.com/zdhelp/win_help/win98_help.html.*

- **Mecklemedia**: This company maintains a site that serves as a computer and Internet dictionary, located at *http: //www.webopedia.com.*

CHAPTER SUMMARY

- If you are troubleshooting in an organization, you need a systematic and documentable set of tools to help you define a problem, theorize as to the cause, and test solutions. This sequence, based on the traditional scientific method, is one way to make sure that your approach to troubleshooting can be understood by your colleagues.

- In Chapter 10, you learned about a number of tools to maintain your system. To minimize the problems that you may have, it is important to run Microsoft System Information and disk management tools on a regular basis.

- The Windows 98 Setup wizard is designed to bypass any problems that it encounters. For example, if it cannot find a driver for your printer, it will bypass this step in the process and go on to the next step. But it does not address every possible combination of devices and drivers. Whatever happens during the setup, the wizard documents everything that it attempts to install in a series of text files, which you can use to troubleshoot your Windows 98 installation. Particular problems may occur during installation if your hard disk is compressed, or your available conventional memory is inadequate.

- The options in the Startup and Shutdown troubleshooter are extensive. If you have problems booting Windows 98, your Windows 98 Emergency Startup Disk includes a number of troubleshooting utilities. Some of these utilities are set up on a RAMDrive, in random access memory. Among other things, these utilities allow you to check the integrity of your disk, restore old versions of your Registry, and restore system files to your root directory. Another series of startup and shutdown problems relates to conflicts with drivers and startup files. You can troubleshoot your startup files with the System Configuration Utility. You can check the integrity of your Windows 98 system files with System File Checker.

- When you have a problem, the first place to go is the troubleshooter wizards available in the Help menu. While this chapter does not cover the troubleshooting wizards themselves, it does cover the tools called up by these wizards, to help you understand what you are doing. These tools include a broad range of features that help you define the problem, isolate the cause, and test a solution.

- If you are having problems with your printer, monitor, or hard disk, there are a number of adjustments that can be made to help optimize your system. Each printer has a Properties dialog box with an extensive series of options. If you are having problems getting files from your system, you may need to use the maintenance utilities on your hard disk. You can also use some of an extensive series of adjustments to check your file system. Be aware that some of these adjustments can be permanent. Others should be used only on a temporary basis, to help you identify a problem and give you time to work out a solution.

- You learned about some of the Microsoft System Information tools in Chapter 10. Others include the Automatic Skip Driver agent, which can tell you if drivers did not load properly. MSInfo also includes a Windows Report Tool, which consolidates a user's system configuration along with his or her trouble report.

- Windows 98 includes a number of network troubleshooting tools for solving network connectivity problems. You learned about the TCP/IP tools in Chapter 13. You can use a number of other tools to troubleshoot connections with the NetBEUI and IPX/SPX-compatible protocols.

- Additional troubleshooting resources are available from a number of sources. The manufacturers of most peripherals have updated drivers available for download on their Web sites. Microsoft TechNet is a good source of detailed technical information on all Microsoft operating systems, including Windows 98. A number of Web sites have been dedicated to Windows 98; only some of these are affiliated with Microsoft, so it is possible to get a balanced view of various features.

KEY TERMS

- **Automatic Skip Driver (ASD) agent** — This is the utility that detects any critical failures in the startup sequence for Windows 98.

- **Bootlog.txt** — The file that records the drivers that did and did not load successfully during the installation of Windows 98.

- **Detlog.txt** — The list of hardware drivers and devices found by the Windows 98 Setup wizard.

- **Netlog.txt** — The file that records the network components that were detected during the installation of Windows 98.

- **RAMDrive** — A part of your random access memory (RAM) that has been configured to look like a hard drive. When you boot your computer with the Windows 98 ESD, it sets up a RAMDrive with a number of DOS-style utilities.

- **Setuplog.txt** — A list of what has and has not been successfully copied and implemented by the Windows 98 Setup wizard.

- **tunneling** — The process by which some older programs and operating systems use standard filenames with 8 characters in the name and 3 characters in the extension (abcdefgh.ijk). When they are used in place of long filenames, they are known as aliases. Programs and operating systems can associate long Windows 98 filenames with aliases.

REVIEW QUESTIONS

1. Why is a consistent approach important in troubleshooting?
    a. because Windows 98 remembers the approach that you take in each troubleshooting session and uses it to help determine how to defragment the hard disk
    b. Windows 98 has a limited number of troubleshooting tools, which limits the troubleshooting methods that can be used.
    c. A consistent approach is critical if you are working with others on a problem. Without methods that can be easily documented, it is difficult for someone else to take over when necessary.
    d. A consistent approach helps you avoid version conflicts in device drivers.

2. In what utility can you find information on drivers and easy access to a number of other troubleshooting tools?
    a. Microsoft System Information
    b. My Computer, Properties, Device Driver tab
    c. Control Panel, System, Tools menu
    d. Control Panel, Drivers, Tools menu

3. Suppose it takes a long time to access your files. Why would you want to run the Windows 98 version of Disk Defragmenter?
    a. It can be set to split up every executable file and intersperses them with parts of their associated dynamic-link libraries.
    b. It can be set to make every file contiguous on the hard disk for easy continuous retrieval.
    c. It corrects all errors in hard disk organization.
    d. It cleans up and deletes all temporary and otherwise unneeded files from the hard disk.

4. Which of the following files can you use to examine and troubleshoot the progress of a Windows 98 installation? (Choose all correct answers.)
    a. Setuplog.txt
    b. Detlog.txt
    c. Hdwrlog.txt
    d. Netlog.txt

5. Which of the following troubleshooting operations can you perform with the Windows 98 Emergency Startup Disk? (Choose all correct answers.)
    a. ScanDisk
    b. Chkdsk
    c. restore Registry
    d. restore system files to the root directory

6. If your Windows 98 installation stops during the initial real-mode ScanDisk operation, which of the following could be the problem?
   a. more than five errors on the hard drive
   b. You are trying to install Windows 98 from MS-DOS. You can install Windows 98 only from Windows 95.
   c. Your free conventional memory is less than 432 KB.
   d. Your hard disk is larger than 6 GB, and ScanDisk cannot handle a partition of that size. You need to reformat your hard disk before installing Windows 98.

7. Which of the following statements about TSR programs and the Windows 98 installation process are true? (Choose all correct answers.)
   a. As long as you have sufficient free extended memory, TSRs are generally not a problem.
   b. As long as you have sufficient free conventional memory, TSRs are generally not a problem.
   c. You need to deactivate all TSR programs before installing Windows 98.
   d. As long as you are installing Windows 98 from Windows 95, TSRs are not a concern.

8. Which of the following is the most likely reason that a network installation of Windows 98 may not be working?
   a. You have the wrong commands set up in Msbatch.inf. Even though you've tested it on two different configurations, your Msbatch.inf file may not work with the Windows 98 Setup wizard on all systems.
   b. There is a physical break somewhere in the system between your computer and the server where the Windows 98 installation files are stored.
   c. There is a protocol mismatch on your network. Your Microsoft Client has been set up to use token ring, while the server where the Windows 98 installation files are stored is sending out Ethernet packets.
   d. You don't know, but you know that ScanDisk will always clean up the network system sufficiently to allow the Windows 98 installation to work.

9. When you load Windows 98 in safe mode, which of the following drivers may be installed? (Choose all correct answers.)
   a. VGA driver
   b. DriveSpace driver
   c. modem driver
   d. scanner driver

10. How does System File Checker use cyclic redundancy checks on Windows 98 system files?

   a. The cyclic redundancy check cycles each of the Windows 98 system files through the Disk Defragmenter.

   b. The cyclic redundancy check makes sure that the Windows 98 video drivers work at a level that is readable to the human eye.

   c. The cyclic redundancy check is a number based on some combination of binary data from within a system file. If it matches the number in a file installed during the installation of Windows 98, you know that the file is still good.

   d. The cyclic redundancy check is a number based on some combination of binary data from within a system directory. If it matches the number in a directory installed during the installation of Windows 98, you know that the file is still good.

11. The System Configuration Utility is used to check for various problems with which of the following? (Choose all correct answers.)

   a. RAM memory

   b. hard disk compatibility with 32-bit protected-mode drivers

   c. flaws in the Windows 98 fast shutdown sequence

   d. program faults

12. With which files can you experiment in the System Configuration Utility to find problems with your startup sequence? (Choose all correct answers.)

   a. Config.sys

   b. Autoexec.bat

   c. System.ini

   d. Drvspace.dll

13. In which of the following programs will you find a series of troubleshooting utilities to help you to locate various problems?

   a. Microsoft System Information has a series of tools.

   b. The Device Driver tab from the Properties sheet of "My Computer" is the key in troubleshooting various devices.

   c. The troubleshooting wizards available from the Help menu include a series of utilities for all sorts of problems.

   d. Windows 98 includes Web-based wizards for all conceivable problems. The Windows Report Tool allows all such problems to be reported to Microsoft.

14. Which of the following commands or procedures might you use if you suspect that you have a printing problem with your spool? (Choose all correct answers.)

   a. net use //servername/sharename lpt1:

   b. copy /b filename.txt lpt1:

c. Activate the System File Check utility. In the settings, focus the utility on the system files in the spool directory.

d. Activate the MSInfo utility. In the left-hand pane, click on components. In the right-hand pane, click on drivers, then on user mode. Look for the revision level on the driver of the spool, to make sure that it is 4.00 or above.

15. Which of the following is among the first steps that you take when troubleshooting a hard disk problem?

    a. examine the Device Driver tab from the Properties sheet of "My Computer"

    b. look through MSInfo for conflicts under the resources setting in the left-hand pane

    c. Perform a ScanDisk utility. Follow up by defragmenting the hard disk.

    d. Disconnect and reconnect the cables to your hard disk. Most hard disk problems are the result of bad physical connections.

16. You are troubleshooting your file system via the File System button of the System applet Performance tab. Suppose you find an adjustment that works; why shouldn't you make this a permanent setting?

    a. Troubleshooting settings in this tab only last for three restarts of Windows 98. After that time, the troubleshooting settings are inactive, and you will want to remove the settings to avoid confusion when you need to do some future troubleshooting.

    b. All of these settings will degrade the performance of your system, even if they address the problem at hand.

    c. You want to use a file system setting until you can reset your computer to perform standard disk maintenance utilities.

    d. There is no penalty for making any of these settings permanent.

17. You are having problems with multimedia performance on your system. Which of the following could improve performance? (Choose all correct answers.)

    a. Reallocate a greater percentage of your VCACHE to your video driver.

    b. In the Display applet, reduce the number of colors that are displayed.

    c. In the Display applet, reduce the number of pixels required to 640 x 480.

    d. Reallocate a greater percentage of RAM to your video driver.

18. Why is the version of your video driver important?

    a. It is not all that important. Windows 3.1, Windows 95, Windows NT 4.0, and Windows 98 share common video drivers.

    b. Windows 95 drivers will work in a Windows 98 computer, as long as the version number of the driver is 4.00 or greater.

    c. Windows NT Workstation drivers will work in a Windows 98 computer, as long as the version number on the driver is 4.00 or greater.

    d. You can install drivers from Microsoft TechNet on a Windows 98 computer, as long as the version number on the driver is 4.00 or greater.

19. When troubleshooting a NetBEUI network, which of the following utilities can you use to make sure that you are connected to the network?

   a. Net Connect
   b. Net PING
   c. Net Use
   d. Net Check

20. Which of the following is the most common problem relating to a Windows 98 computer on a Novell NetWare network?

   a. mismatch in frame types
   b. Drivers were not loaded properly.
   c. Source routing has not been enabled.
   d. conflict with TCP/IP frames

21. Match the following tools to their intended function:

Utility	Function
1. ScanDisk	A. Trial and error for startup files
2. Windows Report Tool	B. Backup for older versions of the Registry
3. System File Checker	C. File scanner to determine duplicate drivers
4. Automatic Skip Driver agent	D. Disk repair
5. Version Conflict Manager	E. Reporting the problem to Microsoft
6. Registry Checker	F. Check the startup sequence for problems
7. System Configuration Utility	G. File scanner to determine the integrity of the operating system files

Hands-on Projects

Project 14-1

In this project, assume that you just had problems getting into Windows 98 and had to go into safe mode. For example, if you accidentally deleted your display adapter driver, you would go into safe mode to use the default VGA display adapter driver, reinstall the correct driver, and restart your computer. In the following steps you will experiment with a variety of troubleshooting techniques. Although you can do these steps in Windows 98 normal mode, safe mode is preferred to help accustom you to its limitations. (Read through this chapter for some of the ways to restart your computer in safe mode.) First of all, you will run System File Checker to verify the integrity of your Windows 98 system files. Next, you will verify the integrity of your Registry. Finally, you will use the Automatic Skip Driver agent to check for critical system failures. To complete this project, you need a computer with Windows 98 installed.

1. Click **Start**, point to **Programs**, point to **Accessories**, point to **System Tools**, and click **System Information**. The MSInfo window opens.
2. Click **Tools** on the menu bar, and then click **System File Checker**. This opens the System File Checker dialog box. Before actually running System File Checker, you need to set the criteria for what the System File Checker will check.
3. Click **Settings**. This opens the System File Checker Settings dialog box. Click the **Search Criteria** tab.
4. Review the folders in the "Select the folders you want to check" list box. Make sure that the files in your Windows and Windows/system directories are included in the list. If they are not included, use the Add Folder button to add them to the list.
5. Once you are satisfied with the list on the Search Criteria tab, click **OK**. You return to the System File Checker dialog box.
6. Click the **Scan for altered files** option button to select it, and then click **Start**. System File Checker begins checking your Windows 98 system files for integrity. As discussed in the chapter, this check is based on a comparison of CRC numbers. Note that this process could take several minutes.
7. If System File Checker detects a problem with any of your files, it prompts you to reinstall the flawed files from your Windows 98 Installation CD. Follow the prompts to reinstall the files, and then skip to Step 9. If System File Checker does not find any problems, you see the Finished dialog box, in which case you can proceed to the next step.
8. If System File Checker found no errors in your system files, click **OK** in the Finished dialog box, and then click **Close** in the System File Checker dialog box. You return to the MSInfo window.
9. Next, you need to verify the integrity of your Registry. Click **Tools** on the MSInfo menu, and then click **Registry Checker**. The Registry Checker examines your computer's Registry. If it detects a problem, the Registry Checker will ask you if you want to restore a previous version of the Registry. Otherwise, it will ask if you want to back up your current Registry. Choose the appropriate response, depending on the results for your system. Note that, in general, you shouldn't back up your current Registry unless you are fully satisfied that everything is working in an acceptable manner.
10. Finally, you need to check for critical system failures. Click **Tools** on the MSInfo menu bar, and then click **Automatic Skip Driver Agent**. Unless you have just encountered a critical system failure, a dialog box will appear indicating that everything is in working order.
11. Click **OK** to close the Automatic Skip Driver dialog box, and then close the MSInfo window.

PROJECT 14-2

In this project, you will use a multimedia presentation to check the quality of your display hardware and software setup. At the end of this project, if your computer shows multimedia presentations in a "jerky" fashion, you may want to consider upgrading your video graphics hardware card. This depends on whether you really need smooth multimedia on your computer. To complete this project, you need a computer (with a working monitor) with Windows 98 installed. In addition, it would be helpful if you actually had access to a system with problems displaying multimedia presentations.

1. Click **Start**, point to **Settings**, click **Control Panel**, and then double-click the **Display** icon. The Display Properties dialog box opens.

2. Click the **Settings** tab. In the next few steps you will maximize the demand on your display adapter, to help you assess whether it is good enough for your needs. Write down the settings that you currently see in the Colors list box and the Screen area box. You will restore these settings at the end of this project.

3. Use the Colors list box to make sure that the maximum number of colors is active. The actual maximum will vary depending on your display adapter. To find your maximum, click the arrow next to the Colors list box.

4. Drag the Screen Area bar all the way to the right, to maximize the number of pixels displayed on your screen.

5. Click **OK**. If prompted to do so, restart your computer to activate your new settings. Now that you have maximized the demands on your display adapter, you can test it with a multimedia presentation.

6. Open a multimedia presentation on your computer. If you do not have one available, do a search for "AVI files" on the Internet using Internet Explorer. One option is to download crash test videos from the US National Highway Transportation Safety Administration at *http://www.nhtsa.dot.gov/airbags*. Once the presentation starts running, right-click the picture. On the shortcut menu, point to **Zoom** or click **Full Screen** to maximize the requirements on your system. (If you choose Full Screen, press the Esc key when you are ready to exit this mode.)

7. Run the multimedia presentation. Watch it closely, especially for any jerkiness in the motion. If you notice some, the memory and acceleration in your graphics card may not be sufficient for full multimedia. You need to check this, as described in the next step.

8. Right-click the picture again. Point to **Zoom** again on the shortcut menu, then click **50%** to reduce the requirements on your system.

9. Open the **Settings** tab of the Display applet again. Now you will reduce the demands on your display adapter. This often improves the performance of multimedia, at the cost of color contrast and picture size.

10. Use the Screen area bar to reduce the screen area as much as possible. In most cases, this results in a setting of 640 × 480.

11. Click **OK**. If prompted to do so, restart your computer to activate the new setting.

12. Run your multimedia presentation again. Watch it closely and compare its performance to its previous performance. If there is a difference, it should be possible to improve your display by reducing the number of colors required in your display. In the next few steps you will verify this by reducing the number of colors required in your display. But you also need to restore your maximum screen area settings. In this way, you will be able to determine which change makes more of a difference.

13. Open the **Settings** tab of the Display applet again.
14. Use the Screen area bar to restore the screen area to the setting you specified in Step 4.
15. Use the Colors list box to restore the colors to a minimum (probably 16 or 256 colors).
16. Click **OK** to close the Display Properties dialog box. Restart your computer if prompted.
17. Repeat Step 11. Since you have reduced the number of colors on your system, you will want to check whether or not the color contrast is acceptable for your purposes. This is a subjective judgment, based on your opinion as well as the opinion of your users.
18. Restore the settings in your Colors list box and Screen area box that you recorded in Step 2 of this project.

PROJECT 14-3

In this project, you will resolve a hardware conflict on your computer. With Windows 98, this is unlikely to be necessary, if you have all Plug and Play components. So before you solve a problem, you first need to introduce a problem into your system. For this project, you will need a computer with Windows 98 installed, as well as access to your Windows 98 installation CD. This project also assumes that you have a sound card installed in your computer. If you are installing new hardware in your computer, complete the process, including rebooting, before starting this project.

1. First, you need to inspect the list of components in your computer. You will do this in two ways. To start, open the **Device Manager** tab of the Systems applet, and click the **View devices by type** option. This shows the types of devices that you currently have installed in your computer.
2. Now check this information again through the MSInfo utility. Click **Start**, point to **Programs**, point to **Accessories**, point to **System Tools**, and then click **System Information**. In the left-hand pane, click the **plus** sign adjacent to Hardware Resources, and then click **DMA**. Review the list in the right-hand pane. Highlight **IRQs**. Review the list in the right-hand pane. Highlight **Memory**. Review the list in the right-hand pane. This is the list of resources that your hardware components are currently using.
3. Now you will introduce a conflict. Open the **Add New Hardware** applet. In the first Add New Hardware dialog box, click **Next**. Then click **Next** again to allow the wizard to begin searching for new Plug and Play hardware.
4. If you already have a conflict, you will see the question, "Is the device you want to install listed below?" Make sure No is highlighted, and then click **Next**. (You will be able to use the techniques you practice here to fix this problem too.) Otherwise, skip to Step 5.
5. On the next page, you will see options that allow Windows to search for hardware that is not Plug and Play. Highlight **No** and click **Next**.
6. In the Select the type of hardware you want to install box, highlight **Sound, video, and game controllers**, and click **Next**.

7. Now you will choose hardware for another sound card. For the purposes of this project, it should *not* be Plug and Play. Choose a manufacturer in the left-hand pane, a model in the right-hand pane, and click **Next**. You should also be sure that this is a component that is not already on your computer. One example that works for this project is the Compaq Business Audio sound card. You do not need the physical sound card to install its drivers.

8. If the next page states that "The hardware you are installing is Plug and Play compatible," click **Back**, and repeat Step 7. Otherwise, depending on what you chose in Step 7, you may need to click Next or Finish to install your drivers. If you had to click Next, you need to click Finish when your drivers are installed.

9. If your Windows 98 Installation CD is not already in your CD-ROM drive, you will see the Insert Disk dialog box. Insert the CD and click **OK**. When you are notified that your drivers are loaded, click **Finish**.

10. The System Settings Change dialog box opens. Click **Yes**. Depending on what you installed, either this restarts your computer or instructs you to install the card while the computer is off. Turn your computer back on if required.

11. When your computer restarts, repeat Step 1 and Step 2. If you have successfully created a conflict, you will see a yellow exclamation point in the Device Manager tab. If you see the exclamation point, skip to Step 14.

12. If you do not see a yellow exclamation point, you will now attempt to create a conflict again. Click the **plus** sign next to Sound, video, and game controllers. Find the card that you just installed. Click **Properties**. (Note, if you installed a Plug and Play device, contrary to the instructions in this project, there will be no Resources tab in the Properties dialog box for your new card.)

13. In the Properties dialog box for your new card, click the **Resources** tab. Highlight **Interrupt Request**, and click **Change Setting**. This opens the Edit Interrupt Request dialog box. Click the up or the down arrow adjacent to the Value box, until you see a conflict in the Conflict Information text box. When you do, click **OK**. Click **OK** again in the Properties dialog box for your new card, and click **OK** in the System Properties dialog box. When prompted by the System Settings Change dialog box, click **Yes** to restart your computer. Repeat Step 1, Step 2, and Step 12.

14. Return to MSInfo. Highlight **Conflicts/Sharing**. The conflict you created should be listed in the right-hand pane. Do not close MSInfo at this time. You will now "fix" the conflict.

15. Return to the Device Manager tab, highlight the device that you just installed, and click **Properties**.

16. In the Properties dialog box for your new device, click the **Resources** tab. Under Resource type, highlight the resource with the conflict listed in MSInfo. (Sometimes "No conflicts" will be listed in the Conflicting Device List. Ignore it. You still have a conflict.) Click **Change Setting**. The resulting dialog box will be named for the resource that you are changing.

17. Now go back to MSInfo. Highlight the resource that you are changing. Whether the resource is memory, DMA, IRQ, or I/O, some part of the resource should be free. Look for the free part of that resource. (If you do not have free areas in any of these resources, your computer has too much equipment installed. You need alternate equipment such as that developed to USB or FireWire standards.)
18. Go back to the dialog box for the resource that you are changing. Change the value to one that is not taken by any device, as shown in MSInfo. Click **OK**.
19. If MSInfo shows more than one conflict, repeat Step 16, Step 17, and Step 18. Otherwise click **OK** in the Properties dialog box for your "new" device.
20. Click **OK** in the System Properties dialog box. In the System Settings Change dialog box, click **Yes**. If this does not restart your computer, do it manually.
21. When Windows 98 restarts, open the **Device Manager** tab again. The conflict you created earlier should no longer exist.
22. To complete this project, remove the device that you installed. Click the **plus** sign adjacent to Sound, video, and game controllers. Highlight the device. Click **Remove**.

CASE PROJECTS

1. You are responsible for setting up a help desk to answer computer-related questions within your company 24 hours a day, 7 days a week. When company machines are upgraded to Windows 98, you expect that the number of questions directed to the help desk will increase dramatically. To help standardize routines on the help desk, you want to create a protocol for troubleshooting procedures for several different categories of problems, including:

   - File and disk systems
   - Monitors
   - Printers

   Which of the Windows 98 tools and utilities would you use for each of these categories? In what order would you use each of these tools? This last question is somewhat subjective, depending on which tools you consider easier or more difficult to use.

2. As a network engineer who is now familiar with Windows 98, you want to be able to explain the available troubleshooting tools to others. How would you describe the following troubleshooting tools? What roles do they play in the troubleshooting process?

   - Microsoft System Information (MSInfo)
   - Device Driver tab
   - Disk maintenance tools

3. Your organization has recently upgraded its computers to Windows 98. You are the supervisor for the network administrators for your organization. They are not satisfied with most of the literature available on Windows 98. Besides a copy of this book, what other options could you recommend? Of the available resources over the Internet, what would you recommend, and why?

APPENDIX A

ONLINE RESOURCES AND BIBLIOGRAPHY

The Internet offers a wide array of material on Windows 98. This appendix lists a few of the Web sites dedicated to various aspects of Windows 98. The second half of this section lists some helpful books devoted to the topic.

WEB SITES

There are a substantial number of Web sites with information on Windows 98. A query through any of the major Internet search engines for "Windows 98" may yield literally thousands of Web pages. The following lists contain the Web sites of computer-based media, and other general sites. If you are working from somewhere outside the USA, or if English is not your first language, you might find that Web sites based in other parts of the world are useful because of the speedier connections and different languages they offer. Also, keep in mind that Microsoft and some of the major PC magazines include details and discussions in different languages.

Most of these sites are listed in alphabetical order by URL. Microsoft and non-US sites are at the end of each list. Web site URLs change often; if you do not find a site using the full address, such as *http://www.cnet.com/Content/Features/Techno/Win98/index.html*, try connecting to the basic domain name, such as *http://www.cnet.com*.

Please keep in mind that this book does not endorse the Web sites listed in this appendix. This is not a comprehensive listing of Web sites discussing Windows 98. As for the non-English language sites, the list here is just a sampling of the early Web sites with material on the Windows 98 operating system.

MEDIA-BASED WINDOWS 98 WEB SITES

CNET addresses a number of the basic aspects of Windows 98 through 20 questions, at *http://www.cnet.com/Content/Features/Techno/Win98/index.html*.

Course Technology has a series of Windows 98 articles at *http://www.course.com/news/features/win98/techtrends_win98.html*.

The InsidePC series on Windows 98 can be found at *http://www.insidepc.com/articles/software/windows98.htm*.

A newsletter focusing on different Windows operating systems, including Windows 98, is available at *http://www.lockergnome.com/*.

Macmillan Computer Publishing articles on Windows 98 can be found at *http://www.mcp.com/resources/opsys/win98/*.

NetPropensity has set up an extensive Windows 98 information site at *http://netpropensity.com/windows98/index.html*.

The Techmall is an alternative to ZDnet and Windows magazine for Windows 98 stories at *http://techmall.com/index.html*. You may need to use the internal Techmall search feature to find stories on Windows 98.

The MyDesktop network has put together a series of reports through their Windows Central site at *http://www.windowscentral.com/features/reports/win98/*.

The Windows online magazine has a storehouse of Windows 98 information at *http://www.winmag.com/win98*.

You can find the Ziff-Davis Windows 98 help site at *http://www.zdnet.com/zdhelp/win_help/win98_help.html*.

The Australian PC magazine runs an information site at *http://apcmag.com/features/win98.htm*.

Ziff-Davis also maintains a French site, dedicated to Windows 98 news and tools, at *http://www.zdnet.fr/fr/98.html*.

The Microsoft site tends to focus nearly as much on marketing as it does on Windows 98 itself. Because Windows 98 is in part an amalgamation of different upgrades and programs, search terms are not by any means limited to "Windows 98." The Microsoft Windows 98 site can be found at *http://www.microsoft.com/windows98*.

For users outside North America, Microsoft maintains a European Windows 98 mirror site in London at *http://www.eu.microsoft.com/windows98*. The Asian mirror site, based in Tokyo, is located at *http://www.asia.microsoft.com/windows98*. Although Microsoft maintains over 50 country sites, Windows 98 information in non-English languages appears to be updated less often than that at the U.S. site.

General Windows 98 Web Sites

A site focused on the degree to which Active Web is integrated with Windows 98 can be found at *http://www.activewin.com*.

A site that has made a reputation based on identifying Windows 98 problems and documenting alternatives can be found at *http://www.annoyances.org/win98/*.

World Builder Technology Services has set up a "Windows Galore – Windows 98 Tips and Tricks" site at *http://www.blarg.net/~wrldbuld/win98/index.htm*.

A general tutorial designed for less experienced users can be found at *http://www.geekgirls.com/windows_9598_menu.htm*.

A long list of tips is available at *http://home.att.net/~gunn1/tips_from_gager.htm*.

A fact sheet on Windows 98, entitled "Windows 98, Fact and Fiction," can be found at *http://members.aol.com/gurucps/windows98/new.html*.

A general Windows 98 site that has collected information since Windows 98 was known as "Memphis" can be found at *http://www.memphis97.com/windows98/index.html*.

Another collection of resources can be found at *http://www.stefan98.com/*. The focus here is largely on Windows 98 related news and reviews.

An extensive set of resources can be found at *http://www.windows98.org/home.html*. Despite the name, this site does not appear to be affiliated with Microsoft.

Another set of tips and tricks can be found at *http://www.windows-help.net*.

A comprehensive site of features, tips, news, drivers, and downloads for all Windows operating systems can be found at *http://www.winfiles.com/*.

An extensive Canadian site, entitled "Tech User Tips," is located at *http://tcp.ca/gsb/PC/win98tips.htm*.

Parlez-vous Francais? A Windows 98 site in French is available at *http://www.mygale.org/07/megaland/win98/*. It takes a broad-brush look at topics from installation requirements to the latest bugs.

Sprechen Sie Deutsch? One Windows 98 site that looks fairly comprehensive is available at *http://rover.wiesbaden.netsurf.de/~kevinopoly/*.

Parla Italiano? An Italian site is available at *http://billow.pair.com/*. Go to the FAQ menu, then click on the "Win98" menu.

A Korean FAQ site can be found at *http://skyhawk.i.ml.org/win98/faq/index.html*.

A general Windows 98 site based in the United Kingdom can be found at *http://freespace.virgin.net/dhirajlal.shah/features/w98features.html*.

MCSE Web Sites

There are a substantial number of Web sites dedicated to helping anyone interested in passing the different Microsoft certification exams. A few of them are listed here. Most of them have links to other MCSE sites. If you search the Web for MCSE help, remember that some of the best sites are based and/or developed outside the USA.

The main source for Microsoft exam objectives is located at *http://www.microsoft.com/mcp*.

You can get to a site known as the "braindump heaven" by navigating to *http://www.bnla.baynet.de/bnla01/members/robsch19/*. This site was developed in Germany.

A site dedicated to user questions is at *http://www.saluki.com*.

There are a number of study guide outlines at *http://www.cramsession.com*.

A couple of excellent sites developed in the Netherlands can be found at *http://people.a2000.nl/denneman/index.html* and *http://www.shine1.com/pdeboer.mcse/*.

Books

A number of publishers and authors operate on the "bleeding edge," writing books during the beta and early releases of Windows 98. These expert users have taken the lessons of Windows 95 to heart, and are ready to help others learn and manage Windows 98 based on their experiences. Books published through Microsoft Press are collected in the next section.

Bailes, Lenny. *Maximizing Windows 98*. Berkeley: Osborne/McGraw-Hill, 1998. List price: $34.99. ISBN 0-07882-539-3.

Bott, Ed, and Ron Person. *Platinum Edition Using Windows 98*. Indianapolis: Que Education & Training, 1998. List price: $60.00. ISBN 0-78971-513-9.

Calabria, Jane. *Windows 98 6-in-1*. Indianapolis: Que Education & Training, 1998. List price: $29.99. ISBN 0-78971-486-8.

Casad, Joe, and Bruce Hallberg. *Windows 98 Professional Reference*. Indianapolis: New Riders Publishing, 1998. List price: $49.99. ISBN 1-56205-786-3.

Cowart, Robert. *Mastering Windows 98*. Alameda, CA: Sybex Network Press, 1998. List price: $34.99. ISBN 0-78211-961-1.

Davis, Fred, and Kip Crosby. *The Windows 98 Bible*. Berkeley: Peachpit Press, 1998. List price: $34.95. ISBN 0-20169-690-8.

Ezzell, Ben. *Windows 98 Developer's Handbook*. Alameda, CA: Sybex Network Press, 1998. List price: $59.99. ISBN 0-78212-124-1.

Hergert, Douglas A. *The Big Basic Book of Windows 98*. Indianapolis: Que Education & Training, 1998. List price: $19.99. ISBN 0-78971-513-9.

Honeycutt, Jerry. *Windows 98 Administrator's Bible*. San Mateo, CA: IDG Books Worldwide, 1997. List price: $49.99. ISBN 0-76453-181-6.

Ivens, Kathy. *Using Windows 98*. Indianapolis: Que Education & Training, 1998. List price: $29.99. ISBN 0-78971-594-5.

Jamsa, Ph.D, Kris. *1001 Windows 98 Tips.* Las Vegas: Jamsa Press, 1988. List price $44.95. ISBN 1-88413-361-4.

Koers, Diane, and Elaine Marmel. *Essential Windows 98 Book*. Rocklin, CA: Prima Publishing, 1988. List price $24.99. ISBN 0-76150-967-4.

Leinecker, Richard C., Ruth Maran, and Tom Archer. *Windows 98 Programming Bible*. San Mateo, CA: IDG Books Worldwide, 1997. List price: $49.99. ISBN 0-76453-185-9.

Livingston, Brian, and Davis Straub. *Windows 98 Secrets*. San Mateo, CA: IDG Books Worldwide, 1997. List price: $49.99. ISBN 0-76453-186-7.

Mansfield, Ron. *Windows 98 for Busy People*. Berkeley: Osborne/McGraw-Hill, 1998. List price: $24.99. ISBN 0-07882-398-6.

Maran, Ruth. *Master Windows 98 Visually*. San Mateo, CA: IDG Books Worldwide, 1997. List price: $39.99. ISBN 0-76450-034-4.

McFedries, Paul. *Complete Idiot's Guide to Windows 98*. Indianapolis: Que Education & Training, 1998. List price: $14.99. ISBN 0-78971-493-0.

McFedries, Paul. *Windows 98 Unleashed, Professional Reference Edition*. Indianapolis: SAMS Publishing, 1998. List price: $54.99. ISBN 0-67231-224-7.

Meadhra, Michael, and Tom Barich. *Learn Windows 98 in a Weekend*. Rocklin, CA: Prima Publishing, 1988. List price: $19.99. ISBN 0-76151-296-9.

Minasi, Mark, and Robert Cowert. *The Ultimate Windows*. Alameda, CA: Sybex Network Press, 1998. List price: $69.98. ISBN 0-78212-285-x.

Minasi, Mark, Eric Christiansen, and Kristina Shapar. *Expert Guide to Windows 98*. Alameda, CA: Sybex Network Press, 1998. List price: $49.99. ISBN 0-78211-974-3.

Norton, Peter, and John Mueller. *Peter Norton's Complete Guide to Windows 98*. Indianapolis: SAMS Publishing, 1998. List price: $29.99. ISBN 0-67231-230-1.

Rothbone, Andy. *Dummies 101, Windows 98*. San Mateo, CA: IDG Books Worldwide, 1997. List price: $19.99. ISBN 0-76450-208-5.

Russel, Charlie, and Sharon Crawford. *Upgrading to Windows 98*. Alameda, CA: Sybex Network Press, 1998. List price: $19.99. ISBN 0-78212-190-x.

Sagman, Steve. *Windows 98 (Visual Quickstart Guide)*. Berkeley: Peachpit Press, 1998. List price: $16.95. ISBN 0-20169-689-4.

Sheldon, Tom, and Dan Logan. *Windows 98 Made Easy*. Berkeley: Osborne/McGraw-Hill, 1998. List price: $49.99. ISBN 0-07882-407-9.

Simpson, Alan. *Windows 98 Bible*. San Mateo, CA: IDG Books Worldwide, 1997. List price: $39.99. ISBN 0-76453-192-1.

Stewart, James Michael, and Amy Horowitz. *Windows 98 Black Book: The Definitive Guide to Implementation*. Cambridge, MA: International Thomson Publishing, List price: $49.99. ISBN 1-57610-265-3.

Tidrow, Rob. *Windows 98 Installation and Configuration Handbook*. Indianapolis: Que Education & Training, 1998. List price: $39.99. ISBN 0-78971-510-4.

Underdahl, Brian. *Presenting Windows 98: One Step at a Time*. San Mateo, CA: IDG Books Worldwide, 1997. List price: $19.99. ISBN 0-76453-191-3.

MICROSOFT BOOKS

The Microsoft Press has been busy with books on Windows 98. They have prepared material on every anticipated need with respect to the use and development of Windows 98.

Borland, Russell. *Introducing Microsoft Windows 98: The Official First Look at the Next Version of Microsoft Windows*. Redmond, WA: Microsoft Press, 1997. List price: $19.99. ISBN 1-57231-630-6.

Born, Gunter. *Inside the Microsoft Windows 98 Registry*. Redmond, WA: Microsoft Press, 1988. List price: $39.99. ISBN 1-57231-824-4.

Gookin, Dan. *Introducing Windows Scripting Host for Microsoft Windows 98*. Redmond, WA: Microsoft Press, 1988. List price: $34.99. ISBN 1-57231-822-8.

Joyce, Jerry, and Marianne Moon. *Microsoft Windows 98 at a Glance*. Redmond, WA: Microsoft Press, 1988. List price: $16.99. ISBN 1-57231-631-4.

Microsoft Press. *Microsoft Windows 98 Resource Kit: The Professional's Companion to Windows 98*. Redmond, WA: Microsoft Press, 1998. List price: $69.99. ISBN 1-57231-644-6.

Microsoft Press. *Microsoft Windows 98 Training Kit*. Redmond, WA: Microsoft Press, 1998. List price: $99.99. ISBN 1-57231-730-2.

Microsoft Press. *Microsoft Windows 98 Upgrade Training*. Redmond, WA: Microsoft Press, 1998. List price: $49.99. ISBN 1-57231-739-6.

Nelson, Stephen L. *Microsoft Windows 98 Field Guide*. Redmond, WA: Microsoft Press, 1998. List price: $12.99. ISBN 1-57231-684-5.

Stinson, Craig. *Running Microsoft Windows 98*. Redmond, WA: Microsoft Press, 1988. List price: $39.99. ISBN 1-57231-681-0.

APPENDIX B

THE WINDOWS 98 COMMAND-LINE ENVIRONMENT

Not everyone appreciates the Windows 98 graphical user interface (GUI). Devotees of operating systems such as Novell NetWare and UNIX will tell you that you have more control over a system through a command line. Except for the GUI and multimedia features, you can actually manage a good portion of Windows 98 through the command line. The following is only a partial list of available commands and utilities. Because files such as Config.sys are not essential to the operation of Windows 98, the utilities that are used in these files are not discussed here.

AFTER READING THIS APPENDIX YOU WILL BE ABLE TO:

- Understand the advantages of the command-line environment
- Use the command line to call up Windows 98, MS-DOS, network, and system utilities

Command-line Entries for Windows 98 Utilities

In your command-line Windows folder, there are a number of executable utilities. Throughout this book you learned to call up these utilities through the GUI interface. You can also call these up through the MS-DOS command-line window or through the Run command line. To get to the MS-DOS command-line window, click Start, point to Programs, and then click MS-DOS Prompt. To get to the Run command line, click Start, and then click Run. In many cases, using either command line may be more efficient than using the GUI interface.

If you become a devotee of the command-line interface, you can move the MS-DOS Prompt utility to the StartUp menu. At the command-line prompt, navigate to the C:\Windows\start menu\programs directory. Click Start, point to Programs, and then click MS-DOS Prompt. At the prompt, type CD C:\Windows\Start menu\Programs, and press Enter. Then type Copy ms-dos~1.pif StartUp, and press Enter. As long as your startup subdirectory is named "StartUp," this copies the MS-DOS command utility program information file to your StartUp subdirectory/menu. The next time you start Windows 98 in GUI mode, you will have an MS-DOS command-line window ready for any of the following commands:

ASD: Calls up the Automatic Skip Driver agent. All you need to do is click Start, click Run, type ASD in the Open text box, and press Enter. This may be easier than the other way to get to the Automatic Skip Driver: click on Start, point to Programs, point to Accessories, point to System Tools, click System Information, and then click Tools in the menu bar of MSInfo.

Calc: Brings up the Windows 98 calculator

Cdplayer: Activates the audio CD functions for the CD-ROM

Charmap: Calls up the character map utility to associate different characters by font style

Clipbrd: Starts the clipboard viewer

Control: Opens up the Windows 98 Control Panel, with associated icons

Dialer: Enters the Windows 98 phone dialer

Directcc: Goes to the Direct Cable Connection utility

Drvspace: Starts the DriveSpace3 utility

Drwatson: Starts the Windows 98 program debugger

Explorer: Opens Windows Explorer

Faxcover: Opens the Fax Page editor

Filexfer: Starts the file transfer utility between two different computers

Kodakimg: Goes to the Kodak image viewer utility included with Windows 98

Kodakprv: Goes to the Kodak image preview utility included with Windows 98

Mplayer: Brings up the media player utility

Notepad: Opens the Windows 98 text editor

Packager: Goes to the Object Packager utility, which assembles a package of files to insert into a document

Pbrush: Opens the Windows image paint utility

Progman: Opens the Windows 3.x style program manager, complete with program groups

Qfecheck: Starts the Windows 98 Update Information Tool

Regedit: Starts the Windows Registry Editor

Rsrcmtr: Brings up the Windows 98 resource meter to track available system, user, and GDI resources

Sndrec32: Opens the Sound Recorder utility

Sndvol32: Opens the Master Volume utility

Taskman: Opens a task manager in a window, which is a different way to manage the programs in the taskbar

Tour98: Starts the introductory tour to Windows 98

VCMUI: Brings up Version Conflict Manager

Welcome: Starts the Windows 98 welcome screen, which includes registration and maintenance utilities

Winfile: Opens the Windows 3.x style file manager

Winpopup: Starts the windows network message utility

Winrep: Starts the Windows Report Tool

Winver: Calls up the current version of Windows

Wscript: Opens a window you can use to set a time limit on Windows scripting of programming languages

MS-DOS COMMANDS

The Windows 98 version of MS-DOS is 4.10.1998. The following list does not include MS-DOS command settings for startup files such as Config.sys. Before trying an MS-DOS command, go to the MS-DOS prompt, as follows: click Start, point to Programs, and then click MS-DOS Prompt. Then to find out more about a command, type the command, followed by a space and a /?, and then press Enter. For example, to find out more about the Attrib command, type Attrib /?, and press Enter.

Attrib: Allows you to display or set read-only, hidden, system, and archive attributes of a file of your choice

CHCP: Sets or lists the active code page number, which is related to the country keyboard setting. For USA keyboards, CHCP = 437.

CTTY: Changes the port used by the input device. The input device is usually a keyboard.

Debug: Starts an editor that allows files to be inspected and revised at the byte level

Deltree: *This is a very dangerous command.* Deltree deletes all the files in a directory and the subdirectories within that directory.

Dir: Lists all files in the current directory

Diskcopy: Copies the contents of one floppy disk onto another. It does not work with any other type of disk medium.

DOSKEY: Allows your computer to remember what you entered into the command line. You can then use the arrow keys to recall what you entered. The F7 key allows you to go through your whole history of commands. Doskey is a TSR that takes 5 to 64 KB of conventional memory.

Dosrep: The MS-DOS version of the Windows Report Tool discussed in Chapter 14. The Dosrep command can only be run from MS-DOS mode, not in an MS-DOS command-line utility.

Edit: Opens a special editor for MS-DOS. If you were not able to load the Windows 98 GUI because of a mistake in a startup system file, you can use the MS-DOS editor to restore the commands from your original system files.

FC: Starts a utility that compares two files at the binary (/B) or ASCII (/A) levels. It either reports on the differences, line by line, or declares that the two files are identical.

Fdisk: Includes the traditional fdisk options to display and configure your hard disks. For Windows 98, this utility can also enable support of disks larger than 2 GB by converting your files to the FAT32 file system.

Find: Searches through all specified files for a text string, and returns all lines in all files with that string. Wildcards are not allowed.

Format: Formats a disk for use with the native MS-DOS. *This is a dangerous command because it can delete everything on your hard disk.*

Keyb: Starts a utility that specifies a keyboard of a specific type or language. Options are available for everything from Dvorak to Russian.

Label: Specifies a label for your disk volume. Without switches, this command prompts you for the label of your choice.

Lock: Enables direct disk access for an application, superseding the Installable File System Manager. This can be a risk to the integrity of all files in the chosen drive.

Mem: Displays a chart showing the free and occupied conventional (0–640 KB), upper (640 KB–1MB), and extended memory (above 1 MB). If you have a problem with sufficient free conventional memory, the mem /c command will list all resident TSRs.

Memmaker: Starts the MS-DOS conventional memory optimizer

Mode: By itself, the mode utility displays the status of all LPT and COM ports. With appropriate switches, you can redirect data such as printer output to a different port.

More: Displays output one screen at a time. This can be used to display files, e.g. "more filename.txt", or to display output from a different command, e.g. "dir | more".

Move: In DOS 6.22, can be used to move files between directories. In the Windows 98 command line, the Move command can also be used to move entire subdirectories.

Mscdex: The standard real-mode CD-ROM driver. It is also a TSR that takes about 30 KB of conventional memory. In command mode, it is helpful to activate SMARTDrive after running Mscdex, because the SMARTDrive utility can cache CD-ROM data like the protected-mode CDFS.

Nlsfunc: Allows you to load a file containing country-specific information. You might load this from a floppy disk drive with a command such as "nlsfunc a:\germany.dat".

Prompt: Changes the prompt in the command line

Set: Can be used to set or display command-line environment variables. For example, "set copycmd /-y" sets prompts for confirmation before the Copy, Move, or Xcopy commands can overwrite a file.

Setver: If the version of your DOS command does not match the present operating system, the command may not work. The setup of Windows 98 does not update the version of most DOS commands. If a DOS command does not work because of incompatible versions, "setver abc.exe 7.00" can reset that particular command.

Smartdrv: SMARTDrive is a real-mode version of VCACHE. It is a common driver if you boot to the command line. It does not work in the MS-DOS window mode.

Sort: Takes all the lines in a text file and sorts them in alphanumeric order based on the first character in each line

Subst: Substitutes an available drive letter for the directory of your choice. For example, "subst l: d:\windows" allows you to use the l: drive to access your Windows directory.

Sys: Copies boot and system files to the disk of your choice. There are three basic system files: Io.sys, Command.com, and Msdos.sys. If you use a compressed drive, the Drvspace.bin file is included as part of the system files.

Truename: If you have reassigned the name or location of directories or files with the "subst" command, this command shows the actual filenames and paths.

Type: If you type "type filename.ext" that file scrolls on your screen, without interruption.

Ver: Displays the current running version of DOS in the command line

Verify: Toggles command-line verification that a file was written correctly to disk. If Verify is on, your computer reads back all copied files and compares them to the source.

Xcopy32: Copies files and directory trees to the directories of your choice. Similar in functionality to the Move command.

Networking Commands

A number of networking commands can be run from the command line. Some of these commands were discussed in Chapters 5, 13, and 14. Most of these commands use Internet Control Message Protocol (ICMP) packets to gather their information. ICMP is a low-overhead TCP/IP protocol dedicated to getting status information for various stations on the network.

ARP: The Address Resolution Protocol associates IP addresses with the hardware address of the network adapter. With ARP, you can list what is in cache, or modify the cached address table.

FTP: Brings the command line into the File Transfer Protocol command environment. There is a series of commands available in FTP mode for file transfer and system status.

Ipconfig: This is the standard TCP/IP call for the local workstation configuration, which consists of IP address, subnet mask, and default gateway. See the WinIPCfg command for additional information.

Nbtstat: The NetBIOS status command can provide connection and cache information by NetBIOS name or IP address.

Netstat: Lists the status of connections over a network. Try it while you're connected to the Internet and learn from the result.

Net: The net is the header for a series of network commands. Many of these commands will not work from the MS-DOS Prompt window within Windows 98. Therefore, you may need to restart your system in MS-DOS mode.

- **Net config**: Calls up settings for your present network configuration: local name, workgroup, redirector, client, and connections
- **Net diag**: Requests communication with a diagnostic server, for troubleshooting
- **Net init**: Starts or stops a network
- **Net logon/logoff**: Logs on or logs off a local network. Only accessible from a full-screen command mode.
- **Net print**: Requests the queue for a specific computer or printer port
- **Net start/stop**: Starts or stops services
- **Net time**: Synchronizes time between your workstation and the local server
- **Net use**: Allows you to connect to a server share from the command line. An example of this command is "net use F: //servername/sharename", which sets up the drive F: as the local drive to access files on the given share.
- **Net ver**: Displays type and version of your computer redirector
- **Net view**: Lists computers that share a local resource

Netwatch: Starts the Netwatcher utility discussed in Chapter 13

PING: Packet Internet Grouper utility. This is a very useful TCP/IP command for troubleshooting. You can PING IP addresses or NetBIOS names. In this way, you can verify connections to the network as well as the accuracy of the NetBIOS to IP address name cache.

Route: Manually controls network routing tables. You can "route add" or "route delete" the path to an IP address. An entry in a routing table can save your TCP/IP network from having to send out a broadcast request for this information. Protocols such as RIP and OSPF are available to maintain routing tables, normally on routers between networks.

Telnet: This is a terminal emulation program. Remote systems that run a Telnet emulation service allow for time-sharing of the facility, such as a supercomputer.

Tracert: Traces the route, by IP address, to the host of your choice. When your Windows 98 machine is connected to the Internet, go to your MS-DOS command line. Try a command such as "tracert *www.yahoo.com*". Watch how this utility traces the path from your workstation connection to an available IP address connected to that domain name.

WinIPCfg: This is the Windows version of the Ipconfig command, which also includes additional network configuration data such as hardware address, DHCP and WINS server addresses, and NetBIOS settings.

System Commands

These utilities should only be run after you restart your computer in MS-DOS mode. Unless otherwise noted, they do not call up any Windows 98 GUI utilities. Many of these are important for troubleshooting situations in which you have problems getting to the GUI environment.

Chkdsk: A simpler version of ScanDisk. Chkdsk checks for disk usage, checks and displays disk status, and addresses errors in FAT and directory structure.

Cleanmgr: Activates the GUI version of the Disk Cleanup utility, which can help you keep your free disk space as large as possible, by giving you the opportunity to delete unneeded files

Cscript: Calls the ActiveX scripting host. This is the MS-DOS version of the Windows 98 scripting host.

Cvt: This is the command-line FAT16 to FAT32 converter. As with the GUI mode converter, this is a one-way process.

Cvt1: Calls up the Windows GUI FAT16 to FAT32 converter

Defrag: You can run this in the MS-DOS window to call up the Windows 98 GUI defragmentation utility.

Emm386: The extended memory manager allows you to manage the upper memory area (between 640 KB and 1 MB) as well as up to 4 MB of expanded memory to support MS-DOS-based programs.

Extract: Windows 98 setup files are compressed into what are known as cabinet files, with a .cab extension. The extract utility can be used to expand some or all of the files from a cabinet, from the setup files or from the Emergency Startup Disk.

Findramd: Sweeps all possible drive letters to find the RAM drive

Iextract: Internet Explorer backup information extraction tool

Jview: Java command line loader. Installed with Internet Explorer 4.0.

Scandisk: In the command line, this is the real-mode version of the disk error-checking utility.

Scandskw: In the MS-DOS command-line window, this starts the protected-mode version of the disk error-checking utility.

Scanreg: This command-mode utility is used to check the Registry for errors. If errors are found, this can be used to restore any of the last five backed-up copies of the Registry.

Setdebug: Activates the ActiveX debugger for Java in Internet Explorer 4.0

Sysmon: Starts the GUI System Monitor performance measurement utility

Uninstal: Uninstalls Windows 98 from your computer. Because so many of the settings are made within the GUI, the best way to uninstall Windows 98 is through the Control Panel, as discussed in Chapter 2.

SETUP SWITCHES

As discussed in Chapter 2, when you install Windows 98 in a new installation, the Setup wizard actually starts in MS-DOS. If you start your Windows 98 setup from the MS-DOS command line, there are a large number of options available for the Setup command. The options are specified with a forward slash. For example, the "setup /C" command instructs the Setup wizard not to load the SMARTDrive disk cache. The following tables of setup switches are divided into four categories: general settings, disk settings, network switches, and non-USA installations.

Table B-1   General Settings

Switch	Description
?	General help for setup command-line switches
d	Setup does not use the existing version of Windows for the early phases of setup. Defaults are still taken from the previous settings.
IA	Does not load drivers that are normally loaded after the Windows 98 files are copied
IB	Does not load drivers that are normally loaded before the Windows 98 files are copied
IC	Windows 98 does a "clean" boot, without benefit of settings in Autoexec.bat or Config.sys.
IE	Skips the Emergency Startup Disk screen
IF	Windows 98 fast setup
IL	Loads Logitech mouse driver

Table B-2 Disk Settings

Switch	Description
C	Windows 98 does not load the SMARTDrive disk cache.
ID	Skips check for minimum hard disk space required for Windows 98 installation
IH	Runs preinstallation ScanDisk in foreground; allows viewing of any errors that may arise
IQ	Skips ScanDisk quick check. Required for drives compressed by something other than DriveSpace or DoubleSpace

Table B-3 Automated/Network Setup Switches

Switch	Description
IN	Avoids calling up network portion of the Setup wizard
IX	Avoids a character set check
IW	Skips end-user license agreement
Script.inf	A "Setup script.inf" uses the settings in the Script.inf file to automate setup.
SrcDir	Specifies the source directory for Windows 98 installation files
S filename.inf	The Filename.inf script is loaded when starting the Windows 98 setup.
T:tempdir	Specifies location for temporary files. Directory must already exist. Files in that directory will be deleted.

Table B-4 Non-USA Installations

Switch	Description
IJ	NEC Japan version. Windows 98 does not prompt user for boot drive.
IO	NEC Japan version. Windows 98 calls for the exit executable files.
IF	NEC Japan version. Windows 98 does not perform a bootable setup.
A	NEC Japan version. Windows 98 uses AT drive mode.
IY	European version. Windows 98 ignores mismatches in language.

Glossary

8 mm 8 millimeter tape media, used for data backup.

32-bit print subsystem Defines how Windows 98 communicates with printers. The Windows 98 version accommodates newer computer to printer communication technologies such as the extended capabilities port and USB.

32-bit shell The underpinnings for the user interface in the Windows 98 environment, this software provides a default user interface that appears on the desktop after system bootup.

A

ACPI (Advanced Configuration and Power Interface) An extended and enhanced version of the APM originally defined by Intel and Microsoft to improve battery life and power management for laptops and other portable computing devices.

active channels A term for both the content and the delivery mode for specialized content developed for Internet Explorer.

Active Desktop A special view of the Windows 98 desktop that integrates Internet and network resources with purely local resources, and provides single-click access to all resources within its purview.

ActiveMovie The media-streaming component of Windows 98. It permits a computer to play back the front end of an incoming file even while the remainder of the file may be en route from a server elsewhere on the network.

Active Server Pages (ASP) A Web server technology developed by Microsoft that allows the dynamic creation of Web pages by the server, at the moment they are requested by the site visitor. For example the output of a search engine can use ASP technology. ASP may be enabled on Personal Web Server, as well as Internet Information Server (IIS) for Windows NT.

ActiveX Microsoft standards that support interactive content on the Internet. With the Windows Scripting Host, ActiveX can support interactive Web content.

Address Resolution Protocol (ARP) A low-level protocol in the TCP/IP suite that maps numeric IP addresses for a computer to physical addresses for that computer. ARP defines a mapping between a numeric IP address and a specific network interface card, and thus, to the computer to which that card is attached. ARP is described in RFC 826.

.adm files Text-based system policy template files.

ADSL (asymmetrical digital subscriber line) Technology that allows data to flow over ordinary telephone lines at multimegabit speeds.

Advanced Configuration and Power Interface (ACPI) A system BIOS feature that allows the operating system to direct power management activities.

AGP (accelerated graphics port) An Intel-defined specification designed to speed up communications between Pentium processors and the graphics processors usually found on graphics adapter cards, or other specialized image-processing devices.

alignment error A transmission error in which a data packet of incorrect size is received.

API (Application Programming Interface) A set of rules and specifications that permits one computer application to communicate with another, or which allows an application to take advantage of lower-level system services or to gain network access.

APM (Advanced Power Management) A predecessor to the ACPI, the APM represented an initial effort from Microsoft and computer manufacturers to define power-conserving and management interfaces for desktop and portable computers.

applet Literally, this means "a small application." It refers to programs that are run from inside other programs. For example, the Control Panel contains numerous applets.

application programming interface (API) A set of common tools, protocols, and program routines that provide a common interface to a major component such as the Registry.

applications The programs that allow the user to create documents, view Web pages, edit graphics, and so on.

ASCII (American Standard Code for Information Interchange) A standard 7- or 8-bit character-encoding scheme still widely used to represent and exchange character data among computers and applications.

Asynchronous Transfer Mode (ATM) Like Ethernet, ATM is a networking technology for transferring data on a network. ATM is also well-suited to multimedia.

Authenticode A technology that allows digital identification of the publisher of a piece of software and evidence of any tampering.

Autoexec.bat The boot file for 16-bit operating systems such as MS-DOS and Windows 3.x. It also calls up the 16-bit programs that support hardware such as CD-ROM drives and sound cards. It does not load drivers. Windows 98 does not rely directly on this file, but refers to it to configure operating settings for MS-DOS applications.

Automatic Skip Driver (ASD) agent This is the utility that detects any critical failures in the startup sequence for Windows 98.

Autonet The Windows NT 5.0 method for assigning IP addresses, similar to the Dynamic Host Configuration Protocol (DHCP).

B

bandwidth The speed of data transfer.

Banyan DOS/Windows 3.1 Client The real-mode client software created for the Banyan VINES network.

basic input/output system (BIOS) The software that actually gets a computer up and running. A Plug and Play BIOS matches installed hardware with available system resources, such as COM and LPT ports. A Plug and Play BIOS is usually stored in a flash memory chip that can be updated as required.

batch script A file that can substitute for user input. In the context of the Windows 98 Installation Wizard, it can help you automate the installation with a group of customized settings.

binary The number system with two unique digits, 1 and 0. Some Registry keys are described as binary data.

bindery The NetWare database of users, groups, passwords, and rights.

binding An association between network components, such as between an adapter and a protocol, or a protocol and a client. Allows the two components to act as one unit.

BIOS (basic input/output system) The software that defines the most basic set of PC system capabilities that are used during system startup to access a hard drive or floppy disk to load a master boot record, and then to load the operating system that actually makes the computer work. Even after bootup, BIOS routines play a key role in handling basic system input and display behavior.

BIOS translation A technique you can use to overcome size limits on hard disks.

Block I/O Subsystem Handles read and write access to storage disks. One part of it takes the requests sent to it by the file system drivers and interprets these requests, and another does the actual reading and writing.

Bootlog.txt The file that records the drivers that did and did not load successfully during the installation of Windows 98.

boot record The first entry in the boot sector. Tells the computer where to look for key boot information and related programs.

boot sector A special area on a bootable hard disk containing a series of instructions and code that tells a computer where one or more operating systems are located on the disk, and how to start up (boot) each one.

BRI (Basic Rate Interface) The most common ISDN interface. It consists of two B channels (64 Kbps each) and a single D channel (16 Kbps).

bridge Sometimes known as a switch. Bridges are often used to split, or segment, a network into different logical networks. Works at the data-link layer of the OSI model.

browse list A listing of computers on a Microsoft network. Microsoft clients are added to the browse list when you have activated LM Announce on those computers.

browse master The computer that maintains the browse list. Computers refer to the browse master to find other computers on a Microsoft network.

browsing In networking terminology, the process initiated by clicking the Browse button within a Windows application, or the Network Neighborhood icon on a Windows desktop, in My Computer, or in Windows Explorer.

bus A set of connections between your CPU or RAM and other hardware components. On startup, the Registry commands the BIOS to check all buses to identify configured and unconfigured Plug and Play hardware.

C

cabinet file A file that contains a number of other files in a compressed format. A number of cabinet files are used to store Windows 98 Setup wizard and installation files.

cache The process of storing documents or files that are either commonly requested or recently used. For example, proxy server can immediately serve back a file that has been cached without having to send a message out onto the Internet to retrieve it.

CIS (card information structure) Details about a PC Card's purpose and settings.

client A desktop or portable computer used to access network resources.

cluster A storage area on a hard disk consisting of a group of sectors.

CMYK Short for cyan, magenta, yellow, and black. Multimedia developers use CMYK to filter out unwanted colors. This is different from the RGB approach used by ICM to add colors as desired.

CO (central office) A telephone company facility where switching equipment is located.

codec In the multimedia world, short for the compression required to transmit a multimedia signal over many communications lines. This is different from codecs in the networking world.

.com A common Windows or DOS file extension that indicates an executable command file.

Common Gateway Interface (CGI) Similar to dynamic link libraries. Programming code that can be used by multiple applications. The disadvantage of CGI in Microsoft operating systems is that separate copies of a .cgi file are open for every separate program. Commonly stored in Web server directories to work with animated or interactive Web pages.

compact installation One of the options presented by the Windows 98 Setup program. Copies only the minimum files and components necessary to create a working version of Windows 98. Designed to consume as little disk space as possible. Unless disk space is at a premium, this option is not recommended.

computer policy A system policy that applies to a single computer.

Config.pol The standard default name for the system policy file.

Config.sys The configuration file for 16-bit operating systems such as MS-DOS and Windows 3.x. Before Autoexec.bat calls the setup files for hardware, Config.sys loads the associated real-mode drivers. Config.sys cannot be run by itself. Windows 98 does not rely directly on this file, but refers to it to configure real-mode drivers for MS-DOS applications.

Configuration Manager The Windows 98 architectural component that manages all aspects of the computer's general setup, or configuration, including its hardware and software components.

connectionless protocol A networking protocol that exchanges individual messages, one at a time, between sender and receiver, whereby no ongoing relationship between the parties to the communication is assumed, and whereby no information from prior messages impinges on sending or receipt of subsequent messages.

connection-oriented protocol A networking protocol that establishes an ongoing "conversation," usually called a session, between a sender and receiver. Because this creates a connection that persists across multiple message transfers, such protocols are said to be connection-oriented.

context switch When a CPU is allocated to a thread from a process in a new 4 GB virtual memory address space, memory must be switched around. That is known as a context switch.

cookie A way to collect data on the habits of a user on a Web site. Stored on the computer of the user.

cooperative multitasking A method for sharing CPU time, in which Win16 threads listen for other threads and voluntarily give up CPU access after a fixed period of time. Poorly written applications can take over the CPU, which can lead to problems in the Win16 virtual memory address space.

CRC (cyclic redundancy check) A method to check for proper transmission of data packets. CRC numbers are calculated on both sides of a transmission. If they do not match, there is a problem with the transmission, and the data is corrupt.

cross-linked Term used to refer to files that have become corrupted, causing the FAT to point to the same cluster as other files.

custom installation One of the options presented by the Windows 98 Setup program. Allows an expert to examine all of the component categories for Windows 98 (and their constituent files) and then manually select any and all elements that should be included in a particular installation. This option is most often selected for automated installations, or for bulk installations, where testing has permitted an IS professional to select exactly which components to include.

.cvf A compressed volume file. This contains the result when the files in a logical hard disk are compressed.

D

DAT (digital audio tape) High-capacity sequential tape storage media.

datagram A method of sending messages in which sections of a message may be transferred in any order between sender and receiver, and the correct ordering is rebuilt by the receiving computer.

DC 6000 A 5.25-inch cartridge for quarter-inch tape, originally developed by 3M Corporation, able to accommodate as much as 4 GB of data on a single cartridge.

DDS (digital data storage) A form of DAT tape. DDS comes in three versions, DDS1, 2 and 3, each capable of increased storage capacities.

default computer policy A system policy that applies to a computer if a Computer policy is not defined.

default logon The network to which you log on when you start your computer.

default user policy A system policy that applies to a user if a User policy is not defined.

demodulation The process of converting waveforms on a telephone line into the binary code (1s and 0s) that can be read by a computer.

desktop A computer that fits on top of a desk and is used to conduct everyday work. Also used to refer to the main Windows interface, which looks like the top of a desk.

detection The process of searching for legacy hardware. Windows 98 performs detection when you first set up Windows 98 and run the Add New Hardware applet in Control Panel.

Detlog.txt The list of hardware drivers and devices found by the Windows 98 Setup wizard.

device driver A special operating system software component that mediates information exchange between a computer and some attached device, be it a graphics or network adapter; a keyboard, mouse, or other input device; or a CRT, LCD, or some other display device.

device ID Uniquely identifies the make and model of a peripheral such as a printer. When installed on a system for the first time, a Plug and Play peripheral sends its ID to Windows 98. If the ID is found, then the driver is loaded from the appropriate disk or CD.

DHCP (Dynamic Host Configuration Protocol) An IP-based protocol that supports allocation of IP addresses to workstations, for a limited period known as a lease. It is set up as part of a server. A DHCP server has a pool of addresses to lease to workstations. DHCP is defined in RFC 2131.

Dial-Up Networking (DUN) Microsoft's collection of telephony, modem-handling, and remote communications services, designed to make it easy for users to access and interact with online information providers in the Windows 95, Windows 98, and Windows NT operating systems.

Dial-Up Scripting The scripting language supported by Microsoft Dial-Up Networking (DUN), which is used to automate the process of establishing a connection when dialing into a bulletin board, e-mail system, or some other communication provider's online services.

Digital Video Disc (DVD) standard A new standard that promises to revolutionize CD-based information delivery with up to 18 GB of data on a single disc and extremely fast access and transfer rates.

DirectX A series of Application Programming Interfaces (APIs) that simplifies the task of multimedia programming. With the DirectX APIs, multimedia programmers no longer need to create programs to handle every make and model of hardware on the market. The DirectX APIs are organized in a series of layers, also known as a multimedia architecture.

DirectX hardware abstraction layer (HAL) Part of the DirectX multimedia architecture. If multimedia hardware is not available on a computer, the DirectX HAL is able to emulate the functions of that hardware as required.

disk duplexing Similar to disk mirroring, except that each physical drive is connected to your computer through a different hardware controller connection to your motherboard. One of the options with RAID 1.

disk mirroring The process of creating a mirror image of a disk on a second physical drive. One of the options of RAID 1.

disk partition A reserved area on a hard disk that maps to a specific disk structure. Sometimes referred to as a logical drive. In the Windows 98 environment, each recognizable partition will normally be assigned its own drive letter such as C, D, or E.

disk striping with parity A fault-tolerant storage technique; even if you lose one of your hard disks, you still have access to your data. Sometimes known as RAID 5. Requires three or more hard disks.

disk striping without parity A technique for putting different parts of the same file on different hard disks. File retrieval speed is often limited by the hardware controller. Placing portions of files on separate disks means that all the disks can be writing or reading at the same time, speeding up access. Sometimes known as RAID 0.

DLC (Data Link Control) A nonroutable, connection-oriented protocol used to establish host sessions with IBM mainframe and AS/400 computers, but also to connect print servers to certain network-attached printers (clients need not load the DLC protocol to access such printers, only the print server that manages the printer needs to have DLC installed).

.dll (dynamic link library) A Microsoft Windows executable code module that is loaded on demand and is often used to define common or shared system functionality in Windows run-time environments.

DLT (digital linear tape) A magnetic tape medium used for high-capacity data storage.

DMA (direct memory access) A channel between hardware components that does not require routing through the CPU.

DNS (Domain Name Service) The address book of the Internet. Contains a database of Internet names such as *course.com* and their associated IP addresses such as 198.112.168.244

docking Connecting a portable computer to a base station.

docking station A module that a portable computer can be connected to that may contain drive bays, ports, expansion slots, and a power supply.

domain A group of users and computers. Many organizations divide their users and computers according to the internal structure of the company. For example, the Marketing employees might all be assigned to the Marketing domain. Domains are often used to assign different levels of access to confidential data. This definition of a domain is different from the Internet definition of domain, which (in the United States) is the three-letter designator at the end of an Internet address, such as "com". Uses a server such as Windows NT or Novell NetWare to verify user logons.

domain controllers Specialized Windows NT Servers that provide centralized network logon services and control access to resources. *See also* Domain model.

domain name A unique symbolic name that identifies a particular IP network host, plus the type of domain to which that host belongs (.edu = education, .gov = government, .com = commercial, and so forth), where course.com, for instance, identifies a host named course in the commercial domain.

domain model One of two Microsoft models for networking access and security. Depends on the presence of a server called a domain controller that stores a database of user accounts, group information, and access rights to network and server resources, thereby providing a single logon to the domain, and centralized security and access control mechanisms. *Compare to* Workgroup model.

DOS (disk operating system) A generic name for a class of 16-bit PC operating systems made popular by IBM's adoption of Microsoft DOS (*see also* MS-DOS) in the early 1980s.

driver Programming instructions that interface directly with the CPU. Drivers regulate the functions of hardware devices.

DriveSpace 3 An enhanced version of Microsoft's built-in disk compression software, DriveSpace 3 originally shipped with the Microsoft Plus! package for Windows 95. While it is included in the Windows 98 package, drives compressed with this software cannot be translated from FAT to FAT32 formats. They must first be uncompressed before they can be translated. Also, if the Windows boot partition is compressed using DriveSpace 3, the Windows 98 uninstall program will be unable to revert to a prior version of Windows.

.drv A common Windows NT or Windows 98 file extension that indicates a 32-bit device driver.

Dr. Watson A Windows 98 utility that captures information about application faults and errors.

dual boot The ability of a computer to boot into two different operating systems.

DVD (digital video disc) A new, high-density storage medium that uses the same form as a CD-ROM, but that offers up to 18 GB of storage on a two-sided platter, and support for high-resolution digital video data delivery (which gives this technology its name).

DWORD A type of Registry data. A DWORD is a group of bits. There are 4 bits in a nibble, 8 bits in a byte, 16 bits in a word, and 32 bits in a DWORD. In the Registry, a DWORD is represented as eight hexadecimal (base 16) digits.

Dynamic Data Exchange (DDE) A process by which two applications can share the same data. See OLE for the current standard for data sharing.

dynamic key A type of Windows 98 Registry value that is stored in RAM, and is not explicitly written to any of the Registry files. Dynamic Registry keys map the current settings for plug and play hardware, the network and system performance.

E

e-mail account The means by which you send and receive e-mail. Some ISPs allow for multiple e-mail accounts with each ISP account; for example, a family with one ISP account can have separate e-mail accounts for each family member. The name assigned to an e-mail account is not necessarily the same as the user's username.

Emergency Startup Disk (ESD) A disk containing a small set of files required for a minimal boot of the PC after a catastrophic operating system failure or corruption. An option to create this disk is provided during initial Windows 98 installation.

Enhanced Metafile Spooling (EMF) The technique used to simplify the data that is sent to the printer. A TrueType font can be sent as an outline and a command to fill that outline with ink, which takes a lot less data than a character that is filled in pixel by pixel.

enumeration The process of searching all connections (buses and devices) on a PC during startup for Plug and Play (PnP) devices. When a PnP-compatible device or driver is added to or removed from a Windows 98 PC, the Registry uses enumeration to update the system.

ESDI (Enhanced Small Device Interface) A hard disk interface used on small computers. ESDI standard drives have generally been replaced by IDE and SCSI systems. The ESDI Registry subkey contains IDE drive configuration data.

Ethernet The popularized trade name for the first major networking topology, jointly developed by Digital, Xerox, and Intel. Ethernet was so much faster than the modems and terminals of the time that it helped to revolutionize how computers are connected.

.exe A common Windows or DOS file extension for a binary executable file, most often a program of some kind.

F

Fast Infrared A protocol for network communication, in the same category as Ethernet and token ring. Windows 98 is set up to the Infrared Data Association (IrDA) standard 1.1, which accommodates data transfer of up to 4 MBps.

FAT (file allocation table) A table of file names, directory entries, and disk location information known as a file allocation table which gives the FAT file system its name, as well as describing its organization. This file system has been part of Microsoft operating systems since the first implementation of DOS in the 1980s.

FAT file system Any of a number of file systems that use a file allocation table as the primary means of organizing data on a hard disk. MS-DOS and Windows 3.11 through Windows for Workgroups use a simple 16-bit FAT file system (FAT16) that supports only eight-character filenames. A new 16-bit FAT file system called VFAT was introduced with Windows 95 that could also handle long filenames. Today, Windows NT and Windows 95 both support VFAT, as does Windows 98. But Windows 98 also supports a 32-bit implementation of the FAT file system called FAT32.

FAT32 (32-bit FAT) A 32-bit version of the FAT file system.

fault tolerance A computer system's ability to withstand element or component failures. This term also refers to a design and deployment strategy for computer systems that systematically seeks to eliminate any single-factor causes of failure that could lead to system downtime or losses of data.

file and print sharing In Microsoft terminology, the ability of Microsoft network-attached computers to make file system directories (called file shares) and printers available to other users on the network.

file system The overall structure or organization an operating system uses to name, store, and organize files. A file system is a physical disk structure that permits a computer operating system to allocate hard disk storage, to associate storage regions with named entities called files and folders or directories, and to read and write such entities upon user or application demand.

file system driver The software component that permits an operating system like Windows 98 to use a file system in order to store and retrieve data and applications.

FireWire *See* IEEE 1394.

flat address space A single, complete memory address space. Because Windows 98 32-bit programs can use, or point to, 4 GB of information, they require only one, flat address space. *Compare to* Segmented address space.

flush The process by which Registry data is written to the hard disk.

Frame type The type of data transmitted at the OSI Data Link layer.

FrontPage Server Extensions Programs that can be installed with Personal Web Server to facilitate the creation of a Web site home page. Based on the Microsoft Web page creation program FrontPage 98.

FTP (File Transfer Protocol) One of the most common methods of transferring files between local and remote computers via the Internet.

G

gateway An IP-based server that handles all IP packets not addressed to any local segment to which the server is attached. If the IP address on your data is not on your network, your data is sent to the gateway, which then sends it on to the Internet.

GDI (Graphics Device Interface) A special set of programming interfaces used in Windows 3.x, Windows 95, and Windows 98 to represent graphical images and transfer them to monitors and printers.

GPF (General Protection Fault) A response in Windows 3.x and 95 to an unrecoverable error (generally followed by a reboot).

graphical user interface (GUI) Any of a number of windows-oriented user interfaces, commonly associated with modern operating systems such as the Macintosh Operating System (MacOS) and Microsoft Windows. GUI may also be used more generically to describe any program that uses a graphical user interface, irrespective of the operating system involved.

group policy A system policy that applies to each member of a group.

H

hardware The physical devices, such as a disk drive, tape drive, mouse, keyboard, graphics card, or monitor, with which the operating system must communicate. The hardware is at the bottom of the Windows 98 architecture.

hardware profile The set of keys, drivers, and settings associated with each installed component. Windows 98 supports multiple hardware profiles on a single computer. This can accommodate setups such as a laptop that runs in "docked" mode in a docking station or "undocked" mode when you use the laptop out of the office. Different hardware profiles are stored in the HKEY_LOCAL_CONFIG\Config\000n key. The first configuration has a subkey of 0001, the second configuration has a subkey of 0002, and so on.

hierarchical database A database in which information is organized in a tree-like structure, where the lower levels contain successively greater detail. Used to describe the structure of the Registry, because it consists of a set of nested keys, beginning with the root keys.

HiPack compression A technique for file distribution that saves about 10% extra space despite being based on the same compression methods as standard Windows 95 style compression.

hit Any request for content. For example, when you retrieve a Web page from the Internet, that Web page may include nine pictures. That results in 10 hits: one for the Web page, and one for each of the nine pictures. *See also* Request.

HKEY_CLASSES_ROOT A Registry root key that provides backward compatibility information for OLE and 16-bit applications, but also includes Registry values used to control drag-and-drop operations, shortcuts, and various aspects of the Windows 98 GUI. This root key is associated with the HKEY_LOCAL_MACHINE\Software\Classes subkey.

HKEY_CURRENT_CONFIG A Registry root key that contains information about the current hardware and software configuration for a Windows 98 machine. This root key is associated with the HKEY_LOCAL_MACHINE\Config subkey to provide quick, easy access to configuration data for PnP and other hardware management services in Windows 98.

HKEY_CURRENT_USER A Registry root key that defines the desktop settings, menus, shortcuts, and resource mappings in effect for the user currently logged on to the system. This key is associated with the HKEY_USERS subkey for that user's account name. If there is only one user on the local system, this root key maps to the Default subkey.

HKEY_DYN_DATA A Registry root key that stores all its values in RAM to support faster access. It also contains a copy of the current hardware configuration (in the Config Manager subkey) and active performance counters (in the PerfStats) subkey.

HKEY_LOCAL_MACHINE A Registry master root key that is associated with the System.dat Registry file, and stores all hardware- and software-related configuration data.

HKEY_USERS A Registry master root key that is associated with the User.dat Registry file. This key contains elements such as user preferences, desktop settings, shortcuts, menus, and taskbars. Individual user profiles set up as roaming profiles will usually reside on a network server, rather than on an individual machine (although a local copy will be cached to enable access when the network server is down).

.hlp A common Windows file extension for a help system file.

hop The movement of data from one IP address to another, usually from router to router.

host name The portion of a domain name that identifies a specific host within a general domain; for example, the host part of the course.com domain name is course.

hot docking Installing or removing a device while the PC is fully powered.

HTML (HyperText Markup Language) The language used to create basic Web pages.

Hub A repeater that can connect to several computers.

hyperlink A bit of text or an image specially marked with HTML to "link" the user to another Web page.

I

IDE (Integrated Device Electronics) A common, inexpensive hard drive interface technology widely used on many PCs to this day; an enhanced version known as EIDE (Enhanced IDE) is far more common today, because it supports larger, faster drives. One commonly advertised technology is Ultra ATA, which is a version of EIDE.

IEEE 1394 Also known as FireWire. An official standard for a 100 Mbps serial interface specified by the Institute of Electrical and Electronics Engineers (IEEE). Supports 100 Mbps data rates, and can handle cables up to 4.5 meters (approximately 15 feet). This serial interface was designed with high-end consumer electronics, video, and networking requirements in mind.

Image Color Management (ICM) 2.0 A color-matching specification developed by Microsoft to help designers match output colors to digital color values or to other standard color-matching systems.

IMAP (Internet Mail Automation Protocol) A more fully-featured mail-handling protocol than POP.

.inf A common Windows file extension for a file that contains hardware or device driver configuration or installation information.

infrared A means of using light to transmit data between different computers or computer components.

.ini A common Windows 3.x or Windows 95 file extension that indicates a file that contains startup or initialization settings for hardware or software components on a PC.

.ini files Initialization files used by 16-bit applications and operating systems to store settings. Although Windows 98 stores this kind of information in a centralized database called the Registry, .ini files are maintained under Windows 98 for backward compatibility with those Win16 applications which can't retrieve information from the Registry.

Installable File System (IFS) Manager The Windows 98 architectural component that interacts with the various file system drivers and creates a single file system interface for applications and the operating system to use. The IFS Manager allows Windows 98 to support multiple file systems and network access through a single consistent interface.

Installation Wizard A method for Windows 98 to guide the user through the installation process for new components. Simple key questions are asked, and the software performs the rest of the required activities.

Intellimirror A real-time backup technology that supports Windows 98 and Windows NT 5.0 clients, in which client-side file system changes are automatically mirrored on a designated network server.

Internet Directory Service The "white pages" of the Internet. Public or private directories of individuals and their e-mail addresses. Sometimes they also include physical addresses and telephone numbers.

Internet Information Server Similar to Personal Web Server. The Web server application for the Windows NT operating system.

Internet Protocol (IP) One of the two primary protocols in the TCP/IP suite, the Internet Protocol is responsible for managing network routing and outbound message delivery, handling network addresses, and recognizing inbound messages. IP was initially described in RFC 791, and is the subject of numerous follow-up RFCs.

Internet service provider (ISP) An organization that maintains a constant presence on the Internet, and divides up and resells available Internet connections at different speeds to customers who seek to connect through their point of Internet presence to the Internet at large.

InterNIC (Internet Network Information Center) The central Internet domain name and address management facility, located online at *ds.internic.net*.

Interprocess Communication (IPC) A file looking for an object, such as a part of another file, over a network. The actual communication path is known as a named pipe.

intranet Similar to the Internet, an intranet is a TCP/IP network limited in scope, usually to a single organization.

IP address A unique numeric address for a device on an IP-based network that consists of four numbers between 0 and 255, separated by periods, such as 172.16.1.7

IPX/SPX (Internetwork Packet Exchange/ Sequenced Packet Exchange) IPX is a networking protocol used on Novell networks in the file server portion of the operating system. SPX serves as a transport layer on top of IPX for client/server applications.

IRQ An IRQ is an interrupt request to a CPU through a dedicated channel. There are 16 common IRQs allocated by Windows 98.

ISA (Industry Standard Architecture) The adapter card bus introduced with the IBM PC/AT. The 16-bit ISA bus is still a widely used standard PC bus architecture.

ISDN (Integrated Services Digital Network) A completely digital form of telephone connections that is widely used for data and voice communications in Japan, the U.S., and Europe; ISDN offers higher bandwidth (one or two 64 Kbps channels are typical for most end-user implementations) and better signal quality than conventional analog modems. Windows 98 includes built-in ISDN support.

ISP account The means by which you are identified to your Internet service provider. Each ISP account is associated with a username and a password.

J

Jaz A storage media format developed by Iomega Corporation. Disks have capacities of 1 to 2 GB, and are read by proprietary hardware devices.

K

kernel The portion of the operating system that handles the most basic of computing functions, such as managing access to the CPU by the rest of the operating system.

key A named value within the Registry database; in the Windows 98 Registry Editor, keys appear in the left-hand pane of the Registry Editor display.

L

LAN (local area network) A group of computers connected in a manner that allows communication among all connected devices.

LAN emulation A process commonly used to allow an ATM network to simulate the characteristics of a local area network.

LAN Manager (LM) Microsoft client software originally used on MS-DOS and Windows 3.x systems.

LDAP (Lightweight Directory Access Protocol) A protocol for client applications to query and handle information from an Internet directory service.

legacy Hardware or software that wasn't specifically designed to work with the current operating system. In Windows 98, backward compatibility is maintained for most legacy items.

Link Control Protocol (LCP) A TCP/IP protocol that works with PPP at the data-link layer to connect to several different protocols for checking encrypted passwords.

LM Announce The technique by which Microsoft clients announce their presence to other computers on a Microsoft client-server network.

LMHOSTS file A database that associates NetBIOS names with IP addresses.

local area network (LAN) A group of connected computers in a small area such as an office. Often, all the computers on a LAN will access the Internet through one computer (often a server), which is referred to as the gateway.

local-only users Users who only have access to the local computer, with no access to a network.

local profile A user profile that exists only on a local client. By default, all profiles are initially local profiles.

locked memory Some programs require a certain amount of dedicated RAM. This area is known as locked memory, because the information within cannot be moved out to a swap file on a hard disk.

logical database A single contiguous source of information. The Windows 98 Registry is a logical database. Although it resides in multiple physical files, it behaves like a single, coherent collection of information.

logical drive The software counterpart of a physical disk drive. Each logical drive is assigned a letter (such as C, D, or E). Physical disk drives can be split into partitions, each with their own File Allocation Table (FAT). Partitions can be split into multiple logical drives.

logon method The process of supplying a user account name and a password when prompted for such information, when a user tries to gain access to a Windows computer; the addition of third-party software may impose additional checks or input requirements (such as thumbprint or retinal scans, multiple password checks, and so forth).

logon script A series of commands that runs automatically when a user logs on to a network.

long filenames Filenames of up to 255 characters (with a total of 260 characters for the complete path name).

loopback address Used in reference to a specific TCP/IP address, 127.0.0.1. If you can contact your loopback address with the PING utility, you have confirmed that you are properly connected to a network.

LRU (least recently used) A means of identifying blocks in VCACHE that are used least often. LRUs are the first blocks that are recycled when new candidates for VCACHE are identified.

M

mail server The server to which an ISP directs all e-mail. The Internet name of the server often depends on the mail protocol in effect. For example, your ISP's mail server might be named smtp.*yourISP*.com

Maintenance Wizard A Windows 98 utility that schedules and runs maintenance tasks.

mandatory profiles A user profile that does not record user environment changes. To create a mandatory profile, rename User.dat to User.man.

Microsoft Data Access Components 1.5 Programs that can be installed with Personal Web Server that allow access to powerful databases such as Oracle, Microsoft Access, and SQL Server.

Microsoft Message Queue (MSMQ) Programs that can be installed with Personal Web Server that provide for guaranteed delivery of messages over the TCP/IP protocol.

Microsoft System Information A utility that presents information gleaned from the Configuration Manager and the Windows 98 Registry, thus providing a comprehensive overview of hardware and software installed on a particular Windows 98 PC. Sometimes known as MSInfo.

Microsoft Transaction Server (MTS) Programs that can be installed with Personal Web Server that provide for guaranteed delivery of database change requests before those changes are written to disk.

minidrivers Dynamically loaded drivers that usually take data only from hardware-specific functions. Windows 98 minidrivers are designed to work with Windows NT 5.0. They can also contain more than one type of interface, such as audio and video.

MMX technology Multimedia technology, developed originally by Intel to add multimedia processing instructions to the CPU.

modulation The process of converting from a digital signal of binary code (1s and 0s) to waveforms that resemble sound on a telephone line.

Most Recently Used (MRU) Term used to refer to the most recently accessed folders on local and networked computers. The InstallLocationsMRU Registry key stores the drive or network address where the Windows 98 Setup program last found installation files.

MS-DOS The Microsoft version of the DOS operating system (*see* DOS).

MS-DOS mode A Windows 98 environment that simulates the MS-DOS operating system, and in which most of Windows 98 is shut down.

MSInfo *See* Microsoft System Information.

multiboot The ability of a computer to boot into multiple operating systems.

multiboot machine A computer that can boot to three or more operating systems.

multilink A process that enables a dial-up connection using two or more modems or ISDN connections.

multitasking The ability to run more than one program at the same time.

multithreaded A term used to describe 32-bit programs, which can run multiple threads simultaneously, in competition for CPU time.

multithreading The ability of a computer's operating system and hardware to execute multiple pieces of code (or threads) from a single application simultaneously; this is what permits applications like MS Word to manage text input on the display while performing spelling or grammar checks in the background.

multiuser operating system A software product that integrates the functions and interactions between hardware components in separate environments for multiple users.

My Computer One of two primary resource navigation tools that are included in the default shell for Windows 95, Windows 98, and Windows NT.

N

Named pipe The channel for interprocess communication over a network, usually between a file and an object.

NDIS (Network Device Interface Specification) The interface for network drivers used in Microsoft Windows operating systems.

NetBEUI (NetBIOS Enhanced User Interface) A simple, fast, but nonroutable networking protocol included as one of the three major networking protocols in most modern Windows implementations; Microsoft no longer recommends using NetBEUI except for small, single-segment networks.

NetBIOS (network basic input/output system) A set of simple network services originally defined by IBM in the early 1980s, NetBIOS has become a popular networking API in many environments, and still plays a key role on Microsoft networks, especially for name resolution, browsing, and other important network services.

Netlog.txt The file that records the network components that were detected during the installation of Windows 98.

Net use A command to link a Microsoft client to a folder on a server connected through a network.

NetWare Directory Service (NDS) NetWare 4 and 5 database that is used to manage network resources on a Novell NetWare network.

NetWatcher A system administration tool that allows administrators to monitor and control usage of and access to the Internet.

Network control blocks (NCB) The generic term for the means by which a redirector prepares data for a network. In Windows 98, Client for Microsoft Networks uses the server message block (SMB) type of NCB, while Client for NetWare Networks uses the NetWare Core Protocol (NCP) type of NCB.

Network interface card (NIC) The hardware card that connects your computer to the network.

network protocols The rules that govern message formats and sequences that computers use to communicate with one another over a network. Examples of network protocols include NetBEUI and TCP/IP, which will be discussed in later chapters.

network users User accounts defined by a domain controller that can log on to any workstation within the network, including Windows 98.

networking model The kind of network access and security controls that apply to specific Microsoft network implementations; the models supported include the workgroup model and the domain model.

NETX The real-mode Novell Workstation Shell client, version 3.x.

New Technology File System (NTFS) Like FAT, a system for formatting and organizing a hard disk. Can only be done with and read by the Windows NT operating system. NTFS files cannot be read by Windows 98.

news account The means by which you post and view messages on an Internet newsgroup. Similar to an ISP e-mail account.

newsgroup An electronic bulletin board where users share information on common topics. The most common series of newsgroups is known as Usenet. When you post a message to a newsgroup, the contents of that message are often accessible through search engines to the entire Internet.

news server Similar in function and address to a mail server. A common Internet name for a news server would be NNTP.*yourISP*.com, where *yourISP* stands for the name of your ISP.

null modem A specialized parallel or serial cable between two computers. Two of the wires in the cable are crossed, which makes the cable appear to be a modem to each computer.

NWLink A Microsoft designation for the IPX/SPX-compatible network protocol.

O

object linking and embedding (OLE) A means by which two programs can share the same data. For example, when you import a picture into a Microsoft Word document, OLE links the picture to the designated picture-editing program. If you make a change to the picture, OLE allows Microsoft Word to reflect the change.

OGL (Open Graphics Language) Legacy graphical system that is included in the DirectX multimedia architecture model. OGL allows a multimedia application to interface directly with the hardware.

OLE (object linking and embedding) The method by which file types are associated with certain programs.

Open Datalink Interface (ODI) The Novell version of NDIS, for network driver interfaces.

operating system (OS) Software that makes it possible for a computer to run applications, store data, and communicate across a network.

P

packet A unit of data of a fixed size separated for transmission.

page A 4 KB area in which user data is stored. Memory can be swapped from the virtual memory address space to RAM (and vice versa) in pages.

paging The process by which data is transferred between RAM and virtual memory, or between RAM and a swap file.

partition A section of a hard drive. Each partition has its own File Allocation Table (FAT). Partitions can be further divided into logical drives.

pass-through security The process of passing responsibility for authentication from a local operating system to a server elsewhere on the network.

password cache *See* password list file (.pwl).

Password List Editor A simple tool used to remove passwords from the Windows 98 password list file.

password list file (.pwl) The files stored in the main Windows 98 subdirectory where all passwords are stored. This file is encrypted.

password policy Refers to Windows NT rules on passwords for age, content, and repetition. Applies to Windows 98 systems that verify logons through a Windows NT- based network.

password security The use of a password to grant access to some specific resources; in the domain model for security, the domain controller requires a valid account name and password before a user is permitted to log on to a machine or access any domain resources, and handles all authentication requests thereafter; in the workgroup model for security, individual resources carry password checks, and users must remember and use individual passwords on a per resource basis.

PC card A removable device intended to be plugged into a PCMCIA slot. The term PC Card is a trademark of the PCMCIA.

PCI (Peripheral Component Interconnect) A 32-bit local PC adapter bus designed by Intel; since PCI is much faster and more capable than ISA, it is the more common bus for video and network adapter cards.

PCMCIA (Personal Computer Memory Card International Association) The international association that sets the standards for functionality in PC Card devices.

PDA (personal digital assistant) Small computing devices most often used for contact and task management activities, e-mail, and even Web browsing. Examples include the PalmPilot and Rexx.

peer-to-peer network A type of networking in which each computer can be a client to other computers, and act as a server as well.

PerfStats A dynamic Registry key used to store real-time counters and performance data about the current state of a Windows 98 system.

Personal Web Server A desktop Web server included in Windows 98. Intended for personal home page publication on a small intranet, or for testing and development purposes prior to publication.

pixel One of the dots that make up the image on a computer monitor. Each pixel requires its own unique address, and depending on your monitor and graphics card, carries anywhere from 1 to 32 bits worth of color information.

Plug and Play (PnP) A design specification created to permit a properly equipped PC BIOS and operating system to automatically detect and configure PnP-compatible devices. PnP works during system installation and startup, or as devices are added to or removed from an active system.

Glossary

.pol files System policy files created by the System Policy Editor.

POP (Post Office Protocol) One of the TCP/IP application layer protocols. An ISP usually designates a POP server to receive your e-mail from the Internet. A common Internet name for your news server is pop.*yourISP*.com, where *yourISP* stands for the name of your ISP.

POP account Synonymous with e-mail account; the account used to access the mail server.

port A socket used to connect devices such as printers and modems to the PC via a cable.

port driver A component of the Installable File System Manager that communicates with a specific disk device, such as a hard disk controller. In Windows 98, all communication with IDE and ESDI drivers is handled with a port driver.

portable installation One of the options presented by the Windows 98 Setup program. Tailored for use on a portable or laptop computer, and therefore omits certain items that may not be of interest to portable computer users, while including a complete collection of communications and remote access tools.

PPP (Point-to-Point Protocol) A communications protocol used in modem-based communications.

PPTP (Point-to-Point Tunneling Protocol) A secure connection, made by tunneling encrypted data through a traditional PPP connection to the Internet or a LAN.

preemptive multitasking A method of multitasking in which all threads have a preset time to run before ceding control of the CPU to another thread. DOS and Win32 applications use preemptive multitasking under Windows 98.

protected mode A mode of DOS operation in which memory addresses beyond the 1 MB "high-water" mark required for real-mode operation may be accessed; protected-mode operation is the norm for newer versions of Windows NT and Windows 95.

protocol A standard, or set of rules, for data communications; among other things, protocols govern how data travels over modems and network adapters.

protocol stack A group of network protocol layers that work together, such as the seven layers of the Open Systems Interconnect (OSI) model.

proxy server A server that intercepts requests headed for the Web and tries to fulfill the requests itself, before passing them on to the Internet for completion. Proxies help save bandwidth and can speed up perceived system performance.

pull installation An installation technique in which a user initiates the steps required to install a program such as Windows 98. The user may be allowed to input some of the program settings.

push installation An installation technique in which the installation of a program such as Windows 98 happens automatically with a minimum of user input.

Q

QIC *See* TR1

R

RAID (redundant array of independent disks) A series of different techniques for using multiple hard disks on a single computer. Some versions of RAID emphasize speed, while others emphasize fault tolerance. Windows NT supports RAID levels 0, 1, and 5.

RAM (random access memory) RAM provides the working storage that computers use to manipulate programs and data while they're executing; in many ways, the amount of RAM on a PC, also known as physical memory, helps to determine its overall performance and multitasking capabilities.

RAMDrive A part of your random access memory (RAM) that has been configured to look like a hard drive. When you boot your computer with the Windows 98 ESD, it sets up a RAMDrive with a number of DOS-style utilities.

RAW Printer data that has not been processed by the Windows 98 system.

real mode A mode of DOS operation in which the original constraints of the 80286 processor architecture are rigidly enforced, and in which only the lower 1 MB of RAM may be directly addressed. This distinction is important because it relates to the method in which certain device drivers operate, and because switching between real and protected mode, or vice versa, is a time-consuming and therefore "expensive" operation in terms of system overhead and performance.

Redirector Also known as a client, such as Client for Microsoft Networks or Client for NetWare Networks. Software that prepares your message in your computer for the network.

Regedit Another name for the Registry Editor.

Registry The hierarchical database that stores all user, hardware, software, and operating system configuration information about a Windows 98 system.

Registry API (or 32-bit Registry API) The standard programming interface that allows for consistency among system tools, install wizards, setup programs, and other software that interacts with the Registry.

Registry Checker The application that checks the integrity of the Registry. Each time Windows 98 starts up, Registry Checker can back up, restore, or repair the Registry as directed, or if damage or corruption is detected during startup. There are two versions of Registry Checker: the Windows 98 DOS version, Scanreg.exe, is more powerful than the GUI version, Scanregw.exe.

Registry Editor The high-risk tool used to directly inspect and edit the Registry. Regedit.exe can be found in the Windows 98 root directory, usually C:\Windows.

remote access Used to refer to a connection to a computer from a distant location. Sometimes implemented by Remote Access Server for Windows 98.

remote procedure call (RPC) A Windows 98 feature that allows a program on one computer to use a different program on another computer connected through a network. Microsoft RPCs allow a network administrator to remotely manage a remote Registry through a local Registry Editor.

Remote Registry Services A Windows 98 utility that allows a system administrator to make use of system management tools, to use setup scripts to configure new machines, and to control an entire enterprise remotely.

repeater A device that regenerates a network signal. As signals travel over distance, they degenerate. An amplifier turns up the volume on a signal, but a repeater actually interprets what it receives and regenerates the binary code of 1s and 0s that make up the signal. Works at the physical layer of the OSI model of networking.

request A hit that successfully retrieves content. Not all hits actually bring a file, such as a picture, into a browser. All requests actually make it into a browser.

RGB (red, green, and blue) The three primary colors of the television spectrum. Used by ICM 1.0, as supported by Windows 95.

Ring architecture The type of design incorporated into Intel processors. Intel processors include four rings. Ring 0 (kernel level) interacts directly with the CPU. If there is a problem with something running at Ring 0, the computer may be shut down. Therefore, Microsoft has set up most applications in Windows 98/NT 4.0 to run in Ring 3, as far away from the CPU as possible.

roaming profile A user profile that is stored on a network share so that it can be used on any network client.

routable Term used to describe a protocol that can be used to communicate between different networks.

router A device that divides networks into segments. Although the term "router" is often used interchangeably with "gateway," they are not the same. While a router works at the network layer of the OSI model, a gateway works at the application layer of the OSI model.

roving profile Another term for a roaming profile.

S

SAP (Service Advertising Protocol) A protocol used by a Windows 98 computer to announce its presence to Novell NetWare client computers.

ScanDisk A management utility that scans hard disks to check FAT integrity, verify folder/directory structures, and check files to ensure their proper sequence and construction.

Scanreg.exe The 16-bit DOS-based implementation of Registry Checker that runs each time Windows 98 starts up. If you are in the Windows 98 GUI, you need to restart your computer in MS-DOS mode to execute this program. You can use it to back up, restore, or repair a Registry.

Scanregw.exe The 32-bit Windows implementation of Registry Checker that may be run from the standard Windows 98 desktop. It is not as powerful as Scanreg.exe.

SCSI layer The portion of the Block I/O Subsystem that communicates with SCSI devices. It's a general interface for dealing with all SCSI devices—the specifics for a particular device are handled by a miniport driver.

sector A portion of a hard drive.

segmented address space A memory address space divided into separate pieces, known as segments. 16-bit programs can point directly to only 64 KB of memory. To address all of a virtual memory address space, you need to specify a segment (64 KB) and an offset (64 KB) for a total of 64 KB $\times$ 64 KB = 4 GB of memory.

segments Distinctly different local area networks. Different network segments can be joined with a router, or a bridge.

server A networked computer that responds to client requests for network resources.

service An operating system process that provides the ability to share resources such as files and printers. When you enable File and Printer Sharing, you are providing a service to the computers that are connected through a network.

Setuplog.txt A list of what has and has not been successfully copied and implemented by the Windows 98 Setup wizard.

share-level security A security model that uses passwords assigned to individual resources that may be shared on the network.

SIPC (Simply Interactive Personal Computer) Microsoft's PC of the future. The PC would become the heart of the family entertainment center, almost as easy to use as a toaster.

Site Server The Windows NT level program associated with Internet Information Server that collects data such as requests and hits.

SLIP (Serial Line Interface Protocol) An older and simpler Internet protocol than PPP.

SMARTDrive The 16-bit hard disk caching system on the local RAM. Windows 98 uses the successor to SMARTDrive, known as VCACHE.

SMB (Server Message Block) The basic unit of transmission on NetBIOS networks.

SMTP (Simple Mail Transfer Protocol) One of the TCP/IP protocols, at the application layer. An ISP usually uses an SMTP server to send your e-mail on to the Internet. A common Internet name for an SMTP server is SMTP.*yourISP*.com, where *yourISP* stands for the name of your ISP.

SPA (Secure Password Authentication) An encrypted means of exchanging password information between client and server.

standalone workstation A workstation that operates without any kind of connection to a network.

Start menu The main menu, which appears when you click the Start button in the lower-left corner of the Windows 95, Windows 98, or Windows NT display. Applications, documents, services, and other system management activities may be launched at will from this menu.

swap file A reserved area on a hard disk that Windows 98 uses to store elements of virtual memory that are not currently in active use. Data constantly moves back and forth from this file, into and out of RAM. The continual swapping of information gives the swap file its name.

subkey A Registry key one or more levels down from another Registry key.

subnet A network, such as a LAN, that shares part of the same networking address. In most cases, a TCP/IP subnet includes all IP addresses with the same prefix. One example of a TCP/IP subnet might be all addresses that start with 133.133.133.

system bootup The process that occurs when a computer is first powered on, such as when Windows 98 starts. A PnP BIOS will check the system for existing and new PnP devices. This information is reflected in the hardware configuration in the Registry.

System File Checker A utility that checks the integrity and consistency of the Windows 98 system files, including files that end with extensions such as .dll, .com, .vxd, .drv, .ocx, .inf, and .hlp.

System Monitor The Windows 98 utility used to monitor various performance characteristics in an operating PC.

system policy A set of restrictions on user access, resources, desktop attributes, and application access that may be applied on a per user, per computer, or per group basis. Windows 98 includes a tool called the System Policy Editor, which must be used to create or modify such policies.

System Policy Editor The administrative tool used to create and modify system policies.

System Virtual Machine The one virtual machine in which all Windows programs run together. Since Windows programs can share resources, they only need the one System Virtual Machine.

System.dat One of two primary Windows 98 Registry files. The System.dat file includes data on operating system configuration, hardware components, and installed software. This file is always stored on the local computer.

T

TAPI (Telephony Application Programming Interface) A method of communication between application software, the operating system, and telephony hardware (telephones, modems, ISDN adapters, etc).

taskbar A special desktop construct within Windows 98 that appears within the Start menu frame at the bottom of the display, and provides an immediate method to toggle among active applications (the Alt-Tab key combination represents an equivalent keyboard shortcut).

TCP/IP (Transmission Control Protocol/ Internet Protocol) The standard set of networking protocols used on the Internet, originally developed in the late 1970s and early 1980s, now used on many, if not most, networks all over the world. Installed by default with Windows 98.

Telephony Application Programming Interface (TAPI) A standard devised to help develop integration between computers and telephones.

terminate-and-stay-resident program (TSR) A special type of DOS program, such as a driver, that loads into memory and remains present even when not in use, so as to be available whenever it's needed. (For example, to handle incoming data from a network interface, or to send outgoing data through such an interface.) One of the greatest advantages of Windows 98 is that it can load and unload drivers as they're needed, rather than consuming precious system resources with TSRs.

Terminate-and-stay-resident (TSR) MS-DOS-based programs that are run to load real-mode components in the first MB of RAM.

thread One part of a process devoted to performing a single task. CPU time is allocated to individual threads.

thunking The communications process between 16-bit and 32-bit programs at the Windows core user layer.

Timeslice In multitasking, a predetermined period of CPU time allotted to a thread, after which the thread has to cede the CPU to another thread.

TR-1 through **TR-4** A family of tape format designations normally associated with Travan tapes that are backward compatible with QIC tape cartridges. TR1 is used with QIC-80, TR2 with QIC-3010, and TR3 with QIC-3020. TR4 is Travan only.

Travan (TR) An extended-capacity magnetic tape format developed by 3M Corporation.

tunneling The process by which some older programs and operating systems use standard filenames with 8 characters in the name and 3 characters in the extension (abcdefgh.ijk). When they are used in place of long filenames, they are known as aliases. Programs and operating systems can associate long Windows 98 filenames with aliases.

TWAIN A set of software standards devised to incorporate image capture directly into applications such as Microsoft Office without the need for intermediate, proprietary programs.

Typical installation The default installation option presented by the Windows 98 Setup program. Should suffice for most ordinary users, for either desktop or laptop computers.

U

UltraPack The compression option in DriveSpace 3 that saves the most possible space. Uses a compression method different from Standard or HiPack compression.

Unimodem V A TAPI protocol that allows the multiplexing of more than one telephone number on one telephone line. Thanks to Unimodem V, Windows 98 can make use of distinctive ringing to determine which number is being called. Windows 98 can then send the phone call to the correct telephone appliance (e.g., modem, fax, or voice telephone).

universal serial bus (USB) A medium-speed serial bus designed to handle up to 127 peripheral devices through a single port, including mice, keyboards, modems, telephones, scanners, and joysticks.

URL (Uniform Resource Locator) A special naming convention used to identify transport protocols and information resources available through a Web browser. Sometimes referred to as a Web page address.

USB *See* universal serial bus.

Usenet A newsgroup hierarchy on the Internet. Tens of thousands of topic-related groups are available in the system.

user accounts Logical identifiers used by the operating system to identify specific individuals, associate their user environments with them, and track and control their resource access.

User Datagram Protocol (UDP) A lightweight, connectionless transport protocol used to provide best-effort, but not guaranteed, delivery services within the TCP/IP protocol suite.

user environment The collection of user preferences and administrative limitations that determine how the user interface looks and operates.

user interface tools The part of the 32-bit shell with which the user interacts. Provides a standard set of graphical items, such as browsers, toolbars, taskbars, icons, and so forth, that the user can manipulate in order to interact with utilities, applications, and the operating system. These items are used consistently by all utilities and applications, and give all software running under Windows 98 a common look and feel.

user-level security A security model that assigns a username and password to each individual person who will be accessing the network. Access to individual resources is then assigned to specific users.

user policy A system policy that applies to a single user.

user profile A collection of files containing preferences and configuration settings specific to a single user.

User.dat One of two primary Windows 98 Registry files, User.dat contains user profile information for all users known to a system. It also includes default settings and related information for new users.

user.man The filename that applies to a mandatory user profile (instead of User.dat).

V

VCACHE The Windows 98 32-bit protected-mode driver for hard disk caching in RAM.

virtual device driver A 32-bit device driver that manages a resource such as hardware so that more than one application can use the resource at a time. Virtual device drivers (VxDs) are 32-bit and operate in protected mode. The VxDs used with Windows 95 and Windows 98 are dynamically loaded and unloaded, requiring less memory.

virtual directories The directories in a Web site manager such as Personal Web Server do not necessarily correlate to folders on a physical hard disk. Thus these directories are virtual.

Virtual Machine Manager The Windows 98 architectural component that sets up private workspaces, called virtual machines, for all applications that run on a Windows 98 computer.

virtual memory A software component that acts like an extension to physical RAM and resides in a reserved space on the hard disk. Virtual memory is a hallmark of most modern operating systems, including Windows 95, Windows 98, and Windows NT.

virtual memory address space The specific portion of virtual memory allocated to an active program or group of programs. 32-bit programs can use, or address, 2^{32} (4 GB) bits of information. Thus, Windows 98 allocates one 32-bit virtual memory address space to each 32-bit program, as well as to each MS-DOS program. All 16-bit Windows programs together share the same 32-bit virtual memory address space.

visit A single session on a Web site. Usually consists of a series of hits and requests.

Visual InterDev A tool for creating dynamic Web applications.

VLM The real-mode Novell Workstation client, version 4.x.

VxD *See* Virtual device driver.

W

WDM Driver Manager The Windows 98 architectural component that allows 32-bit Windows drivers that adhere to the Windows Driver Model (and therefore work with both Windows 98 and Windows NT) to communicate with the computer's hardware.

Win16 applications Applications originally written to operate in the 16-bit Windows 3.x environment. They are supported under Windows 98 and will look like Win32 applications, although they don't run quite as Win32 applications do.

Win32 applications Applications originally written to operate in a 32-bit environment, whether Windows 95, Windows NT, or Windows 98. Win32 applications are those most able to take advantage of all the internal and external advances of Windows 98.

Win32 Driver Model (WDM) Part of the DirectX multimedia architecture. The WDM is a series of APIs designed to minimize the multimedia data that gets transmitted between the application and the CPU.

Windows 3.x A generic way to refer to various implementations of Windows version 3, including Windows 3.0, Windows 3.1, Windows 3.11, and Windows for Workgroups.

Windows 98 The latest iteration of Microsoft's most popular desktop operating system, and the primary focus of this book.

Windows 98 core The heart of the operating system; controls and coordinates all system activity. Consists of user, GDI, and kernel layers.

Windows Driver Model (WDM) A common 32-bit device driver architecture that permits vendors to write a single device driver that will work both for Windows 98 and Windows NT 5.0 without alteration. Also referred to as Win32 Driver Model.

Windows NT Server The highest-powered version of Windows NT currently available from Microsoft. Includes a broad range of network services and applications that make it uniquely well-suited to deliver file, print, and application services to network clients of many kinds.

Windows NT Workstation The most powerful desktop operating system currently available from Microsoft. Windows NT Workstation shares a common fundamental architecture with Windows NT Server, but lacks the collection of network services and applications that would make it able to function as a general-purpose network server on its own (Windows NT Workstation is also subject to a maximum of 10 simultaneous logged-in users, while Windows NT Server is subject to no such limitation, except for user licensing considerations).

Windows_Passthru account An account on a NetWare server that allows a Windows 98 computer to use the username and password data on that server. A Windows 98 computer that is set up for File and Print Sharing for NetWare Networks uses a Windows_Passthru account on a NetWare server with a bindery.

Windows Scripting Host (WSH) A scripting facility included with Windows 98. WSH makes it possible to automate and schedule routine tasks of all kinds, including command lines sequences, keystrokes, and mouse events.

Windows Update The automatic, Internet-based software update utility included as a part of the Windows 98 operating system. Windows Update makes it possible to keep Windows 98 current at all times with only minimal effort.

WINS (Windows Internet Name Service) A Microsoft name resolution service that translates between NetBIOS names and IP addresses.

WINUNDO.DAT A kind of "suitcase file" (that is, a file that contains multiple original files in a restorable format) that is created when the Uninstall option is selected when installing Windows 98 as an upgrade. Contains the complete set of files that constituted the previous version of Windows.

WINUNDO.INI A map file that records the contents of WINUNDO.DAT and the original locations of the files it contains. Should you ever choose to uninstall Windows 98, this file unpacks the contents of WINUNDO.DAT and indicates where its component files should reside.

workgroup model One of two security models supported for Windows 98, the workgroup model depends on share-level security and peer-to-peer interaction to make network resources available to users. This model works best for small groups of users who normally work together. *Compare to* domain model.

workstation A synonym for user computer. The term "workstation" also carries more of a connotation of power and capability than does the term "client." Historically, hardware vendors differentiated between workstation computers and personal computers, to emphasize a difference in speed, power, and cost. Today, this distinction is almost meaningless.

Z

Zip A medium developed by Iomega Corporation. A Zip disk capable of storing up to 100 MB of data. Requires a special drive unit.

INDEX

3½ Floppy window, 204
3.3 Volt operation, 10
8mm, 394
16-bit applications, 296
   backward compatibility to, 77–78
   communicating with 32-bit applications, 307
   cooperative multitasking, 302
   initialization files, 305
   storing settings, 305
   virtual memory address space, 299, 301
   VM (virtual machine), 296
16-bit components *versus* 32-bit components, 306
16-bit configuration files, 305
16-bit operating system, 4
32-bit applications
   communicating with 16-bit applications, 307
   threads, 301–302
   virtual memory address space, 296, 299, 301
   VM (virtual machine), 296
32-bit CD-ROM file system, 318
32-bit components *versus* 16-bit components, 306–307
32-bit drivers, 5, 7, 295
32-bit FAT file system, 318
32-bit file system, 295
32-bit kernel, 295
32-bit memory, 67
32-bit operating system, 4
32-bit print subsystem, 260–261, 282
32-bit processes and threads, 297
32-bit protected-mode drivers, 308
32-bit Registry API, 87
32-bit shell, 7, 17
802.3 standard, 259
16550 UART standard, 187

A

access rights
   assigning to shared folders, 255–257
   users or groups, 255, 256–257
ACPI (Advanced Configuration and Power Interface), 9, 17, 201–202, 206, 270, 277
ACPI subkey, 81
active application priority, 302
active channels, 161, 167
active desktop, 17, 107
Active Server, 221
Active Server Pages (.asp), 227
ActiveMovie, 10–11, 18
ActiveX, 18
Add Item dialog box, 303, 541–542
Add New Hardware Control Panel applet, 77
Add New Hardware Wizard, 185, 201, 388
Add New User wizard, 110
Add Printer Wizard, 263–264
Add Printer Wizard dialog box, 421
Add Service to Profile dialog box, 258
Add Users dialog box, 257
Add/Remove Hardware Wizard, 278

Add/Remove Programs applet
   Installed Programs tab, 363
   installing/uninstalling Win32 applications, 306
   Install/Uninstall Tab, 413, 414
   Windows Setup tab, 106, 363, 387
Add/Remove Programs Properties dialog box, 128, 199
   Setup tab, 233
   Windows Setup tab, 203, 491, 508
Address Book, 107
addresses, 296
.adm files, 120–124, 133
   adding or removing, 123–124
   Default Computer dialog box, 127
   Default User dialog box, 127
ADSL (asymmetrical digital subscriber line), 148, 197–198, 206
Advanced Connection Settings dialog box, 196
Advanced Graphics Settings dialog box, 365
Advanced Program Settings dialog box, 309
Advanced Troubleshooting Settings dialog box, 511, 520–522
AGP (accelerated graphics port), 10, 18
aliases and long filenames, 307
alignment errors, 342, 370
Alto, 2
Andressen, Marc, 161
antivirus software installation, 43–44
AOL (America Online), 12, 153
API (application programming interface), 84, 184, 206, 274, 282
APM (Advanced Power Management), 18, 201–202, 277
   1.2 extensions, 9
   driver, 270
AppEvents subkey, 79
Apple computers, 2–3, 262
applets, 68–69, 84, 240
Application Data folder, 107
applications, 7, 18
   See also programs
   active, 302
   compiling information on currently running, 353–354
   default folder, 108
   hardware request, 316
   management terms, 296–298
   memory caching, 347
   multiple using resources, 316
   protected mode, 296
   virtual memory address space, 299
Appsini.adm file, 120
architecture, 6
Area Code Rules dialog box, 189
ARP (Address Resolution Protocol), 146–147, 168, 477
ASCII (American Standard Code for Information Interchange), 145, 168
ASD (Automatic Skip Driver) agent, 539, 551
ASP (Active Server Pages), 240
ASPI (DOS Advanced SCSI Programming Interface) Manager, 356
ATM (Asynchronous Transfer Mode), 148, 282, 486
   FireWire, 278
   LAN emulation, 487
AT&T WorldNet Service, 12, 153

Attrib.exe file, 517
audio, 279
Authenticode technology, 163, 168
Autoexec.bat file, 305, 320, 412
  displaying contents, 523–524
  modifying commands executed by, 368
automated backup and restore, 67
Automatic Configuration dialog box, 164
Automatic Skip Driver, 507
Autonet, 426, 447

B

Backup Job Options dialog box, 388–389
Backup utility, 14
backups, 384
  all files, 388
  automated, 67
  differential, 388
  DLT (digital linear tape), 389
  excluding files report, 388
  FAT32 boot sector, 385
  floppy-based backup, 390
  formats hardware devices, 389
  incremental, 388
  magnetic tapes, 389
  new or changed files, 388
  password-protecting, 388
  performing, 388
  Registry, 72–73, 389
  removable media, 389–90
  storing off-site, 391
  system recovery, 390–392
  tape drives, 389–400
  verifying quality, 388
bandwidth, 152, 168
Banyan DOS/Windows 3.1 Client, 430, 447
baseline configuration, 338
  printing, 334
  saving, 334
  troubleshooting, 506
Batch 98 - Advanced Options dialog box
  Additional Files tab, 435–436
  Windows Update tab, 436–437
Batch 98 - General Setup Options dialog box
  Desktop tab, 422–423
  Install Info tab, 416
  MRU locations tab, 420
  Printers tab, 421–422
  Regional Settings tab, 419
  Setup Prompts tab, 418–419
  User Info tab, 417
  User Profiles tab, 420
Batch 98 - Internet Explorer Options dialog box
  Browser tab, 433–434
  Desktop tab, 431–432
  Display tab, 432–433
  Proxy Settings tab, 435
  Security tab, 434–435
Batch 98 - Multiple Machine-Name Save dialog box, 438
Batch 98 - Network Options dialog box
  Access Control tab, 428–429
  Additional Clients, 429

Clients tab, 427–428
Protocols tab, 423–426
Services tab, 426
Batch 98 - Optional Components dialog box, 431
Batch 98 - TCP/IP Options dialog box, 425
batch files, 438–439
batch mode installation
  advanced options, 435–437
  automating installation process, 418–419
  basic target computer information, 416
  collecting Registry settings, 415–416
  desktop look and feel, 422–423
  general setup options, 416–423
  installation directory, 416
  Internet Explorer options, 431–435
  keyboard layout, 419
  language, 419
  MRU (Most Recently Used) locations, 420
  multiple computers, 417
  multiple machine-name files, 437
  network options, 423–431
  optional components, 431
  printers, 421–422
  product ID, 416
  Registry or policy files for target computers, 435–436
  saving batch settings, 438
  source folder, 419
  time zone, 419
  uninstall information, 416
  updating drivers and software, 436–437
  user and network information, 417
  user profiles, 420
  viewing batch file, 439
  Windows 98, 414–415
batch programs, 311
batch scripts, 407, 414, 447
  See Also batch mode installation
  .reg files, 436
binary, 84
binary code, 145
binary data type, 79
bindery, 493
binding, 168, 463, 493
  protocol stacks, 146
  redirector, 463
BIOS (basic input/output system), 18, 84, 206
  PnP (Plug and Play), 80
BIOS specification, 201
BIOS subkey, 81
BIOS translation, 447
Block I/O Subsystem, 319–320
books, 566–568
boot disks
  accessing, 410
  Fdisk.com file, 413
  Format.com file, 413
  MS-DOS, 411
  Scandisk.exe file, 413
  Sys.com file, 413
  testing, 410
  usage, 412–412
  Windows 3.x, 411

Windows 95, 410
Windows 98, 411
boot record, 56
boot sector, 56
Bootdisk.bat utility, 411
Bootlog.txt file, 509, 511–512, 551
bottlenecks, 338
BRI (Basic Rate Interface), 206
bridges, 485, 493
Briefcase, 203–204
briefcases, 116
  additional, 203
  on floppy disks, 203–204
  transferring over network, 203
Browse dialog box, 414
browse list, 426, 447, 489
browse master, 426
browsers, 161
  configuring Windows 98 computer as, 489–490
  sharing information, 230
browsing, 168
bus class driver, 317
bus class minidrivers, 317
Bus Enumeration, 409
Bus Enumerator, 409
buses, 77, 84

C

C:Windows spool printers folder, 261
cabinet files, 408, 447
cable modems, 148, 197–198
cables and connections troubleshooting, 528
cache, 168
  management, 340–341
  minimizing, 275
caching, 67, 84
Call Forwarding service, 186
Calling Card dialog box, 189
Cancel (CTRL-C) keyboard combination, 52
Cardbus, 10
CDFS (CD-ROM File System), 340
CD-ROM drives
  optimizing, 364–365
  performance, 339
CGI (Common Gateway Interface), 227, 241
Change Access Control access, 256
Change Access Rights dialog box, 257
Change File Attributes access, 256
Change Password dialog box, 105
Change Windows Password dialog box, 105
channels, active, 161
CHAP (Challenge Handshake Authentication Protocol), 239
Chat.adm file, 120
check boxes, 126
Checking Your System dialog box, 53
Chkdsk.exe file, 517
CIS (card information structure), 201, 206
clean boot, 44
client, 18
Client for Microsoft Networks, 112, 113, 237, 462
  configuring, 464–465

NDIS (Network Device Interface Specification), 462
SMBs (Server Message Blocks), 464
Client for Microsoft Networks Properties dialog box, 465
Client for NetWare Networks, 112, 114, 462, 466–468
　Advanced tab, 467
　bindery, 468
　configuring, 466–467
　configuring computer to logon, 467
　ODI (Open Datalink Interface), 462
　Service for NDS (NetWare Directory Services), 468
　shared folders from server, 467
Client for NetWare Networks Properties dialog box, 114, 466
clients, 2
　Microsoft networks, 427
　NetWare 3.x/4.x networks, 427
　Windows 98 installation, 511
　Windows NT, 427
client-server networks, 144
client/server technology, 254
Close Application dialog box, 306
clusters, 33–34, 56, 359
CMYK (cyan, magenta, yellow, and black), 262, 282
CO (central office), 197, 206
codecs, 280–282
cold reboot, 392
Collected Information dialog box, 539
color display, 544
.com files, 13, 18
COM port, 186
Command.com file, 310, 314
command-line entries for Windows 98 utilities, 570–571
Common.adm file, 120, 124
communication ports, 335
communications architecture, 206
Communications dialog box, 199
communications protocols, 36
compact installation, 43, 56
compacting Registry, 73
components
　establishing baseline, 338
　input/output port address, 335
compressed partitions, 269
compression
　hard disks, 270–271, 512, 537
　incompatible schemes, 512
　telecommunication devices, 195–196
Compression Agent, 385
CompuServe, 12, 153
computer policies, 72, 119, 133
computers
　Apple, 2–3
　changing name, 39
　configuring as WINS client, 474
　finding name of, 224
　OSs (operating systems), 2
　sharing files, 203
　working configuration, 76–77

WYSIWYG (What You See Is What You Get) display, 2
computer-specific policy, 130
Conf.adm file, 120
Config Manager, 84
Config Manager subkey, 78
Config subkey, 77
Config.pol file, 119, 124–125, 129, 133
Config.sys file, 305, 320, 412
　displaying contents, 523
　editing commands, 368
Configuration Manager, 7–8, 18
Configure LPT Port dialog box, 264
configuring
　global modem properties, 185–188
　ISDN devices, 193–195
　modem dialing properties, 188–190
　printers, 263–264
　TCP/IP (Transmission Control Protocol/Internet Protocol), 149–151, 160
　Windows 98 RAS (Remote Access Server), 234
configuring Windows 98
　file systems, 32–42
　networking model, 36–39
　security strategies, 40–42
Connect to dialog box, 199, 488
connecting Web sites, 231–232
connection description dialog box, 199
Connection Properties dialog box, 196
connection type, 156
connectionless protocol, 147, 168
connection-oriented protocol, 147, 168
consistent client-server interface, 113
context switch, 302, 320
Control Panel applets, 82
Control Panel Passwords applet, 113
Control Panel subkey, 79
conventional memory
　MS-DOS applications, 313
　requirements, 513
cookies, 107, 163, 168
Cookies folder, 107
cooperative multitasking, 297, 302, 320
Copy Profile dialog box, 117
CPU (central processing unit)
　32-bit protected-mode substitutes, 356–357
　access, 302–304
　flawed older Pentium, 522
　lower levels of access, 275
　optimizing, 356–357
　performance, 338
　real-mode operations, 356
　rings, 356
CPU time and threads, 302
CRC (cyclic redundancy check), 343, 352, 370, 526, 528
Create access, 256
cross-linked files, 370
CSMA/CD (Carrier Sense Multiple Access/Collision Detection), 485
CTI (computer-telephony integration), 259
CTRL-ALT-DEL keyboard combination, 392
current user profile data, 78

custom installation, 43, 56
Custom Setup dialog box, 220
customized user environments, 102
.cvf (compressed volume file) files, 270, 282

D

DAT (digital audio tape), 394
data, moving between computers, 145
data bits, 187
data quality line, 197
Data Sources dialog box, 220
databases, 220–221
datagram, 168
DC 6000, 394
DCC (direct cable connection), 205
DDE (dynamic data exchange), 78, 84
DDS (digital data storage), 389, 394
Debug.exe file, 517
DEC PrintServer bidirectional communication, 261
Default Computer dialog box, 127
Default Computer policy, 126–127, 131, 133
Default Computer Properties dialog box, 126
default Logon, 447
default policy, 133
.Default subkey, 78
default system policies, 124–127
Default User dialog box, 127
Default User policies, 130, 133
default user profiles, 108
Default.asp file, 225, 228
Default.htm file, 225, 228
deferred printing, 261–262
defragmenting
　hard disks, 272–273
　logical drives, 361–362
Delete access, 256
deleting
　files, 273–274
　passwords, 42
　system policies, 129
demand paging, 296
demodulation, 184, 206
desktop, 2, 3, 18, 127
　displaying Web-related content on, 433
　modifying look and feel, 69
　Windows 95, 4
desktop computers, 148
Desktop folder, 107
Detcrash.log file, 409, 509–511
detection, 84
Detlog.txt file, 409, 551
device class driver, 317
device class minidrivers, 317
device drivers, 5, 6, 18
　disabling, 118
　file systems, 317
　listing changes, 336
　virtual, 315–316
device ID, 264, 282
Device Manager, 337
devices
　not operating properly, 336
　range of memory addresses used, 335

Index

troubleshooting, 539
USB (Universal Serial Bus), 278
DHCP (Dynamic Host Configuration Protocol), 151, 168, 425, 472
diagnosing problems, 341
Dialing Properties dialog box, 188–189, 200
dial-up connections and passwords, 240
Dial-Up Networking Password dialog box, 234, 235
Dial-Up Networking window, 160, 190, 234
Dial-Up networking window, 191
Dial-Up Scripting, 12, 18
Dial-Up Server, 232, 235
Dial-Up Server dialog box, 234, 235
different environments, 102
differential backup, 394
digital color, 262
digital video, 279
Direct3D RM (Retained Mode), 279–280
DirectAnimation, 280
DirectDraw, 279
DirectInput, 279
DirectMusic, 279
directory permissions, 227
DirectPlay, 280
DirectShow, 280
DirectSound, 279
DirectX architecture, 275, 279–280, 282
DirectX/WDM model, 275–277
disk caches, 344–346, 348
Disk Cleanup, 386, 537
  automatically running, 385
  regular maintenance, 508
Disk Compression Settings dialog box, 271
disk compression utilities, 270
Disk Defragmentation tool, 14
Disk Defragmenter, 272–273, 361–362, 385–386, 508, 536
disk duplexing, 393–394
disk management, 265–274
disk mirroring, 393, 394
disk optimization tools, 14
disk partitions, 282
disk reads and writes, 345
disk spindown, 9
disk striping with parity, 393–394
disk striping without parity, 392, 394
disk thrashing, 357
display
  changing scheme, 69
  settings and controls, 11
  troubleshooting, 544–545
display adapter, 545
Display applet, 69, 82
  Appearance tab, 69
  Settings tab, 544–545
Display Properties dialog box, 279
Distinctive Ring service, 186
DLC (Data Link Control) protocol, 144, 169, 470, 482
.dll (dynamic link library) files, 13, 19, 227
DLLs (dynamic-link libraries), 336, 340, 370
DLT (digital linear tape), 389, 394
DMA (direct memory access), 334, 370

DNS (Domain Name Service), 169, 425, 472, 474
DNS servers, 151, 157
docking, 207
docking stations, 116, 202–203, 207
documenting security plan, 381
domain controllers, 38, 57
domain model, 38, 40, 57
domain name, 169, 474
domains, 38, 56, 68, 84, 110, 492
DOS (disk operating system), 2, 19
DOS programs, 3
DOSKEY, 310
DoubleSpace, 512
downloaded program files, 362
downloading files, 200
DPMI (MS-DOS protected-mode interface) memory, 314
Dr. Watson, 14, 19, 353–354, 507, 548
Drive Converter, 9
Drive Converter (FAT32) Wizard, 269
drivers, 5, 19, 207, 370
  32-bit, 5, 7
  accessing INT 13, 356
  ASPI (DOS Advanced SCSI Programming Interface) Manager, 356
  conflicts, 354–355
  input devices, 547
  installing, 185
  interrupt request ports, 335
  MS-DOS version 5.0 (or higher), 356
  not strictly necessary, 512
  performance, 340
  startup and shutdown processes, 519
  troubleshooting, 539
  unsuccessful loading of, 511–512
  updating, 436–437
  WDM (Windows Driver Model), 5
drivers and controllers, 336
DriveSpace 3, 36, 270–271, 282, 362, 370, 512
.drv files, 19
DSOUND driver, 512
dual-boot computers, 219
dual-boot machines, 57, 444–445, 447
  configurations, 54–55
dual-boot or multiboot machines, 444–446
dual-protocol clients and redirectors, 468
DUN (Dial-Up Networking), 12, 19, 190–192, 195–196, 206
DUN Wizard, 12
DVD (Digital Video Disc) drives
  optimizing, 364–365
  performance, 339
DVDs (digital video discs), 10, 18, 280, 283, 340, 370
DWORD data type, 79, 84
dynamic keys, 69, 85
dynamic memory allocation, 314

E

EBIOS driver, 512
ECP (extended capabilities port), 260
Edit Alias dialog box, 230

Edit Directory dialog box, 227
Edit Extra Device dialog box, 195
Edit.com file, 517
e-mail accounts, 152, 157, 169
e-mail server names and types, 157
Emergency Startup Disk dialog box, 49–50
EMF (Enhanced Metafile Spooling), 283
EMF (Enhanced Metafile) spooling, 370
EMS (enhanced Metafile spooling), 260
encrypting passwords, 239
encryption, 163
Enum subkey, 77
enumeration, 66, 85
ESD (Emergency Startup Disk), 12, 19, 44, 50, 391, 394
  checking TEMP directory parameters, 518
  Command.com, 518
  creation of, 408
  multiple computer, 418
  real-mode CD-ROM drivers, 411–412
  Registry, 519
  startup and shutdown processes, 517–519
  system files, 518
  testing, 411–412
  troubleshooting, 517–519
  verifying integrity of hard disk, 519
  Windows 95 upgrade, 53
ESDI (Enhanced Small Device Interface), 81, 85
ESDI subkey, 81
Establishing Your Location dialog box, 49
Ethernet, 148, 197, 259, 283, 485–486
even-length packets, 543
.exe files, 12, 19
Execute permission, 227
expanded memory, 314
Explorer bars, 169
extended DOS partition, 266
extended memory, 33
  MS-DOS applications, 314
Ext.exe file, 517

F

Fast Infrared protocol, 144, 470, 483, 494
Fast Infrared Protocol Properties dialog box, 483
fast shutdown, disabling, 522
FAT (file allocation table), 19, 32–33, 370
  backups, 35
  clusters, 33, 359
  converting to FAT32, 9
  cross-linked, 359
FAT (file allocation table) file system, 32–33, 57
FAT16 drives, 33
FAT16 file system, 33–35
  drive partition size, 268
  partitions, 54–55
FAT32 Drive Converter, 269
FAT32 drives, 33
FAT32 file system, 4, 8–9, 19, 33–35
  backups, 35
  boot sector backups, 35, 385
  cluster sizes, 34

converting FAT to, 9
disk size, 35
DriveSpace 3 disk compression utility, 36
ESD (Emergency Startup Disk), 50
expanding boot record information, 35
hardware failure, 35
installed software and, 36
large hard disk support, 268
largest partition, 33
operating system compatibility, 35
relocating root directory, 35
reversibility, 35
small clusters, 34
utility software, 35
virus protection software, 36
Windows NT 5.0, 269
FAT32 partitions, 270
fault tolerance, 57, 395
  backups, 384–393, 387–390
  disk duplexing, 393
  disk mirroring, 393
  disk striping with parity, 393
  disk striping without parity, 392
  earlier versions of Windows, 392
  FAT32 boot sector backups, 385
  Intellimirror, 393
  no touch maintenance, 393
  PC mirroring, 393
  preventative maintenance utilities, 385–386
  RAID (redundant array of independent disks), 392–393
  simplified policy support, 393
  system recovery, 390–392
  Windows NT, 392–393
favorites, 107, 161
Favorites folder, 107
Fax Modem Properties dialog box, 259
fax modems, 258–259
Fdisk, 266–268, 444
Fdisk command, 413
Fdisk.com file, 413
file and print sharing, 283
  NetWare networks, 426, 490
File and Print Sharing dialog box, 237
File and Printer Sharing for Microsoft Networks Properties dialog box, 489–490
File and Printer Sharing for NetWare Networks, 490
file corruption, 67
file requests, 462–463
file sharing, 236–238
  DCC (direct cable connection), 205
  disabling, 537
File System Properties dialog box, 358, 364–365
file systems, 5, 19, 32–36, 57
  choosing, 35–36
  device drivers, 317
  disk sizes, 35
  drivers, 5, 19, 318
  FAT (file allocation table), 32–33
  FAT16, 33–35
  FAT32, 33–35
  installed software and, 36
  number of red operations, 345

number of write operations, 345
operating system compatibility, 35
performance monitoring, 345
protected-mode, 33
reads and writes, 319
real mode VFAT, 33
reversibility, 35
troubleshooting, 537–538
WDM (Win32 Driver Model), 315–319
filenames, 33
files
  contiguous, 361
  deleting, 273–274
  linking to home page, 226
  Registry, 67–68
  removing those with absolute information, 362–364
  scanning for problem, 352
  shortcut to last accessed, 108
  transferring, 165–167
  transferring between home and work computers, 232
  undeleting, 273
  uploading and downloading, 200
FireWire, 9, 19, 185, 278
flat address space, 297, 301, 320
FLOP subkey, 81
floppy-based backup, 390
flush, 85
folder Properties dialog box, 230, 237
folders
  contiguous, 361
  sharing files, 237–238
fonts and MS-DOS applications, 308, 313
format command, 413
Format.com file, 413, 518
Four11, 158
frame type, 424, 447
  mismatch, 543
Front Page Express, 220
Front Page Server Extensions, 241
FTP (File Transfer Protocol), 160, 165–167, 169
  common commands, 166
  graphical FTP client, 167
  proxy servers, 159
full-screen mode, 314

G

game card information, 335
gateways, 151, 169, 471, 485
GDI (Graphics Device Interface), 7, 275–276, 283
general virtual device drivers, 305
general Windows 98 Web sites, 565–566
global policy, 72
Gopher protocol, 160
  proxy servers, 159
GPF (General Protection Fault), 392, 395
graphics, 365, 367
graphics cards, 278
group access rights, 255–257
group policies, 72, 119, 128, 130, 133, 134
Group Priority dialog box, 130

A Guide to Microsoft Windows NT Server 4.0, 393, 440, 445
A Guide to Microsoft Windows NT Server 4.0 in the Enterprise, 128
A Guide to Networking Essentials, 144
A Guide to TCP/IP on Microsoft Windows NT 4.0, 145, 472, 473
A Guide to Windows NT 4.0 in the Enterprise, 489, 492
A Guide to Windows NT Server 4.0 in the Enterprise, 38, 68
GUIs (graphical user interfaces), 2–3, 19

H

HAL (DirectX hardware abstraction layer), 276, 282
Hands-On NetWare: A Guide to NetWare 4.1 and IntranetWare 4.11 with Projects, 430
hang, 392
hard disk management
  Disk Cleanup utility, 362–364
  Disk Defragmenter, 361–362
  DriveSpace 3, 362
  ScanDisk, 358–361
hard disks
  accessing through real-mode driver, 521
  appropriate file system, 35
  attempts to reboot after failure, 391
  bad sectors, 359
  boot sector backup, 385
  cleaning up, 537
  clusters, 33
  compressing, 270–272, 362, 512, 537
  converting partition from FAT16 to FAT32, 269–270
  correct settings for BIOS, 519
  defragmenting, 272–273
  deleting files, 273–274
  disabling interrupt handling, 537
  disabling synchronous buffer commits, 538
  disk management, 265–274
  dynamically allocating pages, 340
  extended DOS partition, 266
  FAT16 partition, 269
  FAT32 Drive Converter, 269–270
  Fdisk utility, 266
  inoperable, 391
  large hard disk support, 268
  logical DOS partition, 266
  non-MS-DOS partition, 266
  organizing files and folders, 361–362
  partitioning, 33–34, 266–267, 268, 413
  performance, 339
  primary DOS partition, 266
  purging Recycle Bin, 273–274
  reformatting, 413
  removing partitions, 266
  repartitioning, 266
  sectors, 33
  slow performance, 341
  space requirements, 32
  storing files on bad sectors, 391
  swap file, 32
  troubleshooting, 536–537

Index 605

undeleting files, 273
VCACHE, 340
verifying with ESD (Emergency Startup Disk), 519
write-behind caching, 538
hardware, 6, 20
  AGP (accelerated graphics port), 10
  automatic configuration, 80
  backups, 389
  basic information, 336
  compression, 195–196
  detection during Setup, 409
  detection process, 80
  DVD (Digital Video Disc) standard, 10
  enumeration process, 80
  failure and FAT32 file system, 35
  information about, 335–336
  installed, 337
  key features, 8–11
  legacy devices, 80
  listing changes, 336
  manual installation, 80
  matching to hardware profiles, 117
  network cards, 484
  networks, 485
  next-generation, 9–10
  overview, 13
  Plug and Play, 510
  PnP-compatible, 80
  settings, 82
  Setup Wizard, 80
  updated drivers, 409
  VxDs, 316
  Windows 98 interactions, 77
hardware cards, 521
hardware controller, 393
hardware detection, 510–511
hardware interface layers, 275
hardware profiles, 67, 70, 85, 116–118, 134
Hardware subkey, 77
Hardware Troubleshooting Agent dialog box, 539
hardware-related Registry data, 68
hardware-specific information, 79
HD IRQ (hard disk interrupt requests), 521
Hewlett-Packard JetAdmin, 261
hierarchical database, 66, 85
high memory area, 298
HiPack compression, 283
History folder, 108
hits, 228, 241
HKEY_CLASSES_ROOT root key, 75, 77–78, 85
HKEY_CURRENT_CONFIG root key, 75, 77, 85
HKEY_CURRENT_USER root key, 75, 78–79, 85, 118
HKEY_DYN_DATA root key, 75, 78, 80, 85
HKEY_LOCAL_MACHINE root key, 75–77, 80, 86
HKEY_USERS root key, 75, 78, 86
.hlp files, 13, 20
Home Page Wizard, 224, 225
home pages, 224–226, 228
hops, 478, 494

host, 278
host name, 169, 474
Hosts.sam file, 223–224
hot docking, 202–203, 207
hot-swappable components, 116
HTML (Hypertext Markup Language), 241
  displaying home page code, 225
  use with mail and news messages, 122
HTTP (Hypertext Transfer Protocol), 159, 163
hubs, 278, 485, 494
hyperlinks, 241
HyperTerminal, 199–200

I

ICM (Image Color Management), 262–263
  2.0 standard, 283
IDE (Integrated Device Electronics), 86
IDE (Integrated Device Electronics) controllers, 81
Identification dialog box, 49
identifying problem, 506–507
IE (Internet Explorer)
  History Explorer bar, 163
  restricting Web site access, 163
IE (Internet Explorer) 4.0, 161, 218, 225
  Active Channels, 161
  advanced features, 15
  assigning security level, 162
  Authenticode technology, 163
  batch mode installation options, 431–435
  browsing options double or single-clicking, 433
  cache files, 108
  cookie control, 163
  display options, 432–433
  displaying Web-related content on desktop, 433
  Explorer bars, 161
  Favorites, 15
  Favorites Explorer bar, 161
  files making up home page, 225
  History Explorer bar, 161
  Internet and Web standards support, 15
  Microsoft Wallet, 163
  most recently accessed sites, 108
  navigation histories, 15
  PICS (Platform for Internet Content Selection) content ratings, 164
  Product update, 15
  proxy server settings, 435
  Quick Launch toolbar icons, 431–432
  Search Explorer bar, 161
  secure channel services, 163
  secure data transfer, 163
  security, 161–164
  target computer default pages, 433–434
  viewing home page, 225
  Web searching tools, 15
  Web Sharing, 230
  Web site security, 434–435
  zones, 162
IEEE 802.3 standard, 259, 485
IEEE 1284 bidirectional standard, 530

IEEE 1394, 9, 20
IEEE (Institute of Electrical and Electronics Engineers), 147, 259
IFS (Installable File System) Manager, 6, 20, 317–319, 321, 462–463
IIS (Internet Information Server), 217–218, 219, 241
IMAP (Internet Mail Automation Protocol), 157, 169
incompatible compression schemes, 512
incremental backups, 388, 395
Inetresm.adm file, 120
Inetsetm.adm file, 120
.inf files, 13, 20
Inf Installer, 431
.inf setup files, 438
infrared, 207
infrared communications devices, 335
Infrared subkey, 81
.ini files, 20, 305, 320
initial environment, 314
input devices, 335, 546–547
input/out supervisor, 319
Insert Disk dialog box, 49–50
Install From Disk dialog box, 383
Install New Modem Wizard, 185
installation process, 42–44, 52, 54–55, 408–413
  batch mode, 414–439
  Setup Wizard, 43–55, 408
Installation Wizard, 82, 185, 207, 419
installed
  hardware, 337
  printers, 335
  storage devices, 336
InstallLocationsMRU subkey, 79
Install/Uninstall utility, 519
Integrated Internet Shell, 11
Intellimirror, 393, 395
Internet
  advanced browsing, 15
  communication tools, 15–16
  connecting Web site to, 231–232
  connections, 151–167
  history, 160–161
  increase integration, 15–16
Internet Configuration Wizard, 199
Internet Connection Wizard, 154–161, 422
  default Web page, 437
  news server connection, 164
Internet connections
  installing modems, 156
  Internet Connection Wizard, 154–161
  ISP (Internet Service Provider) terminology, 152–153
  options, 153
  TCP/IP (Transmission Control Protocol/Internet Protocol), 144
Internet Directory Service, 158, 169
Internet Information Server for Windows NT Server, 218
Internet LAN gateway access, 196
Internet Properties dialog box, 162–164
Internet system update, 13

InterNIC (Internet Network Information Center), 147, 170
interrupt request ports, 335
intranets, 217, 241
IP addresses, 145–147, 151, 156, 170, 207, 426
  loopback address, 224
  mapping, 473
IP (Internet Protocol), 147, 169
IPX/SPX (Internetwork Packet Exchange/Sequenced Packet Exchange), 144, 170
  Remote Registry Services, 383
  sending request, 462
IPX/SPX-compatible protocol, 424, 470, 479–482, 541–543, 543
IPX/SPX-Compatible Protocol dialog box, 543
IPX/SPX-compatible Protocol Properties dialog box, 480–482
IrDA (Infrared Data Association) 1.1 standard, 470, 483
IRQ, 370
IS (information systems), 43
ISA (Industry Standard Architecture), 81, 86
ISAPNP subkey, 81
ISDN adapters, 193–194, 232
ISDN Configuration Wizard, 193, 194
ISDN devices, 193–195
ISDN (Integrated Services Digital Network), 12, 20, 148, 193, 207
ISDN telephone lines, 193194
ISP account, 152, 170
ISPs (Internet Service Providers), 10, 20, 147, 169, 207
  accounts, 152
  bandwidth, 152
  changing settings for, 156–157
  connecting by telephone, 155
  connecting to existing account, 155–158
  connection type, 156
  dial-up adapter, 149
  DNS server address, 157
  e-mail accounts, 152, 157
  Internet Connection Wizard, 153
  IP address, 156
  LAN (local area network), 152, 155, 158–160
  LDAP (Lightweight Directory Access Protocol), 157
  logon commands, 156
  mail servers, 152
  news accounts, 152
  news servers, 152
  newsgroups, 152
  POP (Post Office Protocol), 152–153
  preconfigured online service, 153
  proxy servers, 152
  scripts, 156
  signing up with, 154–155
  SMTP (Simple Mail Transfer Protocol), 153
  specializing in supporting Web sites, 231
  TCP/IP and Dial-Up Networking, 153
  terminology, 152–153
  unable to use Internet Connection Wizard, 160
  UNIX, 153

J
Jaz drives, 390, 395
Jobs, Steven, 2

K
kernel, 7, 20, 207, 297, 302–303, 345–346
Keyboard layout subkey, 79
keys, 66, 86

L
LAN emulation, 487, 494
LAN Manager, 426
LANs (local area networks), 152, 170, 207
  connecting to ISP with, 158–160
  gateway, 196
  proxy servers, 158–159
laptops, 9
  ACPI (Advanced Configuration and Power Interface), 81, 201–202
  APM (Advanced Power Management) BIOS specification, 201–202
  BIOS (basic input/output system), 201
  Briefcase, 203–204
  DCC (direct cable connection), 204–205
  deferred printing, 261
  docking station, 202–203
  hardware profiles, 70
  hot docking, 202–203
  installing cards, 149
  managing files, 203–204
  PC Cards, 81, 149, 201–202
  port replication support, 202–203
  portable installation, 43
  synchronizing files, 203
  up-to-date files, 203
large hard disk support, 268
layout.css file, 225
LCP (Link Control Protocol), 239, 241
LDAP (Lightweight Directory Access Protocol), 157, 170
legacy, 207
  devices, 80
  VxDs, 317
level resource sharing, 42
LFN (long filename) support, 112
Linotype-Hell Color Management engine, 262
Linux, 446
List access, 256
LM Announce, 448
LM (LAN Manager), 447
LMHOSTS file, 425, 473
Lmhosts.sam file, 473
local print devices, 336
local profiles, 134
local user accounts, 110
local user profiles, 112
local-only users, 110, 134
locked memory, 346, 371
lockup, 392
logical database, 67, 86
logical DOS partition, 266
logical drives, 34, 57, 266, 361–362
logon commands, 156

logon method, 40, 57
logon requirements, 133
logon script, 414, 440, 448
long filename support, 33, 57, 307, 321, 537
loopback address, 472, 478, 494
loopback connector, 546
LRU (Least recently used), 371
LSL (Link Support Layer), 484
Lycos, 161

M
magnetic tapes, 389
mail account name, 157
mail logon name and password, 157
mail servers, 152, 170
Maintenance Wizard, 385–386, 395
Make New Connection dialog box, 488
Make New Connection Wizard, 190–191, 193
mandatory profiles, 115–116, 134
mapping, 297, 473
Maximum.pol file, 124
MCSE Web site, 566
measuring performance, 341
Mecklermedia Web site, 550
Media Player, 280–281
media-based Windows 98 Web sites, 564–565
memory
  32-bit, 67
  addresses, 521
  allocation, 346
  autotuning, 357–358
  available to Command.com, 314
  extended, 33
  instance faults, 347
  limiting, 522
  locked, 346
  management, 301–302, 357–358
  MS-DOS applications usage, 313–314
  optimizing, 357–358
  page faults
  paging, 296
  performance, 339
  printers, 531–532
  segment/offset model addressing, 301
  TSR (terminate-and-stay-resident) programs, 300–301
  Win32 applications usage, 306
memory address space, 297
memory faults, 346–348
memory leaks, 341, 345
memory protection, 302
  MS-DOS applications, 309–310
  TSR (terminate-and-stay-resident) programs, 309
message queues and threads, 307
Microsoft 32-bit DLC, 424
Microsoft 32-bit DLC Properties dialog box, 482
Microsoft Backup, 387–88, 391–392
Microsoft Batch 98 dialog box, 415–416
Microsoft Batch 98 Setup dialog box, 414
Microsoft books, 568
Microsoft Channel Guide, 161

Index

Microsoft Client for NetWare Networks, 348, 443, 466, 469, 542
Microsoft Data Access Components 1.5, 220, 241
Microsoft Fax, 258
Microsoft Fax dialog box, 258
Microsoft Fax Properties dialog box, 258
Microsoft FrontPage Express, 15
Microsoft FTP site, 166
Microsoft Knowledge Base, 549
Microsoft NetMeeting, 15
Microsoft NetShow, 15
Microsoft Network, 153
    case insensitivity, 467
    clients, 427
    network home directory, 112
Microsoft operating systems, 2
Microsoft Outlook Express, 15, 258
Microsoft Personal Web Server Setup Wizard, 221
Microsoft Referral Network, 154–155
Microsoft TechNet, 549
Microsoft Transaction Server installation directory, 222
Microsoft Wallet, 163
Microsoft Web site, 55, 161, 549
Mini.cab file, 408
minidrivers, 261, 321
miniport driver, 319
mirroring, 393
MMX technology, 283
mobile computing, 189, 200–205
Modem applet, 343
modem Properties dialog box, 185–188, 191–192, 196
modems, 148, 184–200
    16550 UART standard, 187
    actual inbound transmission, 343
    actual outbound transmission, 343
    adjusting settings, 191
    advanced connection settings, 187–188
    area code rules, 189
    buffer overruns, 343
    buffers, 342
    bytes, 343
    Call Forwarding service, 186
    calling card, 189, 192
    communications port, 186
    complete frame, 343
    compression, 196
    connection preferences, 187
    connection speed, 343
    CRC (cyclic redundancy check), 343
    data bits, 187
    demodulation, 184
    dial tone and connection time limits, 187
    dialing properties, 188–190
    different geographical locations, 189
    Distinctive Ring service, 186
    external speaker volume, 186
    frames, 343
    functionality, 342–343
    global properties, 185–188
    incomplete frame, 343
    installing, 156, 185
    listening during connection, 187
    locations, 188–189
    manually changing settings, 185
    manually dialing phones, 192
    maximum speed, 186–187
    modulation, 184
    multilink connections, 195
    operator-assisted dialing, 192
    parity, 187
    performance monitoring, 3242–343
    PnP (Plug and Play) feature, 185
    powering down, 9
    remote access, 190–192
    special command sequences, 192
    transmission ends unexpectedly, 343
    UART (universal asynchronous receiver-transmitter), 187, 343
modulation, 184, 207
Monitor subkey, 81
monitoring performance
    MSInfo tools, 351–355
    servers, 349
monitoring Web site traffic, 228–229
monitors
    improving performance, 351
    information, 335
    support for multiple, 278–279
More Info dialog box, 187
Mosaic, 161
Mouse applet, 547
MRU (most recently used), 79, 86, 448
    folders, 416
    locations, 420
Msbatch.inf file, 438–440, 444
Mscdex.exe file, 518
MS-CHAP (Microsoft Challenge Handshake Authentication), 239
MS-DOS, 2, 4, 20
    boot disks, 411
    commands, 571–573
    dual boot, 55, 444–445
    file system compatibility, 35
    managing look and feel, 314
    Prompt utility, 570
    redirector, 463
    running Setup from, 43
    typical screen, 3
    Windows 98 and, 305
    Windows NT push installation, 442
MS-DOS applications, 298, 308–315, 312
    operational defaults, 310–315
    preemptive multitasking, 302, 315
    TSR (terminate-and-stay resident), 300
    virtual machines failure of, 298
    virtual memory address space, 299, 308
    window-related properties, 311–313
MS-DOS mode, 308–309, 321
    configuring operating environment, 313
    MS-DOS applications, 309, 311
MS-DOS-based programs, 296
Msdos.sys file, 444
MSI (Microsoft System Information), 13, 20
MSInfo (Microsoft System Information), 334–337, 371
    ASD (Automatic Skip Driver) agent, 539
    boot process always opening Start Menu, 511–512
    categories, 333
    Dr. Watson, 353–354
    Hardware Resource category, 529
    printing baseline configuration, 334
    printing problems, 529
    Registry Checker, 353
    regular maintenance, 508
    saving baseline configuration, 334
    ScanReg, 353
    ScanRegW, 353
    SFC (System File Checker), 352
    Signature Verification Tool, 352–353
    subcategories, 333
    System Configuration Utility, 354
    tools, 351–355
    troubleshooting, 538–540
    VCM (Version Conflict Manager), 354–355
    Windows Report Tool, 539–540
MSMQ (Microsoft Message Queue), 221, 241
MSN (Microsoft Network), 12
Msprint2.inf file, 264
msprint.inf file, 264
MTS (Microsoft Transaction Server), 221, 241
multiboot, 444, 448
multiboot machine, 54, 57
multifunction card support, 10
multilink, 195, 207
multimedia
    APIs (DirectX Application Programming Interfaces), 274
    architecture, 275–277
    audio support, 279
    codecs, 280–281
    digital video support, 279
    DirectX, 275, 279, 280–281
    DirectX/WDM model, 275–277
    FireWire, 278
    GDI (Graphics Device Interface), 275–276
    HAL (DirectX Hardware Abstraction Layer), 276
    hardware interface layers, 275
    HDTV (high-definition TV), 280
    Media Player, 280–281
    MMX technology, 274
    multiple monitor support, 278–279
    OGL (Open Graphics Language), 275–276
    Plug and Play, 277–278
    TV Viewer, 280
    USB (Universal Serial Bus), 277–278
    WDM (Win32 Driver Model), 276
multiplexed phone lines, 259
multitasking, 5, 20, 308
multitasking operating system, 296
multithreaded, 5, 20, 302, 321
multiuser operating system, 102, 134
My Briefcase window, 204
My Computer, 7, 20
My Documents folder, 108

N

NCB (network control blocks), 494
NDIS (Network Device Interface Specification), 36, 170, 462, 483–484, 494

Ndis2sup.vxd drive, 512
NDS (NetWare Directory Service), 428, 448
Net Watcher, 382, 395, 490–491
NetBEUI (NetBIOS Extended User Interface) protocol, 144, 170, 424, 470, 482–483
   Remote Registry Services, 383
   sending request, 462
   troubleshooting, 540–541
NetBEUI Properties dialog box, 483
NetBIOS (network basic input/output system), 170
   SMBs (server message blocks), 348
NetHood folder, 108
Netlog.txt file, 409, 509, 551
Netscape Communicator 4.0, 218
Netscape Navigator, 161
NetShow, 280
NetWare 3.x networks, 467
NetWare 3.x/4.x networks, 427
NetWare 4.x networks, 467
NetWare 32-bit Client for NetWare 5.0, 469
NetWare clients, 469–470
NetWare networks
   bindery, 468
   case sensitivity, 467
   configuring computer to logon, 467
   domain services, 38
   file and printer sharing, 426, 490
   NDS (NetWare Directory Service), 428
   network home directory, 112
   roaming profiles, 114–115
   workgroup advertising, 426
NetWare servers and user-level security, 39
network adapters, 335, 511
Network Administrator: NetWare 4.1, 468, 484
Network applet
   Configuration tab, 110, 149–150, 236, 383, 480, 482–483, 487, 490, 542
   Identification tab, 224
network cards, 149
network clients, 462
   as redirectors, 463–470
   Windows 98 installation, 511
Network dialog box, 465–466
   Access Control tab, 234, 256, 467
   Configuration tab, 113–114, 193, 195, 205, 466–468, 479
   Identification tab, 39, 128
network interface, 148–149
network protocols, 20
   Windows 95, 4
   Windows 98 installation, 511
network redirector, 318, 341
network resources, 257–265
network server, 153
network services, 511
Network subkey, 77, 79, 81
network transport protocols, 36
network users, 110, 134
networked printer, 482
networking
   basics, 145–146
   client/server technology, 254
   codecs, 281

commands, 574–575
DLC (Data Link Control), 144
Fast Infrared, 144
IPX/SPX (Internetwork Packet Exchange/Sequenced Packet Exchange), 144
model, 36–39, 57
NetBEUI (NetBIOS Extended User Interface), 144
network interface, 148–149
OSI (Open Systems Interconnection) model, 145–146
packets, 144
programs and layers, 145–146
protocols, 144
TCP/IP (Transmission Control Protocol/Internet Protocol), 144
networks
   access rights, 428–429
   ATM (Asynchronous Transfer Mode), 486–487
   Banyan DOS/Window 3.1 client, 430
   batch mode installation options, 423–431
   bridges, 485
   briefcases, 203
   browse list, 426
   clients, 2
   combining computer and telephone, 184
   current session number, 348
   default logon, 428
   default protocol, 424
   deferred printing, 261
   describing components and services, 78
   domains, 68, 492
   drive mapping, 108
   Ethernet, 485–486
   file requests, 462–463
   gateways, 485
   hardware, 485
   home directory, 112
   hub, 485
   IFS (Installable File System) Manager, 462–463
   installation basics, 440–444
   integrating telephones into, 259–260
   measuring performance, 69
   minimizing protocols, 367
   network adapters, 367–368
   Novell NetWare (Workstation Shell 3.x [NETX]), 430
   Novell NetWare (Workstation Shell 4.x [VLM]), 430
   number connected to, 348
   number of open files, 348
   opening files, 462–463
   optimizing, 367–368
   passwords, 103
   performance, 340
   permissions, 103
   policy files, 68
   printer port problems, 532
   printing, 261, 366
   protocols, 423–426
   reconnecting to shares, 465
   remote management, 67

repeaters, 485
resources in use, 348
roaming profiles, 67
routers, 485
segments, 485
share-level security, 103
sharing files, 218
sharing files or computers, 426
SMBs (server message blocks), 348
speed baseline, 340
Token Ring, 486
troubleshooting configuration, 540–543
types, 485–488
user accounts, 110
user-level security, 103
VPN (virtual private networking), 487–488
workgroups, 492
Networks Properties dialog box, 467
NETX (3.x), 443, 448, 469
NETX real-mode client, 429–431
new installation
   already-installed Windows 98 components, 46
   computer description, 44
   computer name, 44
   copying Windows 98 files, 50–51
   country for channels, 49
   detecting hardware, 51
   directory for installation, 46
   directory name for, 44
   directory structure, 46
   Emergency Startup Disk, 44
   enter Windows Password dialog box, 52
   ESD (Emergency Startup Disk), 50
   free disk space, 46
   identifying computer to network, 49
   interrupting, 51
   license agreement, 46
   Microsoft site license, 46
   MS-DOS driver, 44
   predefined Windows 98 components, 47
   product ID number, 46
   real-mode CD driver, 44
   Setup Wizard, 45
   steps, 45–52
   user information, 48
   Windows 98 components, 48
   workgroup name, 44
news accounts, 152, 157–158, 170
news servers, 152, 170
newsgroups, 152, 157–158, 164–165, 170
Newsgroups dialog box, 164–165
next-generation
   hardware, 9–10
   USB (universal serial bus), 9
NIC (network interface card), 484, 494
no touch maintenance, 393
non-MS-DOS partition, 266
non-Plug-and-Play devices
   conflicts, 334
   recording settings, 408
   Windows 95 update, 54
Norton's System Information, 337
notebook computers, 9, 116
Notepad, 223

Index

Novell Client for Windows 95/98, 443, 469
Novell IP, 479
Novell NetWare
  based domain, 382
  IPX/SPX-compatible protocol, 424
  Mail092user_id directory, 129
  Mail/user_id directory, 129
  point and print capabilities, 261
  policy files, 436
  push installation, 443
  real-mode clients, 429–431
  SPAP (Shiva Password Authentication Protocol), 239
  Sys\Public directories, 129
Novell NetWare (Workstation Shell 3.x [NETX]), 430
Novell NetWare (Workstation Shell 4.x [VLM]), 430
NT Server, 129
NTFS (New Technology File System), 4, 254, 283
Ntkern.vxd, 317
NTKERN.VXD driver, 8
null modem, 204, 207
NWLink, 383, 448, 479

O

.ocx files, 13, 21
ODI (Open Datalink Interface), 462, 484, 494
Oem.adm file, 120, 121–123
off-site backup storage, 391
OGL (Open Graphics Language), 275–276, 283
OLE (object linking and embedding), 77–78, 86, 336–337, 371
online resources, 563–566
online services folder, 12
Open dialog box, 383
Open Policy dialog box, 129
Open Template File dialog box, 124
opening files, 462–463
operational defaults, 310–315
optimizing Windows 98
  CD-ROM and DUDs (Digital Video Disc) drives, 364–365
  CPU, 356–357
  graphics, 365
  hard disk management, 358–364
  memory management, 357–358
  networks, 367–368
  printing, 366–367
  removable media, 365
  System Configuration utility, 368
OS/2, 446
OSI (Open Systems Interconnect), 145–146, 348
  Data Link layer, 146
  Physical layer, 146
OSs (operating systems), 2, 21
  16-bit, 4
  32-bit, 4
  architecture, 6
  DOS (disk operating system), 2
  GUIs (graphical user interfaces), 2–3

MS-DOS, 2
PnP (Plug and Play), 80
small cluster size, 34
Outlook Express, 121–122, 159, 164–165

P

packets, 144, 170, 543
pages, 301
paging, 296, 321, 339, 347, 371
PAP (Password Authentication Protocol), 239
PARC (Palo Alto Research Center), 2
parity, 187
partitioning hard disks, 266, 413
  converting from FAT16 to FAT32, 269–270
  third-party utilities, 266–267
partitions, 33–34, 57, 444
pass-through security, 381, 395
Password applet, 108, 257
password cache, 41–42, 58, 104, 106, 134
Password Confirmation dialog box, 238
Password List Editor, 42, 106, 134
password lists, 103–106
Password Properties applet, 104–105
password-protecting backups, 388
passwords
  additional requirements, 41
  changing resource, 105
  deleting, 42
  dial-up connections, 240
  encryption, 239
  logging on, 52
  matching logon, 105
  minimum requirements, 103
  networks, 103, 105
  password cache, 104
  policies, 134
  resources, 105
  restrictions, 103
  same local and network, 104
  security, 41, 58, 103–104
  share-level security, 38, 42, 234
  storing, 42
  user-level security, 41
  usernames and, 102
  validation, 40
  Windows NT policy, 106
Passwords applet
  Remote Administration tab, 382
  User Profiles tab, 109, 420
Passwords Properties dialog box, 71
PC Card32, 10
PC Cards, 10, 21, 115, 207
  CIS (card information structure), 201
  PnP (Plug and Play) feature, 201
  power management, 9
  skipping, 419
  standards, 149
  support, 201
PCI devices, 81
PCI (Peripheral Component Interconnect), 86
PCI subkey, 81
PCMCIA (Personal Computer Memory Card International Association), 10, 21, 201, 207

PCMCIA subkey, 81
PCs (personal computers), 2
  multiple graphics cards, 9
PDAs (personal digital assistants), 201, 208
peer-to-peer network, 8, 21
performance, 338–341
performance monitoring
  disk cache, 344–345
  disk reads and writes, 345
  file systems, 345
  kernel, 345
  memory faults, 346–348
  modems, 342–343
  System Monitor, 342–349, 349–351
  trail and error, 351
PerfStats, 86
PerfStats subkey, 78
Personal Web Manager, 223–224
Personal Web Server for Windows 98, 218
Personal Web Server for Windows NT Workstation 4.0, 218, 229
personalized information delivery, 16
Personalized Items Settings dialog box, 71, 110
PFX (Personal Information Exchange), 163
Phone Dialer, 200
phone line switches, 197
phone line transmission problems, 197
PICS (Platform for Internet Content Selection) content ratings, 164
PING (Packet Internet Groper), 147–148, 478
pixels, 260, 283
PnP (Plug and Play) feature, 8, 11, 21, 66, 77, 86, 208
  BIOS (basic input/output system), 80
  closest match printer driver, 264
  disabling, 334
  FireWire, 278
  hardware, 510
  installing new hardware, 69
  ISDN adapters, 194
  modems, 185
  motherboard, 80
  multimedia, 277–278
  network cards, 149
  not installing printer driver, 265
  OS (operating system), 80
  PC Cards, 201
  PnP-compatible hardware, 80
  printer support, 264–265
  Registry, 79–81
  subkey relationships, 81
  updated Windows 98 printer driver, 264
  USB (Universal Serial Bus), 277–278
  Windows 95, 4
.pol (policy) files, 82–83, 120, 134
  saving system policies as, 128–129
  System Policy Editor, 120
  target computers, 435–436
Policy Template Options dialog box, 124
Policy.pol file, 68, 72, 83
POP account, 153, 171
POP (Post Office Protocol), 152–153, 157, 171
portable installation, 43, 58
ports, 208
  drivers, 319, 321

replication support, 202–203
posting to Web Site, 226
power and usability, 11–12
Power Management Properties dialog box, 202
PPP (Point-to-Point) capable server, 239
PPP (Point-to-Point Protocol), 147, 171, 195, 241
PPTP (Point-to-Point Tunneling Protocol), 10, 21, 241, 487
Precopy1.cab file, 408
Precopy2.cab file, 408
preemptive multitasking, 297, 302, 315, 321
preferred Web sites, 107
Preparing Directory dialog box, 46–47
primary DOS partition, 266
primary kernel scheduler, 297
print jobs stored on disk, 261
print servers, 261
Print Spooler, 260–261
printer drivers, 261
 archival or compressed formats, 263
 closest match, 264
 minidrivers, 261
 not installing, 265
 universal driver, 261
 updated, 264
 Windows NT 4.0, 261
printer Properties dialog box
 Details tab, 366, 532–533
 Device Options tab, 367, 534
 General tab, 532
 Graphics tab, 367, 535
 Paper tab, 533
 Sharing tab, 238
Printer Setup Wizard, 421
printer sharing, 236–237
 DCC (direct cable connection), 205
printers
 batch mode installation, 421–422
 closest match printer driver, 264
 comments, 532
 configuring, 263–264
 device ID, 264
 driver problems, 532–533
 ECP-capable sending instructions to, 260
 graphics, 367
 IEEE 1284 bidirectional standard, 530
 installed, 335
 installing, 263
 LPT1 port, 264
 manually setting memory, 534
 memory, 531–532
 memory tracking option, 367
 name of, 421
 networked, 482
 not installing printer driver, 265
 paper source, 533
 Plug and Play support, 264–265
 port problems, 532
 properties, 532–535
 specifying port, 264
 spooling problems, 533
 troubleshooting, 529–535
 updated Windows 98 driver, 264
Printers window, 262

printing
 32-bit print subsystem, 260–261
 baseline configuration, 334
 deferred, 261–262
 EMF (enhanced metafile) format, 351
 format, 366
 ICM (image color matching), 262–263
 installing and configuring printers, 263
 MS-DOS applications, 308
 networks, 261, 366
 optimizing, 366–367
 performance, 340
 to printer or spooler, 366
 problems and MSInfo, 529
 raster graphics, 535
 RAW format, 351
 spooler problems, 530–531
 trial and error, 351
 TWAIN standards, 263
 vector graphics, 535
problem files, 352
problems and diagnostics, 341
processes, 297, 301
 multithreaded, 302
 threads, 297
processor requirements, 32
Prodigy, 12
Prodigy Internet, 153
Product Identification dialog box, 46
Product Key dialog box, 46
Profiles directory, 41
programs
 See also applications
 associating file extensions with, 82
 authorized copy of, 352–353
 automatically running resident in memory, 336
 backward compatibility to 16-bit, 77–78
 diagnosing and logging software related problems, 353–354
 installed and file systems, 36
 links to file types, 77–78
 modifying automatic startup, 525–526
 overview, 13
 settings, 82
 translating for protocols, 145
 updating, 436–437
 virtual memory, 299–301
Properties dialog box, 127–128
 Advanced Program settings, 312
 Font tab, 313
 General tab, 310–311
 Global tab, 273
 Memory tab, 310, 313–314
 Misc tab, 315
 Program tab, 309, 311–313
 Screen tab, 314
 Sharing tab, 205, 257, 420
 Tools tab, 14, 272
Property dialog box, 309
protected mode, 58
 applications, 274–275, 296
 disk drives, 538
 file system, 33
 rings, 274–275

protected-mode
 clients and Novell NetWare push installation, 443
protecting Win16 applications, 306
protocol stacks, 144, 171
 binding, 146
protocols, 144, 171, 335, 470–484
 binding, 463, 471
 configuring, 473
 connectionless, 147
 connection-oriented, 147
 default, 144, 424
 DLC (Data Link Control) protocol, 482
 Fast Infrared, 483
 installing multiple, 146
 IPX/SPX-compatible protocol, 479–482
 minimizing, 367
 NDIS (Network Driver Interface Specification), 483–484
 NetBEUI (NetBIOS Extended User Interface), 482–483
 networks, 423–426
 ODI (Open Datalink Interface), 484
 TCP/IP (Transmission Control Protocol/Internet Protocol), 471–479
 translating programs for, 145
proxy servers, 152, 158–159, 171
 changing settings, 164
 settings, 435
pull installation, 439, 448
purging Recycle Bin, 273–274
push installation, 439–440, 448
 Windows NT, 440–442
.pwl (password list file), 104, 134
PWM (Personal Web Manager), 218
 Advanced icon, 226
 home page creation, 224–225
 Home Page Wizard, 224, 225
 Monitoring Web site traffic, 228–229
 posting to Web site, 226
 Publish icon, 226
 Web Site icon, 223
PWS (Personal Web Server), 8, 15, 218–223, 241
 Active Server, 221
 animating Web pages database changes, 221
 Common Program Files, 220
 comparative features, 218
 dynamic Web applications, 222
 Edit Directory dialog box, 227
 hard disk space, 219
 Home Page Wizard, 225
 installing, 219–223
 linking to Front Page Express databases accessible by, 220
 message receipt acknowledgement, 221
 MTS (Microsoft Transaction Server), 221
 permissions settings, 226
 publishing to same directory as Internet Information Server, 219
 services, 222
 uninstalling, 223
 uninstalling earlier version, 219

Index

Visual InterDev RAD (Rapid Application Development) Remote Deployment Support, 222
Web Sharing, 230
WWW Service, 222
PWS (Personal Web Server) for Windows 98, 218
PWS (Personal Web Server) for Windows NT Workstation, 218
PWS Setup Wizard, 220

Q

Quick Launch toolbar, 107

R

RAID (redundant array of independent disks), 392–393, 395
RAM cache, 344
RAM (random access memory), 5, 21
  elements assigned within, 346
  free, 346
  performance, 339
  requirements, 32
RAMDrive, 517–518, 551
RAS (Remote Access Server), 217, 232
raster graphics, 535
RAW, 371
Read access, 256
Read permission, 227
reading data, 345
real mode, 58
  applications and rings, 274–275
  CD-ROM drivers, 44, 411–412
  clients and Novell NetWare push installation, 443
  file system, 33
real-mode drivers, 149, 538
  configuring for MS-DOS applications, 305
  unsafe, 357
Recent folder, 108
Recycle Bin, 273–274, 363
redirectors, 321, 348, 371, 462, 494
  amount of data read through, 348
  amount of data sent through, 348
  binding, 463
  Client for Microsoft Networks, 348, 464–465
  Client For NetWare Networks, 466–468
  dual-protocol clients, 468
  message preparation, 464
  MS-DOS, 463
  network clients, 463–470
reformatting hard disks, 413
Regedit, 86
Registry, 7, 21, 86
  access and usage, 68–70
  APIs (application programming interfaces), 66
  applet modification of, 69
  automated backup and restore, 67
  backing up, 72–73, 389
  batch mode settings collection, 415–416
  benefits, 66–67
  better protection against corruption, 67

changes taking effect, 70
changing settings, 40
checking for problems, 73
compacting, 73
computer performance, 75
Control Panel applets, 82
corruption, 353
customizable, 67
data types, 78–79
database of installed hardware, 66
directly modifying, 119
dynamic keys, 69
editing, 74, 383–384
efficient file size, 67
ESD (Emergency Startup Disk), 72
files, 67–68
hardware configuration, 75
hardware listing, 69
hardware profiles, 70
hardware-relatch information, 68
hardware-specific information, 79
HKEY_CLASSES_ROOT root key, 75, 77–78
HKEY_CURRENT_CONFIG root key, 75, 77
HKEY_CURRENT_USER root key, 75, 78
HKEY_DYN_DATA root key, 75, 78
HKEY_LOCAL_MACHINE root key, 75, 76–77
HKEY_USERS root key, 75, 78
improved caching, 67
improved system performance, 67
inconsistent file structure, 353
Installation Wizards, 82
keys, 66
loading programs, 69
managing, 72–74
modifying, 120–124
more reliable code sharing, 67
new features, 66
overview, 66–72
PnP (Plug and Play), 79–81
policies, 68
Policy.pol file, 68
Registry Checker, 73
Registry Editor, 74, 82
remote control, 382
remote management, 67
repairing, 73
restoring, 72
restoring with ESD (Emergency Startup Disk), 519
restrictions on values, 72
roles of, 66
root keys, 74, 75
safety, 72–73
scanning for errors, 72
Setup programs, 82
size, 66
storing settings, 305
structure, 74–79
subkeys, 74
system policies, 72, 118
System Policy Editor, 82

System.dat file, 68
target computers, 435–436
user profiles, 66, 70–71, 75
user snapshot, 66
User.dat file, 68
user-specific information, 68
user-specific parts, 107
variables, 66
Windows 95 update, 54
Windows 98, 305
Registry API, 87
Registry Checker, 67, 72, 73, 87, 353
  regular Maintenance, 509
Registry Editor, 72, 74, 76, 82, 87
Registry Scanner, 54
regular maintenance, 508–509
regular phone service, 193
relevant group policies, 130
remote
  management, 67
  Registry control, 382
remote access, 190–192, 217, 241
Remote Administration tools, 381
Remote Registry Services, 383, 395
RemoteAccess subkey, 79
removable media, 365, 389
Remove Item dialog box, 303
renaming MS-DOS programs, 312
repartitioning hard disks, 266
repeaters, 485, 494
requests, 228–229, 242
Resource Meter, 507–508
resources
  managing, 315–316
  more than one application using, 316
  passwords assigned to, 255
  shared-level permissions, 255
  sharing, 254, 426
  user-level permissions, 255
restoring
  Command.com, 518
  Registry, 72
  system files, 518
Restricted Sites Zone dialog box, 163
resume on ring or keyboard/mouse events, 9
RGB (red, green, and blue), 262, 283
ring architecture, 274–275, 283, 371
roaming profiles, 67, 112–115, 134
ROM (read-only memory) problems, 520
root directory, 35
root keys, 74–75
Root subkey, 81
rotation, 390
routable, 424, 448
routers, 471, 485, 494
roving profiles, 112, 134
RPC (remote procedure call), 74, 87
Run dialog box, 267
Run Installation Program dialog box, 414

S

Safe Mode, 514
  startup and shutdown processes, 516–517
SAP (Service Advertising Protocol), 426, 448

Save As dialog box, 129, 540
Save System Files dialog box, 52
ScanDisk, 14, 21, 45, 53, 358–361, 386, 536
  automatically running, 385
  bad sectors, 359
  checking files and folders after failure, 391
  checking for specific problems, 360
  compressed drives, 361
  cross-linked files, 360
  deleting old files, 363
  disabling after bad shutdown, 522
  file system structure, 359
  log file, 507
  long filenames, 361
  lost file fragments, 360
  protected mode, 408
  real-mode version, 408
  regular maintenance, 508
  ScanDisk Advanced Options dialog box, 360–361
  standard scan, 359–360
  summary of activity log file, 360
  surface check, 391
  Surface Scan Options dialog box, 360
Scandisk.exe file, 413, 518
scanning for problem files, 352
Scanreg.exe file, 73, 87
Scanregw.exe file, 73, 87
Scheduled Tasks folder, 386
scripts, 156, 227, 414
SCSI drives, 521
SCSI layer, 319, 321
SCSI (Small Computer Systems Interface) devices, 81
SCSI (Small Computer Systems Interfaces) devices
  troubleshooting, 546
SCSI subkey, 81
SCSI/CD-ROM troubleshooting, 546
SCU (System Configuration Utility)
  Autoexec.bat tab, 523–524
  Config.sys tab, 523
  Diagnostic startup, 520
  General tab, 520–522
  Normal startup, 520
  Selective startup, 520
  Startup tab, 525–526
  System.ini tab, 524
  Win.ini tab, 524
search engines, 161
secondary kernel scheduler, 297
sectors, 33, 58
secure
  data transfer, 163
  proxy servers, 159
security, 40–42
  administrating user-level, 381–384
  Internet Explorer 4.0, 161–164
  logon method, 40
  master access plan, 381
  overview, 380–384
  pass-through, 381
  password cache, 41–42, 104
  password validation, 40
  passwords, 104
  plan documentation, 381
  share-level permissions, 37, 255, 380
  system policies, 40–41
  third-party tools, 384
  user profiles, 41
  user-level permissions, 38, 255, 380
  username validation, 40
  Web sites, 434–435
Security subkey, 77
segmented address space, 297, 321
segment/offset model of memory addressing, 301
segments, 485, 494
Select a Target Directory dialog box, 438
Select Components dialog box, 48
Select Network Adapters dialog box, 194, 488
Select Network Client dialog box, 237, 466
Select Network Component Type dialog box, 113, 194, 237, 383, 466, 468, 479, 487
Select Network dialog box, 383
Select Network Protocol dialog box, 487
Select Network Service dialog box, 383, 468
Select Password dialog box, 105
Server Types dialog box, 235–236
servers, 2, 21
  amount of memory required, 349
  buffer number, 349
  configuring Windows 98 as, 489–491
  network buffer, 349
  number of threads used by processes, 349
  operating system, 2
  performance monitoring, 349
  reading rate, 349
  writing rate, 349
services, 426, 448, 511
Settings Properties dialog box, 258
setup msbatch.inf command, 440
Setup Options dialog box, 47
Setup Wizard, 12, 43, 45, 58, 82, 219, 408, 412
  automated documentation, 509–512
  batch mode Windows 98, 414
  boot disks, 409–411
  Bootlog.txt file, 509, 511–512
  CD-ROM drivers, 411–412
  copying files, 408
  Detcrash.log file, 509, 510–511
  detecting hardware, 409
  driver database, 409
  Emergency Startup Disk dialog box, 49–50
  Establishing Your Location dialog box, 49
  hardware, 80
  hardware combinations, 509, 510
  hardware detection, 510–511
  Identification dialog box, 49
  Insert Disk dialog box, 49–50
  installation, 414–415
  license agreement, 46
  Netlog.txt file, 509, 511
  network adapters, 511
  network clients, 511
  network protocols, 511
  network services, 511
  options, 409
  parameters, 408
  Preparing Directory dialog box, 46, 47
  problems and, 510
  Product Identification dialog box, 46
  Product Key dialog box, 46
  recording non-Plug-and-Play devices settings, 408
  restarting computer, 51–52
  routine check of system, 45
  running from MS-DOS, 43
  running from Windows 95, 43
  ScanDisk protected mode, 408
  ScanDisk real mode version, 408
  ScanReg, 408
  Select Components dialog box, 48
  Select Directory dialog box, 46
  Setup Options dialog box, 47
  Setuplog.txt file, 510
  smart recovery, 409
  Smart Recovery feature, 408
  starting system, 511–512
  switches, 576–577
  User Information dialog box, 47–48
  user input, 408
  Welcome screen, 45
  Windows 95 upgrade, 53–54
  Windows Components dialog box, 48
  Windows Registry Checker (ScanRegW), 408
Setup.exe file, 440
Setuplog.exe file, 551
Setuplog.txt file, 409, 509–510
SFC (System File Checker), 13, 21, 352, 507–508, 526–528
  CRC (cyclic redundancy check), 352
  regular maintenance, 508
shared
  fax modems, 258–259
  files access types, 237–238
  folders access permissions, 255–257
  folders user-level security, 257
  printers user-level security, 257
  resources, 236–239, 254–257, 426
share-level security, 37, 58, 103, 133, 255, 381, 395, 429
  advantages and disadvantages, 38, 380
  full access, 380
  passwords, 38, 42, 234
  read-only access, 380
  remote administration, 382
  resource sharing, 42
  shared resources, 254
  small peer-to-peer networks, 39
  user ID, 42
  workgroups, 492
Shellm.adm file, 120
Signature Verification tool, 508
simplified policy support, 393
SIPC (Simply Interactive Personal Computer), 253, 274, 284
Site Server, 217, 229, 242
Site Server Enterprise, 229
Site Server Express, 229
sleep mode, 9
SLIP (Serial Line Internet Protocol), 147, 171, 195
slower performance, 341

Index

SMARTDrive, 310, 341, 371
SMB (Server Message Blocks) protocol, 348, 371, 462, 464
SMTP (Simple Mail Transfer Protocol), 145, 153, 171
Socks servers, 159
software components required to run programs, 336
Software subkey, 77, 79
sound cards, 335
source folder, 419
source routing, 543
SPA (Secure Password Authentication), 157, 171
SPAP (Shiva Password Authentication Protocol), 239
SPE (System Policy Editor), 40
SPID (Service Profile Identifier), 194
Spool Setting dialog box, 366
SSL (Secure Sockets Layer), 163
stack, 144
stand alone systems, 102
standalone, 58
standalone workstation, 36–37, 58
standard Windows 98 VGA-mode driver, 521
Standard.pol file, 124
Start Copying Files dialog box, 50–51
Start menu, 21
   enhancements, 12
   Windows 95, 4
   Windows Update option, 13
Start Menu folder, 108
startup and shutdown processes
   conflicts, 519
   drivers, 519
   ESD (Emergency Startup Disk), 517–519
   modifying programs automatically starting, 525–526
   SCU (System Configuration Utility), 520–526
   SFC (System File Checker), 526–528
   Startup and Shutdown troubleshooter, 514–516
   Startup Menu and Safe Mode, 516–517
   troubleshooting, 513–528
Startup and Shutdown troubleshooter, 514–516
startup configuration files, 354
   at startup, 368
StartUp folder, 525–526
Startup Menu, 516–517, 521
startup programs, modifying, 368
Startup Wizard, 50–51
storage devices, 336
storing system policies, 129
subkeys, 74, 87
   HKEY_CURRENT_USER root key, 79
   HKEY_LOCAL_MACHINE root key, 77
   PnP (Plug and Play) relationships, 81
subnets, 147, 171
Subsm.adm file, 120
SuperStor, 512
surface check, 391
suspend mode, 9
suspending parts of system, 201

swap files, 32, 58, 296, 339, 346–347, 371
   problems, 357
SwitchBoard, 158
synchronizing files, 203
Sys.com file, 413, 518
system
   bootup, 87
   commands, 575–576
   failure and recovery, 390–392
   failure and warm reboot, 392
   measuring performance, 69
   minimizing crashes, 275
   recovery, 390–392
   settings, 82
   snapshot of configuration, 78
System applet
   Device Manager tab, 118
   Hardware Profiles tab, 70, 117–118
   Performance tab, 364, 365, 537
System Commander, 445
System Commander Special Edition for Windows 98, 445
System Configuration, 354, 368, 508
System Configuration dialog box, 511
System File Checker Settings dialog box, 527
system files
   compiling information on, 353–354
   corrupt, 526–527
   limiting search of, 527
system freeze, 392
system hibernation, 270
system hooks, 336
system inventory, 13, 332–337
System Monitor, 14, 21, 371
   Add Item dialog box, 342, 357
   Dial-Up adapter category, 342–343
   Disk Cache category, 344–345
   features, 342–349
   File System category, 345
   Kernel category, 345–346
   log file, 349–350
   Memory Manager category, 346–348
   Microsoft Network Client category, 348
   Microsoft Network Server category, 349
   modem functionality, 342–343
   number of threads and virtual machines, 303
   Options dialog box, 349–350
   Save As dialog box, 349
   Sysmon.log file, 349
   usage, 349–351
   viewing, 304
   viewing list of items that can be monitored, 342
system policies, 40–41, 58, 67, 72, 82–83, 87, 118–131, 134
   caching, 106
   changing settings, 128–129
   computer policies, 119
   creation, 119–124, 125, 127–128
   default, 124–127
   Default Computer icon, 124
   Default User icon, 124
   deleting, 129
   denying users access, 41
   deployment, 131

disabling password, 106
disabling password caching, 106
editing, 119–124
group policies, 119
limitations, 119
mandatory, 41
networked environment, 40
order of application of, 130–131
organizing listing of, 126
password minimum requirements, 103
password security, 41
Registry, 118
saving as .pol file, 128–129
saving changes to, 129
standard and custom, 40
storing, 129
testing, 131
user policies, 119
System Policy Editor, 72, 82–83, 119–124, 128–129, 134, 395
   .adm files, 120–124
   Connect dialog box, 383
   deactivating .adm files, 123
   Default Computer icon, 125–126
   Default User icon, 125
   editing Registry, 383–384
   Group Priority dialog box, 130
   Open Registry command, 119
   .pol (policy) files, 120–124
   prioritizing group policies, 130
system profile, 332–337
System Properties dialog box
   Device Manager, 337
System Security Check dialog box, 205
System Settings Change dialog box, 234
System subkey, 77
System Tools dialog box, 387, 491, 508
System Virtual Machine, 296, 298, 304–307, 321
System.dat file, 68, 83, 87
   root keys, 75
System.ini file, 305, 442
   editing or disabling, 524
   modifying commands, 368

T

T1 connections, 198
T3 connections, 198
tape drives, 389–400
TAPI (Telephony Application Program Interface)
   version 2.1, 259
TAPI (Telephony Application Programming Interface), 184, 208, 284
target computers, 435–436
Task Monitor, 361
Task Scheduler, 302
taskbars, 4, 11, 22
tasks, listing, 336
TCP (Transmission Control Protocol), 147
TCP/IP Properties dialog box, 149–151
   Advanced tab, 151
   Bindings tab, 151
   DNS Configuration tab, 151, 157, 474, 476

Gateway tab, 151
IP Address tab, 151, 156, 473
NetBIOS tab, 151
WINS Configuration tab, 151, 474
TCP/IP Settings dialog box, 196
TCP/IP (Transmission Control Protocol/Internet Protocol), 144, 171, 424, 470–479
ARP (Address Resolution Protocol), 147
Autonet, 426
configuring, 149–151, 160
as default protocol, 144, 151
DHCP (Dynamic Host Configuration Protocol), 472
DNS (Domain Name System), 425, 472, 474, 476
gateways, 425, 471
IP address, 145, 426, 472
IP (Internet Protocol), 147
NetBIOS name, 151
PING (Packet Internet Groper), 147–148, 478
port numbers, 159
PPP (Point-to-Point Protocol), 147
Remote Registry Services, 383
sending request, 462
SMTP (Simple Mail Transfer Protocol), 145
TCP (Transmission Control Protocol), 147
Tracert, 478
troubleshooting connections, 476–478
UDP (User Datagram Protocol), 147
Winipcfg file, 477
WINS (Windows Internet Name Service), 472–474
WINS (Windows Internet Naming Service), 425
telecommunication devices
compression, 195–196
faster connections, 197–198
installation wizards, 185
troubleshooting connection problems, 198–199
telephones integrating into networks, 259–260
TEMP directory parameters, 518
templates, 120–124
temporary files, 363
temporary Internet files, 362
Temporary Internet Files folder, 108
terminator, 546
testing
boot disks, 410
deployment, 131
ESD (Emergency Startup Disk), 411–412
solution, 508
system policies, 131
text data type, 79
theorizing about problem, 507
third-party
boot managers, 445–446
file system drivers, 318
security tools, 384
utilities, 266–267
threads, 297, 301–303, 307, 321, 341
thunking, 322
time-sensitive data, 78

timeslice, 302, 322
Token Ring, 486
toolbars, 11
TR (Travan), 395
TR-1 through TR-4, 395
Tracert, 478
transferring files, 165–167
transmitting data, 200
Travan technology389
trial-and-error performance monitoring, 351
troubleshooting
automated Setup documentation, 509–512
baseline, 506
cables and connections, 528
conflicts and startup and shutdown processes, 519
connection problems, 198–199
conventional memory requirements, 513
devices, 539
disk and file systems, 536–538
display, 544–545
Dr. Watson, 548
drivers, 539
ESD (Emergency Startup Disk), 517–519
identifying problem, 506–507
incompatible compression schemes, 512
input devices, 546–547
IPX/SPX-compatible protocol, 541–543
MSInfo (Microsoft System Information), 538–540
NetBEUI protocol, 540–541
network configuration, 540–543
printers, 529–535
regular maintenance, 508–509
SCSI/CD-ROM, 546
startup and shutdown processes, 513–528
Startup and Shutdown troubleshooter, 514–516
Startup Menu and Safe Mode, 516–517
testing solution, 508
theorizing about problem, 507
Windows 98 installation, 509–513
TSR (terminate-and-stay-resident) programs, 59, 300, 321, 513
installation, 43–44
memory protection, 309–310
memory used by, 300–301
Tune-Up Wizard, 14
tunneling, 551
TWAIN, 284
TWAIN Web site, 263
typical installation, 43, 59

U

UART (universal asynchronous receiver-transmitter), 343
FIFO (first in, first out) buffers, 187
UDF (Universal Disk File) file system, 340, 522
UDP (User Datagram Protocol), 147, 171
UltraPack, 284
undeleting files, 273
Unimodem V, 284
driver, 259
operator agent, 260

Uninstall.exe file, 518
uninstalling
PWS (Personal Web Server), 223
Windows 98, 54, 413
universal driver, 261
universal printer driver, 261
UNIX operating system, 153
SLIP (Serial Line Interface Protocol), 147
Untitled - Microsoft Batch 98 window, 415
Update My Briefcase dialog box, 204
uploading files, 200
URLs (Uniform Resource Locators), 22
USB (Universal Serial Bus), 9, 22, 185, 208, 277–278, 284, 336, 371
Usenet, 171
Usenet newsgroups, 157–158
user, 7
user accounts, 102, 110–111, 134
user environments, 110, 134
limits, 118–131
user profiles, 107–116
User Information dialog box, 47–48, 540
user input needs and threads, 302
user interface tools, 7, 22
user name length, 102
user policies, 72, 119, 133, 135
user profiles, 41, 59, 66, 75, 87, 107–116, 133, 135
Application Data folder, 107
batch mode installation, 420
Cookies folder, 107
customizing, 71
default, 108
Desktop folder, 107
Favorites folder, 107
History folder, 108
local, 112
mandatory, 41, 115–116
multiple, 108–109
My Documents folder, 108
NetHood folder, 108
network users, 110
Recent folder, 108
Recent folder, 108
roaming, 112
roaming profiles, 113
Start Menu folder, 108
storing, 41, 108
Temporary Internet Files folder, 108
troubleshooting, 116
User.dat file, 107
user settings, 82
User Settings applet, 110
User.dat file, 68, 70–71, 87, 107, 115, 134
keys, 75
user-level permissions, 255–256, 429
user-level security, 38, 59, 103, 133, 381, 396
administrating from, 381
administration rights, 257
advantages, 39
backup capabilities, 382
dial-up network access, 382
domains, 492
groups, 380
larger networks, 39

Index

Net Watcher, 382
  passwords, 41
  performance-monitoring utilities, 382
  Registry, 382
  remote administration, 382
  remote management rights, 382
  resources managed by administrator, 382
  rights, 380
  setting up, 255–256
  shared resources, 254
  sharing folders, 257
  sharing printers, 257
  sharing resources, 256–257
  user accounts, 380
  usernames, 41
  Windows 98, 39
  Windows 98 computer, 381–384
User.man file, 115, 135
usernames, 41, 102–103
user-related Registry data, 68
users
  access rights, 255–257
  administration rights, 257
  multiple group policies, 130
Users applet, 112
user-specific policies, 130
utilities, 570–571
utility software, 35, 59

V

VCACHE, 371
  amount of data needing to be written, 345
  DVD (Digital video discs), 340–341
  dynamically adjusting disk cache, 344
  dynamically allocating pages, 340
  hard disks, 340
  Network Redirector, 341
  number of searches, 345
VCM (Version Conflict Manager), 354–355, 507, 508
VDDs (Video Display Drivers), 314
VDMs (virtual DOS machines), 298, 308
vector graphics, printing, 535
VFAT file system, 33
video cards, 335
virtual device drivers, 315–316, 322
virtual directories, 226–227, 242
Virtual Machine Manager, 6, 22
virtual memory, 5, 22, 296, 299–301
virtual memory address space, 296, 299, 301, 308, 322, 392
virus protection software, 36
visits, 229, 242
Visual InterDev, 242
  RAD (Rapid Application Development)
  Remote Deployment Support, 222
VLM (4.x), 443, 448, 469
VLM real-mode client, 429–431
VM (virtual machines), 6, 296, 298, 303
voice calls, 200
VPN (virtual private networking), 487–488
.vxd files, 13, 22
VXDs (virtual device drivers), 8
VxDs (virtual device drivers), 322
  paging, 316

W

warm reboot, 392
WDM Driver Manager, 7, 22
WDM (Win32 Driver Model), 5–8, 22, 276, 316–317, 384
  file system, 315–319
  kernel streaming, 279
Web applications, 222
Web browsers, 161
Web guides, 161
Web pages and animation, 221
Web Publishing Wizard, 15
Web Sharing, 230
Web sites
  adding to zones, 162–163
  Authenticode, 163
  connecting, 231–232
  data on visitor preferred pages, 229
  default, 437
  excluding proxy server from, 159
  Execute permission, 227
  favorites, 161
  fully-qualified Internet domain name, 231
  general Windows 98, 565–566
  hits, 228
  home directory, 226
  home page creation, 224–225
  listing explored, 161
  managing, 223–229
  managing small, 218–223
  MCSE, 566
  media-based Windows 98, 564–565
  monitoring traffic, 228–229
  most recently accessed, 108
  number of persons connecting to, 231–232
  pinging, 147–148
  posting to, 226
  preferred, 107
  rating, 164
  Read permission, 227
  requests, 228–229
  restricting access, 163
  Scripts permission, 227
  security, 434–435
  stable IP address, 231
  upgrading Web server program, 229
  viewing directories, 227
  virtual directories, 226–227
  visits, 229
WebTV, 280
Welcome screen, 107
Welcome to Windows 98 Setup dialog box, 53
Welcome to Windows dialog box, 102
welcome to Windows dialog box, 102
Who Where, 158
Win16 applications, 298, 304–307, 322
Win32 applications, 298, 306–307, 322
Win386.swp file, 32
WinAlign utility, 347
WinBench, 337
Windows
  history, 2–4
  update, 23

Windows 3.1, 4
  dual boot, 55
  file system compatibility, 35
Windows 3.x, 4, 22
  boot disks, 411
  drivers, 5
  fault tolerance, 392
  upgrade, 52
  D, 52
Windows 95, 2
  boot disks, 410
  boot loader, 54
  desktop, 4
  drivers, 5
  ESD (Emergency Startup Disk), 410
  fault tolerance, 392
  network protocols, 4
  OSR2 file system compatibility, 35
  Plug and Play technology, 4
  running Setup from, 43
  Start menu, 4
  taskbars, 4
  update, 54
  upgrade, 53–54
  upgrading requirements, 32
  VFAT file system, 33
  Windows NT push installation upgrade, 441
Windows 98, 2, 4, 22
  16-bit programs, 296
  32-bit components, 306–307
  32-bit file system, 295
  32-bit kernel, 295
  as 32-bit operating system, 4
  32-bit protected-mode drivers, 308
  architecture, 6–8
  basics, 4–5
  batch mode installation, 414–415
  benefits for MS-DOS applications, 308
  boot disks, 411
  boot loader, 54
  client-server networks, 144
  commonalities with Windows NT, 5
  compatibility with Win16 applications, 305
  configuring, 32–42
  configuring as server, 489–491
  core, 7, 22
  deleting uninstall information, 363
  desktop, 3
  display settings and controls, 11
  drivers, 5, 316
  enhanced power management, 9
  file system, 5, 35
  hardware and architectural, 8–11
  increased Internet integration, 15–16
  installation process, 408–413
  installation troubleshooting, 509–513
  Integrated Internet Shell, 11
  Internet and Web standards support, 15
  Internet communication tools, 15–16
  Internet connections, 144
  key features, 8–16
  MS-DOS mode, 308–309
  multiple displays, 9
  multitasking, 5, 296
  multithreading, 5

multiuser operating system, 102
network installation, 439–444
next-generation hardware, 9–10
online services folder, 12
optimizing, 356–369
personalized information delivery, 16
Plug and Play feature, 8
power and usability, 11–12
printing, 260–265
RAM (random access memory), 5
reclaiming used memory and system resources, 5
Registry, 7, 305
robustness and reliability, 12–14
Setup program, 12
simultaneous applications, 4
Start menu enhancements, 12
Startup Menu, 507
supporting more powerful applications, 4
switching between programs, 314
system requirements, 32
taskbars, 11
toolbars, 11
uninstalling, 54, 413
user interface tools, 7
user-level security, 39
virtual memory, 5
Windows 98 computer, 382, 489–490
Windows 98 RAS (Remote Access Server), 232
   authentication and access controls, 239–240
   configuring, 234
   features, 233
   installing, 233–234
   ISDN adapter, 232
   LCP (Link Control Protocol), 239
   password encryption, 239–240
   PPP (Point-to-Point) capable server, 239
   as remote PPTP client, 233
   sharing resources, 236–239
   simultaneous remote connections, 233
Windows CE, 201
Windows Components dialog box, 48

Windows directory, 41, 68, 71
Windows Explorer, 7, 22, 203–204
Windows for Workgroups, 441–442
Windows Help dialog box, 514
Windows Internet Naming Service, 151
Windows NT
   boot loader, 54
   clients, 427
   as domain controller, 38
   dual boot, 55, 445
   fault tolerance, 392–393
   MS-CHAP (Microsoft Challenge Handshake Authentication), 239
   network mandatory profiles, 115
   Password Policy, 106
   policy files, 436
   protective isolation between virtual memory address spaces, 392
   push installation, 440–442
   RAS (Remote Access Server) features, 233
   roaming profiles, 113–114
   routing TCP/IP messages between LANs (local area networks), 233
   Service Pack 3, 106
   Site Server versions, 229
   VFAT file system, 33
   workgroup-based and domain-based computers, 39
Windows NT 3.1, 4
Windows NT 4.0, 4
   file system compatibility, 35
   printer drivers, 261
Windows NT 5.0, 4
   driver compatibility with Windows 98, 316
   drivers, 5
   FAT32 file system, 269
   file system compatibility, 35
Windows NT based domain, 382
Windows NT Server, 2, 23, 217
Windows NT Workstation, 2, 23
Windows online magazine Web site, 550
Windows Report Tool, 539–540

Windows TAPI, 184
   Distinctive Ring service, 186
Windows Tune-Up Wizard, 14
Windows.adm file, 120, 124
Windows_Passthru account, 490, 494
   directory, 71
   subdirectories, 68
Win.ini file, 305
   editing or disabling, 524
   modifying commands, 368
Winipcfg., 477
WINS (Windows Internet Name Service), 171, 472
WINS (Windows Internet Naming Service), 425
Winsock, 335
Winstart.bat file, 520
WINUNDO.DAT file, 54, 59
WINUNDO.INI file, 54, 59
workgroup model, 37, 40, 59
workgroups, 492
   changing names, 39
   share-level security, 492
workstation operating system, 2
workstations, 2, 23
Write access, 256
writing data, 345
WSH (Windows Scripting Host), 11, 23
WWW Service, 222
WYSIWYG (What You See Is What You Get) display, 2

X

XtraDrive, 512

Y

Yahoo! People Search, 158

Z

Ziff Davis Web site, 550
Zip disks, 396
Zip drives, 390
zones, 162–163